ARCO Scholarship Exam Series

AP/CLEP

Advanced Placement and College Level Examinations in ENGLISH-Analysis and Interpretation of Literature

James W. Morrison

with the assistance of

Julia Reiss, Dorothy S. Ryan, and Stanley Gorskey, Jr.

ARCO PUBLISHING COMPANY, INC.
NEW YORK

Published by Arco Publishing Company, Inc.
219 Park Avenue South, New York, N.Y. 10003

Library of Congress Cataloging in Publication Data

Morrison, James Warner, 1940-
Advanced placement and college level examinations in English—analysis and interpretation of literature.

Bibliography: p. 454
1. English literature—Examinations, questions, etc. 2. American literature—Examinations, questions, etc. 3. College-Level Examination Program. I. Title.

PR87.M68 378.1'66'4 77-14209
ISBN 0-668-04406-3 (Paper Edition)

Printed in the United States of America

FOR

JULIA REISS - A BLESSED NAOMI

PREFACE

Each year more than 25,000 students take the Advancement Placement Examination in English, and thousands more take the CLEP Subject Examination in the Analysis and Interpretation of Literature. These College Entrance Examination Board tests require a rigorous study of literature. This book presents units on poetry, drama, prose (short story and novel), practice examinations of multiple-choice with explained answers and free-response essays. There are several actual student examination essays as well as other essays on poetry, novels and plays to illustrate good literary criticism.

To get the greatest help from this book, please understand that it has been carefully organized. You must, therefore, plan to use it accordingly. Study this concise, readable book earnestly and your way will be clear. You will progress directly to your goal. You will not be led off into blind alleys and useless fields of study.

This book will tell you exactly what to study by presenting in full every type of CLEP or AP question you will get on the actual test. You'll do better merely by familiarizing yourself with them.

This book will help you find your weaknesses and find them fast. Once you know where you're weak you can get right to work (before the test) and concentrate your efforts on those soft spots. This is the kind of selective study which yields maximum test results for every hour spent.

This is most important for you in the light of recent findings in the theory of learning. Gestalt (meaning configuration or pattern) psychology stresses that true learning results in a grasp of the entire situation. Gestaltists also tell us that we learn by "insight." One of the salient facets of this type of learning is that we succeed in "seeing through" a problem as a consequence of experiencing previous similar situations. This book contains hundreds and hundreds of "similar situations". . . as you will discover when you take the actual examination.

Almost all our sample and practice questions are taken from similar, related AP and CLEP exams. Since relevant exams are not always available for inspection by the public, these sample test questions are quite important for you. The day you take your exam you'll see how closely this book follows the format of the real test.

This book will give you confidence now, while you are preparing for the test. It will build your self-confidence as you proceed. It will beat those dreaded before-test jitters that have hurt so many other test-takers. Your confidence will arise naturally, as a result of getting the "feel" of the exam.

"The learned become more learned." In going over the practice questions in this book, you will not--if you use this book properly--be satisfied merely with the answer to a particular question. You will want to find out why the other choices are incorrect. In this way, you will broaden your background to be adequately prepared for the exam to come. It is quite possible that a question on the exam may require your knowing the meaning of one of these other choices. Thorndike's principle of "identical elements" explains this important phase of learning--particularly as it applies to examination preparation. It explains how you help yourself when you jog your memory, bring back much you thought you had forgotten.

Remember, to score high on the CLEP or AP English Examination you must read the essays, novels, poems, and plays of acknowledged literary merit, and afterwards, you must be able to write your own well-organized essay about the reading or some related literary question.

This volume represents the works of many. The students of Trinity High School Advanced Placement English, over the years, have made an important contribution with their sample essays--a grade of 5 is a sign of excellence--the actual, free-response essays are appreciated. The poetry analysis of Dorothy S. Ryan is acknowledged and shows a love for the subject. The drama unit has been well organized by Stanley Gorski, Jr. As teacher of AP English courses he has tried to provide the correct orientation to the discipline at hand.

Julia Reiss, an English honors graduate, has given of herself and family in her essays on plays, novels, and short stories. This book came into final form with the assistance of Blanche E. Duval, Marsha Glance, and Janet Lord; the theatre drawings were completed by Cathryn F. Morrison.

J.W.M.

CONTENTS

Part I

Introductory Material

HOW TO USE THIS BOOK

Students are too often disastrously surprised when they find out their results from a CLEP Literature Test or an Advanced Placement Exam in English. To many it will unfortunately be something the likes of which they have never seen before, and the students more often than not defeat themselves before they get started. The idea of this book is to assert the aspiring AP student, the honors student, or just the interested student with as many typical questions and answers as time will allow thereby acclimating him/her to hopefully any possible situation. It is important that you take the practice examinations under the recommended, simulated conditions; know the time constraints of the multiple-choice and free-response essay sections.

To be "trite" for a second HOW TO PREPARE FOR THE CLEP-AP ENGLISH EXAMINATIONS attempts to make all this second nature for you. You should attempt plowing through as much of the material as possible realizing some will rub off, some won't, but over all an impression will be made. You will need to practice and study if you expect a score of three or higher on the AP test.

A point to keep in mind is that one of the most important things is to read. Once again, in order not to score the student, we will not say that it is a necessary prerequisite. But, if reading is not something that has interested you, the road will be "rocky" but not an impossible one. Literature is the result of someone having something to say, and this will in time give any interested person much to talk about - if he reads, then reads some more, and finally never stops reading. The guidelines are drawn for you. They will not make you successful unless you want to be. The final decision is yours. With this book you will:

- Gain familiarity with your examination;
- Improve your skill in analyzing and answering questions involving reasoning, judgment, comparison, and evaluation; and
- Improve your speed and skill in reading and understanding what you read--an important ability in learning, and an important component of most tests

This book will pinpoint your study by presenting the types of questions you will get on the actual exam. It will help you find your weaknesses and show you how to concentrate on those soft spots. Come exam-day you'll see how closely the book conforms. This book will build your self-confidence and elminiate those before-test jitters. By creating the "climate" of typical tests, this book will give you an accurate picture of what is involved and what you have to do to succeed.

You should read through sample questions and answers, multiple-choice and free-response essays. Check the answer key. Then, do the succeeding planned questions yourself trying to justify what you put down. Your teacher may have additional comments. You may or may not agree, but you've at least said something and if you can substantiate it, how can you be all wrong.

Remember, your first need is to have something to say. This comes with reading and more reading. You can think all you want but if you don't have the information or material to funnel into your "thought machine", nothing can come out. This book will help you put it all together.

COLLEGE-LEVEL EXAMINATION PROGRAM

The College-Level Examination Program (CLEP) was conceived to enable nontraditional and traditional students to earn college credit by examination. Underlying the Program are the beliefs that the future calls for more education for all citizens; that flexibility, innovation, and independent study are essential in education; that what a person knows is more important than how he came to know it; and that academic credit by examination is one key to a more flexible educational system.

The College-Level Examination Program was established in 1965 as a new activity of the College Board. Developed with the broad purpose of establishing a national system of awarding college credit by examination, the Program has grown in many different directions. Some of the ways CLEP is being used are:

To enable adults and unaffiliated students to demonstrate their knowledge and validate their learning by receiving college credit on the basis of examinations.

To enable enrolled students to get credit by examination.

To assist transfer and continuing students in the transition to upper-division study.

To provide measures of college equivalency for use by business, industry, and other noncollegiate organizations.

To help meet licensing and certification requirements and to provide a means of qualifying for job advancement.

Candidate volume has grown dramatically since the CLEP began in 1971-72 with 80,134 to 252,671 in 1975-76.

The College-Level Examination Program offers you the opportunity to obtain college credit by examination. On-the-job experience, purposeful reading, adult school or corresponding courses, or television or taped courses may have prepared you to earn college credit. No matter where or how you have learned, you can take CLEP tests. If the results are acceptable to your college, you can receive credit.

Many American institutions encourage students to take CLEP tests for credit in subjects they have mastered. People of all ages interested in pursuing a college education have reduced costs in time and money by successfully completing CLEP tests.

Colleges and universities that award such credit are listed in <u>CLEP Test Centers and other Participating Institutions</u>. Each institution decides which CLEP tests it will accept for credit and the amount of credit it will award. If you intend to take tests for credit, first consult the college you wish to attend to learn its policy on CLEP scores and its other admission requirements.

The services of the program are also available to people asked to take the tests by an employer, a professional licensing or certifying agency, or other groups that recognize college equivalency on the basis of satisfactory CLEP scores. And of course you may take the test solely for your own information.

Three states, Connecticut, New Jersey, and New York, offer external degree programs that enable individuals to earn degrees by passing examinations, including CLEP tests, and demonstrating in other ways that they have satisfied the educational requirements. No classroom attendance is required. Out-of-state as well as in-state residents are eligible.

Prospective candidates for these degree programs should write for full information, before taking the examinations, to the following addresses:

Board for State Academic Awards
340 Capitol Avenue
Hartford, Connecticut 06115

Thomas A. Edison College
Forrestal Center, Forrestal Road
Princeton, New Jersey 08540

Regents External Degrees
99 Washington Avenue
Albany, New York 12210

There are two types of examinations: the General Examinations designed to provide a comprehensive measure of undergraduate achievement in five basic areas of liberal arts (English composition, mathematics, natural sciences, humanities, social sciences-history) and the Subject Examinations designed to measure achievement in specified undergraduate courses (Afro-American history; American government; American history; American literature; analysis and interpretation of literature; anatomy, physiology, microbiology; behavioral sciences for nurses; biology; calculus with analytic geometry; clinical chemistry; college algebra; college algebra-trigonometry; college composition; college French - levels 1 and 2; college German - levels 1 and 2; college Spanish - levels 1 and 2; computers and data processing; dental materials (available May 1977); educational psychology; elementary computer programming-Fortran IV; English literature; freshman English; fundamentals of nursing; general chemistry; general psychology; head, neck, and oral anatomy; hematology; history of American education; human growth and development; immunohematology and blood banking; introduction to business management; introductory accounting; introductory business law; introductory macroeconomics; introductory microeconomics; introductory micro- and macroeconomics; introductory marketing; introductory sociology; medical-surgical nursing; microbiology; money and banking; oral radiography; statistics; tests and measurements; tooth morphology and functioning; trigonometry; Western civilization).

CLEP is a program of the College Entrance Examination Board, administered with the help of Educational Testing Service. The Program has been supported by grants from the Carnegie Corporation of New York and the National Institutes of Health. More than 1,700 colleges and universities have agreed to award credit to candidates submitting CLEP scores.

The examinations are given at test centers during the third week of each month. Candidates should register for them three weeks before the test date. More than 1,000 test centers are located on college and university campuses throughout the country. Information concerning the establishment of test centers is available to institutions through the College Board regional offices.

The fee at the test centers for one examination is $20; for two, $30; for three to five, $40.

Publications about the College-Level Examination Program are available on request to individual candidates wishing to take the examinations and to institutions wishing to participate in the Program. CLEP May Be for You describes generally how the Program works and what each examination consists of. The CLEP registration packet has two parts: CLEP Registration Guide and CLEP Test Centers and Other Participating Institutions. CLEP General and Subject Examinations ($1) gives detailed information about the examinations themselves; and What Your Scores Mean gives information to individuals who have taken the tests. CLEP Scores: Interpretation and Use ($2.50), available to faculty and administrators only, is a detailed evaluation of General and Subject Examination scores. To order publications write to: College Board Publication Orders, Box 2815, Princeton, New Jersey 08540.

SUBJECT TESTS
COLLEGE-LEVEL EXAMINATION PROGRAM

The College-Level Examination Program (CLEP) provides an opportunity for both traditional and nontraditional students to obtain college credit by examination. Anyone may take the CLEP Subject tests to demonstrate college-level competency, no matter where or how this knowledge was acquired: through formal study and training, private reading, employment or on the job training, noncredit courses, TV/radio/cassette courses, or advanced work in regular high school courses. Nearly 2000 American colleges and universities honor CLEP test scores for credit. The CLEP Subject Examinations, now available in 47 subjects, measure achievement in specific college-level courses and can be used to grant exemption from and/or credit for these courses. The CLEP Examinations are not based on particular syllabus, but a collection of principles, concepts, relationships and applications of course material. The Subject Examinations contain questions of varying difficulty and an individual does not need to be able to answer, or even attempt, every question in order to demonstrate competence in the subject. Each Subject Examination is a 90-minute multiple-choice objective test. Most Subject Examinations include a separate 90-minute essay section, which some colleges and universities require as part of their validating process for awarding credit. These essays are sent, for faculty grading, to the institutions to which candidates submit their scores.

The 47 College-Level Subject Examinations now offered are comparable to the final, or end-of-course, examinations in particular undergraduate courses. A student who has completed one of these courses successfully in college can probably earn satisfactory scores on the corresponding CLEP Subject Examination. So can the person who has learned the subject in some other way, such as by independent study.

The Subject Examinations are given in the following subjects:

Business:
Computers and Data Processing
Elementary Computer Programming - FORTRAN IV
Introduction to Business Management
Introductory Accounting
Introductory Business Law
Introductory Marketing
Money and Banking

Dental Auxiliary Education:
Dental Materials
Head, Neck, and Oral Anatomy
Tooth Morphology and Function
Oral Radiography

Education:
Educational Psychology
History of American Education
Human Growth and Development
Tests and Measurements

Humanities:
American Literature
Analysis and Interpretation of Literature
College Composition
College French - Levels 1 and 2
College German - Levels 1 and 2
College Spanish - Levels 1 and 2
English Literature
Freshman English

Mathematics:
Calculus with Analytic Geometry
College Algebra
College Algebra - Trigonometry
Statistics
Trigonometry

Medical Technology:
Clinical Chemistry
Hematology
Immunohematology and Blood Banking
Microbiology

Nursing:
Anatomy, Physiology, Microbiology
Behavioral Sciences for Nurses
Fundamentals of Nursing
Medical - Surgical Nursing

Sciences:
Biology
General Chemistry

Social Sciences:
Afro-American History
American Government
American History
General Psychology
Introductory Macroeconomics
Introductory Micro- and Macroeconomics
Introductory Sociology
Western Civilization

Each Subject Examination is made up of multiple-choice questions and has a time limit of 90 minutes. In addition, each examination, except the ones in nursing, college algebra and trigonometry, and modern language, has an optional 90-minute essay section which is ordinarily taken only if it is required by a college from which you are seeking credit. The essay section is based, as a rule, on the same subject matter and objectives as the multiple-choice examination.

It is not necessary to answer all the CLEP questions on a test correctly in order to get an acceptable or even a high score.

Colleges that use the College-Level Examinations differ greatly from one another in the scores they designate as passing and the total amount of credit they allow.

A person taking an examination may have his scores sent only to himself if he wishes. He can have them sent to someone else if he so decides.

The examination may be repeated once within a 12-month period under certain conditions. A request for permission to do so, accompanied by a Registration Form, must be sent to the College Board at least four weeks in advance of the new test date. The Subject Examinations after six months. Written permission to repeat a test must be received by the test taker from the College Board before the new test date. Scores on tests repeated without advance authorization will be canceled and test fees forfeited.

The College-Level Examinations are given during the third week of each month at more than 1,000 CLEP centers in the United States.

Each CLEP Subject Examination yields a total score reported on a 20 to 80 scale. In addition to total scores, some Subject Examinations provide subscores on the same scale of 20 to 80. A score or subscore acquires meaning when it is related to the performance of others who took the same test. The CLEP Subject score itself does not say whether one has passed or failed; it can provide for a fair comparison between one candidate and another or between one student and a group of students, e.g. percentile ranks for total scores of students who took subject examinations at the end of a college course in the subject, or how total scores or subscores compare with final grades earned in corresponding college courses. Further information about CLEP scores is given in "What Your Scores Mean," a booklet sent with each score report.

Candidates should understand that the College Board provides only the CLEP examinations. The colleges and their faculty determine what degree credit will be awarded for the score(s). Post-secondary institutions usually will have developed explicit policies of credit-by-examination which match the various tests with specific courses or area requirements and establish cutting scores that are reasonable in terms of their enrolled students.

The American Council on Education's Commission on Educational Credit has recommmended that the minimum score required for credit for Subject Examinations be the average score of students in the norming group who earned a grade of C in the comparible college subject. Usually the Development Committee, college faculty members who designed the Subject Examinations, determine the amount of credit to be given for satisfactory performance on the tests. In terms of typical course length, the semester credit, e.g. 3 semester credits, is given in the description for each Subject Examination.

The preceding information of the CLEP examinations are intended to tell you what examinations are being offered at this time and give you some idea of what they are like.

Perhaps you found one or more that you are ready to take right now, and you want to know how to register.

Maybe you found one or more that you might be ready to take, but you're not sure, so you want more information about them.

Perhaps you are ready for one or more of the examinations, but first you want to know more about when and where they are given, or about colleges that give credit for them.

Your next step is the same, no matter which of these statements fits you. It is to study the printed information that CLEP has prepared for the person who reads this booklet and wants to know more. In includes:

CLEP General and Subject Examinations: Descriptions and Sample Questions. This booklet discusses the objectives of the program and gives specific descriptions of, and sample questions from each of the General and Subject Examinations. ($1 per copy)

Registration Information Material. This consists of a booklet, Test Centers and Other Participating Institutions, and a leaflet, CLEP Registration Guide, which includes a registration form. (Free)

Public libraries are supplied with these items, too, for the convenience of their readers.

College Placement and Credit by Examination, 1975 lists the Advanced Placement and College-Level Examination Program policies of more than 1,600 colleges throughout the country.* Each entry gives the name of the college and the lowest Advanced Placement Examination grades and CLEP scores the college will normally accept for advanced placement or credit, or both, in each of the Advanced Placement and CLEP subjects, and the use of these examinations toward immediate sophomore standing. Also listed is the name of the person at each college to whom inquiries may be directed. ($3.50 per copy)

A final word to help you decide. It is natural to be hesitant, but remember that the program works, the savings in time and money can be substantial, and you are only deciding to learn more if you send for the materials. After you study them there is a bigger decision: should you take CLEP tests? You alone can decide that, but thousands of men and women who have tried have been rewarded.

CLEP PUBLICATIONS**

Item Number	Title	Price
2006324	CLEP General and Subject Examinations: Descriptions and Sample Questions	$1.00
2181827	CLEP Registration Guide	free
2181800	CLEP Test Centers and Other Participating Institutions	free
239460X	The College Handbook	$6.95
2181584	College Placement and Credit by Examination, 1975	$3.50
2386585	How to Decide: A Guide for Women	$5.95
2198509	I Can Be Anything (paperbound)	$4.50
2179423	Student Expenses at Postsecondary Institutions, 1976-77	$2.50

* 1977 publications is planned for Fall 1977.
**Order from College Board Publication Orders, Box 2815, Princeton, New Jersey 08540.

ADVANCED PLACEMENT PROGRAM
COLLEGE ENTRANCE EXAMINATION BOARD

A program of college-level courses and exams for secondary school students. Over 90 percent of the nation's colleges that most AP candidates attend give credit and/or advanced placement ot students whose AP examination grades are considered acceptable.

The courses offered in the AP Program are:

- English
- American History
- European History
- Calculus (two courses)
- Biology
- Chemistry
- Physics (three courses)
- Music
- Studio Art
- History Art
- Classics (two courses)
- French Language
- French Literature
- German Literature
- Spanish Language
- Spanish Literature

Individual "Course Description: booklets describing the essential content of each course are prepared by committees of college professors and AP teachers. These booklets also contain sample exam questions.

About 15 percent of the nation's 21,000 secondary schools have college-level AP course work, and they offer only those AP classes most appropriate for their college preparatory students; the average is three or four courses.

An "AP course" is a special college-level learning experience that most often takes a full academic year. It can take the form of an honors class, a strong regular course, a tutorial, or independent study. It is usually challenging and thought-provoking and--compared to other high school courses--it often takes more time, requires more work, gives greater opportunity for individual progress and accomplishment, goes into greater depth, and is more stimulating.

In a study of 400 former AP students interviewed at their colleges, more than 90 percent ranked their AP experiences as the most valuable of their high school studies As one student said: "I wasn't just learning facts and more facts...he (the AP teacher) taught us the tools and techniques of scholarship so you could see what facts you need and how to get them...." To get your own idea, ask other students about their experiences with AP.

AP Exams, like Art, contain both multiple-choice questions and free-response questions that require essay writing, problem solving, and so forth. In History of Art there are only essay questions - some based on projected color slides - and there is an option between an essay based on a required text and an individual study. In Studio Art there is no exam; rather, students submit portfolios of their work. Tape recordings are used with certain portions of the Music and foreign language exams.

Most of the examinations are three hours long, but some take only an hour and a half or two hours. They are given every year in the third week of May, at your school or one nearby.

The best way to describe the exams is "tough but fair." Each one is carefully developed to match the AP course description by a committee of examiners made up of college professors and AP teachers who specialize in that field. It ordinarily takes between one and two years to develop a single AP Examination.

The multiple-choice answer sheets are scored by special scoring equipment. The essays are evaluated by more than 550 carefully selected professors and AP teachers who spend a week each June grading answers in the more than 100,000 essay booklets. No matter how many answers there may be in a booklet, each is graded by a different person who has been especially trained to assess this question; the typical booklet is evaluated by four professors and teachers. No grader ever knows the scores given by another grader.

Every examination receives an overall grade on a five-point scale; 5 (extremely well qualified), 4 (well qualified), 3 (qualified), 2 (possibly qualified), and 1 (no recommendation). An AP Grade Report is sent in early July to each student at his or her home address, school, and if the student requested it, to his or her college.

Each college decides what AP Examination grades it will accept for credit and/or advanced placement. The great majority of colleges and universities accept grades of 3 and above, and there are quite a few that will consider grades of 2. If you wish to know what AP grades are considered acceptable by the colleges you are interested in, write to the Director of Admission of the college or ask your AP Coordinator to let you see the latest edition of College Placement and Credit Examination.

More than 90,000 students take the AP Exams each year, and while the percentages vary from subject to subject, a rough breakdown of the grades received is as follows:

93 percent of AP students get a grade of 2 or higher
71 percent of AP students get a grade of 3 or higher
33 percent of AP students get a grade of 4 or higher
13 percent of AP students get a grade of 5

To obtain a score comparable to a grade of 3 on the multiple-choice section of the typical exam, a student needs to answer about half the questions correctly. Of course, he or she also must do acceptable work on the broader questions in the free-response section to get a grade of 3 or higher.

The fee is $32 for each exam taken. (A limited number of fee reductions that reduce the cost to as little as $15 per exam are available to students with financial need.)

Advanced placement means that in college you can avoid the boredom of repeating work you've already done. You can also take advanced courses in your AP subject, explore other subjects that interest you, and join honors and other special programs. If you earn the required grade on an AP Exam, you may receive the equivalent of 6-8 semester hours or 10-12 quarter hours of credit, probably worth between $300 and $600. If you're granted a full year of college credit, the savings could be anywhere from $2,500 to $6,000.

Some of the most selective colleges are among the approximately 400 institutions that consider acceptable grades on three or more AP Exams as evidence that the student has done work comparable to a year's academic program at college. More than 6,000 AP students are potentially eligible for sophomore standing each year.

Studies undertaken by individual colleges have shown repeatedly that AP students who take advanced courses in their first year of college do as well as or better than upperclassmen. Most AP students do extremely well throughout their college careers, and a good number graduate with honors.

It's unlikely that an AP course or an AP Exam could work against you - regardless of the grade you get in either - for the following reasons:

At many secondary schools the grades received in AP courses are weighted to reflect the quality of work undertaken; for example, a "B" in an AP or honors course counts for more in a student's grade point average than the same grade in a regular course.

Even if no adjustment is made to a grade, college admissions officials know the value of AP-level work and judge students accordingly.

Remember, too, that if you take an AP Exam, your AP Grade Report is usually sent to a college after you are admitted, and only if you request it. Even so, it is improbable that you would be disadvantaged by having any AP grade, no matter how low, reported to the college you plan to attend.

Finally, it is generally to your benefit to submit all evidence of your college-level work to the colleges you're interested in.

While several studies show that AP Exams are the most generally accepted college-level examinations, they are not the only good tests around. Certain colleges have their own placement tests, and the College-Level Examination Program (CLEP) of the College Board offers a number of tests, many covering subjects not included in AP.

AP Exams differ from these others tests in two major ways: (1) They are based on the content of specific courses, and (2) they offer essay components that are graded under controlled conditions. Further, AP Examination grades are nationally recognized and are, therefore, widely transferable among institutions.

If you decide to explore alternatives to the AP Exams, the first thing to do is ask the colleges you're interested in about their placement and credit-by-examination policies. (Your counselor or AP Coordinator can give you an idea of the kinds of questions to ask.) After you have the facts, compare the various options and choose the one that offers the best credit and placement opportunities. Whatever test you choose, you should plan to take it as close to the end of your course as possible. Remember, however, that you have only one chance at the AP Exams each year.

Talk to your principal, department chairman, teacher, counselor, AP Coordinator - whoever knows about AP at your school. He or she can fill you in on the AP Program and help you decide which AP courses may be for you. It's a good idea to plan ahead - even in the ninth or tenth grade - so you will have the appropriate background courses for the AP experience in your junior or senior year. You don't have to take an AP course to be able to take an AP Exam, but - however you prepare - you should be sure your study fits the appropriate AP course description.

If you want further information about AP, request a free copy of the <u>Guide to the Advanced Placement Program</u> from: College Board, Publication Orders, Box 2815, Princeton, New Jersey 08540.

AP/CLEP ENGLISH EXAMINATION

The College Entrance Examination Board (CEEB) offers a number of examinations in literature; this book deals with CLEP Subject Examination in Analysis and Interpretation of Literature and the Advanced Placement Examination in English. These CEEB tests are useful in helping colleges respond to the widely varied backgrounds of entering students. The CLEP-AP Literature Examinations provide a means of assessing students' academic achievement so that they can be placed appropriately in a college course or can receive credit for having already acquired learning equivalent to that usually gained through the regular campus curriculum.

ANALYSIS AND INTERPRETATION OF LITERATURE EXAMINATION

The CLEP Examination in Analysis and Interpretation of Literature measures how well a student has met the objectives of a one-year undergraduate course (or its equivalent) in literature. It is not a test of information about specific works, although it is based on the assumption that you have read perceptively poems, plays, essays, and works of prose fiction. There are other subject CLEP tests in American and English literature.

The test includes approximately 100 multiple-choice questions and has a time limit of 90 minutes. All the questions are based on passages supplied in the test, and the passages have been so selected that no previous experience with them or knowledge of their background is required to answer the questions. The passages reflect nineteenth- and twentieth-century American literature and each of the major periods of English literature from the Renaissance to the present.

There are on the average 20 passages (poetry, prose and drama) of varying lengths, each accompanied by a set of multiple-choice questions. Many sets contain approximately 5 questions, but some have as few as 2 or as many as 10. English literature is emphasized (67 per cent) but almost one-third of the questions are based on passages from American literature. Approximately three per cent of the test deals with world literature. The specific chronology of this CLEP subject is:

18th and 19 Centuries	40%
20th Century	30%
Renaissance & 17th Cent.	25%
Classical and Pre-Renaissance	3%

Approximately 40 per cent of the questions are poetry analysis, 40 per cent prose analysis (of both narrative and critical writing), and 20 per cent analysis of passages from plays.

The examination tests the student's ability to read prose and poetry with understanding. You will be expected to analyze the elements of a literary passage and to respond to nuances of meaning, tone, mood, imagery, and style. Therefore, the most relevant preparation that one can bring to this examination is the habit of attentive and reflective reading of the various literary forms. The only formal knowledge required is familiarity with the basic terminology used to discuss literary texts, such as terms that describe verse forms or figures of speech that contribute to the meaning and effectiveness of prose and poetry.

This CLEP test explores one's ability to read and understand works of literature and to demonstrate a knowledge of the means by which literary effects are achieved. Thus, there are questions that test not only comprehension and understanding of paraphrase but also ability to interpret metaphors, to recognize rhetorical and stylistic devices, to perceive relationships between parts and wholes, and to grasp the speaker's or author's attitudes.

This test is designed to be fair to people who have been prepared in different ways or have taken courses at different colleges, it is not expected that everyone taking the test will be able to answer every question. For example, at the conclusion of appropriate courses at 17 colleges, the typical "A" student (scaled score: 61) on the average answered approximately 66 per cent of the questions correctly, while the typical "C" student (scaled score: 49) answered approximately 51 per cent correctly.

The optional essay section allows the students the opportunity to demonstrate the ability to write well-organized critical essays on given passages of poetry and on general literary questions. Students are asked to write two essays, the first analyzing a poem supplied in the test book and the second discussing a particular technique in relation to a novel, story, or play of their choosing. Any student may elect to take the essay section; some institutions require the student to take it. The student's essays are sent directly to the college or university to which the students submit their scores and are graded by the faculty of that institution according to their own standards.

Although the evaluation of the responses will take into account many things, generally speaking, the emphasis will be on the following: the quality of the writing (organization, sentence structure, diction, clarity, and general effectiveness), the relevance of illustrations to the questions asked, and the critical perception that the answers demonstrate. In the answers, it is expected that there will be a discussion of the works of recognized literary merit and to avoid vague generalities, irrelevant philosophizing, and unnecessary plot summaries.

The CLEP Subject Examination in Analysis and Interpretation of Literature was designed to aid in awarding credit by examination and cover a full academic year of course work (the equivalent of six semester hours of credit). The amount of credit actually awarded to an individual student is determined by the institution that is granting the credit after it determines which of its courses parallels the material covered on the test.

The Commission on Educational Credit of the American Council on Education recommends that college-level credit be awarded to all students who earn a score at or above the mean score achieved by students in the national norms sample who earned a grade of C in a regular college course in the subject. For the Analysis and Interpretation of Literature test, the average (mean) score would be 49; scale used for reporting is 20-80. Each college or university will establish its own policies based on their campus norms.

AP EXAMINATION IN ENGLISH

The Advanced Placement program is organized around the fact that many young people can, with profit and delight, complete college-level studies in their secondary schools, and represents a desire of schools and colleges to foster such experiences. Advanced Placement serves those students who wish to go ahead with college-level studies while still in secondary school, the schools that desire to offer these students the opportunity to do so, and the colleges that wish to encourage and recognize such achievement. It does this by providing practical descriptions of college-level courses to interested schools and the results of examinations based on these courses to the colleges of the students' choice. Participating institutions, in turn, grant credit and appropriate placement, or one of these, to students who have done well on the examinations. The Advanced Placement program is an important way to promote educational opportunities by effectively relating college-level courses at thousands of schools to appropriate credit and placement at the colleges that the students eventually attend.

This College Board test assumes the students' deliberate preparation in college-level work in English. In addition to being skilled in reading literature, students should be able to write critical and, on occasion, creative essays related to literary topics. Although many students qualify for the examination by taking one or more years of Advanced Placement or honors English courses, a number of successful students have prepared independently. The guide for the course work and for the examination is the course description published annually by the Advanced Placement Program, which also provides the booklet Beginning an AP English Course. (See list of publications.)

All the questions in the multiple-choice section are based on passages of poetry, drama or prose provided in the examination. The passages are usually drawn from English and American literature from the Renaissance to the present. The 60-minute multiple-choice section contains sets of questions based on approximately 4 passages, usually 3 free-response questions.

In addition, there is a required essay section which is centrally graded by secondary school and college English teachers according to scoring guidelines established by the Chief Reader and the Development Committee for AP English. (The booklet Grading The AP English Examination explains how the examination is read.) The AP exam, therefore, tests not only students' ability to analyze passages of literature, but also the ability to write critically about their own reading.

The AP test is designed for placement/exemption/credit. Because preparation for the examination involves work equivalent to that of full-year introductory college courses in composition and in literature, the Development Committee for AP English recommends that colleges consider awarding qualified candidates units of credit commensurate with that achievement and admitting them to appropriately advanced courses in literature. The candidates' composite score--multiple-choice plus essay--is reported as a grade of 1 (low) to 5 (high), with credit recommended for grades of 3, 4, and 5.

AP and CLEP questions that measure skills in analyzing and interpreting literature cover areas such as understanding figurative language and its effects; recognizing allusions; discerning syntactical relationships; grasping the meaning of words in particular contexts; paraphrasing difficult lines or sentences; perceiving structure and organization; summarizing; making inferences and recognizing implications; identifying tone, attitude, and point of view; understanding the effect of using particular words, phrases, structures, or rhetorical devices. These questions are generally in sets based on passages supplied in the text.

The AP English Examination, and the CLEP Analysis and Interpretation of Literature Examination primarily assess skills; only a few of their multiple-choice questions might require students to demonstrate knowledge of specific authors, styles, or periods.

College Board examinations in literature can be viewed in two ways: those emphasizing specific points of information and familiarity with major works of literature (CLEP Subject Examinations in English Literature and American Literature) and those emphasizing the skills of analyzing and interpreting selections from literary works (AP English and CLEP Analysis and Interpretation of Literature).

The AP and CLEP examinations assume that students have done college-level work and does attempt to determine whether they deserve exemption or credit and are usually taken by choice to gain credit or exemption. AP differs from CLEP in that it is designed specifically for secondary school students. It provides a course description as a guide for teachers and students and bases the examination on the skills students are expected to have developed in such a course. AP aids students by encouraging schools to offer advanced programs and by providing students with the opportunity to demonstrate that they have done college-level work. CLEP, on the other hand, is not related to a high school curriculum; rather, it attempts to cover those areas of college-level work that are common to a variety of institutions and that students might reasonably be expected to have mastered, through independent study or work experience, school classes, or other nontraditional means. Students of all ages can, and do, take the CLEP examinations; the program was developed for adult learners as well as for more traditional students.

AP and CLEP examinations assume a familiarity with terminology, although neither examination relies heavily on such knowledge, i.e., "speaker," "tone," and "image" type questions.

The AP English Examination, for example, often includes long and complex passages and has a large number of questions on them. The CLEP Analysis and Interpretation of Literature Examination sometimes uses passages drawn from literary criticism or passages that rely on some familiarity with literary background; such passages would probably not be selected for either of the other examinations.

Another important difference is that only the Advanced Placement English Examination requires students to write essays. Therefore, it measures both how well students can read literature and how well they can write about it, drawing on their own reading. The writing requirement necessitates special student preparation. This emphasis on writing makes preparation for the examination equivalent to introductory college courses in composition as well as in literature.

Substantial overlap in content and in method exists between the multiple-choice sections of the AP and the CLEP examinations. But, although a particular multiple-choice question or set of questions from one of these examinations might fit another examination equally well, no one of the examinations is completely comparable to any of the others in terms of content, difficulty, or potential use.

It is significant to understand the knowledge and abilities tests in either the CLEP or AP English Examinations. These examinations use two distinctive kinds of questions: those that test a knowledge of literature and those that test skills of analyzing literature (poetry, prose and drama). CEEB questions that measure the extent of knowledge cover areas such as literary background; content of major works; chronology; identification of authors, periods, and styles; metrical patterns; literary reference and a number of other types of discrete points of literature.

An Advanced Placement course requires the study and practice of writing. You will learn to respond to language with sensitivity and discrimination, and to develop the ability to write in various forms. Through speaking, listening, and reading, but chiefly through the experience of their own writing, you will become more aware of the resources of language: connotation, metaphor, irony, syntax, and tone. You should learn to identify characteristic forms of discourse and the assumptions underlying rhetorical strategies.

Your writing assignments might include practice in exposition, argument, critical analysis, personal narrative, and fictional or poetic forms. Speaking and writing about many experiences (not only those of literature) should develop the students' sense of the relationships among style, subject, and audience. The desired goals are the honest, concise, and effective use of language, and the organization of ideas in a clear, coherent, and persuasive way.

In your Advanced Placement course in English, you should be engaged in perceptive reading and critical analysis of literature. They study the individual work: its language, characters, action, and themes. They consider its structure, meaning, and value. They may consider its relationship to contemporary experience as well as to the times in which it was written.

You should study intensively a few representative works from several genres and periods. Advanced Placement courses do concentrate on the study of challenging works of recognized literary merit, worthy of careful scrutiny, and should avoid the shallow and faddish. Most of the assigned reading should be in texts originally written in English, though reading in translations can be helpful.

Remember--the CEEB Committee of Examiners for English prepares a three-hour examination that gives students the opportunity to demonstrate their mastery of the competencies described above. Like other nationally administered tests used to make decisions regarding advanced placement and credit, the Advanced Placement Examination in English employs multiple-choice questions that test the student's reading of selected passages. But the Advanced Placement Examination is unique in certain respects. It is the only national college-level test that requires writing as a direct measure of the student's ability to read and interpret literature and to use other forms of discourse effectively. The free-response essay part of the examination is scored by college and Advanced Placement English teachers. Although the skills tested in the examination remain essentially the same from year to year, each year's examination is comprised of new questions.

FURTHER INFORMATION

More detailed descriptions of each of these examinations, some with sample questions, can be found in the following:

<u>About the Achievement Tests.</u> Free. 205328
<u>Advanced Placement English Course Description</u>. $1 per copy. 2013061
<u>Beginning an Advanced Placement English Course</u>. Free. 2089297
<u>Grading the Advanced Placement English Examination</u>. Free. 2354233
<u>CLEP General and Subject Examinations</u>. $1 per copy. 2006324
<u>Testing Academic Achievement</u>. Free. 2090694

Copies of these publications may be obtained by writing to:

College Board Publication Orders
Box 2815
Princeton, New Jersey 08540

SAMPLE AP EXAMINATION
FREE-RESPONSE ANSWERS

The 1973 AP Section II Test of three questions and five selected student responses (actual answers) is presented below without reference to the students' actual grades. The grades ranged from 0 to 5 in the sample responses. AP candidates should test themselves. AP teachers will have a copy of the actual test questions in his/her files.

Question 1 (Suggested time - 45 minutes)

The 1973 Section II, Question 1, contained a prose passage which had certain details, structures, ideas and attitudes about Coketown. Write an essay in which you develop or explain how the author's presentation of details helps the reader to understand the prose selection, i.e., Coketown and the caves. In your essay specific thought should be devoted to the diction, phrasing, imagery and like items in the passage. Your essay should also include the second passage on the caves.

Response (1):

In order for the author to express his attitude successfully, he must write in a manner to bring his point across. Coketown and the caves reveal the author's attitude through innumerable descriptions, appropriate word use, abstract and concrete images, and drawn-out sentences. This all goes to further the author's point of view of sameness, commonplace and dull.

Both authors stress the identical qualities of people, things, and caves in both passages by continually repeating that everything is the same, by using the same words such as "fact." They use images as "the piston of the steam-engine worked monotonously up and down" and "The two flames approached and strive to unite, but cannot because one of them breathes air, the other stone," through which the reader can get a true picture of what the author is trying to convey. To make sure he has got his point across, the author uses as many adjectives as he can dig up to describe what he sees.

Description has its greatest effect when the right words are chosen. The words "black," "dark," and "dull" relate to the author's feelings of the dreary places where these passages are situated. These word choices can illustrate the image the author is trying to get across.

Imagery is the tool the author uses to give the reader a comparision to go by. A phrase like "interminable serpents of smoke trailed themselves forever and ever" gives the impression of the situation being unstoppable, which is exactly what the author is trying to convey. Images as the two flames approach suggest only meaningless relationships can be found in these caves.

Finally, as the clincher, the author uses long drawn out sentences which tend to bore the reader adding to the detestability of these places.

The most important factor in the success of the author to get his attitude across is the fact that rather than using just one literary device, he uses many to be sure that his point is firmly entrenched in our minds.

Response (2):

The two excerpts included are very good examples of how a reader's attitude toward that which the author is describing can be detected through his choice of words, use of imagery, phrasing, and sentence structure.

It is obvious that both the caves and Coketown are ordinary places without exceptional qualities. The caves can be seen once of twenty-four times and a difference won't be found from the first to the last. If you've seen one house in Coketown, you've seen them all, and if you have met one citizen, you have met them all. The writings don't stop here, however. Though the two authors are writing about basic places, their feelings toward these places are different. By simply studying the word usage one may conclude that the author's, then the reader's attitudes differ. Within the passage on caves, the author makes use of words like marvelous, radiance, smooth, windless -- all words which show approval on the author's part. Yet when Coketown is being described only words like severe, black, ill-smelling, and serpents surface. We can readily assume that this reader obtains an unfavorable attitude relative to this town.

The difference in attitude doesn't end here. The use of imagery in the prose passages is another point through which the reader may sense the optimistic or pessimistic views of the author. The image of the flame rising from within the stone walls of the cave is written so as to convey the author's true love for these dark chambers. The flame from the match touches that of the wall, they kiss, then expire -- this iamge of love and beauty is in great contrast to the images found in the passage on Coketown. One is presented with an image of pious warehouses of brick when the author is speaking about the churches. We are also presented with the image of a sick elephant in relation to the steam-engines. It is very obvious that these harsh images express the author's negative feelings toward Coketown in comparison to the positive reaction of the author writing about the caves.

There are yet two other elements present in these writings which further shape the author's attitude and in turn mold the reader's feelings. As one reads the two passages, a sharp difference in phrasing and sentence structure is apparent. The caves are described with a descriptive, yet moving manner; the reader is not overwhelmed with this type of phrasing. I feel that a harsh attitude is reinforced through the violent phrasing in the Coketown passage. The sentences seem to run on and on with harsh descriptions.

The final difference in sentence structure is readily noticeable. The caves are described in brief, yet informative sentences while Coketown contains several sentences of over fifty words. The colons, semi-colons, and commas are a bit overly used and so the reader becomes a bit aggravated with their length. Short, concise descriptions keep the action moving and provide the reader with a more positive attitude than that type of description used in the writing about Coketown.

The two articles, caves and Coketown, are excellent examples of how an author can make use of imagery, words, phrasing, and sentence structure to develop specific attitudes in the reader.

Response (3):

In the first passage, the caves are physically described as being "eight feet long, five feet high, and three feet wide." This is the extent of detail that the author presents. It is implied that there is little or no distinctive qualities between any two caves; that having seen one cave, one has seen them all. Choice words such as distinguishes, interesting, and extraordinary are used to achieve this feeling of commonplace, of uniformity, which makes a visit to these caves a most uninteresting experience. In much the same way, the author of Coketown uses choice words in his description to express the idea of total conformity and lack of innovation. Repetition of key words such as red brick, material, and most particularly fact places emphasis upon the lesser aspects of this town, its inability to accept change, its partisan thinking, its biased way of living. Here there can be no hope of change; conformity is an institution held in the utmost esteem, from which there can be no deviation. Imagery is utilized to more closely attract the reader's attention to the depravity of the situation that exists here, as the "interminable serpents of smoke trailed themselves forever and ever." Coketown is not merely one solitary place; it is a state of mind that can be adopted by any city, town, or individual that may choose to live there. In each passage, therefore, the author harnesses his words, makes them work for him, to achieve his wanted effect and to shape the reader's attitude towards the place he describes.

Response (4):

In describing their respective topics, both authors employ similar styles which favorably lend to the descriptions. The authors begin each paragraph with a general statement dealing with their subject. The author of the caves passage uses very blunt sentences and goes into great detail from that point on. This is also true of the Coketown passage. That author states a major idea and then takes a paragraph to follow the idea with details. This sentence structure, therefore, leads the reader on to the details in a very orderly progression.

Word choice also lends to the effectiveness of the passages. The words "tunnel" and "circular chamber" give the reader a clear idea of the caves. The idea that the experience can't be decided on to be interesting or dull puts the idea across even further.

The Coketown passage is overflowing with adjectives. "Red brick," "purple river," and a "stuccoed edifice" are a few examples, making the imagination work hard. Using colors, the authors convey a similar atmosphere - dark and alike in the caves and drab and monotonous in Coketown.

Imagery is very abundant in the passages, revealing the author's tone. The author of the caves writes about birds proclaiming "extraordinary" to mankind. This makes it clear to the reader that this author sees something special in these caves. This is further exemplified in the image of the flame. The picture becomes very clear and the reader can feel the author's excitement in these strange "circular chambers."

Just as a feeling of excitement comes from the first passage, monotony stems out of the second's imagery. The serpent smoke winding forever, the mad elephant-piston, and the bell in a birdcage leave the reader feeling bored and uninterested, just as the author intends. His long chains of phrase after phrase also lend to this feeling.

Using these devices, in similar manners, the first author has conveyed a positive, enjoyable attitude and the second author a deflated, bored feeling.

Response (5):

In the two passages, the authors' usage of specific details establishes a definite conception in the reader's mind of the fundamental natures of Coketown and the caves. Examination of the authors' methods of presentation of those details brings to light a number of common factors. The author of the first passage describes the caves as an essentially dull natural phenomenon, in the first paragraph. Coketown, in the second passage, assumes much the same character, and that character is developed in a similar way to the caves.

In order to establish that dull tone, the authors very carefully selected words which would best convey that attitude. Thus, in the first passage's first sentence, the use of the word "readily" immediately indicates to the reader that the caves are not extraordinary. The author of the second passage also promotes an initial feeling about the town when he notes that "it had no greater taint of fancy in it than Mrs. Gradgrind..." The use of "taint" with regard to "fancy" implies that "fancy" is an undesirable attribute as far as Mrs. Gradgrind is concerned, and that its use also adds an ironic touch to both the lady and the town.

After their initial comments, both authors proceed to graphically describe their subjects. The author of the first passage resorts to an exacting account of the dimensions of a cave and thus substantiates his claim that the caves can be "readily described." He then immediately applies that dimensional description to all the Marabar Caves and thus shows the underlying significance of his initial observation; he demonstrates that the caves are dull in that they are all the same.

The author of the second passage also uses graphic description in order to manifest to the reader that the town is purely functional, cold and dirty, and that everyone in it has little personal identity. In order to establish that attitude, the author uses images to illustrate dirt, pollution, monotony, and order. His word choice in imagery is also very important. He describes the "ill-smelling" dye and the dirty red brick buildings with words that appeal directly to the senses. He thus causes the reader to apply those images to the town and its inhabitants. In describing the steam engine, the author stresses the monotonous image with the phrase "up and down" and with the elephant image. At the same time, the elephant being "in a state of melancholy madness" provides the reader with the allusion that the humdrum nature of Coketown is much the same as madness.

Question 2 (Suggested time - 40 minutes)

There is always some concern on how, why or the way a literary work ends (or concludes). Some critics argue that all good literature must have an adequate, even a significant closure. This may not be the case. In an essay, discuss the ending of a play or novel of acknowledged literary merit. You should not write a summary of the plot. Your essay should explain how and why the "closure" is appropriate or inappropriate as the case may be.

Response (1):

In order for a novel to have a significant "closure" some questions must be answered, an idea which the author wants to generate for the reader. A book with such an ending is East of Eden by John Steinbeck.

At the end of the book we find Adam Trask dying, having been shocked with his son's death which he blames on his other son, Caleb. At this point, the reader does not know what is going to happen to Caleb, who blames himself completely. In the closing scene, Lee forces Adam to answer whether or not he forgives his son. At the last moment he whispers the word "Tishmet," meaning "you may."

This ending is addressed to everyone, that you can be what you want to be. It is these final words that the author wants to leave us with. Not only does it answer Caleb's question, but our question sometime in the future.

Response (2):

"Portrait of a Lady" by Henry James is a novel that does not merely close; the reader is given the pleasure of significant closure.

Throughout the novel, the reader follows Isabel Archer throughout her development as a functioning woman and her search for a man who will fulfill her and whom she can fulfill. Isabel is never satisfied with the men who profess faith to her -- they always have some sort of fault in her eyes. The fault, I believe, lies in Isabel. She doesn't seem capable of the love professed to her. When dear Isabel finally marries, it is to a rather poor Gilbert Osmond.

Isabel discovers that this marraige wasn't what she bargained for and at the near end of the novel one can sense that Isabel yearns to break away from her ties to Osmond and Pansy, his daughter. She even goes away, and is separated from Gilbert and all he represents, but at the conclusion, Isabel returns to him and his daughter. The mere fact that Isabel returns is a significant conclusion but even more so because the reader is left with a deep-rooted feeling of uncertainty. One begins to wonder if Isabel will ever be able to cope with the problems that will arise if she remains as Gilbert's wife. Will she be able to succumb to the monotonous life she now must lead?

There are many other reasons which make this conclusion effective. Throughout "The Portrait of a Lady," Isabel has no responsibilities and no one to look out for but herself. Up until Gilbert Osmond, Isabel's men friends gave in to her every wish and made her feel superior. But this relationship was different; Gilbert would put her in her place and not let her feel superior in any way. I believe that this was precisely what Isabel was searching for in life -- someone to tell her to do something; someone she could really look up to and admire. Making Isabel return to Gilbert at the conclusion actually helped her development.

Yet another point relative to this effective conclusion is the fact that Isabel would not have to face her duties -- her duties both to her husband and his child. Isabel could no longer exist for herself; she would have to develop a sense of obligation to others, not only to herself.

If Isabel had not returned to Gilbert, the plot of the novel would have been defeated. Isabel, somehow, had to be overcome. She was overcome by her return to Gilbert Osmond.

I feel that Henry James very appropriately concludes his novel. The reader is not only left with an effective sense of conclusion but with a further feeling of uncertainty. The hows and whys of James' concluding actions are many, yet I feel I am justified in saying that they are all elements which add to his effective conclusion.

Response (3):

In response to question 2, I choose to discuss Thomas Hardy's "Tess of the D'Urbervilles." Tess is a victim, not only of her Victorian environment, but of other people as well. Tess is an example of a very real and natural heroine, a perfect illustration of getting down to basics. Tess is victimized not only by her cruel seducer Alex, but by many others among whom are her husband Angel, morally rigid and prudish by nature, and her parents, whose shiftless qualities have Tess in a state of uncertainty and turmoil. Misused by Alec, disowned by her family, and abandoned by her husband, Tess remains strong and noble-minded, yet she is quite sadly destined to tragedy. Tess' fall is determined not only by the mistreatment and abuse she received from those she comes into contact with, but by her fate, namely, her D'Urberville lineage. It is this fate, coupled with her own supreme act of fulfillment in killing Alec, that brings about her ultimate end. Nothing could be more appropriate. Despite any feelings that one may develop for Tess throughout the book, despite any feelings of sorrow or of loss, one realizes that there could be no other end for Tess, that this is the only appropriate fini that could be expected. As the novel closes, it is said that fate has played its last with Tess. Nothing could be a more appropriate conclusion.

Response (4):

John Steinbeck's novel, "East of Eden," is a novel of development -- a Bildungsroman -- for many of the characters. These characters are all brought to suitable ends and the theme is brilliantly brought out at the conclusion of the novel.

The last scene in the book finds the characters all standing around Adam Trask's deathbed. Adam was introduced as a young man who had little self-confidence and has risen -- not without many downfalls -- to an intelligent old man who has found the secret happiness he looked for. The servant, Lee, is quitely begging Adam to forgive his son for a mistake he has made. Adam opens his eyes, embraces his son, and says one word - timshel. This word means "thou mayest" and has special significance.

The Oriental servant, Lee, once told his philosophy of life to Adam. He said that life was a choice and in the end you received what you chose. Since this choice was so important, Lee lived for his timshel and was a very peaceful man.

When Adam said this one word, his forgiveness was clear. He was telling his son that although he would be gone, the son had to choose what he felt was right for his life.

The utterance also showed that Adam was at peace with himself. He realized that he had made a few poor choices in his life, but felt that his good outweighed the evil.

This ending is very appropriate for the novel. The character's conflicts are brought to an end and the reader is confident that they are on a peaceful trail. The theme which was somewhat clear throughout the novel is once again stated, but very obviously. Timshel becomes a whole philosophy of life to remember.

John Steinbeck has brought his characters through the novel developing them as they go and has concluded with a very meaningful scene.

Response (5):

In the prologue to his book "For Whom the Bell Tolls," Ernest Hemmingway quotes John Donne in noting that "No man is an island." In simplest terms, that statement seems to fairly summarize the theme of the novel, and Hemmingway utilizes the work to discuss the fine points of that idea.

After presenting that philosophy, the author then introduces the main character, Robert Jordan, who, at the outset, is seen to be an opponent of a very broad interpretation of John Donne's observation. The reader begins to understand that Jordan is essentially an introvert who does not prescribe to Donne's philosophy. He feels that, in order to survive in the type of business in which he is, he must not allow his emotions or other convictions to interfere with his life. Jordan's indifference toward women and people in general is felt by the reader almost immediately, and Hemmingway sets about to reconcile Jordan's beliefs with the prologue's observation.

By attempting to bring those two opposing philosophies to a common ground, the author makes up the plot of the novel; and, if he succeeds in reconciling them, it seems that he will have effected a satisfactory conclusion to the work. Examination of the ending of "For Whom the Bell Tolls" demonstrates the propriety of the author's conclusion. Toward the end of the work, the reader begins to understand that Jordan loves Maria. This love represents an emotional attachment that Jordan had heretofore avoided. By recognizing in himself a need for Maria, Jordan begins to realize that his philosophy was wrong. When they finally blow the bridge, they do so with Pablo's aid, and thus Jordan must discard, or at least ignore, the cold, hard rules which would have admonished him to execute the dangerous rebel.

Jordan's eventual renunciation -- within himself -- of the street rules of war and of the rigid precepts that required him to remain emotionless, is climaxed by the last scene where he is left to die, at his own demand, by the fleeing saboteurs. This is the ultimate resolution of the novel, because Jordan is fully giving himself -- his life -- in order to save his friends. In doing so, he also realizes finally that Pablo, Pilar, Maria, and the rest all rely solely on him for their safety, and that his life is integrally bound within theirs.

Question 3 (Suggested time - 50 minutes)

Develop a dialogue on a significant issue between two characters who have incompatible points of view of the specific topic. It is important to reveal the qualities and attitudes of your characters in what they say and how them demonstrate their respective positions. The characters in the dialogue should not exchange random remarks; exchange should be sharp, have coherence, and focus on a single issue.

Response (1):

"Can we go now, Rena?"

"No, you know the wake doesn't end until nine."

"So what, these silly things serve no purpose anyway."

"Bite your tongue, think of poor Henry there. Don't you have any respect for the dead?"

"Oh, come on. How is sitting around discussing what a nice job they did on Henry, when Henry could care less."

"You know better than that, George. It's the principle."

"What principle?"

"It's the principle that all good Christians have a wake for the one they have lost."

"Now, where did you dig that one up? Ha, ha, ha!"

"Do you think you're funny? Have you ever heard the priest say that a Christian doesn't have to have a wake?"

"Have you ever heard that one had to have one?"

"Come on, let's be serious. Do you see anyone else crabbing? Anyong trying to sneak out?"

"Are you kidding? Everyone here is too chicken to leave before they're supposed to. They're all dying to get out. Ha, ha, ha!"

"How would you feel, if when you died, you had a wake and nobody showed up or if no one bothered to arrange one at all?"

"It wouldn't bother me in the least. What do I care what you do down here for me; it's just a waste of time. In fact, when I die, it will say in my will that I forbid anyone to give me a wake. Why should people waste time and money on such a foolish thing?"

"George, you know that you'd want your friends and relatives to pray for your everlasting happiness."

"Look around! Do you see anyone praying for Henry? This is just an excuse for all the old biddies to get together to exchange all the juicy gossip they've acquired over the years."

"I don't want to discuss this any further. Now, sit still and be quiet."

"Oh, alright."

"Is that Sonny Richardson and his wife?"

"Hey, Sonny, how's the kid? What have you been up to? It's a shame about poor old Henry. But they did a great job fixing him up and ... "

Response (2):

The Question of Granting Amnesty
pro - X; con - Y

X - The government is in the position to either grant amnesty or not. It is up to these officials to decide whether someone has the right to return to these United States as a free citizen or as a prisoner.

Y - Exactly, and I do hope that the White House has enough backbone to choose the proper alternative of the two - don't let them back unless they pay, and pay dearly for the wrong they have committed to you, to me, to each and every American citizen.

X - The wrong they have committed! Is it wrong to decide what you want out of life -- is it wrong to have the right to live?

Y - A man's first duty in life is to his country, his country makes him what he is; and if that country tells him to go to war whether it be in Vietnam or in New York City, there lies his obligation.

X - A man's first duty is to himself, or how else could he survive from day to day?

Y - Did you ever hear of J.F. Kennedy?

X - Why?

Y - Maybe this will sound familiar - "Ask not what your country can do for you; ask what you can do for your country."

X - Do you think dying in Vietnam is doing anything for my country? No, it's not -- all it is doing is creating more harm and hatred than before. Why should an eighteen-year-old man have to face torture when the war isn't even close to American interests. Vietnam wasn't "our" war; it was theirs -- but we had to lose so many. If a young man feels he can't face such a crisis, why should he be punished for it now? Besides, the war's over!

Y - The war's over -- nice excuse. So all those who were afraid or unwilling to face what thousands had to should be permitted to return. I say no, they should return with their tails between their legs and ready to be persecuted.

X - The army is on a volunteer basis now; the government has finally come to its senses. They realize that not everyone can cope with the trials and tribulations of war.

Y - It's volunteer now, but it wasn't when all our friends in Canada took flight. They were chickens - not men.

X - I do realize that some left the United States for reasons not totally related to the conscientious objector attitude.

Y - There were no conscientious objectors.

X - I'll disregard that and continue with what I was saying. Those who did flee without reasonable cause should probably be forced to work in hospitals and in government agencies like the Peace Corps or Vista. The time they should have spent in the service could be made up in this manner.

Y - Making beds and teaching children how to read are quite different than marching in mud up to your knees on a battlefield.

X - Alright, you have your point but I've got mine, too. Maybe the best way to solve the problem of amnesty is to have each and every case brought before the courts and be decided upon individually.

Y - Why give a break to a guy who's turned his back on "my" country.

X - But . . .

Response (3):

Miss Libby and Mr. C. Atlas have just met at a dinner party held at the Brown's. Mr. C. Atlas is a business associate of Mr. Brown (John), while Miss Libby is a close friend of Mrs. Brown (Mary). The following is a dialogue held between Miss Libby and Mr. C. Atlas.

Mr. A: Another Scotch and soda, Miss, Miss, pardon me, but what was your name again?

Ms. L: Libby, Ms. Gloria Libby.

Mr. A: Ah, yes, I remember you had pronounced Miss as Ms. before; its quite charming how you do that, you know.

Ms. L: What wit, Mr. Atlas! Surely you know the difference between Ms. and Miss.

Mr. A: Oh, of course, my dear. Ms. stands for all that Fem Lib nonsense. I've known that for years, every since all that foolishness began. Forgive me for confusing it so, my dear.

Ms. L: Just what do you mean by foolishness, MR. ATLAS; you see, I ...
Mr. A: Oh, you know, all those crazy women running around, leading protest marches, demanding equal rights with men, all so foolish; why half of them are just love-starved idiots looking to be recognized, and where does it get them -- nowhere, I tell you. Why I ...
Ms. L: Now just a minute, Mr. C. Atlas, I happen to be one of those love-starved, no, I mean one of those women who stands for equality, who's willing to work for what she believes in, in battles against such chauvinistic hash as you speak now!
Mr. A: I speak only what is right; woman is the lesser of the two sexes, her role is to be submissive and receptive to the male's wants and desires.
Ms. L: Pig! Chauvanistic degenerate! Why I have more potential, more stamina in my little finger than you have in your entire body. Look at you, a fine example of the 9-5 blob. Tweed suit, pencils in your pocket, gold lighter, shined shoes, ha! And what for, to live a life that is shallow, empty, and unfulfilled, while you condemn and exploit any woman's efforts to make a better place for herself in this world. Go, get out of my signt, Mr. Business World, before I show you a few things with my black belt in karate!
Mr. A: (sarcastically) Oh, please, please don't hurt me, Miss Libby. I couldn't bear it!
Ms. L: You, you Sexist!!!
Mr. A: (rising) You sexless ...

(Enter Jim and Mary Brown)

Jim: You two getting along fine?
Ms. L: Jim, where's the closet, I'm getting my coat. Would you like yours, Mr. Atlas?
Mr. A: Yes, by all means, but over my dead body will you get it for me.
Ms. L: As you wish!
Mary: Charlie, Gloria, what's happening?
Ms. L: Nothing, Mary, only that there can never be peace while monsters like him are allowed to run loose!
Mr. A: Remember, dear Miss Libby, you're part of the reason I'm here. It takes two to tango!

Response (4):

Man: They're finally going to get rid of that crazy man who shot his wife to death.
Lady: So they are.
Man: I'll be so glad. He'll get what he's got coming to him.
Lady: And just exactly what do you think he deserves?
Man: He should suffer just as she did. I wish they'd torture him a little before they put him in that gas chamber. Capital punishment is great.
Lady: What harm would it be to just lock him up for life? Oh, that would really disappoint you, wouldn't it?
Man: Do you think I like having to explain to my kids about the terrible people in this world? I will not pay taxes to feed this man for life. He should be killed and go to Hell where he belongs.
Lady: You really believe that he's doomed, don't you? He should never be forgiven, right?
Man: Someone who does such a terrible thing to an innocent woman could never be forgiven. Who's forgiven her?
Lady: Who do you think gives us the right to take this man's life?
Man: What do you mean? If he could do such a terrible thing to her, he deserves to die.

Lady: Would you turn on the switch for the gas?
Man: Um, of course ... well, why not? ... anyway, the man who does is only doing his job.
Lady: Sure, that's a fine answer. But wouldn't you feel guilty?
Man: Why?
Lady: Just because the man has made a mistake, we have no right to take his life. We can't judge others. Two wrongs don't make a right. Even in prison that man could be made useful. He could literally find a cure for cancer while locked up, which might help even your wife. The possibilities are infinite and you're saying we can just say the word and his life will be snuffed out.
Man: Well,... he deserves it ... I never looked at it that way ... but I don't want my money used to support that no-good bum ... my wife is really sick ... you don't really believe that cancer stuff, do you?
Lady: I most certainly do.
Man: Maybe you're right ... but I sure don't want him walking the streets.
Lady: I agree. There are rehabilitation programs you know. You might volunteer some time.
Man: I have no time for those bums. I play golf every night.
Lady: Did you ever make a mistake?
Man: Um ... well, ... gee, it's time for my supper... Be seeing you ...

Response (5):

(1. is character 1; 2. is character 2)

1. Catholic high schools are teaching religion in an outrageous fashion these days!
2. Why is that?
1. Do you know what they are teaching my child? She is in a class called "Sexual Development and Marriage!" She's only 14 years old! But it's not so much that as she just doesn't learn anything! Religion classes should teach about God, about her religion, not about biology. My daughter was in a course last month where the students discussed how hell must be like! Now I ask you, who cares? I want my daughter to learn about her religion, not to dream idle thoughts that could never help her in this life. They're all stupid! Everyone of those damn teachers is a crazy, radical communist.
2. I understand your point of view completely, madam, and I am sure that if I were you, I would feel the same way. But don't you think you are being a little harsh on the religion program -- and teachers -- in our schools? It seems to me, although I may be wrong, that the program is really quite effective.
1. What! You can't be serious. Our children are in school debating whether or not God exists, and you say that the religion program is good?
2. You know, I really don't understand exactly what you object to. Maybe if you explained just what it is that you feel the program lacks we could come to a better understanding of one another.
1. Very well. I feel that they should be taught the fundamentals of the Roman Catholic faith. They should learn its rules and regulations and be taught to accept them and they should examine the Bible to learn how to emulate Christ's life. The program now teaches them nothing but new theory, new theory that may be fine, but they cannot learn to accept it until they understand just what the old is. The worst part about the curriculum is that the subject matter - including "new theories" -- is so new that the Church does not officially sanction it. Therefore, the program should stay within the realm of the traditional religious philosophies.
2. I believe I understand you better now. Don't you think that our children should decide for themselves just what they want to believe in, just as they may decide for whom to vote on election day?

1. Yes, I do. But their decision should come at a mature age -- when they are intelligent enough to evaluate life.
2. I think that if we look at the religion program in light of what you just said, we may find that it is not quite so bad after all. It seems to me that the courses dealing with Life and Death, New Theory, and even Hell, allow our children to more fully develop their conscience before they step into the real world. They can toy with ideas about Hell, and if they decide it does exist, they will more fully appreciate the concept of a good life. They can argue about the existence of God and, if they decide He exists, will come to a better understanding of their own faith through their own reasoning.

AP ENGLISH
READING LIST OF RECOMMENDED WORKS OF LITERARY MERIT

NOVELS

THE DUBLINERS - James Joyce

PORTRAIT OF THE ARTIST AS A YOUNG MAN - James Joyce

TESS OF THE D'URBERVILLES - Thomas Hardy

INVISIBLE MAN - Ralph Ellison

THE GRAPES OF WRATH - John Steinbeck

ANIMAL FARM - George Orwell

1984 - George Orwell

LORD OF THE FLIES - William Golding

THE ANTHEM - Ayn Rand

MADAME BOVARY - Gustave Flaubert

THE RED AND THE BLACK - Stendahl

PORTRAIT OF A LADY - Henry James

A PASSAGE TO INDIA - E. M. Forster

LIGHT IN AUGUST - William Faulkner

ALL THE KING'S MEN - R. Penn Warren

MAN'S FATE - Andre Malraux

SLAUGHTERHOUSE FIVE - Kurt Vonnegut

CRIME AND PUNISHMENT - Fyodor Dostoevsky

JANE EYRE - Charlotte Bronte

AN AMERICAN TRAGEDY - Theodore Dreiser

CATCH-22 - Joseph Heller

GULLIVER'S TRAVELS - Jonathan Swift

DARKNESS AT NOON - Arthur Koestler

THE CASTLE - Franz Kafka

SONS AND LOVERS - D. H. Lawrence

NATIVE SON - Richard Wright

POETRY

DOVER BEACH - Matthew Arnold

MUSEE des BEAUX ARTS - W. H. Auden

THE PERSIAN VERSION - Robert Graves

BASE DETAILS - Siegfried Sassoon

ODE TO THE WEST WIND - Percy B. Shelley

COME UP FROM THE FIELDS, FATHER - Whitman

MUSEUM PIECE - Richard Wilbur

THE SLAUGHTER HOUSE - Alfred Hayes

ODE TO A GRECIAN URN - John Keats

LYCIDAS - John Milton

THE LOVE SONG OF J. ALFRED PRUFROCK - T. S. Eliot

THE FURY OF AERIAL BOMBARDMENT - Richard Eberhart

ANDREW MARVEL - Archibald MacLeish

TO HIS COY MISTRESS - Andrew Marvel

DRAMAS

WAITING FOR GODOT - Samuel Beckett

THE SEA GULL - Anton Chekhov

THE WAY OF THE WORLD - William Congreve

THE WILD DUCK - Henrik Ibsen

RHINOCEROS - Eugene Ionesco

VOLPONE - Ben Jonson

DEATH OF A SALESMAN - Arthur Miller

JUNO AND THE PAYCOCK - Sean O'Casey

THE SCHOOL FOR SCANDAL - R. Brinsley Sheridan

THE GLASS MENAGERIE - Tennessee Williams

ROSENCRANTZ AND GUILDENSTERN ARE DEAD - Tom Stoppard

SHORT STORIES

SILENT SNOW, SECRET SNOW - Conrad Aiken

THE EGG - Sherwood Anderson

THE SECRET SHARER - Joseph Conrad

THE BEAR - William Faulkner

THE PROCURATOR OF JUDEA - Anatole France

THE KILLERS - E. Hemingway

THE SHORT HAPPY LIFE OF FRANCIS MCCOMBER

THE HUNTER GRACCHUS - Franz Kafka

THE HORSEDEALER'S DAUGHTER - D. H. Lawrence

THE ROCKINGHORSE WINNER - D. H. Lawrence

THE FLY - Katherine Mansfield

MARIO AND THE MAGICIAN - Thomas Mann

FLOWERING JUDAS - Katherine Anne Porter

BILLY BUDD - Herman Melville

THE DEATH OF IVAN ILYCH - Leo Tolstoy

A VISIT OF CHARITY - Eudora Welty

* Also recommended for preparation of the CLEP Literature Examination.

AP/CLEP ENGLISH
OUTSIDE READING LIST *

FRESHMEN

A TALE OF TWO CITIES - Dickens

CALL OF THE WILD - London

THE PEARL/THE RED PONY - Steinbeck

LORD OF THE FLIES - Golding

ANIMAL FARM/1984 - Orwell

OF MICE AND MEN - Steinbeck

THE PURLOINED LETTER
THE FALL OF THE HOUSE OF USHER
THE GOLD BUG - Poe

WALDEN - H.D. Thoreau

THE BRIDGE OF SAN LUIS REY - Wilder

TO KILL A MOCKINGBIRD - Lee

A BELL FOR ADANO - Hersey

INVISIBLE MAN - Ralph Ellison

A SEPARATE PEACE - Knowles

SOPHOMORES

THE SCARLET LETTER - Hawthorne

LEATHERSTOCKING TALES - Cooper
- a. THE DEERSLAYER
- b. THE PATHFINDER
- c. THE LAST OF THE MOHICANS
- d. THE PIONEERS
- e. THE PRAIRIE

HUCKLEBERRY FINN/TOM SAWYER - Twain

*For summer and academic year

THE SPY/THE PILOT - Cooper

THE RED BADGE OF COURAGE - Crane

AN AMERICAN TRAGEDY - Dreiser

MAGGIE: A GIRL OF THE STREETS - Dreiser

THE GRAPES OF WRATH - Steinbeck

THE OLD MAN AND THE SEA - Hemingway

DEATH BE NOT PROUD - Gunther

THE GOOD EARTH - Buck

THE GREAT GATSBY - F. Scott Fitzgerald

ALICE IN WONDERLAND - Carroll

BRAVE NEW WORLD - Huxley

THE TURN OF THE SCREW - James

THE DUBLINERS - Joyce

PYGMALION - Shaw

TWO YEARS BEFORE THE MAST - Dumas

THE GLASS MENAGERIE - Williams

THE HOBBIT - Tolkien

REBECCA - Du Maurier

ALL MY SONS - Miller

OUTCASTS OF POKER FLAT - Harte

FAHRENHEIT 451 - Bradbury

TESS OF THE D'URBERVILLES - Hardy

JUNIORS AND SENIORS

GULLIVER'S TRAVELS - Swift

CATCHER IN THE RYE - Salinger

A FAREWELL TO ARMS - Hemingway

SWISS FAMILY ROBINSON - Wyss

DEAD SOULS - Gogol

THE CHERRY ORCHARD/THE SEA GULL - Chekhov

THE PROPHET - Gibran

SIDDHARTHA - Hesse

MOLL FLANDERS/ROBINSON CRUSOE - Defoe

DRACULA - Stoker

FRANKENSTEIN - Shelley

BILLY BUDD - Melville

THE HAIRY APE - O'Neill

CYRANO de BERGERAC - Rostand

THE OXBOW INCIDENT - W.T.V. Clark

LE MISANTHROPE - Molière

PHAEDRA - Racine

ANNA KARENINA - Tolstoy

CRIME AND PUNISHMENT - Dostoevsky

JULIUS CAESAR
HAMLET
MACBETH
ROMEO AND JULIET
LOVE'S LABORS LOST
HENRY IV - I, II -Shakespeare

MADAME BOVARY - Flaubert

VANITY FAIR - Thackeray

PRIDE AND PREJUDICE - Austen

WUTHERING HEIGHTS - Emily Bronte

LORD JIM/THE SECRET SHARER - Conrad

ILIAD
THE ODYSSEY - Homer

THE AENEID - Virgil

THE CANTERBURY TALES - Chaucer

DON QUIXOTE - Cervantes

LES MISERABLES
TOILERS OF THE SEA
THE HUNCHBACK OF NOTRE DAME - Hugo

ANTIGONE - Sophocles

MEDEA - Euripedes

ANTHEM - Ayn Rand

METAMORPHOSES - Kafka

COACH: A SEASON WITH LOMBARD - Dowling

THE JIM THORPE STORY - Schoor

THE OEDIPUS PLAYS - Sophocles

A STREETCAR NAMED DESIRE - Williams

RIDERS TO THE SEA - Synge

SHORT STORIES OF de MAUPASSANT

A PASSAGE TO INDIA - E. M. Forster

PORTRAIT OF A LADY - James

AP/CLEP EXAMINATION IN LITERATURE
ILLUSTRATED QUESTIONS
ENGLISH, SECTION I

All questions are of the multiple-choice type; this has proven to be an effective and reliable way of providing a measure of a student's developed ability. The AP-CLEP Test in Literature consists of selections from literary works and questions on their content, form, and style. After reading each passage, choose the best answer to each question. Read each of the sample passages carefully several times before you choose your answers.

Answer questions 1-2 by referring to the following selection:

> The Niobe of nations! there she stands,
> Childless and crownless, in her voiceless woe;
> An empty urn within her wither'd hands,
> Whose holy dust was scatter'd long ago;
> The Scipios' tomb contains no ashes now;
> The very sepulchres lie tenantless
> Of their heroic dwellers: dost thou flow,
> Old Tiber! through a marble wilderness?
> Rise, with they yellow waves, and mantle her distress.

1. The "Niobe of nations" referred to is ancient

   (A) Athens
   (B) Carthage
   (C) Rome
   (D) Jerusalem
   (E) Persia

2. The lines are outstanding for their

   (A) delicacy
   (B) simplicity
   (C) lilt
   (D) word choice
   (E) vigor

Answer question 3 by referring to the following selection:

> King Francis was a hearty king, and loved a royal sport,
> And one day, as his lions fought, sat looking on the court;
> The nobles filled the benches, with the ladies in their pride,
> And 'mongst them sat the Count de Lorge, with one for whom he sighed.

And truly 'twas a gallant thing to see that crowning show,
Valor and love, and a king above, and the royal beasts below.

3. If you were to rearrange this stanza, instead of six lines how many lines would you have?

   (A) 4
   (B) 8
   (C) 12
   (D) 14
   (E) 16

Answer question 4 with reference to the following stanza:

The boast of heraldry, the pomp of pow'r,
   And all that beauty, all that wealth e'er gave,
Awaits alike th' inevitable hour.
   The paths of glory lead but to the grave,

4. "The boast of heraldry" is an allusion to

   (A) ancient Greece
   (B) the Middle Ages
   (C) the newspaper profession
   (D) a Teutonic myth
   (E) none of the above

5. Each of the following types of reference book is correctly matched with its author or editor <u>except</u>

   (A) an anthology of poetry--Brewer
   (B) a book of familiar quotations--Bartlett
   (C) a dictionary of synonyms--Merriam-Webster
   (D) an American college Dictionary--Barnhart
   (E) a dictionary of slang--Partridge

Answer questions 6, 7, 8 with reference to the following passage:

If a man were called to fix the period in the history of the world, during which the condition of the human race was most happy and prosperous, he would, without hesitation, name that which elapsed from the death of Domitian to the accession of Commodus (96-180 A.D.). The vast extent of the Roman empire was governed by absolute power, under the guidance of virtue and wisdom. The armies were restrained by the firm but gentle hand of four successive emperors, whose characters and authority commanded involuntary respect. The forms of the civil administration were carefully preserved by Nerva, Trajan, Hadrian, and the Antonines, who delighted in the image of liberty, and were pleased with considering themselves as the accountable ministers of the laws. Such princes deserved the honour of restoring the republic, had the Romans of their days been capable of enjoying a rational freedom.

The labours of these monarchs were overpaid by the immense reward that inseparably waited on their success; by the honest pride of virtue, and by the exquisite delight of beholding the general happiness of which they were the authors. A just, but melancholy reflection embittered, however, the noblest of human enjoyments. They must often have recollected the instability of a happiness which depended on the character of a single man. The fatal moment was perhaps approaching, when some licentious youth, or some jealous tyrant, would abuse, to the destruction, that absolute power, which they had exerted for the benefit of their people. The ideal restraints of the senate and the laws might serve to display the virtues, but could never correct the vices, of the emperor. The military force was a blind and irresistible instrument of oppression; and the corruption of Roman manners would always supply flatterers eager to applaud, and ministers prepared to serve, the fear or the avarice, the lust or the cruelty, of their masters.

These gloomy apprehensions had been already justified by the experience of the Romans. The annals of the emperors exhibit a strong and varied picture of human nature, which we should vainly seek among the mixed and doubtful characters of modern history. In the conduct of those monarchs we may trace the utmost lines of vice and virtue; the most exalted perfection, and the meanest degeneracy of our own species. The golden age of Trajan and the Antoines had been preceded by an age of iron. It is almost superfluous to enumerate the unworthy successors of Augustus. Their unparalled vices, and the splendid theater on which they were acted, have saved them from oblivion. The dark unrelenting Tiberius, the furious Caligula, the feeble Claudius, the profligate and cruel Nero, the beastly Vitellius, and the timid inhuman Domitian, are condemned to everlasting infamy. During fourscore years (excepting only the short and doubtful respire of Vespasian's reign) Rome groaned beneath an unremitting tyranny, which exterminated the ancient families of the republic, and was fatal to almost every virtue and every talent that arose in that unhappy period.

6. According to the author, Roman emperors are unique in that

   (A) they represent greater variety of moral conduct than any other group of leaders
   (B) they are unmatched for their cruelty
   (C) their life spans were shorter than those of any other group of rulers
   (D) they were the most capable leaders in all history
   (E) they encouraged the building of roads and temples

7. It can be inferred that the author believes which of the following about the dictatorial government of ancient Rome?

   I. It caused great hardship.
   II. It was the best possible form of government.
   III. It created a time of greatest human happiness.

   (A) I only
   (B) II only
   (C) I and III only
   (D) II and III only
   (E) I, II, and III

8. According to the passage, Vespasian's reign can best be characterized as

   (A) violent
   (B) prosperous
   (C) victorious
   (D) democratic
   (E) short

Answer questions 9 and 10 with reference to the following passage:

Do students learn from programed instruction? The research leaves us in no doubt of this. They do, indeed, learn. They learn from linear programs, from branching programs built on the Skinnerian model, from scrambled books of the Crowder type, from Pressey review tests with immediate knowledge of results, from programs on machines or programs in texts. Many kinds of students learn--college, high school, secondary, primary, preschool, adult, professional, skilled labor, clerical employees, military, deaf, retarded, imprisoned--every kind of student that programs have been tried on. Using programs, these students are able to learn mathematics and science at different levels, foreign languages, English language correctness, the details of the U. S. Constitution, spelling, electronics, computer science, psychology, statistics, business skills, reading skills, instrument flying rules, and many other subjects. The limits of the topics which can be studied efficiently by means of programs are not yet known.

For each of the kinds of subject matter and the kinds of student mentioned above, experiments have demonstrated that a considerable amount of learning can be derived from programs; this learning has been measured either by comparing pre- and post-tests or the time and trials needed to reach a set criterion of performance. But the question, how well do students learn from programs as compared to how well they learn from other kinds of instruction, we cannot answer quite so confidently.

Experimental psychologists typically do not take very seriously the evaluative experiments in which learning from programs is compared with learning from conventional teaching. Such experiments are doubtless useful, they say, for school administrators or teachers to prove to themselves (or their boards of education) that programs work. But whereas one can describe fairly well the characteristics of a program, can one describe the characteristics of a classroom teaching situation so that the result of the comparison will have any generality? What kind of teacher is being compared to what kind of program? Furthermore, these early evaluative experiments with programs are likely to suffer from the Hawthorne effect: that is to say, students are in the spotlight when testing something new, and are challenged to do well. It is very hard to make allowance for this effect. Therefore, the evaluative tests may be useful administratively, say many of the experimenters, but do not contribute much to science, and should properly be kept for private use.

These objections are well taken. And yet, do they justify us in ignoring the evaluative studies? The great strength of a program is that it permits the student to learn efficiently by himself. Is it not therefore important to know how much and what kind of skills, concepts, insights, or attitudes he can learn by himself from a program as compared to what he can learn from a teacher? Admittedly, this is a very difficult and complex research problem, but that should not keep us from trying to solve it.

9. According to the passage, experimental psychologists typically view the results of experiments comparing programed instruction to conventional teaching methods with

   (A) scepticism
   (B) distaste
   (C) great interest
   (D) complete acceptance
   (E) extreme annoyance

10. The author's main purpose is to point out that programed instruction

   (A) deserves further investigation
   (B) is a superior method of teaching
   (C) comes in a variety of forms
   (D) is criticized by educators
   (E) is the teaching method that is most effective

ANSWERS TO SAMPLE LITERATURE TEST QUESTIONS

1. C	6. A
2. E	7. B
3. C	8. E
4. B	9. A
5. A	10. A

AP/CLEP EXAMINATION IN LITERATURE
ILLUSTRATED QUESTIONS
ENGLISH, SECTION II

All of the questions in Section II are Free-response essay questions. An actual example answer from a previously administered AP Examination in included. It is significant to note that the quality of composition will affect the grading of all essay questions. The essay will be judged on its clarity and effectiveness in dealing with the topics. In Section II it is important to select only works of acknowledged literary merit in the essay response.

Question 1 (Suggested time - 40 minutes)

Directions: Authors frequently use the same character successfully in their writings. Choose an acknowledged literary merit and, in a well-written essay, demonstrate how stereotyped or conventional characters function and achieve author's purpose. You may wish to use a work from the list below or any work of comparable literary excellence.

Response:

The novel Pride and Prejudice by Jane Austen is filled with conventional characters. For example, Mrs. Bennet is the typical mother who wishes to see all her daughters married so that she can brag to her neighbors about her success in getting them a husband. This and her love of gossip seem to be the only outstanding features about her. Then there is Jane. She is pretty, quiet, and good with nothing unusual in her character or appearance. In another daughter, Mary, we see the typical "bookworm" and the two youngest Bennets, Lydia and Kitty, are devoted entirely to thoughts of soldiers and balls.

The stereotyped characters are not restricted to the women in the novel only. Mr. Bennet we find to be someone who takes only slight interest in his children and spends the rest of the time in his study. As for Mr. Collins, he is the typical minister. He tries always to please everyone and does what is proper and correct at all times. Another conventional character is Bingley who is a good-natured, young man, well-off financially and pleasing to everyone. However, he allows himself to be ruled by others with no definite opinions of his own.

These characters all help to call attention to the characters of Elizabeth and Darcy. These two alone stand out as individuals. They are the only characters whose actions cannot be accurately guessed in advance. Thus the reader can put to the background the other people and concentrate on how Elizabeth and Darcy act, react and eventually change. The stereotyped characters create the situations and Elizabeth and Darcy find the solutions. One example of this is when Lydia and Wickham run off together. Darcy arranges the matter so that a huge scandal is not created. Elizabeth tells her mother of Darcy's generous help but Mrs. Bennet is concerned only with the fact that at last she has one daughter safely married. Before Darcy's intercession the Bennets and their relatives think that a suitable outcome is impossible. As they lack ideas on how to get out of the situation they show indecision on how to act. Darcy is not held back in the least. He acts quickly and decisively. Only Elizabeth can appreciate what Darcy has done because it is how she would have acted had she· the opportunity. The other characters dismiss what has happened and concern themselves only with the result. The farsightedness of Elizabeth and Darcy is revealed by the other characters' concern with only the present. The stereotyped characters achieve the author's purpose by allowing Elizabeth and Darcy to control the action of the story. They also emphasize the complexity of Elizabeth and Darcy making the story both interesting and worthwhile.

Question 2 (Suggested time - 40 minutes)

Directions: Read a short story from THE MARRIAGE FEAST (Farrar, Straus & Grroux, 1954) carefully about "Father and I." Then write a well-organized essay in which there is a discussion of the reading. Your essay should deal with significance of the events, and when possible, make references to the short story text. The actual examination reprints the 180-line reading.

Response:

The short story Father and I is about two people and how they are both similar and different. The father and son are close but there are many things which separate them. Each is also a stranger to the other. In the first paragraph the narrator emphasizes the link between them. ". . . we were sound, sensible people, Father and I, brought up with nature and used to it." Then begin the references to the superiority of the father. "We walked along the railway line, where people are not allowed to go as a rule, but Father worked on the railway and so he had a right to." This superiority is seen when the father makes remarks about the weather and when he scans a field of oats. The boy accepts this and even expects it. "Father just looked to see that the semaphore was right--he thought of everything." It is after this point that the author reminds us of their closeness again, "... throwing pebbles out into the water to see who could throw the farthest, we were both gay and cheerful by nature, Father and I."

With the fall of darkness a change in the mood comes about. The boy and his father no longer seem close. "Under one of them was a glowworm. . . I squeezed Father's hand, but he didn't see the strange glow, just walked on." Again we see this when the boy thinks that his father will carry him across the stream but he does not. The boy has difficulty in understanding his father and feels lonely when his father does not adequately comfort him. There is no communication of feelings between them. "It was so strange that only I was afraid, not Father, that we didn't think the same."

The end of the story with the near accident of the strange train emphasizes the difference between the two by the importance attached to the incident by each. To the father it is a strange incident but something that will be forgotten. However, to the boy it is a momentous event in which he sees the relationship between his father and himself as something which would not be of great value to him in the real world.

Question 3 (Suggested time - 40 minutes)

Directions: Select a play you have studied or read; write an essay in which you explain some of the techniques the playwright must use to guide his audience's responses to the central focus and figures. Remember that a playwright does not use his own voice to guide the audience's responses to character and action. In your essay you should consider all of the play elements, i.e., setting, use of comparable characters, and employment of contrasting characters. Develop your essay with specific reference to the play of your choice. The play you use should be of acknowledged literary merit. Do not give a plot summary.

Response:

In Hamlet, Shakespeare uses many devices to call attention to Hamlet and the main action of the play. One way in which this is done is by costuming. Hamlet is still dressed in mourning colors while the rest of the court have gone back to gay ones because of the queen's wedding. This has the effect of making Hamlet stand out which is important to his major role in the story. Another point where costumes are important is when Hamlet has different clothes on his return from the captivity of the pirates. This leads the audience to expect a change in Hamlet and a climax as a result of his change.

A second way in which the audience is drawn to the main action is the conflict between Hamlet and Claudius. These two characters contrast not only in the way they are dressed but also in the way they act. Claudius is seen to be a diplomat in his dealings with Fontibras. Hamlet acts on impulse and is only held back by his intellect from getting immediate revenge for his father's death. Claudius does not show a great deal of emotion while Hamlet's feelings are deep and lasting. These things intensify the conflict between them and also hold the audience's attention to the major issue.

A final technique used by Shakespeare is the unique play within a play. In this scene the audience is brought to a realization of the horrible crime Claudius has committed by seeing it enacted before their eyes. When Hamlet is furnished with proof of Claudius' guilt by his reaction, the audience begins to anticipate the final vengeance to be wrought on Claudius.

It is in these ways and others that the audience is drawn to the main action in the story.

1 Ⓐ Ⓑ Ⓒ Ⓓ Ⓔ	26 Ⓐ Ⓑ Ⓒ Ⓓ Ⓔ	51 Ⓐ Ⓑ Ⓒ Ⓓ Ⓔ	76 Ⓐ Ⓑ Ⓒ Ⓓ Ⓔ	101 Ⓐ Ⓑ Ⓒ Ⓓ Ⓔ	126 Ⓐ Ⓑ Ⓒ Ⓓ Ⓔ
2 Ⓐ Ⓑ Ⓒ Ⓓ Ⓔ	27 Ⓐ Ⓑ Ⓒ Ⓓ Ⓔ	52 Ⓐ Ⓑ Ⓒ Ⓓ Ⓔ	77 Ⓐ Ⓑ Ⓒ Ⓓ Ⓔ	102 Ⓐ Ⓑ Ⓒ Ⓓ Ⓔ	127 Ⓐ Ⓑ Ⓒ Ⓓ Ⓔ
3 Ⓐ Ⓑ Ⓒ Ⓓ Ⓔ	28 Ⓐ Ⓑ Ⓒ Ⓓ Ⓔ	53 Ⓐ Ⓑ Ⓒ Ⓓ Ⓔ	78 Ⓐ Ⓑ Ⓒ Ⓓ Ⓔ	103 Ⓐ Ⓑ Ⓒ Ⓓ Ⓔ	128 Ⓐ Ⓑ Ⓒ Ⓓ Ⓔ
4 Ⓐ Ⓑ Ⓒ Ⓓ Ⓔ	29 Ⓐ Ⓑ Ⓒ Ⓓ Ⓔ	54 Ⓐ Ⓑ Ⓒ Ⓓ Ⓔ	79 Ⓐ Ⓑ Ⓒ Ⓓ Ⓔ	104 Ⓐ Ⓑ Ⓒ Ⓓ Ⓔ	129 Ⓐ Ⓑ Ⓒ Ⓓ Ⓔ
5 Ⓐ Ⓑ Ⓒ Ⓓ Ⓔ	30 Ⓐ Ⓑ Ⓒ Ⓓ Ⓔ	55 Ⓐ Ⓑ Ⓒ Ⓓ Ⓔ	80 Ⓐ Ⓑ Ⓒ Ⓓ Ⓔ	105 Ⓐ Ⓑ Ⓒ Ⓓ Ⓔ	130 Ⓐ Ⓑ Ⓒ Ⓓ Ⓔ
6 Ⓐ Ⓑ Ⓒ Ⓓ Ⓔ	31 Ⓐ Ⓑ Ⓒ Ⓓ Ⓔ	56 Ⓐ Ⓑ Ⓒ Ⓓ Ⓔ	81 Ⓐ Ⓑ Ⓒ Ⓓ Ⓔ	106 Ⓐ Ⓑ Ⓒ Ⓓ Ⓔ	131 Ⓐ Ⓑ Ⓒ Ⓓ Ⓔ
7 Ⓐ Ⓑ Ⓒ Ⓓ Ⓔ	32 Ⓐ Ⓑ Ⓒ Ⓓ Ⓔ	57 Ⓐ Ⓑ Ⓒ Ⓓ Ⓔ	82 Ⓐ Ⓑ Ⓒ Ⓓ Ⓔ	107 Ⓐ Ⓑ Ⓒ Ⓓ Ⓔ	132 Ⓐ Ⓑ Ⓒ Ⓓ Ⓔ
8 Ⓐ Ⓑ Ⓒ Ⓓ Ⓔ	33 Ⓐ Ⓑ Ⓒ Ⓓ Ⓔ	58 Ⓐ Ⓑ Ⓒ Ⓓ Ⓔ	83 Ⓐ Ⓑ Ⓒ Ⓓ Ⓔ	108 Ⓐ Ⓑ Ⓒ Ⓓ Ⓔ	133 Ⓐ Ⓑ Ⓒ Ⓓ Ⓔ
9 Ⓐ Ⓑ Ⓒ Ⓓ Ⓔ	34 Ⓐ Ⓑ Ⓒ Ⓓ Ⓔ	59 Ⓐ Ⓑ Ⓒ Ⓓ Ⓔ	84 Ⓐ Ⓑ Ⓒ Ⓓ Ⓔ	109 Ⓐ Ⓑ Ⓒ Ⓓ Ⓔ	134 Ⓐ Ⓑ Ⓒ Ⓓ Ⓔ
10 Ⓐ Ⓑ Ⓒ Ⓓ Ⓔ	35 Ⓐ Ⓑ Ⓒ Ⓓ Ⓔ	60 Ⓐ Ⓑ Ⓒ Ⓓ Ⓔ	85 Ⓐ Ⓑ Ⓒ Ⓓ Ⓔ	110 Ⓐ Ⓑ Ⓒ Ⓓ Ⓔ	135 Ⓐ Ⓑ Ⓒ Ⓓ Ⓔ
11 Ⓐ Ⓑ Ⓒ Ⓓ Ⓔ	36 Ⓐ Ⓑ Ⓒ Ⓓ Ⓔ	61 Ⓐ Ⓑ Ⓒ Ⓓ Ⓔ	86 Ⓐ Ⓑ Ⓒ Ⓓ Ⓔ	111 Ⓐ Ⓑ Ⓒ Ⓓ Ⓔ	136 Ⓐ Ⓑ Ⓒ Ⓓ Ⓔ
12 Ⓐ Ⓑ Ⓒ Ⓓ Ⓔ	37 Ⓐ Ⓑ Ⓒ Ⓓ Ⓔ	62 Ⓐ Ⓑ Ⓒ Ⓓ Ⓔ	87 Ⓐ Ⓑ Ⓒ Ⓓ Ⓔ	112 Ⓐ Ⓑ Ⓒ Ⓓ Ⓔ	137 Ⓐ Ⓑ Ⓒ Ⓓ Ⓔ
13 Ⓐ Ⓑ Ⓒ Ⓓ Ⓔ	38 Ⓐ Ⓑ Ⓒ Ⓓ Ⓔ	63 Ⓐ Ⓑ Ⓒ Ⓓ Ⓔ	88 Ⓐ Ⓑ Ⓒ Ⓓ Ⓔ	113 Ⓐ Ⓑ Ⓒ Ⓓ Ⓔ	138 Ⓐ Ⓑ Ⓒ Ⓓ Ⓔ
14 Ⓐ Ⓑ Ⓒ Ⓓ Ⓔ	39 Ⓐ Ⓑ Ⓒ Ⓓ Ⓔ	64 Ⓐ Ⓑ Ⓒ Ⓓ Ⓔ	89 Ⓐ Ⓑ Ⓒ Ⓓ Ⓔ	114 Ⓐ Ⓑ Ⓒ Ⓓ Ⓔ	139 Ⓐ Ⓑ Ⓒ Ⓓ Ⓔ
15 Ⓐ Ⓑ Ⓒ Ⓓ Ⓔ	40 Ⓐ Ⓑ Ⓒ Ⓓ Ⓔ	65 Ⓐ Ⓑ Ⓒ Ⓓ Ⓔ	90 Ⓐ Ⓑ Ⓒ Ⓓ Ⓔ	115 Ⓐ Ⓑ Ⓒ Ⓓ Ⓔ	140 Ⓐ Ⓑ Ⓒ Ⓓ Ⓔ
16 Ⓐ Ⓑ Ⓒ Ⓓ Ⓔ	41 Ⓐ Ⓑ Ⓒ Ⓓ Ⓔ	66 Ⓐ Ⓑ Ⓒ Ⓓ Ⓔ	91 Ⓐ Ⓑ Ⓒ Ⓓ Ⓔ	116 Ⓐ Ⓑ Ⓒ Ⓓ Ⓔ	141 Ⓐ Ⓑ Ⓒ Ⓓ Ⓔ
17 Ⓐ Ⓑ Ⓒ Ⓓ Ⓔ	42 Ⓐ Ⓑ Ⓒ Ⓓ Ⓔ	67 Ⓐ Ⓑ Ⓒ Ⓓ Ⓔ	92 Ⓐ Ⓑ Ⓒ Ⓓ Ⓔ	117 Ⓐ Ⓑ Ⓒ Ⓓ Ⓔ	142 Ⓐ Ⓑ Ⓒ Ⓓ Ⓔ
18 Ⓐ Ⓑ Ⓒ Ⓓ Ⓔ	43 Ⓐ Ⓑ Ⓒ Ⓓ Ⓔ	68 Ⓐ Ⓑ Ⓒ Ⓓ Ⓔ	93 Ⓐ Ⓑ Ⓒ Ⓓ Ⓔ	118 Ⓐ Ⓑ Ⓒ Ⓓ Ⓔ	143 Ⓐ Ⓑ Ⓒ Ⓓ Ⓔ
19 Ⓐ Ⓑ Ⓒ Ⓓ Ⓔ	44 Ⓐ Ⓑ Ⓒ Ⓓ Ⓔ	69 Ⓐ Ⓑ Ⓒ Ⓓ Ⓔ	94 Ⓐ Ⓑ Ⓒ Ⓓ Ⓔ	119 Ⓐ Ⓑ Ⓒ Ⓓ Ⓔ	144 Ⓐ Ⓑ Ⓒ Ⓓ Ⓔ
20 Ⓐ Ⓑ Ⓒ Ⓓ Ⓔ	45 Ⓐ Ⓑ Ⓒ Ⓓ Ⓔ	70 Ⓐ Ⓑ Ⓒ Ⓓ Ⓔ	95 Ⓐ Ⓑ Ⓒ Ⓓ Ⓔ	120 Ⓐ Ⓑ Ⓒ Ⓓ Ⓔ	145 Ⓐ Ⓑ Ⓒ Ⓓ Ⓔ
21 Ⓐ Ⓑ Ⓒ Ⓓ Ⓔ	46 Ⓐ Ⓑ Ⓒ Ⓓ Ⓔ	71 Ⓐ Ⓑ Ⓒ Ⓓ Ⓔ	96 Ⓐ Ⓑ Ⓒ Ⓓ Ⓔ	121 Ⓐ Ⓑ Ⓒ Ⓓ Ⓔ	146 Ⓐ Ⓑ Ⓒ Ⓓ Ⓔ
22 Ⓐ Ⓑ Ⓒ Ⓓ Ⓔ	47 Ⓐ Ⓑ Ⓒ Ⓓ Ⓔ	72 Ⓐ Ⓑ Ⓒ Ⓓ Ⓔ	97 Ⓐ Ⓑ Ⓒ Ⓓ Ⓔ	122 Ⓐ Ⓑ Ⓒ Ⓓ Ⓔ	147 Ⓐ Ⓑ Ⓒ Ⓓ Ⓔ
23 Ⓐ Ⓑ Ⓒ Ⓓ Ⓔ	48 Ⓐ Ⓑ Ⓒ Ⓓ Ⓔ	73 Ⓐ Ⓑ Ⓒ Ⓓ Ⓔ	98 Ⓐ Ⓑ Ⓒ Ⓓ Ⓔ	123 Ⓐ Ⓑ Ⓒ Ⓓ Ⓔ	148 Ⓐ Ⓑ Ⓒ Ⓓ Ⓔ
24 Ⓐ Ⓑ Ⓒ Ⓓ Ⓔ	49 Ⓐ Ⓑ Ⓒ Ⓓ Ⓔ	74 Ⓐ Ⓑ Ⓒ Ⓓ Ⓔ	99 Ⓐ Ⓑ Ⓒ Ⓓ Ⓔ	124 Ⓐ Ⓑ Ⓒ Ⓓ Ⓔ	149 Ⓐ Ⓑ Ⓒ Ⓓ Ⓔ
25 Ⓐ Ⓑ Ⓒ Ⓓ Ⓔ	50 Ⓐ Ⓑ Ⓒ Ⓓ Ⓔ	75 Ⓐ Ⓑ Ⓒ Ⓓ Ⓔ	100 Ⓐ Ⓑ Ⓒ Ⓓ Ⓔ	125 Ⓐ Ⓑ Ⓒ Ⓓ Ⓔ	150 Ⓐ Ⓑ Ⓒ Ⓓ Ⓔ

1 Ⓐ Ⓑ Ⓒ Ⓓ Ⓔ	26 Ⓐ Ⓑ Ⓒ Ⓓ Ⓔ	51 Ⓐ Ⓑ Ⓒ Ⓓ Ⓔ	76 Ⓐ Ⓑ Ⓒ Ⓓ Ⓔ	101 Ⓐ Ⓑ Ⓒ Ⓓ Ⓔ	126 Ⓐ Ⓑ Ⓒ Ⓓ Ⓔ
2 Ⓐ Ⓑ Ⓒ Ⓓ Ⓔ	27 Ⓐ Ⓑ Ⓒ Ⓓ Ⓔ	52 Ⓐ Ⓑ Ⓒ Ⓓ Ⓔ	77 Ⓐ Ⓑ Ⓒ Ⓓ Ⓔ	102 Ⓐ Ⓑ Ⓒ Ⓓ Ⓔ	127 Ⓐ Ⓑ Ⓒ Ⓓ Ⓔ
3 Ⓐ Ⓑ Ⓒ Ⓓ Ⓔ	28 Ⓐ Ⓑ Ⓒ Ⓓ Ⓔ	53 Ⓐ Ⓑ Ⓒ Ⓓ Ⓔ	78 Ⓐ Ⓑ Ⓒ Ⓓ Ⓔ	103 Ⓐ Ⓑ Ⓒ Ⓓ Ⓔ	128 Ⓐ Ⓑ Ⓒ Ⓓ Ⓔ
4 Ⓐ Ⓑ Ⓒ Ⓓ Ⓔ	29 Ⓐ Ⓑ Ⓒ Ⓓ Ⓔ	54 Ⓐ Ⓑ Ⓒ Ⓓ Ⓔ	79 Ⓐ Ⓑ Ⓒ Ⓓ Ⓔ	104 Ⓐ Ⓑ Ⓒ Ⓓ Ⓔ	129 Ⓐ Ⓑ Ⓒ Ⓓ Ⓔ
5 Ⓐ Ⓑ Ⓒ Ⓓ Ⓔ	30 Ⓐ Ⓑ Ⓒ Ⓓ Ⓔ	55 Ⓐ Ⓑ Ⓒ Ⓓ Ⓔ	80 Ⓐ Ⓑ Ⓒ Ⓓ Ⓔ	105 Ⓐ Ⓑ Ⓒ Ⓓ Ⓔ	130 Ⓐ Ⓑ Ⓒ Ⓓ Ⓔ
6 Ⓐ Ⓑ Ⓒ Ⓓ Ⓔ	31 Ⓐ Ⓑ Ⓒ Ⓓ Ⓔ	56 Ⓐ Ⓑ Ⓒ Ⓓ Ⓔ	81 Ⓐ Ⓑ Ⓒ Ⓓ Ⓔ	106 Ⓐ Ⓑ Ⓒ Ⓓ Ⓔ	131 Ⓐ Ⓑ Ⓒ Ⓓ Ⓔ
7 Ⓐ Ⓑ Ⓒ Ⓓ Ⓔ	32 Ⓐ Ⓑ Ⓒ Ⓓ Ⓔ	57 Ⓐ Ⓑ Ⓒ Ⓓ Ⓔ	82 Ⓐ Ⓑ Ⓒ Ⓓ Ⓔ	107 Ⓐ Ⓑ Ⓒ Ⓓ Ⓔ	132 Ⓐ Ⓑ Ⓒ Ⓓ Ⓔ
8 Ⓐ Ⓑ Ⓒ Ⓓ Ⓔ	33 Ⓐ Ⓑ Ⓒ Ⓓ Ⓔ	58 Ⓐ Ⓑ Ⓒ Ⓓ Ⓔ	83 Ⓐ Ⓑ Ⓒ Ⓓ Ⓔ	108 Ⓐ Ⓑ Ⓒ Ⓓ Ⓔ	133 Ⓐ Ⓑ Ⓒ Ⓓ Ⓔ
9 Ⓐ Ⓑ Ⓒ Ⓓ Ⓔ	34 Ⓐ Ⓑ Ⓒ Ⓓ Ⓔ	59 Ⓐ Ⓑ Ⓒ Ⓓ Ⓔ	84 Ⓐ Ⓑ Ⓒ Ⓓ Ⓔ	109 Ⓐ Ⓑ Ⓒ Ⓓ Ⓔ	134 Ⓐ Ⓑ Ⓒ Ⓓ Ⓔ
10 Ⓐ Ⓑ Ⓒ Ⓓ Ⓔ	35 Ⓐ Ⓑ Ⓒ Ⓓ Ⓔ	60 Ⓐ Ⓑ Ⓒ Ⓓ Ⓔ	85 Ⓐ Ⓑ Ⓒ Ⓓ Ⓔ	110 Ⓐ Ⓑ Ⓒ Ⓓ Ⓔ	135 Ⓐ Ⓑ Ⓒ Ⓓ Ⓔ
11 Ⓐ Ⓑ Ⓒ Ⓓ Ⓔ	36 Ⓐ Ⓑ Ⓒ Ⓓ Ⓔ	61 Ⓐ Ⓑ Ⓒ Ⓓ Ⓔ	86 Ⓐ Ⓑ Ⓒ Ⓓ Ⓔ	111 Ⓐ Ⓑ Ⓒ Ⓓ Ⓔ	136 Ⓐ Ⓑ Ⓒ Ⓓ Ⓔ
12 Ⓐ Ⓑ Ⓒ Ⓓ Ⓔ	37 Ⓐ Ⓑ Ⓒ Ⓓ Ⓔ	62 Ⓐ Ⓑ Ⓒ Ⓓ Ⓔ	87 Ⓐ Ⓑ Ⓒ Ⓓ Ⓔ	112 Ⓐ Ⓑ Ⓒ Ⓓ Ⓔ	137 Ⓐ Ⓑ Ⓒ Ⓓ Ⓔ
13 Ⓐ Ⓑ Ⓒ Ⓓ Ⓔ	38 Ⓐ Ⓑ Ⓒ Ⓓ Ⓔ	63 Ⓐ Ⓑ Ⓒ Ⓓ Ⓔ	88 Ⓐ Ⓑ Ⓒ Ⓓ Ⓔ	113 Ⓐ Ⓑ Ⓒ Ⓓ Ⓔ	138 Ⓐ Ⓑ Ⓒ Ⓓ Ⓔ
14 Ⓐ Ⓑ Ⓒ Ⓓ Ⓔ	39 Ⓐ Ⓑ Ⓒ Ⓓ Ⓔ	64 Ⓐ Ⓑ Ⓒ Ⓓ Ⓔ	89 Ⓐ Ⓑ Ⓒ Ⓓ Ⓔ	114 Ⓐ Ⓑ Ⓒ Ⓓ Ⓔ	139 Ⓐ Ⓑ Ⓒ Ⓓ Ⓔ
15 Ⓐ Ⓑ Ⓒ Ⓓ Ⓔ	40 Ⓐ Ⓑ Ⓒ Ⓓ Ⓔ	65 Ⓐ Ⓑ Ⓒ Ⓓ Ⓔ	90 Ⓐ Ⓑ Ⓒ Ⓓ Ⓔ	115 Ⓐ Ⓑ Ⓒ Ⓓ Ⓔ	140 Ⓐ Ⓑ Ⓒ Ⓓ Ⓔ
16 Ⓐ Ⓑ Ⓒ Ⓓ Ⓔ	41 Ⓐ Ⓑ Ⓒ Ⓓ Ⓔ	66 Ⓐ Ⓑ Ⓒ Ⓓ Ⓔ	91 Ⓐ Ⓑ Ⓒ Ⓓ Ⓔ	116 Ⓐ Ⓑ Ⓒ Ⓓ Ⓔ	141 Ⓐ Ⓑ Ⓒ Ⓓ Ⓔ
17 Ⓐ Ⓑ Ⓒ Ⓓ Ⓔ	42 Ⓐ Ⓑ Ⓒ Ⓓ Ⓔ	67 Ⓐ Ⓑ Ⓒ Ⓓ Ⓔ	92 Ⓐ Ⓑ Ⓒ Ⓓ Ⓔ	117 Ⓐ Ⓑ Ⓒ Ⓓ Ⓔ	142 Ⓐ Ⓑ Ⓒ Ⓓ Ⓔ
18 Ⓐ Ⓑ Ⓒ Ⓓ Ⓔ	43 Ⓐ Ⓑ Ⓒ Ⓓ Ⓔ	68 Ⓐ Ⓑ Ⓒ Ⓓ Ⓔ	93 Ⓐ Ⓑ Ⓒ Ⓓ Ⓔ	118 Ⓐ Ⓑ Ⓒ Ⓓ Ⓔ	143 Ⓐ Ⓑ Ⓒ Ⓓ Ⓔ
19 Ⓐ Ⓑ Ⓒ Ⓓ Ⓔ	44 Ⓐ Ⓑ Ⓒ Ⓓ Ⓔ	69 Ⓐ Ⓑ Ⓒ Ⓓ Ⓔ	94 Ⓐ Ⓑ Ⓒ Ⓓ Ⓔ	119 Ⓐ Ⓑ Ⓒ Ⓓ Ⓔ	144 Ⓐ Ⓑ Ⓒ Ⓓ Ⓔ
20 Ⓐ Ⓑ Ⓒ Ⓓ Ⓔ	45 Ⓐ Ⓑ Ⓒ Ⓓ Ⓔ	70 Ⓐ Ⓑ Ⓒ Ⓓ Ⓔ	95 Ⓐ Ⓑ Ⓒ Ⓓ Ⓔ	120 Ⓐ Ⓑ Ⓒ Ⓓ Ⓔ	145 Ⓐ Ⓑ Ⓒ Ⓓ Ⓔ
21 Ⓐ Ⓑ Ⓒ Ⓓ Ⓔ	46 Ⓐ Ⓑ Ⓒ Ⓓ Ⓔ	71 Ⓐ Ⓑ Ⓒ Ⓓ Ⓔ	96 Ⓐ Ⓑ Ⓒ Ⓓ Ⓔ	121 Ⓐ Ⓑ Ⓒ Ⓓ Ⓔ	146 Ⓐ Ⓑ Ⓒ Ⓓ Ⓔ
22 Ⓐ Ⓑ Ⓒ Ⓓ Ⓔ	47 Ⓐ Ⓑ Ⓒ Ⓓ Ⓔ	72 Ⓐ Ⓑ Ⓒ Ⓓ Ⓔ	97 Ⓐ Ⓑ Ⓒ Ⓓ Ⓔ	122 Ⓐ Ⓑ Ⓒ Ⓓ Ⓔ	147 Ⓐ Ⓑ Ⓒ Ⓓ Ⓔ
23 Ⓐ Ⓑ Ⓒ Ⓓ Ⓔ	48 Ⓐ Ⓑ Ⓒ Ⓓ Ⓔ	73 Ⓐ Ⓑ Ⓒ Ⓓ Ⓔ	98 Ⓐ Ⓑ Ⓒ Ⓓ Ⓔ	123 Ⓐ Ⓑ Ⓒ Ⓓ Ⓔ	148 Ⓐ Ⓑ Ⓒ Ⓓ Ⓔ
24 Ⓐ Ⓑ Ⓒ Ⓓ Ⓔ	49 Ⓐ Ⓑ Ⓒ Ⓓ Ⓔ	74 Ⓐ Ⓑ Ⓒ Ⓓ Ⓔ	99 Ⓐ Ⓑ Ⓒ Ⓓ Ⓔ	124 Ⓐ Ⓑ Ⓒ Ⓓ Ⓔ	149 Ⓐ Ⓑ Ⓒ Ⓓ Ⓔ
25 Ⓐ Ⓑ Ⓒ Ⓓ Ⓔ	50 Ⓐ Ⓑ Ⓒ Ⓓ Ⓔ	75 Ⓐ Ⓑ Ⓒ Ⓓ Ⓔ	100 Ⓐ Ⓑ Ⓒ Ⓓ Ⓔ	125 Ⓐ Ⓑ Ⓒ Ⓓ Ⓔ	150 Ⓐ Ⓑ Ⓒ Ⓓ Ⓔ

FIRST PRACTICE AP/CLEP ENGLISH TEST
SECTION I

Directions: Select from the lettered choices that choice which best completes the statement or answers the question. Indicate the letter of your choice on the answer sheet.

THE SICK ROSE

O rose, thou art sick!
The invisible worm
That flies in the night,
In the howling storm

Has found out thy bed
Of crimson joy,
And his dark secret love
Does thy life destroy.

1. "Love," "bed," and "crimson joy" are images that connote

   (A) death in nature
   (B) sexuality in humans
   (C) nature's storms
   (D) man's need for intellectual understanding
   (E) none of the above

2. A literal reading of the poem would indicate that

   (A) death has devoured the rose
   (B) life is an unweeded garden
   (C) a worm has devoured the rose
   (D) the rose was destroyed by the howling storm
   (E) none of the above

3. One theme of the poem may well be the

   (A) harsh life that flowers undergo
   (B) loss of innocence
   (C) fear of death
   (D) ephemeral quality of life
   (E) all of the above

4. A good writing follow-up assignment would require the students to write about

   (A) man's inhumanity to man
   (B) nature's storms
   (C) their reactions to experience
   (D) a history of symbolic poetry
   (E) (C) and (D) above

5. The teacher should be prepared in the teaching of this poem to

   (A) accept a wide variety of interpretation
   (B) do away with class discussion because of the poem's difficulty
   (C) develop one strong thematic approach
   (D) disregard the study of imagery
   (E) (B) and (D) above

Questions 6 through 11 are based on the reading passage below.

While we were enjoying the unlimited vistas, we noticed a commotion on the water at some distance to our left and, somewhat nearer on our right, a rock rising out of the sea; one was Charybdis, the other Scylla. Because of the considerable distance in nature between these two objects which the poet has placed so close together, people have accused poets of fibbing. What they fail to take into account is that the human imagination always pictures the objects it considers significant as taller and narrower than they really are, for this gives them more character, importance and dignity. A thousand times I have heard people complain that some object they had known only from a description was disappointing when seen in reality and the reason was always the same. Imagination is to reality what poetry is to prose: the former will always think of objects as massive and vertical, the latter will always try to extend them horizontally.

6. Scylla and Charybdis are famous in classic lore because

   (A) they were the home of the gods
   (B) they were the site of religious rites
   (C) many mariners were wrecked between them
   (D) lovers eloped to them in spring
   (E) none of the above

7. The writer believes

   (A) that poets lie
   (B) that travel is disappointing
   (C) that human imagination distorts reality
   (D) that the poet extends objects horizontally
   (E) all of the above

8. In line 5 the poet to whom the author refers is probably

   (A) Homer
   (B) Shakespeare
   (C) Robert Frost
   (D) W. H. Auden
   (E) Robert Browning

9. The author believes that reality is often disappointing because

   (A) reality is always dull and uninteresting
   (B) we enhance reality through imagination
   (C) we are escapists at all times
   (D) poets usually avoid facts
   (E) poets live in an imaginary world

10. "Imagination is to reality what poetry is to prose" is an example of

    (A) hendiadys
    (B) litotes
    (C) analogy
    (D) apostrophe
    (E) homology

11. Scylla and Charybdis are

    (A) a rock and a whirlpool
    (B) two rocks near Greece
    (C) two Greek gods in Malta
    (D) names of purely imaginary places
    (E) two mountains in Greece

Questions 12 through 16 refer to the following passage:

The following homework assignment was submitted by a ninth grade pupil in response to the teacher's question: "Describe what Golding means by 'survival of the fittest' in Lord of the Flies:

Lord of the Flies is a book that tells why only the fittest will survive when people are forced to live like savages in the jungle. All that you have to do is to look at what happened to some of the characters to know that this is true, if you ask yourself who made it and why you will also find the answer, but it's not easy.
Now Ralph lived and Fatty didn't and Jack survived and Roger didn't, that proves that the strong survive and the weak don't. A man on television once said that if you have guts and courage you will be able to make it anywhere, after all why do the strongest and fastest animals live so long?

Select from the four choices offered in each of the following the one which is correct or most nearly correct. Mark on the answer sheet the number corresponding to that choice.

12. Most noticeable in the student's sentences is the repeated use of

    (A) sentence fragments
    (B) run-on sentences
    (C) dangling participles
    (D) misplaced modifiers
    (E) adjectives

13. The homework fails to answer the teacher's question because

    (A) the student is not clear as to what "survival of the fittest" means
    (B) the student does not provide sufficient specific references from the novel
    (C) the student is illiterate in his use of English
    (D) the student is unable to come to a conclusion
    (E) the student did not read the book

14. The most helpful comment that a teacher might place on this student's homework is

    (A) "Improve your sentences."
    (B) "Get to the point."
    (C) "Which of the events in the book could help you prove your point?"
    (D) "Not very convincing!"
    (E) "Get some help."

15. In order to improve the thought in the opening line of paragraph 2, the teacher should write in the margin

    (A) "But do the strong survive?"
    (B) "Why did Ralph and Jack survive?"
    (C) "Tell me more."
    (D) "Not a bad idea at all."
    (E) "Why didn't Roger survive?"

16. Homework assignments requiring written response will improve writing ability if they are

    (A) based on outlines worked out in class
    (B) limited to short sentences
    (C) developed into three paragraphs
    (D) always rated for both content and style
    (E) all long sentences

Questions 17 through 22 are based on the following poem.

THE NEW COLOSSUS

Not like the brazen giant of Greek fame,
With conquering limbs astride from land to land;
Here at our sea-washed, sunset gates shall stand
A mighty woman with a torch, whose flame
Is the imprisoned lightning, and her name
Mother of Exiles. From her beacon-hand
Glows world-wide welcome; her mild eyes command
The air-bridged harbor that twin cities frame.

"Keep, ancient lands, your storied pomp!" cries she
With silent lips. "Give me your tired, your poor,
Your huddled masses yearning to breathe free,
The wretched refuse of your teeming shore.
Send these, the homeless, tempest-most to me.
I lift my lamp beside the golden door!"

17. Of the following items the best choice for use by a teacher wishing to make the main idea of this poem clearer to a class is

    (A) make a replica of the Statue of Liberty
    (B) a cassette recording of an interview with a recent immigrant
    (C) large pictures of the Statue of Liberty and of the Colossus of Rhodes
    (D) a recording of the song beginning, "Give me your tired, your poor"
    (E) a display photograph of Emma Lazarus

18. Bright sophomores might be expected to discover all of the following about the form of this poem <u>except</u> its

    (A) use of octave and sestet
    (B) typical rhyme scheme
    (C) identity as a Shakespearean sonnet
    (D) iambic pentameter
    (E) loss of stress because of the beat

19. Of the following figures of speech, the one that is used most frequently in this poem is

    (A) onomatopoeia
    (B) apostrophe
    (C) alliteration
    (D) simile
    (E) dangling participles

20. The first word of the poem, <u>not</u>, has special significance in that it

    (A) sets the negative mood of the whole
    (B) emphasizes the contrast implied in the title
    (C) loses all stress because of the iambic beat
    (D) echoes the unspoken nautical word <u>knot</u>
    (E) indicates a negation reaction

21. A word that should be taught as having an intentionally ambiguous meaning in this poem is

    (A) teeming, meaning both "crowded" and "raining"
    (B) silent, meaning both "quiet" and "sighing"
    (C) limbs, meaning both "legs" and "tree branches"
    (D) brazen, meaning both "brass" and "bold"
    (E) gates, meaning both "fences" and "forts"

22. The expression closest in its form and structure to "sea-washed gates" is

    (A) world-wide welcome
    (B) air-bridged harbor
    (C) beacon-hand glows
    (D) homeless, tempest-most
    (E) teeming shore

Questions 23 through 31 are based on the following selection.

The civilization round Concord today is an odd distillation of city, village, farm, and manor. The houses, yards, fields look not quite suburban, not quite rural. Under the bronze beech and the blue spruce of the departed baron grazes the milch goat of the heirs. Under the porte-cochere stands the reconditioned station wagon; under the grape arbor sit the puppies for sale.

It was June and everywhere June was publishing her immemorial stanza; in the lilacs, in the syringa, in the freshly edged paths and the sweetness of moist beloved gardens, and the little wire wickets that preserve the tulips' front. Farmers were already moving the fruits of their toil into their yards, arranging the rhubarb, the asparagus, the strictly fresh eggs on the painted stands under the little shed roofs with the patent shingles. And though it was almost a hundred years since you had taken your ax and started cutting out your home on Walden Pond, I was interested to observe that in the center of a vacant lot some boys were assembling the framework of a rude shelter, their whole mind and skill concentrated in the rather inauspicious helter-skeleton of studs and rafters. They too were escaping from town, to live naturally, in a rich blend of savagery and philosophy.

23. The you in line 13, "and though it was almost one hundred years since you had taken your ax and started cutting out your home on Walden Pond," is

    (A) Nathaniel Hawthorne
    (B) Ralph Waldo Emerson
    (C) Henry David Thoreau
    (D) James Fenimore Cooper
    (E) Henry Wadsworth Longfellow

24. The phrase June was publishing her immemorial stanza is an example of

    (A) oxymoron
    (B) simile
    (C) apostrophe
    (D) personification
    (E) hyperbole

25. The phrase "an odd distillation of city, village, farm, and manor" (lines 1-2) is an example of

    (A) personification
    (B) metaphor
    (C) oxymoron
    (D) simile
    (E) apostrophe

26. The author does all the following in the passage except

    (A) use descriptive details
    (B) point out contrasts
    (C) include an anecdote
    (D) note similarities
    (E) has run-on sentences

27. The author's attitude toward the boys' "escaping from town" is one of

(A) contempt
(B) bewilderment
(C) approval
(D) indifference
(E) satisfaction

28. The repetition of vowel sounds in a phrase like "philosophical spirit was still alive" is an example of

(A) alliteration
(B) onomatopoeia
(C) assonance
(D) hyperbole
(E) metaphor

29. The sentence "Under the porte-cochere stands the reconditioned station wagon; under the grape arbor sit the puppies for sale" (lines 4-6) is an example of a

(A) loose sentence
(B) complex sentence
(C) balanced sentence
(D) run-on sentence
(E) unbalanced sentence

30. The expression "helter-skeleton" (line 17) is an example of a (an)

(A) anachronism
(B) oxymoron
(C) euphemism
(D) pun
(E) personification

31. During the lifetime of the baron mentioned in the first paragraph, he probably lived in (on) the

(A) city
(B) village
(C) farm
(D) manor
(E) castle

Questions 32 through 35 are based on the following poem

To one who has been long in city pent,
'Tis very sweet to look into the fair
And open face of heaven,--to breathe a prayer
Full in the smile of the blue firmament.
Who is more happy, when, with heart's content
Fatigued he sinks into some pleasant lair
Of wavy grass, and reads a dobonair
And gentle tale of love and languishment?

Returning home at evening with an ear
Catching the notes of Philomel,--an eye
Watching the sailing cloudlet's bright career,
He mourns that day so soon has glided by,
E'en like the passage of an angel's tear
That falls through the clear ether silently

32. Concerning the poem all the following information is true <u>except</u> that

(A) it is iambic
(B) the predominant meter is trochaic
(C) its rhyme scheme is abba, abba, cde cde
(D) it is a sonnet
(E) it is the work of John Keats

33. The poet regrets that

(A) he does not live in the country
(B) he does not live in the city
(C) his day in the country passes so rapidly
(D) the quiet of night is broken by the song of a bird
(E) his day in the country has fatigued him

34. The poet alludes to the song of the

(A) nightingale
(B) thrush
(C) swallow
(D) whippoorwill
(E) meadowlark

35. In the poem the poet compares

(A) the sky with a woman's smile
(B) a bird with a tear
(C) a bird with an eye
(D) a day with a tear
(E) a day with an eye

Answer questions 36 through 39 with reference to the following passage:

The Arthurian cycle of legends is perhaps the most varied and widely known of all romances. These legends have been widely circulated since 1400 in most European literature: French, German, Spanish, Italian, English, and Welsh. Wagner's musical dramas also refer to the legends. Historical material upon which these legends may have been based is extremely sketchy. There was an Arthur who was a captain of the Britons in successful repulses of the Saxons. The victories, however, were short-lived, and the Saxons returned in greater numbers to crush the Britons. Some early chroniclers mentioned Arthur, and later imaginative writers told stories about him in a highly interpretative and colored fashion, so that it is difficult to tell where the truth, if any, ends, and the fiction begins. Sir Thomas Malory, who wrote Morte D'Arthur in the 1400's is recognized as the greatest writer of Arthurian romance. The material for the Idylls in general was written over a period of more than forty years, but the development of a single theme binds them together: the destruction of a noble ideal by the ever-increasing consequences of a single sin. Although the Idylls end upon a gloomy note, a note of great hope exists for the future with a promise of even greater glory for Arthur in the next world because of his loyalty to the heroic ideal.

36. The first writings about the Arthurian legend placed the chieftain in

(A) France
(B) Spain
(C) Germany
(D) Italy
(E) none of the above

37. The earliest record of the events which concern the Arthurian cycle goes back to the

(A) first century
(B) sixth century
(C) twelfth century
(D) thirteenth century
(E) fourteenth century

38. Originally, Arthur was a

(A) Norman hero
(B) Saxon hero
(C) Celtic hero
(D) Roman hero
(E) Greek hero

39. The book most widely recognized as the best Arthurian story was done

(A) in free verse
(B) as a group of ballads
(C) in prose form
(D) partly in verse, partly in metrical form
(E) in none of the above

Answer questions 40, 41, and 42 with reference to the following passage:

Hamlet lives and moves by and through a series of conflicts and contrasts to ultimate resolutions. Among these conflicts is the central action, the duel of wits between Hamlet and Claudius, which sweeps all lesser interlopers away (for, as Hamlet says of Rosencrantz and Guildenstern's going to their deaths: " 'Tis dangerous when the baser nature comes / Between the pass and fell incensed points / Of mighty opposites.") Then there is the physical duel between Laertes and Hamlet, the verbal duel between Polonius and Hamlet (e.g., about the "shape" of the cloud--part of the larger duel of Polonius and the King with the Prince to ascertain the cause of his madness) and the duel on many levels between Hamlet and Rosencrantz / Guildenstern. The larger physical conflict between Norway and Denmark hovers over the play. Implicit and explicit character contrasts abound, such as those between Claudius and the elder Hamlet, between incestuous Gertrude and innocent Ophelia. Psychological conflict expresses itself at times in terms of reason vs. passion. The colorful splendor of the opening court scene contrasts with Hamlet's sable garb (a conflict in clothes which is echoed in clothes-imagery and diction throughout the play). The antic disposition of Hamlet contrasts with the real madness of Ophelia. And there are the contrasts within the structural parallels of Laertes, Fortinbras, and Hamlet--three sons with fathers to avenge. These and many other covert and overt clashes are the substance of the play as drama.

40. It is not true that

(A) in addition to the external conflicts in Hamlet, there are various internal ones
(B) Hamlet is cast in the role of avenger in a world he never made
(C) the thematic conflict of "reality vs. appearance" echoes throughout Hamlet
(D) Hamlet like almost all great dramatic works consists of conflicts
(E) as a play, Hamlet has little emotional involvement

41. Hamlet and Macbeth have much in common, but not the following:

(A) the feeling of a supreme power who is destined to avenge a crime
(B) the appearance of a ghost
(C) the milieu of royalty
(D) the importance placed on the loyalty of a friend
(E) the element of plotting

42. The figure of speech used in the parenthetical quote (lines 4-5) is

(A) hyperbole
(B) personification
(C) simile
(D) alliteration
(E) none of the above

Answer questions 43 - 44 by referring to the following selection:

I met a traveller from an antique land
Who said: Two vast and trunkless legs of stone
Stand in the desert. Near them, on the sand,
Half sunk, a shattered visage lies, whose frown,
And wrinkled lip, and sneer of cold command,
Tell that its sculptor well those passions read
Which yet survive, stamped on these lifeless things,
The hand that mocked them, and the heart that fed:
And on the pedestal these words appear:
'My name is Ozymandias, king of kings:
Look on my works, ye Mighty, and despair!'
Nothing beside remains. Round the decay
Of that colossal wreck, boundless and bare
The lone and level sands stretch far away.

43. The principal thought is that

(A) there is no frigate like a book to take you lands away
(B) art is long and time is fleeting
(C) the paths of glory lead but to the grave
(D) the meek shall inherit the earth
(E) royalty, to be worshipped, must be humble

44. The words "hand" and "heart" refer, respectively, to

(A) the traveller--the antique land
(B) the sculptor--the king
(C) the statue--the sculptor
(D) the king--the traveller
(E) none of the pairs above

Answer questions 45 - 47 with reference to the following passage:

For common gifts, necessity makes pertinences and beauty every day, and one is glad when an imperative leaves him no option, since if the man at the door has no shoes you have not to consider whether you could procure him a paint-box. And as it is always pleasing to see a man eat bread, or drink water, in the house or out of doors, so it is always a great satisfaction to supply these first wants. Necessity does everything well. In our condition of universal dependence, it seems heroic to let the petitioner be the judge of his necessity, and to give all that is asked, though at great inconvenience. If it be a fantastic desire, it is better to leave to others the office of punishing him. I can think of many parts I should prefer playing to that of the Furies. Next to things of necessity, the rule for a gift, which one of my friends prescribed, is, that we might convey to some person that which properly belonged to his character, and was easily associated with him in thought. But our tokens of compliment and love are for the most part barbarous. Rings and other jewels are not gifts, but apologies for gifts. The only gift is a portion of thyself. Thou must bleed for me. Therefore the poet brings his poem; the shepherd, his lamb; the farmer, corn; the miner, a gem; the sailor, coral and shells; the painter, his picture; the girl, a handkerchief of her own sewing. This is right and pleasing, for it restores society in so far to its primary basis, when a man's biography is conveyed in his gift, and every man's wealth is an index of his merit. But it is a cold, lifeless business when you go to the shops to buy me something, which does not represent your life and talent, but a goldsmith's. This is fit for kings, and rich men who represent kings, and a false state of property, to make presents of gold and silver stuffs, as a kind of symbolical sin-offering, or payment of blackmail.

45. One thing that we may say about the style of writing of this passage is that

(A) the unit of thought is the sentence, not the paragraph
(B) sparkle, humor, and originality prevail
(C) it is dramatic and emotional
(D) it is direct, yet pessimistic
(E) it is vibrant and free-flowing

46. The Furies (line 10) refer to

(A) dancing comedians on the Elizabethan stage
(B) people who are angry with their lot in life
(C) a clan that was involved in a bitter feud
(D) beings who punished the wicked
(E) none of the above

47. The writer believes that

(A) a gift should be given only if it has little material value
(B) a ring made by a craftsman would be an appropriate gift--provided he himself offers it
(C) the most meaningful gift is that which one has made himself for someone else
(D) a painting is a better gift than food
(E) gift-giving is a barbaric custom

Answer questions 48 - 51 by referring to the following selections:

The world is too much with us; late and soon,
Getting and spending, we lay waste our Powers:
Little we see in Nature that is ours;
We have given our hearts away, a sordid boon!
This Sea that bares her bosom to the moon;
The winds that will be howling at all hours,
And are up-gathered now like sleeping flowers;
For this, for everything, we are out of tune;
It moves us not.--Great God! I'd rather be
A Pagan suckled in a creed outworn;
So might I, standing on this pleasant lea,
Have glimpses that would make me less forlorn;
Have sight of Proteus rising from the sea;
Or hear old Triton blow his wreathed horn.

48. The verse meter is

(A) trochaic hexameter
(B) dactylic tetrameter
(C) iambic pentameter
(D) spondaic heptameter
(E) none of the above

49. The central idea is that

(A) we are not using our talents to full capacity
(B) there are values in other religions
(C) loneliness can be, and should be overcome
(D) commercialism is eclipsing spiritual values
(E) present-day religions stem from myths

50. The poet expresses a desire to

(A) be a child again
(B) appreciate natural beauty
(C) desert the city for the country
(D) play harmonious music
(E) do none of the above

51. Proteus and Triton are

(A) sea monsters
(B) forms of fish
(C) human beings
(D) sea gods
(E) none of the above

Answer questions 52 - 54 with reference to the following passage:

For the first day or two I felt stunned, overwhelmed. I could only apprehend my felicity; I was too confused to taste it sincerely. I wandered about, thinking I was happy, and knowing that I was not. I was in the condition of a prisoner in the Old Bastille, suddenly let loose after a forty years' confinement. I could scarce trust myself with myself. It was like passing out of Time into Eternity--for it is a sort of Eternity for a man to have his Time all to himself. It seemed to me that I had more time on my hands than I could ever manage. From a poor man, poor in Time, I was suddenly lifted up into a vast revenue; I could see no end of my possessions; I wanted some steward, or judicious bailiff, to manage my estates in Time for me. And here let me caution persons grown old in active business, not lightly, nor without weighing their own resources, to forego their customary employment all at once, for there may be danger in it. I feel it by myself, but I know that my resources are sufficient; and now that those first giddy raptures have subsided, I have a quiet home feeling of the blessedness of my condition. I am in no hurry. Having all holidays, I am as though I had none. If Time hung heavy upon me, I could walk it away; but I do not walk all day long, as I used to do in those old transient holidays, thirty miles a day, to make the most of them. If Time were troublesome, I could read it away, but I do not read in that violent measure, with which, having no Time my own but candle-light Time, I used to weary out my head and eyesight in bygone winters. I walk, read, or scribble (as now) just when the fit seizes me. I no longer hunt after pleasure; I let it come to me.

52. Charles Lamb's attitude toward retirement is one of

(A) boredom
(B) indecision
(C) satisfaction
(D) ecstasy
(E) disgust

53. The writing style of the passage is both

(A) mild and trenchant
(B) stilted and imaginative
(C) informal and human
(D) satiric and formal
(E) fast-moving and abstruse

54. The reader may infer that Lamb

(A) has just been released from prison
(B) has just left the hospital and is now recuperating
(C) has quite a bit of money
(D) is accustomed to hard work
(E) is sick and tired of work

Answer questions 55 - 57 with reference to the following passage:

Length is about the only thing that Pope's The Rape of the Lock and Keats' The Eve of St. Agnes have in common. Both works, the Neo-Classical and the Romantic, employ the devices of poetry--meter and rhythm, image and metaphor, together with the narrative conventions which are the property of both novelists and poets, to create words of illusion. The narrative materials constitute the subject, while the poetic devices define an attitude or set of attitudes toward the subject. There are obvious contrasts both of subject and tone in the two poems. Pope's subject is drawn from the contemporary world of fashion, a world with which he had an immediate relationship; which he could observe directly. Keats' subject is drawn from the remote world of the feudal Middle Ages, which he could observe directly only by looking, say, at architectural remains (and note the detailed attention given to the "carved angels, ever eager-eyed," etc.), or by the "direct observation" of research; but there is no evidence that Keats made use of the latter expedient. The world of The Eve is made up almost entirely of materials furnished by the imagination, of poetic suggestions, hints, culled from the poet's reading of the older English poetry, not chroniclers like Froissart. The story is both simple and familiar: the Romeo-Juliet lovers belonging to feuding baronial houses, the dangerous visit of Porphyro to the house of Madeline, the St. Agnes Eve revelry in the great hall contrasted with the maiden's vigil alone in her chamber, the union there effected by Angela, the go-between (Juliet's nurse), and the escape. Some slight claim to historical validity is made--"ages long ago / These lovers fled away into the storm." But it is not so much "belief" in the story that is called for as belief in an illusion, the illusion of art, which creates an unreal world in which age, death, ugliness, and hatred exist, but in which two lovers, set over against those "realities," persuade us that they will forever love "and she be fair" in the world across the moors to which they flee. The art is contrived solely to create this "belief," this illusion--the verbal orchestration, the rich stained-glass coloring, the "argent revelry" of the trumpets. All is designed to impel the reader to "melt" into the illusion as Porphyro melts, swooning, into Madeline's dream. And it is precisely this that most clearly distinguishes Keats' poem from Pope's. Pope's art discourages such "melting"; it is designed to put the reader off. In the poetic world of The Rape of the Lock illusion is created, and with great skill; but is created only to be ruthlessly, although gayly, destroyed. Example: the effect of the two "realistic" lines which follow immediately upon the dream-speech of Ariel in Canto I: "He said; when Shock, who thought she slept too long, / Leaped up, and waked his mistress with his tongue." Between this rude awakening and the lute melody of La Belle Dame Sans Merci which awakens Madeline, lies the whole difference between the two poets and (forgetting Byron for the moment) their different literary periods: Age of Disillusionment; Age of Illusion Regained.

55. Pope and Keats are

(A) Neo-Classical but not Romantic
(B) Romantic but not Neo-Classical
(C) Romantic and Neo-Classical respectively
(D) Neo-Classical and Romantic respectively
(E) not any of the above

56. The Rape of the Lock and The Eve of St. Agnes have the following in common:

(A) chronological source of material
(B) actual contact with subject
(C) choice of subject
(D) purpose of illusion created
(E) use of poetic technique

57. We may justifiably say that, in regard to poetic response to similar situations,

(A) Keats accepted human limitations --Pope did not.
(B) Keats tried to keep passion under control--Pope did not.
(C) Keats cultivated the primitive--Pope did not.
(D) Keats enjoyed the graces of urbanity--Pope did not.
(E) none of the above is true

Answer questions 58 - 60 with reference to the following passage:

Mr. Hooper had the reputation of a good preacher, but not an energetic one; he strove to win his people heavenward by mild, persuasive influences, rather than to drive them thither by the thunders of the Word. The sermon which he now delivered was marked by the same characteristics of style and manner as the general series of his pulpit oratory. But there was something, either in the sentiment of the discourse itself, or in the imagination of the auditors, which made it greatly the most powerful effort that they had ever heard from their pastor's lips. It was tinged, rather more darkly than usual, with the gentle gloom of Mr. Hooper's temperament. The subject had reference to secret sin, and those sad mysteries which we hide from our nearest and dearest, and would fain conceal from our own consciousness, even forgetting that the Omniscient can detect them. A subtle power was breathed into his words. Each member of the congregation, the most innocent girl, and the man of hardened breast, felt as if the preacher had crept upon them, behind his awful veil and discovered their hoarded iniquity of deed or thought. Many spread their clasped hands on their bosoms. There was nothing terrible in what Mr. Hooper said, at least no violence; and yet, with every tremor of his melancholy voice, the hearers quaked. An unsought pathos came hand in hand with awe. So sensible were the audience of some unwonted attribute in their minister, that they longed for a breath of wind to blow aside the veil, almost believing that a stranger's visage would be discovered, though the form, gesture, and voice were those of Mr. Hooper.

58. The style of the minister's delivery may be described as

(A) forceful and direct
(B) amusing and convincing
(C) effective through delayed reaction
(D) replete with examples
(E) free-flowing, but complicated

59. Mr. Hooper was

(A) esoteric
(B) willful
(C) ingenuous
(D) penetrative
(E) none of the above

60. The pulpit delivery of the preacher reminds one of the influence of

(A) Billy Sunday
(B) Svengali
(C) Pershing
(D) Babe Ruth
(E) Theodore Roosevelt

ANSWER KEY

1. B	16. A	31. D	46. D
2. C	17. B	32. C	47. B
3. D	18. C	33. C	48. C
4. A	19. C	34. A	49. D
5. A	20. B	35. D	50. B
6. C	21. D	36. E	51. D
7. C	22. B	37. B	52. C
8. A	23. C	38. C	53. C
9. B	24. D	39. C	54. D
10. C	25. C	40. E	55. D
11. A	26. C	41. D	56. E
12. B	27. C	42. B	57. C
13. B	28. C	43. C	48. C
14. C	29. C	44. B	59. D
15. B	30. D	45. A	60. B

FIRST PRACTICE AP/CLEP ENGLISH TEST
SECTION II

Question 1 (Suggested time - 30 minutes)

Directions: Read the following poem carefully and then write an essay in which you discuss how the poet's diction (choice of words) represents a dramatic monologue.

SNAKE

D.H. Lawrence

A snake came to my water trough
On a hot, hot day, and I in my pajamas for the heat,
To drink there.

In the deep, strange-scented shade of the great dark carob-tree
I came down the steps with my pitcher and must wait,
must stand and wait, for there he was at the trough before me.

He reached down from a fissure in the earth-wall in the gloom
And trailed his yellow-brown slackness soft-bellied down,
   over the edge of the stone trough
And rested his throat upon the stone bottom,
And where the water had dripped from the tap, in a small clearness,
He sipped with his straight mouth
Softly drank through his straight gums, into his slack long body,
Silently.

Someone was before me at my water-trough,
And I, like a second comer, waiting.

He lifted his head from his drinking, as cattle do,
And looked at me vaguely, as drinking cattle do,
And flickered his two-forked tongue from his lips, and mused a moment,
And stooped and drank a little more,
Being earth-brown, earth-golden from the burning bowels of the earth
On the day of Sicilian July, with Etna smoking.
The voice of my education said to me
He must be killed,
For in Sicily the black, black snakes are innocent, the gold are venomous.

And voices in me said, If you were a man
You would take a stick and break him now, and finish him off.

But must I confess how I liked him,
How glad I was he had come like a guest in quite, to drink at my
water-trough
And depart peaceful, pacified, and thankless,
Into the burning bowels of this earth?

Was it cowardice that I dared not kill him?
Was it perversity, that I longed to talk to him?
Was it humility, to feel so honoured?
I felt so honoured.

And yet those voices: If you were not afraid, you would kill him!

And truly I was afraid, I was most afraid,
But even so, honoured still more that he should seek my hospitality
From out the dark door of the secret earth.

He drank enough
And lifted his head, dreamily, as one who has drunken,
And flickered his toungue like a forked night on the air, so
black.

Seeming to lick his lips,
And looked around like a god, unseeing, into the air,
And slowly turned his head, And slowly, very slowly, as if thrice adream,
Proceeded to draw his slow length curving round
And climb again the broken bank of my wall-face.

And as he put his head into that dreadful hole,
And as he slowly drew up, snake-easing his shoulders, and entered farther,
A sort of horror, a sort of protest against his withdrawing into that
horrid black hole,
Deliberately going into the blackness, and slowly drawing himself after,
Overcame me now his back was turned.

I looked around, I put down my pitcher,
I picked up a clumsy log And threw it at the water-trough with a clatter.

I think it did not hit him,
But suddenly that part of him that was left behind convulsed
in undignified haste,
Writhed like lightning, and was gone
Into the black hole, the earth-lipped fissure in the wallfront,
At which, in the intense still noon, I stared with fascination.

And immediately I regretted it.
I thought how paltry, how vulgar, what a mean act!
I despised myself and the voices of my accursed human education.

And I thought of the albatross,
And I wished he would come back, my snake.

For he seemed to me again like a king,
Like a king in exile, uncrowned in the underworld,
Now due to be crowned again.

And so, I missed my chance with one of the lords
Of Life.
And I have something to expiate;
A pettiness.

Response (1):

The Snake by D.H. Lawrence is a dramatic monologue dealing with an important moment in the poet's life. It comments on how man, through his education and inherent weaknesses, sometimes loses touch with nature, and disrupts what he cannot fully understand. The speaker's attitude is one of regret: he is sorry for the "mean act" he committed, and ashamed at his human pettiness.

Lawrence uses contrasting imagery and sound to compare the snake, which represents the harmony of nature, and man (himself). The snake has come to drink at the watering trough at the speaker's home. The grace of the snake is portrayed by the use of the "s" sound ("soft-bellied," "softly drank through his straight gums into his slack long body, silently"). He is "like a god," perfect in his simplicity of purpose and intent. The snake is aware of the man, but continues to drink. The man, on the other hand, must wait while the snake is drinking. He feels like a "second-comer" in his own home. Dressed in his pajamas, waiting, the man seems out of place. Emotionally, two opposing forces pull at him. All of his upbringing and years of education tell him that the snake should be killed because it is poisonous. The voices prod him by saying, "If you were a man, you would take a stick and break him now." But inside, the man feels honoured at the snake's presence. He is attracted to the snake because it comes from deep within the ground ("burning bowels of the earth"). He is both fascinated and wary of the mysteriousness of this creature that lives beneath the smoking Mr. Etna. Lawrence admires the qualities of his guest -- "quite," "peacebul," "pacified" -- qualities that are gentle, both in meaning and in sound. But he is also afraid, not so much by the physical danger as by being afraid that he is really a coward for not immediately killing the snake. By his decision to let the snake alone, he has gone against his education and the superstitions of his society. The man feels close to nature at this point.

While the image of the man is one of inner turmoil, the snake has remained an image of tranquility and deliberateness: "and lifted his head dreamily, . . . and looked around . . . unseeing into the air." As he turns to enter his hole, all of the snake's movements are slow and deliberate. The repetition of the word "slowly" adds to the flowing rhythm of the poem, as does the phrase "snake-easing his shoulders," all using the soft "s" sound. By contrast, the man's next actions are awkward, and impulsive. On seeing the snake withdrawing into the "dark door of the most secret earth," the hole and his fear of the unknown make it seem dreadful and "horrid." To protest the snake's departure, the man picks up a log and chucks it at the retreating figure, missing widely. The words used to describe this scene involving the man are also awkward: "clumsy," "clatter," "convulse," "undignified." They use hard sounds. By disrupting the pattern of the snake, man has also disrupted nature. He has let his learning and human weaknesses and fear influence his actions. The books say you must kill poisonous snakes. Society demands that a "real" man would kill the snake unless he is a coward.

Lawrence regrets what he has done. He despises himself and the "voices of my accursed human education." He makes an allusion to the albatross in Samuel Taylor

Coleridge's Rime of the Ancient Mariner. In that poem, man's fear and superstition caused him to kill the albatross, thus bringing down on his head misfortune and death. In the poem by Lawrence, the man is afraid of the snake returning to the unknown, dark hole in the ground. The man is led partly by the Sicilian superstition that gold snakes are harmful, also. Lawrence infers that perhaps man should accept more of his own feelings, and not let our lives be ruled by the dictates of society, for we can miss out on many new experiences -- "And so, I missed my chance with one of the lords of life." He also suggests man makes too little effort to understand nature, and perhaps he could learn a few things from the simple animals. Man can only lose when he chooses to think himself superior to nature. In his poem, the snake displayed much more admirable qualities than the man. Because of his encounter with the snake, Lawrence has changed, and now realizes and wishes to atone for his weakness and pettiness.

Response (2):

"Snake" is a poem in which D.H. Lawrence tells of a personal experience of his. One day he goes to the water-trough and when he gets there he sees a snake who seems to be thoroughly enjoying the cool, clear water. At the beginning of the poem, Lawrence describes the actions of the snake and then gets the notion that it should be killed because it is venomous. The middle of the poem has the author debating over whether to kill the snake or to leave it to it's peaceful existence. He seems to be listening to someone, most likely his conscience, and yet there are voices telling him, "If you were not afraid, you would kill him." Towards the end, the speaker throws a log at the snake but doesn't kill it. I think that he is happy the snake lived but he's a little worried about having given in and tried to kill the snake.

According to "The Reader's Companion to World Literature," a dramatic monologue is "a poem in which one character speaks throughout but the presence, actions, and even words of other characters are implied." Also the speaker is usually caught at a dramatic moment or crisis and often reveals his innermost character, his "soul in action." This is very true in "The Snake" as all these conditions are present.

The aspects of dramatic monologue are easily seen in Lawrence's poem. We observe the author caught in a dramatic moment in his life, a time when he must make a big decision for himself. This decision may not seem that great at first, but when you realize that it involves his feelings towards cowardice and honour you can see that it is.

There are not actually any other characters in "Snake," but the speaker hears some kind of voices, probably those of people he has known and also his own thoughts. We also most definitely see Lawrence's soul in action making up his mind whether to even try to kill the snake or to just leave it alone and let it be on its way.

As you read this poem you can see these things that help make it a dramatic monologue and a very interesting poem. A poem that is about more than just a snake but about an important decision in a man's life. A decision about what is probably most important in every man's life: his own innermost feelings about life and living.

Question 2 (Suggested time - 50 minutes)

Directions: Select a satire of recognized literary merit and write a critical essay. In your essay analyze the conflict and discuss the moral implications for the individuals involved.

Response:

Don Juan, a satire of seventeen cantos written by Lord Byron between 1818 and 1824, is a mock epic of the adventures of Don Juan. The first canto is the story of his life until he reaches the age of sixteen. His father, Don Jose, died when Juan was a small child. Because of this, he was brought up by his overly-possessive mother, Donna Inez, who was an intelligent but impractical woman.

Juan's early life was very simple. When he wasn't studying with his tutors he was in his mother's company. The first change in his life occurred at the age of sixteen when he was influenced by Donna Julia, a friend of his mother. She was twenty-three but was attracted to Juan because she was tired of her husband, Don Alfonso, who was fifty-one.

The section I have chosen to analyze is taken from the last part of the first canto. It is the scene where Julia is suspected by Alfonso of having a man in her room. She flatly denied it and he believed her until --

CLXXXI

A pair of shoes! -- what then? not much, if they
Are such as fit with ladies' feet, but these
(No one can tell how much I grieve to say)
Were masculine; to see them, and to seize,
Was but a moment's act. -- Ah! well-a-day!
My teeth begin to chatter, my veins freeze --
Alfonso first examined well their fashion,
And then flew out into another passion.

CLXXXII

He left the room for his relinquish'd sword,
And Julia instant to the closet flew.
'Fly, Juan, fly! for heaven's sake -- not a word --
The door is open -- you may yet slip through
The passage you so often have explored --
Here is the garden-key -- Fly -- fly -- Adieu!
Haste -- haste! I hear Alfonso's hurrying feet --
Day has not broke -- there's no one in the street.'

CLXXXIII

None can say that this was not good advice
The only mischief was, it came too late;
Of all experience 't is the usual price,
A sort of income-tax laid on by fate:
Juan had reach'd the room-door in a trice,
And might have done so by the garden-gate,
But met Alfonso in his dressing-gown,
Who threatened death -- so Juan knocked him down.

By using this passage I would like to show how important word choice and sentence structure is to Byron's satiric writing style. Critics have called Don Juan the greatest satire ever written. By pointing out different lines that are comical where they would be serious, I will show that it is a satire.

Byron first introduces a controversial subject, the pair of shoes, which he emphasizes with an exclamation point. Instead of telling us why they are so important he builds suspense by first asking the question "what then?". He answers part of the question then takes a pause to make a personal comment before revealing the fact that they are masculine. After this is brought out he reverts back to his attitude of nonchalance saying that they are right in front of Alfonso and about to be discovered. It is as though Alfonso knows they are there but plans to make nothing of it. The narrator then tries to tell us that something terrible is going to happen but Alfonso remains very passive in his examination of the style of the shoe. Then, quite suddenly, he went into a rage.

In the next stanza Byron is emphasizing the fact that Julia went quickly to the closet by placing the word instant directly after her name. He added a comical effect by using the word fly to describe the actions of both Julia and Juan. The choice of words in the next three lines is very important. On first reading it you understand that Julia is giving the garden key to Juan so that he might leave quickly as he has done often enough. But on close examination you can see the sexual connotations that are expressed because of his choice of words.

Byron warns us that Juan must really hurry by having Julia repeat the words fly and haste. In the line "I hear Alfonso's hurrying feet," the choice of words gives us a humorous image. Instead of telling us that she hears Alfonso coming, Julia speaks only of his feet.

The narrator says that Julia's advice to Juan is good but that it came too late. He says that getting good advice too late is the price paid in many circumstances. Then he uses an anachronism as a side note to add humor to the poem. Juan runs to the door but is met there by Alfonso who is carrying a sword. Instead of picturing him carrying his sword in a fit of anger the reader gets an image of Alfonso as an old man in a dressing gown because of the words used to describe him. Byron then tries to make him seem tough by saying that he threatened death. The fact that Juan just knocked him down pokes fun at Alfonso.

Question 3 (Suggested time - 40 minutes)

Directions: Select a novel of your choice and develop the character conflicts. Focus on the evolution of roles and resolution; do not summarize the plot or action of the work you choose.

Response:

"There Were Some Changes Made"

> "Everyone is disgusted by his pride. You will not find him . . . favorably spoken of by anyone."
>
> "I love him. Indeed he has no improper pride. He is perfectly amiable."

Both of the above quotes were made by Elizabeth Bennett at different times in Jane Austen's "Pride and Prejudice." It is obvious that there was quite a change somewhere in between. It will be the purpose of this paper to show how that change took place and to show that the main event in this change is the scene in which Elizabeth visits Darcy's estate at Pemberley.

It is obvious that Miss Austen does not intend for her reader to particularly admire Darcy at the beginning. A mere three lines after he is first introduced amid favorable reports of glamor and wealth, he is brought down sharply;

> ". . . his manners gave a disgust which turned the tide of his popularity; for he was discovered to be proud, to be above his company, and above being pleased."

She tells us that he has "a most forbidding, disagreeable countenance;" this could not possibly be the best way to introduce a man who the reader is intended to like.

And we do not like him at the beginning; neither does Elizabeth. In fact, it does not take her long to learn to hate him, as he hurts her pride by referring to her as "tolerable." Miss Lucas asks her not to dance with him, even if approached by him, to which she replies:

> "I believe, ma'am, I can safely promise you never to dance with him."

Such is the hate which is already harbored in her soul for Mr. Darcy. She will not even think of dancing with him. When the question of his pride and whether he has a right to it comes up, we find the reason for her contempt.

> "I could easily forgive <u>his</u> pride, if he had not mortified <u>mine</u>."

There are two main plots in "Pride and Prejudice." The Darcy/Elizabeth plot is the major one, and the Bingley/Jane plot is the minor one, although it must be considered a main plot. The only characters in the book which change in the story are those involved in the former plot. Those whose primary concern is with the latter plot stay the same (i.e., retain the same character) throughout the novel. They are also constantly being driven by the influence of others. A prime example of this is Bingley moving back to London because his friend Darcy feels that Jane is "indifferent" to him.

A major plot connection lies in Wickham, who not only plays a major role in the Darcy/Elizabeth plot but also plays an equally important part in the minor plot, which takes in all sub-plots, hence all minor characters. Wickham does not change during the novel (which is why I believe that he does not belong entirely in the major plot) although his character as viewed by others undergoes major surgery. He is introduced as a good man who was taken advantage of by Darcy and reduced to a state of relative poverty. This sob story he tells to Elizabeth, which she readily believes, and hates Darcy even more (if that is possible) than previously.

This hatred continues until the first turning point halfway through the book. Elizabeth is sitting alone, pondering what a horrible man Darcy is, when he enters her room, and in a totally confident and conceited manner, he asks for her hand in marriage. His manner makes her hate him even more. She tells him in a fit of anger,

> "You could not have made me the offer of your hand in any way that would have tempted me to accept it."

citing his abuse of Wickham and his treatment of Jane as her chief reasons.

But this, her strongest hatred, is short-lived. He writes her a letter which explains his reasoning in the matter of Bingley and Jane and he also tells her the true story of Wickham, which she at first does not believe, but it is easily verified. This letter sets her mind in motion. But although she becomes convinced that he means well in what he does, she cannot help disliking him still for his pride is intolerable. But she wants (although she won't admit it to herself) to discover that even this is false. And she wishes that she had not spoken so harshly about him before. To Jane she says:

> "The misfortune of speaking with bitterness is a most natural consequence of the prejudices I had been encouraging."

The one step which was needed in order to completely change her feelings about him was to come quite unexpectedly in Chapter 43. Traveling with her aunt and uncle, Elizabeth is brought (to her horror and above her protests) to see Darcy's Pemberley estate.

It is the housekeeper who presents the news that Elizabeth has waited to hear. She can hardly believe it when she hears it, yet her desire to believe it overcomes all doubts. Darcy, to this servant, is the most wonderful man on earth. He is a kind man, "affable to the poor," and "the sweetest-tempered, most generous-hearted boy in the world." With the phrase "sweetest-tempered," she catches Elizabeth's attention. Her main conviction had been that Darcy was ill-tempered. And yet the housekeeper said:

> "I have never heard a cross word from him in my life."

Elizabeth listened intently to all the praise the housekeeper had for Darcy, and new thoughts flowed through her mind:

> "Can this be Mr. Darcy? . . . In what an amiable light does this place him!"

When she takes leave of his housekeeper to see the grounds, she is shocked to run right into the man of whom she has thought so often lately, returning a day early from his trip. She was totally embarassed but pleased and surprised to find Darcy exactly as the housekeeper had said he was. Something, everything, about him had changed. He had undergone a complete character reversal (something he later attributed to her bitter refusal to marry him), and was not as sweet, gentle, and tender as he could get. Even the thing that had bothered him most, her relations, did not bother him now. It was at this point that Elizabeth was falling in love with him.

It was not yet love, but it was something like it. She needed first to be acknowledged that he still loved her before she would let her heart get the best of her. But at Pemberley the change had come. She herself later said when asked by Jane when she had first loved Darcy:

> "It has been coming on so gradually, that I hardly know when it began. But I believe I must date it from my first seeing his beautiful grounds at Pemberley."

She was joking, of course, but still there is no denying that it was at Pemberley that her mind was changed. It was at Pemberley where all of her negative beliefs about Darcy were rebutted. It was at Pemberley that the two major changes were made in the two major characters. And it was at Pemberley where the gears were set in motion that led to the marriage of Elizabeth Bennett and Fitzwilliam Darcy.

Part II

English Review

POETRY

INTRODUCTION

No one has adequately defined poetry. The poets speak abstractly and romantically when defining their domain. For example, Samuel Taylor Coleridge rather egotistically called poetry, "the best words in the best order." J. S. Eliot spoke as an idealist when he explained poetry as "not the assertion that something is true, but the making of that truth more fully real to us." The average reader sees poetry as, "the literature that is written in some kind of verse form." Perhaps it is sufficient to say that poetry is literature that is not prose.

Yet, most people recognize that some literature labelled poetry is not so and that some prose is poetic. Merely setting sentences in verse form does not make poetry. Therefore, poetry must have some requisites.

Aside from the basic demand that poetry "say something," poetry is characterized by the following elements: a musical effect created by rhythm and sounds, a precise and fresh imagery, and multiple levels of interpretation suggested by the connotation of the closer words and by allusions.

A poem, however, should not be regarded as a marriage of technical devices and ideas. The devices should enhance or expose the poem's meaning(s). But, for convenience's sake, the elements of poetry will be focused on separately in this unit so that the student can devote his/her attention to the effects achieved by certain poetic conventions.

THE MUSICAL EFFECT OF POETRY

Poetry has its roots in song. The earliest poetic forms were the epics and ballads sung by travelling bards and minstrels. Though no longer sung, poems retain their musical quality. This section deals with the elements of poetry which create that musicality.

A. Meter--loosely defined meter is the "beat" or rhythm of the poem. It is the pattern of stressed and unstressed syllables used in the poem.

Meter is shown by a visual code. The accent mark (/) indicates the stressed syllable, the mark (◡) indicates an unstressed syllable.

Certain combinations of these syllables are most frequently employed in English verse. One unit, or combination, is called a foot. The following are the basic metric feet.

NOTE: There are other metric terms to name variations in metric feet, but these are relatively obscure terms used only by the most technical of critics. Most analyzers of poetry merely refer to an extra unstressed syllable at a line's end as just that and not a catalexis.

Meter is also influenced by pauses. Most metrical poetry evolves into a pattern of pauses at lines' ends. A caesura, or pause within a line (usually indicated by a mark of punctuation), can alter, usually slow down, the meter. An enjambement, or run-on line, can speed up the flow of the poem.

Caesura--Be that as may be, she was in their song.

(Robert Frost, "Never Again Would Birds' Song Be the Same")

Enjambement--This living hand, now warm and capable
Of earnest grasping, . . .

(Keats, "This living hand,")

B. Rhyme--(or rime)--the repetition of similar (or duplicate) sounds at regular intervals. (Usually this repetition occurs at the ends of lines.)

Types of Rhyme

1. End rhyme--rhyme found at the ends of verse lines.

   Ex: Thou ill-formed offspring of my feeble brain,
   Who after birth did'st by my side remain,

   (Anne Bradstreet, "The Author to Her Book")

   End rhyme follows, usually, a pattern that is repeated throughout the stanzas of the poem. The rhyme scheme is denoted by small case letters, each letter representing a specific rhyme-sound. Once a pattern for one stanza is established the analyzer need not continue with his lettering. Thus a poem following a scheme of abac has the first and third lines only of each stanza rhyming.

2. Internal rhyme--this is rhyme contained within a line of verse.

   Ex: "The long light shakes across the lakes"

   (Tennyson, "Blow, Bugle, Blow")

3. Slant rhymes--an inexact rhyme where the final consonant sounds are the same but the vowel sounds are different.

   "And by his smile, I knew that sullen hall,
   By his dead smile I knew we stood in Hell."

   (Wilfred Owen, "Strange Meeting")

   (Also called "near rhyme," "half rhyme," or "partial rhyme.")

4. Eye rhyme--the rhyming of two words which look as if they'd rhyme, but do not, such as "move" and "love."

5. Feminine rhyme--rhyme in which two consecutive syllables of the rhyme-words match. The first syllable carries the stress. Feminine rhyme adds lightness to a poem.

   We poets in our youth begin in gladness,
   But thereof come in the end despondency and madness.

   (Wm. Wordsworth, "Resolution and Independence")

6. Masculine rhyme--the rhyme of one-syllable words or, in the case of words of more than one syllable, the rhyming of stressed final syllables.

   A sweet disorder in the dress
   Kindles in clothes a wantonness.

   (Robert Herrick, "Delight in Disorder")

C. Other musical devices: the use of sounds

1. Assonance--the repetition of two or more vowel sounds within a line.

   Our echoes roll from soul to soul.

2. Consonance--the repetition of two or more consonant sounds within a line.

   The splendor falls on castle walls

   And snowy summits old in story;

   (Tennyson, "The splendor falls . . .")

3. Alliteration--repetition of two or more initial consonants sounds in words within a line.

   He clasps the crag with crooked hands

   (Tennyson, "The Eagle")

4. Onomatopoeia--the use of a word whose sound suggests its meaning or which imitates the sound made by an object or creature.

   I heard a fly buzz when I died,

   (Emily Dickinson)

   The <u>moan</u> of doves in immemorial elms,
   And murmuring of innumerable bees.

   (Tennyson, "Come down, O maid")

5. Euphony and Cacophony--euphony is the use of harmonies, melodious sounds in a poem. Cacophony is the use of harsh, irritating sounds.

Stanzas are the "paragraphs" of poems. Stanzas can range in length from two lines to an unlimited number of lines. However, few poems use stanzas of more than eight lines. For convenience of reference, the stanzas have been titled according to line length.

Number of Lines in the Stanza	Stanza Name
2	Couplet
3	Tercet
4	Quatrain
5	Cinquain
6	Sestet
7	Septet
8	Octabe (octet)

For stanzas of 9 or more lines, merely refer to them as "nine-line stanzas," etc.

ANNABEL LEE

It was many and many a year ago,
In a kingdom by the sea,
That a maiden there lived whom you may know
By the name of Annabel Lee;
And this maiden she lived with no other thought
Than to love and be loved by me.

I was a child and *she* was a child,
In this kingdom by the sea,
But we loved with a love that was more than love--
I and my Annabel Lee
With a love that the winged seraphs of heaven
Coveted her and me.

And this was the reason that, long ago,
In this kingdom by the sea,
A wind blew out of a cloud, chilling
My beautiful Annabel Lee;
So that her highborn kinsmen came
And bore her away from me,
To shut her up in a sepulchre
In this kingdom by the sea.

The angels, not half so happy in heaven,
Went envying her and me--
Yes! that was the reason (as all men know,
In this kingdom by the sea)
That the wind came out of the clouds by night,
Chilling and killing my Annabel Lee.

But our love it was stronger by far than the love
Of those who were older than we,
Of many far wiser than we;
And neither the angels in heaven above,
Nor the demons down under the sea,
Can ever dissever my soul from the soul
Of the beautiful Annabel Lee;

For the moon never beams, without bringing me dreams
  Of the beautiful Annabel Lee;
And the stars never rise, but I feel the bright eyes
  Of the beautiful Annabel Lee;
And so, all the night-tide, I lie down by the side
Of my darling--my darling--my wife and my bride
  In the sepulchre there by the sea,
  In her tomb by the sounding sea.

Edgar Allan Poe

In this last poem written by Poe, the subject, Annabel Lee, and her sad fate haunt the poet. He grieves for the loss of his darling whom he describes as a princess, "In the kingdom by the sea," born away in death by "her highborn kinsmen." This girl whose life ended all too soon was taken by angels envious of the love she shared with the poet. Her death and his response are made more touching by the knowledge that this was a childhood romance.

The real strength to this poem, however, does not lie in the narrative but rather in the musical delivery of it. The poem's alternation of lines of iambic pentameter and anapestic dimeter terminated by a single iamb creates a rhythm imitative of the ebb and flow of the sea, the site of their shared kingdom and of her burial place. This almost rolling beat also suggests the sing-songiness of a child's ditty. The incongruity of the tuneful versification of the child's vision of the cause for her death and the adult loss of a love establishes a strange, unreal aura.

Contributing to the fluid rhythm is the preponderance of rhyme. The rhyme scheme is not the same throughout the poem, although in all but the fourth stanza the second, fourth, and sixth lines rhyme with a long e sound--sea, Lee, me, we. The one sound unifies the poem, pervading it with the echo of the sea. Interspersed with this basic rhyme are various other end rhymes, such as "ago"/"know." Internal rhyme, too, is found giving melody to the poem, as in line 26 "Chilling and killing my Annabel Lee," or line 32 "Can <u>ever</u> dis<u>sever</u> my <u>soul</u> from the <u>soul</u>." The final stanza is abundantly rich in internal rhyme--"beams"/"dreams," "rise"/"eyes," "tide"/"side"/"bride." This superfluity of rhyme, all of which is bold masculine rhyme, imprints itself in the reader's mental ear.

Poe uses a great deal of repetition to give a ballad quality to "Annabel Lee." The line, "In a kingdom by the sea," appears five times in the poem. The name Annabel Lee resounds in every stanza, haunting the reader as her memory haunts the poet. Phrases are reiterated throughout. This repetition not only creates the effect of a lyric refrain, the poet's repetitiveness indicates his anguished, perhaps irrational, state of mind; he is almost mad with despair for his Annabel Lee.

So the poet, touching the reader with his compulsion to find this ghost that torments his thoughts, lies down by her "sepulchre there by the sea."

THE TYGER

Tyger! Tyger! burning bright
In the forests of the night,
What immortal hand or eye
Could frame thy fearful symmetry?

In what distant deeps or skies
Burnt the fire of thine eyes?

On what wings dare he aspire?
What the hand dare seize the fire?

And what shoulder, and what art,
Could twist the sinews of thy heart?
And when thy heart began to beat,
What dread hand? and what dread feet?

What the hammer? What the chain?
In what furnace was thy brain?
What the anvil? What dread grasp
Dare its deadly terrors clasp?

When the stars threw down their spears
And watered heaven with their tears,
Did he smile his work to see?
Did he who made the Lamb make thee?

Tyger! Tyger! burning bright
In the forests of the night,
What immortal hand or eye
Dare frame thy fearful symmetry?

William Blake

"The Tyger" is one of Blake's most potent musings on the nature of God, or whatever creative force or deity Blake realizes. In asking the tiger, a beast of sheer strength and cunning fierceness, what hands formed it, Blake is implying that a force of equal strength and ferocity must have been the creator. Yet, when he questions,

"Did he who made the Lamb make thee?"

Blake is pondering the possible myriad faces of a God. Is this God both fierce and gentle, making animals to suit his moods? Is this brutal artifice of the tiger the same kindly father who sent His Son (the Lamb, as Christ was often called) as man's salvation? Or is this God a mere brute who fashions vicious beasts and sends His Son, the Lamb, to slaughter? Blake does not answer any of these questions for the reader. Yet, from the images evoked by his questions, the reader feels that whatever force it is that created the tiger, it is a powerful, and fearless, one that "Dare frame thy (the tiger's) symmetry."

The "music" of this poem, however, may shed some light on the poet's own vision of the creative God. The poem is written primarily in lines of trochaic trimeter ending with an extra accented syllable.

Tyger! Tyger! burning bright,

In the forests of the night,

What immortal hand or **eye**

Could frame thy fearful symmetry?

This metric pattern is that commonly used by most nursery rhymes and chants. Readily eliminating the possibility of Blake's wishing to be cute, one must conclude that he utilized the chantlike aspect of trochaic trimeter. Indeed, this poem eerily intones the haunting melody of a witches' song. Compare this poem's musical quality to that of the famous refrain of Shakespeare's well-known triad of witches.

> "Double, double, toil and trouble,
> Fire burn, and cauldron bubble."

Here, too, is that haunting chanting in trochaic meter. Since chants are associated with praying, occasionally to God, more often to a pagan deity or demon, one might suspect that Blake's chant is to his God, and in this case, a diabolical God. Moreover, "The Tyger" is versed with closely spaced rhymes which are also characteristic of chants and songs. As each line's final syllable forms half of a strong, masculine rhyme, the reader hears the beat of that accented syllable. When the rhyme is completed, again on an accented final syllable, the reader hears the ring, almost as if that hammer were beating on that anvil. The meter, reinforced with this rhyme scheme, is ominous sounding in the same way beating tom-toms and tolling bells are.

Alliteration plays a definite role in creating the essence of "The Tyger." the tiger is "burning bright." Those bright eyes perhaps came from "distant deeps" and the creator soars on "what wings" to find the light, maybe stars, for those eyes. When the tiger's heart "began to beat," who, asks Blake, "dare its deadly terror clasp?" In both the first and last stanzas, besides the alliterated b's, there are repeated f's in "frame thy fearful symmetry." This alliteration, beyond yielding the usual musicality to the poem, conveys a threatening quality in those hard b's and d's and those spitting f's.

Blake takes advantage of repetition in this poem. The most obvious example is the almost perfect repetition of the first stanza at the poem's end. The alteration of "Could" to "Dare" suggests the poet's conclusion--that God, or whatever force Blake is depicting, is not capable of creating a ferocious creature, but is dauntless enough to put such ferocity into existence. The frequent use of the word "dread" repeatedly reminds the reader that whatever molded the tiger is to be feared, dreaded. The pattern of the questions, too, is insistently repeated.

> What dread hand? and what dread feet?
>
> What the hammer? What the chain?
> In what furnace was thy brain?
> What the anvil? What dread grasp
> Dare its deadly terrors clasp?

The total effect of all this repetition is to strengthen that illusion of chanting, of re-emphasizing the invocation.

In conclusion, the metric pattern, the rhyme scheme, and the memorable sounds of this poem support the hypothesis that Blake intended this poem to be a chant, demanding that the tiger's being give him the truth of its creator's nature. This chant, eerie and rich with images of strength, speaks to a creator that is equally dreadful and powerful, not to a creator that is gentle. Perhaps the same hand created the Tyger and the Lamb, but Blake can only see the "dread hand" in the tiger's creation.

(NOTE: This poem could also be analyzed through imagery. For the purposes of this section the focus has been on the structural elements of meter, rhyme, and sound.)

Type	Pattern	Example
Iambic	∪ /	control
Trochaic	/ ∪	tiger
Anapestic	∪ ∪ /	contradict
Dactylic	/ ∪ ∪	foolishness
Spondaic	/ /	moonstone

Thus, the number of syllables in a line is relevant, but the number of stresses is more important in determining the pace of the poem. The more stresses in a line the more weighty and slow-moving is it. Alternately, a preponderance of unstressed syllables gives lightness and guideness to a poem.

These metrical feet, in repetition, build the rhythm of the poem. When a line of poetry is divided into metrical feet, the line is named after the number of feet contained therein. The types of lines are:

Monometer:	one foot per line
Dimeter	two feet per line
Trimeter	three feet per line
Tetrameter	four feet per line
Pentameter	five feet per line
Hexameter	six feet per line
Heptameter	seven feet per line
Octometer	eight feet per line

(Rarely does a line contain eight feet or more)

The process of marking these feet off in a poem is called scansion.

Ex: From Thomas Gray's "Elergy Written in a Country Churchyard"

The curfew tolls the knell of parting day,

The lowing herd wind slowly o'er the lea,

The plowman homeward plods his weary way,

And leaves the world to darkness and to me.

The basic pattern, as seen in lines one and three, is iambic, and since five feet are regularly used, the lines are pentameter. Thus, the poem is said to be written in iambic pentameter.

Most poems are not written rigidly in one metric pattern. Monotony would ensure otherwise. The variety of a new foot interspersed among a set of regular feet can call attention to the words of those irregular feet or can obscure unimportant words. For example, in line two above a spondaic foot (wind slow) not only draws attention to that action, but also weighs down that line a bit to imitate the lumbering of the herd. In line four extra unstresses minimize the insignificant words "and to." This Gray passage, moreover, is more regular than many. Intentionally, Gray is creating a somewhat monotonous rhythm to emphasize the weary plodding of the man.

IMAGERY

Imagery is the use of descriptive language to re-create sensory experiences. An image is a verbal picture of an object, action, abstract idea, or sensation.

Examples:

1. Ezra Pound, "In a Station of the Metro"

   The apparition of these faces in the crowd;
   Petals on a wet, black bough.

2. They are yellow forms
   Composed of curves
   Bulging toward the base.
   They are touched red.

   (Wallace Stevens, "Study of Two Pears")

3. I cannot see what flowers are at my feet,
   Nor what soft incense hangs upon the boughs,
   But, in embalmed darkness, guess each sweet
   Wherewith the seasonable month endows
   The grass, the thicket, and the fruit tree wild;
   White hawthorne, and the pastoral eglantine;
   Fast fading violets covered up in leaves;
   And mid-May's eldest child
   The coming musk rose, full of dewy wine,
   The murmurous haunt of flies on summer eves.

   (John Keats, "Ode to a Nightingale")

Images often are created by utilizing figures of speech. These are ways of making an idea or picture come clearer into focus by relating the idea or experience to another that may be more familiar to the reader.

Some figures of speech are:

1. Metaphor--a comparison of unlike items. This comparison is directly stated as in

   "All the world's a stage"
   --Shakespeare

   or implied as in,

   That time of year thou mayest in me behold
   When yellow leaves, or none, or few, do hang
   Upon those boughs which shake against the cold,
   Bare ruin'd choirs, where late the sweet birds sang:

   The metaphor is a device in which one object is substituted for another, or an idea is identified by a concrete object.

2. Simile--the direct comparison of two unlike items, using the words "like" or "as" to complete the comparison.

Helen, thy beauty is to me
Like those Nicear barks of yore,

(Poe, "To Helen")

This is the forest primeval.
The murmuring pines and hemlocks
Stand like Druids of old
With beards, sad and prophetic.

(Longfellow, "Evangeline")

3. Extended metaphor--a metaphor that is carried and embellished for a lengthy duration in a poem. Also called a conceit.

4. Personification--the figure of speech which assigns human qualities to inanimate objects or abstractions.

Because I could not stop for Death--
He kindly stopped for me--

(Emily Dickinson)

    The moon doth with delight
Look round her when the heavens are bare.

(William Wordsworth, "Ode on the Intimations of Immortality")

5. Metonymy--literally "a change of name;" a figure of speech in which the name of some object or idea is substituted for another name to which it has some relation (as a cause for an effect, a writer for his work).

When I consider how my light is spent,

(John Milton) ("light" is substituted for "vision")

The serpent that did sting the father's life
Now wears his crown.

(Shakespeare, <u>Hamlet</u>)

("serpent" stands for Claudius)

6. Synecdoche--a figure of speech in which a part of an object is used to represent the whole object or idea.

Not marble, nor the gilded monuments
of princes, shall outlive this powerful rhyme. . .

(Shakespeare, Sonnet 55)

("Rhyme" is used to represent the entire poem.)

7. Apostrophe--a figure of speech in which an inanimate object, a dead person, or an abstract idea is addressed directly. (The object or idea is thereby personified.)

   Hail to thee, blithe spirit!
   Bird thou never went--

   (Percy Bysshe Shelley, "To a Skylark")

   Rhodora! if the sages ask thee why
   This charm is wasted on the earth and sky,
   Tell them, dear, that if eyes were made for seeing,
   Then Beauty is its own excuse for being:

   (Ralph Waldo Emerson, "The Rhodora")

8. Hyperbole--an exaggration used to give emphasis.

   The brain is wider than the sky--

   (Emily Dickinson)

9. Litotes--a figure of speech in which an idea is expressed by understatement or by denying its opposite.

   --feelings too,
   Of unremembered pleasure: such, perhaps,
   As have <u>no slight or trivial influence</u>
   On that best portion of a good man's life,

   (William Wordsworth, "Tintern Abbey")

   (Wordsworth in the underlined section minimizes the great influence feelings have upon man.)

10. Paradox--a statement which is an apparent contradiction contains a basis of truth which, when considered, reconciles the seeming opposites.

   <u>I'm nobody</u>! Who are you?

   (Emily Dickinson)

   My youth is spent, and yet I am not old,

   (C. Tichbarne, "Elergy, Written with his Own Hand in the Tower Before His Execution")

   (oxymoron is a poetical paradox--"O loving hate!")

11. Pun (paronomasia)--a play on words; this can be a wordplay on a word with two different meanings or a play on the similarity of meanings in two words spelled differently but pronounced the same or a play on two words pronounced somewhat alike but differing in meanings.

   John Donne, "Hymn to God the Father"; speaking to God

But swear by Thyself, that at my death Thy Son
  Shall shine as he shines now, and heretofore;
And, having done that, Thou hast done;

In the Donne selection, he is toying with the pun "Son"/"sun" and with the play on his name and the word "done". ("Thou hast done (Donne)").

12. Epithet--a descriptive name or fille; rosy-fingered Dawn, Ivan the Terrible.

Images also can be created by other devices. Two of the most frequent are symbolism and allusion.

Symbolism is the use of an object, person, reason, animal or other concrete item to represent an abstract idea or an emotion. A symbol does not have one stock meaning. A symbol can represent a summary of ideas or attitudes.

Odysseus' journey to find his homeland after the Trojan War is symbolic of each man's quest to find his niche in society.

"Home" frequently is a symbol for a safe place, a place where one fits it, or any of a number of such related ideas.

An allusion is a reference to an outside event, person, or fact. Most allusions in pre-Twentieth century poetry referred to events in people from classical Greek mythology or the Bible. More often in the twentieth century poets one finds allusions to current events or personages.

Then felt I like some watcher of the skies
When a new planet swims into his ken;
Or like stout Cortez when with eagle eyes
He stared at the Pacific--

(Keats, "On First Looking into Chapman's Homer")

(Actually the allusion to Cortez is faulty. Balboa was the first to see the Pacific.)

Sophocles long ago
Heard it on the Aegean, and it brought
Into his mind the turkid ebb and flow
Of human misery;

Images can be suggested by the connotations of words. The denotation of a word is its literal meaning. The connotations of a word are those suggestions of additional meaning that are attached to a word. Thus "home" denotes merely a place where one lives; it may connote warmth, love, shelter, or a number of other meanings.

Gerard Hanley Hopkins is noted for his coercetive imagery and unique use of figurtive language.

"The Windhover."
To Christ Our Lord

I caught this morning morning's minion, king-
   dom of daylight's dauphin, dapple-dawn-drawn Falcon, in his riding
      Of the rolling level underneath him steady air, and striding
High there, how he rung upon the rein of a wimpling wing
In his ecstasy! then off, off forth on swing,
   As a skate's heel sweeps smooth on a bowbend; the hurl and gliding
   Rebuffed the big wind. My heart in hiding
Stirred for a bird,--the achieve of, the mastery of the thing!

Brute beauty and valor and act, oh, air, pride, plume, here
   Buckle! And the fire that breaks from thee then, a billion
Times told lovelier, more dangerous, O my chevalier!
   No wonder of it: sheer plod makes plough down sillion
Shine, and blue-bleak embers, ah, my dear,
Fall, gall themselves, and gash gold-ver million.

"The Windhover" is Hopkins' celebration of the force and beauty of a living creature, and therefore a celebration of God. The poet finds the magnificence of this flesh and blood bird is meager when compared to the brilliance of its soul, the God within. "The Windhover" is a sonnet which moves from the poet's contemplation of a winging bird to the contemplation of the force which propels the life within that creature.

In the octave of this sonnet, which describes the experience of viewing the windhover, the rhyme sound "ing" is repeated in all eight lines. In the first, fourth, fifth and eighth lines the rhyme is masculine, while the remaining four lines end in feminine rhyme. The octave is resonant with the lingering sounds of this rhyme. As the poem stirs with this echoing "ing" syllable, the poet is stirred by the victory of the bird over the wind. The description of this experience begins with a series of three epithets for the windhover. The first, "morning minion," signals the bird as a favorite of the personified morning. The bird is, therefore, immediately characterized as one that inspires affection. The second epithet, "kingdom of daylight's dauphin," suggests that the windhover is regal, a crown prince of the kingdom of daylight. "Dapple-dawn-drawn Falcon" is an unusual title. Hopkins condensed a number of images into "dapple-dawn-drawn." The dawn is mottled with color; thus it is "dappled"--hence, "dapple-dawn." The bird is drawn to the skies by the call of day's opening; thus he is "dapple-dawn-drawn." "Falcon" connotes a more noble and powerful image than does windhover. This windhover, a variety of falcon, merits the capitalization of "Falcon" by virtue of his regality. The first two lines, then, evoke a picture of a majestic bird answering an instinctive call to the challenge of the skies. The abundance of alliteration used in these epithets--the resonant m's of "morning morning's minion" and the explosive d's of "daylight's dauphin, dapple-dawn-drawn"--touches the poem with a powerful rhythm that heralds the windhover.

The poet moves on to depict the flight of the windhover. This kestrel rides the currents of the air. The ambiguous phrase, "the rolling level underneath him steady air," expresses the changing movement of the bird. At one moment the bird seems to roll with the air flow. Then he balances himself so that he appears to be on a level plane. Then he hovers on the "steady air" that is "underneath him." The juxtaposition of these words gives the reader both a sense of the bird's changing tactics and a sense of the poet's multiple, and simultaneous, impressions. The windhover "striding/High there" is a picture of bold flight. However, the bird's free, joyous soaring is held in check by the limits of his rippling, or unfolding, wings.

   How he rung upon the rein of a wimpling wing
In his ecstasy!

Then the falcon ceases his hovering and sails off, "As a skate's heel sweeps smooth on a bow-bend." This simile vivifies for the reader the exact motion of the bird. Then the bird emerges victorious over the "big wind," which he defeats with both power ("hurl") and finesse ("gliding"). Thus description of the flying windhover is made active and immediate, simulating movement, by the use of present progressive verbs--"riding," "rolling," "striding," "wimpling," and "gliding." The consonance of these lines utilizes sounds that stretch on and glide, the r's, l's, w's and s's, thus emphasizing the fluid motion of the bird.

The poet is deeply moved by the bird's victory because it represents an achievement.

> My heart in hiding
> Stirred for a bird,--the achieve of, the mastery of the thing!

The poet's heart is "in hiding;" an image is created of a man who doesn't often allow himself to vent his feelings. The man is then awakened to splendor by this experience.

In lines 9-11 the poet addresses the elements that comprise the windhover.

> Brute beauty and valor and act, oh, air, pride, plume; here Buckle!

He requests that these elements split apart into their essences. The force of these elements straining against each other and then bursting into a release of energy is indicated by the strong sounds of the alliterated b's and p's.

The poet, still addressing the windhover, announces that the "fire" or energy which this falcon's spirit contains is much greater, "a billion/Times told lovelier, more dangerous," than the force of the physical bird. It is this spirit within that is the embodiment of God. Hopkins says that the essence of this creature is both beautiful and awful. These two adjectives, or rather Hopkins' own, "lovelier" and "dangerous," apply to a force that embraces opposites. The implication that the "fire" is God, or God's vitality, within the bird is suggested by the power of the "fire" and its ability to reconcile opposites. Again alliteration punctuates the lines with sounds of power--b's and t's. The assonance of long, bold o's accentuates the illusion of strength. The apostrophe, "O, my chevalier," reveals that the poet, in crying out to the bird, is honoring the creature as a lord (chevalier) or superior on whom he gratefully bestows his awe and love.

The poet concludes, however, that it is not incomprehensible that this mere bird contains such Godly glory. Hopkins uses two examples to explain metaphorically this phenomenon. Any furrow (sillion), he says, contains the shine of rich earth; the furrow has only to be patiently plowed to achieve this beauty. Secondly, he tells us that a charred ember, when it falls and strikes something, can release the brilliant red and gold fire hidden under blackened ash. Hopkins' word choice in these last three lines is vivid and musical. The alliteration and assonance of "shéer plód makes plough down sillion/Shine" is mellifluous. The image of dreary work creating the lusciousness of plowed earth is teasingly ironical. The hyphenated word, "blue-bleak," coined by Hopkins, creates a precise picture of the ember's color. This word is also a pun on the common epithet "blue-black," thus suggesting, through association, the black tint of the ash. The last line, too, echoes with alliteration--"gall," "gash," "gold"--and internal rhyme--"fall"/"gall." Hopkins manufactures another word, "gold-vermilion," to capture that duality of color the eye assimilates all at once.

Once again Hopkins addresses the bird--"ah, my dear." But in this apostrophe the windhover is not the regal conqueror, but rather the fond love, of Hopkins' heart. The windhover has come to symbolize the beauty and energy that is the soul, the gift of God. For this reason Hopkins reveres and loves the windhover, as he does God.

THE TYPES OF POETRY

A. The Lyric Poem

A *lyric* poem is a poem of limited length, expressing the thoughts and feelings of a single speaker. The lyric has a regular metrical pattern and a regular rhyme scheme. It is characterized by its intensely personal tone and imagery.

There are a number of more specific categories of lyrics.

1. The *elegy*--this is a dignified lyric poem lamenting the death of an individual 'among all men'.

2. The *ode*--this is a lyric poem of considerable length. The ode is serious in subject and formal in style.

3. The *sonnet*--this is a lyric poem of fourteen lines which follow a designated rhyme scheme. The sonnet is written in iambic pentameter. The two basic types of sonnets are the Petrarchan (or Italian) and the Shakespearian (or English).

   The Petrarchan sonnet follows the rhyme scheme

   a
   b
   b
   a
   a
   b
   b
   a

c		c
d		d
e		c
c	or	c
d		d
e		c

   The Petrarchan sonnet is divided into two sections, the octave (first eight lines) and the sestet (the final six lines). The octave usually proposes a question, develops a narrative, or delineates an idea. The accompanying sestet will answer the question, comment on the story, or countermand the idea. This thought-division is often signalled by an enjambement in line 9.

   The Shakespearean sonnet follows the rhyme scheme

   a
   b
   a
   b
   c
   d
   c
   d
   e

f
e
f
g
g

The Shakespearean sonnet's thought-division is a 4-4-4-2 plan. There are four sections--three quatrains and a final couplet. In the Shakespearean sonnet each quatrain deals with a different aspect of the subject and the couplet either summarizes the theme or makes a final, sometimes contradictory, comment.

Two variations of these sonnets are the Miltonic and the Spenserian sonnets. John Milton followed the Petrarchan rhyme scheme, but made his sestet merely a continuation of his original octave, not an answer or comment to it. His unique sonnet has been utilized by a number of poets. Edmund Spenser's original sonnet rhyme scheme has been passed down to us also, although it has not been commonly used by anyone but Spenser. Spenser followed the English thought-division of three quatrains and a couplet. However, he altered the rhyme scheme to abab bcbc cdcd ee, thus linking the quatrains.

The sonnet is a rigid form, imposing strict rules on its practitioners. Many poets have chosen to accept the challenge of the sonnet, calling upon their skills as poets.

Examples--

1. The lyric--

TO HIS COY MISTRESS

Had we but world enough, and time,
This coyness, lady, were no crime.
We would sit down and think which way
To walk, and pass our long love's day.
Thou by the Indian Ganges' side
Should'st rubies find; I by the tide
Of Humber would complain. I would
Love you ten years before the Flood,
And you should, if you please, refuse
Till the conversion of the Jews.
My vegetable love should grow
Basker than empires, and more slow.
An hundred years should go to praise
Thine eyes, and on thy forehead gaze,
Two hundred to adore each breast,
But thirty thousand to the rest.
An age at least to every part,
And the last age should show your heart.
For, lady, you deserve this state,
Nor would I love at lower rate.
   But at my back I always hear
Time's winged chariot hurrying near;
And yonder all before us lie
Deserts of vast eternity.

Thy beauty shall no more be found,
Nor in thy marble vault shall sound
My echoing song; then worms shall try
That long preserved virginity,
And your quaint honor turn to dust,
And into ashes all my lust.
The grave's a fine and private place,
But none, I think, do there embrace.
  Now therefore, while the youthful hue
Sits on thy skin like morning glew, (glow)
And while thy willing soul transpires
At every port with instant fires,
Now let us sport us while we may;
And now, like am'rous birds of prey,
Rather at once our time devour,
Than languish in his slow-chapped power,
Let us roll all our strength, and all
Our sweetness, up into one ball;
And tear our pleasures with rough strife
Thorough the iron gates of life. (through)
Thus, though we cannst make our sun
Stand still, yet we will make him run.

Andrew Marvell

A. Situation and Theme--

This lyric is in the form of a <u>monologue</u>. Browning named this form the "dramatic lyric."

Marvell is urging his mistress to relinquish her modesty and to allow herself the luxury of physical love. His persuasive, and flattering, argument has three distinct sections. In the first, Marvell states that if they had an eternity to spend together on earth he could understand her reluctance. If they had an eternity, then he would assuredly cultivate slowly their love, devoting ample time to praising and appreciating her beauty. Yet, he says in the second section, they do not have much time. Life is a brief encounter. So they should use their time together well, for there is no love, no embraces, beyond the grave. So, in the third part, says Marvell, come and enjoy deeply and now the pleasures of love while we are young enough to achieve passion.

Besides the entreaty, the poem deals with the transcience of life. His philosophy, while seemingly selfish, is also pragmatic. Life is short and postponing its enjoyment is wasting it.

B. Meter and Rhyme Scheme--

The basic meter is iambic tetrameter. Of course, many of the lines do not scan perfectly--how monotonous! The regularity of the meter is also broken up by frequent caesuras (lines 1, 4, 6, 12, 27; for example) and enjambements (lines 3 to 4, 6 to 7, 9 to 10, 23 to 24; for example). These stops prevent the lines from becoming sing-songy. The rhyme scheme is aa--or every two lines rhyming in couplets. With this close rhyme scheme, a poem could tend to turn nursery rhymish. Marvell deftly avoids this by the manipulation of meter. The result is a musical plea.

C. Tone--

The tone of a poem is, metaphorically speaking, the tone of voice in which the poet is speaking. The tone is inferred by the reader through the word choice, the connotations of those words, the verse form, the rhyme, the figurative language, and the allusions.

In "To His Coy Mistress" Marvell's tone is one of a passionate plea. His tone is touched, though, with humor, as if the poet, anticipating rejection, is preparing himself to accept it. The tone in the first two-thirds is more light-hearted than that of the final third of the poem, where Marvell makes his final, moving plea.

In the first section the poet, in a series of hyperboles, states that if he had ample time he could adequately appreciate his mistress. The exaggerated times necessary for adequate loving of her are indicative of the playfulness with which the poet begins his case.

> I would
> Love you ten years before the Flood,
>
> My vegetable love should grow
> Vaster than empires, and more slow.
> An hundred years should go to praise
> Thine eyes, and on thy forehead gaze.

Also suggesting his opening lightheartedness is the relatively simple diction and syntax. The sentence structure and vocabulary approximate natural speech.

> We would sit down and think which way
> To walk, and pass our long love's day.

The poet is not yet earnest. His fairly regular meter and the rhyme couple to make the lines, such as those two immediately preceeding, cute.

The allusion to walking by the Ganges where rubies would be hers to find is one of fantasy. The reference to the local Humber River adds a touch of commonness to him, as compared to her exoticness as typified by the Ganges River. He is still teasing her. The allusion to the Flood shows the long span of time his love could encompass; it also playfully shows Marvell's sense of the ridiculous.

The second stanza is touched by less humor and more serious intent. The meter is less regular, so the lilt of rhyme is less noticeable. Some of the rhymes are slant rhymes--"lie"/"eternity" or "try"/"virginity." The effect of these devices is to weigh down the poem's rhythm.

The images are no longer comical. They depict gloom or the melancholy of wasted life.

> And yonder all before us lie
> Deserts of vast eternity.

In these empty "Deserts" of time will be found her virginity "turned to dust" and his passion burned out, in ashes. Mockingly and bitterly, Marvell calls her honor "quaint," implying it is a foolish bit of old-fashioned honorableness. Blackly humorous and rollicking are the two lines that end this section.

The grave's a fine and private place,
But none, I think, do there embrace.

In the final lines, Marvell drops the tone of sarcasm and bitterness to state how exquisite their love could be. The meter becomes more regular and the rhyme more pronounced as Marvell's spirits rise.

In a series of sensual images Marvell conveys his eagerness. The tone is passionate and hopeful.

While the youthful hue
Sits on thy skin like morning glow,
And while they willing sound transpires
At every port with instant fires.

The above passage shows the sensualness of his images. The picture of the soul being extinguished by passion's fires is not only a physical reference but a spiritual one. Marvell's love is deep, not superficial.

Marvell concludes with a desire to "tear" through life roughly squeezing pleasure from it. This is not the playful Marvell of section one, nor the bitter Marvell of part two. It is the eager, exuberant lover, who daringly will live each day fully since he cannot "make our sun/Stand still."

2. <u>The elegy</u>--

Elegy, Written with His Own Hand in the Tower Before His Execution

My prime of youth is but a frost of cares,
My feast of joy is but a dish of pain,
My crop of corn is but a field of tares,
And all my good is but rain hope of gain:
The day is past; and yet I saw no sun,
And now I live, and now my life is done.

My tale was heard, and yet it was not told,
My fruit is fallin, and yet my leaves are green,
My youth is spent, and yet I am not old,
I saw the world, and yet I was not seen:
My thread is cut, and yet it is not spun,
And now I live, and now my life is done.

I sought my death, and found it in my womb,
I looked for life, and saw it was a shade,
I trod the earth, and knew it was my tomb,
And now I die, and now I was but made:
My glass is full, and now my glass is run,
And now I live, and now my life is done.

Chidiock Tichborne

A. Situation and Theme--

The poet, who is awaiting his death, laments his all-too-soon departure from life. He is not whining or snivelling. Rather, he sadly regrets the waste of his life. Through a series of metaphors and paradoxes the poet expresses the irony of a young death,

My thread is cut, and yet it is not spun.

B. Form--

The poem follows a rhyme scheme of ab abcc. The rhyme is neither pronounced or lilting. This is because of (1) the serious subject of the poem, (2) the definite caesuras in most lines, slowing the rhythm, (3) the rhythm established mid-line by the balanced, parallel halves of lines, and (4) the simple, sad diction.

The meter is iambic pentameter, and stolidly regular. The longish line minimizes the effect of frequent rhyme. The regularity of the meter tolls the death bell-slow and inevitable.

The repetition of the line--

And now I live, and now my life is done.

adds the effect of finality to the poem. Repeated as it is, the line seems to be the haunting knowledge that Tichborne cannot escape.

C. Imagery--

The first stanza begins with a metaphor--

My prime of youth is but a frost of cares.

This image of a youth grown cold (deathlike and old) with cares reveals Tichborne's regret. His "feast" is only a "dish," an image conveying the picture of unfulfilled expectations. The feaster was to have been served joy, but disappointing receives pain. This metaphor where the feast is Tichborne's life which he cannot glut himself on, reveals the mind of a man who has had his hopes blighted. The subsequent metaphor--

My crop of corn is but a field of tares,

suggests the same idea--blighted dreams. Tichborne's life (his crop) is not as he wished (of corn), but is rather a disappointment (a field of tares).

Tichborne uses a series of parodoxes to explain his situation. Each paradox makes a statement, then contradicts it. Often these contradictions are negatives, leaving the reader with an impression of a life denied.

The day is past, and yet I saw no sun.

Here Tichborne reflects that a day has gone by in which he, in the Tower of London, did not glimpse the sunlight. But metaphorically is he saying that his life (day) is all past and in it he experienced no bright spots (sun)? The second stanza continues with these paradoxes.

My tale was heard, and yet it was not told,
    My fruit is fall'n, and yet my leaves are green.
My youth is spent, and yet I am not old,
    I saw the world, and yet I was not seen:

The dominant image is that of waste--wasted effort, symbolized by a tale not told, but heard--and wasted life, symbolized by a green fruit tree that has untimely lost its fruit. His youth is wasted; his mark on the world will not be made; and the thread of his life has been cut before its natural conclusion.

In the third stanza Tichborne despairingly says that all he sought for was found in its opposite. This negation seems a negation of what is natural. He found death in the womb, the source of life. He found life, but it was his destiny that his early death was the result of his living. Earth is his tomb, not his home.

In the final three lines, Tichborne states in three paradoxes, one of which is presented metaphorically, that he is about to die just when he should be in the midst of living. At this moment his lifetime is over, "now my life is done," but he still exists, "And now I live." This is what Tichborne mourns most--that he must exist in this frustrated state, alive but not living. He repeats this line three times; he repeats the idea of being in limbo--neither one definite, such as young, nor its opposite, old--in every image.

3. <u>The Petrarchan sonnet</u>--

THE SOUND OF THE SEA

The sea awoke at midnight from its sleep,
   And round the pebbly beaches far and wide
   I heard the first wave of the rising tide
   Rush onward with uninterrupted sweep;
A voice out of the silence of the deep,
   A sound mysteriously multiplied
   As of a cataract from the mountain's side,
   Or roar of winds upon a wooded steep.
So comes to us at times, from the unknown
   And inaccessible solitudes of being,
   The rushing of the sea-tides of the soul;
And inspirations, that we deem our own,
   And some divine foreshadowing and foreseeing
   Of things beyond our reason or control.

Henry Wadsworth Longfellow

A. Sonnet form--

The rhyme scheme is abba abba cde cde. The meter is fairly regular iambic pentameter:

The sea awoke at midnight from its sleep,

And round the pebbly beaches far and wide

I heard the first wave of the rising tide

The 8-6, octave-sestet, division is very clear in this sonnet. In the octave, Longfellow develops a picture of the sea and an impression of the sound the incoming waves make. In the sestet he compares the rush and roar of the sea to the inspirations or the innate knowledge man receives from "the divine". Just as the sea rolls into shore, instintual "foreshadowing and foreseeing" sweeps into our souls, sent by God, of course.

B. Imagery--

Longfellow vividly portrays the sea's movement and voice. Through this clear image, the reader can visualize the abstract; he can see how spiritual enlightenment comes to the soul.

In the octave Longfellow personifies the sea. The sea "awoke" and has a voice. This being's voice comes from "The silence of the deep." The picture of the deep the reader creates is akin to the "solitudes of being" from whence come the soul's inspiration. The lines which describe the sound of the sea,

> A sound mysteriously multiplied
> As of a cataract from the mountain's side,
> Or roar of winds upon a wooded steep.

are perfect. The similes tell of the volume and speed of the sound, that of a waterfall or a roaring wind. Though these are not strikingly unusual comparisons, they are clear. Furthermore they are enhanced by the reverberating sounds of the alliterated m's, the hushing consonance of s's and the whispering of the w's. The sound is "mysteriously multiplied." This element of mystery is picked up in the sestet which states that the inspirations come from the "unknown" and "inaccessible" regions in our souls.

The lines depecting the movement of the ocean are also good. They, too, resound with the echoes of sea sounds--s's, r's, and elongated vowels.

C. Rhyme--

The rhyme-words are almost all masculine rhymes with long vowel sounds. Since the long vowels convey a tonal quality of strength and flow, these rhymes accent the sea's rhythm. The only feminine rhyme--"being"/"foreseeing" --ends with a lingering consonant blend. Thus, all the rhymes are melodic and haunting, conspiring with the alliteration and consonance to imitate the sea roar.

4. <u>The Shakespearean sonnet</u>--

SONNET

That time of year thou mayst in me behold
When yellow leaves, or none, or few, do hang
Upon those boughs which shake against the cold,
Bare ruined choirs where late the sweet birds sang.
In me thou see'st the twilight of such day
As after sunset fadeth in the west,
Which by-and-by black night doth take away,
Death's second self that seals up all in rest.
In me thou see'st the glowing of such fire
That on the ashes of his youth doth lie,
As the deathbed whereon it must expire,
Consumed with that which it was nourished by.
    This thou perceiv'st, which makes thy love more strong,
    To love that well which thou must leave ere long.

William Shakespeare

Thy rhyme scheme of this Shakespearean (English) sonnet is the typical abab cdcd efef gg. When scanned, the poem reveals its basic iambic pentameter.

The 4-4-4-2 division is obvious. In a series of three distinct conceits, one for each quatrain, the poet paints himself as a man in his declining years. He is not mourning this fact. Rather, he faces the brevity of life with good humor. The three images are sharp and somewhat romantic, as if the poet finds beauty in his advancing years. In the first quatrain Shakespeare compares his stage of life to autumn. The season which marks the beginning of the year's end. The picture of fall's trees, barren of leaves and choirs of birds, seems to remind one of the withering body of a man. In the second conceit, Shakespeare's period of life is suggested by twilight, the time just prior to black night, symbolically death. Thirdly, the poet is the allegorical equivalent of a dying fire. As the fire is quenched by the ashes that it created, so the poet is worn out by the life he has spent. In the final couplet the poet speaks his purpose. After telling the "thou," revealed in the couplet as someone that loves the poet, that he is nearing his death, Shakespeare comments that this realization of the shortness of life makes love the more valuable. Since Shakespeare must leave his friend or love soon, he is, therefore, more precious.

5. <u>The ode</u>--

Odes are usually addressed to someone, some abstraction, or some object. More often in odes dating from the seventeenth century on the addressed subject is not a person but an inanimate object. The contemplation of the object or the picture of the viewed scene causes the poet to speculate on life.

TO AUTUMN

Season of mists and mellow fruitfulness,
    Close bosom-friend of the maturing sun;
Conspiring with him how to bad and bless
    With fruit the vines that round the thatch-eaves run;
To bend with apples the mossed cottage-trees
    And fill all fruit with ripeness to the core,
        To swell the gourd, and plump the hazel shells
    With a sweet kernel; to set budding more,
And still more, later flowers for the bees,
Until they think warm days will never cease,
        For Summer has o'er-brimmed their clammy cells.

Who hath not seen thee oft amid thy store?
    Sometimes whoever seeks abroad my find
Thee sitting careless on a granary floor,
    Thy hair soft-lifted by the winnowing wind;
Or on a half-reaped furrow sound asleep,
    Drowsed with the fume of poppies, while they hook
        Spares the next swath and all its twined flowers;
And sometimes like a gleaner thou dost keep
    Steady thy laden head across a brook;
    Or by a cider-press, with patient look,
        Thou watchest the last oozings, hours by hours.

Where are the songs of Spring? Ay, where are they?
    Think not of them, thou has thy music too,--
Until barred clouds bloom the soft-dying day,
    And touch the stubble plains with rosy hue;
Then in a wailful choir, the small gnats mourn
    Among the river sallows, borne aloft
        Or sinking as the light wind lives or dies;
And full-grown lambs loud bleat from hilly bourn;
    Hedge-crickets sing; and now with treble soft
    The redbreast whistles from a garden-croft,
        And gathering swallows twitter in the skies.

John Keats

This ode is a celebration of Autumn, a song to Autumn's beauty and vitality. In the first stanza Keats opens with an apostrophe, hailing fall the "Season of mists and mellow fruitfulness." The personified Autumn of this stanza conspires with fellow soulmate, the sun, to load the vines, branches and stalks of the vegetation with ripening fruits. The autumn days of these first eleven lines are the left-overs of the summer, hot and humidity-ladened, so summer-like, in fact, that the bees,

. . . think warm days will never cease,
For Summer has o'er-brimmed their clammy cells.

To suggest the languid air of this opening of Autumn, the poet has "o'er-brimmed" this stanza with slow-moving, lingering sounds. The stanza is stocked with the sounds of resonant b's, m's, r's, and s's. There is hardly a line that has no consonance or alliteration. For example:

Line one: consonance----season, mists, fruitefulness--s
alliteration--mists, mellow

Line two: consonance----close, bosom, sun
alliteration--bosom, maturing

Line three: consonance----conspiring, bless
alliteration--him, how

Line four: consonance----fruit, round, run
alliteration--the, that, thatch

Line six: consonance----ripeness, core/fill, all
alliteration--fill, fruit

And the list could go on. Besides the languidity of the sounds used, the odd combinations of words--combinations utilizing tongue-tying syllables--elongates the lines. Hyphenated words such as "thatch-eaves" or "cottage-trees" and phrases such as "o'er-brimmed their clammy cells" are not sound patterns that can be rapidly pronounced.

The mixture of the vivid sight imagery such as,

        To swell the gourd, and plump the hazel shells
    With a sweet kernel; to set budding more,
And still more, later flowers for the bees,

and the sound imagery of the poem's consonance creates a "mellow" atmosphere. The movement of the stanza is slow, as if weighted down by heavy-ripe fruits.

The second stanza shows a personified Autumn moving among its crops. This personage visits the granary, the "half-reaped furrow", the mowed fields or the cider-born. The images in this stanza are of work--the reaping, gleaning and harvesting of the crops. This character of Autumn is a bit more lively than the character of stanza one. This is shown by the somewhat quicker pace of the lines in stanza two. The sounds of s's, w's, and r's still predominate. Many of the vowel sounds are long--"thee," "store," "seeks," "find," "asleep" and so on. Yet the syntax approximates normal speech patterns, thus making the lines easier, and faster, reading. More quick sounds pepper the stanza--p's and k's. Odd word combinations are not used. Enough of the luscious slowness of stanza one remains in images such as,

Drowsed with the fume of poppies

or

Thou watchest the last oozings, hours by hours.

The total effect of this stanza is one of mellowed vigor. This is a season of action, but it is tempered by the sloth brought on by the sun's heat.

In the third stanza the poet inquires, "Where are the songs of Spring?" He is implying that for him autumn's sublimity has dispelled any remembrances of spring's glory. In repeating "Ay, where are they?" he seems to be saying that spring is not the only season worthy to be touted by poets. When he says, "thou has thy music too," Keats is telling the reader that he has been trying to capture the rhythms, as well as the sights, of fall. The final lines re-emphasize those rhythms. The slow pace of the lines--again created by the echoings of the consonants and the Mouth-convolting sound-combinations--suggest the motion of this season that is born of lazy summer and sinks to the death of winter. Autumn is a season of leisurely activity. This activity, from stanza two, subsides to death, in stanza three. The day dies, the wind diminishes, the lambs are full-grown, and the swallows are gathering to leave for winter. All these are hints of the coming winter; all are pictures of the beginning of the dying.

Iambic pentameter is used throughout the poem. This meter maintains a steady pace that adapts itself well to the languid feeling and the elegaic tone of the ode. This elegaic touch is most prominent in that last stanza, where Keats accepts the finality that is suggested by the "soft-dying day" and the "wailful choir" of insects.

The rhyme scheme is not precisely the same in all three stanzas. In stanza one the scheme is a b ab cde d cce; in the other two the pattern is abab cde cdde. The effect of this scheme is harmony. The rhyme gives music and unity to the poem. The toying with five rhyme sounds per stanza adds variety of sounds. The stanzas are a bit reminiscent of sonnets, thus giving a formal and lyric tone to the ode.

In all, "To Autumn" is a beautiful poem. Carefully constructed, it, however, has the feel of a spontaneous reaction to the season's glory.

B. The Narrative Poem

The narrative poem tells a story. This story can be simple or complicated, long or short. Often the story is non-dramatic, the events of the tale being arranged in mere chronological order not in a dramatic sequence building to a climax. Narrative verse is objective, rarely revealing any of the poet's philosophy. The narrative verse appears to come from the tales of an impartial narrator.

1. The ballad--

Ballads are the traditional narrative songs, or poems. The traits of a ballad are:

1) A ballad tells a story; often the story is not fully developed. The ballad story frequently gives no motives for a character's actions. The story is usually tragic, focusing most likely on love or death.

2) A ballad has a simple meter, quite often very regular iambic or trochaic tetrameter.

3) Because ballads are sing-songy, they often use nonsense syllables in refrain.

4) Ballads utilize quite a bit of repetition. Sometimes this repetition takes the form of a refrain, or chorus. Often a pattern is repeated; for example, in the old English ballad "Lord Randall" the pattern is a series of similarly phrased questions and answers. Sometimes the repetition is <u>incremental</u>, that is a line or lines is/are repeated but with a variation on that line.

5) Ballads deal with local history, folklore, or escapades of a hero.

6) Ballads rhyme. The traditional ballad stanza is a quatrain which rhymes abcb.

7) Ballads frequently are written in dialect.

8) Superstitions, or the supernatural, often play a role in ballads.

SIR PATRICK SPENS

The King sits in Dumferline town,
    Drinking the blood-red wine:
"O whar will I get a good sailor
    To sail this ship of mine?"

Up and spoke an ancient knight,
    Set at the king's right knee:
"Sir Patrick Spens is the best sailor
    That sails upon the sea."

The king has written a bread letter
    And signed it wi' his hand,
And sent it to Sir Patrick Spens,
    Was walking on the sand.

The first line that Sir Patrick read,
    A loud laugh laughed he;
The next line that Sir Patrick read,
    The tear blinded his ee*. *eye

"O who is this has done this deed,
    This ill deed done to me,
To send me out this time o' the year,
    To sail upon the sea.

"Make haste, make haste, my merry men all,
    Our good ship sails the morn."
"O say not so, my master dear,
    For I fear a deadly storm.

"Late, late yestre'en I saw the new moon
    Wi' the old moon in her arm,
And I fear, I fear, my dear master,
    That we will come to harm."

O our Scots nobles were right loath,
    To wet their cork-heeled shoon*, *shoes
But long before the play were play'd
    Their hats they swan aboon*. *above

O long, long may their ladies sit,
    Wi' their fans into their hand,
Or e'er they see Sir Patrick Spens
    Come sailing to the land.

Long, long may the ladies stand,
    With their gold combs in their hair,
Waiting for their own dear lords,
    For they'll see them no mair.

Half o'er, half o'er to Aberdour
    It's fifty fathom deep,
And there lies good Sir Patrick Spens
    Wi' the Scots lords at his feet.

The ballad "Sir Patrick Spens" (above) is a classic example of a ballad. It fulfills many of the requirements of a ballad.

1. The traditional ballad stanza--abcb--is employed.

2. The meter is highly regular--iambic in most stanzas, trochaic in the second stanza.

3. The story is very simple. The king of Scotland needed a sailor. An old knight tells him that Sir Patrick is "the best sailor/that sails upon the sea." So the king sends a letter to Sir Patrick, requesting him to undertake a voyage. At first Sir Patrick laughs at the idea of a seatrip; then he cries to think he has to attempt a journey in the stormy season. The crew also is afraid, having seen an omen for a storm. On the voyage the ship is wrecked and all the crew lost.

4. The story is tragic, concerning itself with death.

5. The story contains superstition in the warning of a crewman.

> "Late, late yestre'en I saw the new moon
> Wi' the old moon in her arm,
> And I fear, I fear, my dear master,
> That we will come to harm."

6. The poem contains much repetition, mainly incremental. Stanza three repeats a pattern--"The first line that Sir Patrick read," . . . "The next line that Sir Patrick read." Stanzas 9 and 10 use incremental repetition. Other stanzas merely repeat words--"Half o'er, half o'er" or "Make haste, make haste."

7. The ballad "Sir Patrick Spens" deals with a bit of folklore about a local hero.

8. "Sir Patrick Spens" is written in a slight Scottish dialect.

Modern ballads adhere less strictly to the content requirements of a ballad, utilizing the format merely to tell a folksy tale.

2. The epic--

The epic is a lengthy narrative poem which deals with a hero, a man of historical or legendary significance. The epic is formal in style. It follows a fairly well-established format. The poet opens with a question, an inquiry into the tale of some great personage or event. The answer to the question follows as the narrative of the epic. During the singing of the hero's praises the poet usually catalogues and describes the other main characters and their backgrounds. Deeds of valor are recounted. Battles usually are the main sources of action.

Epics are of two types--the folk epic and the art epic. The folk epic is one that was born of the oral tradition, the tale being handed down from generation to generation sung by travelling bards. Finally some poet wrote the folk epic down. The Anglo-Saxon Beowulf and the Greek Odyssey are examples of folk epics. The art epics are more tightly organized than many of the folk epics. Virgil's Aeneid and Dante's Divine Comedy are examples of art epics.

C. Blank Verse

Blank verse is the term applied to poetry written in unrhymed iambic pentameter. This type of verse was first employed by the English poet Surrey. It is reasonable for an English poet to adopt this mode since English, unlike many of the Romance languages, is a language of such a variety of sounds that rhymes are not easily come by. Many English words rhyme with no others.

Blank verse was popularized by Elizabethan playwrights, notably Christopher Marlowe and William Shakespeare. These Elizabethan poets found that blank verse solved a problem of theirs as dramatists. Since poetry was the only accepted mode for writing anything but instructive essays, the Elizabethan playwrights had to struggle with creating reasonable dialogue in verse. The limiting nature of rhyme made the task difficult. The playwright had two options. He could create good poetry, but his dramatic style suffered. Or he could pen a play with a cohesive plot and meaningful dialogue, but in shoddy poetry. Blank verse offered these sixteenth century dramatists a compromise. The verse is regular in meter, but not confined by the convention of rhyme. Also, the elimination of rhyme released much of the serious dialogue from the musicality, cuteness, or lightness of rhymed verse.

In later centuries blank verse has been used in a variety of poems. Quite often a poet who is contemplating a serious subject will write in blank verse. Since spoken English has been scanned and consequently found to be fairly iambic in its cadence, blank verse is used frequently in poems which imitate spoken English. Blank verse, because of the absence of rhyme, can be used to convey either a formal or a conversational tone. The word choice determines which.

Blank verse is not easy to do well. Because of its freeness, blank verse can deteriorate into mere sentences split at 10-syllable intervals. Therefore, a blank versist must pay particular attention to imagery, symbolism, and sound effects.

The following excerpt from Shakespeare's A Mid-Summer Night's Dream will demonstrate blank verse at its best.

Lovers and madmen have such seething brains,
Such shaping fantasies that apprehend
More than cool reason ever comprehends.
The lunatic, the lover and the poet
Are of imagination all compact:
One sees more devils than vast hell can hold,
That is, the madman: the lover, all as frantic,
Sees Helen's beauty in a brow of Egypt:
The poet's eye, in a fine frenzy rolling,
Doth glance from heaven to earth, from earth to heaven;
And as imagination bodies forth
The forms of things unknown, the poet's pen
Turns them to shapes and gives to airy nothing
A local habitation and a name.
Such tricks hath strong imagination,
That, if it would but apprehend some joy,
It comprehends some bringer of that joy;
Or in the night, imagining some fear,
How easy is a bush supposed a bear!

This short passage memorably, and humorously, discuss the similarity between poets (like Shakespeare himself), lovers, and madmen. All three have minds so governed by strong imaginations that reality is oftentimes converted, or perverted, into personal fantasies. The madman sees devils, or personified fears. The lover sees beauty where there is more. The poet creates new and strange objects or places from sheer visions.

Yet how much more powerful is Shakespeare's statement than a simple paraphrase. The passage has music created by a number of means. Shakespeare sprinkles alliteration and consonance throughout. The first two lines echo with s's. Other examples occur in line four with "lunatic" and "lover" or line six with "hell can hold." The lover

"Sees Helen's beauty in a brow of Egypt".

All three might see "a bush supposed a bear." Repeated sounds, almost rhymes, occur in lines two and three, "apprehends" and "comprehend." In lines 17 and 18 "joy ends each. The repeating in "from heaven to earth from earth to heaven," is also lyrical.

Stronger than the music of the passage are the vivid images. The three have "seething brains" that are "shaping fantasies." This active image causes one to see minds boiling over with wild visions, as bubbles overflowing a cauldron. The madmad "sees more devils than vast hell can hold." Certainly that is a lot of devils. The lover is "frantic," a nice word, depicting him as mad as the before-mentioned lunatic. Thus the similarity between lover and lunatic is re-emphasized. This lover sees beauty in one not beautiful. The image of a man seeing the magnificence of Helen of Troy in a Cleopatran face is evocative of mythology's magic. The poet, though, is most picturesque; he is "in a fire frenzy rolling." The idea of madness is echoed here. The reader, also, can "see" an excited man, his eyes rolling rapidly as he thinks, creating mind-spun fantasies. The last line is a contrast to the images of the earlier lines. Most of the passage shows those three wild minds as envisioning splendid and unusual things. Yet imagining, in the dark, that a bush is a bear is very common. The three men are, by this vision, brought back to the reader as real, not fantastic, beings. The commonness of this image is also human--for we've all imagined something similar.

This passage is not serious, but it has a lyrical beauty even though it does not have a lyric's rhyme. The creation of this feel of a lyric is proof of Shakespeare's mastery of blank verse.

D. Free Verse

It is difficult to define free verse by telling what it is. It is easier to say what free verse is not. Free verse is not rhymed. It does not have a regular meter, but rather relies on the "ebb and flow" or cadences of speech. Free verse is not written in definite stanzas. It is exactly as its name implies--free, free to wander the printed page at the poet's will, free to create pictures in random order.

Free verse, or vers libre, has been extremely popular in the twentieth century, although it is not that new. In the nineteenth century French poets experimented with free verse. The King James Bible employed free verse.

Free verse is not as easy to write as people suppose. Because it has even less form then blank verse, it more easily can turn into prose written in verse form. Because free verse lacks the obvious music of rhyme and meter, it has to rely on other sound devices and phrasing for rhythm. Imagery is very important in free verse since the poem has to capture the reader's imagination with words alone, unaided by these old favorites rhyme and meter.

NOTE: You should obtain a copy of Ezra Pound's "The Study in Aesthetics" in order to better follow the next few paragraphs.

In the free verse poem THE STUDY IN AESTHETICS the title is significant for an understanding of the poem's theme. The poet is pleased that the children appreciate the beauty of the passing woman. He feels that these ragamuffins, despite their ages and social positions, have a sense of aesthetics. He indicates this in line two when he says the youngsters are "smitten with an unusual wisdom." Yet three years later he watches as a boy repeats the same appreciative phrase, "Ch' è be' a" (That's beautiful), while surveying packed sardines. "Midly abashed," the poet realizes that both the children and the Dante boy have a very simple criterion for determining beauty--beauty is pleasant to look at. Snobbishly, the poet had attached a more profound meaning to "beautiful" since to him beauty is an aesthetic value, not merely a descriptive quality. Thus, the poet's title, "The Study in Aesthetics" is midly sarcastic, revealing that the poet has been learning about those aesthetics.

The poem has a conversational quality. This is especially pronounced in lines seven and eight where the poet pauses to tell us parenthetically that there are many Dantes and Catullis in this Italian town. This tone is effective in creating the illusion that the poet is confiding to the reader an anecdotal lesson. The tone is created by the rhythm of free verse.

The images are simple and clear. The children in their "patched clothing" are real as they play on the cobbled street. The poet's vision of them as astute viewers of beauty, however, is unrealistic. The words he chooses to describe their "wisdom" are less realistic. These children are "smitten." This old-fashioned word is reminiscent of sentimental poems about "smitten" loves. It seems incongruous applied to street urchins ogling a local beauty. "Wisdom" also does not seem accurate to describe these children's thought processes. The image of the boy leaping about, "snatching at the bright fish" is visually precise. It is also suggestive of fish themselves, leaping to snatch bait. A correspondence between boy and fish is implied. When the boy then strokes the packed sardines, murmuring, "Ch' 'e be' a," the reader feels that the boy loves these fish. The words "stroke" and "murmur" are words of love poems, just as "smitten" is. The suggestion is that both the children and the Dante boy appreciate, with a feeling close to love, simple beauties.

Through his choice of words, Pound shows us his own lack of wisdom. He has learned that beauty need not be a sublime quality. It exists in everyday experiences. It is truly "in the eyes of the beholder." Thus, when Pound first thought the children had "wisdom" in their choice of an admired sight, he was wrong. He thought they saw the quality he termed "beauty." Yet the children, in simply admiring a pretty woman, had a different wisdom. They understood better the meaning of "beautiful," as did the Dante boy. Beauty attracts.

Pound is gently laughing at himself and the notion of beauty he held. His playful use of images adds to the tone of humor.

His toying with the word "wisdom" is part of this mockery. The choice of Dante as the boy's last name is sarcastic. The boy is hardly a genius or poet as Dante was. The poet might first have laughed at the boy's name as unfitting his station as two fish-packers' son. Yet, in his new frame of mind, the poet might find the name appropriate, the boy, in his simple appreciation of the world, being as much a poet as Dante. This joke is carried further when the poet says there are twenty-eight young Dantes and thirty-two Catullis in town. Why, the town is chock full of young poets, savoring the unacclaimed beauties of Italy!

The free verse style is well chosen and well done in "The Study of Aesthetics." This style enabled Pound to talk to the reader. It also allowed him to be both Cryptic, in the first section or in the punning with "Dante", or imagistic, as in the description of the boy enjoying the fish. Pound can move freely from tone to tone since he is not tied to a structural meter.

In the free verse poem "Buffalo Bill's" by e.e.cummings, it shows a more unorthodox use of the style. The poet shows the reader an image of the famous and fabulous Buffalo Bill as he once was. But in questioning, "how do you like your blue-eyed boy/Mister Death," cummings implies that the once-great Buffalo Bill is no better than dust when relegated to the grave.

The interest in this poem is not thermatic, however. The visual impression that the poem gives the reader is the most memorable quality of the verse. It appears that cummings realizes that poetry is no longer a spoken art; it is a literary form that reaches most people via the printed page. So, he uses the medium of print to create images. The sprawling of the poem's lines conveys a feeling of freedom and movement. Perhaps this is suggestive, especially in the opening lines, of Buffalo Bill's riding of that stallion. The crushing together of "onetwothreefourfive pigeonsjustlikethat" is imitative of the speed with which Bill shot down those clay pigeons. The solitary word "defunct," meriting its own line, is potent. It is preceded by a pause, caused by the change from one line to another, and followed by a pause, for the same reason. No matter how often a reader hears that he should read to the punctuation not merely to the ends of lines, he still is affected by the switches from line to line. Capitalizing on that knowledge, cummings gives "defunct" a deliberate emphasis and finality. This is powerful in conveying the death of Buffalo Bill. The use of "defunct" to mean "dead" is strange, also. "Defunct" is a term from the world of business. It is impersonal and cold. Somehow Buffalo Bill is turned into an inanimate commodity by the use of this word. The expletive "Jesus" also stands out because of the spatial arrangement of the poem. A reader cannot help, therefore, but make an emphatic declaration with this word. Thus, the tone of the lines, "Jesus/he was a handsome man" is one of positive appreciation, even wonder. This makes his death, and the question at the end, bitter. The poet is angry at, perhaps disappointed with, the fate of Buffalo Bill. Sarcastically, he spits out the question at Death, mocking the idea that Death chose a favorite (blue-eyed boy).

The form of e.e.cummings' poem, in conclusion, defines exactly how it is to be read--fast, slow, with emphasis here or with finality there.

ANALYZING A POEM

The following questions may help a student learn what to look for in a poem, what to ask about the poem.

1. Who is the speaker? What is the speaker like?

2. To whom is he speaking? What kind of person is this?

3. What is the situation in the poem?

4. What is the setting of the poem (if any)?

5. What is the central idea, theme, of the poem?

6. What is the tone of the poem? How is this tone created--by diction, images, rhyme, etc.?

7. How does the poem develop?

8. Paraphrase the poem.

9. Discuss the images in the poem. How do they affect you? What do they suggest?

10. What symbols are used in the poem?

11. Symbolically, could the poem have a second level of meaning? What is it?

12. Check for figures of speech. How are they used? Why might they have been used?

13. What allusions are used? What do these contribute to the poem?

14. What sound devices--alliteration, onomatopoeia, assonance, consonance, rhyme, or repetition--are used? What effects do these have on the poem's tone or meaning?

15. What is the poem's meter? What effect does it have on the poem?

Obviously all these questions will not apply to every poem. The student should recognize that some of these questions--such as #3 or #5--will apply to every poem. Some questions--such as #10 or #13--apply only to selected poems.

When writing an analysis of a poem, a student can approach the task in a number of ways.

1. Begin by selecting a facet of the poem to focus on. For example, you might wish to discuss the use of imagery in the poem. Then, open with a brief statement of what the analysis intends to prove. Then prove it.

2. Begin with a general introduction to the poem, its core situation and theme. Then begin to show how that theme is arrived at. You could move chronologically through the poem, explicating lines and developing the theme. Or you could organize your analysis into areas that develop the theme--imagery, sound, etc.

3. Attack the poem as a statement of a poet's philosophy. In this type of analysis you are trying to demonstrate what type of person or philosophy creates such a work. Most likely you will begin with a general statement summarizing what you believe that philosophy is. Then by explicating sections of the poem, you would prove your thesis.

EXAMPLES OF AP/CLEP POETRY ANALYSIS

Sample (1):

OZYMANDIAS

I met a traveller from an antique land
Who said: Two vast and trunkless legs of stone
Stand in the desert . . . Near them, on the sand,
Half sunk, a shattered visage lies, whose frown,
And wrinkled lip, and sneer of cold command
Tell that its sculptor well those passions read
Which yet survive, stamped on these lifeless things.
The hand that mocked them and the heart that fed:
And on the pedestal these words appear:
"My name is Ozymandias, king of kings:
Look on my works, ye Mighty, and despair!"
Of that colossal wreck, boundless and bare
The lone and level sands stretch far away.

Percy Bysshe Shelley

Response (1)

As you read the poem, a picture of desolation and ruin forms itself in your mind, an image depicting a decaying state in the midst of the barren waste of the desert. The details revolving about the scene give it a special meaning and significance. Here, Shelley relies heavily on symbolism to relate his ideas to the discerning reader. The poem is written in blank verse.

The poem carries a very important message throughout its fourteen lines. We must always remember that the greatest names and their accomplishments do not last forever. As time marches on, the memory and the works of the most powerful men become meaningless as they fall in ruin and are forgotten.

Ozymandias is the Greek name for Ramses II, the powerful ruler of Egypt during the thirteenth century B.C. He ruled for over sixty years and brought great prosperity to the people of Egypt. He was also extrememly vain with respect to his deeds. From this information, the "traveller from an antique land" can only have come from Egypt, which is based on ancient civilizations and is associated with a large amount of desert.

The face of the statue embodies a frown, a wrinkled lip, and a "sneer of cold command." Shelley sees these emotions as characterizing people in power as "its sculptor well those passions read." The sculptor correctly interpreted the character of the king, the one in power, as he made the statue. Through the sculptor, Shelley airs his disapproval of the ruling class, "The hand that mocked them and the heart that fed," the hand being that of the artist, mocks them, referring to the king's passions, and the heart, that of the king, which fed his passions.

As the "Two vast and trunkless legs of stone/Stand in the desert," they support nothing, which is all that remains of the "king of kings" and his works. This is further emphasized as "Nothing beside remains. Round the decay/Of that colossal wreck" there exists nothing but "the lone and level sands." The ozymoron of "colossal wreck" again establishes the once great power of the king to have dissipated with his demise. The statue, like the king, had been great and imposing, colossal, but in time, the king's power and memory were buried along with him and the statue decayed to the level of a wreck. The "shattered visage" appears "half sunk," again symbolizing the memory of the once mighty king to be forgotten and put aside. It is ironic to note that a section of the inscription reads: "Look on my works, ye Mighty, and despair," when in fact Ozymandias and his works other than the decrepit statue no longer exist. All that survives are those passions etched on the face of inanimate stone, "which yet survive, stamped on these lifeless things," to mock all those who wield power, past, present, and future. A sense of endless time is created with the words "boundless and bare/The lone and level sands stretch far away." Since the statue is situated in the midst of this setting of endless time, we can understand that time will obliterate all memory of the great ruler and his works just as the desert will do to the statue.

Response (2)

Ozymandias is a rather simple poem. The theme is apparent upon first perusal. The theme, the transitory nature of man, is presented by the character of Ozymandias, the ruined statue in the desert, and the structure of the poem. In this thesis, I will discuss how the above elements combine to achieve the previously stated theme.

The major character, Ozymandias, was actually the Egyptian Pharaoh Ramses II. Ramses was known for his vast architectural programs which included the construction of some of the largest temples in Egypt. In the quote:

> "My name is Ozymandias, King of Kings:
> Look on my works, ye Mighty, and despair!"

Ozymandias reveals qualities of vanity and greatness. He had done great works and ruled a long time. However, he thought too highly of himself. Power and renown don't last forever. He called himself the "King of Kings", but like all other Kings, he was popular for awhile and then forgotten when the new King came around.

The sculptor built a "colossal" statue of Ozymandias, reputed to be the largest in Egypt. This parallels the large temples of Ozymandias, some of which were supposed to be among the largest in Egypt.

The sculptor captured the real essence of the man and ruler. He believed that he would endure forever, but he wouldn't have if there hadn't been a statue of him. The statue was all that remained, an enduring testimony of his existence. "Nothing beside remains."

The decayed statue shows the futility of Ozymandias' feelings. His words did not incite anyone to do greater deeds than he had done. Instead, everything was left to decay. If there had been some productive result from the saying, the statue would not have been a decaying wreck in the middle of a desolate desert. The adjectives describing the statue are negative and show the decrease in status between Ozymandias' past and present. The shattered effect is used in the lines to describe the statue. Most of the description is written in one sentence and broken up by commas placed after every few words. Alliteration is the major poetic device used in the final sentence. They make the sentence flow smoothly, matching the "level sands" of the desert. The last few sentences isolate the statue from civilization.

Ozymandias' recognition was limited by two elements-time and nature. The first image in the poem is of a "traveler from an antique land". The word "antique" refers to ancient Egypt. Ozymandias' fame was limited to the time he was alive and a few following generations. Over a long period of time, men are soon forgotten, and that is what happened to Ozymandias.

The last image in the poem is "the lone and level sands." The image of nature is the second and final limit put on Ozymandias. The statue was isolated in a place where people aren't liable to seet it.

Shelley shows that art can preserve the past. The story of Ozymandias was preserved by the poet (traveler) who recounted it to the narrator, the sculptor who built the statue, and the statue itself. Man can keep all the knowledge he wishes to retain through art, whether it be writing or sculpting.

Art can also be used as a means for reform. He uses this poem to show the futility of Ozymandias' sentiments. This enables him to change people who have these sentiments He was a firm believer in human perfectibility and universal goodness. He wrote his poetry to reform the world.

Response (3)

Shelley's Ozymandias is an example of a romantic, lyric poem. It is brief, subjective, and strongly marked by various tendencies that create for the reader a single, unified impression.

The strongest aspect of romanticism which is contained in Ozymandias is the turning back to the past. The poem itself is based on a story recounted by Diordorus Siculus, a Greek historian of the first century A.D. He reported that the statue was of Ozymandias (it was actually of the Egyptian Pharoah Ramses II) and that it was the largest in Egypt. It was said to bear the inscription: "I am Ozymandias, King of Kings. If any man wishes to know who I am and where I am buried, let him surpass me in some of my achievements." Shelley uses the story to emphasize how futile and vain such sentiment actually is. There is a strong irony in the fact that a once-powerful king is now only remembered by passerbys in the barren desert who haphazardly view this crumbling, broken down relic. His once mighty accomplishments have literally turned to dust, faded from memory with the passage of time.

The poem is also romantic in the imagery that the author employs. By using the "antique land" of Egypt as a setting, Shelley stirs in the reader feelings of the mysterious and the exotic.

There is sheer music in Shelley's verse. There is a clear-flowing melody found within it, as well as the suggestion of a sublime world beyond the physical which man cannot see but is sure exists. When reading the poem, questions concerning this run through the readers mind: Is Ozymandias, and other power-seekers like him, in this other world? Are their lives really worthwhile, considering the effects of the passage of time?

The author smoothly and subtly switches the mood in his poem. In the first portion of it, strong, descriptive words such as "sneer" and "cold command" are present. They are not pleasant, and those reading the poem can clearly sense the power and arrogance seeping from them. In the latter portions of Ozymandias, words like "barren," "decay," and "lone" evoke only feelings of nothingness, waste, and the sad effects of time.

Sample (2)

LYCIDAS

In this monody the author bewails a learned friend, unfortunately drowned in his passage from Chester on the Irish Seas, 1637. And by occasion foretells the ruin of our corrupted clergy, then in their height.

Yet once more, O ye laurels, and once more,
Ye myrtles brown, with ivy never sere,
I come to pluck your berries harsh and crude,
And with forced fingers rude
Shatter your leaves before the mellowing year.
Bitter constraint and sad occasion dear
Compels me to disturb your season due;
For Lycidas is dead, dead ere his prime,
Young Lycidas, and hath not left his peer.
Who would not sing for Lycidas? he knew
Himself to sing, and build the lofty rhyme.
He must not float upon his wat'ry bier
Unwept, and welter to the parching wind,
Without the meed of some melodious tear.
  Begin, the, Sisters of the Sacred Well[1]
That from beneath the seat of Jove doth spring,
Begin, and somewhat loudly sweep the string.
Hence with denial vain and coy excuse:
So may some gentle Muse
With lucky words favor my destined urn,
And, as he passes, turn
And bid fair peace be to my sable shroud!
For we were nursed upon the self-same hill,
Fed the same flocks, by fountain, shade, and rill;
  Together both, ere the high lawns appeared
Under the opening eyelids of the Morn,
We drove a-field, and both together heard
What time the gray-fly winds her sultry horn,
Battening our flocks with the fresh dews of night,
Oft till the star that rose at evening bright
Towards Heaven's descent had sloped his westering wheel.
Meanwhile the rural ditties were not mute,
Tempered to the oaten flute,
Rought Satyrs danced, and Fauns with cloven heel
From the glad sound would not be absent long;
And old Damaetas[2] loved to hear our song.
  But, O the heavy change, now thou art gone,
Now thou art gone, and never must return!
Thee, Shepherd, thee the woods and desert caves,
With wild thyme and the gadding vine o'er grown,
And all their echoes mourn.

[1]the muses, who dwelt at the Pierian spring
[2]conventional pastoral name for an older man

The willows, and the hazel copses green,
Shall now no more be seen
Fanning their joyous leaves to thy soft lays.
As killing as the canker to the rose,
Or taint-worm to the weanling herds that graze
Or frost to flowers, that their gay wardrobe wear
When first the white thorn blows;
Such, Lycidas, thy loss to shepherd's ear.
  Where were ye, Nymphs, when the remorseless deep
Closed o'er the head of your loved Lycidas?
For neither were ye playing on the steep
Where your old bards, the famous druids, lie,
Nor yet on the shaggy top of Mona[3] high,
Nor yet where Deva[4] spreads her wizard stream.
Ay me! I fondly dream
"Had ye been there"...for what could that have done?
What could the Muse herself that Orpheus bore,[5]
The Muse herself, for her enchanting son,
Whom universal Nature did lament,
When, by the rout that made the hideous roar,
His gory visage down the stream was sent,
Down the swift Hebrus to the Lesbian shore?
  Alas! what boots it with uncessant care
To tend the homely, slighted, shepherd's trade,
And strictly mediate the thankless Muse?
Were it not better done, as others use,
To sport with Amaryllis in the shade,
Or with the tangles of Neaera's[6] hair?
Fame is the spur that the clear spirit doth raise
(That last infirmity of noble mind)
To scorn delights and live laborious days;
But the fair guerdon when we hope to find,
And think to burst out into sudden blaze,
Comes the blind Fury with the abhorred shears,
And slits the thin-spun life. "But not the praise,"
Phoebus replied, and touched my trembling ears:
"Fame is no plant that grows on mortal soil,
Nor in the glistering foil.
Set off to the world, nor in broad rumor lies,
But lives and spreads aloft by those pure eyes
And perfect witness of all-judging Jove;
As he pronounces lastly on each deed,
Of so much fame in Heav'n expect thy meed."
  O fountain Arethuse,[7] and thou honored flood,
Smooth-sliding Mincius,[8] crowned with vocal reeds,
That strain I heard was of a higher mood:
But now my oat proceeds,

[3]island of Anglesey, off Wales
[4]river Dee
[5]Calliope could not prevent a mob of Thracian women from murdering Orpheus. They threw his head into the river Hebrus, whence it floated out to the island of Lesbos in the Aegean Sea.
[6]conventional pastoral names for shepherdesses
[7]a nymph, transformed into a fountain in Sicily
[8]river in Lombardy. Like Arethuse, it represents pastoral poetry.

And listen to the Herald of the Sea,[9]
That came in Neptune's plea.
He asked the waves, and asked the felon winds,
What hard mishap hath doomed this gentle swain?
And questioned every gust of rugged wings
That blows from off each beaked promontory:
They knew not of his story;
And sage Hippotades[10] their answer brings,
That not a blast was from his dungeon strayed:
The air was calm, and on the level brine
Sleek Panope[11] with all her sisters played.
It was the fatal and perfidious bark,
Built in the eclipse, and rigged with curses dark,
That sunk so low that sacred head of thine.
  Next, Camus,[12] reverend sire, went footing slow,
His mantle hairy, and his bonnet sedge,
Inwrought with figures dim, and on the edge
Like to that sanguine flower inscribed with woe.
"Ah! who hath reft," quoth he, "my earest pledge?"
Last came, and last did go,
The pilot of the Galilean lake;[13]
Two massy keys he bore of metals twain
(The golden opes, the iron shuts amain).
He shook his mitered locks, and stern bespake:-
"How well could I have spared for thee, young swain,
Enow of such, as for their bellies' sake,
Creep, and intrude, and climb into the fold!
Of other care they little reckoning make
Than how to scramble at the shearers' feast,
And shove away the worthy bidden guest.
Blind mouths! that scare themselves know how to hold
A sheep-hook, or have learned aught else the least
That to the faithful herdsman's art belongs!
What recks it them. What need they. they are sped;
And, when they list, their lean and flashy songs
Grate on their scrannel pipes of wretched straw;
The hungry sheep look up, and are not fed,
But, swollen with wind and the rank mist they draw,
Rot inwardly, and foul contagion spread;
Besides what the graim wolf with privy paw
Daily devours apace, and nothing said;
But that two-handed engine at the door
Stands ready to smite once, and smite no more."
  Return, Alpheus;[14] the dead voice is past
That shrunk thy streams; return, Sicilian Muse,
And call the vales, and bid them hither cast
Their bells and flowerets of a thousand hues.

---

[9] Triton, who here pleads Neptune's innocence
[10] Aeolus, god of the winds
[11] the principal sea nymph
[12] god of the river Cam; hence Cambridge University
[13] St. Peter, to whom Christ gave the keys of Heaven; who, as the first bishop, is pictured here as wearing a miter
[14] god of a river in Arcadia, representing pastoral poetry

Ye valleys low, where the mild whispers use
Of shades, and wanton winds, and gushing brooks,
On whose fresh lap the swart star sparely looks,
Throw hither all your quaint enameled eyes,
That on the green turf suck the honied showers,
And purple all the ground with vernal flowers.
Bring the rathe primrose that forsaken dies,
The tufted crow-toe, and pale jessamine,
The white pink, and the pansy freaked with jet,
The flowing violet,
The musk-rose, and the well-attired woodbine,
With cowslips wan that hang the pensive head,
And every flower that sad embroidery wears;
Bid Amaranthus all his beauty shed,
And daffadillies fill their cups with tears,
To strew the laureate hearse where Lycid lies.
For so, to interpose a little ease,
Let our frail thoughts dally with false surmise,
Ay me! whilst thee the shores and sounding seas
Wash far away, where'er thy bones are hurled;
Whether beyond the stormy Hebrides,
Where thou, perhaps, under the whelming tide
Visit'st the bottom of the monstrous world;
Or whether thou, to our moist vows denied,
Sleep'st by the fable of Bellerus[15] old,
Where the great Vision of the guarded mount
Looks toward Namancos and Bayona's[16] hold:
Look homeward, angel, now, and melt with ruth;
And, O ye Dolphins, waft the hapless youth.
  Weep no more, woeful shepherds, weep no more,
For Lycidas, your sorrow, is not dead,
Sunk though he be beneath the watery floor:
So sinks the day-star in the ocean bed,
And yet anon repairs his drooping head,
And tricks his beams, and with new-spangled ore
Flames in the forehead of the morning sky:
So Lycidas sunk low, but mounted high,
Through the dear might of Him that walked the waves,
Where, other groves and other streams along,
With nectar pure his oozy locks he laves,
And hears the unexpressive nuptial song,
In the blest kingdoms meek of Joy and Love.
There entertain him all the Saints above,
In solemn troops, and sweet societies,
That sing, and singing in their glory move,
And wipe the tears forever from his eyes.
Now, Lycidas, the shepherds weep no more;
Henceforth thou art the Genius of the shore,
In thy large recompense, and shalt be good
To all that wander in that perilous flood.

  Thus sang the uncouth swain to the oaks and rills,

---

[15]a giant of fable, said to be buried at Land's End, Cornwall
[16]Spanish strongholds of Catholic power

While the still Morn went out with sandals gray;
He touched the tender stops of various quills,
With eager thought warbling his Doric lay:
And now the sun had stretched out all the hills,
And now was dropped into the western bay.
At last he rose, and twitched his mantle blue:
Tomorrow to fresh woods and pastures new.

John Milton

Discussions on Johnson's Criticisms of "Lycidas"

Response (1)

Upon reading "Lycidas," the reader comes across some problems. These are voiced in a criticism of the poem by Samuel Johnson. He in effect states that the two main problems are the awkward technique used and the apparent insincerity of the author. I agree to a certain extent with Johnson on both charges. "Lycidas" was written by Milton upon the death of his friend Edward King, a young clergyman and scholar. Johnson maintains that the poem, which is billed as an elegy, is not what it professes to be. He states that "It's form is that of a pastoral, essay, vulgar, and therefore disgusting; whatever images it can supply are long ago exhausted, and its inherent improbability always forces dissatisfaction on the mind."

The work is supposedly a lament of the death of King and a show of grief that his companionship will no longer be a comfort to Milton. The author, as Johnson further states, has some other motive behind his poem. It is not merely a compliment of King and an expression of grief at his death. Milton launches a very definite attack upon the clergy and their preachings in the work. This is best illustrated in lines 103 - 131. Milton does not wish to blindly accept the fate of mankind as the sheep do theirs. In this section also the awkwardness of his technique comes out. He moves from this tirade of St. Peter to the shepherd to recalling the "Sicilian Muse." Throughout the poem, Milton has chosen to use an often strange mixture of Christianity and paganism. In this instance it seems as if the show of anger by the Christian has frightened the pagan away. Milton has the pagans mourn Lycidas throughout the course of the poem and he speaks of Lycidas' life with the pagan faction in the fields. Towards the end of the poem, however, the narrator goes on to say that Lycidas has not died, he has moved beyond them to another world - the Christian concept of heaven. With this it is apparent that, as far as Milton is concerned, the Christian will win and has won out over the pagan.

Another point of awkwardness is that Milton at times has difficulty in trying to keep the poem at a pastoral level. The point of interest here is between lines 75 - 85. Apollo was one of the higher gods, and his words were recognized as being of a "higher strain," as the narrator tries to put the poem once again on a pastoral note. The same problem can be seen in the appearance of St. Peter and the recalling of the Muse previously mentioned. One of Johnson's main objections to the poem was that it had no real unity in its form. It has no definite rhyme scheme that can be picked up right away. The only section of the poem that shows any signs of being part of a conventional poem is the last eight lines. In this one part there is a complete turn about from what has preceded it. Here there is a definite rhyme scheme; the point of view changes from first person to third person; and I think that the content of this section is also very different from what came before. I will use this section and the three points just mentioned to present a short possible counter-argument to Johnson's criticisms.

In the book Understanding Poetry, it is suggested that the final eight lines of the poem are used by Milton to clear up the disunity that precedes the section. In this passage, there is a definite rhyme scheme: ab, ab, ab, cc. The swain's lament is no longer seen as subjective, but objective, and the author seems to be admitting to the insincerity of the elegy. After the "uncouth" swain has finished his song, Milton hits upon the key phrases for this argument: "At last he rose, and twitched his mantle blue: Tomorrow to fresh woods and pastures new." The swain will not continue to mourn Lycidas, but will go on to a new life elsewhere. I do not totally agree with either of these theories, but I feel that a cross between the two would be more suitable in dealing with this poem.

Response (2)

"Lycidas" is a pastoral elegy in that it is both a poem of lamentation for the dead and a representation of rural life in which the poet portrays himself as a shepherd. The poem was written in memorium to Edward King, a prospective parish priest who, on a voyage to Ireland, perished in a shipwreck. Despite the confines of the conventional form, there is a great deal of passion and energy locked between the lines. The question is who receives the energy and passion - the corrupt clergy he denounces or Edward King? Little is known of the relationship between Milton and King. There is speculation as to whether a special friendship which seemed to cause such acute personal grief actually existed. Perhaps the elegy is an artifical front to condemn the clergy for the passage certainly clashes with the tone of lamentation which preceeds. Milton had been training for the clergy for five years before his friend's death - perhaps he wonders if it is worthwhile to 'scorn delights and live laborious days' (Line 72) to answer the high calling. Where is the justice of God in taking one honest man and allowing the corrupt to continue polluting?

Milton utilized a great deal of literary wealth available to him combining it with his own original ideas. "Lycidas" begins with an invocation of the Muses, a classical move imitated from the ancients, ie: Virgil. Eclogue IV: 'The Messiah' a famous pastoral poem - 'Scilian Muses, begin a loftier strain!' (Line 1). Milton invokes the Muses to sing the praises of Lycidas, a name borrowed from Theocritus, a composer of pastorals. The use of Grecian images is common in pastorals and is well suited for elegies for it serves to augment the melancholy mood and heighten and idealize the poet's grief.

> Yet once more, O ye laurels, and once more,
> Ye myrtles brown, with ivy never sear,
> I come to pluck your berries harsh and crude,
> And with forced fingers rude
> Shatter your leaves before the mellowing year.
> Bitter constraint and sad occasion dear
> For Lycidas is dead, dead ere his prime,
> Young Lycidas, and hath not left his peer.
> Who would not sing for Lycidas? He knew
> Himself to sing, and build the lofty rime.
> He must not float upon his watery bier
> Unwept, and welter to the parching wind,
> Without the meed of some melodious tear.
>
> (Lines 1-14)

The first fourteen lines deal with the brutal plucking of the laurel bush's berries before their prime which can be likened to the premature death of a man. Much as the plucking shatters the plant's leaves so does King's early death shake Milton. Milton feels compelled to write a memoriam, 'melodious tear', in that he hopes some 'gentle muse' or poet will in turn 'with lucky words favor my destined urn' (Line 20).

In the Lines 23-32 the pastoral images of shepherds is employed. Milton reflects on their life together at Cambridge. For a moment the tone lightens as he speaks of happier times. 'But, oh! the heavy change, now thou art gone, Now thou art gone, and never must return!' (Lines 37-38) quickly plunges us back into a melancholy mood. The lamentation continues as Milton compares his loss to rural scenes 'as killing as the canker to the rose, Or taint-worm to the weanling herds that graze, of frost to the flowers...such, Lycidas, thy loss to Shepherd's (Milton's) ear.' (Lines 45-48) Where were the Muses? Couldn't they have prevented it? People frequently ask God why He allowed a thing to happen, so too does Milton. Where the justice? He wonders if it would have been better to sport as the others did before 'comes the blind fury (Anthropos, one of the three Fates who cuts the thread of life) with the abhorred shears, And slits the thin-spun life." (Lines 75-76) Instead the pursuit fame' the spur that the clear spirit doth raise (That last infirmity of the noble mind) To scorn delights, and live laborious days.' (Lines 69-72) occupied their time. To rue the past life is not uncommon for one often regrets time wasted in fruitless or worthless pursuits which might not seen as valuable once attained. Fame does not burst out in 'sudden flame' but rather is witnessed in 'all-judging Jove; as he pronounces lastly on each deed. Of such fame in heav'n expect thy meed.' (Lines 82-84)

The elegy becomes more melancholy as Milton seeks to ascertain the physical side of King's death. A sudden break in the melodious rhythm introduces the passage denonuncing the corrupt clergy. The lines become either very long or very abrupt and the rhyme scheme - which is very Italian - becomes obscure. After speaking of clergymen who 'for their bellies' sake, Creep and intrude, and climb into the fold!' Milton quickly retreats back to pastoral scenes invoking melancholy. In the final passage the eternal hope of man-life after death-is realized for Lycidas. The mourner is soothed with the image of Lycidas being entertained by saints.

Although "Lycidas" is definitely an elegy, what it mourns is a mystery which only Milton can solve. Perhaps he mourns for what King could have accomplished, perhaps he mourns him as a friend, perhaps he mourns the time he wasted seeking fame, or more likely perhaps he mourns the imminent downfall of the Catholic Church. The poem was written in 1637 when Milton was twenty-nine. It still reflects the work of a fortunate youth who had never known trouble or doubt, who viewed the world with a pure and confident air. "Lycidas" springs from the first real shock substained by his religious and moral being. I believe that the poem is a disguised attack on the clergy for, again, little is known of King and Milton's relationship. Thus, on the surface the poem may be an elegy but it is much more complex and diverse. It contains many pastoral scenes but eliminates the conventional features ie: the refrain and it swells particularly in the passage dealing with Saint Peter, to an ode-like intensity. Milton seems to have created a new form of elegy blending many styles.

Response (3)

In his poem "Lycidas" Milton mourns the death of one of his friends. The death of his friend came suddenly and unexpectedly - he drowned while sailing on the Irish Sea. In the first few opening lines Milton lets the reader know how ultimately this death was. He points out that Lycidas died "ere his prime." His death came much too soon. He compares this death to the leaves of the myrtle and laurel trees. The speaker of the poem picks those leaves before they have had a chance to grow and become green. Both Lycidas and the leaves have had their lives prematurely taken away from them.

The speaker of the poem then tells the reader how close the two friends were. They were brought up together and shared each other's experiences. They were also both shepherds. They lead their flocks to the same fields and watched over them.

While Lycidas was alive "Satyrs danced, and Fauns with cloven heel From the glad sound would not be absent long." Everything seemed joyous and full of merriment while Lycidas could never return, the satyrs would never dance again. Everything mourned the death of Lycidas - "and desert caves, With wild thyme and the gadding vine o'er grown, And all their echoes, mourn."

The speaker then asks the nymphs where they were when Lycidas was drowning. He feels that they should have protected and saved him. But then he realizes that nothing, not even the nymphs, could have saved Lycidas from his death.

Milton says that all during a person's life there are many goals he wishes to achieve. He tries to attain these goals and the rewards that go along with them. But suddenly death can come and bring an end to all the dreams, goals, and achievements a person has. Milton says, "Comes the blind Fury with the abhorred shears, And slits the thin - spun life." He compares life to a thread, so thin that it can break at any time. Death can come unexpectedly and often it comes too soon.

For most of the poem Milton is sad and bewails the death of his friend. After much thought though he realizes that Lycidas is physically dead, but that is all. He did drown and was engulfed by the waters of the Irish Sea but that does not matter. Milton then gives the reader an image of the sun. It too has sunk into the water and does so every day. Every morning, though, it makes a glorious return when rising. Lycidas has sunk, but has risen also. He is now in heaven. The angels entertain him and make him happy - "There entertain him all the Saints above...That sing...And wipe the tears forever from his eyes." It may have taken him a long time to realize it, but his attitude toward death had changed a lot.

AP/CLEP PRACTICE EXERCISES IN POETRY

1. Read the five poems by William Wordsworth below, and answer these questions in a well-organized essay. Discuss the essay with your AP teacher.

(1) "Lines Written in Early Spring" contains some of Wordsworth's important ideas about nature and man--ideas that are developed in many of his longer poems. What is the theme of "Lines"? What is "Nature's holy plan"? What has "man . . . made of man"?

(2) "To My Sister," "Expostulation and Reply" and "The Tables Turned" might be considered anti-intellectual. What kind of life and learning process does Wordsworth advocate in the poems? Why does he object to the intellectual inquiry of science?

(3) What is your interpretation of "wise passiveness" ("Expostulation and Reply")?

(4) In "The Tables Turned" Wordsworth says "we murder to dissect". Is this true? Why does Wordsworth think it is?

(5) The sixth stanza of "The Tables Turned" (lines 21-24) is considered by many readers of the poem to be a grotesque exaggeration. Attempt to relate the meaning of the stanza to the theme of "Lines Written in Early Spring" (see, especially, stanza two).

(6) Obviously the poet in "A Poet's Epitaph" wants only the common man to approach his grave (i.e., his poems). What are his specific objections to the scientist (the physician of lines 17-24)?

FIVE POEMS BY WILLIAM WORDSWORTH

Lines Written in the Early Spring

I heard a thousand blended notes,
While in a grove I sate reclined,
In that sweet mood when pleasant thoughts
Bring sad thoughts to the mind.

To her fair works did Nature link
The human soul that through me ran
And much it grieved my heart to think
What man has made of man.

Through primrose tufts, in that green bower,
The periwinkle trailed its wreaths;
And 't is my faith that every flower
Enjoys the air it breathes.

The birds around me hopped and played,
Their thoughts I cannot measure: --
But the least motion which they made
It seemed a thrill of pleasure.

The budding twigs spread out their fan,
To catch the breezy air;
And I must think, do all I can,
That there was pleasure there.

If this belief from heaven be sent,
If such be Nature's holy plan,
Have I not reason to lament
What man has made of man?

To my Sister

It is the first mild day of March:
Each minute sweeter than before
The redbreast sings from the tall larch
That stands beside our door.

There is a blessing in the air,
Which seems a sense of joy to yield
To the bare trees, and mountains bare,
And grass in the green field.

My sister! ('t is a wish of mine)
Now that our morning meal is done,
Make haste, your morning task resign;
Come forth and feel the sun.

Edward will come with you; -- and, pray,
Put on with speed your woodland dress;
And bring no book: for this one day
We'll give to idleness.

No joyless forms shall regulate
Our living calendar:
We from to-day, my Friend, will date
The opening of the year.

Love, now a universal birth,
From heart to heart is stealing,
From earth to man, from man to earth:
--It is the hour of feeling.

One moment now may give us more
Than years of toiling reason:
Our minds shall drink at every pore
The spirit of the season.

Some silent laws our hearts will make,
Which they shall long obey:
We for the year to come may take
Our temper from to-day.

And from the blessed power that rolls
About, below, above,
We'll frame the measure of our souls:
They shall be tuned to love.

Then come, my Sister! come, I pray,
With speed put on your woodland dress;
And bring no book: for this one day
We'll give to idleness.

Expostulation and Reply

"Why, William, on that old grey stone,
Thus for the length of half a day,
Why, William, sit you thus alone,
And dream your time away?

"Where are your books? -- that light bequeathed
To Beings else forlorn and blind!
Up! up! and drink the spirit breathed
From dead men to their kind.

"You look round on your Mother Earth,
As if she for no purpose bore you;
As if you were her first-born birth,
And none had lived before you!"

One morning thus, Esthwaite lake,
When life was sweet, I knew not why,
To me my good friend Matthew spake,
And thus I made reply:

"The eye -- it cannot choose but see;
We cannot bid the ear be still;
Our bodies feel, where'er they be,
Against or with our will.

"Nor less I deem that there are Powers
Which of themselves our minds impress;
That we can feed this mind of ours
Is a wise passiveness.

"Think you, 'mid all this mighty sun
Of things for ever speaking,
That nothing of itself will come,
But we must still be seeking?

"--Then ask not wherefore, here, alone,
Conversing as I may,
I sit upon this old grey stone,
And dream my time away."

The Tables Turned

An Evening Scene on the Same Subject

Up! up! my Friend, and quit your books;
Or surely you'll grow double:
Up! up! my Friend, and clear your looks;
Why all this toil and trouble?

The sun, above the mountain's head,
A freshening lustre mellow
Through all the long green fields has spread,
His first sweet evening yellow.

Books! 't is a dull and endless strife:
Come, hear the woodland linnet,
How sweet his music! on my life,
There's more of wisdom in it.

And hark! how blithe the throstle sings!
He, too, is no mean preacher:
Come forth into the light of things,
Let Nature be your teacher.

She has a world of ready wealth,
Our minds and hearts to bless --
Spontaneous wisdom breathed by health,
Truth breathed by cheerfulness.

One impulse from a vernal wood
May teach you more of man,
Of moral evil and of good,
Than all the sages can.

Sweet is the lore which Nature brings;
Our meddling intellect
Mis-shapes the beauteous forms of things: --
We murder to dissect.

Enough of Science and Art;
Close up those barren leaves;
Come forth, and bring with you a heart
That watches and receives.

A Poet's Epitaph

Art thou a Statist in the van
Of public conflicts trained and bred?
--First learn to love one living man;
Then may'st thou think upon the dead.

A Lawyer art thou? -- draw not nigh!
Go, carry to some fitter place
The keenness of that practiced eye,
The hardness of that sallow face.

Art thou a Man of purple cheer?
A rosy Man, right plump to see?
Approach; yet, Doctor, not too near,
This grave no cushion is for thee.

Or art thou one of gallant pride,
A Soldier and no man of chaff?
Welcome! -- but lay thy sword aside,
And lean upon a peasant's staff.

Physician art thou? one, all eyes,
Philosopher! a fingering slave,
One that would peep and botanise
Upon his mother's grave?

Wrapt closely in thy sensual fleece,
O turn aside, -- and take, I pray,
That he below may rest in peace,
Thy ever-dwindling soul, away!

A Moralist perchance appears;
Led, Heaven knows how! to this poor sod:
And he has neither eyes nor ears;
Himself his world, and his own God;

One to whose smooth-rubbed soul can cling
Nor form, nor feeling, great or small;
A reason, self-sufficing thing,
An intellectual All-in-all!

Shut close the door; press down the latch;
Sleep in thy intellectual crust;
Nor lose ten tickings of thy watch
Near this unprofitable dust.

But who is He, with modest looks,
And clad in homely russet brown?
He murmurs near the running brooks
A music sweeter than their own.

He is retired as noontide dew,
Or fountain in a noon-day grove;
And you must love him, ere to you
He will seem worthy of your love.

The outward shows of sky and earth,
Of hill and valley, he has viewed;
And impulses of deeper birth
Have come to him in solitude.

In common things that round us lie
Some random truths he can impart, --
The harvest of a quiet eye
That broods and sleeps on his own heart.

But he is weak; both Man and Boy,
Hath been an idler in the land;
Contented if he might enjoy
The things which others understand.

--Come hither in thy hour of strength;
Come, weak as is a breaking wave!
Here stretch thy body at full length;
Or build thy house upon this grave.

2. THE CHARGE OF THE LIGHT BRIGADE

Half a league, half a league,
  Half a league onward,
All in the valley of Death
  Rode the six hundred.
'Charge' was the captain's cry;
Their's not to reason why,
Their's not to make reply,
Their's but to do or die,
Into the valley of Death

Cannon to right of them,
Cannon to left of them,
Cannon in front of them
  Volley'd and thunder'd;
Storm'd at with shot and shell,
Boldly they rode and well,
Into the jaws of Death,
Into the mouth of Hell
  Rode the six hundred.

Alfred Lord Tennyson

Write an essay on the markedly public rhythm in Tennyson's "The Charge of the Light Brigade;" demonstrate in your writing the connections between rhythmic effect and meaning of the poem.

3. THE POPLAR FIELD

The poplars are fell'd, farewell to the shade
And the whispering sound of the cool colonnade,
The winds play no longer, and sing in the leaves,
Nor Ouse on his bosom their image receives.

Twelve years have elaps'd since I first took a view
Of my favorite field and the bank where they grew,
And now in the grass behold they are laid,
And the tree is my seat that once lent me a shade.

The blackbird has fled to another retreat
Where the hazels afford him a screen for the heat,
And the scene where his melody charm'd me before
Resounds with his sweet-flowing ditty no more.

My fugitive years are all hasting away,
And I muse ere long lie as lowly as they,
With a turf on my breast, and a stone at my head,
Ere another such grove shall arise in its stead.

'Tis a sight to engage me, if anything can,
To muse on the perishing pleasures of man;
Though his life be a dream, his enjoyments, I see,
Have a being less durable even than he.

William Cowper

Write an essay on the rhythm and meaning of Cowper's poem. In your essay consider these questions in your analysis:

(1) What main point do the last two verses make?

(2) What kind of feeling does Cowper attempt to convey in the last two verses?

(3) Describe the effect of the rhythm of these final verses in one or two adjectives (gay, pensive, etc.)

(4) Does the rhythm contribute to, or detract from, the total effect intended in the last two verses? Give your reasons briefly.

4. PITY FOR POOR AFRICANS

I own I am shock'd at the purchase of slaves
And fear those who buy them and sell them are knaves;
What I hear of their hardships, their tortures, and groans,
Is almost enough to draw pity from stones.

I pity them greatly, but I must be mum,
For how could we do without sugar and rum?
Especially sugar, so needful we see?
What? give up our deserts, our coffee, and tea!

Besides, if we do, the French, Dutch and Danes,
Will heartily thank us, no doubt, for our pains;
If we do not buy the poor creatures, they will,
And tortures and groans will be multiplied still.

If foreigners likewise would give up their trade,
Much more in behalf of your wish might be said;
But while they get riches by purchasing blacks,
Pray tell me why we may not also go snacks?

William Cowper

Write another essay of a Cowper poem with these questions as the focus of your writing:

(1) The poem's speaker claims to be shocked at the purchase of slaves. Is this the case?

(2) What opinion of the speaker do these verses suggest Cowper wants us to have?

(3) Do these verses tell us anything about Cowper's attitude to the slave-trade?

5. LONDON

I wander thro' each charter'd street,
Near where the charter'd Thames does flow,
And mark in every face I meet
Marks of weakness, marks of woe.

In every cry of every Man,
In every Infant's cry of fear,
In every voice, in every ban,
The mind-forg'd manacles I hear.

How the Chimney-sweeper's cry
Every black'ning Church appals;
And the hapless Soldier's sigh
Runs in blood down Palace walls.

But most thro' midnight streets I hear
How the youthful Harlot's curse
Blasts the new born Infant's tear,
And blights with plagues the Marriage hearse.

William Blake

Read William Blake's "London" several times, until you are sure you understand it, at least in its general meaning; and write a well-organized essay on how you understand the poem. Specially consider these questions:

(1) What does the word 'charter'd' in the first stanza mean;

(2) What does the phrase 'the mind-forg'd manacles' mean;

(3) What do you understand by the lines:

"How the Chimney-sweeper's cry
Every black'ning Church appals;"

(4) How can a sigh run in blood down a wall; and

(5) What seems to you to be the point of the final image of the poem: the 'marriage hearse'?

6. DOVER BEACH

The sea is calm to-night.
The tide is full, the moon lies fair
Upon the straits; on the French coast the light
Gleams and is gone; the cliffs of England stand,
Glimmering and vast, out in the tranquil bay.
Come to the window, sweet is the night-air!
Only, from the long line of spray
Where the sea meets the noon-blanched land,
Listen! you hear the grating roar
Of pebbles which the waves draw back, and fling,
At their return, up the high strand,

Begin, and cease, and then again begin,
With tremulous cadence slow, and bring
The eternal note of sadness in.

Sophocles long ago
Heard it on the Aegaean, and it brought
Into his mind the turbid ebb and flow
Of human misery; we
Find also in the sound a thought,
Hearing it by this distant northern sea.

The Sea of Faith
Was once, too, at the full, and round earth's shore
Lay like the folds of a bright girdle furled.
But now I only hear
Its melancholy, long, withdrawing roar,
Retreating, to the breath
Of the night-wind, down the vast edges drear
And naked shingles of the world.

Ah, love, let us be true
To one another! for the world, which seems
To lie before us like a land of dreams,
So various, so beautiful, so new,
Hath really neither joy, nor love, nor light,
Nor certitude, nor peace, nor help for pain;
And we are here as on a darkling plain
Swept with confused alarms of struggle and flight.
Where ignorant armies clash by night.

Matthew Arnold

Matthew Arnold wrote "Dover Beach" (1867) - what is conveyed in the first fourteen lines of this poem? In your practice essay you can also discuss this and what precisely do we learn about "the eternal note of sadness" in the rest of the poem. You should try to write what this poem is essentially about. What do you make of the poem's ending? What is the relationship of the author of "Dover Beach" to his society - would you describe this poem as the work of a committed man or does Arnold turn away from the world he sees?

DRAMA

ALL LITERATURE IS A REPRESENTATION OF THE LIFE OF THE TIMES DURING WHICH IT WAS WRITTEN.

INTRODUCTION

Drama, quite unlike other types of literature, is not written to be read by the individual reader, but primarily to be presented on stage by actors and in this way first of all entertaining and secondarily seeking responses to any number of questions from a mass of people. These prerequisites condition the nature and structure of drama. Like all literature, drama tries to instill in its audience some values. These values may be of a low nature perhaps with main concern in an hour's worth of humor or on a higher scale drama may be used to keynote or order some aspect of the audience's existence. Since the time of the ancient Greeks, drama has been a prime instrument with which man has attempted to explore and explain his existence. Man's nature has changed in 2500 years and drama has kept more than accurate account of these changes. Drama gives us no less a picture of individual man, good man, evil man, social man than any other literary genre. It has a certain appeal, perhaps the same as music to the savage beast. It can be experienced even by those who don't understand the words. To see how drama gives us insight into man and his existence, it is necessary to check briefly into its history, nature and structure. This insight will rely not merely upon the witnessed performance but also upon an analyzation of the written work to determine if action, characters, and techniques are properly employed giving us some picture of the life of the times during which it was written.

WHY DRAMA?

Why act things out? The purpose of art--any art--is to arouse emotion in an observer. No doubt that religion rituals will effect their participants emotionally, and if properly designed and executed will achieve the same effect in onlookers.

But why drama? Why not poetry, or song, or narration? One answer to this is that drama did include poetry, song, and narration, but with a bit more.

With the ancient Greeks drama gave its spectators the feeling of being present at the scene of a myth: Isis didn't revive Osiris a long time ago; she is doing it now, in our midst, even as we watch--poetry (Homer) was past; it served the need for identity. Drama was present; it served present needs.

THE THEATER OF DIONYSUS AT ATHENS
(350 - 325 B.C.)

The Athenian Theater presentations were held twice a year in honor of Dionysus, the god of fertility, vegetation and wine. The dramatic festivals, a three day event, would include the performers, patron-producers and poet-playwrights in a public ceremonies prior to the performing of the play. Finally, the play began at daybreak with the Athenians converging on the Theater of Dionysus (a seating capacity of 15,000). The following are some of the terms used to describe the Greek Theater of Dionysus (350 - 325 B.C.).

SKENE or stage house (modern word - scene) is the dressing areas for the players.

PARASKENA or projecting sidewing of the skenes was not available prior to 500 B.C.

PROSKENION were the wooden stage sets attached directly the skene giving a background for the action of the play.

THREE DOORS were located in the skene; the actors entered and exited by these doors.

SCENERY was used to suggest rather than represent reality.

PARADOS is a corridor for passage of chorus to the orchestra.

PARADOI was an arch for entry of the chorus to the parados.

CHORUS helped represent typical Athenian by its conversation and provided the underlined action and unity for the story.

ALTAR had a deep religious significance and was in honor of Dionysus.

ORCHESTRA was the area between the stage platform and the theatron where actors and chorus performed.

THEATRON was viewing place from which the Athenians watched their plays.

THEATER OF DIONYSUS, ATHENS

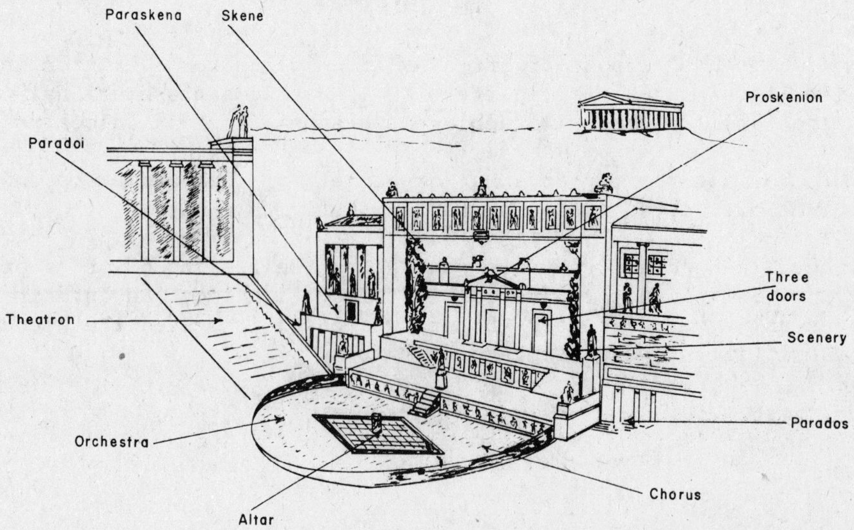

Then drama became a celebration, still religious, but with the performances becoming more original. This allowed drama to reach its full potential. The question was no longer one of what man or his Gods had done but rather what he would, could, and did do. New situations could be developed in this new medium and new insights on man gained. Something new could be learned, instead of the old being related.

Poetry and prose fiction also do this. Yet, somehow they are lacking. To understand what it is they are lacking would perhaps be to answer the question, "What is the nature of drama?"

Drama allows us to say to ourselves, "Look, those are real people doing things that real people can do," and we are all sharing the experience. A novel or poem, no matter how good, still allows us to think, "Those are not real people." Furthermore, reading such a work is a solitary experience, and thus lacks the impact of group involvement. But, a play hits us in the face; we must admit that real people can do these things because there they are doing them. Added to this is the fact that the dramatist must reach his audience quickly; a novelist may have a thousand pages, but the playwright has only two to three hours. The result of these factors is an emotional experience much more intense than that achieved by a poem or a story, and thus a successful play is perhaps the most successful of art forms. It causes us most easily and most strongly to experience emotions. Hopefully the ones the playwright intended.

This then is the answer to the question "What is the nature of drama?" It is to cause us to feel what drama's creators feel through presenting us with an intensified slice of reality (or unreality--drama isn't fussy). It has been doing this successfully for over two thousand years, and whether we like it or not, it appears to be with us to stay.

HISTORY OF DRAMA

Drama first arose out of fundamental human needs in the dawn of civilization and has continued to express things for man for thousands of years. It shows man in moments of joy and sadness, tension and ease, conflict and resolution, and tries to resolve his problems or portray his comfort. It talks, not to man, but to an assembly of mankind. History tells us it was one of the first recorders of man's trials, tribulations, and resolutions. In retracing drama time, the validy of this becomes undeniable.

Most agree that the "urge" to mimic or to ape was inherent in primitive man. Being more flexible, physically and mentally, than an animal he exhibited this whether preparing for battle, a hunt, or mere play. The problem, however, with primitive man was that he had too many other problems, namely those dealing with survival, to let this mimicry manifest itself.

Drama first comes of age in the classicism of Greece and Rome. For whatever reason, leisure time, education or lack of it, or just plain out and out luck, the ancient Greeks start to formulate a literary genre similar to ours. It is ironic that the acknowledged "Father of tragedy," Aeschylus (525-456 BC), be quite familiar with the politics and culture of his day and quite eager to tell the contemporary Athenian about them. It is not important whether what he had to talk about was good or bad but simply that he saw the need to talk about it, and used drama as the medium to get it across. We should be thankful that this first dramatist ranks with the foremost. Most assuredly he set the wheels in motion.

The door was opened to his successors. They deleted and added molding drama into the most popular of the literary forms. They were quick to follow. Sophocles (496-406 BC) added a third speaking actor (limited to two previously). He also did away with the trilogic form (Aeschylus used three tragedies to tell a story and often his works "drag" in the middle). Sophocles used only one plot per play and therefore localized all of the action in it. Aeschylus had spread it too thin.

Euripides (484-406 BC) had much to say. So much so, that he was more or less forced to spend much of his time in exile. We generally assume this as the reason that so much of his work just sort of leaves the reader in suspension. He doesn't moralize whether he is right or wrong but rekindles dying embers regarding topics that are contemporary Athenian social criticisms. Euripides and his Medea were probably one of the first examples of our present twentieth century women's lib movement.

It is here in time that Greece started to wane and the Roman Empire came to the front. The Roman Seneca was influenced by Euripides. It was no fault of the Greeks and Euripides that Seneca's and the Roman mis-use of this art form eventually degenerated it into oblivion but rather its too frequently obscene rhetoric, monotonous verse and crude dramatic situations.

With Aristophanes (445-385 BC) we have the birth of comedy. His social satires about the degeneration of contemporary Athenian life enabled man to grin at his follies and foibles. Menander (c. 343 BC) followed Aristophanes with his New Comedy. Rather than the biting social satire of Aristophanes, we now had a commonplace outlook on life. Romantic love, parents and their children, servants helping or hindering each other, these were laughed at and ridiculed. Though not the most popular, Menander, considered the "father of modern comedy" must be considered the best.

Once again the Romans made a futile attempt to capture and promulgate drama as a literary form. Plautus (c. 254 BC) and Terence (c. 190 BC) were Romans who were quick to follow Aristophanes' and Menander's guidelines. Whether on the seduction of innocents or slaves or common thieves, the end result was a mirth arousing experience, a feeling of ease, that probably could be accounted for by the corresponding growth of the Roman Empire as a world power. They were quick to speak of representative experiences of contemporary life as they transpired. Unfortunately with Terence's death, the last vestiges of Euripides and Menander disappeared and Roman comedy quickly deteriated. Pantominists and travelling acrobats and jugglers, commonly known as mimes, who were nothing more than vagabonds, soon remained as the only means of entertainment for the culturally waning Romans. The total fall of the Roman Empire brought any hope of a drama revival to a screeching halt. History tells us that it would have to be cradled anew in the rites of religion.

Modern drama as we know it today, ideally may be said to have its beginning with the Mass. Each Mass after the first is actually a reenactment of the Last Supper. Realistically, the church of two thousand years ago had problems similar to the church of today. Attendance at Christian Mass was sparse. Empty seats were in abundance. In order to "stir" interest someone came up with the idea of "acting" out parts of the mass. Originally intended for holidays and special feasts, it caught on quickly and became a common event. Perhaps a donkey or a camel would be present at mass or an occasional angel swinging by on a rope, or a herd of sheep being flocked through, these were eye openers and interest makers. These acted out "bits" were called tropes and they worked. Attendance at mass quickly reverted itself. Churches were no longer large enough to contain the people. They were bursting at the seams. Cries went out for more tropes and more room. To accommodate the people the Mass was moved out of the church into the courtyard. From the courtyard it was a short wait until they reached the street corners. The rejuvenation of drama was happening and unknowingly uncontrollable. Of note, however, is the fact that wherever these "tropes" went the subject matter was still orientated around the teachings of the church or of Christ. (Don't mistakingly think that this was an overnight process. From the time of the First Mass to this point of time, six or seven centuries have transpired).

From the street corners these portrayals very soon found themselves headed for the countryside. Transportation was provided by wagons known as pagonds (hence our modern word pageant). They attracted crowds wherever they set up. The size or number of pagonds depended on how long or how many parts there were to the presentation. Some of them were spectacular. The largest of these, the fourteenth century Wakefield Drama Festival, which lasted three days during the feast of the Corpus Christi, the principal holiday of the fourteenth century, reportedly had fifty-eight of these pagonds. Representative presentations up to this time were miracle and mystery plays (See Glossary of Literary Types). In the late fourteenth century these developed into morality plays and they in turn into interludes (See Glossary of Types). This was rather momentous because for the first time since its revival, the subject matter of drama had to do with something other than teachings of the church. The interludes advent the university wits (Lyly, Webster & Ford, Greene, etc.) who are contemporary to Shakespeare, who in turn directly influences modern drama as we know it today.

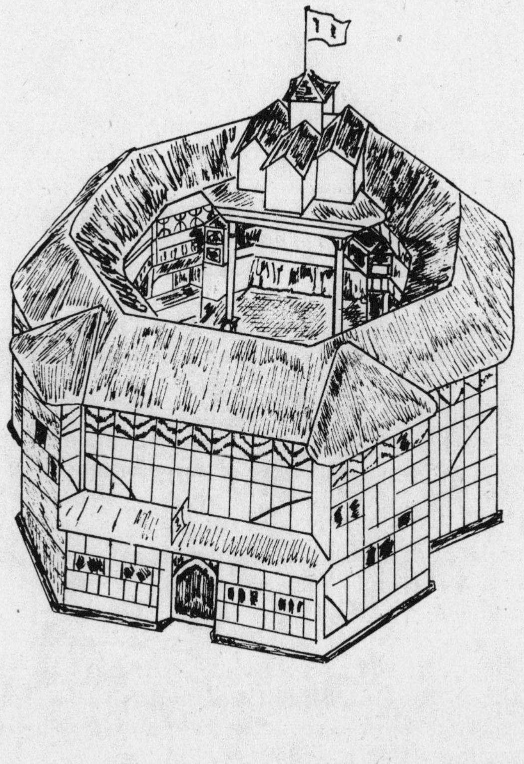

ELEMENTS OF DRAMA

Drama is comprised of three interdependent forces. The first is the element which builds the event on the stage, second is the way in which they are put together, and third is the reaction of the audience to the values within the play.

The elements are comprised of the essential, technical tools that bring about the action, character traits, diction, irony, imagery, and symbolism--the totality of the play. The elements are employed in a cooperative union with the actor. The word is sometimes ineffective without the actor's voice, movement, and gesture and conversely the actor is dependent upon the written word. The more ambiguous elements such as tempo and character are developed when the smaller elements are joined. The organization in turn affects the meaning and values within the play which hopefully will be revealed by the audience's participation.

The unity of the elements is structured into acts and scenes. This format can be traced from the five act Greecian plays to the Twentieth Century two and three act plays. Some modernists have eliminated the concept of acts altogether.

Freytag's Pyramid (by the German critic Gustov Freytag, in his 1863 Technique of the Drama) is a theoretical outline that can be applied to most five act plays.

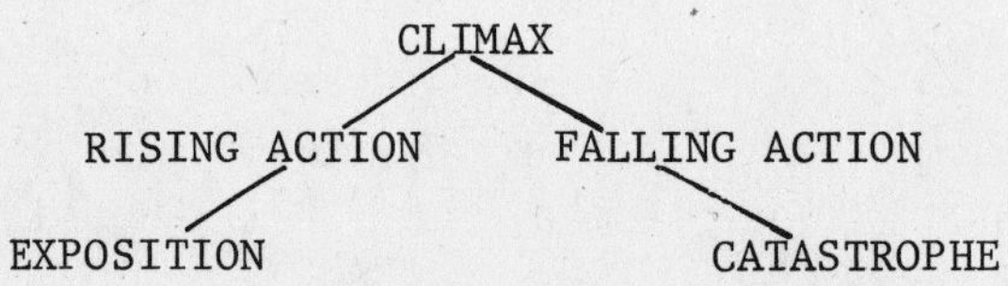

The structure is divided into an exposition, rising action, climax, falling action, and catastrophe. The exposition or introduction supplies important information dealing with the characters or conflicts that have occured before the plays commencement (historical background). The characters are then introduced in the rising action or complication scenes. Conflicts are apparent and the plot begins. The action rises, growing in intensity and interest as the opposing forces inter-react. The climax occurs at the height of the action; usually it is represented by an insight or awareness gained by the hero either about himself, or others, or events. Upon arriving at this highest point of interest, the action then changes direction.

The falling action usually depicts the protagonists inability to resolve the conflicts. Of course it is highlighted by increased antagonistic activities. Just as the rising action is initiated with an incited movement so to the falling action has to be initiated.

The catastrophe resolves the conflicts. It demonstrates tragic failure and usually involves the death of the hero(s) and the antagonist. The result is a logical conclusion to the preceding events.

Whether or not the play succeeds rests in those who witness it, audience participation depends upon both the written word and technical plays. If the people and values employed are much like our own, the greater the response. The audience will always be busy making personal comparisons. In order to bridge the gap between character and audience the author requires the most delicate judgement. Thus, we have come full circle to the elements involved in creating drama.

THREE MAJOR FORMS OF DRAMA

TRAGEDY

To the classic Greeks tragedy was originally a ritual song. From the fifth century BC and onward, it meant serious drama, generally based on heroism (heroes of epic stature). In the middle ages as long as the ending was unhappy it was considered a tragedy. Today, it has become more or less "serious drama" rather than "tragedy." According to Aristotle:

1. It is an imitation of a single, unified action that is serious, complete, probable, and of a certain magnitude.

2. It concerns the fall of a man whose character is good, believable, and consistent.

3. The fall is caused in part by some error or frailty in the protagonist and not by a vice or depravity.

4. The language is embellished with each kind of artistic ornament.

5. The tragedy is presented in the form of action, not narrative.

6. It arouses in the audience the emotions of pity and terror resulting in a catharsis of these emotions.

COMEDY

Once again we can trace this form back to the ancient classic Greeks. It originated in the Dionysian Festivals most likely by those who led the songs of travellers and partiers. The plays of Aristo Phanes are concrete evidence. While the classical form of the Greeks disappeared in the Christian era, the element of comedy remained as evidenced by the Italian forms of the Middle Ages.

It is simply a dramatic form intended to amuse and often to instruct through some form of ridicule. This amusement and this ridicule exposes absurdity, foolishness, the not-so-perfect world, abnormal existence, or whatsoever happens that goes against accepted norms of society. These follies are usually brought out through caricature, gesture, and disguise. On the whole comedy will usually end happily.

TRAGI-COMEDY

Tragi-comedy is a form that combines both tragic and comic elements. Originally, tragic-comedy included any work that did not end in death but brought characters near to it. It contained sudden reversals and averted catastrophes. Today, generally, tragi-comedy concerns itself with not-so-glorious topics (death, aging, infirmities) and it treats them jocundity. Man does not look forward to these things but the tragi-comics treatment of them reawakens their reality. Tragi-comedies usually end happily.

M. William Shak-ſpeare:

HIS
True Chronicle Hiſtorie of the life and death of King LEAR and his three Daughters.

With the vnfortunate life of Edgar, *ſonne* and heire to the Earle of Gloſter, and his ſullen and aſſumed humor of TOM of Bedlam:

As it was played before the Kings Maieſtie at Whitehall vpon S. Stephans *night in Chriſtmas Hollidayes.*

By his Maieſties ſeruants playing vſually at the Gloabe on the Bancke-ſide.

LONDON,
Printed for *Nathaniel Butter*, and are to be ſold at his ſhop in *Pauls* Church-yard at the ſigne of the Pide Bull neere St. *Auſtins* Gate. 1608.

DRAMATIS PERSONÆ

Lear, king of Britain.
King of France.
Duke of Burgundy.
Duke of Cornwall.
Duke of Albany.
Earl of Kent.
Earl of Gloucester.
Edgar, son to Gloucester.
Edmund, bastard son to Gloucester.
Curan, a courtier.
Old Man, tenant to Gloucester.
Doctor.
Fool.
Oswald, steward to Goneril.
A Captain employed by Edmund.
Gentleman attendant on Cordelia.
A Herald.
Servants to Cornwall.

Goneril, ***Regan,*** ***Cordelia,*** } daughters to Lear.

Knights of Lear's train, Captains, Messengers, Soldiers, and Attendants.

Scene—*Britain.*

KING LEAR

ACT I.

SCENE I. KING LEAR'S PALACE.

Enter ***Kent, Gloucester,*** *and* ***Edmund.***

Kent. I thought the king had more affected the Duke of Albany than Cornwall.

Glou. It did always seem so to us : but now, in the division of the kingdom, it appears not which of the dukes he values most ; for equalities are so weigh'd, that curiosity in neither can make choice of either's moiety.

Kent. Is not this your son, my lord ?

Glou. His breeding, sir, hath been at my charge : I have so often blushed to acknowledge him, that now I am brazed to it.

Kent. I cannot conceive you.

Glou. Sir, this young fellow's mother could : whereupon she grew round-wombed, and had, indeed, sir, a son for her cradle ere she had a husband for her bed. Do you smell a fault ?

Kent. I cannot wish the fault undone, the issue of it being so proper.

Glou. But I have, sir, a son by order of law, some year elder than this, who yet is no dearer in my account : though this knave came something saucily into the world before he was sent for, yet was his mother fair ; there was good sport at his making, and the whoreson must be acknowledged. Do you know this noble gentleman, Edmund ?

Edm. No, my lord.

Glou. My lord of Kent : remember him hereafter as my honourable friend.

Edm. My services to your lordship.
Kent. I must love you, and sue to know you better.
Edm. Sir, I shall study deserving.
Glou. He hath been out nine years, and away he shall again.
The king is coming.

Sennet. Enter ***King Lear, Cornwall, Albany, Goneril, Regan, Cordelia,*** *and* ***Attendants.***

Lear. Attend the lords of France and Burgundy, Gloucester.
Glou. I shall, my liege. [*Exeunt* ***Gloucester*** *and* ***Edmund.***
Lear. Meantime we shall express our darker purpose.
Give me the map there. Know that we have divided
In three our kingdom: and 'tis our fast intent
To shake all cares and business from our age;
Conferring them on younger strengths, while we
Unburthen'd crawl toward death. Our son of Cornwall,
And you, our no less loving son of Albany,
We have this hour a constant will to publish
Our daughters' several dowers, that future strife
May be prevented now. The princes, France and Burgundy,
Great rivals in our youngest daughter's love,
Long in our court have made their amorous sojourn,
And here are to be answer'd. Tell me, my daughters,—
Since now we will divest us, both of rule,
Interest of territory, cares of state,—
Which of you shall we say doth love us most?
That we our largest bounty may extend
Where nature doth with merit challenge. Goneril,
Our eldest-born, speak first.
Gon. Sir, I love you more than words can wield the matter;
Dearer than eye-sight, space, and liberty;
Beyond what can be valued, rich or rare;
No less than life, with grace, health, beauty, honour;
As much as child e'er loved, or father found;
A love that makes breath poor, and speech unable;
Beyond all manner of so much I love you.
Cor. [*aside.*] What shall Cordelia do? Love, and be silent.
Lear. Of all these bounds, even from this line to this,
With shadowy forests and with champains rich'd,

With plenteous rivers and wide-skirted meads,
We make thee lady: to thine and Albany's issue
Be this perpetual. What says our second daughter,
Our dearest Regan, wife to Cornwall? Speak.
Reg. Sir, I am made
Of the self-same metal that my sister is,
And prize me at her worth. In my true heart
I find she names my very deed of love;
Only she comes too short: that I profess
Myself an enemy to all other joys,
Which the most precious square of sense possesses;
And find I am alone felicitate
In your dear highness' love.
Cor. [*aside.*] Then poor Cordelia!
And yet not so; since, I am sure, my love's
More richer than my tongue.
Lear. To thee and thine hereditary ever
Remain this ample third of our fair kingdom;
No less in space, validity, and pleasure,
Than that conferr'd on Goneril. Now, our joy,
Although the last, not least; to whose young love
The vines of France and milk of Burgundy
Strive to be interess'd; what can you say to draw
A third more opulent than your sisters? Speak.
Cor. Nothing, my lord.
Lear. Nothing!
Cor. Nothing.
Lear. Nothing will come of nothing: speak again.
Cor. Unhappy that I am, I cannot heave
My heart into my mouth: I love your majesty
According to my bond; nor more nor less.
Lear. How, how, Cordelia! mend your speech a little,
Lest it may mar your fortunes.
Cor. Good my lord,
You have begot me, bred me, loved me: I
Return those duties back as are right fit,
Obey you, love you, and most honour you.
Why have my sisters husbands, if they say
They love you all? Haply, when I shall wed,
That lord whose hand must take my plight shall carry

Half my love with him, half my care and duty:
Sure, I shall never marry like my sisters,
To love my father all.
Lear. But goes thy heart with this?
Cor. Ay, good my lord.
Lear. So young, and so untender?
Cor. So young, my lord, and true.
Lear. Let it be so; thy truth, then, be thy dower:
For, by the sacred radiance of the sun,
The mysteries of Hecate, and the night;
By all the operation of the orbs
From whom we do exist, and cease to be;
Here I disclaim all my paternal care,
Propinquity and property of blood,
And as a stranger to my heart and me
Hold thee, from this, for ever. The barbarous Scythian,
Or he that makes his generation messes
To gorge his appetite, shall to my bosom
Be as well neighbour'd, pitied, and relieved,
As thou my sometime daughter.
Kent. Good my liege,—
Lear. Peace, Kent!
Come not between the dragon and his wrath.
I loved her most, and thought to set my rest
On her kind nursery. Hence, and avoid my sight!
So be my grave my peace, as here I give
Her father's heart from her! Call France; who stirs?
Call Burgundy. Cornwall and Albany,
With my two daughters' dowers digest this third:
Let pride, which she calls plainness, marry her.
I do invest you jointly with my power,
Pre-eminence, and all the large effects
That troop with majesty. Ourself, by monthly course,
With reservation of an hundred knights,
By you to be sustain'd, shall our abode
Make with you by due turns. Only we still retain
The name, and all the additions to a king;
The sway, revenue, execution of the rest,
Beloved sons, be yours: which to confirm,
This coronet part betwixt you. [*giving the crown.*

Kent. Royal Lear,
Whom I have ever honour'd as my king,
Loved as my father, as my master follow'd,
As my great patron thought on in my prayers,—
Lear. The bow is bent and drawn, make from the shaft.
Kent. Let it fall rather, though the fork invade
The region of my heart: be Kent unmannerly,
When Lear is mad. What wilt thou do, old man?
Think'st thou that duty shall have dread to speak,
When power to flattery bows? To plainness honour's bound.
When majesty stoops to folly. Reverse thy doom;
And, in thy best consideration, check
This hideous rashness: answer my life my judgement,
Thy youngest daughter does not love thee least;
Nor are those empty-hearted whose low sound
Reverbs no hollowness.
Lear. Kent, on thy life, no more.
Kent. My life I never held but as a pawn
To wage against thy enemies; nor fear to lose it,
Thy safety being the motive.
Lear. Out of my sight!
Kent. See better, Lear; and let me still remain
The true blank of thine eye.
Lear. Now, by Apollo,—
Kent. Now, by Apollo, king,
Thou swear'st thy gods in vain.
Lear. O, vassal! miscreant!
[*laying his hand on his sword.*
Alb. / ***Corn.*** } Dear sir, forbear.
Kent. Do;
Kill thy physician, and the fee bestow
Upon thy foul disease. Revoke thy doom;
Or, whilst I can vent clamour from my throat,
I'll tell thee thou dost evil.
Lear. Hear me, recreant!
On thine allegiance, hear me!
Since thou hast sought to make us break our vow,
Which we durst never yet, and with strain'd pride,

To come between our sentence and our power,
Which nor our nature nor our place can bear,
Our potency made good, take thy reward.
Five days we do allot thee, for provision
To shield thee from diseases of the world;
And on the sixth to turn thy hated back
Upon our kingdom: if, on the tenth day following,
Thy banish'd trunk be found in our dominions,
The moment is thy death. Away! by Jupiter,
This shall not be revoked.

Kent. Fare thee well, king: sith thus thou wilt appear.
Freedom lives hence, and banishment is here.
[*to* ***Cordelia.***] The gods to their dear shelter take thee, maid,
That justly think'st, and hast most rightly said!
[*to* ***Regan*** *and* ***Goneril.***] And your large speeches may your deeds approve,
That good effects may spring from words of love.
Thus Kent, O princes, bids you all adieu;
He'll shape his old course in a country new. [*exit.*

Flourish. Re-enter ***Gloucester,*** *with* ***France, Burgundy,*** *and* ***Attendants.***

Glou. Here's France and Burgundy, my noble lord.

Lear. My lord of Burgundy,
We first address towards you, who with this king
Hath rivall'd for our daughter: what, in the least,
Will you require in present dower with her,
Or cease your quest of love?

Bur. Most royal majesty,
I crave no more than what your highness offer'd,
Nor will you tender less.

Lear. Right noble Burgundy,
When she was dear to us, we did hold her so;
But now her price is fall'n. Sir, there she stands:
If aught within that little seeming substance,
Or all of it, with our displeasure pieced,
And nothing more, may fitly like your grace,
She's there, and she is yours.

Bur. I know no answer.

Lear. Will you, with those infirmities she owes,
Unfriended, new-adopted to our hate,
Dower'd with our curse, and stranger'd with our oath,
Take her, or leave her?

Bur. Pardon me, royal sir;
Election makes not up on such conditions.

Lear. Then leave her, sir; for, by the power that made me,
I tell you all her wealth. [*to* ***France.***] For you, great king,
I would not from your love make such a stray,
To match you where I hate; therefore beseech you
To avert your liking a more worthier way
Than on a wretch whom nature is ashamed
Almost to acknowledge hers.

France. This is most strange,
That she, that even but now was your best object,
The argument of your praise, balm of your age,
Most best, most dearest, should in this trice of time
Commit a thing so monstrous, to dismantle
So many folds of favour. Sure, her offence
Must be of such unnatural degree,
That monsters it, or your fore-vouch'd affection
Fall'n into taint: which to believe of her,
Must be a faith that reason without miracle
Could never plant in me.

Cor. I yet beseech your majesty,—
If for I want that glib and oily art,
To speak and purpose not; since what I well intend,
I'll do't before I speak,—that you make known
It is no vicious blot, murder, or foulness,
No unchaste action, or dishonour'd step,
That hath deprived me of your grace and favour;
But even for want of that for which I am richer,
A still-soliciting eye, and such a tongue
As I am glad I have not, though not to have it
Hath lost me in your liking.

Lear. Better thou
Hadst not been born than not to have pleased me better.

France. Is it but this,—a tardiness in nature
Which often leaves the history unspoke
That it intends to do? My lord of Burgundy,

What say you to the lady? Love's not love
When it is mingled with regards that stand
Aloof from the entire point. Will you have her?
She is herself a dowry.

Bur. Royal Lear,
Give but that portion which yourself proposed,
And here I take Cordelia by the hand,
Duchess of Burgundy.

Lear. Nothing: I have sworn; I am firm.

Bur. I am sorry, then, you have so lost a father
That you must lose a husband.

Cor. Peace be with Burgundy!
Since that respects of fortune are his love,
I shall not be his wife.

France. Fairest Cordelia, that art most rich, being poor;
Most choice, forsaken; and most loved, despised!
Thee and thy virtues here I seize upon:
Be it lawful I take up what's cast away.
Gods, gods! 'tis strange that from their cold'st neglect
My love should kindle to inflamed respect.
Thy dowerless daughter, king, thrown to my chance,
Is queen of us, of ours, and our fair France:
Not all the dukes of waterish Burgundy
Can buy this unprized precious maid of me
Bid them farewell, Cordelia, though unkind:
Thou losest here, a better where to find.

Lear. Thou hast her, France: let her be thine; for we
Have no such daughter, nor shall ever see
That face of hers again. Therefore be gone
Without our grace, our love, our benison.
Come, noble Burgundy.

[*Flourish. Exeunt all but* **France, Goneril, Regan,** *and* **Cordelia.**

France. Bid farewell to your sisters.

Cor. The jewels of our father, with wash'd eyes
Cordelia leaves you: I know you what you are;
And like a sister am most loath to call
Your faults as they are named. Use well our father:
To your professed bosoms I commit him:
But yet, alas, stood I within his grace,

I would prefer him to a better place.
So, farewell to you both.

Reg. Prescribe not us our duties.

Gon. Let your study
Be to content your lord, who hath received you
At fortune's alms. You have obedience scanted,
And well are worth the want that you have wanted.

Cor. Time shall unfold what plaited cunning hides:
Who cover faults, at last shame them derides.
Well may you prosper!

France. Come, my fair Cordelia.

[*Exeunt* **France** *and* **Cordelia.**

Gon. Sister, it is not a little I have to say of what most nearly appertains to us both. I think our father will hence to-night.

Reg. That's most certain, and with you; next month with us.

Gon. You see how full of changes his age is; the observation we have made of it hath not been little: he always loved our sister most; and with what poor judgement he hath now cast her off appears too grossly.

Reg. 'Tis the infirmity of his age: yet he hath ever but slenderly known himself.

Gon. The best and soundest of his time hath been but rash; then must we look to receive from his age, not alone the imperfections of long-engraffed condition, but therewithal the unruly waywardness that infirm and choleric years bring with them.

Reg. Such unconstant starts are we like to have from him as this of Kent's banishment.

Gon. There is further compliment of leave-taking between France and him. Pray you, let's hit together: if our father carry authority with such dispositions as he bears, this last surrender of his will but offend us.

Reg. We shall further think on't.

Gon. We must do something, and i' the heat. [*exeunt.*

SCENE II. THE EARL OF GLOUCESTER'S CASTLE.

Enter **Edmund,** *with a letter.*

Edm. Thou, nature, art my goddess ; to thy law
My services are bound. Wherefore should I
Stand in the plague of custom, and permit
The curiosity of nations to deprive me,
For that I am some twelve or fourteen moonshines
Lag of a brother? Why bastard? wherefore base?
When my dimensions are as well compact,
My mind as generous, and my shape as true,
As honest madam's issue? Why brand they us
With base? with baseness? bastardy? base, base?
Who, in the lusty stealth of nature, take
More composition and fierce quality
Than doth, within a dull, stale, tired bed,
Go to the creating a whole tribe of fops,
Got 'tween asleep and wake? Well, then,
Legitimate Edgar, I must have your land:
Our father's love is to the bastard Edmund
As to the legitimate: fine word,—legitimate!
Well, my legitimate, if this letter speed,
And my invention thrive, Edmund the base
Shall top the legitimate. I grow; I prosper:
Now, gods, stand up for bastards!

Enter **Gloucester.**

Glou. Kent banish'd thus! and France in choler parted!
And the king gone to-night! subscribed his power!
Confined to exhibition! All this done
Upon the gad! Edmund, how now! what news?
Edm. So please your lordship, none. [*putting up the letter.*
Glou. Why so earnestly seek you to put up that letter?
Edm. I know no news, my lord.
Glou. What paper were you reading?
Edm. Nothing, my lord.
Glou. No? What needed, then, that terrible dispatch of it into your pocket? the quality of nothing hath not such need to hide itself. Let's see: come, if it be nothing, I shall not need spectacles.

Edm. I beseech you, sir, pardon me: it is a letter from my brother, that I have not all o'er-read; and for so much as I have perused, I find it not fit for your o'er-looking.
Glou. Give me the letter, sir.
Edm. I shall offend, either to detain or give it. The contents, as in part I understand them, are to blame.
Glou. Let's see, let's see.
Edm. I hope, for my brother's justification, he wrote this but as an essay or taste of my virtue.
Glou. [*reads.*] 'This policy and reverence of age makes the world bitter to the best of our times; keeps our fortunes from us till our oldness cannot relish them. I begin to find an idle and fond bondage in the oppression of aged tyranny; who sways, not as it hath power, but as it is suffered Come to me, that of this I may speak more. If our father would sleep till I waked him, you should enjoy half his revenue for ever, and live the beloved of your brother, EDGAR.' Hum—conspiracy!—'Sleep till I waked him,—you should enjoy half his revenue,'—My son Edgar! Had he a hand to write this? a heart and brain to breed it in?—When came this to you? who brought it?
Edm. It was not brought me, my lord; there's the cunning of it; I found it thrown in at the casement of my closet.
Glou. You know the character to be your brother's?
Edm. If the matter were good, my lord, I durst swear it were his; but, in respect of that, I would fain think it were not.
Glou. It is his.
Edm. It is his hand, my lord; but I hope his heart is not in the contents.
Glou. Hath he never heretofore sounded you in this business?
Edm. Never, my lord: but I have heard him oft maintain it to be fit, that, sons at perfect age, and fathers declining, the father should be as ward to the son, and the son manage his revenue.
Glou. O villain, villain! His very opinion in the letter! Abhorred villain! Unnatural, detested, brutish villain!

worse than brutish! Go, sirrah, seek him; I'll apprehend him: abominable villain! Where is he?

Edm. I do not well know, my lord. If it shall please you to suspend your indignation against my brother till you can derive from him better testimony of his intent, you shall run a certain course; where, if you violently proceed against him, mistaking his purpose, it would make a great gap in your own honour, and shake in pieces the heart of his obedience. I dare pawn down my life for him, that he hath wrote this to feel my affection to your honour, and to no further pretence of danger.

Glou. Think you so?

Edm. If your honour judge it meet, I will place you where you shall hear us confer of this, and by an auricular assurance have your satisfaction; and that without any further delay than this very evening.

Glou. He cannot be such a monster—

Edm. Nor is not, sure.

Glou. To his father, that so tenderly and entirely loves him. Heaven and earth! Edmund, seek him out: wind me into him, I pray you: frame the business after your own wisdom. I would unstate myself, to be in a due resolution.

Edm. I will seek him, sir, presently: convey the business as I shall find means, and acquaint you withal.

Glou. These late eclipses in the sun and moon portend no good to us: though the wisdom of nature can reason it thus and thus, yet nature finds itself scourged by the sequent effects: love cools, friendship falls off, brothers divide: in cities, mutinies; in countries, discord; in palaces, treason; and the bond cracked 'twixt son and father. This villain of mine comes under the prediction; there's son against father: the king falls from bias of nature; there's father against child. We have seen the best of our time: machinations, hollowness, treachery, and all ruinous disorders, follow us disquietly to our graves. Find out this villain, Edmund; it shall lose thee nothing; do it carefully. And the noble and true-hearted Kent banished! his offence, honesty! 'Tis strange. [*exit.*

Edm. This is the excellent foppery of the world, that, when we are sick in fortune,—often the surfeit of our own

behaviour,—we make guilty of our disasters the sun, the moon, and the stars: as if we were villains by necessity; fools by heavenly compulsion; knaves, thieves, and treachers, by spherical predominance; drunkards, liars, and adulterers, by an enforced obedience of planetary influence; and all that we are evil in, by a divine thrusting on: an admirable evasion of whoremaster man, to lay his goatish disposition to the charge of a star! My father compounded with my mother under the dragon's tail; and my nativity was under Ursa major; so that it follows, I am rough and lecherous. Tut, I should have been that I am, had the maidenliest star in the firmament twinkled on my bastardizing. Edgar—

Enter **Edgar.**

and pat he comes like the catastrophe of the old comedy: my cue is villanous melancholy, with a sigh like Tom o' Bedlam. O, these eclipses do portend these divisions! fa, sol, la, mi.

Edg. How now, brother Edmund! what serious contemplation are you in?

Edm. I am thinking, brother, of a prediction I read this other day, what should follow these eclipses.

Edg. Do you busy yourself about that?

Edm. I promise you, the effects he writes of succeed unhappily; as of unnaturalness between the child and the parent; death, dearth, dissolutions of ancient amities; divisions in state, menaces and maledictions against king and nobles; needless diffidences, banishment of friends, dissipation of cohorts, nuptial breaches, and I know not what.

Edg. How long have you been a sectary astronomical?

Edm. Come, come; when saw you my father last?

Edg. Why, the night gone by.

Edm. Spake you with him?

Edg. Ay, two hours together.

Edm. Parted you in good terms? Found you no displeasure in him by word or countenance?

Edg. None at all.

Edm. Bethink yourself wherein you may have offended him:

and at my entreaty forbear his presence till some little time hath qualified the heat of his displeasure; which at this instant so rageth in him, that with the mischief of your person it would scarcely allay.

Edg. Some villain hath done me wrong.

Edm. That's my fear. I pray you, have a continent forbearance till the speed of his rage goes slower; and, as I say, retire with me to my lodging, from whence I will fitly bring you to hear my lord speak: pray ye, go; there's my key: if you do stir abroad, go armed.

Edg. Armed, brother!

Edm. Brother, I advise you to the best; go armed: I am no honest man if there be any good meaning towards you: I have told you what I have seen and heard; but faintly, nothing like the image and horror of it: pray you, away.

Edg. Shall I hear from you anon?

Edm. I do serve you in this business. [*Exit* **Edgar**.
A credulous father! and a brother noble,
Whose nature is so far from doing harms,
That he suspects none; on whose foolish honesty
My practices ride easy! I see the business.
Let me, if not by birth, have lands by wit:
All with me's meet that I can fashion fit. [*exit.*

SCENE III. THE DUKE OF ALBANY'S PALACE.

Enter **Goneril,** *and* **Oswald,** *her steward.*

Gon. Did my father strike my gentleman for chiding of his fool?

Osw. Yes, madam.

Gon. By day and night he wrongs me; every hour
He flashes into one gross crime or other,
That sets us all at odds: I'll not endure it:
His knights grow riotous, and himself upbraids us
On every trifle. When he returns from hunting,
I will not speak with him; say I am sick:
If you come slack of former services,
You shall do well; the fault of it I'll answer.

Osw. He's coming, madam: I hear him. [*Horns within.*

Gon. Put on what weary negligence you please,
You and your fellows; I'ld have it come to question:
If he dislike it, let him to our sister,
Whose mind and mine, I know, in that are one,
Not to be over-ruled. Idle old man,
That still would manage those authorities
That he hath given away! Now, by my life,
Old fools are babes again; and must be used
With checks as flatteries,—when they are seen abused.
Remember what I tell you.

Osw. Well, madam.

Gon. And let his knights have colder looks among you;
What grows of it, no matter; advise your fellows so:
I would breed from hence occasions, and I shall,
That I may speak: I'll write straight to my sister,
To hold my very course. Prepare for dinner. [*exeunt.*

SCENE IV. A HALL IN THE SAME.

Enter **Kent,** *disguised.*

Kent. If but as well I other accents borrow,
That can my speech defuse, my good intent
May carry through itself to that full issue
For which I razed my likeness. Now, banish'd Kent,
If thou canst serve where thou dost stand condemn'd,
So may it come, thy master, whom thou lovest,
Shall find thee full of labours.

Horns within. *Enter* **Lear, Knights,** *and* **Attendants.**

Lear. Let me not stay a jot for dinner; go get it ready. [*Exit an* **Attendant.**] How now! what art thou?

Kent. A man, sir.

Lear. What dost thou profess? what wouldst thou with us?

Kent. I do profess to be no less than I seem; to serve him truly that will put me in trust; to love him that is honest; to converse with him that is wise, and says little; to fear judgement; to fight when I cannot choose; and to eat no fish.

Lear. What art thou?

Kent. A very honest-hearted fellow, and as poor as the king.

Lear. If thou be as poor for a subject as he is for a king, thou art poor enough. What wouldst thou?

Kent. Service.

Lear. Who wouldst thou serve?

Kent. You.

Lear. Dost thou know me, fellow?

Kent. No, sir; but you have that in your countenance which I would fain call master.

Lear. What's that?

Kent. Authority.

Lear. What services canst thou do?

Kent. I can keep honest counsel, ride, run, mar a curious tale in telling it, and deliver a plain message bluntly: that which ordinary men are fit for, I am qualified in; and the best of me is diligence.

Lear. How old art thou?

Kent. Not so young, sir, to love a woman for singing, nor so old to dote on her for any thing: I have years on my back forty eight.

Lear. Follow me; thou shalt serve me: if I like thee no worse after dinner, I will not part from thee yet. Dinner, ho, dinner! Where's my knave? my fool? Go you, and call my fool hither. [*Exit an* **Attendant.**

Enter **Oswald.**

You, you, sirrah, where's my daughter?

Osw. So please you,— [*exit.*

Lear. What says the fellow there? Call the clotpoll back. [*Exit a* **Knight.**] Where's my fool, ho? I think the world's asleep.

Re-enter **Knight.**

How now! where's that mongrel?

Knight. He says, my lord, your daughter is not well.

Lear. Why came not the slave back to me when I called him.

Knight. Sir, he answered me in the roundest manner, he would not.

Lear. He would not!

Knight. My lord, I know not what the matter is; but, to my judgement, your highness is not entertained with that ceremonious affection as you were wont; there's a great abatement of kindness appears as well in the general dependants as in the duke himself also and your daughter.

Lear. Ha! sayest thou so?

Knight. I beseech you, pardon me, my lord, if I be mistaken; for my duty cannot be silent when I think your highness wronged.

Lear. Thou but rememberest me of mine own conception: I have perceived a most faint neglect of late; which I have rather blamed as mine own jealous curiosity than as a very pretence and purpose of unkindness: I will look further into't. But where's my fool? I have not seen him this two days.

Knight. Since my young lady's going into France, sir, the fool hath much pined away.

Lear. No more of that; I have noted it well. Go you, and tell my daughter I would speak with her. [*Exit an* **Attendant.**] Go you, call hither my fool. [*Exit an* **Attendant.**

Re-enter **Oswald.**

O, you sir, you, come you hither, sir: who am I, sir?

Osw. My lady's father.

Lear. 'My lady's father!' my lord's knave: you whoreson dog! you slave! you cur!

Osw. I am none of these, my lord; I beseech your pardon.

Lear. Do you bandy looks with me, you rascal? [*striking him.*

Osw. I'll not be struck, my lord.

Kent. Nor tripped neither, you base foot-ball player. [*tripping up his heels.*

Lear. I thank thee, fellow; thou servest me, and I'll love thee.

Kent. Come, sir, arise, away! I'll teach you differences: away, away! If you will measure your lubber's length again, tarry: but away! go to; have you wisdom? so. [*pushes* **Oswald** *out.*

Lear. Now, my friendly knave, I thank thee: there's earnest of thy service. [*giving* **Kent** *money.*

Enter **Fool.**

Fool. Let me hire him too: here's my coxcomb.

[*offering* **Kent** *his cap.*

Lear. How now, my pretty knave! how dost thou?

Fool. Sirrah, you were best take my coxcomb.

Kent. Why, fool?

Fool. Why, for taking one's part that's out of favour: nay, an thou canst not smile as the wind sits, thou'lt catch cold shortly: there, take my coxcomb: why, this fellow has banished two on's daughters, and did the third a blessing against his will; if thou follow him, thou must needs wear my coxcomb. How now, nuncle! Would I had two coxcombs and two daughters!

Lear. Why, my boy?

Fool. If I gave them all my living, I'ld keep my coxcombs myself. There's mine; beg another of thy daughters.

Lear. Take heed, sirrah; the whip.

Fool. Truth's a dog must to kennel; he must be whipped out, when Lady the brach may stand by the fire and stink.

Lear. A pestilent gall to me!

Fool. Sirrah, I'll teach thee a speech.

Lear. Do.

Fool. Mark it, nuncle:

Have more than thou showest,
Speak less than thou knowest,
Lend less than thou owest,
Ride more than thou goest,
Learn more than thou trowest,
Set less than thou throwest;
Leave thy drink and thy whore,
And keep in-a-door,
And thou shalt have more
Than two tens to a score.

Kent. This is nothing, fool.

Fool. Then 'tis like the breath of an unfee'd lawyer; you gave me nothing for't. Can you make no use of nothing, nuncle?

Lear. Why, no, boy; nothing can be made out of nothing.

Fool. [*to* ***Kent.***] Prithee, tell him, so much the rent of his land comes to: he will not believe a fool.

Lear. A bitter fool!

Fool. Dost thou know the difference, my boy, between a bitter fool and a sweet fool?

Lear. No, lad; teach me.

Fool.
That lord that counsell'd thee
To give away thy land,
Come place him here by me,
Do thou for him stand:
The sweet and bitter fool
Will presently appear;
The one in motley here,
The other found out there.

Lear. Dost thou call me fool, boy?

Fool. All thy other titles thou hast given away; that thou wast born with.

Kent. This is not altogether fool, my lord.

Fool. No, faith, lords and great men will not let me; if I had a monopoly out, they would have part on't: and ladies too, they will not let me have all fool to myself; they'll be snatching. Give me an egg, nuncle, and I'll give thee two crowns.

Lear. What two crowns shall they be?

Fool. Why, after I have cut the egg i' the middle, and eat up the meat, the two crowns of the egg. When thou clovest thy crown i' the middle, and gavest away both parts, thou borest thy ass on thy back o'er the dirt: thou hadst little wit in thy bald crown, when thou gavest thy golden one away. If I speak like myself in this, let him be whipped that first finds it so.

[*singing.*] Fools had ne'er less wit in a year;
For wise men are grown foppish,
They know not how their wits to wear,
Their manners are so apish.

Lear. When were you wont to be so full of songs, sirrah?

Fool. I have used it, nuncle, ever since thou madest thy daughters thy mother: for when thou gavest them the rod, and put'st down thine own breeches,

[*singing.*] Then they for sudden joy did weep,
And I for sorrow sung,
That such a king should play bo-peep,
And go the fools among.

Prithee, nuncle, keep a schoolmaster that can teach thy fool to lie: I would fain learn to lie.

Lear. An you lie, sirrah, we'll have you whipped.

Fool. I marvel what kin thou and thy daughters are: they'll have me whipped for speaking true, thou'lt have me whipped for lying; and sometimes I am whipped for holding my peace. I had rather be any kind o' thing than a fool: and yet I would not be thee, nuncle; thou hast pared thy wit o' both sides, and left nothing i' the middle: here comes one o' the parings.

Enter ***Goneril.***

Lear. How now, daughter! what makes that frontlet on?
Methinks you are too much of late i' the frown.

Fool. Thou wast a pretty fellow when thou hadst no need to care for her frowning; now thou art an O without a figure: I am better than thou art now; I am a fool, thou art nothing. [*to* ***Gon.***] Yes, forsooth, I will hold my tongue; so your face bids me, though you say nothing.
Mum, mum,
He that keeps nor crust nor crum,
Weary of all, shall want some.
[*pointing to* ***Lear.***] That's a shealed peascod.

Gon. Not only, sir, this your all-licensed fool,
But other of your insolent retinue
Do hourly carp and quarrel; breaking forth
In rank and not-to-be-endured riots. Sir,
I had thought, by making this well known unto you,
To have found a safe redress; but now grow fearful,
By what yourself too late have spoke and done,
That you protect this course, and put it on
By your allowance; which if you should, the fault
Would not 'scape censure, nor the redresses sleep,
Which, in the tender of a wholesome weal,
Might in their working do you that offence,

Which else were shame, that then necessity
Will call discreet proceeding.

Fool. For, you know, nuncle,

The hedge-sparrow fed the cuckoo so long,
That it had it head bit off by it young.

So, out went the candle, and we were left darkling.

Lear. Are you our daughter?

Gon. Come, sir,
I would you would make use of that good wisdom,
Whereof I know you are fraught; and put away
These dispositions, that of late transform you
From what you rightly are.

Fool. May not an ass know when the cart draws the horse?
Whoop, Jug! I love thee.

Lear. Doth any here know me? This is not Lear:
Doth Lear walk thus? speak thus? Where are his eyes?
Either his notion weakens, his discernings
Are lethargied—Ha! waking? 'tis not so.
Who is it that can tell me who I am?

Fool. Lear's shadow.

Lear. I would learn that; for, by the marks of sovereignty, knowledge, and reason, I should be false persuaded I had daughters.

Fool. Which they will make an obedient father.

Lear. Your name, fair gentlewoman?

Gon. This admiration, sir, is much o' the savour
Of other your new pranks. I do beseech you
To understand my purposes aright:
As you are old and reverend, you should be wise.
Here do you keep a hundred knights and squires;
Men so disorder'd, so debosh'd and bold,
That this our court, infected with their manners,
Shows like a riotous inn: epicurism and lust
Make it more like a tavern or a brothel
Than a graced palace. The shame itself doth speak
For instant remedy: be then desired
By her, that else will take the thing she begs,
A little to disquantity your train;
And the remainder, that shall still depend,

To be such men as may besort your age,
And know themselves and you.

Lear. Darkness and devils!
Saddle my horses; call my train together.
Degenerate bastard! I'll not trouble thee:
Yet have I left a daughter.

Gon. You strike my people; and your disorder'd rabble
Make servants of their betters.

Enter **Albany.**

Lear. Woe, that too late repents,—[*to* **Alb.**] O, sir, are you come?
Is it your will? Speak, sir. Prepare my horses.
Ingratitude, thou marble-hearted fiend,
More hideous when thou show'st thee in a child
Than the sea-monster!

Alb. Pray, sir, be patient.

Lear. [*to* **Gon.**] Detested kite! thou liest:
My train are men of choice and rarest parts,
That all particulars of duty know,
And in the most exact regard support
The worships of their name. O most small fault,
How ugly didst thou in Cordelia show!
That, like an engine, wrench'd my frame of nature
From the fix'd place; drew from my heart all love,
And added to the gall. O Lear, Lear, Lear!
Beat at this gate, that let thy folly in, [*striking his head.*
And thy dear judgement out! Go, go, my people.

Alb. My lord, I am guiltless, as I am ignorant
Of what hath moved you.

Lear. It may be so, my lord.
Hear, nature, hear; dear goddess, hear!
Suspend thy purpose, if thou didst intend
To make this creature fruitful!
Into her womb convey sterility!
Dry up in her the organs of increase;
And from her derogate body never spring
A babe to honour her! If she must teem,
Create her child of spleen; that it may live,
And be a thwart disnatured torment to her!

Let it stamp wrinkles in her brow of youth;
With cadent tears fret channels in her cheeks;
Turn all her mother's pains and benefits
To laughter and contempt; that she may feel
How sharper than a serpent's tooth it is
To have a thankless child! Away, away! [*exit.*

Alb. Now, gods that we adore, whereof comes this?

Gon. Never afflict yourself to know the cause;
But let his disposition have that scope
That dotage gives it.

Re-enter **Lear.**

Lear. What, fifty of my followers at a clap!
Within a fortnight!

Alb. What's the matter, sir?

Lear. I'll tell thee: [*to* **Gon.**] Life and death! I am ashamed
That thou hast power to shake my manhood thus;
That these hot tears, which break from me perforce,
Should make thee worth them. Blasts and fogs upon thee!
The untented woundings of a father's curse
Pierce every sense about thee! Old fond eyes,
Beweep this cause again, I'll pluck ye out,
And cast you, with the waters that you lose,
To temper clay. Yea, is it come to this?
Let it be so: yet have I left a daughter,
Who, I am sure, is kind and comfortable:
When she shall hear this of thee, with her nails
She'll flay thy wolvish visage. Thou shalt find
That I'll resume the shape which thou dost think
I have cast off for ever: thou shalt, I warrant thee.
[*Exeunt* **Lear, Kent,** *and* **Attendants.**

Gon. Do you mark that, my lord?

Alb. I cannot be so partial, Goneril,
To the great love I bear you,—

Gon. Pray you, content. What, Oswald, ho!
[*to the* **Fool.**] You, sir, more knave than fool, after your master.

Fool. Nuncle Lear, nuncle Lear, tarry and take the fool with thee.

A fox, when one has caught her,
And such a daughter,
Should sure to the slaughter,
If my cap would buy a halter:
So the fool follows after. [*exit.*

Gon. This man hath had good counsel:—a hundred knights!
'Tis politic and safe to let him keep
At point a hundred knights: yes, that, on every dream,
Each buzz, each fancy, each complaint, dislike,
He may enguard his dotage with their powers,
And hold our lives in mercy. Oswald, I say!
Alb. Well, you may fear too far.
Gon. Safer than trust too far:
Let me still take away the harms I fear,
Not fear still to be taken: I know his heart.
What he hath utter'd I have writ my sister:
If she sustain him and his hundred knights,
When I have show'd the unfitness.—

Re-enter **Oswald.**

How now, Oswald!
What, have you writ that letter to my sister?
Osw. Yes, madam.
Gon. Take you some company, and away to horse:
Inform her full of my particular fear;
And thereto add such reasons of your own
As may compact it more. Get you gone;
And hasten your return. [*Exit* **Oswald.**] No, no, my lord,
This milky gentleness and course of yours
Though I condemn not, yet, under pardon,
You are much more attask'd for want of wisdom
Than praised for harmful mildness.
Alb. How far your eyes may pierce I cannot tell:
Striving to better, oft we mar what's well.
Gon. Nay, then—
Alb. Well, well; the event. [*exeunt.*

SCENE V. COURT BEFORE THE SAME.

Enter **Lear, Kent,** *and* **Fool.**

Lear. Go you before to Gloucester with these letters. Acquaint my daughter no further with any thing you know than comes from her demand out of the letter. If your diligence be not speedy, I shall be there afore you.

Kent. I will not sleep, my lord, till I have delivered your letter. [*exit.*

Fool. If a man's brains were in 's heels, were 't not in danger of kibes?

Lear. Ay, boy.

Fool. Then, I prithee, be merry; thy wit shall ne'er go slip-shod.

Lear. Ha, ha, ha!

Fool. Shalt see thy other daughter will use thee kindly; for though she's as like this as a crab's like an apple, yet I can tell what I can tell.

Lear. Why, what canst thou tell, my boy?

Fool. She will taste as like this as a crab does to a crab. Thou canst tell why one's nose stands i' the middle on's face?

Lear. No.

Fool. Why, to keep one's eyes of either side's nose; that what a man cannot smell out, he may spy into.

Lear. I did her wrong—

Fool. Canst tell how an oyster makes his shell?

Lear. No.

Fool. Nor I neither; but I can tell why a snail has a house.

Lear. Why?

Fool. Why, to put his head in; not to give it away to his daughters, and leave his horns without a case.

Lear. I will forget my nature. So kind a father! Be my horses ready?

Fool. Thy asses are gone about 'em. The reason why the seven stars are no more than seven is a pretty reason.

Lear. Because they are not eight?

Fool. Yes, indeed: thou wouldst make a good fool.

Lear. To take't again perforce! Monster ingratitude!
Fool. If thou wert my fool, nuncle, I'ld have thee beaten for being old before thy time.
Lear. How's that?
Fool. Thou shouldst not have been old till thou hadst been wise.
Lear. O, let me not be mad, not mad, sweet heaven!
Keep me in temper: I would not be mad!

Enter **Gentleman.**

How now! are the horses ready?
Gent. Ready, my lord.
Lear. Come, boy.
Fool. She that's a maid now, and laughs at my departure,
Shall not be a maid long, unless things be cut shorter.
[*exeunt.*

ACT II.

SCENE I. THE EARL OF GLOUCESTER'S CASTLE.

Enter **Edmund,** *and* **Curan** *meets him.*

Edm. Save thee, Curan.
Cur. And you, sir. I have been with your father, and given him notice that the Duke of Cornwall and Regan his duchess will be here with him this night.
Edm. How comes that?
Cur. Nay, I know not. You have heard of the news abroad; I mean the whispered ones, for they are yet but ear-kissing arguments?
Edm. Not I: pray you, what are they?
Cur. Have you heard of no likely wars toward, 'twixt the Dukes of Cornwall and Albany?
Edm. Not a word.
Cur. You may do, then, in time. Fare you well, sir. [*exit.*
Edm. The duke be here to-night? The better! best!
This weaves itself perforce into my business.
My father hath set guard to take my brother;
And I have one thing, of a queasy question,

Which I must act: briefness and fortune, work!
Brother, a word; descend: brother, I say!

Enter **Edgar.**

My father watches: O sir, fly this place;
Intelligence is given where you are hid;
You have now the good advantage of the night:
Have you not spoken 'gainst the Duke of Cornwall?
He's coming hither; now, i' the night, i' the haste,
And Regan with him: have you nothing said
Upon his party 'gainst the Duke of Albany?
Advise yourself.
Edg. I am sure on't, not a word.
Edm. I hear my father coming: pardon me;
In cunning I must draw my sword upon you:
Draw; seem to defend yourself; now quit you well.
Yield: come before my father. Light, ho, here!
Fly, brother. Torches, torches! So, farewell.
[*Exit* **Edgar.**
Some blood drawn on me would beget opinion
[*wounds his arm.*
Of my more fierce endeavour: I have seen drunkards
Do more than this in sport. Father, father!
Stop, stop! No help?

Enter **Gloucester,** *and* **Servants** *with torches.*

Glou. Now, Edmund, where's the villain?
Edm. Here stood he in the dark, his sharp sword out,
Mumbling of wicked charms, conjuring the moon
To stand auspicious mistress,—
Glou. But where is he?
Edm. Look, sir, I bleed.
Glou. Where is the villain, Edmund?
Edm. Fled this way, sir. When by no means he could—
Glou. Pursue him, ho! Go after. [*Exeunt some* **Servants.**]
By no means what?
Edm. Persuade me to the murder of your lordship;
But that I told him, the revenging gods
'Gainst parricides did all their thunders bend;
Spoke, with how manifold and strong a bond

The child was bound to the father ; sir, in fine,
Seeing how loathly opposite I stood
To his unnatural purpose, in fell motion,
With his prepared sword, he charges home
My unprovided body, lanced mine arm :
But when he saw my best alarum'd spirits,
Bold in the quarrel's right, roused to the encounter,
Or whether gasted by the noise I made,
Full suddenly he fled.

Glou. Let him fly far :
Not in this land shall he remain uncaught ;
And found—dispatch. The noble duke my master,
My worthy arch and patron, comes to-night :
By his authority I will proclaim it,
That he which finds him shall deserve our thanks,
Bringing the murderous coward to the stake ;
He that conceals him, death.

Edm. When I dissuaded him from his intent,
And found him pight to do it, with curst speech
I threaten'd to discover him : he replied,
'Thou unpossessing bastard ! dost thou think,
If I would stand against thee, would the reposal
Of any trust, virtue, or worth in thee
Make thy words faith'd ? No : what I should deny,—
As this I would ; ay, though thou didst produce
My very character,—I 'ld turn it all
To thy suggestion, plot, and damned practice :
And thou must make a dullard of the world,
If they not thought the profits of my death
Were very pregnant and potential spurs
To make thee seek it.'

Glou. Strong and fasten'd villain !
Would he deny his letter ? I never got him. [*Tucket within*
Hark, the duke's trumpets ! I know not why he comes.
All ports I 'll bar ; the villain shall not 'scape ;
The duke must grant me that : besides, his picture
I will send far and near, that all the kingdom
May have due note of him ; and of my land,
Loyal and natural boy, I 'll work the means
To make thee capable.

Enter **Cornwall, Regan,** *and* **Attendants.**

Corn. How now, my noble friend ! since I came hither,
Which I can call but now, I have heard strange news.

Reg. If it be true, all vengeance comes too short
Which can pursue the offender. How dost, my lord ?

Glou. O, madam, my old heart is crack'd, is crack'd !

Reg. What, did my father's godson seek your life ?
He whom my father named ? your Edgar ?

Glou. O, lady, lady, shame would have it hid !

Reg. Was he not companion with the riotous knights
That tend upon my father ?

Glou. I know not, madam : 'tis too bad, too bad.

Edm. Yes, madam, he was of that consort.

Reg. No marvel, then, though he were ill affected :
'Tis they have put him on the old man's death,
To have the expense and waste of his revenues.
I have this present evening from my sister
Been well inform'd of them ; and with such cautions,
That if they come to sojourn at my house,
I 'll not be there.

Corn. Nor I, assure thee, Regan.
Edmund, I hear that you have shown your father
A child-like office.

Edm. 'Twas my duty, sir.

Glou. He did bewray his practice ; and received
This hurt you see, striving to apprehend him.

Corn. Is he pursued ?

Glou. Ay, my good lord.

Corn. If he be taken, he shall never more
Be fear'd of doing harm : make your own purpose,
How in my strength you please. For you, Edmund,
Whose virtue and obedience doth this instant
So much commend itself, you shall be ours :
Natures of such deep trust we shall much need ;
You we first seize on.

Edm. I shall serve you, sir,
Truly, however else.

Glou. For him I thank your grace.

Corn. You know not why we came to visit you,—

Reg. Thus out of season, threading dark-eyed night:
Occasions, noble Gloucester, of some poise,
Wherein we must have use of your advice:
Our father he hath writ, so hath our sister,
Of differences, which I least thought it fit
To answer from our home; the several messengers
From hence attend dispatch. Our good old friend,
Lay comforts to your bosom; and bestow
Your needful counsel to our business,
Which craves the instant use.

Glou. I serve you, madam:
Your graces are right welcome. [*exeunt.*

SCENE II. BEFORE GLOUCESTER'S CASTLE.

Enter **Kent** *and* **Oswald**, *severally.*

Osw. Good dawning to thee, friend: art of this house?

Kent. Ay.

Osw. Where may we set our horses?

Kent. I' the mire.

Osw. Prithee, if thou lovest me, tell me.

Kent. I love thee not.

Osw. Why, then, I care not for thee.

Kent. If I had thee in Lipsbury pinfold, I would make thee care for me.

Osw. Why dost thou use me thus? I know thee not.

Kent. Fellow, I know thee.

Osw. What dost thou know me for?

Kent. A knave; a rascal; an eater of broken meats; a base, proud, shallow, beggarly, three-suited, hundred-pound, filthy, worsted-stocking knave; a lily-livered, action-taking knave, a whoreson, glass-gazing, super-serviceable, finical rogue; one-trunk-inheriting slave; one that wouldst be a bawd, in way of good service, and art nothing but the composition of a knave, beggar, coward, pandar, and the son and heir of a mongrel bitch: one whom I will beat into clamorous whining, if thou deniest the least syllable of thy addition.

Osw. Why, what a monstrous fellow art thou, thus to rail on one that is neither known of thee nor knows thee!

Kent. What a brazen-faced varlet art thou, to deny thou knowest me! Is it two days ago since I tripped up thy heels, and beat thee before the king? Draw, you rogue: for, though it be night, yet the moon shines; I'll make a sop o' the moonshine of you: draw, you whoreson cullionly barber-monger, draw. [*drawing his sword.*

Osw. Away! I have nothing to do with thee.

Kent. Draw, you rascal: you come with letters against the king; and take vanity the puppet's part against the royalty of her father: draw, you rogue, or I'll so carbonado your shanks: draw, you rascal; come your ways.

Osw. Help, ho! murder! help!

Kent. Strike, you slave; stand, rogue, stand; you neat slave, strike. [*beating him.*

Osw. Help, ho! murder! murder!

Enter **Edmund**, *with his rapier drawn*, **Cornwall, Regan, Gloucester**, *and* **Servants.**

Edm. How now! What's the matter?

Kent. With you, goodman boy, an you please: come, I'll flesh ye; come on, young master.

Glou. Weapons! arms! What's the matter here?

Corn. Keep peace, upon your lives:
He dies that strikes again. What is the matter?

Reg. The messengers from our sister and the king.

Corn. What is your difference? speak.

Osw. I am scarce in breath, my lord.

Kent. No marvel, you have so bestirred your valour. You cowardly rascal, nature disclaims in thee: a tailor made thee.

Corn. Thou art a strange fellow: a tailor make a man?

Kent. Ay, a tailor, sir: a stone-cutter or a painter could not have made him so ill, though he had been but two hours at the trade.

Corn. Speak yet, how grew your quarrel?

Osw. This ancient ruffian, sir, whose life I have spared at suit of his gray beard,—

Kent. Thou whoreson zed! thou unnecessary letter! My lord, if you will give me leave, I will tread this unbolted villain into mortar, and daub the walls of a jakes with him. Spare my gray beard, you wagtail?

Corn. Peace, sirrah!
You beastly knave, know you no reverence?

Kent. Yes, sir; but anger hath a privilege.

Corn. Why art thou angry?

Kent. That such a slave as this should wear a sword,
Who wears no honesty. Such smiling rogues as these,
Like rats, oft bite the holy cords a-twain
Which are too intrinse t'unloose; smooth every passion
That in the natures of their lords rebel;
Bring oil to fire, snow to their colder moods;
Renege, affirm, and turn their halcyon beaks
With every gale and vary of their masters,
Knowing nought, like dogs, but following.
A plague upon your epileptic visage!
Smile you my speeches, as I were a fool?
Goose, if I had you upon Sarum plain,
I'ld drive ye cackling home to Camelot.

Corn. What, art thou mad, old fellow?

Glou. How fell you out? say that.

Kent. No contraries hold more antipathy
Than I and such a knave.

Corn. Why dost thou call him knave? What's his offence?

Kent. His countenance likes me not.

Corn. No more, perchance, does mine, nor his, nor hers.

Kent. Sir, 'tis my occupation to be plain:
I have seen better faces in my time
Than stands on any shoulder that I see
Before me at this instant.

Corn. This is some fellow,
Who, having been praised for bluntness, doth affect
A saucy roughness, and constrains the garb
Quite from his nature: he cannot flatter, he,
An honest mind and plain, he must speak truth!
An they will take it, so; if not, he's plain.
These kind of knaves I know, which in this plainness
Harbour more craft and more corrupter ends

Than twenty silly ducking observants
That stretch their duties nicely.

Kent. Sir, in good sooth, in sincere verity,
Under the allowance of your great aspect,
Whose influence, like the wreath of radiant fire
On flickering Phœbus' front,—

Corn. What mean'st by this?

Kent. To go out of my dialect, which you discommend so much. I know, sir, I am no flatterer: he that beguiled you in a plain accent was a plain knave; which for my part I will not be, though I should win your displeasure to entreat me to 't.

Corn. What was the offence you gave him?

Osw. I never gave him any:
It pleased the king his master very late
To strike at me, upon his misconstruction;
When he, conjunct, and flattering his displeasure,
Tripp'd me behind; being down, insulted, rail'd,
And put upon him such a deal of man,
That worthied him, got praises of the king
For him attempting who was self-subdued;
And, in the fleshment of this dread exploit,
Drew on me here again.

Kent. None of these rogues and cowards
But Ajax is their fool.

Corn. Fetch forth the stocks!
You stubborn ancient knave, you reverend braggart,
We'll teach you—

Kent. Sir, I am too old to learn:
Call not your stocks for me: I serve the king;
On whose employment I was sent to you:
You shall do small respect, show too bold malice
Against the grace and person of my master,
Stocking his messenger.

Corn. Fetch forth the stocks! As I have life and honour,
There shall he sit till noon.

Reg. Till noon! till night, my lord; and all night too.

Kent. Why, madam, if I were your father's dog,
You should not use me so.

Reg. Sir, being his knave, I will.

Corn. This is a fellow of the self-same colour
Our sister speaks of. Come, bring away the stocks!
[*Stocks brought out.*

Glou. Let me beseech your grace not to do so:
His fault is much, and the good king his master
Will check him for 't: your purposed low correction
Is such as basest and contemned'st wretches
For pilferings and most common trespasses
Are punish'd with: the king must take it ill,
That he 's so slightly valued in his messenger,
Should have him thus restrain'd.
Corn. I 'll answer that.
Reg. My sister may receive it much more worse,
To have her gentleman abused, assaulted,
For following her affairs. Put in his legs.
[***Kent*** *is put in the stocks.*
Come, my good lord, away. [*Exeunt all but* **Glou.** *and* **Kent.**
Glou. I am sorry for thee, friend; 'tis the duke's pleasure,
Whose disposition, all the world well knows,
Will not be rubb'd nor stopp'd: I 'll entreat for thee.
Kent. Pray, do not, sir: I have watched and travell'd hard;
Some time I shall sleep out, the rest I 'll whistle.
A good man's fortune may grow out at heels:
Give you good morrow!
Glou. The duke 's to blame in this; 'twill be ill taken. [*exit.*
Kent. Good king, that must approve the common saw,
Thou out of heaven's benediction comest
To the warm sun!
Approach, thou beacon to this under globe,
That by thy comfortable beams I may
Peruse this letter! Nothing almost sees miracles
But misery: I know 'tis from Cordelia,
Who hath most fortunately been inform'd
Of my obscured course; and shall find time
From this enormous state, seeking to give
Losses their remedies. All weary and o'er-watch'd,
Take vantage, heavy eyes, not to behold
This shameful lodging.
Fortune, good night: smile once more; turn thy wheel!
[*sleeps.*

SCENE III. A WOOD.

Enter **Edgar.**

Edg. I heard myself proclaim'd;
And by the happy hollow of a tree
Escaped the hunt. No port is free; no place,
That guard, and most unusual vigilance,
Does not attend my taking. Whiles I may 'scape,
I will preserve myself: and am bethought
To take the basest and most poorest shape
That ever penury, in contempt of man,
Brought near to beast: my face I 'll grime with filth;
Blanket my loins; elf all my hair in knots;
And with presented nakedness out-face
The winds and persecutions of the sky.
The country gives me proof and precedent
Of Bedlam beggars, who, with roaring voices,
Strike in their numb'd and mortified bare arms
Pins, wooden pricks, nails, sprigs of rosemary;
And with this horrible object, from low farms,
Poor pelting villages, sheep-cotes, and mills,
Sometime with lunatic bans, sometime with prayers,
Enforce their charity. Poor Turlygod! poor Tom!
That 's something yet: Edgar I nothing am. [*exit.*

SCENE IV. BEFORE GLOUCESTER'S CASTLE. KENT IN THE STOCKS.

Enter **Lear, Fool,** *and* **Gentleman.**

Lear. 'Tis strange that they should so depart from home,
And not send back my messenger.
Gent. As I learn'd,
The night before there was no purpose in them
Of this remove.
Kent. Hail to thee, noble master!
Lear. Ha!
Makest thou this shame thy pastime?

Kent. No, my lord.

Fool. Ha, ha! he wears cruel garters. Horses are tied by the heads, dogs and bears by the neck, monkeys by the loins, and men by the legs: when a man's over-lusty at legs, then he wears wooden nether-stocks.

Lear. What's he that hath so much thy place mistook
To set thee here?

Kent. It is both he and she;
Your son and daughter.

Lear. No.

Kent. Yes.

Lear. No, I say.

Kent. I say, yea.

Lear. No, no, they would not.

Kent. Yes, they have.

Lear. By Jupiter, I swear, no.

Kent. By Juno, I swear, ay.

Lear. They durst not do't;
They could not, would not do't; 'tis worse than murder,
To do upon respect such violent outrage:
Resolve me, with all modest haste, which way
Thou mightst deserve, or they impose, this usage,
Coming from us.

Kent. My lord, when at their home
I did commend your highness' letters to them,
Ere I was risen from the place that show'd
My duty kneeling, came there a reeking post,
Stew'd in his haste, half breathless, panting forth
From Goneril his mistress salutations;
Deliver'd letters, spite of intermission,
Which presently they read: on whose contents,
They summon'd up their meiny, straight took horse;
Commanded me to follow, and attend
The leisure of their answer; gave me cold looks:
And meeting here the other messenger,
Whose welcome, I perceived, had poison'd mine,—
Being the very fellow that of late
Display'd so saucily against your highness,—
Having more man than wit about me, drew:
He raised the house with loud and coward cries.

Your son and daughter found this trespass worth
The shame which here it suffers.

Fool. Winter's not gone yet, if the wild-geese fly that way.

Fathers that wear rags
Do make their children blind;
But fathers that bear bags
Shall see their children kind.
Fortune, that arrant whore,
Ne'er turns the key to the poor.

But, for all this, thou shalt have as many dolours for thy daughters as thou canst tell in a year.

Lear. O, how this mother swells up toward my heart!
Hysterica passio, down, thou climbing sorrow,
Thy element's below! Where is this daughter?

Kent. With the earl, sir, here within.

Lear. Follow me not;
Stay here. [*exit.*

Gent. Made you no more offence but what you speak of?

Kent. None.
How chance the king comes with so small a train?

Fool. An thou hadst been set i' the stocks for that question, thou hadst well deserved it.

Kent. Why, fool?

Fool. We'll set thee to school to an ant, to teach thee there's no labouring i' the winter. All that follow their noses are led by their eyes but blind men; and there's not a nose among twenty but can smell him that's stinking. Let go thy hold when a great wheel runs down a hill, lest it break thy neck with following it; but the great one that goes up the hill, let him draw thee after. When a wise man gives thee better counsel, give me mine again: I would have none but knaves follow it, since a fool gives it.

That sir which serves and seeks for gain,
And follows but for form,
Will pack when it begins to rain,
And leave thee in the storm.
But I will tarry; the fool will stay,
And let the wise man fly:
The knave turns fool that runs away;
The fool no knave, perdy.

Kent. Where learned you this, fool?
Fool. Not i' the stocks, fool.

Re-enter **Lear,** *with* **Gloucester.**

Lear. Deny to speak with me? They are sick? they are weary?
They have travell'd all the night? Mere fetches;
The images of revolt and flying off.
Fetch me a better answer.
Glou. My dear lord,
You know the fiery quality of the duke;
How unremoveable and fix'd he is
In his own course.
Lear. Vengeance! plague! death! confusion!
Fiery? what quality? Why, Gloucester, Gloucester,
I'ld speak with the Duke of Cornwall and his wife.
Glou. Well, my good lord, I have inform'd them so.
Lear. Inform'd them! Dost thou understand me, man?
Glou. Ay, my good lord.
Lear. The king would speak with Cornwall; the dear father
Would with his daughter speak, commands her service:
Are they inform'd of this? My breath and blood!
Fiery? the fiery duke? Tell the hot duke that—
No, but not yet: may be he is not well:
Infirmity doth still neglect all office
Whereto our health is bound; we are not ourselves
When nature, being oppress'd, commands the mind
To suffer with the body: I'll forbear;
And am fall'n out with my more headier will,
To take the indisposed and sickly fit
For the sound man. Death on my state! wherefore
[*looking on* **Kent.**
Should he sit here? This act persuades me
That this remotion of the duke and her
Is practice only. Give me my servant forth.
Go tell the duke and 's wife I'ld speak with them,
Now, presently: bid them come forth and hear me,
Or at their chamber-door I'll beat the drum
Till it cry sleep to death.
Glou. I would have all well betwixt you. [*exit.*

Lear. O me, my heart, my rising heart! but, down!
Fool. Cry to it, nuncle, as the cockney did to the eels when she put 'em i' the paste alive; she knapped 'em o' the coxcombs with a stick, and cried 'Down, wantons, down!' 'Twas her brother that, in pure kindness to his horse, buttered his hay.

Enter **Cornwall, Regan, Gloucester,** *and* **Servants.**

Lear. Good morrow to you both.
Corn. Hail to your grace!
[**Kent** *is set at liberty.*
Reg. I am glad to see your highness.
Lear. Regan, I think you are; I know what reason
I have to think so: if thou shouldst not be glad,
I would divorce me from thy mother's tomb,
Sepulchring an adultress. [*to* **Kent.**] O, are you free?
Some other time for that. Beloved Regan,
Thy sister's naught: O Regan, she hath tied
Sharp-tooth'd unkindness, like a vulture, here:
[*points to his heart.*
I can scarce speak to thee; thou'lt not believe
With how depraved a quality—O Regan!
Reg. I pray you, sir, take patience: I have hope
You less know how to value her desert
Than she to scant her duty.
Lear. Say, how is that?
Reg. I cannot think my sister in the least
Would fail her obligation: if, sir, perchance
She have restrain'd the riots of your followers,
'Tis on such ground, and to such wholesome end,
As clears her from all blame.
Lear. My curses on her!
Reg. O, sir, you are old;
Nature in you stands on the very verge
Of her confine: you should be ruled and led
By some discretion, that discerns your state
Better than you yourself. Therefore, I pray you,
That to our sister you do make return;
Say you have wrong'd her, sir.
Lear. Ask her forgiveness?

Do you but mark how this becomes the house:
'Dear daughter, I confess that I am old; [*kneeling.*
Age is unnecessary: on my knees I beg
That you'll vouchsafe me raiment, bed, and food.'
Reg. Good sir, no more; these are unsightly tricks:
Return you to my sister.
Lear. [*rising.*] Never, Regan:
She hath abated me of half my train;
Look'd black upon me; struck me with her tongue,
Most serpent-like, upon the very heart:
All the stored vengeances of heaven fall
On her ingrateful top! Strike her young bones,
You taking airs, with lameness!
Corn. Fie, sir, fie!
Lear. You nimble lightnings, dart your blinding flames
Into her scornful eyes! Infect her beauty,
You fen-suck'd fogs, drawn by the powerful sun,
To fall and blast her pride!
Reg. O the blest gods! so will you wish on me,
When the rash mood is on.
Lear. No, Regan, thou shalt never have my curse:
Thy tender-hefted nature shall not give
Thee o'er to harshness: her eyes are fierce; but thine
Do comfort and not burn. 'Tis not in thee
To grudge my pleasures, to cut off my train,
To bandy hasty words, to scant my sizes,
And in conclusion to oppose the bolt
Against my coming in: thou better know'st
The offices of nature, bond of childhood,
Effects of courtesy, dues of gratitude;
Thy half o' the kingdom hast thou not forgot,
Wherein I thee endow'd.
Reg. Good sir, to the purpose.
Lear. Who put my man i' the stocks? [*Tucket within*
Corn. What trumpet's that?
Reg. I know't, my sister's: this approves her letter,
That she would soon be here.

Enter **Oswald.**

Is your lady come?

Lear. This is a slave, whose easy-borrow'd pride
Dwells in the fickle grace of her he follows.
Out, varlet, from my sight!
Corn. What means your grace?
Lear. Who stock'd my servant? Regan, I have good hope
Thou didst not know on't. Who comes here? O heavens,

Enter **Goneril.**

If you do love old men, if your sweet sway
Allow obedience, if yourselves are old,
Make it your cause; send down, and take my part!
[*to* **Gon.**] Art not ashamed to look upon this beard?
O Regan, wilt thou take her by the hand?
Gon. Why not by the hand, sir? How have I offended?
All's not offence that indiscretion finds
And dotage terms so.
Lear. O sides, you are too tough;
Will you yet hold? How came my man i' the stocks?
Corn. I set him there, sir: but his own disorders
Deserved much less advancement.
Lear. You! did you?
Reg. I pray you, father, being weak, seem so.
If, till the expiration of your month,
You will return and sojourn with my sister,
Dismissing half your train, come then to me:
I am now from home, and out of that provision
Which shall be needful for your entertainment.
Lear. Return to her, and fifty men dismiss'd?
No, rather I abjure all roofs, and choose
To wage against the enmity o' the air;
To be a comrade with the wolf and owl,—
Necessity's sharp pinch! Return with her?
Why, the hot-blooded France, that dowerless took
Our youngest born, I could as well be brought
To knee his throne, and, squire-like, pension beg
To keep base life afoot. Return with her?
Persuade me rather to be slave and sumpter
To this detested groom. [*pointing at* **Oswald.**
Gon. At your choice, sir.
Lear. I prithee, daughter, do not make me mad:

I will not trouble thee, my child; farewell:
We'll no more meet, no more see one another:
But yet thou art my flesh, my blood, my daughter;
Or rather a disease that's in my flesh,
Which I must needs call mine: thou art a boil,
A plague-sore, an embossed carbuncle,
In my corrupted blood. But I'll not chide thee;
Let shame come when it will, I do not call it:
I do not bid the thunder-bearer shoot,
Nor tell tales of thee to high-judging Jove:
Mend when thou canst; be better at thy leisure:
I can be patient; I can stay with Regan,
I and my hundred knights.

Reg. Not altogether so:
I look'd not for you yet, nor am provided
For your fit welcome. Give ear, sir, to my sister;
For those that mingle reason with your passion
Must be content to think you old, and so—
But she knows what she does.

Lear. Is this well spoken?

Reg. I dare avouch it, sir: what, fifty followers?
Is it not well? What should you need of more?
Yea, or so many, sith that both charge and danger
Speak 'gainst so great a number? How, in one house,
Should many people, under two commands,
Hold amity? 'Tis hard; almost impossible.

Gon. Why might not you, my lord, receive attendance
From those that she calls servants or from mine?

Reg. Why not, my lord? If then they chanced to slack you,
We could control them. If you will come to me,—
For now I spy a danger,—I entreat you
To bring but five and twenty: to no more
Will I give place or notice.

Lear. I gave you all—

Reg. And in good time you gave it.

Lear. Made you my guardians, my depositaries;
But kept a reservation to be follow'd
With such a number. What, must I come to you
With five and twenty, Regan? said you so?

Reg. And speak't again, my lord; no more with me.

Lear. Those wicked creatures yet do look well-favour'd,
When others are more wicked; not being the worst
Stands in some rank of praise. [*to* ***Gon.***] I'll go with thee:
Thy fifty yet doth double five-and-twenty,
And thou art twice her love.

Gon. Hear me, my lord:
What need you five and twenty, ten, or five,
To follow in a house where twice so many
Have a command to tend you?

Reg. What need one?

Lear. O, reason not the need: our basest beggars
Are in the poorest thing superfluous:
Allow not nature more than nature needs,
Man's life's as cheap as beast's: thou art a lady;
If only to go warm were gorgeous,
Why, nature needs not what thou gorgeous wear'st,
Which scarcely keeps thee warm. But, for true need,—
You heavens, give me that patience, patience I need!
You see me here, you gods, a poor old man,
As full of grief as age; wretched in both!
If it be you that stir these daughters' hearts
Against their father, fool me not so much
To bear it tamely; touch me with noble anger,
And let not women's weapons, water-drops,
Stain my man's cheeks! No, you unnatural hags,
I will have such revenges on you both,
That all the world shall—I will do such things,—
What they are, yet I know not; but they shall be
The terrors of the earth. You think I'll weep;
No, I'll not weep:
I have full cause of weeping; but this heart
Shall break into a hundred thousand flaws,
Or ere I'll weep. O fool, I shall go mad!

[*Exeunt* ***Lear, Gloucester, Kent,*** *and* ***Fool.***

Storm and tempest.

Corn. Let us withdraw; 'twill be a storm.

Reg. This house is little: the old man and his people
Cannot be well bestow'd.

Gon. 'Tis his own blame; hath put himself from rest,
And must needs taste his folly.

Reg. For his particular, I 'll receive him gladly,
But not one follower.
Gon. So am I purposed.
Where is my lord of Gloucester?
Corn. Follow'd the old man forth: he is return'd.

Re-enter **Gloucester.**

Glou. The king is in high rage.
Corn. Whither is he going?
Glou. He calls to horse; but will I know not whither.
Corn. 'Tis best to give him way; he leads himself.
Gon. My lord, entreat him by no means to stay.
Glou. Alack, the night comes on, and the bleak winds
Do sorely ruffle; for many miles about
There 's scarce a bush.
Reg. O, sir, to wilful men,
The injuries that they themselves procure
Must be their schoolmasters. Shut up your doors:
He is attended with a desperate train;
And what they may incense him to, being apt
To have his ear abused, wisdom bids fear.
Corn. Shut up your doors, my lord; 'tis a wild night:
My Regan counsels well: come out o' the storm. [*exeunt.*

ACT III.

SCENE I. A HEATH.

Storm still. Enter **Kent** *and a* **Gentleman,** *meeting.*

Kent. Who 's there, besides foul weather?
Gent. One minded like the weather, most unquietly.
Kent. I know you. Where 's the king?
Gent. Contending with the fretful element;
Bids the wind blow the earth into the sea,
Or swell the curled waters 'bove the main,
That things might change or cease; tears his white hair,
Which the impetuous blasts, with eyeless rage,
Catch in their fury, and make nothing of;
Strives in his little world of man to out-scorn

The to-and-fro-conflicting wind and rain.
This night, wherein the cub-drawn bear would couch,
The lion and the belly-pinched wolf
Keep their fur dry, unbonneted he runs,
And bids what will take all.
Kent. But who is with him?
Gent. None but the fool; who labours to out-jest
His heart-struck injuries.
Kent. Sir, I do know you;
And dare, upon the warrant of my note,
Commend a dear thing to you. There is division,
Although as yet the face of it be cover'd
With mutual cunning, 'twixt Albany and Cornwall;
Who have—as who have not, that their great stars
Throned and set high?—servants, who seem no less,
Which are to France the spies and speculations
Intelligent of our state; what hath been seen,
Either in snuffs and packings of the dukes,
Or the hard rein which both of them have borne
Against the old kind king; or something deeper,
Whereof perchance these are but furnishings;
But, true it is, from France there comes a power
Into this scatter'd kingdom; who already,
Wise in our negligence, have secret feet
In some of our best ports, and are at point
To show their open banner. Now to you:
If on my credit you dare build so far
To make your speed to Dover, you shall find
Some that will thank you, making just report
Of how unnatural and bemadding sorrow
The king hath cause to plain.
I am a gentleman of blood and breeding;
And, from some knowledge and assurance, offer
This office to you.
Gent. I will talk further with you.
Kent. No, do not.
For confirmation that I am much more
Than my out-wall, open this purse, and take
What it contains. If you shall see Cordelia,—
As fear not but you shall,—show her this ring;

And she will tell you who your fellow is
That yet you do not know. Fie on this storm!
I will go seek the king.

Gent. Give me your hand: have you no more to say?

Kent. Few words, but, to effect, more than all yet;
That, when we have found the king,—in which your pain
That way, I'll this,—he that first lights on him
Holla the other. [*Exeunt severally.*

SCENE II. ANOTHER PART OF THE HEATH. STORM STILL.

Enter **Lear** *and* **Fool.**

Lear. Blow, winds, and crack your cheeks! rage! blow!
You cataracts and hurricanoes, spout
Till you have drench'd our steeples, drown'd the cocks!
You sulphurous and thought-executing fires,
Vaunt-couriers to oak-cleaving thunderbolts,
Singe my white head! And thou, all-shaking thunder,
Smite flat the thick rotundity o' the world!
Crack nature's moulds, all germens spill at once,
That make ingrateful man!

Fool. O nuncle, court holy-water in a dry house is better than this rain-water out o' door. Good nuncle, in, and ask thy daughters' blessing: here's a night pities neither wise man nor fool.

Lear. Rumble thy bellyful! Spit, fire! spout, rain!
Nor rain, wind, thunder, fire, are my daughters:
I tax not you, you elements, with unkindness;
I never gave you kingdom, call'd you children,
You owe me no subscription: then let fall
Your horrible pleasure; here I stand, your slave,
A poor, infirm, weak, and despised old man:
But yet I call you servile ministers,
That have with two pernicious daughters join'd
Your high engender'd battles 'gainst a head
So old and white as this. O! O! 'tis foul!

Fool. He that has a house to put's head in has a good head-piece.

The cod-piece that will house
Before the head has any,
The head and he shall louse;
So beggars marry many.
The man that makes his toe
What he his heart should make
Shall of a corn cry woe,
And turn his sleep to wake.

For there was never yet fair woman but she made mouths in a glass.

Lear. No, I will be the pattern of all patience;
I will say nothing.

Enter **Kent.**

Kent. Who's there?

Fool. Marry, here's grace and a cod-piece; that's a wise man and a fool.

Kent. Alas, sir, are you here? things that love night
Love not such nights as these; the wrathful skies
Gallow the very wanderers of the dark,
And make them keep their caves: since I was man,
Such sheets of fire, such bursts of horrid thunder,
Such groans of roaring wind and rain, I never
Remember to have heard: man's nature cannot carry
The affliction nor the fear.

Lear. Let the great gods,
That keep this dreadful pother o'er our heads,
Find out their enemies now. Tremble, thou wretch,
That hast within thee undivulged crimes,
Unwhipp'd of justice: hide thee, thou bloody hand;
Thou perjured, and thou simular man of virtue
That art incestuous: caitiff, to pieces shake,
That under covert and convenient seeming
Hast practised on man's life: close pent-up guilts,
Rive your concealing continents, and cry
These dreadful summoners grace. I am a man
More sinn'd against than sinning.

Kent. Alack, bare-headed!
Gracious my lord, hard by here is a hovel;
Some friendship will it lend you 'gainst the tempest:

Kent. I had rather break mine own. Good my lord, enter.
Lear. Thou think'st 'tis much that this contentious storm
Invades us to the skin: so 'tis to thee;
But where the greater malady is fix'd,
The lesser is scarce felt. Thou'ldst shun a bear;
But if thy flight lay toward the raging sea,
Thou'ldst meet the bear i' the mouth. When the mind's free,
The body's delicate: the tempest in my mind
Doth from my senses take all feeling else
Save what beats there. Filial ingratitude!
Is it not as this mouth should tear this hand
For lifting food to't? But I will punish home:
No, I will weep no more. In such a night
To shut me out! Pour on; I will endure.
In such a night as this! O Regan, Goneril!
Your old kind father, whose frank heart gave all,—
O, that way madness lies; let me shun that;
No more of that.
Kent. Good my lord, enter here.
Lear. Prithee, go in thyself; seek thine own ease:
This tempest will not give me leave to ponder
On things would hurt me more. But I'll go in.
[*to the* **Fool.**] In, boy; go first. You houseless poverty,—
Nay, get thee in. I'll pray, and then I'll sleep.
[**Fool** *goes in.*

Poor naked wretches, wheresoe'er you are,
That bide the pelting of this pitiless storm,
How shall your houseless heads and unfed sides,
Your loop'd and window'd raggedness, defend you
From seasons such as these? O, I have ta'en
Too little care of this! Take physic, pomp;
Expose thyself to feel what wretches feel,
That thou mayst shake the superflux to them,
And show the heavens more just.
Edg. [*within.*] Fathom and half, fathom and half! Poor Tom!
[*The* **Fool** *runs out from the hovel.*
Fool. Come not in here, nuncle, here's a spirit. Help me, help me!
Kent. Give me thy hand. Who's there?

Fool. A spirit, a spirit: he says his name's poor Tom.
Kent. What art thou that dost grumble there i' the straw? Come forth.

Enter **Edgar** *disguised as a madman.*

Edg. Away! the foul fiend follows me!
Through the sharp hawthorn blows the cold wind.
Hum! go to thy cold bed, and warm thee.
Lear. Hast thou given all to thy two daughters? And art thou come to this?
Edg. Who gives any thing to poor Tom? whom the foul fiend hath led through fire and through flame, through ford and whirlipool, o'er bog and quagmire; that hath laid knives under his pillow, and halters in his pew; set ratsbane by his porridge; made him proud of heart, to ride on a bay trotting-horse over four-inched bridges, to course his own shadow for a traitor. Bless thy five wits! Tom's a-cold,—O, do de, do de, do de. Bless thee from whirlwinds, star-blasting, and taking! Do poor Tom some charity, whom the foul fiend vexes: there could I have him now,—and there,—and there again, and there.
[*Storm still.*
Lear. What, have his daughters brought him to this pass?
Couldst thou save nothing? Didst thou give them all?
Fool. Nay, he reserved a blanket, else we had been all shamed.
Lear. Now, all the plagues that in the pendulous air
Hang fated o'er men's faults light on thy daughters!
Kent. He hath no daughters, sir.
Lear. Death, traitor! nothing could have subdued nature
To such a lowness but his unkind daughters.
Is it the fashion, that discarded fathers
Should have thus little mercy on their flesh?
Judicious punishment! 'twas this flesh begot
Those pelican daughters.
Edg. Pillicock sat on Pillicock-hill:
Halloo, halloo, loo, loo!
Fool. This cold night will turn us all to fools and madmen.
Edg. Take heed o' the foul fiend: obey thy parents; keep

Repose you there; while I to this hard house—
More harder than the stones whereof 'tis raised;
Which even but now, demanding after you,
Denied me to come in—return, and force
Their scanted courtesy.

Lear. My wits begin to turn.
Come on, my boy: how dost, my boy? art cold?
I am cold myself. Where is this straw, my fellow?
The art of our necessities is strange,
That can make vile things precious. Come, your hovel.
Poor fool and knave, I have one part in my heart
That 's sorry yet for thee.

Fool. [*singing.*]

He that has and a little tiny wit,—
With hey, ho, the wind and the rain,—
Must make content with his fortunes fit,
For the rain it raineth every day.

Lear. True, my good boy. Come, bring us to this hovel.
[*Exeunt* **Lear** *and* **Kent.**

Fool. This is a brave night to cool a courtezan.
I 'll speak a prophecy ere I go:
When priests are more in word than matter;
When brewers mar their malt with water;
When nobles are their tailors' tutors;
No heretics burn'd, but wenches' suitors;
When every case in law is right;
No squire in debt, nor no poor knight;
When slanders do not live in tongues;
Nor cutpurses come not to throngs;
When usurers tell their gold i' the field;
And bawds and whores do churches build;
Then shall the realm of Albion
Come to great confusion:
Then comes the time, who lives to see 't,
That going shall be used with feet.
This prophecy Merlin shall make; for I live before his time. [*exit.*

SCENE III. GLOUCESTER'S CASTLE.

Enter **Gloucester** *and* **Edmund.**

Glou. Alack, alack, Edmund, I like not this unnatural dealing. When I desired their leave that I might pity him, they took from me the use of mine own house; charged me, on pain of their perpetual displeasure, neither to speak of him, entreat for him, nor any way sustain him.

Edm. Most savage and unnatural!

Glou. Go to; say you nothing. There 's a division betwixt the dukes; and a worse matter than that: I have received a letter this night; 'tis dangerous to be spoken; I have locked the letter in my closet: these injuries the king now bears will be revenged home; there 's part of a power already footed: we must incline to the king. I will seek him, and privily relieve him: go you and maintain talk with the duke, that my charity be not of him perceived: if he ask for me, I am ill, and gone to bed. Though I die for it, as no less is threatened me, the king my old master must be relieved. There is some strange thing toward, Edmund; pray you, be careful. [*exit.*

Edm. This courtesy, forbid thee, shall the duke
Instantly know; and of that letter too:
This seems a fair deserving, and must draw me
That which my father loses; no less than all:
The younger rises when the old doth fall. [*exit.*

SCENE IV. THE HEATH. BEFORE A HOVEL.

Enter **Lear, Kent,** *and* **Fool.**

Kent. Here is the place, my lord; good my lord, enter:
The tyranny of the open night 's too rough
For nature to endure. [*Storm still.*

Lear. Let me alone.

Kent. Good my lord, enter here.

Lear. Wilt break my heart?

thy word justly; swear not; commit not with man's sworn spouse; set not thy sweet heart on proud array. Tom's a-cold.

Lear. What hast thou been?

Edg. A serving-man, proud in heart and mind; that curled my hair; wore gloves in my cap; served the lust of my mistress' heart, and did the act of darkness with her; swore as many oaths as I spake words, and broke them in the sweet face of heaven: one that slept in the contriving of lust, and waked to do it: wine loved I deeply, dice dearly; and in woman out-paramoured the Turk: false of heart, light of ear, bloody of hand; hog in sloth, fox in stealth, wolf in greediness, dog in madness, lion in prey. Let not the creaking of shoes nor the rustling of silks betray thy poor heart to woman: keep thy foot out of brothels, thy hand out of plackets, thy pen from lenders' books, and defy the foul fiend.
Still through the hawthorn blows the cold wind:
Says suum, mun, ha, no, nonny.
Dolphin my boy, my boy, sessa! let him trot by.
[*Storm still.*

Lear. Why, thou wert better in thy grave than to answer with thy uncovered body this extremity of the skies. Is man no more than this? Consider him well. Thou owest the worm no silk, the beast no hide, the sheep no wool, the cat no perfume. Ha! here's three on's are sophisticated! Thou art the thing itself: unaccommodated man is no more but such a poor, bare, forked animal as thou art. Off, off, you lendings! come, unbutton here.
[*tearing off his clothes.*

Fool. Prithee, nuncle, be contented; 'tis a naughty night to swim in. Now a little fire in a wild field were like an old lecher's heart; a small spark, all the rest on's body cold. Look, here comes a walking fire.

Enter **Gloucester**, *with a torch.*

Edg. This is the foul fiend Flibbertigibbet: he begins at curfew, and walks till the first cock; he gives the web and the pin, squints the eye, and makes the hare-lip; mildews the white wheat, and hurts the poor creature of earth

S. Withold footed thrice the old;
He met the night-mare, and her nine-fold;
Bid her alight,
And her troth plight,
And, aroint thee, witch, aroint thee!

Kent. How fares your grace?

Lear. What's he?

Kent. Who's there? What is't you seek?

Glou. What are you there? Your names?

Edg. Poor Tom: that eats the swimming frog, the toad, the tadpole, the wall-newt and the water; that in the fury of his heart, when the foul fiend rages, eats cow-dung for sallets; swallows the old rat and the ditch-dog; drinks the green mantle of the standing pool; who is whipped from tithing to tithing, and stock-punished, and imprisoned; who hath had three suits to his back, six shirts to his body, horse to ride, and weapon to wear;

But mice and rats, and such small deer,
Have been Tom's food for seven long year.

Beware my follower. Peace, Smulkin; peace, thou fiend!

Glou. What, hath your grace no better company?

Edg. The prince of darkness is a gentleman:
Modo he's call'd, and Mahu.

Glou. Our flesh and blood is grown so vile, my lord,
That it doth hate what gets it.

Edg. Poor Tom's a-cold.

Glou. Go in with me: my duty cannot suffer
To obey in all your daughters' hard commands:
Though their injunction be to bar my doors,
And let this tyrannous night take hold upon you,
Yet have I ventured to come seek you out,
And bring you where both fire and food is ready.

Lear. First let me talk with this philosopher.
What is the cause of thunder?

Kent. Good my lord, take his offer; go into the house.

Lear. I'll talk a word with this same learned Theban.
What is your study?

Edg. How to prevent the fiend, and to kill vermin.

Lear. Let me ask you one word in private.

Kent. Importune him once more to go, my lord;
His wits begin to unsettle.
Glou. Canst thou blame him?
[Storm still.
His daughters seek his death: ah, that good Kent!
He said it would be thus, poor banish'd man!
Thou say'st the king grows mad; I'll tell thee, friend,
I am almost mad myself: I had a son,
Now outlaw'd from my blood; he sought my life,
But lately, very late: I loved him, friend;
No father his son dearer: truth to tell thee,
The grief hath crazed my wits. What a night's this!
I do beseech your grace,—
Lear. O, cry you mercy, sir.
Noble philosopher, your company.
Edg. Tom's a-cold.
Glou. In, fellow, there, into the hovel: keep thee warm.
Lear. Come, let's in all.
Kent. This way, my lord.
Lear. With him;
I will keep still with my philosopher.
Kent. Good my lord, soothe him; let him take the fellow.
Glou. Take him you on.
Kent. Sirrah, come on; go along with us.
Lear. Come, good Athenian.
Glou. No words, no words: hush.
Edg. Child Rowland to the dark tower came,
His word was still,—Fie, foh, and fum,
I smell the blood of a British man. *[exeunt.*

SCENE V. GLOUCESTER'S CASTLE.

Enter **Cornwall** *and* **Edmund.**

Corn. I will have my revenge ere I depart his house.

Edm. How, my lord, I may be censured, that nature thus gives way to loyalty, something fears me to think of.

Corn. I now perceive, it was not altogether your brother's evil disposition made him seek his death; but a provoking merit, set a-work by a reproveable badness in himself.

Edm. How malicious is my fortune, that I must repent to be just! This is the letter he spoke of, which approves him an intelligent party to the advantages of France. O heavens! that this treason were not, or not I the detector!

Corn. Go with me to the duchess.

Edm. If the matter of this paper be certain, you have mighty business in hand.

Corn. True or false, it hath made thee earl of Gloucester. Seek out where thy father is, that he may be ready for our apprehension.

Edm. [*aside.*] If I find him comforting the king, it will stuff his suspicion more fully.—I will persevere in my course of loyalty, though the conflict be sore between that and my blood.

Corn. I will lay trust upon thee; and thou shalt find a dearer father in my love. *[exeunt.*

SCENE VI. A CHAMBER IN A FARMHOUSE ADJOINING THE CASTLE.

Enter **Gloucester, Lear, Kent, Fool,** *and* **Edgar.**

Glou. Here is better than the open air; take it thankfully. I will piece out the comfort with what addition I can: I will not be long from you.

Kent. All the power of his wits have given way to his impatience: the gods reward your kindness!
[Exit ***Gloucester.***

Edg. Frateretto calls me; and tells me Nero is an angler in the lake of darkness. Pray, innocent, and beware the foul fiend.

Fool. Prithee, nuncle, tell me whether a madman be a gentleman or a yeoman?

Lear. A king, a king!

Fool. No, he's a yeoman that has a gentleman to his son; for he's a mad yeoman that sees his son a gentleman before him.

Lear. To have a thousand with red burning spits
Come hissing in upon 'em,—
Edg. The foul fiend bites my back.

Fool. He's mad that trusts in the tameness of a wolf, a horse's health, a boy's love, or a whore's oath.

Lear. It shall be done; I will arraign them straight.
[*to* ***Edgar.***] Come, sit thou here, most learned justicer;
[*to the* ***Fool.***] Thou, sapient sir, sit here. Now, you she foxes!

Edg. Look, where he stands and glares!
Wantest thou eyes at trial, madam?
Come o'er the bourne, Bessy, to me,—

Fool.
Her boat hath a leak,
And she must not speak
Why she dares not come over to thee.

Edg. The foul fiend haunts poor Tom in the voice of a nightingale. Hopdance cries in Tom's belly for two white herring. Croak not, black angel; I have no food for thee.

Kent. How do you, sir? Stand you not so amazed:
Will you lie down and rest upon the cushions?

Lear. I'll see their trial first. Bring in the evidence.
[*to* ***Edgar.***] Thou robed man of justice, take thy place;
[*to the* ***Fool.***] And thou, his yoke-fellow of equity,
Bench by his side: [*to* ***Kent.***] you are o' the commission,
Sit you too.

Edg. Let us deal justly.
Sleepest or wakest thou, jolly shepherd?
Thy sheep be in the corn;
And for one blast of thy minikin mouth,
Thy sheep shall take no harm.
Pur! the cat is gray.

Lear. Arraign her first; 'tis Goneril. I here take my oath before this honourable assembly, she kicked the poor king her father.

Fool. Come hither, mistress. Is your name Goneril?

Lear. She cannot deny it.

Fool. Cry you mercy, I took you for a joint-stool.

Lear. And here's another, whose warp'd looks proclaim
What store her heart is made on. Stop her there!
Arms, arms, sword, fire! Corruption in the place!
False justicer, why hast thou let her 'scape?

Edg. Bless thy five wits!

Kent. O pity! Sir, where is the patience now,
That you so oft have boasted to retain?

Edg. [*aside.*] My tears begin to take his part so much,
They'll mar my counterfeiting.

Lear. The little dogs and all,
Tray, Blanch, and Sweet-heart, see, they bark at me.

Edg. Tom will throw his head at them.
Avaunt, you curs!
Be thy mouth or black or white,
Tooth that poisons if it bite;
Mastiff, greyhound, mongrel grim,
Hound or spaniel, brach or lym,
Or bobtail tike or trundle-tail,
Tom will make them weep and wail:
For, with throwing thus my head,
Dogs leap the hatch, and all are fled.
Do de, de, de. Sessa! Come, march to wakes and fairs and market-towns. Poor Tom, thy horn is dry.

Lear. Then let them anatomize Regan; see what breeds about her heart. Is there any cause in nature that makes these hard hearts? [*to* ***Edgar.***] You, sir, I entertain for one of my hundred; only I do not like the fashion of your garments: you will say they are Persian attire; but let them be changed.

Kent. Now, good my lord, lie here and rest awhile.

Lear. Make no noise, make no noise; draw the curtains: so, so, so. We'll go to supper i' the morning. So, so, so.

Fool. And I'll go to bed at noon.

Re-enter ***Gloucester.***

Glou. Come hither, friend: where is the king my master?

Kent. Here, sir; but trouble him not, his wits are gone.

Glou. Good friend, I prithee, take him in thy arms;
I have o'erheard a plot of death upon him:
There is a litter ready; lay him in 't,
And drive towards Dover, friend, where thou shalt meet
Both welcome and protection. Take up thy master:
If thou shouldst dally half an hour, his life,
With thine, and all that offer to defend him,
Stand in assured loss: take up, take up;

And follow me, that will to some provision
Give thee quick conduct.
Kent. Oppressed nature sleeps:
This rest might yet have balm'd thy broken sinews,
Which, if convenience will not allow,
Stand in hard cure. [*to the* **Fool.**] Come, help to bear thy master;
Thou must not stay behind.
Glou. Come, come, away.
[*Exeunt all but* **Edgar.**
Edg. When we our betters see bearing our woes,
We scarcely think our miseries our foes.
Who alone suffers suffers most i' the mind,
Leaving free things and happy shows behind:
But then the mind much sufferance doth o'erskip,
When grief hath mates, and bearing fellowship.
How light and portable my pain seems now,
When that which makes me bend makes the king bow,
He childed as I father'd! Tom, away!
Mark the high noises; and thyself bewray,
When false opinion, whose wrong thought defiles thee,
In thy just proof, repeals and reconciles thee.
What will hap more to-night, safe 'scape the king!
Lurk, lurk. [*exit.*

SCENE VII. GLOUCESTER'S CASTLE.

Enter **Cornwall, Regan, Goneril, Edmund,** *and* **Servants.**

Corn. Post speedily to my lord your husband; show him this letter: the army of France is landed. Seek out the villain Gloucester. [*Exeunt some of the* **Servants.**
Reg. Hang him instantly.
Gon. Pluck out his eyes.
Corn. Leave him to my displeasure. Edmund, keep you our sister company: the revenges we are bound to take upon your traitorous father are not fit for your beholding. Advise the duke, where you are going, to a most festinate preparation: we are bound to the like. Our posts shall be

swift and intelligent betwixt us. Farewell, dear sister: farewell, my lord of Gloucester.

Enter **Oswald.**

How now! where's the king?
Osw. My lord of Gloucester hath convey'd him hence:
Some five or six and thirty of his knights,
Hot questrists after him, met him at gate;
Who, with some other of the lords dependants,
Are gone with him towards Dover; where they boast
To have well-armed friends.
Corn. Get horses for your mistress.
Gon. Farewell, sweet lord, and sister.
Corn. Edmund, farewell.
[*Exeunt* **Goneril, Edmund,** *and* **Oswald.**
Go seek the traitor Gloucester,
Pinion him like a thief, bring him before us.
[*Exeunt other* **Servants.**
Though well we may not pass upon his life
Without the form of justice, yet our power
Shall do a courtesy to our wrath, which men
May blame, but not control. Who's there? the traitor?

Enter **Gloucester,** *brought in by two or three.*

Reg. Ingrateful fox! 'tis he.
Corn. Bind fast his corky arms.
Glou. What mean your graces? Good my friends, consider
You are my guests: do me no foul play, friends.
Corn. Bind him, I say. [**Servants** *bind him.*
Reg. Hard, hard. O filthy traitor!
Glou. Unmerciful lady as you are, I'm none.
Corn. To this chair bind him. Villain, thou shalt find—
[**Regan** *plucks his beard.*
Glou. By the kind gods, 'tis most ignobly done
To pluck me by the beard.
Reg. So white, and such a traitor!
Glou. Naughty lady,
These hairs, which thou dost ravish from my chin,
Will quicken, and accuse thee: I am your host:

With robbers' hands my hospitable favours
You should not ruffle thus. What will you do?
Corn. Come, sir, what letters had you late from France?
Reg. Be simple answerer, for we know the truth.
Corn. And what confederacy have you with the traitors
Late footed in the kingdom?
Reg. To whose hands have you sent the lunatic king?
Speak.
Glou. I have a letter guessingly set down,
Which came from one that's of a neutral heart,
And not from one opposed.
Corn. Cunning.
Reg. And false.
Corn. Where hast thou sent the king?
Glou. To Dover.
Reg. Wherefore to Dover? Wast thou not charged at peril—
Corn. Wherefore to Dover? Let him first answer that.
Glou. I am tied to the stake, and I must stand the course.
Reg. Wherefore to Dover, sir?
Glou. Because I would not see thy cruel nails
Pluck out his poor old eyes; nor thy fierce sister
In his anointed flesh stick boarish fangs.
The sea, with such a storm as his bare head
In hell-black night endured, would have buoy'd up,
And quench'd the stelled fires:
Yet, poor old heart, he holp the heavens to rain.
If wolves had at thy gate howl'd that stern time,
Thou shouldst have said 'Good porter, turn the key,'
All cruels else subscribed: but I shall see
The winged vengeance overtake such children.
Corn. See't shalt thou never. Fellows, hold the chair.
Upon these eyes of thine I'll set my foot.
Glou. He that will think to live till he be old,
Give me some help! O cruel! O you gods!
Reg. One side will mock another; the other too.
Corn. If you see vengeance,—
First Serv. Hold your hand, my lord:
I have served you ever since I was a child:

But better service have I never done you
Than now to bid you hold.
Reg. How now, you dog!
First Serv. If you did wear a beard upon your chin,
I'd shake it on this quarrel. What do you mean?
Corn. My villain! [*They draw and fight.*
First Serv. Nay, then, come on, and take the chance of anger.
Reg. Give me thy sword. A peasant stand up thus!
[*takes a sword, and runs at him behind.*
First Serv. O, I am slain! My lord, you have one eye left
To see some mischief on him. O! [*dies.*
Corn. Lest it see more, prevent it. Out, vile jelly!
Where is thy lustre now?
Glou. All dark and comfortless. Where's my son Edmund?
Edmund, enkindle all the sparks of nature,
To quit this horrid act.
Reg. Out, treacherous villain!
Thou call'st on him that hates thee: it was he
That made the overture of thy treasons to us;
Who is too good to pity thee.
Glou. O my follies! then Edgar was abused.
Kind gods, forgive me that, and prosper him!
Reg. Go thrust him out at gates, and let him smell
His way to Dover. [*Exit one with* **Gloucester.**] How is't, my lord? how look you?
Corn. I have received a hurt: follow me, lady.
Turn out that eyeless villain; throw this slave
Upon the dunghill. Regan, I bleed apace:
Untimely comes this hurt: give me your arm.
[*Exit* **Cornwall,** *led by* **Regan.**
Sec. Serv. I'll never care what wickedness I do,
If this man come to good.
Third Serv. If she live long,
And in the end meet the old course of death,
Women will all turn monsters.
Sec. Serv. Let's follow the old earl, and get the Bedlam
To lead him where he would: his roguish madness
Allows itself to any thing.

Third Serv. Go thou: I'll fetch some flax and whites of eggs
To apply to his bleeding face. Now, heaven help him!
[*Exeunt severally.*

ACT IV.

SCENE I. THE HEATH.

Enter **Edgar.**

Edg. Yet better thus, and known to be contemn'd,
Than still contemn'd and flatter'd. To be worst,
The lowest and most dejected thing of fortune,
Stands still in esperance, lives not in fear:
The lamentable change is from the best;
The worst returns to laughter. Welcome, then,
Thou unsubstantial air that I embrace!
The wretch that thou hast blown unto the worst
Owes nothing to thy blasts. But who comes here?

Enter **Gloucester,** *led by an* **Old Man.**

My father, poorly led? World, world, O world!
But that thy strange mutations make us hate thee,
Life would not yield to age.
Old Man. O, my good lord, I have been your tenant, and your father's tenant, these fourscore years.
Glou. Away, get thee away; good friend, be gone:
Thy comforts can do me no good at all:
Thee they may hurt.
Old Man. Alack, sir, you cannot see your way.
Glou. I have no way, and therefore want no eyes;
I stumbled when I saw: full oft 'tis seen,
Our means secure us, and our mere defects
Prove our commodities. O dear son Edgar,
The food of thy abused father's wrath!
Might I but live to see thee in my touch,
I'ld say I had eyes again!
Old Man. How now! Who's there?
Edg. [*aside.*] O gods! Who is't can say 'I am at the worst'?
I am worse than e'er I was.

Old Man. 'Tis poor mad Tom.
Edg. [*aside.*] And worse I may be yet: the worst is not
So long as we can say 'This is the worst.'
Old Man. Fellow, where goest?
Glou. Is it a beggar-man?
Old Man. Madman and beggar too.
Glou. He has some reason, else he could not beg.
I' the last night's storm I such a fellow saw;
Which made me think a man a worm: my son
Came then into my mind; and yet my mind
Was then scarce friends with him: I have heard more since.
As flies to wanton boys, are we to the gods,
They kill us for their sport.
Edg. [*aside.*] How should this be?
Bad is the trade that must play fool to sorrow,
Angering itself and others.—Bless thee, master!
Glou. Is that the naked fellow?
Old Man. Ay, my lord.
Glou. Then, prithee, get thee gone: if, for my sake,
Thou wilt o'ertake us, hence a mile or twain,
I' the way toward Dover, do it for ancient love;
And bring some covering for this naked soul,
Who I'll entreat to lead me.
Old Man. Alack, sir, he is mad.
Glou. 'Tis the times' plague, when madmen lead the blind.
Do as I bid thee, or rather do thy pleasure;
Above the rest, be gone.
Old Man. I'll bring him the best 'parel that I have,
Come on't what will. [*exit.*
Glou. Sirrah, naked fellow,—
Edg. Poor Tom's a-cold. [*aside.*] I cannot daub it further.
Glou. Come hither, fellow.
Edg. [*aside.*] And yet I must.—Bless thy sweet eyes, they bleed.
Glou. Know'st thou the way to Dover?
Edg. Both stile and gate, horse-way and foot-path. Poor Tom hath been scared out of his good wits: bless thee, good man's son, from the foul fiend! five fiends have been in poor Tom at once; of lust, as Obidicut; Hobbididance,

prince of dumbness; Mahu, of stealing; Modo, of murder; Flibbertigibbet, of mopping and mowing, who since possesses chambermaids and waiting-women. So, bless thee, master!

Glou. Here, take this purse, thou whom the heavens' plagues
Have humbled to all strokes: that I am wretched
Makes thee the happier: heavens, deal so still!
Let the superfluous and lust-dieted man,
That slaves your ordinance, that will not see
Because he doth not feel, feel your power quickly;
So distribution should undo excess,
And each man have enough. Dost thou know Dover?

Edg. Ay, master.

Glou. There is a cliff, whose high and bending head
Looks fearfully in the confined deep:
Bring me but to the very brim of it,
And I'll repair the misery thou dost bear
With something rich about me: from that place
I shall no leading need.

Edg. Give me thy arm:
Poor Tom shall lead thee. [*exeunt.*

SCENE II. BEFORE THE DUKE OF ALBANY'S PALACE.

Enter **Goneril** *and* **Edmund.**

Gon. Welcome, my lord: I marvel our mild husband
Not met us on the way.

Enter **Oswald.**

Now, where's your master?

Osw. Madam, within; but never man so changed.
I told him of the army that was landed;
He smiled at it: I told him you were coming;
His answer was 'The worse': of Gloucester's treachery,
And of the loyal service of his son,
When I inform'd him, then he call'd me sot,
And told me I had turn'd the wrong side out:

What most he should dislike seems pleasant to him;
What like, offensive.

Gon. [*to* **Edm.**] Then shall you go no further.
It is the cowish terror of his spirit,
That dares not undertake: he'll not feel wrongs
Which tie him to an answer. Our wishes on the way
May prove effects. Back, Edmund, to my brother;
Hasten his musters and conduct his powers:
I must change arms at home, and give the distaff
Into my husband's hands. This trusty servant
Shall pass between us: ere long you are like to hear,
If you dare venture in your own behalf,
A mistress's command. Wear this; spare speech;
[*giving a favour.*
Decline your head: this kiss, if it durst speak,
Would stretch thy spirits up into the air:
Conceive, and fare thee well.

Edm. Yours in the ranks of death.

Gon. My most dear Gloucester!
[*Exit* **Edmund.**
O, the difference of man and man!
To thee a woman's services are due:
My fool usurps my body.

Osw. Madam, here comes my lord.
[*exit*

Enter **Albany.**

Gon. I have been worth the whistle.

Alb. O Goneril!
You are not worth the dust which the rude wind
Blows in your face. I fear your disposition:
That nature, which contemns it origin,
Cannot be border'd certain in itself;
She that herself will sliver and disbranch
From her material sap, perforce must wither
And come to deadly use.

Gon. No more; the text is foolish.

Alb. Wisdom and goodness to the vile seem vile:
Filths savour but themselves. What have you done?
Tigers, not daughters, what have you perform'd?
A father, and a gracious aged man,

Whose reverence even the head-lugg'd bear would lick,
Most barbarous, most degenerate! have you madded.
Could my good brother suffer you to do it?
A man, a prince, by him so benefited!
If that the heavens do not their visible spirits
Send quickly down to tame these vile offences,
It will come,
Humanity must perforce prey on itself,
Like monsters of the deep.

Gon. Milk-liver'd man!
That bear'st a cheek for blows, a head for wrongs:
Who hast not in thy brows an eye discerning
Thine honour from thy suffering; that not know'st
Fools do those villains pity who are punish'd
Ere they have done their mischief. Where's thy drum?
France spreads his banners in our noiseless land,
With plumed helm thy state begins to threat;
Whiles thou, a moral fool, sit'st still, and criest
'Alack, why does he so?'

Alb. See thyself, devil!
Proper deformity seems not in the fiend
So horrid as in woman.

Gon. O vain fool!

Alb. Thou changed and self-cover'd thing, for shame,
Be-monster not thy feature. Were't my fitness
To let these hands obey my blood,
They are apt enough to dislocate and tear
Thy flesh and bones: howe'er thou art a fiend,
A woman's shape doth shield thee.

Gon. Marry, your manhood now—

Enter a ***Messenger.***

Alb. What news?

Mess. O, my good lord, the Duke of Cornwall's dead;
Slain by his servant, going to put out
The other eye of Gloucester.

Alb. Gloucester's eyes!

Mess. A servant that he bred, thrill'd with remorse,
Opposed against the act, bending his sword
To his great master; who, thereat enraged,

Flew on him, and amongst them fell'd him dead;
But not without that harmful stroke, which since
Hath pluck'd him after.

Alb. This shows you are above,
You justicers, that these our nether crimes
So speedily can venge! But, O poor Gloucester!
Lost he his other eye?

Mess. Both, both, my lord.
This letter, madam, craves a speedy answer;
'Tis from your sister.

Gon. [*aside.*] One way I like this well;
But being widow, and my Gloucester with her,
May all the building in my fancy pluck
Upon my hateful life: another way,
The news is not so tart.—I'll read, and answer. [*exit.*

Alb. Where was his son when they did take his eyes?

Mess. Come with my lady hither.

Alb. He is not here.

Mess. No, my good lord; I met him back again.

Alb. Knows he the wickedness?

Mess. Ay, my good lord; 'twas he inform'd against him;
And quit the house on purpose, that their punishment
Might have the freer course.

Alb. Gloucester, I live
To thank thee for the love thou show'dst the king,
And to revenge thine eyes. Come hither, friend:
Tell me what more thou know'st. [*exeunt.*

SCENE III. THE FRENCH CAMP NEAR DOVER.

Enter ***Kent*** *and a* ***Gentleman.***

Kent. Why the King of France is so suddenly gone back know you the reason?

Gent. Something he left imperfect in the state, which since his coming forth is thought of; which imports to the kingdom so much fear and danger, that his personal return was most required and necessary.

Kent. Who hath he left behind him general?

Gent. The Marshal of France, Monsieur La Far.

Kent. Did your letters pierce the queen to any demonstration of grief?
Gent. Ay, sir; she took them, read them in my presence;
And now and then an ample tear trill'd down
Her delicate cheek: it seem'd she was a queen
Over her passion; who, most rebel-like,
Sought to be king o'er her.
Kent. O, then it moved her.
Gent. Not to a rage: patience and sorrow strove
Who should express her goodliest. You have seen
Sunshine and rain at once: her smiles and tears
Were like a better way: those happy smilets,
That play'd on her ripe lip, seem'd not to know
What guests were in her eyes; which parted thence,
As pearls from diamonds dropp'd. In brief,
Sorrow would be a rarity most beloved,
If all could so become it.
Kent. Made she no verbal question?
Gent. 'Faith, once or twice she heaved the name of 'father'
Pantingly forth, as if it press'd her heart;
Cried 'Sisters! sisters! Shame of ladies! sisters!
Kent! father! sisters! What, i' the storm? i' the night?
Let pity not be believed!' There she shook
The holy water from her heavenly eyes,
And clamour moisten'd: then away she started
To deal with grief alone.
Kent. It is the stars,
The stars above us, govern our conditions;
Else one self mate and mate could not beget
Such different issues. You spoke not with her since?
Gent. No.
Kent. Was this before the king return'd?
Gent. No, since.
Kent. Well, sir, the poor distressed Lear's i' the town;
Who sometime, in his better tune, remembers
What we are come about, and by no means
Will yield to see his daughter.
Gent. Why, good sir?
Kent. A sovereign shame so elbows him: his own unkindness,

That stripp'd her from his benediction, turn'd her
To foreign casualties, gave her dear rights
To his dog-hearted daughters, these things sting
His mind so venomously, that burning shame
Detains him from Cordelia.
Gent. Alack, poor gentleman!
Kent. Of Albany's and Cornwall's powers you heard not?
Gent. 'Tis so, they are afoot.
Kent. Well, sir, I'll bring you to our master Lear,
And leave you to attend him: some dear cause
Will in concealment wrap me up awhile;
When I am known aright, you shall not grieve
Lending me this acquaintance. I pray you, go
Along with me. [*exeunt.*

SCENE IV. THE SAME. A TENT.

Enter, with drum and colours, **Cordelia, Doctor,** *and* **Soldiers.**

Cor. Alack, 'tis he: why, he was met even now
As mad as the vex'd sea; singing aloud;
Crown'd with rank fumiter and furrow-weeds,
With bur-docks, hemlock, nettles, cuckoo-flowers,
Darnel, and all the idle weeds that grow
In our sustaining corn. A century send forth;
Search every acre in the high-grown field,
And bring him to our eye. [*Exit an* **Officer.**] What can man's wisdom
In the restoring his bereaved sense?
He that helps him take all my outward worth.
Doct. There is means, madam:
Our foster-nurse of nature is repose,
The which he lacks; that to provoke in him,
Are many simples operative, whose power
Will close the eye of anguish.
Cor. All blest secrets,
All you unpublish'd virtues of the earth,
Spring with my tears! be aidant and remediate
In the good man's distress! Seek, seek for him:

Lest his ungovern'd rage dissolve the life
That wants the means to lead it.

Enter a **Messenger.**

Mess. News, madam;
The British powers are marching hitherward.
Cor. 'Tis known before; our preparation stands
In expectation of them. O dear father,
It is thy business that I go about;
Therefore great France
My mourning and important tears hath pitied.
No blown ambition doth our arms incite,
But love, dear love, and our aged father's right:
Soon may I hear and see him! [*exeunt.*

SCENE V. GLOUCESTER'S CASTLE.

Enter **Regan** *and* **Oswald.**

Reg. But are my brother's powers set forth?
Osw. Ay, madam.
Reg. Himself in person there?
Osw. Madam, with much ado:
Your sister is the better soldier.
Reg. Lord Edmund spake not with your lord at home?
Osw. No, madam.
Reg. What might import my sister's letter to him?
Osw. I know not, lady.
Reg. 'Faith, he is posted hence on serious matter.
It was great ignorance, Gloucester's eyes being out,
To let him live: where he arrives he moves
All hearts against us: Edmund, I think, is gone,
In pity of his misery, to dispatch
His nighted life; moreover, to descry
The strength o' the enemy.
Osw. I must needs after him, madam, with my letter.
Reg. Our troops set forth to-morrow: stay with us;
The ways are dangerous.
Osw. I may not, madam:
My lady charged my duty in this business.

Reg. Why should she write to Edmund? Might not you
Transport her purposes by word? Belike,
Something—I know not what: I'll love thee much,
Let me unseal the letter.
Osw. Madam, I had rather—
Reg. I know your lady does not love her husband;
I am sure of that: and at her late being here
She gave strange œillades and most speaking looks
To noble Edmund. I know you are of her bosom.
Osw. I, madam?
Reg. I speak in understanding; you are, I know 't:
Therefore I do advise you, take this note:
My lord is dead; Edmund and I have talk'd;
And more convenient is he for my hand
Than for your lady's: you may gather more.
If you do find him, pray you, give him this;
And when your mistress hears thus much from you,
I pray, desire her call her wisdom to her.
So, fare you well.
If you do chance to hear of that blind traitor,
Preferment falls on him that cuts him off.
Osw. Would I could meet him, madam! I should show
What party I do follow.
Reg. Fare thee well. [*exeunt.*

SCENE VI. FIELDS NEAR DOVER.

Enter **Gloucester,** *and* **Edgar** *dressed like a peasant.*

Glou. When shall we come to the top of that same hill?
Edg. You do climb up it now: look, how we labour.
Glou. Methinks the ground is even.
Edg. Horrible steep
Hark, do you hear the sea?
Glou. No, truly.
Edg. Why, then, your other senses grow imperfect
By your eyes' anguish.
Glou. So may it be, indeed:
Methinks thy voice is alter'd; and thou speak'st
In better phrase and matter than thou didst.

Edg. You're much deceived: in nothing am I changed
But in my garments.
Glou. Methinks you're better spoken.
Edg. Come on, sir; here's the place: stand still. How fearful
And dizzy 'tis, to cast one's eyes so low!
The crows and choughs that wing the midway air
Show scarce so gross as beetles: half way down
Hangs one that gathers samphire, dreadful trade!
Methinks he seems no bigger than his head:
The fishermen, that walk upon the beach,
Appear like mice; and yond tall anchoring bark,
Diminish'd to her cock; her cock, a buoy
Almost too small for sight: the murmuring surge,
That on the unnumber'd idle pebbles chafes,
Cannot be heard so high. I'll look no more;
Lest my brain turn, and the deficient sight
Topple down headlong.
Glou. Set me where you stand.
Edg. Give me your hand: you are now within a foot
Of the extreme verge: for all beneath the moon
Would I not leap upright.
Glou. Let go my hand.
Here, friend, 's another purse; in it a jewel
Well worth a poor man's taking: fairies and gods
Prosper it with thee! Go thou farther off;
Bid me farewell, and let me hear thee going.
Edg. Now fare you well, good sir.
Glou. With all my heart.
Edg. Why I do trifle thus with his despair
Is done to cure it.
Glou. [*kneeling.*] O you mighty gods!
This world I do renounce, and, in your sights,
Shake patiently my great affliction off:
If I could bear it longer, and not fall
To quarrel with your great opposeless wills,
My snuff and loathed part of nature should
Burn itself out. If Edgar live, O, bless him!
Now, fellow, fare thee well. [*He falls forward.*
Edg. Gone, sir: farewell.

And yet I know not how conceit may rob
The treasury of life, when life itself
Yields to the theft: had he been where he thought,
By this, had thought been past. Alive or dead?
Ho, you sir! friend! Hear you, sir! speak!
Thus might he pass indeed: yet he revives.
What are you, sir?
Glou. Away, and let me die.
Edg. Hadst thou been aught but gossamer, feathers, air,
So many fathom down precipitating,
Thou'dst shiver'd like an egg: but thou dost breathe;
Hast heavy substance; bleed'st not; speak'st; art sound.
Ten masts at each make not the altitude
Which thou hast perpendicularly fell:
Thy life's a miracle. Speak yet again.
Glou. But have I fall'n, or no?
Edg. From the dread summit of this chalky bourn.
Look up a-height; the shrill-gorged lark so far
Cannot be seen or heard: do but look up.
Glou. Alack, I have no eyes.
Is wretchedness deprived that benefit,
To end itself by death? 'Twas yet some comfort,
When misery could beguile the tyrant's rage,
And frustrate his proud will.
Edg. Give me your arm:
Up: so. How is't? Feel you your legs? You stand.
Glou. Too well, too well.
Edg. This is above all strangeness.
Upon the crown o' the cliff, what thing was that
Which parted from you?
Glou. A poor unfortunate beggar.
Edg. As I stood here below, methought his eyes
Were two full moons; he had a thousand noses,
Horns whelk'd and waved like the enridged sea:
It was some fiend; therefore, thou happy father,
Think that the clearest gods, who make them honours
Of men's impossibilities, have preserved thee.
Glou. I do remember now: henceforth I'll bear
Affliction till it do cry out itself
'Enough, enough,' and die. That thing you speak of,

I took it for a man; often 'twould say
'The fiend, the fiend': he led me to that place.

Edg. Bear free and patient thoughts. But who comes here?

Enter **Lear,** *fantastically dressed with wild flowers.*

The safer sense will ne'er accommodate
His master thus.

Lear. No, they cannot touch me for coining; I am the king himself.

Edg. O thou side-piercing sight!

Lear. Nature's above art in that respect. There's your press-money. That fellow handles his bow like a crow-keeper: draw me a clothier's yard. Look, look, a mouse! Peace, peace; this piece of toasted cheese will do't. There's my gauntlet; I'll prove it on a giant. Bring up the brown bills. O, well flown, bird! i' the clout, i' the clout: hewgh! Give the word.

Edg. Sweet marjoram.

Lear. Pass.

Glou. I know that voice.

Lear. Ha! Goneril, with a white beard! They flattered me like a dog; and told me I had white hairs in my beard ere the black ones were there. To say 'ay' and 'no' to every thing that I said!—'Ay' and 'no' too was no good divinity. When the rain came to wet me once, and the wind to make me chatter; when the thunder would not peace at my bidding; there I found 'em, there I smelt 'em out. Go to, they are not men o' their words: they told me I was every thing; 'tis a lie, I am not ague-proof.

Glou. The trick of that voice I do well remember:
Is 't not the king?

Lear. Ay, every inch a king:
When I do stare, see how the subject quakes.
I pardon that man's life. What was thy cause?
Adultery?
Thou shalt not die: die for adultery! No:
The wren goes to 't, and the small gilded fly
Does lecher in my sight.
Let copulation thrive; for Gloucester's bastard son
Was kinder to his father than my daughters

Got 'tween the lawful sheets.
To 't, luxury, pell-mell! for I lack soldiers.
Behold yond simpering dame,
Whose face between her forks presages snow;
That minces virtue, and does shake the head
To hear of pleasure's name;
The fitchew, nor the soiled horse, goes to 't
With a more riotous appetite.
Down from the waist they are Centaurs,
Though women all above:
But to the girdle do the gods inherit,
Beneath is all the fiends':
There's hell, there's darkness, there's the sulphurous pit,
Burning, scalding, stench, consumption; fie, fie, fie! pah, pah! Give me an ounce of civet, good apothecary, to sweeten my imagination: there's money for thee.

Glou. O, let me kiss that hand!

Lear. Let me wipe it first; it smells of mortality.

Glou. O ruin'd piece of nature! This great world
Shall so wear out to nought. Dost thou know me?

Lear. I remember thine eyes well enough. Dost thou squiny at me? No, do thy worst, blind Cupid; I'll not love. Read thou this challenge; mark but the penning of it.

Glou. Were all the letters suns, I could not see one.

Edg. I would not take this from report; it is,
And my heart breaks at it.

Lear. Read.

Glou. What, with the case of eyes?

Lear. O, ho, are you there with me? No eyes in your head, nor no money in your purse? Your eyes are in a heavy case, your purse in a light: yet you see how this world goes.

Glou. I see it feelingly.

Lear. What, art mad? A man may see how this world goes with no eyes. Look with thine ears: see how yond justice rails upon yond simple thief. Hark, in thine ear: change places; and, handy-dandy, which is the justice, which is the thief? Thou hast seen a farmer's dog bark at a beggar?

Glou. Ay, sir.

Lear. And the creature run from the cur?
There thou mightst behold the great image of authority: a dog's obeyed in office.
Thou rascal beadle, hold thy bloody hand!
Why dost thou lash that whore? Strip thine own back;
Thou hotly lust'st to use her in that kind
For which thou whipp'st her. The usurer hangs the cozener.
Through tatter'd clothes small vices do appear;
Robes and furr'd gowns hide all. Plate sin with gold,
And the strong lance of justice hurtless breaks;
Arm it in rags, a pigmy's straw does pierce it.
None does offend, none, I say, none; I'll able 'em:
Take that of me, my friend, who have the power
To seal the accuser's lips. Get thee glass eyes;
And, like a scurvy politician, seem
To see the things thou dost not. Now, now, now, now:
Pull off my boots: harder, harder: so.
Edg. O, matter and impertinency mix'd!
Reason in madness!
Lear. If thou wilt weep my fortunes, take my eyes.
I know thee well enough; thy name is Gloucester:
Thou must be patient; we came crying hither:
Thou know'st, the first time that we smell the air,
We wawl and cry. I will preach to thee: mark.
Glou. Alack, alack the day!
Lear. When we are born, we cry that we are come
To this great stage of fools: this' a good block;
It were a delicate stratagem, to shoe
A troop of horse with felt: I'll put't in proof;
And when I have stol'n upon these sons-in-law,
Then, kill, kill, kill, kill, kill, kill!

Enter a **Gentleman,** *with* **Attendants.**

Gent. O, here he is: lay hand upon him. Sir,
Your most dear daughter—
Lear. No rescue? What, a prisoner? I am even
The natural fool of fortune. Use me well;
You shall have ransom. Let me have surgeons;
I am cut to the brains.

Gent. You shall have any thing.
Lear. No seconds? all myself?
Why, this would make a man a man of salt,
To use his eyes for garden water-pots,
Ay, and laying autumn's dust.
Gent. Good sir,—
Lear. I will die bravely, like a bridegroom. What!
I will be jovial: come, come; I am a king,
My masters, know you that.
Gent. You are a royal one, and we obey you.
Lear. Then there's life in't. Nay, if you get it, you shall get it with running. Sa, sa, sa, sa.
[*Exit running;* **Attendants** *follow.*
Gent. A sight most pitiful in the meanest wretch,
Past speaking of in a king! Thou hast one daughter,
Who redeems nature from the general curse
Which twain have brought her to.
Edg. Hail, gentle sir.
Gent. Sir, speed you: what's your will?
Edg. Do you hear aught, sir, of a battle toward?
Gent. Most sure and vulgar: every one hears that,
Which can distinguish sound.
Edg. But, by your favour,
How near's the other army?
Gent. Near and on speedy foot; the main descry
Stands on the hourly thought.
Edg. I thank you, sir: that's all.
Gent. Though that the queen on special cause is here,
Her army is moved on.
Edg. I thank you, sir. [*Exit* **Gent.**
Glou. You ever-gentle gods, take my breath from me;
Let not my worser spirit tempt me again
To die before you please!
Edg. Well pray you, father.
Glou. Now, good sir, what are you?
Edg. A most poor man, made tame to fortune's blows;
Who, by the art of known and feeling sorrows,
Am pregnant to good pity. Give me your hand,
I'll lead you to some biding.
Glou. Hearty thanks:

The bounty and the benison of heaven
To boot, and boot!

Enter **Oswald.**

Osw. A proclaim'd prize! Most happy!
That eyeless head of thine was first framed flesh
To raise my fortunes. Thou old unhappy traitor,
Briefly thyself remember: the sword is out
That must destroy thee.

Glou. Now let thy friendly hand
Put strength enough to 't. [***Edgar*** *interposes.*

Osw. Wherefore, bold peasant,
Darest thou support a publish'd traitor? Hence;
Lest that the infection of his fortune take
Like hold on thee. Let go his arm.

Edg. Chill not let go, zir, without vurther 'casion.

Osw. Let go, slave, or thou diest!

Edg. Good gentleman, go your gait, and let poor volk pass. An chud ha' bin zwaggered out of my life, 'twould not ha' bin zo long as 'tis by a vortnight. Nay, come not near th' old man; keep out, che vor ye, or ise try whether your costard or my ballow be the harder: chill be plain with you.

Osw. Out, dunghill!

Edg. Chill pick your teeth, zir: come; no matter vor your foins. [*They fight, and* ***Edgar*** *knocks him down.*

Osw. Slave, thou hast slain me: villain, take my purse:
If ever thou wilt thrive, bury my body;
And give the letters which thou find'st about me
To Edmund earl of Gloucester; seek him out
Upon the British party: O, untimely death! [*dies.*

Edg. I know thee well: a serviceable villain;
As duteous to the vices of thy mistress
As badness would desire.

Glou. What, is he dead?

Edg. Sit you down, father; rest you.
Let's see these pockets: the letters that he speaks of
May be my friends. He's dead; I am only sorry
He had no other death's-man. Let us see:
Leave, gentle wax; and, manners, blame us not:

To know our enemies' minds, we'ld rip their hearts;
Their papers, is more lawful.

[*reads.*] 'Let our reciprocal vows be remembered. You have many opportunities to cut him off: if your will want not, time and place will be fruitfully offered. There is nothing done, if he return the conqueror: then am I the prisoner, and his bed my gaol; from the loathed warmth whereof deliver me, and supply the place for your labour.

'Your—wife, so I would say—Affectionate servant,
'GONERIL.'

O undistinguish'd space of woman's will!
A plot upon her virtuous husband's life;
And the exchange my brother! Here, in the sands,
Thee I'll rake up, the post unsanctified
Of murderous lechers: and in the mature time
With this ungracious paper strike the sight
Of the death-practised duke: for him 'tis well
That of thy death and business I can tell.

Glou. The king is mad: how stiff is my vile sense,
That I stand up, and have ingenious feeling
Of my huge sorrows! Better I were distract:
So should my thoughts be sever'd from my griefs,
And woes by wrong imaginations lose
The knowledge of themselves.

Edg. Give me your hand:
[*Drum afar off.*
Far off, methinks, I hear the beaten drum:
Come, father, I'll bestow you with a friend. [*exeunt.*

SCENE VII. A TENT IN THE FRENCH CAMP. LEAR ON A BED ASLEEP, SOFT MUSIC PLAYING: GENTLEMAN, AND OTHERS ATTENDING.

Enter **Cordelia, Kent,** *and* **Doctor.**

Cor. O thou good Kent, how shall I live and work,
To match thy goodness? My life will be too short,
And every measure fail me.

Kent. To be acknowledged, madam, is o'er-paid.

All my reports go with the modest truth;
Nor more nor clipp'd, but so.
Cor. Be better suited:
These weeds are memories of those worser hours:
I prithee, put them off.
Kent. Pardon me, dear madam;
Yet to be known shortens my made intent:
My boon I make it, that you know me not
Till time and I think meet.
Cor. Then be 't so, my good lord. [*to the* **Doctor.**] How does the king?
Doct. Madam, sleeps still.
Cor. O you kind gods,
Cure this great breach in his abused nature!
The untuned and jarring senses, O, wind up
Of this child-changed father!
Doct. So please your majesty
That we may wake the king: he hath slept long.
Cor. Be govern'd by your knowledge, and proceed
I' the sway of your own will. Is he array'd?
Gent. Ay, madam; in the heaviness of his sleep
We put fresh garments on him.
Doct. Be by, good madam, when we do awake him;
I doubt not of his temperance.
Cor. Very well.
Doct. Please you, draw near. Louder the music there!
Cor. O my dear father! Restoration hang
Thy medicine on my lips; and let this kiss
Repair those violent harms that my two sisters
Have in thy reverence made!
Kent. Kind and dear princess!
Cor. Had you not been their father, these white flakes
Had challenged pity of them. Was this a face
To be opposed against the warring winds?
To stand against the deep dread-bolted thunder?
In the most terrible and nimble stroke
Of quick, cross lightning? to watch—poor perdu!—
With this thin helm? Mine enemy's dog,
Though he had bit me, should have stood that night
Against my fire; and wast thou fain, poor father,

To hovel thee with swine, and rogues forlorn,
In short and musty straw? Alack, alack!
'Tis wonder that thy life and wits at once
Had not concluded all. He wakes; speak to him.
Doct. Madam, do you; 'tis fittest.
Cor. How does my royal lord? How fares your majesty?
Lear. You do me wrong to take me out o' the grave:
Thou art a soul in bliss; but I am bound
Upon a wheel of fire, that mine own tears
Do scald like molten lead.
Cor. Sir, do you know me?
Lear. You are a spirit, I know: when did you die?
Cor. Still, still, far wide!
Doct. He's scarce awake: let him alone awhile.
Lear. Where have I been? Where am I? Fair daylight?
I am mightily abused. I should e'en die with pity,
To see another thus. I know not what to say.
I will not swear these are my hands: let's see;
I feel this pin prick. Would I were assured
Of my condition!
Cor. O, look upon me, sir,
And hold your hands in benediction o'er me:
No, sir, you must not kneel.
Lear. Pray, do not mock me:
I am a very foolish fond old man,
Fourscore and upward, not an hour more nor less;
And, to deal plainly,
I fear I am not in my perfect mind.
Methinks I should know you, and know this man;
Yet I am doubtful: for I am mainly ignorant
What place this is; and all the skill I have
Remembers not these garments; nor I know not
Where I did lodge last night. Do not laugh at me;
For, as I am a man, I think this lady
To be my child Cordelia.
Cor. And so I am, I am.
Lear. Be your tears wet? yes, 'faith. I pray, weep not:
If you have poison for me, I will drink it.

I know you do not love me; for your sisters
Have, as I do remember, done me wrong:
You have some cause, they have not.
Cor. No cause, no cause.
Lear. Am I in France?
Kent. In your own kingdom, sir.
Lear. Do not abuse me.
Doct. Be comforted, good madam: the great rage,
You see, is kill'd in him: and yet it is danger
To make him even o'er the time he has lost.
Desire him to go in; trouble him no more
Till further settling.
Cor. Will 't please your highness walk?
Lear. You must bear with me:
Pray you now, forget and forgive: I am old and foolish.
[*Exeunt all but* **Kent** *and* **Gentleman.**

Gent. Holds it true, sir, that the Duke of Cornwall was so slain?
Kent. Most certain, sir.
Gent. Who is conductor of his people?
Kent. As 'tis said, the bastard son of Gloucester.
Gent. They say Edgar, his banished son, is with the Earl of Kent in Germany.
Kent. Report is changeable. 'Tis time to look about; the powers of the kingdom approach apace.
Gent. The arbitrement is like to be bloody.
Fare you well, sir. [*exit.*
Kent. My point and period will be throughly wrought,
Or well or ill, as this day's battle's fought. [*exit.*

ACT V.

SCENE I. THE BRITISH CAMP, NEAR DOVER.

Enter, with drum and colours, **Edmund, Regan, Gentlemen,** *and* **Soldiers.**

Edm. Know of the duke if his last purpose hold,
Or whether since he is advised by aught

To change the course: he's full of alteration
And self-reproving: bring his constant pleasure.
[*to a* **Gentleman,** *who goes out.*
Reg. Our sister's man is certainly miscarried.
Edm. 'Tis to be doubted, madam.
Reg. Now, sweet lord,
You know the goodness I intend upon you:
Tell me—but truly—but then speak the truth,
Do you not love my sister?
Edm. In honour'd love.
Reg. But have you never found my brother's way
To the forfended place?
Edm. That thought abuses you.
Reg. I am doubtful that you have been conjunct
And bosom'd with her, as far as we call hers.
Edm. No, by mine honour, madam.
Reg. I never shall endure her: dear my lord,
Be not familiar with her.
Edm. Fear me not:
She and the duke her husband!

Enter, with drum and colours, **Albany, Gonerill,** *and* **Soldiers.**

Gon. [*aside.*] I had rather lose the battle than that sister
Should loosen him and me.
Alb. Our very loving sister, well be-met.
Sir, this I hear; the king is come to his daughter,
With others whom the rigour of our state
Forced to cry out. Where I could not be honest,
I never yet was valiant: for this business,
It toucheth us, as France invades our land,
Not bolds the king, with others, whom, I fear,
Most just and heavy causes make oppose.
Edm. Sir, you speak nobly.
Reg. Why is this reason'd?
Gon. Combine together 'gainst the enemy;
For these domestic and particular broils
Are not the question here.
Alb. Let's then determine
With the ancient of war on our proceedings.

Edm. I shall attend you presently at your tent.
Reg. Sister, you'll go with us?
Gon. No.
Reg. 'Tis most convenient; pray you, go with us.
Gon. [*aside.*] O, ho, I know the riddle.—I will go.

As they are going out, enter **Edgar** *disguised.*

Edg. If e'er your grace had speech with man so poor,
Hear me one word.
Alb. I'll overtake you. Speak.
[*Exeunt all but* **Albany** *and* **Edgar.**
Edg. Before you fight the battle, ope this letter.
If you have victory, let the trumpet sound
For him that brought it: wretched though I seem,
I can produce a champion that will prove
What is avouched there. If you miscarry,
Your business of the world hath so an end,
And machination ceases. Fortune love you!
Alb. Stay till I have read the letter.
Edg. I was forbid it.
When time shall serve, let but the herald cry,
And I'll appear again.
Alb. Why, fare thee well: I will o'erlook thy paper.
[*Exit* **Edgar.**

Re-enter **Edmund.**

Edm. The enemy's in view; draw up your powers.
Here is the guess of their true strength and forces
By diligent discovery; but your haste
Is now urged on you.
Alb. We will greet the time. [*exit.*
Edm. To both these sisters have I sworn my love;
Each jealous of the other, as the stung
Are of the adder. Which of them shall I take?
Both? one? or neither? Neither can be enjoy'd,
If both remain alive: to take the widow
Exasperates, makes mad her sister Goneril;
And hardly shall I carry out my side,
Her husband being alive. Now then we'll use
His countenance for the battle; which being done,
Let her who would be rid of him devise

His speedy taking off. As for the mercy
Which he intends to Lear and to Cordelia,
The battle done, and they within our power,
Shall never see his pardon; for my state
Stands on me to defend, not to debate. [*exit.*

SCENE II. A FIELD BETWEEN THE TWO CAMPS.

Alarum within. Enter, with drum and colours, **Lear, Cordelia,** *and* **Soldiers,** *over the stage; and exeunt.*

Enter **Edgar** *and* **Gloucester.**

Edg. Here, father, take the shadow of this tree
For your good host; pray that the right may thrive:
If ever I return to you again,
I'll bring you comfort.
Glou. Grace go with you, sir!
[*Exit* **Edgar.**

Alarum and retreat within. Re-enter **Edgar.**

Edg. Away, old man; give me thy hand; away!
King Lear hath lost, he and his daughter ta'en:
Give me thy hand; come on.
Glou. No farther, sir; a man may rot even here.
Edg. What, in ill thoughts again? Men must endure
Their going hence, even as their coming hither:
Ripeness is all: come on.
Glou. And that's true too. [*exeunt.*

SCENE III. THE BRITISH CAMP NEAR DOVER.

Enter, in conquest, with drum and colours, **Edmund: Lear** *and* **Cordelia,** *prisoners;* **Captain, Soldiers,** *etc.*

Edm. Some officers take them away: good guard,
Until their greater pleasures first be known
That are to censure them.
Cor. We are not the first

Who, with best meaning, have incurr'd the worst.
For thee, oppressed king, am I cast down;
Myself could else out-frown false fortune's frown.
Shall we not see these daughters and these sisters?
Lear. No, no, no, no! Come, let's away to prison:
We two alone will sing like birds i' the cage:
When thou dost ask me blessing, I'll kneel down,
And ask of thee forgiveness: so we'll live,
And pray, and sing, and tell old tales, and laugh
At gilded butterflies, and hear poor rogues
Talk of court news; and we'll talk with them too,
Who loses and who wins; who's in, who's out;
And take upon's the mystery of things,
As if we were God's spies: and we'll wear out,
In a wall'd prison, packs and sects of great ones,
That ebb and flow by the moon.
Edm. Take them away.
Lear. Upon such sacrifices, my Cordelia,
The gods themselves throw incense. Have I caught thee?
He that parts us shall bring a brand from heaven,
And fire us hence like foxes. Wipe thine eyes;
The good-years shall devour them, flesh and fell,
Ere they shall make us weep: we'll see 'em starve first.
Come. [*Exeunt* **Lear** *and* **Cordelia**, *guarded.*
Edm. Come hither, captain; hark.
Take thou this note [*giving a paper*]; go follow them to prison:
One step I have advanced thee; if thou dost
As this instructs thee, thou dost make thy way
To noble fortunes: know thou this, that men
Are as the time is: to be tender-minded
Does not become a sword: thy great employment
Will not bear question; either say thou 'lt do 't,
Or thrive by other means.
Capt. I'll do 't, my lord.
Edm. About it; and write happy when thou hast done.
Mark, I say, instantly; and carry it so
As I have set it down.
Capt. I cannot draw a cart, nor eat dried oats;
If it be man's work, I'll do 't. [*exit.*

Flourish. *Enter* **Albany, Goneril, Regan,** *another* **Captain,** *and* **Soldiers.**

Alb. Sir, you have shown to-day your valiant strain,
And fortune led you well: you have the captives
That were the opposites of this day's strife:
We do require them of you, so to use them
As we shall find their merits and our safety
May equally determine.
Edm. Sir, I thought it fit
To send the old and miserable king
To some retention and appointed guard;
Whose age has charms in it, whose title more,
To pluck the common bosom on his side,
And turn our impress'd lances in our eyes
Which do command them. With him I sent the queen;
My reason all the same; and they are ready
To-morrow, or at further space, to appear
Where you shall hold your session. At this time
We sweat and bleed: the friend hath lost his friend;
And the best quarrels, in the heat, are cursed
By those that feel their sharpness:
The question of Cordelia and her father
Requires a fitter place.
Alb. Sir, by your patience,
I hold you but a subject of this war,
Not as a brother.
Reg. That's as we list to grace him.
Methinks our pleasure might have been demanded,
Ere you had spoke so far. He led our powers;
Bore the commission of my place and person;
The which immediacy may well stand up,
And call itself your brother.
Gon. Not so hot:
In his own grace he doth exalt himself,
More than in your addition.
Reg. In my rights,
By me invested, he compeers the best.
Gon. That were the most, if he should husband you.
Reg. Jesters do oft prove prophets.

Gon. Holla, holla!
That eye that told you so look'd but a-squint.
Reg. Lady, I am not well; else I should answer
From a full-flowing stomach. General,
Take thou my soldiers, prisoners, patrimony;
Dispose of them, of me; the walls are thine:
Witness the world, that I create thee here
My lord and master.
Gon. Mean you to enjoy him?
Alb. The let-alone lies not in your good will.
Edm. Nor in thine, lord.
Alb. Half-blooded fellow, yes.
Reg. [*to* ***Edmund.***] Let the drum strike, and prove my title thine.
Alb. Stay yet; hear reason. Edmund, I arrest thee
On capital treason; and, in thine attaint,
This gilded serpent [*pointing to* ***Gon.***]. For your claim, fair sister,
I bar it in the interest of my wife;
'Tis she is sub-contracted to this lord,
And I, her husband, contradict your bans.
If you will marry, make your loves to me,
My lady is bespoke.
Gon. An interlude!
Alb. Thou art arm'd, Gloucester: let the trumpet sound:
If none appear to prove upon thy head
Thy heinous, manifest, and many treasons,
There is my pledge [*throwing down a glove*]; I'll prove it on thy heart,
Ere I taste bread, thou art in nothing less
Than I have here proclaim'd thee.
Reg. Sick, O, sick!
Gon. [*aside.*] If not, I'll ne'er trust medicine.
Edm. There's my exchange [*throwing down a glove*]: what in the world he is
That names me traitor, villain-like he lies:
Call by thy trumpet: he that dares approach,
On him, on you, who not? I will maintain
My truth and honour firmly.
Alb. A herald, ho!

Edm. A herald, ho, a herald!
Alb. Trust to thy single virtue; for thy soldiers,
All levied in my name, have in my name
Took their discharge.
Reg. My sickness grows upon me.
Alb. She is not well; convey her to my tent.
[*Exit* **Regan,** *led.*

Enter a **Herald.**

Come hither, herald,—Let the trumpet sound,—
And read out this.
Capt. Sound, trumpet! [*A trumpet sounds.*
Her. [*reads.*] 'If any man of quality or degree within the lists of the army will maintain upon Edmund, supposed Earl of Gloucester, that he is a manifold traitor, let him appear by the third sound of the trumpet: he is bold in his defence.'
Edm. Sound! [*First trumpet.*
Her. Again! [*Second trumpet.*
Her. Again! [*Third trumpet.*
[*Trumpet answers within.*

Enter **Edgar,** *at the third sound, armed, with a trumpet before him.*

Alb. Ask him his purposes, why he appears
Upon this call o' the trumpet.
Her. What are you?
Your name, your quality? and why you answer
This present summons?
Edg. Know, my name is lost;
By treason's tooth bare-gnawn and canker-bit:
Yet am I noble as the adversary
I come to cope.
Alb. Which is that adversary?
Edg. What's he that speaks for Edmund Earl of Gloucester?
Edm. Himself: what say'st thou to him?
Edg. Draw thy sword,
That, if my speech offend a noble heart,
Thy arm may do thee justice: here is mine.
Behold, it is the privilege of mine honours,
My oath, and my profession: I protest,
Maugre thy strength, youth, place, and eminence,

Despite thy victor sword and fire-new fortune,
Thy valour and thy heart, thou art a traitor;
False to thy gods, thy brother, and thy father;
Conspirant 'gainst this high-illustrious prince;
And, from the extremest upward of thy head
To the descent and dust below thy foot,
A most toad-spotted traitor. Say thou 'No,'
This sword, this arm, and my best spirits, are bent
To prove upon thy heart, whereto I speak,
Thou liest.

Edm. In wisdom I should ask thy name;
But, since thy outside looks so fair and warlike,
And that thy tongue some say of breeding breathes,
What safe and nicely I might well delay
By rule of knighthood, I disdain and spurn:
Back do I toss these treasons to thy head;
With the hell-hated lie o'erwhelm thy heart;
Which, for they yet glance by and scarcely bruise,
This sword of mine shall give them instant way,
Where they shall rest for ever. Trumpets, speak!

[*Alarums. They fight.* **Edmund** *falls.*

Alb. Save him, save him!

Gon. This is practice, Gloucester:
By the law of arms thou wast not bound to answer
An unknown opposite; thou art not vanquish'd,
But cozen'd and beguiled.

Alb. Shut your mouth, dame,
Or with this paper shall I stop it: Hold, sir;
Thou worse than any name, read thine own evil:
No tearing, lady; I perceive you know it.

[*gives the letter to* **Edmund.**

Gon. Say, if I do, the laws are mine, not thine:
Who can arraign me for't?

Alb. Most monstrous! oh!
Know'st thou this paper?

Gon. Ask me not what I know. [*exit.*

Alb. Go after her: she's desperate; govern her.

Edm. What you have charged me with, that have I done;
And more, much more; the time will bring it out:
'Tis past, and so am I. But what art thou

That hast this fortune on me? If thou'rt noble,
I do forgive thee.

Edg. Let's exchange charity.
I am no less in blood than thou art, Edmund;
If more, the more thou hast wrong'd me.
My name is Edgar, and thy father's son.
The gods are just, and of our pleasant vices
Make instruments to plague us:
The dark and vicious place where thee he got
Cost him his eyes.

Edm. Thou hast spoken right, 'tis true;
The wheel is come full circle; I am here.

Alb. Methought thy very gait did prophesy
A royal nobleness: I must embrace thee:
Let sorrow split my heart, if ever I
Did hate thee or thy father!

Edg. Worthy prince, I know't.

Alb. Where have you hid yourself?
How have you known the miseries of your father?

Edg. By nursing them, my lord. List a brief tale;
And when 'tis told, O, that my heart would burst!
The bloody proclamation to escape,
That follow'd me so near,—O, our lives' sweetness!
That we the pain of death would hourly die
Rather than die at once!—taught me to shift
Into a madman's rags; to assume a semblance
That very dogs disdain'd: and in this habit
Met I my father with his bleeding rings,
Their precious stones new lost; became his guide,
Led him, begg'd for him, saved him from despair;
Never,—O fault!—reveal'd myself unto him,
Until some half-hour past, when I was arm'd:
Not sure, though hoping, of this good success,
I ask'd his blessing, and from first to last
Told him my pilgrimage: but his flaw'd heart,
Alack, too weak the conflict to support!
'Twixt two extremes of passion, joy and grief,
Burst smilingly.

Edm. This speech of yours hath moved me,
And shall perchance do good: but speak you on;

You look as you had something more to say.
Alb. If there be more, more woeful, hold it in;
For I am almost ready to dissolve,
Hearing of this.
Edg. This would have seem'd a period
To such as love not sorrow; but another,
To amplify too much, would make much more,
And top extremity.
Whilst I was big in clamour came there in a man,
Who, having seen me in my worst estate,
Shunn'd my abhorr'd society; but then, finding
Who 'twas that so endured, with his strong arms
He fasten'd on my neck, and bellow'd out
As he 'ld burst heaven; threw him on my father;
Told the most piteous tale of Lear and him
That ever ear received: which in recounting
His grief grew puissant, and the strings of life
Began to crack: twice then the trumpets sounded,
And there I left him tranced.
Alb. But who was this?
Edg. Kent, sir, the banish'd Kent; who in disguise
Follow'd his enemy king, and did him service
Improper for a slave.

Enter a **Gentleman**, *with a bloody knife.*

Gent. Help, help, O, help!
Edg. What kind of help?
Alb. Speak, man.
Edg. What means that bloody knife?
Gent. 'Tis hot, it smokes;
It came even from the heart of—O, she's dead!
Alb. Who dead? speak, man.
Gent. Your lady, sir, your lady: and her sister
By her is poisoned; she hath confess'd it.
Edm. I was contracted to them both: all three
Now marry in an instant.
Edg. Here comes Kent.
Alb. Produce their bodies, be they alive or dead:
This judgement of the heavens, that makes us tremble,
Touches us not with pity. [*Exit* **Gentleman.**

Enter **Kent.**

O, is this he?
The time will not allow the compliment
Which very manners urges.
Kent. I am come
To bid my king and master aye good night:
Is he not here?
Alb. Great thing of us forgot!
Speak, Edmund, where's the king? and where's Cordelia?
See'st thou this object, Kent?
[*The bodies of* **Goneril** *and* **Regan** *are brought in.*
Kent. Alack, why thus?
Edm. Yet Edmund was beloved:
The one the other poison'd for my sake,
And after slew herself.
Alb. Even so. Cover their faces.
Edm. I pant for life: some good I mean to do,
Despite of mine own nature. Quickly send,
Be brief in it, to the castle; for my writ
Is on the life of Lear and on Cordelia:
Nay, send in time.
Alb. Run, run, O, run!
Edg. To who, my lord? Who hath the office? send
Thy token of reprieve.
Edm. Well thought on: take my sword,
Give it the captain.
Alb. Haste thee, for thy life. [*Exit* **Edgar.**
Edm. He hath commission from thy wife and me
To hang Cordelia in the prison, and
To lay the blame upon her own despair,
That she fordid herself.
Alb. The gods defend her! Bear him hence awhile.
[**Edmund** *is borne off.*

Re-enter **Lear,** *with* **Cordelia** *dead in his arms;* **Edgar, Captain,** *and others following.*

Lear. Howl, howl, howl, howl! O, you are men of stones:
Had I your tongues and eyes, I'ld use them so
That heaven's vault should crack. She's gone for ever!

I know when one is dead, and when one lives;
She's dead as earth. Lend me a looking-glass;
If that her breath will mist or stain the stone,
Why, then she lives.
Kent. Is this the promised end?
Edg. Or image of that horror?
Alb. Fall, and cease!
Lear. This feather stirs; she lives! if it be so,
It is a chance which does redeem all sorrows
That ever I have felt.
Kent. [*kneeling.*] O my good master!
Lear. Prithee, away.
Edg. 'Tis noble Kent, your friend.
Lear. A plague upon you, murderers, traitors all!
I might have saved her; now she's gone for ever!
Cordelia, Cordelia! stay a little. Ha!
What is't thou say'st? Her voice was ever soft,
Gentle, and low, an excellent thing in woman.
I kill'd the slave that was a-hanging thee.
Capt. 'Tis true, my lords, he did.
Lear. Did I not, fellow?
I have seen the day, with my good biting falchion
I would have made them skip: I am old now,
And these same crosses spoil me. Who are you?
Mine eyes are not o' the best: I'll tell you straight.
Kent. If fortune brag of two she loved and hated,
One of them we behold.
Lear. This is a dull sight. Are you not Kent?
Kent. The same,
Your servant Kent. Where is your servant Caius?
Lear. He's a good fellow, I can tell you that;
He'll strike, and quickly too: he's dead and rotten.
Kent. No, my good lord; I am the very man,—
Lear. I'll see that straight.
Kent. That, from your first of difference and decay,
Have follow'd your sad steps.
Lear. You are welcome hither.
Kent. Nor no man else: all's cheerless, dark, and deadly.
Your eldest daughters have fordone themselves,
And desperately are dead.

Lear. Ay, so I think.
Alb. He knows not what he says: and vain it is
That we present us to him.
Edg. Very bootless.

Enter a **Captain.**

Capt. Edmund is dead, my lord.
Alb. That's but a trifle here.
You lords and noble friends, know our intent.
What comfort to this great decay may come
Shall be applied: for us, we will resign,
During the life of this old majesty,
To him our absolute power: [*to* ***Edgar*** *and* ***Kent.***] you, to your rights;
With boot, and such addition as your honours
Have more than merited. All friends shall taste
The wages of their virtue, and all foes
The cup of their deservings. O, see, see!
Lear. And my poor fool is hang'd! No, no, no life!
Why should a dog, a horse, a rat, have life,
And thou no breath at all? Thou'lt come no more,
Never, never, never, never, never!
Pray you, undo this button: thank you, sir.
Do you see this? Look on her, look, her lips,
Look there, look there! [*dies.*
Edg. He faints! My lord, my lord!
Kent. Break, heart; I prithee, break!
Edg. Look up, my lord.
Kent. Vex not his ghost: O, let him pass! he hates him much
That would upon the rack of this tough world
Stretch him out longer.
Edg. He is gone, indeed.
Kent. The wonder is, he hath endured so long:
He but usurp'd his life.
Alb. Bear them from hence. Our present business
Is general woe. [*to* ***Kent*** *and* ***Edgar.***] Friends of my soul, you twain
Rule in this realm, and the gored state sustain.

Kent. I have a journey, sir, shortly to go;
My master calls me, I must not say no.
Alb. The weight of this sad time we must obey;
Speak what we feel, not what we ought to say.
The oldest hath borne most: we that are young
Shall never see so much, nor live so long.
[*exeunt, with a dead march.*

ANALYSIS OF SHAKESPEARE'S KING LEAR

Language and Style

Act I provides an excellent example of the slight differences of language that can occur in Shakespeare and that can help our understanding.

Consider, for example, the daughters' answer to Lear's question "which of you, shall we say, doth love us most?" The dividing of the kingdom seems to depend on the answers to this question and yet the opening lines imply that Goneril's and Regan's shares have been decided. Let us assume this question is mere formal ceremony. Is there evidence to follow this through?

Observe lines 1-33. They are in prose. This is the idle chatter of men at court and sets the contrasting scene of what is to come. It is easy to observe Kent, Gloucester, and Edmund quite relaxed and then very reserved as the king enters, but to read this necessitates imagination. What is there in Lear's first main speech to suggest formality? For one thing, the "we" in 'know, that we have divided' implies total agreement with the act. The sentences are very balanced as 'our son of Cornwall,/and you, Gurnoless loving son of Albany'. Finally, Lear begins with the agenda, division of the kingdom, dowries of the daughters, husband for Cordelia.

Goneril answers quickly and Lear in turn quickly accepts her answer as if it had been expected. Regan follows suit. When it comes to Cordelia we can feel his bias but his tone is still extremely formal and flowering, "The vines of France, and milk of Burgundy." We know he expects more of the same from Cordelia but different in the sense that it will be more loving. He is very disappointed. After these previous stately lines, we only hear:

Cordelia: Nothing, my lord.
Lear: Nothing?
Cordelia: Nothing.

Our formality disappears again. Previously one stately speech after another had followed. Now, however, there is questioning. But once again Lear suppresses his fury by once again returning to formality. He is disappointed in Cordelia and becoming intolerant of Kent but remains "formal" (prim and proper). One would expect Lear's wrath to take over the situation but it doesn't. Why? Perhaps this is to show that Act I, 1 is like no other part of the play. It is used to set the stage for all that is to come. The language of formality makes the distinction of this part of the play being unlike any other.

Shakespeare wrote in blank verse probably quite naturally but why the prose-verse alternations? It is not sound to say that the "higher moments" of a play are reserved for verse and "lows" or "asides" for prose. Goneril and Regan display their pulsomeness in poetry and their shrewdness in prose. They are found using both. Madness is usually given in prose but then again prose is also used to exhibit person's rationality. Maybe there isn't a difference between the two. I think it is safe to say that alternating the tempo (prose-verse) enables us to sense (consciously or unconsciously)

Tone and Meaning

Are there any other ways the play can communicate through its language? Reread Act II .4. ("Vengeance! plague! death! confusion. . . till it cry--SLEEP TO DEATH".) The passage in itself is very dramatic. It is very obvious to us what emotions (physical and emotional) Lear is going through and we don't need asides to explain them to us. Lear's fury and incoherence at Gloucester's 'well, my good Lord, I have informed them so' and his twice repeated 'Gloucester' significantly illustrate Lear's furious impatience. Gloucester, on the other hand, doesn't comprehend the urgency of the situation and in no way intends to be offensive. How do the lines

> 'The king would speak with Cornwall; the dear father
> Would with his daughter speak, commands her service:
> Are they informed of this?--My breath and my blood!--'

illustrate this situation and the urgency Lear is experiencing? When Lear continues his

> 'Are they inform'd of this?--My breath and my blood!--
> Fiery? the fiery duke?--Tell the duke, that--'

he stops. How does the choice of language help us to understand this?

Now turn to Lear's last speech in Act II.4: 'O, reason not the need. . . O' fool, I shall go mad!' This section is a little deeper but surely just as realistic. Like the previous passage we can "get" what is happening. Lear jumps on Regan's 'what need one!' Just as he had jumped on Gloucester's words. Lear tries to remain constant but is so confused that he breaks down into incoherence and vagueness. When he says 'O, fool!' it is perhaps as much about himself as to the actual fool. With his 'I shall go mad!' he feels madness is upon him. The speech was a coherent emotional experience rather than a rational one. Lear didn't explain his "method" or his plan of attack but his emotional experiences developed the mood.

A final example of use of language will be Lear's speech in Act V.3, 'no, no, no, no! . . . that ebb and flow by the moon.' The speech is very beautiful. But why now? A battle has just been lost. The sentences are almost chill-like and the images contain an innocence: 'We two alone will sing like birds in the cage' and'. . . and laugh at gilded butterflies.' An air of incredible purity has been created. Why? The exerpt started out with birds in a cage and ended with the quiet of the moon. These are also the same cliffs where Cordelia is to be hanged and yet to Lear it lends to his peaceful hermit-type existence. Has Lear's vision of the world been transformed?

Perhaps some of these ideas were obvious, perhaps they weren't. It is not absolutely necessary to understand every work in Shakespeare but there are certainly some very key ones. Some words from Shakespeare have retained their essential meaning whereas others need expert interpretation ('abused' in Act IV.3 does not mean to us what it meant to Shakespeare.) Some people underestimate Shakespeare's foresight just as there are those who start their first Shakespeare with the anticipation of un-present difficulties thereby doubling their problems. I still find excitement in a word from Shakespeare meaning the same today as it did over three centuries ago.

Themes

There are three basic ideas that recur throughout Lear. They are NOTHING, NATURE, and BLINDNESS. The question to consider here will be of what importance can Lear be aside from its plot? This meaning is not something of which we are always aware of. By pulling these three ideas apart we are separating something that was meant to exist as a whole. Let us remember this and see if we can add rather than detract from Shakespeare's command of imagination and intellect.

Nothing:

In Act I.4., what is your reaction to Lear's answer to the fool's 'Can you make no use of nothing, Nuncle?' This is in response to all that Lear has given away and should bring back to mind Act I.1:

Cordelia: Nothing, my lord.
Lear: Nothing?
Cordelia: Nothing.
Lear: Nothing can come of nothing: speak again.

Reread Act I.1. How does Shakespeare make sure that we don't forget them? For one thing, in twelve words the word "nothing" recurs twelve times. We are very eager to hear Cordelia's response, especially after her asides, and the word "nothing" is the very word that estranges her from Lear. The word has become omen-like and we can't help but feel that it is telling us something about the world of Lear.

In Act I.2, the beginning of the Gloucester, the word "nothing" is once again emphasized. Reread the dialogue between Edmund and Gloucester. How would you relate the usage of the word "nothing" to the first scene? What differences are there in tone?

By the end of the first act what does the word "nothing" mean? A word in different contexts takes on different meanings. There was even some humor in Act I 'If it be nothing, I shall not need spectacles'. We must ask ourselves not only about the word but the concepts it may be trying to convey. We fully realize Cordelia's love is not "nothing". We also hear Lear say 'nothing will come of nothing' but we know the second "nothing" is something. What about the first? Answers should be obvious. Another example is Lear tries to make Cordelia "nothing" but what has he actually given to Goneril and Regan? What does Cordelia's "nothing" become for Lear at the end of the play? In Act II.3 what have Goneril and Regan, to whom all was given, got? In Act IV. 2 how does Albany describe his wife's value?

"Nothing" is an absolute word. It is presenting a world of moral extremes. Apparently Shakespeare feels Lear and Gloucester both use it too haphazardly not realizing its consequences.

Nature:

Nature is used by Shakespeare and his contemporaries as much as the romantics were to use it in two centuries to come. Some people feel that Shakespeare may have tried to do too much with nature and incapably so. If you agree, whatsoever, on Shakespeare's handling of "nothing" you should readily accept his abilities of deliberation and control that even his simplest of expressions will have an effect on the total impact of the play.

One of the major problems is the dichotomy of meaning that the word "nature" implies: 1) the order and essence of all entities composing the physical universe and 2) the physical world, including living things, natural phenomena, etc.

In Act I.2 Edmund's opening speech should not be overlooked. Reread the scene and try to decide what Gloucester means by natural. You should have been affected by:

'Thou, nature, art my goddess. . .'
'Who in the lusty stealth of nature take. . .'
'Unnatural, detested, brutish villain!'
'. . . The king falls from the bias of nature. . .'
'Unnaturalness between the child and the parent'

To Gloucester it is as much nature for a son to obey his father as a tree shedding its leaves in August, or for a father not to cast off his most beloved daughter. Edmund uses this same in deceiving his brother. Gloucester nature is the whole of creation and the laws which govern it. The deviation is that things which do not follow laws (they are unnatural) do exist in nature. Elizabethans felt that man could react against nature but to do so was to invite destruction. Gloucester does this when he proclaims the illegitimate Edmund heir over Edgar.

Edmund reacts to nature also. By his claims, he is not saying the illegitimate are equal, but that they are superior. Therefore, we see his priority in his animal nature. The only law that governs his actions is that which is to his best interests. Edmund cares not for laws or theories. They have no attraction or meaning for him. He lives by the only thing which has meaning for him--his own nature.

Seeing and Blindness:

I find this theme the most recurrent. Whether it comes across as evidently as Gloucester's loss of his physical blindness or Lear's not "seeing" his face because his nose was in the way to the blindness Gloucester experiences in not "seeing" Edgar and Lear's not realizing Cordelia's true love, the images are extremely consistent. Without reading further, if you were asked to give an approximate number of the "sight" or "blindness" images recurring in Lear, how many would you say? Ten? Twenty? Fifty? Try these on for size!

Act I.1

'Meantime, we shall express our darker purpose.'
'Dearer than eyesight.'
'Hence, and avoid my sight!'
'Out of my sight!'
'See better, Lear; and let me still remain/The true blank of thine eye.'
'A still-soliciting eye'
'Nor shall ever see/That face of hers again'

Act I.2

'Let's see: come, if it be nothing, I shall not need spectacles.'
'For so much as I have perns'd, I find it not fit for your o'er looking.'
'Let's see. Let's see.'

Act I.4

'Do you bandy looks with me, you rascal?'
'So out went the candle, and we were left darkling.'
'Does Lear walk thus? Speak thus? Where are his eyes?'
'Darkness and devils!'
'Old fond eyes,/. . . I'll pluck ye out,'
'How far your eyes may pierce I cannot tell'

Act I.5

'Why, to keep one's eyes of either side's nose,
'That what a man cannot smell out, he may spy into.'

Act II.1

'Light, ho! here. . . torches! torches!'
'Here stood he in the dark'
'Thus out of season, threading dark ey'd night'

Act II.2

'Glass-gazing'
'For though it be night, yet the moonshines'
'Nothing almost sees miracles, but misery'
'Take vantage, heavy eyes, not to behold/This shameful lodging.'

Act II.4

'Fathers that wear rags/Do make their children blind'
'All that follow their noses are led by their eyes but blind men'
'Good sir, no more; these are unsightly tricks'
'She hath. . . look'd black upon me'
'You nimble lightnings, dart your blinding flames into her scornful eyes!'
'Her eyes are fierce, but thine/Do comfort and not burn.'
'Outivarlet, from my sight!'
'Art not ashamed to look upon this beard?'
'You see me here, you Gods, a poor old man'

Act III.1

'The impetuous blasts, with eyeless rage'

Act III.2

'Then comes the time, who lives to see 't/That going shall be us'd with feet.'

Act III.4

'Look! here comes a walking fire.'
'. . . squinies the eye. . .'

Act III.6

'Look where he stands and glares! Want'st thou eyes at trial, madam?'
'I'll see their trial first.'
'When we our betters see bearing our woes. . .'

Act IV.1

'You cannot see your way.'
'I have no way, and therefore want no eyes; I stumbled when I saw.'
'Might I but live to see thee in my touch, I'd say I had eyes again.'
'Bless my sweet eyes, they bleed.'
'There is a cliff, whose high and bending head/Looks fearfully in the confined deep.'

Act IV.2

'See thyself, devil!'
'O! My good Lord, the Duke of Cornwall's dead;/Slain by his servant, Going to put out/The other eye of Gloucester.'
'Where was his son when they did take his eyes?'
'Gloucester, I live/To thank thee for the love thou show'dst the king,/And to revenge thine eyes.'

Act IV.3

'There she shook/The holy water from her heavenly eyes. . .'
'. . . and by no means/Will yield to see his daughter.'

Act IV.4

'. . . bring him to our eye.'
'Soon may I see and hear him!'

Act IV.5

'It was great ignorance, Gloucester's eyes being out,/To let him live; where he arrives he moves/All hearts against us.'

Act IV.6

'This world I do renounce, and in your sights/Shake patiently my great affliction off . . .'
'Look up a-height. . . do but look up.'
'A lack! I have no eyes.'
'O thou side-piercing sight!'
'Look, look! A mouse.'
'Behold yond simp'ring dame. . .'
'Were all thy letters suns, I could not see.'
'What! with the case of eyes?'
'I see it feelingly.'
'There thou might'st behold/The great image of Authority'
'That eyeless head of thine was first fram'd flesh/To raise my fortunes.'

Act IV.7

'Fair daylight?'
'O! Look upon me, Sir.'

Act V.3

'Wipe thine eyes;'
'That eye that told you so look'd but a squint.'
'The dark and vicious place where thee he got/Cost him his eyes.'
'This is a dull sight.'
'O! see, see!'
'Do you see this? Look on her, look, her lips,/Look there, look there!'
'Look up, my Lord.'
'. . . we that are young/Shall never see so much, nor live so long.'

AND THERE ARE MORE! It is hard to overlook the images of sight but their (they are) omnipresence can only be felt by looking at their frequency out of context. Find some more.

Madness:

Some critics feel that the element of madness prevailing in Lear is Shakespeare's way of commenting on a prevalent madness in the society of his day threatening to break it up. Whether it is the fool's professional madness, Edgar's feigned madness, or Lear's "mad" madness, Shakespeare's treatment superceded the professional medicine of his day. Keeping this in mind, what special privilege does the insight of madness retain in this play?

Justice is the obsession of Lear's madness. He observes a world with sin, crime, despair and wanting. Justice is his way of regulating it. But the world does not conform to what he expects of it. All the disappointments and finally the storm (a non-conformity of nature) bring to him problems which he tries to solve with justice. He even has an imaginary trial for Goneril and Regan. Does the fact that the "mad" Lear is the one most preoccupied with justice have anything to say about the pursuit of justice in the supposedly sane world?

Is the imagining of justice madness? Reread Act III.2 'Let the great Gods, . . . More sinn'd against than sinning.', Act III.4 'Pr'y thee, go in thyself; . . . And show the heavens more just,' Act III.6, and Act IV.6. In all of these instances justice is prevalent but its recurrence in the mind of a madman (Lear) must be significant.

With the feigned madness of Edgar and the "professional" madness of the fool, the reader has more problems. We know why Lear is mad. But where and how did Edgar "learn" his madness? Before he became Poor Tom, we didn't see that much of him. Is his state brought about by what has transposed as in Lear's case? Edgar, at times, seems as mad as Lear. Perhaps his asides tell us again of society where to be mad is advantageous. One can learn much when no one wants to deal with him and simply ignores him. He seems to understand what is happening.

How about the fool? He is supposed to have been always mad. He spoke of the madness of Lear before it happened. Is this mad? In a world where Goneril and Regan succeed and are considered sane, is it not better perhaps to be mad? Is this justifying "a reason for madness"?

Once again is the play Lear commenting on a special vision to madness? Make a decision. Would the play have been as effective without it? Is this a commentary on the life of the times during which it was written?

Two Plots

There are many similarities between the plots of Lear and Gloucester. Make a summary of the similarities between them. Most are obvious. Lear and Gloucester are both deceived by evil children and both undergo suffering. They are both rescued for whatever's left by their good children. But as soon as we confront these similarities, we are faced with differences. Edmund directly betrays Edgar while Cordelia brings her problems on herself. Gloucester's pain is physical, Lear goes mad. Lear's mind suffers, Gloucester's body does. Is there any relation between their kind of pain and the causes of it? Lear lacks judgement. Is this why his affliction is mental? Gloucester lost his eyes supposedly because of the sin of adultery. But Lear also lacked in moral judgement. Act II.4 he says to Regan

'. . . if thou shouldst not be glad,
I would divorce me from thy mother's tomb,
Sepulchring an adult'ress.'

And Gloucester, of course, exercises poor judgement in his hasty reaction to Edgar.

There are other reciprical similarities. Can you justify them? How about both Lear and Gloucester suffer dreadfully. Why? Lear's children and Gloucester's children both react to natural instincts. Gloucester for the most part, is passive to his punishment. Why? What about Lear?

Summary

Who but Shakespeare can satisfyingly explain the reasons behind something like Lear. He is the creator, the story teller. The form he uses is drama. He has left us something to follow. He has told us something. But what is this something? It would be all too easy for Shakespeare to explicitly tell us what he tried to do. He didn't and therefore, we will never really know. We must proceed accordingly and assume that his creations are "reflections of the life of the times during which they were written." We see both good and evil. We see life as it really is. We see the comic, the tragic, and the chronicles. We can be sure that in some way the genre reflects some aspect of his life, his society, his mind and he thereby is giving us something to think by, to live by, something to follow to direct our lives and avoid the pitfalls of Lear, Edmund, Gloucester, Cordelia, and the rest. Your "message" may not be the same as mine but you will get one. You should now be aware of the presence of something more than a storm, a family squabble or a physical pain. Look at all literature this way. There is quite often more than meets the eye and that more will usually be a reflection of the life of the times during which it was written.

The tragedy of Lear is deservedly celebrated among the dramas of Shakespeare. There is perhaps no play which keeps the attention so strongly fixed; which so much agitates our passions, and interests our curiosity. The artful involutions of distinct interests, the striking oppositions of contrary characters, the sudden changes of fortune, and the quick succession of events, fill the mind with a perpetual tumult of indignation, pity, and hope. There is no scene which does not contribute to the aggravation of the distress or conduct to the action, and scarce a line which does not conduce to the progress of the scene. So powerful is the current of the poet's imagination, that the mind, which once ventures within it, is hurried irresistibly along.

On the seeming improbability of Lear's conduct, it may be observed, that he is represented according to histories at that time vulgarly received as true. And, perhaps, if we turn our thoughts upon the barbarity and ignorance of the age to which this story is referred, it will appear not so unlikely as while we estimate Lear's manners by our own. Such preference of one daughter to another, or resignation of dominion on such conditions, would be yet credible, if told of a petty prince of Guinea or Madagascar. Shakespeare, indeed, by the mention of his earls and dukes, has given us the idea of times more civilized, and of life regulated by softer manners; and the truth is, that though he so nicely discriminates, and so minutely describes the characters of men, he commonly neglects and confounds the characters of ages, by mingling customs ancient and modern, English and foreign.

There are instances of cruelty which are too savage and shocking, and the intervention of Edmund destroys the simplicity of the story. These objections may be answered by repeating, that the cruelty of the daughters is an historical fact, to which the poet has added little, having only drawn it into a series by dialogue and action. We are not able to apologize with equal plausibility for the extrusion of Gloucester's eyes, which seems an act too horrid to be endured in dramatic exhibition, and such as much always compel the mind to relieve its distress by incredulity. Yet let it be remembered that our author well knew what would please the audience for which he wrote.

The injury done by Edmund to the simplicity of the action is abundantly recompensed by the addition of variety, by the art with which he is made to co-operate with the chief design, and the opportunity which, he gives the poet of combining perfidy with perfidy, and connecting the wicked son with the wicked daughters, to impress this important moral, that villany is never at a stop, that crimes lead to crimes, and at last terminate in ruin.

But though this moral be incidentally enforced, Shakespeare has suffered the virtue of Cordelia to perish in a just cause, contrary to the natural ideas of justice, to the hope of the reader, and what is yet more strange, to the faith of chronicles.

A play in which the wicked prosper, and the virtuous miscarry, may doubtless be good, because it is a just representation of the common events of human life: but since all reasonable beings naturally love justice, that the observation of justice makes a play worse; or that, if other excellencies are equal, the audience will not always rise better pleased from the final triumph of persecuted virtue. In the present case the public has decided. Cordelia, from the time of Tate, has always retired with victory and felicity.

SELECTED BIBLIOGRAPHY ON KING LEAR

Textual Studies

Duthie, G.I., Elizabethan Shorthand and the First Quarto of King Lear. Oxford: Oxford University Press, 1950.

Greg, W.W., The Variants in the First Quarto of "King Lear." London: Oxford University Press, 1940.

Honigmann, E.A.J., The Stability of Shakespeare's Text. Lincoln, Nebr.: University of Nebraska Press, 1965, pp. 121-128.

Kirschbaum, L., The True Text of "King Lear." Baltimore: Johns Hopkins Press, 1945.

VanDam, B.A.P., The Text of Shakespeare's Lear. Louvain: Uystpruyst, 1935.

Walker, A., Textual Problems of the First Folio. Cambridge: Cambridge University Press, 1953.

Sources

Henderson, W.G., "Montaigne's Apologie of Raymond Sebond and King Lear," Shakespeare Association Bulletin, XIV (1939), 209-225; XV (1940), 40-56.

Muir, K., Shakespeare's Sources. London: Methuen, 1957.

Perrett, W., The Story of King Lear. Berlin: Mayer & Muller, 1904.

Stage History

Brooke, C.F.T., "King Lear on the Stage," in Essays on Shakespeare and Other Elizabethans. New Haven: Yale University Press, 1948.

Copeau, Jacques, "King Lear at the Theatre Antoine," Educational Theatre Journal, XIX (1967), 376-381.

Mack, M., King Lear in Our Time. Berkeley: University of California Press, 1965.

Odell, G.C.D., Shakespeare from Betterton to Irving, 2 vols. New York: Columbia University Press, 1920.

Trewin, J.C., Shakespeare on the English Stage: 1900-1964. London: Barrie & Rocliffe, 1964.

Critical Studies

Brooke, N., "The Ending of King Lear," in E.A.Bloom, ed., Shakespeare 1564-1964. Providence, R.I.: Brown University Press, 1964.

Campbell, O.J., "The Salvation of Lear," ELH, (1948), 93-109.

Chambers, R.W., "King Lear." Glasgow University Publications LIX (1940), 20-52.

Empson, W., "Fool in Lear," in The Structure of Complex Words. London: Chatto and Windus, 1951.

Fraser, R., Shakespeare's Poetics in Relation to "King Lear." London: Routledge & Kegan Paul, 1962.

Freud, S., "The Theme of the Three Caskets," in Collected Papers, IV. London: Hogarth Press, 1950, pp. 244-256.

Frye, N., Fools of Time: Studies in Shakespearian Tragedy. Toronto: University of Toronto Press, 1967.

Greg, W.W., "Time, Place and Politics in King Lear," Modern Language Review, XXXV (1940), 431-446.

Heilman, R., "Twere Best Not Know Myself: Othello, Lear, Macbeth," in Shakespeare 400. New York: Holt, Rinehart & Winston, 1964.

James, D.G., The Dream of Learning: An Essay on "The Advancement of Learning," "Hamlet" and "King Lear" Oxford: Clarendon Press, 1951.

Jayne, S., "Charity in King Lear," in Shakespeare 400. New York: Holt, Rinehart & Winston, 1964.

Jorgensen, P., Lear's Self-Discovery. Berkeley and Los Angeles: University of California Press, 1966.
Keast, W.R., "Imagery and Meaning in the Interpretation of King Lear," Modern Philology, XLVII (1949), 45-64.
Kernan, A., "Formalism and Realism in Elizabethan Drama: the Miracles in King Lear," Renaissance Drama, 9 (1966), 59-66.
Knights, L.C., "King Lear as Metaphor," in B. Slote, Ed., Myth and Symbol. Lincoln, Nebr.: University of Nebraska Press, 1963.
Levin, H., "The Heights and the Depths," in J. Garrett, ed., More Talking of Shakespeare. London: Longmans, Green, 1959.
Lothian, J.M., "King Lear": A Tragic Rending of Life. Toronto: Clarke, Irwin & Co., 1949.
Maclean, N., "Episode, Scene, Speech and Word: The Madness of Lear," in R.S.Crane, ed., Critics and Criticism. Chicago: University of Chicago Press, 1952.
Markels, J., "Shakespeare's Confluence of Tragedy and Comedy," in Shakespeare 400. New York: Holt, Rinehart & Winston, 1964.
Muir, E., The Politics of "King Lear." Glasgow University Publication No. 72. Glasgow: Jackson, Son & Co., 1947.
Myrick, Kenneth, "Christian Pessimism in King Lear," in E.A.Bloom, ed., Shakespeare 1564-1964. Providence, R.I." Brown University Press, 1964.
Nowottny, W.M., "Lear's Questions," Shakespeare Survey, 10 (1957), 90-97.
Peck, R.A., "Edgar's Pilgrimage: High Comedy in King Lear," Studies in English Literature, 7 (1967), 219-237.
Ribner, I., "The Gods Are Just," Tulane Drama Review, II (1958), 34-54.
Sewall, R., "King Lear," in The Vision of Tragedy. New Haven: Yale University Press, 1959.
Sitwell, E., "King Lear," Atlantic Monthly, May, 1950, pp. 57-62.
Welsford, E., The Fool. London: Faber & Faber, 1935.
Williams, G.W., "The Poetry of the Storm in King Lear," Shakespeare Quarterly, II (1951), 57-71.

SOME TYPICAL AP QUESTIONS

The first one is accompanied by three possible answers by aspiring Advanced Placement students. Do you agree with what they have to say? Do you agree with their ratings? The suggested time for each is forty minutes.

Directions: Some novels or plays contain parallel or recurring events that prove to be additionally significant. Using a work of recommended literary merit discuss what significance the recurring events may have. Do not merely summarize the plot.

The following samples are all from King Lear.

Sample 1:

In Shakespeare's classic King Lear, we find that paralleling events are an essential part of the work. Shakespeare begins with two separate and distinct families, draws continuous similarities between them through the course of the play, then unites them in a manner which brings the play's theme to light.

The syllabus of the play's action and theme revolves around the two families previously mentioned, the family of Lear and that of Gloucester.

Both men are wealthy, prominent, and ailing in health. Both preside over extravagant estates, and have very eligible heirs standing by to 'cash in' on their share of the fortune.

Let us now examine these heirs, for we may draw further parallels at this sibling level. In Lear's family, Goneril, Cordelia, and Regan are his daughters. Cordelia is sincere, whereas the other two take advantage of the senility which accompanies their father's golden years. The offspring of Gloucester, Edmund and Edgar, are much the same. Edmund is filled with deceit, whereas Edgar serves to protect his father from the pitfalls of his vulnerability.

Returning to Gloucester and Lear, a definite parallel emerges regarding their naievete of their offspring. Lear cannot see through the curtain of deceit that Goneril and Regan have built, and Gloucester is no more aware of Edmund's cunning ways. Both Cordelia and Edgar (through his mad Tom disguise) attempt to be inconspicuous protectors of their respective father's well-being, and their true goodness and loyalty are not realized until late in the course of action.

At one point in the play, an event occurs which draws a revealing parallel between Lear and Gloucester. The feeble Gloucester loses his eyes at the hands of his destructive son, thus making him literally blinded. At the same point in the play, Goneril and Regan had reached their peak regarding their trickery of Lear. This resulted in a literal 'blinding' of Lear's awareness, thereby placing him on the same level as was Gloucester.

Throughout the work, there is a recurring event which seems to herald imminent danger, and that was the weather. At each focal point in the play, a key action was denoted by violence in the atmosphere in the form of storms.

At the conclusion of the play, all received their just fate with one exception: Cordelia. Perhaps her death prevents the play from losing a realistic touch.

Rating: 1-2 Range

Sample 2:

Shakespeare's King Lear contains two distinctly parallel subplots dealing with the fall of a patriach because he misjudged his children and their love for him. First is King Lear himself, who foolishly decides to split up his kingdom and give it to his daughters (this in itself was a mistake; it is unnatural for a king to split up his kingdom). His requirement is that they each tell him how much they love him. The two oldest, Goneril and Regan, deceive him with flowery words. In reality, they don't care about him at all. As we soon find out, they are only after power.

Cordelia, on the other hand, loves her father and is honest enough not to deceive him. Because her speech is truthful, he misses its worth--it is not as faltering as those of her sisters. The sub-plot concerns the Earl of Gloucester, his son Edward, and his bastard son, whom he has taken in, Edmund. Edmund, jealous of Edward, his power and his wealth, devises a scheme to make Edward appear bad. Gloucester believes Edmund's claim that Edward is planning to kill him, and Edward is outlawed. Here again, the father mistakes the false, showy love of one child (as Edmund proclaimed his loyalty to his father, and even injured himself and claimed Edward wounded him) as genuine love. He does not see the quiet loyalty and honesty of the child that really does love him.

This child (Cordelia or Edward) is a victim of the hunger for power of their siblings, who effectively manipulate the father into doing things that he later regrets. Cordelia is perhaps a little more to blame for her exile than Edward. She could have used more tact with her father, and, knowing what her sisters were trying to do, could have given herself some defense. She, in fact, let them have their own way, instead of stopping what she knew to be inevitable--their betrayal of King Lear and his downfall. Edward, on the other hand, did not realize what his brother was really doing. His mistake was trusting Edmund, and therefore not seeing his plot.

As the play progresses, we see both King Lear and the Earl of Gloucester betrayed and turned out by their children. A symbolic parallel can be drawn in regards to Gloucester's blindness. He is caught trying to help King Lear, and the enraged Goneril and Regan, and their cohorts blind him as a punishment. After this, the physically blind Gloucester can "see" the situation as it really is. He realizes that Edward was innocent, and that the villains are Edmund, Cordelia and Regan. He then wants Edward to come back, never realizing that he is the stranger who has been helping him after his impairment. He "sees" right and wrong, but doesn't see what is going on around him. Lear, on the other hand, was able to see physically, had absolutely no insight or common sense. Even when Goneril turns him out, he doesn't "catch on". He goes to Regan, believing that she would take him in. By then, he should have realized that both had the same motives. It is not until the end, shortly before his death, that he too can "see" the situation for what it really is.

Both Lear and Gloucester were to blame for their own downfall. Both were gullible and foolish, too trusting in appearances, and not sensible enough to look deeper. Lear, however, was more responsible for his tragedy. His mistakes began when he wanted to give up his throne and split apart his kingdom. This was against custom, common sense, and political norms. Everything he did after that continued to show that he was a poor judge of characters, even though the situations and their motives were obvious. Gloucester, on the other hand, was taken in by Edmund. His shock is somewhat understandable, and perhaps this is why he did not question Edmund's claims. However, he too lacked the insight and common sense to avoid the tragedy.

Rating: 1-2 Range

Sample 3:

In Shakespeare's play, King Lear, there are many recurring events that take place in the plot and subplot. Direct parallels can be drawn to many of the characters involved.

The play begins with King Lear dividing his land up among his three daughters. This is uncommon practice, and the reader must question himself as to Lear's sanity. The king first calls Goneril, his oldest daughter, to him and asks her to tell him how much she loves him. She goes into great detail, saying she loves her father more than anyone possibly could. This pleases Lear to a great extent and he then proceeds to give her a share of his kingdom. Regan is then asked by her father if it is possible for her to love him as much, if not more than Regan. Regan follows the same pattern Goneril used, and is promptly rewarded with a share in the kingdom. At last, the youngest daughter, and the dearest to her father, Cordelia, is called. When Lear questions her as to her love for him, she says she loves him as a good daughter would love her father, and nothing more. The words "nothing more" are very important in this play. Lear often says, "nothing from nothing will come." Needless to say Lear is deeply hurt by his daughter's statement (which is rather harsh). Both begin to say things that they don't really mean, and soon Cordelia is banished from the kingdom.

There were two suitors of Cordelia in the play, and when Cordelia is banished, the King of France takes her for his wife and the two return to France.

At this same time, the king's faithful servant Kent is also banished from the kingdom for trying to reason with Lear on Cordelia's behalf.

In another part of the kingdom a very similar event is taking place. The Duke of Gloucester is having his own problems with his son Edgar and his bastard son Edmund. During this time, according to custom and law, a bastard son would not receive any benefits from his father while the real son is living. Lear and Gloucester are very much alike in that they allow themselves to be fooled by their children who don't really care for them, and shunning the love of those that do. In a very sly plan, Edmund convinces Gloucester that Edgar is plotting against him for his inheritance and gets Edgar to run off, convincing him that his father is out to get him. From this we can draw a very close parallel from Goneril and Regan to Edmund, and from Cordelia to Edgar.

Both Cordelia and Edgar seem to be victims of circumstance, however, Cordelia seems to bring on some of her own problems. However, these are the two children that truly love their parents, yet they can't express their love in such a way as to convince their fathers of it.

As the story continues the plot and sub-plot are drawn closer and closer together until they become one. The fool has entered the play and seems to represent the missing Cordelia (at least there is a close comparison to be made between the two).

Lear has left the confines of his daughter's castle and is now wandering about. Kent has disguised himself, and has joined the King. Gloucester meets up with them and helps the king escape Goneril and Regan. When the two daughters find out that it was Gloucester who helped their father, they have their husbands, the Duke of Cornwall (Regan's husband) and the Duke of Albany (Goneril's husband), pluck out his eyes. Cornwall takes on most of the details of the event, while Albany tends to stay in the background.

Meanwhile, Edgar has disguised himself as Mad Tom, saying, "I, Edgar, nothing am." The word nothing again comes into the play. He finds Gloucester wandering about and begins to lead the blind man back to the realization that his son, Edgar, is the one who really loves him. This action appears to be closely linked to Kent's leading the blind Lear (blind to the truth) back to love of his daughter Cordelia.

All the characters that are connected to one another seem to reach the same fate. Gloucester and Lear die of broken hearts. The fool and Cordelia are hung. Edmund is slayed by Edgar, and Goneril and Regan kill each other. The only three to remain living at the end of this terrible tragedy are Kent, Edgar, and Cornwall.

As it can now be seen there are many similarities and differences between the two families, yet, their actions all seem to lead to the destruction of the family.

Rating: 2-3 Range

Sample 4:

As the play begins King Lear retires from his throne, which is quite unusual. He divides his kingdom into three divisions among his three daughters, Goneril, Regan, and Cordelia. This family can be paralleled to the family of Gloucester. Gloucester had two sons, Edmund, a bastard son and greedy for the Kingdom, and Edgar, a loyal son. The first of parallels is both Lear and Gloucester must figure out who will get the land.

The Fool is the advisary to King Lear; this person can speak back to the king, put down the king, say anything he wishes. Actually the Fool is not an idiot at all. He knows everything going on around the kingdom and knows what to do about it. Cordelia and the Fool are sometimes thought of as the same person for the reasons they are never seen together and they both have a straight head, meaning they understand their surroundings.

With all the commotion going on trying to decide who the kingdom should be going to and the fact that he retired in the first place we see King Lear gradually growing mad.

Going back to the other family of Gloucester, Edmund and Edgar are having a dispute whereas Edgar must leave the land. Edgar disguised himself as Mad Tom so he may stay around. This situation had also happened to Kent who had disguised himself too. Kent after disguising himself, was only recognized by Cordelia, and the Fool also knows who he is for another similarity between the two.

King Lear is blind to all that is going on around him. He does not see these two in disguise, he does not feel the pressure of Regan and Goneril trying to gain the kingdom for their own, and he does not pick up all the hints the Fool throws at him. This is where we see his sanity breaking down quite rapidly. Gloucester is paralled to this when he physically is blinded and laying on a roadside dying. Gloucester and King Lear have many similarities though Gloucester was not insane.

King Lear, in his madness, dies. Gloucester also dies from his physical being. The kingdom of King Lear went to Regan and Goneril.

The play, King Lear, has two sections: the family of King Lear forming the main plot; and the family of Gloucester forming the sub-plot.

Rating: 3-4 Range

PRACTICE AP ESSAYS

Characters are often helpless in face of their destinies. They have no control over what is to happen. Using a novel or drama of accepted literary merit show how these characters must react.

Dramatic irony is present when one or more of the main characters is totally unaware of a situation of which the audience is well informed. In a novel or drama of recommended literary merit describe such a situation and the effect that would be present with the absence of this dramatic irony.

Characters in literature are often faced with crucial decisions that will directly affect their fate. They may be faced with a choice that they know is morally correct versus one that is demanded by society. Whatever their choice, there will be dire consequences. In a novel or drama of recommended literary merit describe such a situation and the resulting dire consequential effects on the protagonist.

All literature is a representation of the life of the times during which it was written. In a novel or drama of accepted literary merit relate a situation where the superficialness of the plot is secondary to the reality of the underlying "message" the author is very likely to get across.

A SAMPLE AP ESSAY: THE MADWOMAN OF CHAILLOT

This play is a whimsical collection of fancy, farce and flippancy, a great success in the theatre. It does not appear to have social seriousness at first, but if it is not noted, it is due, I think, to the mood and the remoteness of the characters from reality. This lends it a particular charm.

Ironically, the play is a biting satire on the then odious conditions existing in France during the German occupation, but written so cleverly that the state did not take offense and actually subsidized its production. The producer was Louis Jovet, the Theatre de l'Athenee, on the 15th of April, 1945. It was an instant success.

The play was Giraudoux's commitment to the social and political debacle which reigned after the defeat of France by Germany. The script carefully avoided using any German names for the invaders, but the dialogue and the action said more than the names, allowing Giraudoux to blast certain segments of society and get away with it.

One of the themes seems to be the division of society into two races, one of eccentrics, the other of pimps. The Madwoman Aurelie, the real leader of the first race is, "A grande dame. Silk skirt leading to a train, but gathered up by a metal clothespin. Louis XIII slippers. Marie Antoinette chapeau. A lorgnette hanging on a chain. A cameo. A basket..a dinner bell in the bosom of her dress" (stage direction). Supporting the madwoman are the three more madwomen, a streetsinger, a flower girl, a lace merchant, a sewer king, a pair of lovers and the "friends of vegetables." The pimps comprise the enemy army, a nameless, faceless horde of barons, presidents, prospectors, brokers, lobbyists, seeking to get rich on oil. The armies fight a comic war, but like any war it is a fight to the death.

The scheming and plotting takes place in the Cafe de l'Alma in the Chaillot district of Paris. Here the various characters pass through. The good and the evil of Chaillot, citizens of every fibre converge and are judged by their words and behavior. The tycoons and the brokers sit at the table and talk about destroying the city of Paris because petroleum lies in its innards. They whisper and they converse in loud tones about figures...the stock market...buying and selling. They take anybody's money and use it for themselves, contemptuous of the people they take it from.

Giraudoux is using poetic fantasy to relate a very realistic and serious accusation against mankind in general. His bold and exciting, flowing clever dialogue, gives the play a racy atmosphere. But it is obviously a parody of modern high finance policies. It is also a satirical analysis of the political scene. On another level it is a scathing condemnation of the black marketeers, the pimps, who attach themselves to the need and desire of the people and succeed in getting a cut on the exchange.

There are several themes running through this utterly delightful play. One is the adoration of the Golden Calf. The evil ones worship the Calf and are bent on the destruction of the world and mankind if only they succeed in obtaining their goal. This theme runs concurrently with the theme of political concubinage with the German occupying forces. Yet Giraudoux uses his language so cleverly to make his point, that the audience does not feel the sting of insult, so absorbing is the farcical element.

The Madwoman and her friends represent the old inhabitants of the city. The invaders, the enemy army are the intruders. It is they who appear to control everything. They corrupt. They destroy, wantonly. I must include some of the diaglogue. It is just delicious. The enemy are sitting in the cafe scheming and plotting the destruction of Paris so that they could get the oil:

Prospector Well?
The President I need a name.
Prospector I need fifty thousand.
The President For a corporation.
They keep talking until they finally hit upon a name.
Prospector International Substrate of Paris, Inc.
The President And now that we have a name...
Prospector You need a property.
The President Precisely.
and further on: (he knows where to look for oil)
Prospector French.
The Baron In Indo-China?
Broker Morocco?
The President In France?
Prospector In Paris.

The dialogue between the Madwoman and her friends, and between the poor and the madwomen are so full of imagery and axioms, it would be wonderful to write much of it; but then one can read the play, which is much better and more to the point.

The action of the play is not complicated or complex. It consists of the Countess and her friends, upon learning of the nature of the enemy and of their plot to destroy Paris, they hold a mock trial condemning them in absentia, thereby ridding the world of them by sending them down to a bottomless pit, which the sewer king shows her how to open. Into this pit come the invaders, the barons, presidents, brokers, the tycoons, the lobbyists, the press, in short, the army of destruction, led there by insatiable greed.

The invading army are analogous to the occupation forces who are eager to devour France, rob her of her resources, her properties, to destroy her faith in her people. Here Giraudoux shows that the eccentrics and the poor are her defenders of freedom. He defends the simple people, the provincials; a respect for tradition, for history, and for a continuance of the French way of life.

Giraudoux used the theatre to sound an alarm. He was opposed to progress as a means of robbing man of his existing state of things; of industrialization and a mechanized civilization of robots. His play confirmed his thoughts of what man's destiny ought to be. He felt that man should be aware of the futility of gaining wealth and power and of the needless waste in human resources that such a victory entails. He speaks out for tolerance for all mankind, for the end to oppression. Also he sees technological society as a dehumanizing, sterile, mass.

I feel that the pimps in the play are the agents of technological progress. They are the nameless, faceless, agents of anonymity, identical in intent and purpose--destruction in the guise of progress. As the madwoman says: "Men everywhere who seem to be building are secretly involved in destruction. The newest of their buildings is only the mannequin of a ruin...They build quays and destroy rivers (look at the Seine), build cities and destroy the countryside (look at Pre-aux-clercs), build the Palace of Chaillot and destroy the Trocadero...The occupation of humanity is only a universal enterprise of demolition." (Act 11)

The country was debauched and debilitated during the occupation, and Giraudoux made an appeal to Frenchmen to save France for the future. He wrote in Sans Pouvoirs,

> "Our financial policy has become a money game. It has detached money from its real value; and has allowed our great national resources to go

> to waste by detaching money from work, from function and even from the gold itself."

He saw this as an unhealthy aspect of capitalism. The play serves as a concrete affirmation of his political, social, and moral principles. In this play I can see how he makes an appeal to people of sensitivity and sensibility to retain what is good and in man and exterminate what is evil. There is also an appeal to Frenchmen for sobriety, for an evaluation of Franco-German relations; not to succumb to capitulation of becoming Germanic; to retain her individuality, ergo her eccentrics--to remain a haven for her creative artists and retain her liberty as a nation.

His satire against capitalism is justified even today, especially in view of the oil problem created by the same industrialists, capitalists, lobbyists, brokers of today's world. The dilemma still persists--when will man learn from the past to improve the present, the future? In this respect the dialogue between the ragpicker and the Countess is truly pertinent as they say, "You never see them sweat," says the ragpicker. Their motivating source is oil, and their taste for it is sensual, lustful. They find oil under Paris and so will destroy the city to get it." (today it is Saudi Arabia's oil and her tycoons and capitalists who will destroy the world for power and money) "What do they want to make with it?" asks the madwoman. "What one makes with oil--misery, war, ugliness," answers the young lover." (Act 1)

Giraudoux says everything worth saying, says it with verve and vigor. In a comic, farcical, satirical play, he brings home an important lesson--one we might all learn from before it's too late.

A SAMPLE AP ESSAY: A STUDY OF THE CHARACTERS MRS. ALVING IN GHOSTS, AND NORA IN A DOLL'S HOUSE

In choosing to write my paper on the protagonists in Ibsen's Ghosts and A Doll's House, I had in mind the situation that existed in society in the woman's world in the nineteenth century and her place in society in the twentieth century; to examine the mores and tenets the woman of yesteryear had to bow to, and the changes and their effects on the woman of today.

During Ibsen's adult lifetime women were expected to be seen, used, but not heard. Ibsen was well aware of the discrimination that women were subjected to. He did not condone the double standard that existed for men, the perversity of the situation that encouraged it, and the parochial atmosphere that women were expected to live in and suffer.

A play having as its theme the emancipation of women was not a popular theatre piece with men of narrow convictions. In Ghosts, Mrs. Alving comes across as an independent, moralistic woman. She is also a long-suffering wife. Her inhibitions are due to cowardice on her part, a result of conditioning and therefore really not her fault. Because religion played such a strong role in the lives of people, women especially, it behooved Mrs. Alving to seek advice from her Pastor. When she confided to him that her husband was a dissolute character and that she did not wish to live with him, he admonished her to remember her duty as a Christian and a wife and to return to him.

Mrs. Alving had been surfacing from the old beliefs, struggling to free herself from them. Not only did she have to overcome inherited teachings and moral torpidity, she had to face life realistically in the area of the tragedy of Osvald's inherited disease. Mrs. Alving must face the facts, for not only is Osvald's disease her problem, but his half-sister, Regina, is an additonal problem and she must find the right solution. She has a moral obligation to save Regina from moral destruction.

The question of morality is not the only question which Mrs. Alving must answer. She is faced with the prospect of her son's disease, and that she could give him the poison that would put an end to his misery. Here again she is in the clutches of old moral precepts. Ibsen does not provide the audience with a solution in her case. He leaves the question open. As in the case of Nora, she too must overcome awesome problems. In her mind she is sufficiently emancipated to take her place in society in her own way. Even if that means walking out on her husband and her children. She is more resolute than Mrs. Alving who is pathetically standing over her son with the bottle of poison in her hand, restricted spiritually and physically from taking the final step.

Nora presents a picture of a young, unsophisticated, wife. She appears to be happy. Her husband is priggish and pompous, dominates her completely. At least that is the impression one gets at first. Torvald addresses her like a juvenile, using pet names for her, scolding her for being extravagant. He tells her that she has inherited that trait from her father. As a husband he is well-meaning, but he is a small man in mentality.

Nora chirps and sings like a bird, but she acts like a highminded woman when she is faced with an important problem. Unlike Mrs. Alving, who uses Pastor Manders as an excuse for living a miserable life with her husband, Nora reaches out, beyond the authority of Torvald and borrows money to take him to Italy for his health. This is indicative of a strong, not a weak person. She does not ask for help, even from her father who loves her. But she does need money and so she borrows it from Krogstad, an employee at the bank where Torvald works.

that she possessed such a spirit. Had she not, she would have been completely crushed by her beast of a husband, her hypocritical Pastor, and society in general. The circumstances that produced the tragic mental breakdown of Osvald are not as tragic as Mrs. Alving's struggle against the heritage from the past--spiritual and physical.

Ibsen referred to this play as a "modern tragedy." He said further, "A woman cannot be herself in the society of the present day, which is an exclusively masculine society, with laws framed by men and with a judicial system that judges feminine conduct from a masculine point of view."

This remark is noteworthy, and is applicable to Torvald's ethical standards. Nora is not a typical victim of male domination. She is strong-willed, and in a sense, presides over the domestic world she calls her doll's house. She is a squirrel to her husband, but as a woman she takes the initiative when Torvald is ill, going as far as to forge a note in order to get the money for his convalescence. She manages to meet the payments on her loan.

The deception is discovered when Krogstad tries to blackmail Torvald to restore him to his job from which he had been fired. This is also the turning point in the play, for it is only then that Nora realizes that her husband is more concerned with his image in a bourgeois society than he is in understanding her impulse to save his life. Torvald was eager to forget the whole unpleasant crisis, but not Nora. She tells him, "I say that we have never sat down in earnest together to try and get at the bottom of anything."

Ibsen knew the true value of life--understood the soul of man, the individual. He had a deep regard for the dignity of the human being and a sensitivity for portrayal.

He understood theatre, having spent five years, from 1851 until 1856 as a stage manager and official dramatic poet to the theatre in Bergen. The next five years he was director of the Norwegian Theatre in Christiania, Oslo. The exposure was beneficial, for his duties included the writing of at least one play a year. In his capacity of manager-poet-director, he attended all rehearsals which were invaluable to a young playwright.

While discharging his duties as a director in Christiania, two of his plays were presented there, Lady Inger of Ostraat and The Vikings at Helgeland. He vainly tried to raise the level of productions and the quality of the plays presented there, but met with frustration and disappointment. The theatre was forced to close in 1862, but Ibsen's groundwork had been laid.

As a playwright, he introduced a startlingly new concept; women counted for something and needed to be liberated from old conventions; they were more than creatures of comfort. They had intellectual capabilities and strong emotions. Women had a definite place in society, they were not meant to be kept ignorant and subservient. Yet he was not a feminist in the context of that word today.

Ibsen is associated with realism, as his plays indicate, but with romantic overtones. They are considered social plays, for they are about individuals and their problems. But mostly his concern was with women, for they had only him to champion their cause in a society that was blind and deaf to their needs and their desires.

When famous actresses lauded Ibsen for the wonderful roles he created for them, he retorted angrily, "I have never created roles. I have written of human beings and human destinies!"

It was an equitable resolution. Consternation and controversy resulted from it. Ibsen was attacked for disturbing the status quo. But he felt that the time was ripe for a change not only in the institution of marriage, but in society's precepts regarding family, fate and religion; in restoring to women their dignity, and in helping them escape the confines of environment. In presenting his plays in the context of each man and woman in relation to society as a whole, his greater concern lay in the area of women. Both Mrs. Alving and Nora attain a certain nobility and dignity through the decisions they are forced to make.

Mrs. Alving at one point accuses Pastor Manders of being guilty of forcing her to accept an untenable position in her life when he stresses her duty to remain with her husband. When she discloses the story of Regina's birth and Osvald's disease, she points an accusing finger at the inherent hypocrisy of the Pastor. She also accuses herself of being a coward because she did not tell him the whole truth when she should have, and then she kept the shameful secret of her husband's dissolute life from her son.

Unlike Nora, Mrs. Alving's role is not that of a plaything. She is a mature woman who has had to take over the role of business woman and the head of her house. But male chauvinism has had its effect on her. Outwardly Mrs. Alving abides by the tenets of church and society, but inwardly the flames of rebellion are smoldering. She reveals this in the first act when Manders reprimands her for reading some books he doesn't approve of. She replies, "that the books clarify and confirm many things I've thought of about myself." In the course of their discussion Manders assures Mrs. Alving "that sometimes it is better to depend on the opinion of others."

The play impressed me because Ibsen was willing to expose a matter that was calculated to disturb the playgoer and startle him into thought. He used the stratagem of innocently portraying commonplace life, then dealing it a shattering blow. In doing so, the spectator was obliged to see validity of respectability shattered by disclosures of the evil in its fabric, of its inconsistentency and its errors. Added to these, the theme of venereal disease, and the sins of the father being visited on the children did not go very well with a public who were not inclined to being part of the society of which Ibsen wrote. The public outcry was loud, and the plays were not produced without opposition. Ibsen started a revolution not only in the theatre, but in the annals of society. He made a crack in an outworn tradition. He dared to mention the unmentionable.

If A Doll's House became the cry of freedom for women generally, Ghosts symbolizes the tragedy of woman in her struggle to escape from the spiritual and moral heritage of the past. Mrs. Alving tells Paster Manders, "I must work my way to freedom." At the end of the play Mrs. Alving is liberated, but her son loses his sanity. There is stark irony in this ending.

Although Mrs. Alving's liberation was slow in coming, the seeds were beginning to germinate early in the play. At one point in their conversation, Manders upbraids Mrs. Alving about her duties as a mother, telling her, "as a wife and mother you did not do your duty. It is not a wife's part to be her husband's judge." In more dialogue in the same vein, "Just as once you forsook your duty as a wife, so, since then, you have forsaken your duty as a mother."

Manders is quite obviously obsessed with the word Duty! Yet he refuses to believe that he is remiss in performing his duty to Mrs. Alving as a friend and advisor in urging her to live a life of deceit and despondency; to build a monument to hypocrisy in memory of her husband. Manders did not hesitate to remind her that, "all your life you have been possessed by a willful, rebellious spirit." How fortunate for Mrs. Alving

This decision ultimately forces Nora to make a dramatic and drastic change in her life. When her husband learns about the note she has signed he chides her unmercifully. He compares her to her father thus: "What a horrible awakening! All those eight years--she who was my joy and pride--a hypocrite, a liar--worse--a criminal! For shame! I ought to have suspected that something of the sort would happen. I ought to have forseen it. All your father's want of principle has come out in you. No religion, no morality, no sense of duty."

It is this nineteenth century sense of Victorian morality which Ibsen revolted against. So much so that he incurred the displeasure of certain segments of society, which was an attack on smug, conventional minds. His Nora was not to be robbed of her heritage. Women were wronged as wives, daughters, as sisters, robbed of their very spirit. They could suffer silently, but they did not do so by choice.

Ibsen was aroused sufficiently by the plight of women to bring it to the attention of the theatre-going public, where he rightly felt it would make a strong impact. The subject had never been openly aired, but it was a subject that had tormented Ibsen from his youth. It was a human drama, an eternal drama, an obstacle to attaining happiness. But later in his life he concedes that happiness is necessary to progress in human relationships. In Ghosts, Ibsen lets Pastor Manders ask, "What right have we human beings to happiness?" His thoughts on the question of happiness undergo a change and he decides that he does have a right to be happy.

The pessimism that permeates both Ghosts and A Doll's House undoubtedly is due to Ibsen's own experiences. He had had a run-in with the Norwegian Church Department, saying that his son could not graduate law unless he took a second examination for the second degree. He was very angry and promised: "For the black theological band which at present dominates the Norwegian Church Department, I shall, when the opportunity comes, raise a fitting literary memorial." No doubt Pastor Manders was born from his anger. Ibsen was a man of very strong convictions, with a keen sense of justice, and a strong feeling for the individual. He saw the futility of the individual's struggle because the past was so strong; it dominated human life. Ibsen gave much thought to the relation between the past and the future and between society on the one hand and the individual on the other.

With his mind filled with these thoughts, it is inevitable that he should put the plight of the individual first in his plays. Nora's role in society in the nineteenth century is due to the philistine attitude in that time in Europe and on the Continent. Mrs. Alving shared the same fate as Nora, but not for the same reasons. Her obsequious obeisance to Paster Manders, concept of Christian duty, nullifies her rightful role as an individual in society. To be sure she had committed a deadly sin in her youth; she agreed to marry for "external reasons." Christian morality sanctioned the act. She did not marry for love. Therefore she had committed a sin for which she was punished. Osvald was the child born with the disease which he inherited from his dissolute father. Punishment was doled out to Mrs. Alving, not because she married an immoral man, but because she obeyed the immoral ethics of society.

Nora's sin did not stem from acceding to a loveless marriage, but from accepting the role of a doll, a plaything for her father and later her husband. She ran true to the Victorian ideals of feminine dependency. When Nora tells Torvald that she is leaving her home in search of self-development, she abruptly gives the lie to the myth that this act is a destructive one, rather than a constructive one--not negating the sanctity of the marriage ideal, but proving that a woman is essentially a free human being possessing a mind and a will to educate herself, thereby freeing herself from independency.

I have endeavored to make suitable comparisons between Nora, the heroine of A Doll's House, and Mrs. Alving, the heroine of Ghosts. Perhaps I could have said more about the former. In order to substantiate my comments, I have collected a number of critical reviews by several critics. Before I proceed, I should like to add that I do sympathize with the heroine of A Doll's House.

After considerable study and contemplation about Nora's decision to leave her husband and children, I could not, without complete honesty, share her decision with such finality. But, as a member of her sex, I cannot condone the treatment that she received from her overbearing, pompous, super-moralistic, selfish husband. Appearances were more important to him than the hurt he inflicted upon Nora.

Ibsen's thoughts of emancipation for women are commendable and right, but as a woman, and mother of children, were I in the same circumstances, I could leave my husband, but I would not suffer my children to be deprived of their mother.

It is not simple to isolate the protagonist in a drama and concentrate on that person without running the risk of leaving unsaid things that are important to the plot and that have a direct bearing on the behavior of the protagonist. But to relate the story in toto, would be a repetitious bore. However, I have these criticisms which I hope will not be a bore, and will help sustain me in my comments.

1. NBC TV Edwin Newman Jan. 13, 1971

A Doll's House--a forerunner of women's liberation. Ibsen's constant theme was the struggle of the individual against the stultifying pressures of society. In this case it was a woman, a childlike wife, babied and bullied by her husband until she sees him for what he is and leaves him and the children to carry out as she says, her duty to herself. A very worthwhile revival.

2. New York Post, Richard Watts Jan. 14, 1971

Carefully constructed structure, characteristic of Ibsen's technique proficiency, occasionally seems a bit labored.

Nora is not the feather-brained heroine she appears to be, risks much to help Torvald convalesce after his illness. To obtain the money for their trip, Nora forges her sick father's name on the note that she gives to Krogstad. This is the reason for his attempt to blackmail her. This act of Nora's shows a resiliency and spirit that offsets her "childish" quality.

3. Time T. E. Kalem Jan. 25, 1971

Clair Bloom's interpretation exquisite as she moves from puppet to the women who issues an emancipation proclamation to her husband. When threat of exposure lifts, Tovald wants to go on as if nothing had happened. But Nora sees her idealistic love shattered. She feels she has been treated like a doll child by her father in his house and a doll woman in her husband's house. She opts to leave him and her children in order to forge an independent soul and consciousness in the outer world.

Her actions previous to and after the discovery of the damaging letter are on a par with an individual's growth mental, spiritually, and emotionally.

In conclusion, I must admit that what Nora did requires courage, but it also implies selfishness. Still, when one considers that Ibsen wrote this play during the nineteenth century when women were not much more than creatures of comfort or decoration, this was a very revolutionary idea. He surely was the precursor of women's liberation as we know it today.

Bibliography

Ibsen, Henrik. Ghosts. New York: Bantam Books Inc., 1971.

Ibsen, Henrik. A Doll's House. New York: Bantam Books Inc., 1971.

Koht, Halvdan. The Life of Ibsen. New York: W. W. Norton and Co., Inc., 1931.

A SAMPLE AP ESSAY: OTHELLO

Iago appears on the scene clothed in the cloak of friendship and a helpmate to all mankind. He is not what he seems to be, for he is consumed by jealousy and cunning and avarice, and uses his office to turn man against man at every opportunity. His is the art of the doubledealer. For example early in the play, he uses Roderigo to somehow injure Brabantio by telling him about the artifices used by Othello to ensnare Brabantio's daughter Desdemona.

All the while he is appearing as a friend to one, he is planning his next move to do some evil to another. Thus he urges Roderigo to get Othello's ear and tell him that Cassio is having an affair with Desdemona. He lies copiously and swindles Roderigo out of his money. To illustrate his villainy:

> "But I will wear my heart upon my sleeve
> For daws to peck at: I am not what I am".

Othello is respected as a general and Iago is inflamed because Cassio has been chosen to serve him instead of himself. He decides to get the choice job by making Othello suspicious of Cassio. So base is his character, that he is willing to sacrifice Desdemona in his scheme. Iago appears to Othello as an honest and trusting friend and he entrusts Desdemona to Iago's care. The plot thickens and the man who appears to be a saint, turns out to be a sinner. He weaves a web of intrigue and with his talent for appearing a good and honest man, he manages adroitly to turn love to hate, to turn truth into dishonesty. Iago tells Roderigo:

> "For that I do suspect the lusty Moor
> Hath leap'd into my seat: etc.,
> And nothing can or shall content my soul
> Till I am even'd with him, wife for wife,
> Or failing so, yet that I put the Moor
> At least into a jealousy so strong."

It is from this desire on the part of Iago to hurt Othello and to use all possible means at his disposal even if it cause the death of those whom he must use to obtain what he is determined to win.

However, in the end, justice will prevail and the guilty will be punished. For in the act of opening a hole for others to fall into, the hole is filled by the one who has opened it.

Having spun a web so tight that none who are caught in it can escape live, Iago goes on to prove adultery where none exists; such is his double-faced nature that he does not care how he lures men into his web. Eventually all the characters turn against each other and misery and a sense of calamity pervade the whole play. While he talks sweetly to one, he builds uncontrolled passion into their minds and thoughts of revenge are manifest.

Iago is ultimately the loser because the web he had spun also gets him trapped in its vise. The truth will out, and the liar will be found out by his own betrayal of himself.

A SAMPLE AP ESSAY: THE CRUCIBLE

Arthur Miller's The Crucible was a conscious effort to awaken the American public to the parallel between the sinister, notorious Salem trials and the contemporary and equally notorious trials during the McCarthy era of the 1950s. The seventeenth century seemed to overlap the twentieth century and paradoxically Puritanism emerged fully grown in the United States, a country where dissent and lack of conformity was not necessarily a crime. The McCarthy trials were a shocking, unorthodox procedure and affected people who believed in the American experiment, that the witch-hunt was no longer to be tolerated silently. People like Arthur Miller spoke out eloquently against it, and his play explains the sequence of events which started the Salem witch-hunt and follows it to its end.

Miller's sense of moral justice, his regard for the dignity of man, plus his sensitivity to man's problems, makes him a playwright who stands out as an artist and a thinker. He takes to task those paragons of virtue who in the guise of good and just men, bend to the will of a megalomaniac to denounce dissenters and pronounce them guilty, threatening dire consequences unless they recant and conform to the will and word of the accusers. Refusal generally spells disaster for the accused and those close to him. It is this denial of the rights of a man to choose and be master of his own destiny, that impelled Miller to write about the shameful epoch in history when fear walked hand in hand with man.

After considering how the conclusion of the play related to the plot, it became clear to me that in order to justify one's beliefs in certain principles one had to stand fast, never waver, even if that staunch refusal to submit to trumped-up charges and mass hysteria ultimately leads one to his death. That is exactly what happened to John Proctor and his friends when intolerance and deceit took the place of reason and restraint.

The dialogue between the accused and accusers is Miller's way of showing his concern for the manner in which social and/or political justice is meted out to man; when church and state combine to inculcate their theories by coersive measures. Miller deliberately chose the historical incident to present and the spectacle of the calamity which confronts man today as it did in the past. Although the Puritans left England in order to pursue their own type of life, free from persecution, they soon became the very oppressors they sought to escape. The discipline of their theocratic government established a society in which men could destroy one another by word of mouth, not needing proof of accusation or other evidence to substantiate their claims.

The play's ending bears this out very strongly. As recrimination and denial fail to stir the judges, except to further the obvious decision that will be made by the presiding judge, Proctor realizes that no matter what he says at this point he has besmirched his good name. If he is to agree to the false charges, hasn't he lost his pride, honor, assumed guilt and debased himself? If, on the other hand, he clings to his testimony and pleads innocence to the charges, but admitting a moral infraction, he is still the loser, for he has sinned.

So it was with the McCarthy witch-hunt of the 1950s. The liberal element in society who were not timorous, did in fact make waves, cognizant of the hysteria of the conservative faction of the masses. There is a similarity of manner in both the witch-hunt and the subsequent trials. The dissimilarity only rests in the outcome. Death was not the verdict handed down by McCarthy. One other variation on the theme is the basic issue involved. In Salem it hinged on the service to God or to the Devil. In the latter-day trial, the issue involved patriotism and service to one's country, as

McCarthy sought to define it. In both cases the trials served to stifle freedom.

Miller uses the dramatic technique to bring the preceding events in the play to its logical and credible conclusion. The first three acts introduce the characters, put them in their proper perspective within the framework of the play, explain the situation in terms of the behavior of the characters and the events that take place as a direct outcome of the actions and dialogue of the characters. The action rises until it reaches a climax, when near the end of the third act the plot is seen in the answer Elizabeth gives to Danforth about Proctor's leachery. From then on the events lead to the inevitable end of the play with the death of Proctor.

The artistic structure of the play is good and does for the playwright what he intended the play to do. It raises questions in the mind of the viewer. By the time the play ends, the viewer must surely have come up with some answers, to his own questions. Plays of such magnitude cannot leave the viewer untouched.

When reading the title of Miller's play, it occurred to me that "The Crucible" means a "severe test or trial." The play is an indictment against the abuse of our fundamental rights in the pursuit of liberty, freedom and justice; the right to act and think in accordance with our individual precepts of those rights. During the Salem trials the rights of man were non-existent so that theocratic rule could arbitrarily extinquish a man's life while exclaiming that what was done, was done to save a man from damnation. Many conformed, confessed to lies in order to live. Others, men of high character and of high princples, refused to be bullied and died on the gallows to uphold their beliefs. According to the tenets of the church and the opinions held by the authorities, men were either good or evil. Either they lived by the rules laid down for them, or if they proved to non-comformists, then they had to pay for their show of independence.

Had the condemned people of Salem gone along with the practice of publicly admitting that they had sinned, even though it was not true, many lives might have been spared; and some did. But to many it was a far worse sin to admit to a lie than to suffer the consequences that the refusal to admit it brought. The system made spies out of ordinary, hard-working people. They lived in constant dread that a knock on the door might end in disaster. And very often that was the case. No one was really immune to somebody's warped and evil mind. Even children were used to ensnare people. The crying-out was usually done by children, whom the nobler spirits of church and state were prepared to believe.

Due process of law was not invoked in these trials, which of course were nothing more than mock-trials. And in this atmosphere human dignity was swept out the door, much like dust with a broom. It is this nightmare, this infraction of justice and decency that Miller, an artist and a man of high moral principle, wishes to talk about, to enlighten men everywhere and point out the dangers of demagogues and the brutality of mass hysteria.

Miller was so shocked by the McCarthy accusations and harassment of liberal men and women in this country that he chose the historical past to show the parallel of that period of our history with that of the present.

The characters in the The Crucible are prototypes of the real characters who lived in 1692. They are believable because they behave as most people would if confronted with the situation today. The Proctors reacted in typical fashion. They were shocked, dismayed and terrified. Such an unexpected happening left them incredulous. That it was possible was even more incredulous. Yet it can and did happen in the twentieth century too. Liberals were suspect, including Miller. Teachers were required to take an oath of loyalty. Whispering campaigns became debates and engendered hysteria and hate. People suddenly were called upon to defend themselves against things they did not do.

This is the tragedy that Miller must talk about. He does it through Proctor and Elizabeth, through Hale and Danforth and through Abigail, Mary and the others. He tells how vindictiveness and jealousy, corruption and theocracy can ruin a society and forever bear shame in the annals of history. Repressive measures stunt the growth and development of the mind of man. The plausibility of restrictive government being good for man in that it holds society together proved to be the reverse. It let evil-doers have the last word and play into the hands of tyrants.

As Proctor pleads his innocence, the authorities display their power. They taunt him, cajole him to confess and save his life. But they really do not show him true Christian mercy. They are hypocrites and murderers. In their zeal to turn everybody to do God's work, they did the opposite. They were a perverted group of men who persecuted any who did not follow their dictum.

Proctor felt that he had lost his good name, his honor and his pride as well as his wife, children and home. But when he reverses himself in the courtroom and decides to sign the confession, Danforth and Hale are delighted; they have scored a victory! However, Proctor surprises them, for when Danforth stretches out his hand to accept the signed statement, Proctor suddenly snatches it and tears it up. With this act he signs his death warrant. But in the final analysis he has retained his good name, his honor, his pride and above all, his human dignity.

The ending is a Big-Endian, it is dramatic and it tells what it set out to do.

At this point I would like to add this little paragraph from the Overture, Act I: "When one rises above the individual villainy displayed, one can only pity them all, just as we shall be pitied someday. It is still impossible for man to organize his social life without repressions, and the balance has yet to be struck between order and freedom."

DRAMA: READING LIST OF RECOMMENDED WORKS OF LITERARY MERIT

AGAMEMNON	Aeschylus
ANTIGONE	Sophocles
OEDIPUS THE KING	Sophocles
OEDIPUS AT COLONUS	Sophocles
MEDEA	Euripides
THE FROGS	Aristophanes
WAITING FOR GODOT	Beckett, Samuel
THE SEA GULL	Chekhov
THE CHERRY ORCHARD	Chekhov, Anton
THE WAY OF THE WORLD	Congreve, William
THE MASTER BUILDER	Ibsen, Henrik
THE WILD DUCK	Ibsen, Henrik
RHINOCEROS	Ionesco, Eugene
VOLPONE	Ben Jonson
DR. FAUSTUS	Marlowe, Christopher
DEATH OF A SALESMAN	Miller, Arthur
THE MISANTHROPE	Moliere
KING LEAR	Shakespeare, William
THE TEMPEST	Shakespeare, William
OTHELLO	Shakespeare, William
CORIOLANUS	Shakespeare, William
THE SCHOOL FOR SCANDAL	Sheridan, Richard Brinsley
ROSENCRANTZ AND GUILDENSTERN ARE DEAD	Stoppard, Tom
THE GLASS MENAGERIE	Williams, Tennessee
A STREETCAR NAMED DESIRE	Williams, Tennessee

A GLOSSARY OF TYPES OF DRAMA

Drama--a literary form written to be performed on a stage by actors representing the characters. (This may sound simple enough but observe the following examples of how diversified the many types (examples) of drama became.)

Boulevard Drama--originally a body of plays produced in the late 19th century for major theatres in Paris. Presently, this type of drama is usually a comedy or melodrama of some sophistication, designed primarily as a commercial production. (Ex. the plays of Noel Coward).

Bourgeois Drama--a style presenting the aspects of middle class life.

Burletta--a musical farce, popular in 18th and 19th century England. The music evaded the law which limited legitimate drama to patent theatres. (Ex. Life in London by Pierce Egan).

Capa y Espada--("cloak and sword")--comedy dealing with love and intrigue among the aristocracy. Written in the 16th and 17th century by Spanish playwrites such as Calderon de la Barca and Lope de Vega.

Cavalier Drama--decorous and solemn plays which drew their material from Greek Romances. A typical cavalier drama could involve political and/or military conflict between neighboring states, pirates who captured or rescued central characters from sinking ships, beautiful ladies who are in love with valiant and honorable men, and villains and other things which prevent the normal course of marriage. In time all obstacles are removed and the play may end in wedlock. Fluid dialogue is rhythmic prose giving the impression of blank verse. This type of writing basically ended in 1640 with Cromwell. (Ex. Sir John Suckling).

Chronicle Play--a dramatization of historical events taken from the chronicle histories of England, Scotland, and Ireland. (Ex. Edward the fourth by Thomas Heywood).

Closet Drama--a play that has been read rather than performed. (Otho the Great--Keats). Also, a play which, written for the theatre, has been accepted as a dramatic poem. (Shelley's--The Cerci).

Comedie Larmoyante--French, tearful comedy. It was preceded by sentimal comedy and followed by the drama Bourgeois.

Comedy of Humors--a realistic, 16th century play in which "humor" is a personification of some individual passion or tendency. (Ex. Ben Jonson and John Fletcher).

Comedy of Intrigue--a play which subordinates character to plot. It originated in Spain and was practiced in England by Mrs. A. Behn. Her writings include The Rovers and City Heiress.

Comedy of Manners--originated in France with Moliere's Les Precieuses Ridicules. Their basic aim was to satirize fashionable society. (Ex. Congrere's 'Way of the World').

Commedia dell'arte--an Italian improvised comedy of the 16th and 17th century. Performed by professional actors. It developed from character comedies (farces) and included type D characters, masks, and traditional costumes. (Ex. 'The Metamorphoses of a Wandering Minstrel').

Domestic Tragedy--a Latin production which was of house and home (18th century). These plays adapted classical tragedy to the domestic life of the times. (Ex. Elizabethan--Heywood's 'A Woman Kilde with Kindnesse.')

Farce--a comedy which begins with an absurd situation and is then developed through ridiculous or hilarious complications involving exaggerated or far-fetched characters. The farce involves boisterous comic action and ludicrous comedy. (Ex. Twelfth Night and Midsummer Night's Dream).

Heroic Drama--a play written in rhymed couplets, popular in England from 1664-1678. Their theme was of love and honor and the writings of Dryden, Howard, and Otway are examples.

High Comedy--a subtle and articulate play which gives rise to thoughtful laughter.

History Play--similar to the Chronicle Play.

Interlude--a short comic play popular in the 15th and 16th centuries. It succeeded the miracle and morality plays. To bring abstract social and political problems to light, they were performed at court, in the halls of nobles, at colleges, and during intervals at banquets and entertainments.

Kabuki--The Japanese popular theatre, the scenery is elaborate, costumes are fitted to the part, performers are not masked, and the female parts are taken by males.

Liturgical Drama--was used for public worship and originally applied to the mass or the service of the Holy Eucharist. The mystery, miracle, and morality plays were in this category. There is a struggle between good and evil occuring. Biblical figures gave way to personified abstractions. The action was simple and didactic.

Living Newspaper--a stage production which made use of the devices of the cinema. It presented problems of modern social life in a series of short, quick-moving scenes, each putting forth methods of dealing with those problems. During World War II the Federal Theatre of the United States used this in England for the purpose of educating the troops.

Melodrama--originally a stage play with songs and music. Presently, it is a sensational, gruesome play with touches of bathos, violent action, and sometimes a happy ending. Sentiment and passion are sometimes exaggerated for effect.

Mime--a farce in which scenes of real life are expressed by gesture only. Grotesque masks were often worn, as gods and legendary heroes were burlesqued also.

Miracle Play--plays written about the lives of saints.

Morality Play--contained a struggle between good and evil with simple didactic action.

Mystery Play--dramatization of parts of the life of Christ.

New Comedy--of Greek origin in the 3rd and 4th centuries. It was pure comedy of manners. It used to stock characters and conventional turns of plot. Often the scene represented a street where the love intrigues were enacted. (Ex. the Greek, Menander who in turn influenced the Romans, Plautus and Terence).

No Drama--a form of traditional, ceremonial, or ritualistic drama particular to Japan. Being symbolic and spiritual in character, it evolved from the religious rites of Shinto worship. Originally popular from 1652-1868, it was revived as short (1-2 acts) plays written in prose and verse in which the chorus contributes political comments. It can be compared to early Greek drama.

Passion Play--a miracle play representing the passion of Christ.

Problem Play--a drama dealing with social problems. It directs attention to injustices and maladjustments, as well as to preventable evils of many kinds.

Restoration Comedy--comedy which was marked by the return of Charles II in 1660 to the monarchy. (Ex. Dryden, Congreve, Locke).

Revenge Play--a drama in which revenge is the central theme.

Satyric Drama--typical of the ancient Greeks. A semi-mocking, semi-serious presentation of a legendary theme in honor of Dionysus, a God attended by Satyrs. (Ex. 'Cyclops' by Euripides).

Senecan Tragedy--constructed in five acts, this dealt with emotions and catastrophies which were universally intelligible. It was rant and rhetoric and typically contained rattling line by line interchange of dialogue, a chorus, tyrants, ghosts, witches, and was set upon a corpse strewn stage.

Sentimental Comedy--a pathetic play which reflected the false sensibility of the rising middle class in the 18th century. (Ex. Richard Steele's 'The Lying Lover').

Thesis Play--see problem play.

Well-made Play--a play constructed with the utmost neatness and economy.

PROSE

Literature is a form of art similar to painting, music, sculpture, architecture, and dancing. Good literature takes aspects of living and human experience, and develops them in written form in order that we should see things more clearly. Literary writing enables us to see how other people live, appreciate the mistakes and wisdom of others, and develops an understanding of the qualities that make some people outstanding. Through literature we can develop a greater awareness of ourselves, of the world, and learn about new and different peoples, places and events. Literature recreates the exciting events of the past as well as stimulates our intellect with new ideas, and most of all, reading good literature can be an enjoyable and relaxing event in our lives.

Prose or imaginative literature, i.e., plays, stories or novels, as we discuss it here, refers to those works "worth talking about" as good literature and can stand the test of judgement and time. Literature comes about when language is used creatively and creates a new expression of an idea or awareness. The basic element of literary prose is the sentence (and a sentence is a construction of language which has at least a beginning and an end). Sentences provide a self-conscious organization of language that presupposes a relatively sophisticated level of human development, e.g., description of feelings. Prose, unlike poetry, was not developed by the relatively spontaneous sounds and phrases uttered by people in the past. Prose, like poetry, uses for instance, rhythm, and repetition to create better understanding. Before developing the traditional prose units of the short story and novel, a few brief definitions can aid our study.

The novel is a full-length narrative work of fiction involving several characters in a series of events and incidents. These incidents must be closely related and have a continuity that will keep the reader interested until the end. If there is more than one story, the most important is called the main plot. There may be one or more less important stories called subplots which are closely interwoven with the main plot. It usually presents a true-to-life picture of a particular time or area. The characters are fully developed because the reader is told their thoughts and feelings.

While the characters, story or background may be based upon true events, fiction depends upon the imagination of the author. Other elements or ingredients that most examples of fiction have in common are the following.

The plot is the story itself. It is usually composed of a series of related incidents or events that lead to the climax, the incident or event that marks the highest point of the story.

The characters are the people in the story through whose actions, words, and ideas the plot is unfolded.

The conflict is the problem or difficulty that the characters must solve. It may be a struggle between two or more characters. One character may have to settle a problem existing within himself. Or the characters may be obliged to fight to overcome physical obstacles. Whatever the conflict may be, there must be enough suspense to make the reader wish to discover the solution.

The setting is the time and place of the action of the story.

The resolution is the final result of the conflict. If the hero overcomes his obstacles and the ending is happy, the story is called a comedy. Should the hero be defeated or die, the story is a tragedy. The terms comedy and tragedy are usually applied to dramas.

The theme is the moral or main idea which the story illustrates. Unless the story was written merely for entertainment or amusement, there is a message just as there is in Aesop's Fables. Sometimes the author will tell this moral directly; more often he will merely suggest it through the actions and events.

The short story is written so that it may be read at a single sitting. Therefore, the plot must be simpler and more unified than that of a novel. As a result, attention is usually focused on one character, one problem, or one setting. The short story also tries to produce a single emotion or effect. For example, fear, anger, sorrow, love, pity, hope, etc.

The play may be either full-length or one act. The story is told through the dialogue and actions of the characters on the stage. As a result, much that is carefully spelled out in a novel is left to the audience's imagination in a play. While plays may be enjoyably read, they are written to be performed on a stage.

Non-fiction may show great variations because the author must stick to facts. Imagination plays no part unless we can say that giving opinions or evaluating facts is imagination.

Biography is an account of a part or the whole of a person's life. It is called autobiography when the person has written the story of his own life.

The essay is most often a short work in which the author discusses anything of interest to himself from his personal point of view. The subject may be important or trivial. It may be treated humorously or seriously. A speech is an oral essay.

Factual reporting may include any writing from newspaper stories to magazine articles to full-length books. Giving the facts or relating events exactly as they happened is its purpose. It may deal with any subject about which someone may wish to read. For example, current events, art, science, travel, adventure, exploration, history, etc.

Poetry was once the favorite form of literature.* Much great literature from ancient times, such as Homer's Odyssey and Iliad, was originally written in poetic form. It is no accident that Shakespeare's plays are poetry; he was merely giving his audiences what they wanted. Even today, despite what many of us say, we prefer poetry to pure prose. Our political parties realize this when they write poetic campaign slogans such as, Tippecanoe and Tyler too, I like Ike, and All the Way with LBJ. Advertisers spend fortunes of money to develop slogans that rhyme or a catchy rhythm. In making speeches, famous men will switch to a form of poetry to emphasize a great thought or ideal. Abraham Lincoln wrote poetry in the Gettysburg Address: ". . . and that government of the people, by the people, and for the people shall not perish from the earth." John F. Kennedy in his inaugural address did the same with: "Ask not what your country will do for you--ask what you can do for your country." Even children learning to speak prove our natural preference for poetry. They easily and quickly learn nursery rhymes, advertizing slogans, and jingles that have either rhythm or rhyme. Older children delight in playing games accompanied by rhyming and rhythmic jingles.

The enjoyment of poetry, like anything else, requires some understanding. People do not care for what they know little about. Actually, understanding poetry requires little more effort than knowing why poetry is written. Once you know the purpose of poetry, you should be able to decide what poems you like. No person can like all poetry. We all like food, but we vary considerably in our preferences. Some foods we dislike while others may thoroughly delight us. So it is with poetry. Only when you know what it is, can you choose those poems you may enjoy.

Narrative poetry tells a story. It may be any length, from an amusing limerick to an epic like Beowulf or a romance like Scott's The Lady of the Lake.

Lyric poetry expresses the feelings of the author. He uses "word pictures" in rhythm to reveal his emotions, to describe beauty, and to inspire us with his thoughts and ideals. Therefore, lyric poetry is a personal expression of the author's moods and imagination. Literally, a lyric is a song. The lyrics of popular songs today are poems. How often have you liked a song because of its words? There is merely another example of people enjoying poetry today.

Rhythm. The meaning of the words is the first ingredient of poetry. Rhythm is the second. Just as in music, the rhythm of poetry aids in expressing the thought. A stirring story or exciting event calls for a rhythm such as a military band might play. A love story would require any rhythm found in love songs, while a lullaby should have a delicate and dreamy rhythm.

Rhyme is frequently used in poetry. It can add to the musical feeling and help emphasize the rhythm. Still it is not essential. Much great poetry is rhymeless.

Blank verse is poetry that is unrhymed iambic pentameter. Shakespeare's plays are examples of blank verse.

Free verse has no rhyme or regular rhythm. But this does not mean that rhythm is lacking. Usually it is too subtle to be quickly noticed. Free verse tries to develop a natural rhythm that suggests the activity or feeling of the poem. For example, a free verse poem about sounds heard in the woods would employ a different rhythm to suggest the different sounds mentioned in the poem.

---

*We should beware, despite the obvious differences, of making too sharp a distinction between prose and poetry as between two quite different uses of language.

THE NOVEL

What can we say about the novel?

A novel is a prose account of human experiences that are not only unique, but also universal. A novel enables man to see facets of himself, but in doses that are ordered, palatable, entertaining, or symbolic.

A novel should point out something (an experience, a thought, a condition, a possibility) and spotlight it as being worth consideration because not everyone can think of or experience all the things that are worth thinking of or experiencing.

A novel is a book that tells you something. It can give you greater insight into human behavior or about the world around you. It is not some romantic story which is nothing but drivel. A novel can entertain but not just on the level of the romance.

A novel should have a plot, should have complete character development, should have a theme, should have an antagonist and protagonist.

A novel should deal with the entertainment of a person's mind. It doesn't have to be a true to life event to the reader, but should make the reader become interested in it by presenting the reader with thoughts and ideas to expand their day to day life. It shows how everything isn't the same to everyone in the world and the possibilities of something existing that one would never find possible in their life.

A novel should be either a reading to let you escape from reality for awhile, or a reading which will teach you some knowledge about life. A good novel should do both of these; it should hold the reader's attention, provide entertainment, and also make the reader think.

A novel is a piece of life cornered by some person amateur or professional and thoroughly exposed and discussed and looked at. A novel should have some realism in it otherwise it will only amuse and not instruct as most authors wish their novels to do. The novel should have two levels, the amusement level and the hard, deep level where nothing is sacred and everything can be criticized or agreed upon or discussed.

E. M. Forster said: "Prose, because it is a medium for daily life as well as for literature, is particularly sensitive to what is going on, and two tendencies can be noted; the popular, which absorbs what is passing, and secondly, the esoteric, which rejects it, and tries to create something more valuable than monotony and bloodshed. The best work of the period has this esoteric tendency. . ."

Purpose of Reading a Novel

1. Novels are representations of life, of the world, and of the peoples who make up those worlds. The reading of a novel gives a vicarious experience of some facets of the world, thus life. The reading of a novel gives one perhaps added insights or new perspectives on some parts of life.

    a. since they can't experience all life, novels can offer some experience not gotten in everyday world.

    b. since novels explore more deeply into the situation and the minds of the characters the experience can be more full, or more revealing.

2. Because what you understand about a novel, what you "get" from it are dependent on what you already know or have experienced, a novel can give added dimension or understanding to your own conceptions of the world. Novels may change/alter your conceptions or preconceptions.

   a. good novels are psychological documents.

   b. good novels are the depiction of one man's or Man's, or a number of peoples conflicts without life. Their solutions may offer suggestions for one's own solutions; their non-solutions as examples of poor solutions.

   c. good novels show characters who find or do not show their peace without life--again, can offer examples.

   d. every novel should say something to the individual--give him something to fit to his perception of world.

   e. novels should <u>entertain</u>.

<u>Study Guide for Any Novel</u>

1. Theme is the central or dominating idea in a literary work. In a novel it is the abstract concept which is made concrete through its representation in person and action. It is the basic idea or general truth the author is try- to present. In any novel your task is to define what you believe the theme is.

2. Plot or the situation or story itself; what is happening between the characters.

   The author has complete control of the series of actions he depicts. He chooses and arranges his incidents to focus on the theme, to build the characterization of his characters, and to create an effect that dominates the novel.

   Plot is <u>not</u> merely the random ordering of a series of incidents; the series must be unified toward a goal (that of creating a fictive world in which the theme is set forth) to be a plot.

   Plot is the interrelationship of the actions; these interrelationships give unity to the novel.

   Plot sets forth the major and minor conflicts in any novel.

3. Conflict is the "meat" of the plot. Conflict is the struggle which grows out of the interplay of two opposing forces in the novel. <u>Usually</u> one of these forces is a character in the novel.

   The conflict may be the struggle between man and nature. A character may struggle against another person. A character may struggle against society. The conflict may be within the character himself; his good nature may struggle against his tendency to do evil, his jealousy of a friend may be in conflict with his love for that friend, or his desire to run away from a situation may be in opposition to his feeling that to run would be cowardly, for example. Or a character may struggle, most often uselessly, against fate, against his destiny.

For any novel define what struggle, or more probably struggles, is or are going on in the novel. What type of struggles are they? Once you see what conflicts are being presented, you can usually define what the central ideas or themes in the novel are.

For any novel ask how do these conflicts arise from the personality and situations of the characters, how do these characters face and solve, or not solve, these conflicts.

4. Obviously the characters are the persons who act and are acted upon in the novel. The characters serve to carry the author's theme. It is through the actions and feeling of the characters that the theme is presented.

   A character is developed or shown by:

   a. straightforward descriptions of how the character looks.

   b. outright presentations of what the character is feeling.

   c. the author's narration of what the character does.

   d. what the other characters say about him, tell you about him.

   e. how other characters react to him, feel toward him.

   f. how the character himself reacts to other characters, to society, and to the objects in his world.

   For any novel note how the particular author develops his characters and note what information leads you to form the opinions you do about the characters.

5. Setting is the physical, and sometimes spiritual, background against which the action of a narrative takes place. The elements which go to make up a setting are: (1) the actual geographical location, its scenery, its "props"; (2) the occupations and daily manner of living of the characters; (3) the time or period in which the action takes place, and (4) the general environment of the characters, that is, religious, moral, mental, social, and emotional conditions through which the people in the novel move.

   For any novel ask what is the actual location and physical setting, what is the daily manner of living, what is the time period and/or season, and what is the general environment of the characters (religious, moral, social, etc.). Then ask how these relate to the theme or what theme that they could be aiming at. Ask how the <u>whole</u> setting adds to the characterization, plot, theme, etc.

6. The way in which the author views the story; who tells it. The most widely used points of view are:

   a. omniscient (all-knowing), in which the author knows and portrays the thoughts and actions of all the characters--he is always aware of what will happen at every point of the story.

   b. first person, in which the story is told from the limited knowledge of the narrator--all thoughts and actions are seen through his eyes.

c. partial omniscient, in which the author limits his awareness of thoughts and actions to one character.

d. objective, in which the author sees and records without expressing an opinion or comment.

Criteria for Critically Evaluating the Novel

1. A good novel contains action. This action need not be physical, external action; it quite often is internal action.

   a. The action of a good novel is based on a condition of suspense. Suspense in a novel is defined as a means of developing and maintaining interest by creating expectations (through uncertainty and anticipation) in the reader.

2. The major characters of a good novel are believable. This is not to say that they are people who seem familiar to the average reader. A "real" character should grow and change as a personality, yet he must remain a fairly consistent being; an author cannot make you believe in a character if that character suddenly commits an action against his established nature.

   a. The author builds his character carefully, always preparing the way for a major change or decision.

   b. Stereotyped characters are those that are rigid; they never change. A good novelist rarely uses a stereotyped character in a major position.

3. A good novel will build to a climax or climaxes. Climax here shall be defined as a turning point in the situation of the major character(s) or an incident that brings about a crisis in the character's situation. This turning point or crisis sets the way for the outcome of the novel.

   a. The climax may be action-oriented or may be an internal event.

   b. A climax need not be an especially dramatic or exciting point; it need only be significant.

4. A novel of value will have a theme. Any good novel will have an idea, a philosophy, a message to communicate.

   a. This theme is not necessarily world-shaking, but it will be some point that a reader can ponder. This requirement of theme satisfies the intellect of the reader; he wants to find something more than a mere story.

   b. However, a good novel should not obscure its theme, thus leaving the reader wondering exactly what the point of the narrative is. A good novelist will not bludgeon you over the head with his message, yet he also will not beat around the bush.

5. A satisfying novel will have a "good ending." Loosely defined, a good ending is one that seems appropriate to the action that has preceded it.

   a. The ending should fit the mood of the novel. If the novel has been extremely pessimistic, the famous "happily-ever-after" ending may seem wrong or ridiculous.

b. The surprise ending will be appropriate only if there have been some hints that this surprise could happen. Otherwise the reader may feel that the author has used a gimmick to merely make his novel "different."

c. The "leave-you-hanging" ending will satisfy only if the novelist has previously given enough information to let the reader piece together his own ending. Otherwise the reader may feel that the author himself didn't have any idea of an ending.

d. The novelist therefore must always prepare the way for his ending or the ending will not be believable.

6. An effective novelist will always be conscious of his style. If his style is not appropriate to his subject matter, the novel will not satisfy the reader.

a. The language the author uses should fit the characters; the dialogue should be part of the character. Thus the author must make his words fit the economic background, the social environment, and the age of the characters.

(1) the language of the novel should always be consistent with the mood of the novel.

b. The amount of description an author will use will depend partly on the author's preference for prose description. Yet a good novelist also realizes that there are guidelines to the amount of description that is satisfying to the reader.

(1) the amount of description should be enough to let the reader "see" the environment and "feel" the mood. Once this has been accomplished any more may clog the novel. Thus exotic places and unusual environments will warrant more elaboration than the commonplace.

(2) the amount of description should be parallel to the emphasis the novelist wants to place on the places/things described. Thus if a novelist emphasized the appearance of a certain place, it should contain some importance to the narrative. For example, Lewis, in Babbitt, wanted to show how "thing-conscious" George Babbitt was, so he detailed a description of Babbitt's bathroom.

(3) description should not be hung on the reader all at once; it gets weighty. A good novelist will interweave his description with his action.

c. A good novelist will be careful to project a tone that is consistent with the story. An experienced novelist can find that his choice of words or arrangement of events has projected an attitude he never meant to give; a reader will sense this.

AP/CLEP FREE-RESPONSE ESSAYS: THE NOVEL

The suggested topics in the AP Examination around the novel should include: the structure of the novel, i.e., concepts of character, techniques of characterization, and psychological perspectives. Other topics , such as structual topics, follow.

Setting:

1. Social milieu
2. Physical and historical setting
3. Symbolic elements

Points of View:

1. Shifting or complex points of view
2. Centers of consciousness
3. Embedded points of view

Patterns of Plot:

1. Biographical
2. Mythic
3. Chronicle
4. Picturesque

The tone of the novel should include the philosophical perspectives (existentialism, puritanism), historical and social background, and the special techniques for conveying meaning, i.e., allegory, authorial intrusion or overt philosophizing.

Sample Essay Responses on Novels:

<u>Realism As Seen In the Character of Elizabeth Bennet</u>

The novel <u>Pride and Prejudice</u> is a very realistic novel. The majority of the characters are normal men and women. They are very believable and they don't act in any way that is unreal. The author, Jane Austen, makes each character a very real and convincing individual. In this paper I will attempt to show the realistic character of the heroine, Elizabeth Bennet, as seen in her relation with Fitzwilliam Darcy.

Jane Austen depicts Elizabeth as a very real person. Elizabeth in no way appears as a storybook character. She behaves and reacts in different situations as most credible, true to life people do.

In making decisions, Elizabeth carefully ponders every side of an issue. She doesn't regard anything as being unimportant. She knows that any decision she makes must be carefully thought out. I think this is best seen in the length of time she takes to decide how she feels about Darcy. She receives his proposal and his letter just a little further than midway through the story. It isn't until quite near the end of the story that Elizabeth makes up her mind in favor of Darcy. It is Elizabeth's final admission of her love for Darcy and the results of this that bring the story to an end.

After Lizzy receives the letter she doesn't become immediately infatuated with Darcy. She reads and rereads the letter. "Her feelings as she read were scarcely to be refined. Astonishment, apprehension, and even horror, appeased her." She refused to accept and believe many parts of the letter. She took her time deciding what course she would follow. She didn't jump into anything blindly, and didn't believe it to be something written in a moment of rashness which would later hold no meaning. "She studied every sentence and her feelings toward its writer were at times widely different." As any normal person would have done, Lizzy changed and rechanged her ideas and opinions. She didn't merely read Darcy's letter and become convinced of his fairness. It definitely took time.

More of Elizabeth's realistic character shows through when she confides her problem to Jane. "Elizabeth's impatience to acquaint Jane with what had happened could no longer be overcome. . ." As anyone that finds themselves in a dilemma, Elizabeth wanted to speak with Jane, her older sister, about it. Elizabeth needed to be comforted and listened to. She needed someone to be close to.

> (Elizabeth): "I was uncomfortable enough. I was very uncomfortable, I may say unhappy. And with no one to speak to of what I felt, no Jane to comfort me and say that I had not been so very weak and vain and nonsensical as I knew I had! Oh! how I wanted you!"

The convincingly real feelings and emotions of Lizzy are seen in this quotation. She is troubled and confused. She needs some reassurance that her courses of action have been right. She needed someone to tell her that everything would be all right.

Jane Austen also gives Elizabeth an imagination as you or I must surely have. As Lizzy is strolling around the grounds at Pemberly with her aunt and uncle she imagines what it might be like to be the mistress of such a grand place. She felt "that to be mistress of Pemberly might be something."

Elizabeth is also a very open-minded and inquisitive character. She is always open for new bits of information which will help her to formulate her opinions. Her opinion of Darcy is challenged by the letter she receives from him. Her opinion is again challenged when she is residing at Pemberly. Darcy's housekeeper speaks very highly of him. "He is the best landlord, and the best master that ever lived." Elizabeth's curiosity is aroused and she wishes to know more.

> "This was perhaps, of all others most extraordinary, most opposite to her ideas. That he was not a grand-tempered man had been her firmest opinion. Her keenest attention was awakened; she longed to hear more."

Standing before a large painting of Darcy "a more gentle sensation towards the original than she had ever felt in the height of their acquaintance" filled Elizabeth's mind. She thought of his regard "with a deeper sentiment of gratitude than it had ever raised before; she remembered his warmth." Here Elizabeth's very real emotions are again being seen. She is being sentimental and dreamy. She is beginning to think that there possibly is a place in her heart for Darcy.

> "She certainly did not hate him. No; hatred had vanished long ago and she had almost as long been ashamed of ever feeling a dislike against him. . . She respected, she esteemed, she was grateful to him. She felt a real interest in his welfare. . .!!

Elizabeth's feelings continued on in this trend until they developed into love for Darcy. Once Darcy realizes what Lizzy's feelings are they become engaged. They later marry and the novel ends on a happy note.

The characteristics of Elizabeth which I have presented in this paper, and many other characteristics, all add up and present us with a very convincingly, real character. Elizabeth is portrayed as such an ordinary person that you wouldn't be surprised to find people similar to her in any walk of life.

The Convert

Ever since the time Alec D'Urberville had been introduced into the novel, he was always conspiring to have Tess. He wronged her, yet the knowledge of this didn't stop him from pursuing her. In Phase the Sixth, Tess recognizes a traveling preacher to be none other than her cruel seducer Alec D'Urberville. I plan to focus on this phase of the novel to prove that this brief conversion resulted in his pursuit and subsequent capture of Tess.

The phase commences with Tess' description of the man behind the pulpit. She states that "his dress was half-clerical; a modification which had changed his expression sufficiently to abstract the dandyism from his features". The phrase "half-clerical" raised doubt in my mind as to whether he had totally reformed. He appeared to have changed, but was it only a facade that he presented? In actuality, it was a facade.

Tess states, "It was less a reform than a transfiguration." Alec had undergone a physical change. That was apparent by his attire. However, it was ironical that a man who was so corrupt and cruel should be preaching the Scriptures. In order for him to have sincerely reformed, he would have had to change his character completely. This was impossible for him to do for even his nature rejected it. Tess relates this through her description of Alec as he is preaching from the pulpit.

> "The lineaments, as such, seemed to complain. They had been diverted from their hereditary connotation to signify impressions for which nature did not intend them. Strange that their very elevation was a misapplication, that to raise seemed to falsify."

Then Alec detects Tess, and he becomes totally unnerved. "The effect upon her lover was electric". Alec was very upset. He stumbled over his words and could barely speak. There is no doubt that she still had a great amount of influence on him. This line not only informs you that he is not acting as a preacher would, but that he also has feelings for Tess. The key word in the phrase is "lover". The narrator did not describe Alec as a minister, but as Tess' lover.

When they meet in the road, Tess remarks: "The inferior man was certainly quiet in him now, but it was surely not extracted, nor even entirely subdued." Alec's former personality was certainly not subdued. From then on, Alec's former self started to emerge. He had Tess cover her face with her veil so that he could not gaze upon her good looks, which were reviving his old feelings for her. He had her swear on the stone at the spot known as "Cross-in-Hand", that she would not tempt him with her charms and ways. He requested that she see him again, but she declined.

Already, he started his pursuit of her. He told her that he wanted to see her again so that he could save her soul. He visited her against her wishes and asked her to marry him. Had he sincerely wanted to help her, he would have sent another preacher to see her, and stayed out of her life. However, he did not. He visited her many times after this, and tormented her by continually asking her to go away with him. In Phase the Seventh, you will discover that he achieves his aim.

Toward the end of the phase, the narrator introduces other elements that provide insight on Alec's reformation. Previously, Tess had referred to Alec as a saint: "The greater the sinner, the greater the saint." Yet as the phase progresses, the above comparison was contradicted.

In the aforementioned scene, Tess overtakes a stranger and asks him the meaning of the stone. She was told that it was an ill omen. The man who was buried there had sold his soul to the devil. Tess had sworn to Alec as the man had sworn to the devil. Alec becomes a devil image, something of evil. The narrator uses words such as "tempt", to describe his advances toward Tess. Alec also compares himself to Satan when he relates a version of the devil tempting Eve.

> "You are Eve, and I am the old Other One come to tempt you in the disguise of an inferior animal. I used to be quite up in that scene of Milton's when I was theological. Some of it goes--'Empress, the way is ready, and not long. . . . If thou accept
> My conduct, I can bring thee thither, soon.' 'Lead then, said Eve."

Alec does lead on. He led Tess to believe that she should trust him. He convinced her that Angel would not return and that she should let him take care of her. He achieved this and only got her deeper into trouble.

Alec's brief conversion and final actions depict Hardy's philosophies of life. Hardy believed that life is shaped by chance, not by moral design. Fate was the deciding factor, and in no way could you change the final outcome. Therefore, Alec could not reform because he was destined to be an evil character. He was to be the administrant of Tess' downfall and his own destruction.

Reflections on The Portrait of a Lady

In "The Portrait of a Lady" characters are seen, for the most part, through their association with Isabelle Archer. They are often described through her eyes. At first she gives an impression of them; then, as the novel progresses, she goes deeper into their characters. In this way I feel she reveals her own personality through her changing views of others. I would like to show how Isabelle's traits are brought out through her views of others then go on to show how her changing views of Casper Goodwood reflect her changing personality.

When Casper is first introduced into the novel he is described by Isabelle. "He was tall, strong, and somewhat stiff. He was not romantically but rather obscurely, handsome; but his physiognomy had an air of requesting your attention, which it rewarded according to the charm you found in blue eyes of remarkable fixedness, the eyes of a complexion other than his own, and a jaw of somewhat angular mould which is supposed to bespeak resolution." It is the last fact, his air of resolution, that seems to bother Isabelle because it conflicts with her personality. In her thoughts about Casper she is showing us one of her traits. The fact that she doesn't like resolution is brought out in this passage. Later, when speaking to Mr. Touchett, this fact is revealed more clearly. Isabelle says "I don't like everything settled beforehand. I like more unexpectedness."

A few months after her arrival in Europe Isabelle's gradual character change is observed by Henrietta Stackpole. On their first encounter, Henrietta said, "Yes, you've changed; you've got new ideas over here." In America she had been independent in spirit but being "out in the world" has helped her to express these feelings more noticeably. When Isabelle was at home in Albany she encouraged Casper but when she was on her own she wanted to hear nothing of him.

Isabelle's most appealing quality to others is her sense of independence. She thought very highly of it, "If there's a thing in the world I'm fond of, it's my personal independence," and it was because of her liberty that she rejected both Lord Warburton and Mr. Goodwood. When speaking of Casper she said, "Sometimes Casper Goodwood had seemed to range himself on the side of her destiny, to be the stubbornest fact she knew: she said to herself at such moments that she might evade him for a time, but that she must make terms with him at last--terms which would be certain to be favourable to himself." She had high respect for him but she also felt that he would limit her if she were to marry him.

After Isabelle went off to Europe, Casper followed her there. At this point she really didn't know what she wanted most in life but she was sure that her plans didn't include Casper. She asked him to go away, to leave her alone. When he asked if he must stay away forever she answered "Indefinitely is more than I ask. It's more even than I should like." In this last sentence and through her actions after his departure Isabelle revealed the fact that her mind was confused and that she really didn't know what her future might be.

In Chapter 21 Isabelle began to doubt her actions. She knew that her reasons for telling Casper to go were good but, in her thoughts, "she reflected that she herself might know the humiliation of change, might really, for that matter come to the end of the things that were not Casper and find rest in those very elements of his presence which struck her now as impediments to the finer respiration." She admitted that her feelings about Casper may some day change. This helps to show that Isabel did doubt her actions and ideas and that she wasn't as secure as she had led others to believe.

After hearing of Isabel's engagement in a letter she wrote to him, Mr. Goodwood wasted no time in getting to Europe. Isabel knew that he would most probably travel to Italy but she really didn't know how he would act or what he would say. She tried to tell herself that her actions were right but her thoughts conveyed a different message. Isabel had wanted Casper to tell her how badly she had treated him and how unjust her actions were. "She had wished his visit would be short; it had no purpose, no propriety; yet now that he seemed to be turning away she felt a sudden horror of his leaving her without uttering a word that would give her an opportunity to defend herself. . ." The fact that she had to defend herself against something she didn't do implies that she wasn't sure her actions were in her best interest.

In her first year of marriage Isabel heard nothing of Casper and thought of him very little. "As time went on Isabel had thought of him oftener, and with fewer restrictions: she had had more than once the idea of writing to him." With our knowledge of how Isabel's marriage was after their first year, we can see how her feelings toward Casper reflect the changes in her own life.

Isabel's life in Italy with Osmond was very unreal. She tried to convince everyone including Casper that she was happy. It was not until just before he left with Ralph that Isabel revealed her feelings to him. She began to treat Casper with more understanding and compassion. After he tells of his love for her he asked if he could pity her. Isabel's reply is "Don't give your life to it; but give a thought to it every now and then." This left Casper with a feeling that there was some hope in what he was striving for.

In the closing scenes of the book Casper tried to convince Isabel to trust him. When Goodwood asked her why she should go back to Rome her reply is "To get away from you! But this expressed only a little of what she felt. The rest was that she had never been loved before." Although her actions are quite harsh there is a meaning behind them that is not obviously seen. What her true feelings are is a more difficult question to answer. Her feelings toward herself and toward Casper are questionable. She has changed throughout the novel and so have her feelings toward Casper. In the end when Casper meets with Henrietta he is left with the "key to patience." I feel that this ends the novel on a note of hope for Casper and Isabel.

Student Essays on the Novel, Scarlet Letter

These essays deal with the structure of the novel and tone in the literary work; the essays are uncorrected and not graded. Students are encouraged to read the essays critically and to practice with additional character analyses in other novels.

Sample 1

In Nathaniel Hawthorne's novel, THE SCARLET LETTER, Roger Chillingworth is the character who is most evil. Hester Prynne, Roger's wife, committed the sin of adultery. Roger Chillingworth always knew that she did not love him. He married her with the hope that she would grow to love him. He was much older than Hester, but he still married her. This was essentially Chillingworth's first mistake. However, Chillingworth was fully aware of what he was doing.

When Roger finally comes to the town where Hester is living, he finds his wife the disgrace of the town. Chillingworth was not surprised; he knew Hester never loved him. Instead of announcing who he is, he takes a false name and occupation, that of a doctor named Chillingworth. This name seems to fit him well as he certainly has a cold heart, never feeling love. Chillingworth decides to avenge this injustice. It does not take Roger long to learn that Hester's paramour is the Reverend Arthur Dimmesdale. Chillingworth does not say anything to Dimmesdale. He knows that he is being tortured by his own conscience. Roger pretends to be the Reverend's best friend and protector, with nothing else in mind but the Reverend's health. Poor Arthur did not know he was befriending an evil friend.

Roger Chillingworth was tormenting Arthur Dimmesdale because of the injustice Hester and Arthur had committed. However, Roger knew that the sin Hester had committed could hardly be called an injustice to him. However, he responds to this dishonor with intellect, since that is all he has--he has no feelings. He uses his intelligence to torture Dimmesdale. Hester even speaks to him and asks him to stop. This has no effect on Roger. Roger knows what he is doing and what he is. He states,

> "Better had he died at once! Never did mortal suffer what this man has suffered. And all, all, in the sight of his worst enemy! . . . With the superstitions common to his brotherhood, he fancied himself given over to a fiend, to be tortured with frightful dreams, and desperate thoughts, the sting of remorse, and despair of pardon; as a foretaste of what awaits him beyond the grave. But it was the constant shadow of my presence!--the closest propinquity of the man whom he had most vilely wronged!--and who had grown to exist only by this perpetual poison of the duest revenge! Yea, indeed!--he did not err!--there was a fiend at his elbow! A mortal man, with once a human heart, has become a fiend for his especial torment!"

Chillingworth knows that he is a fiend. The sin he commits is that of revenge. However, Roger enjoys watching Dimmesdale suffer. Chillingworth knows that Dimmesdale is close to death, but he keeps him alive with herbs and other medicines. He thinks that death would be too good for Arthur. He wants him alive so he can torture him.

Although Hester was as guilty as Arthur, Roger seems to forgive her. He does not torment her; he thinks the scarlet letter is enough. He even leaves Hester and Pearl a more than substantial amount of property. He does not show any hatred to either Hester or her daughter. He realizes Hester has been punished enough. However, he does not think Dimmesdale has gone through enough, so he continues to torture him. Roger also feels partially to blame for Hester's sin. If he had not trapped her in a loveless marriage, she may not have transgressed.

Roger Chillingworth does not have the right to torture Arthur Dimmesdale. Evidently, Roger does not realize this. However, he does realize his evilness. He does not appear human. He has a passion for tormenting Roger to seek revenge. The three major characters, Hester, Roger, and Arthur have all committed sins. However, Roger is the worst one of all three. He realizes his evilness, but does not stop being evil.

Sample 2

In the novel THE SCARLET LETTER, written by Nathaniel Hawthorne, there are several involved interactions between the main characters. One example of such interactions is the relationship between the supposed physician, Roger Chillingworth and the minister Arthur Dimmesdale.

Chillingworth gradually undergoes the metamorphasis from a gentler, kind scholar into a demon entity. This transformation is brought on by Dimmesdale's failure to confess his guilt. When Chillingworth first meets Dimmesdale, there is a fire in his soul which burns brighter with every chance he obtains to carry out his vendetta towards the minister. After some time, the physician obtains his will of existence from Dimmesdale's suffering.

As Chillingworth is carrying out his torture on the unknowing minister, there comes a change in his overall appearance. His face is twisted into a grimace of horror and evil. The townspeople notice him and remark that their minister has a devil in his midst but that this devil will not overtake the local saint.

Later on in the book, Chillingworth tells Hester directly that his evil stems from Dimmesdale. He relates the fact that he survives on Arthur's torment and suffering. However, as he is relating his discourse, he cowers back in repulsion as he sees himself turning into a devilish creature. Chillingworth has to blame someone else for his condition just as Dimmesdale places his grievances as Hester's and Chillingworth's faults. This unfortunate occurence in Roger does take place because of Arthur. Chillingworth's evil manifests itself in Dimmersdale's emancipated being, but as Dimmesdale slowly dies, so too does Chillingworth.

Sample 3

In THE SCARLET LETTER, the decoration on Hester's bosom influenced all who knew of it in New England. It benefited many people, including Hester Prynne, her daughter Pearl, and the notorious Arthur Dimmesdale.

Hester Prynne, by wearing the red A, elaborately embroidered, on her at all times after her infamy, could face the truth of her sin. She did not have to conceal the secret, thereby inflicting extreme pain onto herself. By letting others know, she released some of the burden she felt.

In the conference between Hester and the governor, Hester stated "this badge hath taught me--it daily teaches me--it is teaching me at this moment--lessons whereof my child may be the wiser and better." Hester's daughter Pearl was influenced greatly by her mother. Her strangeness resulted from their seclusion from others because of the fate of Hester. But the lurid A set an example for Pearl and made her aware of the strictness of the Puritan Age they lived in. This difference in Pearl could have helped her to grow up independently and not as somberly as the others.

In the chaos of Pearl's lonely life there appeared in her "principles of an inflicting courage,--an uncontrollable will,--a sturdy pride, which might be disciplined into self-respect,--and a bitter scorn of many things, found to have a taint of falsehood in them."--which made it easy to believe Pearl may become a noble woman.

The discussion between Roger Chillingworth and the minister emphasizes the comfort of not hiding away the bad deeds one has done.

"There goes a woman," resumed Roger Chillingworth, after a pause, "who, be her dements what they may, hath none of that mystery of hidden sinfulness which you deem so grievous to be borne. Is Hester Prynne the less miserable, think you, for that scarlet letter on her breast?"

"I do verily believe it," answered the clergyman. "Nevertheless I cannot answer for her. There was a look of pain in her face, which I would gladly have been spared the sight of. But still, methinks, it must be better for the sufferer to be free to show his pain, as this poor woman Hester is, than to cover it all up in his heart."

Arthur Dimmesdale, in seeing Hester daily exhibiting her symbol of adultery, was constantly reminded of why she was wearing it. He wished to announce the fact that he was Hester's paramour, but never seemed to get the courage to. Finally, after his eloquent speech at the procession, he ascended the scaffold where Hester had displayed her shame publicly, and released his agonizing secret, escaping the evilness of hypocrisy deep within his heart, and also destroying Chillingworth's constant punishment.

"Hads't thou sought the whole world over," said Roger Chillingworth, "there was no one place so secret,--no high place nor lowly place, where thou couldst have escaped me,--save on this very scaffold!"

The scarlet letter benefitted the townspeople by being true, which meant life and reality to them. They also became more aware of their own sins hidden deep within them.

The final opinion of the necessity of the scarlet letter was in the conclusion of THE SCARLET LETTER.

"Be true! Be true! Be true! Show freely to the world, if not your worst, yet some trait whereby the worst may be inferred!"

A SAMPLE AP ESSAY: CRIME AND PUNISHMENT

The scope and complexity of Dostoevsky's novel is of such magnitude, that upon serious reflection, I question my ability to write a comprehensive book report.

This is a pyschological novel and also a kind of detective story, but without the ramifications that are present in the typical detective story. In this story, we are presented with a young man of superior intellect who is convinced that he has been destined to do something noble and majestic for mankind. Thus the hero, Raskolnikov, becomes obsessed with his idea and from that idea springs the story which embodies realism, irrationality, pathos, philosophy, symbolism and religion and nihilism.

The story's appeal, to me, is its subject matter; not only its subject matter, but the style, the tone and the structure all combine in making this a book of unusual dimensions for study and artistic entertainment. As the novel progresses, the reader can see a unity in action: all the parts contribute to the whole, but before one can understand the parts one must be aware of the whole.

The drama unfolds bit by bit, revealing the philosophical and pyschological thinking of the characters. They engage in lengthy dialogues, drawing on politics, economics, history, law, and mankind in general. Raskolnikov is the central figure in this tale of good and evil. From his inner dialogues and his spoken dialogues the author's point of view via narrative exposition brings into sharp focus the social motifs--the extreme poverty of the Marmeladovs, the poverty of Raskolnikov and his family, and the squalor and filth in St. Petersburg; the overcrowded slums, the drunkenness, the evil and misery that exist in a big city.

Dostoevsky's novel deals with double exposures, that is, split personalities. Because of the dual nature of his characters, the drama is expressed in terms of conflict between opposite poles of self-sacrifice and self-assertion, spirit and mind, passiveness and agressiveness, good and bad. To make the conflict plausible, Dostoevsky supplies his characters with alter egos, or doubles, each projecting the extreme manifestation of that trait which is embodied in the mind of the split personality. Svidrigaylov is the alter ego of Raskolnikov. He is a man who has chosen to satisfy his appetities and greed, yet he also must satisfy a need to do good. Raskolnikov is the epitome of God-Man, the good and the bad. This clash of conscious and the sub-conscious results in the self-appointed role of benefactor of mankind; he sets his sights on a par with Napoleon, he will storm the ramparts. Raskolnikov exhibits an extraordinary pride, arrogance and contempt for society. In reality, I feel in his ideas those of a true despot, a man goaded by the wish to become powerful enough to wield his will on society.

The hero is exceedingly young, being only twenty-three years of age, and it is remarkable that at this age is capable of engaging in such profound dialogue with men many years his senior in age and in experience. The dialogue between Raskolnikov and Porfiry in the police office that brings out the caliber of Raskolnikov's mentality as well as his deep seated hatred of people, of life itself. He has such contempt for Porfiry's accurate insight of his involvement in the murder of the old pawnbroker, Alena Ivanova and her sister Lizaveta. Although one would relate his crime to madness, it is difficult to consider this to be the case in the light of his ability to debate theory.

Because of his personality, his egoism, and his depression, his theory does not stand on solid ground, it becomes apparent that it is counter to all the valid values rational men could abide by. In his argument in support of his theory, he refutes the Christian moral precepts that sacrifice and suffering enoble the spirit and that it is God's will that man accept this dictum as naturally right. It is his inability to accept this as a truism that enrages him and torments him beyond description. It is too abstract a reason for Raskolnikov. For whatever else he appears to be, one thing is certain; he is at times too rational, although from his point of view, only a man gifted with the talent to lead, a man of stature and power of his convictions, would hesitate to carry out an act of murder, if by that act the perpetrator of such a crime would rid the world of a useless "louse" who contributed nothing but grief and misery, who robbed the needy for self-gain.

It is this struggle that goes on within himself, that sparks the bulk of the inner dialogue in which Raskolnikov proves to be an extreme individualist, where he begins to formulate his idea. In this state he reaches a new level of consciousness. The idea is repulsive to him, but Reason takes over and embraces the idea, and he becomes desperate in his attempt to shake off the newly formulated idea. He becomes feverish, delirious, subject to violent emotions, and I began to look upon him as a man suffering from an extreme pathological condition. The contradiction exists in his anguished feelings about the Marmeladovs. His conscious reflections result in an aura of indefiniteness as to his motives in pursuing the course of action he has been building up to in his mind. After he had murdered the women and taken the loot to the spot where he had buried it, he suddenly stops in the street to ponder the question he asks of himself: "If it had all really been done deliberately and not idiotically, if I really had a certain and definite object, how is it that I did not even glance into the purse and didn't know what I had there. Then why have I undergone these agonies and have deliberately undertaken this dirty and degrading business?" There are several passages in which Raskolnikov loses sight of his motives.

From the very outset of the novel, Raskolnikov is disturbed by his idea. He wonders why he is thinking about that act--wondering whether he is really capable of it--such fantastic nonsense. "Am I really serious? No, of course I'm not serious. Yes, perhaps I am only play a game." In this conscious encounter with his subconscious, the ambiguity and incongruity is a forerunner of the psychological torments that beset him from the moment he gives birth to his idea.

As his idea formulates into theories, and thence to the overt act, apart from the philosophical and psychological nuances, one can understand the author's indictment of the social injustice the Russian masses were victims of. He uses his characters with such dexterity and purposefulness, that each character becomes an adjunct to the novel in its totality. There is the preoccupation with the self, the self in relation to his mother and sister, to Sonya, her family and his friend Razumikhin. On the other side of the coin his relationship with the police chief Zametov and the examiner, Porfiry is filled with an almost diabolical hatred of them.

Dostoevsky plays upon the reader's senses and emotions with unequivocal intent. It becomes clearly understood that Svidgigaylov is the essence of evil in the hero; Sonya supplies the spiritual chord for his eventual regeneration. It is she who brings him back from lifelessness to life. Her father, Marmeladov, opens for him the window into his soul and his intellect--from him he realizes that man suffers a needless tyrannical existence. His isolation, self-containment, and withdrawal from life experiences, due perhaps to his split personality, does not make him devoid from a reasonable trait of humanitarianism. This is what makes him resolve to save Dunya from sacrificing herself to Luzhin for his benefit. His mother's letter serves as the turning point in his life. It spurs him to action and results in the act that makes Raskolnikov and the rest of humanity share the guild equally; all humanity is--one man.

A SAMPLE AP ESSAY: A CRITICAL REVIEW OF FATHERS AND SONS

Turgenev's novel is more than a story about the conflicts between younger and older generations. It is a novel based on the socio-psychological-philosophical tenor of that time in history, prior to the emancipation of serfdom in Russia. It was also the decade when Western philosophers, scientists, writers of literature on humanism made a great wave in all segments of intellectual society. They attacked the old traditions and their mouldy conventions; held up to ridicule the stagnant mentality of the peasants conditioned and kept in abeyance by the Orthodox Church.

The conflict is directly concerned with these issues and a foreshadowing of the political upheaval concomitant to the views held by the Sons. Profound changes in a state of euphoria in which the Fathers existed, (and preferred to remain), irritated the Sons. Bazarov in particular. This hero is the antithesis to the dreams and beliefs the older generation clings to. He is not easy to like, mainly because he rejects and refutes in short, clipped sentences arguments on the subjects concerning art, music, poetry, and nature. Bazarov is a scientist, an empiricist. Yet with his penchant for belief in only those things that could be seen, touched, heard, smelled and tasted, it is a paradox that he could dismiss nature in all her glorious facets as just so much drivel.

Bazarov is disinclined to waste time, be it in conversation, or action in the form of trying to educate people he condescended to talk to, that he was a man of ideas, ideas he accepted from the radical critics Dobrolyubov and Chernyshevsky who were the proponents of "realism" and progressive ideas. Turgenev has incorporated in Bazarov the 'new man' of the nineteenth century. When Arkady describes him to his father and to his uncle Pavel, he calls him a nihilist, taken from the Latin which equates with 'nothing'. This establishes Bazarov as a man who believes in nothing and accepts nothing. Arkady tells them that Bazarov "regards everything from a critical point of view." Bazarov accepts nothing on faith, does not bow down to or before any authority.

Early in their relationship, both Nikolai and Pavel are conscious of the polarity that exists between them and Bazarov. They feel that the Sons are creating and living in a vacuum, and that the world which they wish to destroy would be meaningful if they could produce a significantly better world for the universal man. Turgenev has imbued his hero with both good and bad qualities; he possesses in his character elements of honesty and he is just, also he is a democrat; he is coarse, sharp and dry, exhibits a heartlessness. Bazarov is a man of strong mind and character. His aspirations are those of the younger generation, and at variance with the older, a notable representative of the disciples of the new political and psychological logic.

Bazarov is the central character in the book. He is in every chapter and thus enables the reader to measure the worth and significance of the other characters. This figure dominates everybody and everything. He is an isolationist and prefers it that way. When words annoy him or it becomes clear that his adversaries cannot match his mental and intellectual prowess, his remarks are sharp, curt, and he discontinues all talk and stalks away to his own room. Fatuity he cannot abide.

One may be inclined to dislike Bazarov, but one cannot in all justice divorce him from sincerity. He believes in the reality of the uneducated and superstitious peasants. He believes that romanticizing the past abrogates the future. In the dialogue between Pavel and himself, when the former tells him that Nikolai enjoys the poetry of Schiller and Goethe, he adds sarcastically that they are no longer considered worthwhile because in the present time "they are all some sort of chemists and materialists..." to which Bazarov replies, "A good chemist is twenty times as useful as any poet."

Pavel continues. "You don't recognize art then, I suppose?" And Bazarov's typical answer, "The art of making money or of 'shrink hemorrhoids'!"

There is no common ground upon which the old and the young can stand. Bazarov is pure negation--the Kirsanovs relics of a past that extolled all the arts and loved the land and nature. Although Bazarov came from the land himself, he identified not with the country, but with the city, where for the intellectual it represented life and ideas. The ideas make no allowance for sentimentality or romanticism. They are radical ideas that stress change in the old system and a new evaluation of the universe and of life itself; where and how man will fit into the scheme of things.

Bazarov has a high opinion of himself. He feels that he stands way above most men. It is that attitude that at once repels and delights one. Although Turgenev does not give an account of his hero's life prior to the reader's meeting him, it is still obvious that he must have been poor as a student and that whatever he accomplished he had to do by his own mettle. His father was a poor district doctor who could not help his son if he had wanted to. Bazarov knew and understood poverty. Perhaps because of the harshness life imposed upon him during his youth, he had not time to develop the capacity to enjoy the simple pleasures derived from painting, poetry, music or nature. It may also be the reason that life is devoid of dreams. He is also devoid of feelings of love.

In his encounter with the beautiful and intelligent Anna Odintsov, Bazarov admits to her that he has indeed fallen in love with her. His reaction to that feeling is akin to hatred. Her answer is a blow to his ego. But he does not plead--he walks out. Odintsov was also incapable of love. He tells Arkady when they have taken leave of their hostess, that "it's better to break stones on the highroad than to let a woman have the mastery of even the end of one's little finger." The only other love interest in the story is the affair between Arkady and Katya. This is traditional and conventional in its resolution.

Bazarov does not go out of his way to make his parents happy either. He cannot understand their emotions and their anguish when he informs them that he does not intend to stay with them more than a few days. His father is so impressed with his son's degree in science and medicine, that he gets into Bazarov's way when he tries to work. But Bazarov is true to his character, he must be honest even when it causes pain. The father is brokenhearted. He says, "He has cast us off; he has forsaken us; he was bored with us." The old are left behind while the young take off for parts unknown.

Turgenev artfully and beautifully brings into clear focus the chasm that exists between dreams and reality. The Pavels and the Bazarovs may represent different aspects of nature, but in a sense they are alike. Both are strong in their convictions and neither will accept what each stands for, for one believes nothing and the other cherishes his ideals.

Bazarov speaks in aphorisms and proverbs. He lives by calculation. He does only that which is advantageous to himself. Turgenev draws attention to his hero in an honest, if unflattering manner. A case in point is this dialogue between the two friends about the peasants. Arkady is indignant about the poverty and the miserable huts the peasants have and says, "Russia will attain perfection when the poorest peasant has a clean hut." And Bazarov replies, "and I felt such a hatred for this poorest peasant, this Philip or Sidor, for whom I'm ready to jump out of my skin, and who won't even thank me for it...and what do I need his thanks for?" There is cynicism, expressed and internal.

The story is replete with scenes and incidents. There does not seem to be a plot or a denouement. One is left with a feeling that Bazarov died in vain. He accomplished nothing; all he left behind of himself was a plethora of ideas. The conflict was not resolved. The Fathers' values will always be incompatible with the Sons'. Radical changes are never brought about peacefully. Nikolai and Pavel are the guardians of the older Culture; they belong to the past. Arkady the sentimentalist represents the Present although he is not aware of it. Bazarov is the champion of the future. The older generation represents the family; and it is ironical that this is what the nihilists were destroying, this and all it stood for, without offering a substantial change or modification for its loss. It is also true that the old could not be made over to fit the new, for they could not fit the deeds or ideas of their children to their own life styles.

When the novel is set aside, meditation takes over for one realizes that the theme of conflict is as old as time itself--solution impossible.

Turgenev's portraits of his characters makes them come to life. It is not difficult to picture Pavel extolling the virtues of the anglophile, both by dress and by act. Or Kuksin's appearance and her dishevelled apartment, papers in disarray. His description of both Bazarov and Vassily are interwoven with the background. And the picture of Sitnikov is verified by his antics around Bazarov. He delineates his characters with such exactitude, but not without feeling, and with great artistry.

The reader can visualize the people and what they hold dear by the language Turgenev uses to describe interiors of rooms, dress, feelings and one can get a picture of a part of Russia itself.

THE SHORT STORY

Romances

These are stories whose authors believe art should be a combination of imagination and feeling.

A. Traits

1. A romance makes life appear more exciting, more strange, or more noble than it is.

2. Often exotic, faraway settings are used.

3. The author glamorizes everyday life.

4. The story is sentimental; love is emphasized, but not only love for a person but also love for country, and, work, and ideal.

5. The author sees man as a noble creature and life as a noble experience; noble ideas are emphasized, such as patriotism, or brotherhood.

6. Nature is glorified.

7. The work is often optimistic; the author sees men as good.

8. Often there is a hero.

B. Local color stories often fall into this category since local color authors tend to exaggerate and glamorize their settings.

C. Humorous stories tend to be romances since they are usually optimistic and make life appear more interesting, more funny, than it really is.

Realistic

Realistic authors want to show life as it really is. They want to be fair and they see art's purpose as that of revealing life to people.

A. Traits

1. The author does not paint life as either good or bad; rather he makes life seem a bit of both.

2. Often the settings are everyday places and the incidents are ordinary happenings.

3. The characters are usually recognizable as people you could know.

Naturalistic

Naturalistic writers also want to show life as it really is. But naturalistic writers believe that life is not at all good, but is a constant struggle against evil and hardships. They feel the purpose of art is to force people into wanting to change bad conditions.

A. Traits

1. A gloomy picture of life.

2. Settings that are miserable and depressing.

3. Characters that seem to suffer constantly.

4. No relief in the story from the hardness of life.

5. Hardly any humor.

6. A reality that is almost too real, no glamorizing at all.

Plot in the Short Story

A. Plot is in simplest terms the incidents which form the story and the arrangement in which these incidents are ordered.

A plot is good only as long as its series of incidents is unified toward a goal, a dramatic conclusion.

B. A plot maintains interest through building up conflicts.

1. Conflict is the "meat" of the plot. It is the struggle or struggles which grow out of the relationships between two opposing forces or elements in the story. One of these forces, or elements, is a major character.

Conflicts may be struggles between:

(1) a man and himself

(2) a character and another character

(3) a character and Nature

(4) a character and society

(5) a character and fate or destiny

2. In a story the major character with whom we relate or sympathize is the <u>protagonist</u>.

The force or person against whom our protagonist struggles is the <u>antagonist</u>.

C. Plot revolves around characters facing problems. How the characters go about solving or failing to solve problems makes up the central issue of a plot. These problems the major characters face are the sources of these conflicts.

D. Every plot is essentially structured the same way. It follows the pattern of:

1. An introduction to the main characters and the basic situation they are faced with.

2. The rising action--this is the building up of conflicts within the story; the action increases in dramatic interest as the story moves along.

3. The climax--this is the point in the story of the highest dramatic interest; it is the exciting point in the story to which the previous action has been building. Usually the climax is a turning point in the story. From this point on the reader can see an approaching solution or end to the conflicts.

4. The dénouement--this is the untying or unravelling of all the conflicts; sometimes known as the falling action of the story where all the earlier questions and problems are resolved.

5. The conclusion is the final outcome of the story.

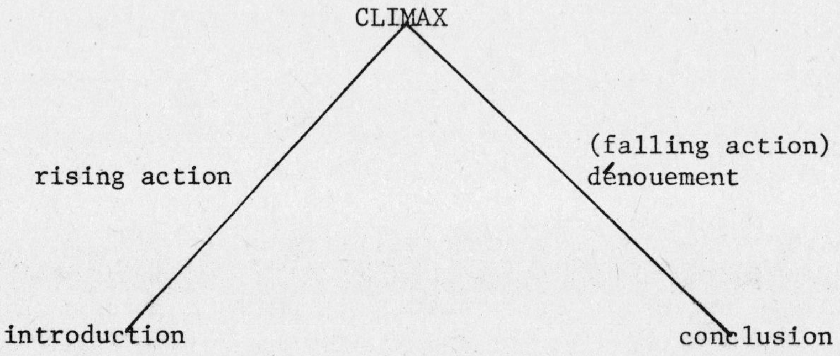

E. Discovering the theme in a short story.

1. Define the interactions and ultimate relationship between the qualities of the forces allied and against the man, and the qualities of the man.

2. Find the connections between the qualities, i.e., man is confident, courageous, persistent, optimistic and are in conflict with cold, powerful, lethal, relentless.

3. Outcome of the conflict says that the man is dead.

4. Theme is defined by the interactions and ultimate relationship between the qualities of man and the qualities of the forces allied or against him as he strives in a given situation to act as he wishes to attain what he wants.

5. Theme is also a generalization or conclusion about Man and Human Nature.

6. The theme may be: "Human courage and determination are not enough when matched against the powerful forces of nature."

BOOK OF RUTH[1]

CHAPTER ONE

Elimelech driven by famine into Moab, dieth there. 4 His two sons, having married wives of Moab, die also. 6 Naomi returning homeward, 8 dissuadeth her two daughters in law from going with her. 14 Orpah leaveth her, but Ruth cleaveth unto her. 19 They two come to Bethlehem.

1 Now it came to pass in the days when the judges ruled, that there was a famine in the land. And a certain man of Beth-lehem-judah went to sojourn in the country of Moab, he, and his wife, and his two sons.

2 And the name of the man was Elimelech, and the name of his wife Naomi, and the name of his two sons Mahlon and Chilion, Ephrathites of Beth-lehem-judah. And they came into the country of Moab, and continued there.

3 And Elimelech Naomi's husband died; and she was left, and her two sons.

4 And they took them wives of the women of Moab; the name of the one was Orpah, and the name of the other Ruth: and they dwelt there about ten years.

5 And Mahlon and Chilion died also both of them; and the woman was left of her two sons and her husband.

6 Then she arose with her daughters in law, that she might return from the country of Moab: for she had heard in the country of Moab how that the LORD had visited his people in giving them bread.

7 Wherefore she went forth out of the place where she was, and her two daughters in law with her; and they went on the way to return unto the land of Judah.

8 And Naomi said unto her two daughters in law, Go, return each to her mother's house: the LORD deal kindly with you, as ye have dealt with the dead, and with me.

9 The LORD grant you that ye may find rest, each of you in the house of her husband. Then she kissed them, and they lifted up their voice, and wept.

10 And they said unto her, Surely we will return with thee unto thy people.

11 And Naomi said, Turn again, my daughters: why will ye go with me? are there yet any more sons in my womb, that they may be your husbands?

12 Turn again, my daughters, go your way; for I am too old to have a husband. If I should say, I have hope, if I should have a husband also to night, and should also bear sons;

13 Would ye tarry for them till they were grown? would ye stay for them from having husbands? nay, my daughters; for it grieveth me much for your sakes that the hand of the LORD is gone out against me.

14 And they lifted up their voice, and wept again: and Orpah kissed her mother in law; but Ruth clave unto her.

1. The Holy Bible, New York: American Bible Society, 1860.

15 And she said, Behold, thy sister in law is gone back unto her people, and unto her gods: return thou after thy sister in law.

16 And Ruth said, Entreat me not to leave thee, or to return from following after thee: for whither thou goest, I will go; and where thou lodgest, I will lodge: thy people shall be my people, and thy God my God:

17 Where thou diest, will I die, and there will I be buried: the LORD do so to me, and more also, if aught but death part thee and me.

18 When she saw that she was steadfastly minded to go with her, then she left speaking unto her.

19 So they two went until they came to Beth-lehem. And it came to pass, when they were come to Beth-lehem, that all the city was moved about them, and they said, Is this Naomi?

20 And she said unto them, Call me not Naomi, call me Mara: for the Almighty hath dealt very bitterly with me.

21 I went out full, and the LORD hath brought me home again empty: why then call ye me Naomi, seeing the LORD hath testified against me, and the Almighty hath afflicted me?

22 So Naomi returned, and Ruth the Moabitess, her daughter in law, with her, which returned out of the country of Moab: and they came to Beth-lehem in the beginning of barley harvest.

CHAPTER TWO

Ruth gleaneth in the fields of Boaz. 4 Boaz inquireth concerning her, 8 and sheweth her great favour. 18 That which she gleaneth she carrieth to Naomi.

1 And Naomi had a kinsman of her husband's, a mighty man of wealth, of the family of Elimelech; and his name was Boaz.

2 And Ruth the Moabitess said unto Naomi, Let me now go to the field, and glean ears of corn after him in whose sight I shall find grace. And she said unto her, Go, my daughter.

3 And she went, and came, and gleaned in the field after the reapers: and her hap was to light on a part of the field belonging unto Boaz, who was of the kindred of Elimelech.

4 And, behold, Boaz came from Beth-lehem, and said unto the reapers, The LORD be with you. And they answered him, The LORD bless thee.

5 Then said Boaz unto his servant that was set over the reapers, Whose damsel is this?

6 And the servant that was set over the reapers answered and said, It is the Moabitish damsel that came back with Naomi out of the country of Moab:

7 And she said, I pray you, let me glean and gather after the reapers among the sheaves: so she came, and hath continued even from the morning until now, that she tarried a little in the house.

8 Then said Boaz unto Ruth, Hearest thou not, my daughter? Go not to glean in
another field, neither go from hence, but abide here fast by my maidens:

9 Let thine eyes be on the field that they do reap, and go thou after them: have I
not charged the young men that they shall not touch thee? and when thou art
athirst, go unto the vessels, and drink of that which the young men have drawn.

10 Then she fell on her face, and bowed herself to the ground, and said unto him,
Why have I found grace in thine eyes, that thou shouldest take knowledge of me,
seeing I am a stranger?

11 And Boaz answered and said unto her, It hath fully been shewed me, all that thou
hast done unto thy mother in law since the death of thine husband; and how thou
hast left thy father and thy mother, and the land of thy nativity, and art come
unto a people which thou knewest not heretofore.

12 The LORD recompense thy work, and a full reward be given thee of the LORD God of
Israel, under whose wings thou art come to trust.

13 Then she said, Let me find favour in thy sight, my lord; for that thou hast comforted me, and for that thou hast spoken friendly unto thine handmaid, though I
be not like unto one of thine handmaidens.

14 And Boaz said unto her, At mealtime come thou hither, and eat of the bread, and
dip thy morsel in the vinegar. And she sat beside the reapers: and he reached
her parched corn, and she did eat, and was sufficed, and left.

15 And when she was risen up to glean, Boaz commanded his young men, saying, Let her
glean even among the sheaves, and reproach her not:

16 And let fall also some of the handfuls of purpose for her, and leave them, that
she may glean them, and rebuke her not.

17 So she gleaned in the field until even, and beat out that she had gleaned: and
it was about an ephah of barley.

18 And she took it up, and went into the city; and her mother in law saw what she
had gleaned: and she brought forth, and gave to her that she had reserved after
she was sufficed.

19 And her mother in law said unto her, Where hast thou gleaned today? and where
wroughtest thou? blessed be he that did take knowledge of thee. And she shewed
her mother in law with whom she had wrought, and said, The man's name with whom
I wrought today is Boaz.

20 And Naomi said unto her daughter in law, Blessed be he of the LORD, who hath not
left off his kindness to the living and to the dead. And Naomi said unto her,
The man is near of kin unto us, one of our next kinsmen.

21 And Ruth the Moabitess said, He said unto me also, Thou shalt keep fast by my
young men, until they have ended all my harvest.

22 And Naomi said unto Ruth her daughter in law, It is good, my daughter, that thou
go out with his maidens, that they meet thee not in any other field.

23 So she kept fast by the maidens of Boaz to glean unto the end of barley harvest
and of wheat harvest; and dwelt with her mother in law.

CHAPTER THREE

By Naomi's instruction, 5 Ruth lieth down at the feet of Boaz. 8 He acknowledgeth the duty of a kinsman; 14 and sendeth her away with six measures of barley.

1 Then Naomi her mother in law said unto her, My daughter, shall I not seek rest for thee, that it may be well with thee?

2 And now is not Boaz of our kindred, with whose maidens thou wast? Behold, he winnoweth barley to night in the threshingfloor.

3 Wash theyself therefore, and anoint thee, and put they raiment upon thee, and get thee down to the floor: but make not thyself known unto the man, until he shall have done eating and drinking.

4 And it shall be, when he lieth down, that thou shalt mark the place where he shall lie, and thou shalt go in, and uncover his feet, and lay thee down; and he will tell thee what thou shalt do.

5 And she said unto her, All that thou sayest unto me I will do.

6 And she went down unto the floor, and did according to all that her mother in law bade her.

7 And when Boaz had eaten and drunk, and his heart was merry, he went to lie down at the end of the heap of corn: and she came softly, and uncovered his feet, and laid her down.

8 And it came to pass at midnight, that the man was afraid, and turned himself: and, behold, a woman lay at his feet.

9 And he said, Who art thou? And she answered, I am Ruth thine handmaid: spread therefore thy skirt over thine handmaid; for thou art a near kinsman.

10 And he said, Blessed be thou of the LORD, my daughter: for thou hast shewed more kindness in the latter end than at the beginning, inasmuch as thou followedst not young men, whether poor or rich.

11 And now, my daughter, fear not; I will do to thee all that thou requirest: for all the city of my people doth know that thou art a virtuous woman.

12 And now it is true that I am thy near kinsman: howbeit there is a kinsman nearer than I.

13 Tarry this night, and it shall be in the morning, that if he will perform unto thee the part of a kinsman, well; let him do the kinsman's part: but if he will not do the part of a kinsman to thee, then will I do the part of a kinsman to thee, as the LORD liveth: lie down until the morning.

14 And she lay at his feet until the morning: and she rose up before one could know another. And he said, Let it not be known that a woman came into the floor.

15 Also he said, Bring the vail that thou hast upon thee, and hold it. And when she held it, he measured six measures of barley, and laid it on her: and he went into the city.

16 And when she came to her mother in law, she said, Who art thou, my daughter? And
she told her all that the man had done to her.

17 And she said, These six measures of barley gave he me; for he said to me, Go not
empty unto thy mother in law.

18 Then said she, Sit still, my daughter, until thou know how the matter will fall:
for the man will not be in rest, until he have finished the thing this day.

CHAPTER FOUR

Boaz calleth the next kinsman before the elders; 6 but he refuseth
to redeem the inheritance of Elimelech according to the manner in
Israel. 9 Boaz buyeth it. 10 He marrieth Ruth. 13 She beareth
Obed the grandfather of David. 18 The generations of Pharez.

1 Then went Boaz up to the gate, and sat him down there: and, behold, the kinsman
of whom Boaz spake came by; unto whom he said, Ho, such a one! turn aside, sit
down here. And he turned aside, and sat down.

2 And he took ten men of the elders of the city, and said, Sit ye down here. And
they sat down.

3 And he said unto the kinsman, Naomi, that is come again out of the country of
Moab, selleth a parcel of land, which was our brother Elimelech's:

4 And I thought to advertise thee, saying, Buy it before the inhabitants, and before
the elders of my people. If thou wilt redeem it, redeem it: but if thou wilt not
redeem it, then tell me, that I may know: for there is none to redeem it besides
thee; and I am after thee. And he said, I will redeem it.

5 Then said Boaz, What day thou buyest the field of the hand of Naomi, thou must
buy it also of Ruth the Moabitess, the wife of the dead, to raise up the name of
the dead upon his inheritance.

6 And the kinsman said, I cannot redeem it for myself, lest I mar mine own inheritance: redeem thou my right to thyself; for I cannot redeem it.

7 Now this was the manner in former time in Israel concerning redeeming and concerning changing, for to confirm all things; a man plucked off his shoe, and gave it
to his neighbour: and this was a testimony in Israel.

8 Therefore the kinsman said unto Boaz, Buy it for thee. So he drew off his shoe.

9 And Boaz said unto the elders, and unto all the people, Ye are witnesses this day,
that I have bought all that was Elimelech's, and all that was Chilion's and
Mahlon's, of the hand of Naomi.

10 Moreover Ruth the Moabitess, the wife of Mahlon, have I purchased to be my wife,
to raise up the name of the dead upon his inheritance, that the name of the dead
be not cut off from among his brethren, and from the gate of his place: ye are
witnesses this day.

11 And all the people that were in the gate, and the elders, said, We are witnesses.
The LORD make the woman that is come into thine house like Rachel and like Leah,
which two did build the house of Israel: and do thou worthily in Ephratah, and
be famous in Beth-lehem:

12 And let thy house be like the house of Pharez, whom Tamar bare unto Judah, of the
seed which the LORD shall give thee of this young woman.

13 So Boaz took Ruth, and she was his wife: and when he went in unto her, the LORD
gave her conception, and she bare a son.

14 And the women said unto Naomi, Blessed be the LORD, which hath not left thee this
day without a kinsman, that his name may be famous in Israel.

15 And he shall be unto thee a restorer of thy life, and a nourisher of thine old
age: for thy daughter in law, which loveth thee, which is better to thee than
seven sons, hath borne him.

16 And Naomi took the child, and laid it in her bosom, and became nurse unto it.

17 And the women her neighbours gave it a name, saying, There is a son born to Naomi;
and they called his name Obed: he is the father of Jesse, the father of David.

18 Now these are the generations of Pharez: Pharez begat Hezron,

19 And Hezron begat Ram, and Ram begat Amminadab,

20 And Amminadab begat Nahshon, and Nahshon begat Salmon,

21 And Salmon begat Boaz, and Boaz begat Obed,

22 And Obed begat Jesse, and Jesse begat David.

AP/CLEP SAMPLE QUESTIONS FOR BOOK OF RUTH
MULTIPLE CHOICE—SECTION I

Directions: These questions are comparable to Section I of an AP Examination or CLEP Literature Test. Select the correct answer as a practice exercise; the correct response follows:

1. Why did Elimelech and Naomi leave Bethlehem for the country of Moab in the time of judges.

   A. Wanted a vacation
   B. Because of persecution
   C. Because of famine
   D. For the sake of discovery
   E. Because of relative dying

2. Why did Naomi decide to return to Bethlehem after Elimelech's death?

   A. Because of a good harvest
   B. Because she was homesick
   C. Needed to settle the estate
   D. Because of persecution
   E. None of the above

3. What is the relationship between Boaz and Naomi?

   A. A brother
   B. A cousin
   C. A brother-in-law
   D. A kinsman
   E. None of the above

4. Which one of the following statements does not indicate Boaz's good-will towards Ruth when she went gleaning?

   A. By instructing the young men to drop barley specially for her
   B. By telling to eat and drink with his folks
   C. By telling the young men to let her glean and not molest her in any way
   D. By permitting her to glean in his fields
   E. All of the above are correct expressions of Boaz's good-will towards Ruth

5. Why was Naomi especially glad to learn of Boaz's interest in Ruth?

   A. Because he was wealthy
   B. Because she wanted to see Ruth married
   C. Because she hoped to see Ruth bear the line of Elimelech
   D. Because Ruth needed a home
   E. Because Ruth was lonely

6. Why did Elimelech hesitate about marrying Ruth?

   A. Because she was already married before
   B. Because she behaved immodestly
   C. Because there was a nearer relation with better rights
   D. Because she was a Moabitess
   E. None of these reasons

7. Why didn't the next-of-kin want to buy Elimelech's land?

   A. At first he did, but he changed his mind when he realized this would mean marrying Ruth
   B. He did not know God's will
   C. Marrying Ruth was not a consideration in selling the land
   D. He could get a fair price by selling in the family
   E. He wanted to develop the land in the wrong way

8. In the story why did the kinsman pull off his shoe?

   A. He had a sore foot
   B. Because this was a way of sealing a bargain at that time
   C. Because he was not sure if the deal was properly adjusted
   D. No reason
   E. None of the above

9. Why was the marriage of Ruth to Boaz particularly gratifying to Naomi?

   A. Because this marriage was made in heaven
   B. Because King David approved
   C. Because the marriage secured the continuity of the family and property of Elimelech, and gave her an assured old age and a "grandson" to look after
   D. Because she was needed in the family at the time
   E. None of the above

10. Naomi's son's name was

   A. David
   B. Jesse
   C. Obed
   D. Pharez
   E. Salmon

ANSWERS

1. B	6. C
2. A	7. A
3. D	8. B
4. E	9. C
5. C	10. C

AP/CLEP SAMPLE QUESTIONS FOR BOOK OF RUTH
FREE-RESPONSE—SECTION II

Directions: These questions are comparable to Section II of an AP Examination or CLEP Literature Test. You should answer the questions in your own words based on the passage from The Book of Ruth.

1. Read the words of Ruth as she speaks to her mother-in-law, Naomi. Having decided to return from Moab to Bethlehem-judah, Naomi has tried to persuade Ruth to stay in Moab which is her own nation, but Ruth replies:

   > . . . Entreat me not to leave thee, or to return from following after thee: for whither thou goest, I will go; and where thou lodgest, I will lodge; thy people shall be my people, and thy God my God. Where thou diest, will I die, and there will I be buried.
   >
   > Ruth, ii, 16-17

   What do you feel about the syntax of these sentences in Ruth, and what is the relationship between the sentence synthax and the over-all effect of the passage?

2. Using the above passage from the Book of Ruth, what do you think gives these words their importance?

3. What kind of story is the Book of Ruth? Write a general literary criticism of the Book of Ruth, i.e., a love story, historical document, a traditional prose.

Suggested Free-Response Answers

1. The word-order or syntax refers to the arrangement of words and the ways that phrases are joined together to give meaning. There are several illustrations of closely related syntactical structures giving meaning to "I" (Ruth) and "thy" (Naomi):

   A. Whither thou goest, I will go
   B. Where thou lodgest, I will lodge
   C. Thy people shall be my people
   D. Thy God (shall be) my God
   E. Where thou diest, will I die
   F. will I be buried

There are several examples of identical syntactical structure.

In viewing the relationship between the sentence syntax and the over-all effect of Ruth ii, 16-17, there is a succession of sentences which promote a growing spirit between "I" and "thy". The passage establishes the point of why agrue anymore--as Ruth expresses her determination to go to Bethlehem with Naomi. The arrangement of these words here is a powerful mechanism for explaining God's will.

2. This passage makes effective use of rhythm and repetition:

   "goest - go"
   "lodgest - lodge"

This expresses a sense of feeling, simply by stressing in the structure of the language that two people are united in one experience, e.g., "Thy people shall be my people"--the voice naturally stresses the "thy" and "my" are identical. The rhythms of the phrases in Ruth's statement of loyalty in themselves expresses a sense of continuity, of the relationship of the two women continuing as life itself. The phrase "Whither thou goest, I will go" establishes a balance of structure and ends with "and there will I be buried" which continues the close relationship. It is possible to judge the sincerity in the death reference; there is also the importance by the marriage phrase. This passage speaks of "life and death" considerations and growth of a relationship of two women.

3. We know from the start that Ruth is not an adventure or mystery story, or we would think of this work as an allegory. The Book of Ruth is an important historical document, but this is incidental to the deeper sociological and literary impact. The Book of Ruth to some extent is a love story without the traditional meanings as in Romeo and Juliet. Ruth is a love story without reference to personal love. Ruth is a "love" of mankind and the growth of a people in the Old Testament. From the story we know what Ruth and Naomi and Boaz feel towards each other, and the eventual love of Ruth and Boaz. In the reading of Ruth, it is apparent that the story is not the traditional religious story. The Jewish God is involved and it is significant that Ruth should take him as her god, and what Ruth joins is not a church but a nation or a new society of mankind. This new relationship and spirit of community is expressed almost entirely in terms of her feelings towards her mother-in-law and of her actions which are in strict conformity to the social customs of the time of judges.

BOOK OF RUTH—SHORT STORY
LITERATURE ANALYSIS AND INTERPRETATION

The version of Ruth that we shall be reviewing in this chapter is the American Bible Society (New York) translation which was published as THE HOLY BIBLE, containing the Old and New Testament in 1860. You may want to read or study a more recent American edition with a contemporary translation for "The Book of Ruth" or The New English Bible (pp. 298-301), 1970. The value of this comparison will be to show the "old style" of the earlier translation.

The Book of Ruth is named for the Moabite woman who was joined to the Israelite people by her marriage with the influential Boaz of Bethlehem. The story of Ruth is a beautiful example of Lilial piety, pleasing to the Hebrews especially because of its connection with King David, and useful both to Hebrews and to Gentiles. The Book of Ruth aims to demonstrate the divine reward for such piety even when practiced by a stranger. Ruth's piety, her spirit of self-sacrifice, and her moral integrity were pleasing to God with the gift of faith and an illustrious marriage whereby she became the ancestress of David and of Christ. In this, the universality of the messianic salvation is foreseen. It is possible to characterize the literary form of The Book of Ruth as dramatic, since about two-thirds of it is in dialogue. Notwithstanding, there is every inclination that the story contains true history. There is no certainty about the author of the story, but it was written long after the events had passed, which occurred in the time of the judges. As a traditional Jewish love story, probably written in the fourth century B.C., was passed on orally and existed in some form like a poem before it was written down; the probable writer of Ruth was a literary editor producing simply a story of already established material. It is possible according to some scholars that the last chapters linking Ruth with King David were added to popular writing, thus providing a place in the Holy Bible.

The Language of Ruth

It is essential to get the feel of the story and to understand the writer's choice of words. A way to learn what the story is about is to look at the words and see what they say. "Now it came to pass in the days when the judges ruled,. . ." How does the opening sentence work? The word "now" establishes a reasonable mystery of beginning what is a traditional Jewish love story. A modern way would be to write "Once in the time of the judges, . . ." or "long ago, in the time of judges, . . ." Many times to the modern mind there will be archaic and biblical phrases, e.g., "it came to pass;" the formal language reminds us of the dialogues of Elizabethan plays and how the Bible could have been read, in the 1970s, aloud at the table. The translations are written to read as literature today; the hearer of yesterday is the modern reader today. ". . . so a man from Bethlehem of Judah departed with his wife and two sons to reside on the plateau of Moab," rather than the 1860 translation ". . . a certain man of Beth-lehem--Judah went to sojourn in the country of Moab, he, and his wife, and his two sons." All of this reminds us of the very differences in oral and written literature. These distinctions continue through The Book of Ruth. ". . . Obed begat Jesse, and Jesse begat David;" the modern form would say ". . . Obed was the father of Jesse, and Jesse became the father of David." Even in the archaic flavor it is possible to feel the meaning of this story. Ruth as liberative takes aspects of family life in written form and enables us to see these ordinary experiences more clearly in Biblical times.

It is impossible here to completely analyze each sentence in The Book of Ruth, nor should we want to undertake such an activity. But it is important to become sensitive to the story and to obtain a literary sense or impression of the literature under study. In reading rapidly The Book of Ruth, it is possible to obtain a feel of the language and the way the writer (editor) wanted you to know the story.

Most certainly The Story of Ruth is presented in a leisurely style; you are given the essential facts without rushing. The book is not melodramatic but there are moments of tension and crisis, i.e., when Boaz finds Ruth at his feet. The story is not full of suspense but a growing love story whereby Ruth's piety, her heroic fidelity, and spirit of self-sacrifice as well as her moral integrity grew into an illustrious marriage. ". . . the Lord makes the woman that is come into thine (my) house like Rachel and like Leah, which two did build the house of Israel: and do thou worthily in Ephratah, and be famous in Beth-lehem." This was the beginning of the marriage at the gate with the elders.

The Book of Ruth in an unhurried narrative-texture gives us a "social realism" in the time of judges; Ruth and Boaz have acted in good social conduct and seem to be true to history.

AP/CLEP EXAMPLES OF STUDENT-WRITTEN SHORT STORIES

MOURNING

It was a room which you could never leave--which never left your mind. The walls were only structures holding in the pain and fear of death-ridden people--people in search of an atmosphere other than the real one. The bleakness and filth; the ether; the feeling of sterility too, was inside to add to the loneliness.

Down the hall there was a woman screeching in desperation, a man was choking in his vomit, and, across from me, someone was administered his "last rights."

But I sat alone listening in distress. How can you express that feeling of death? You can't.

A group of nuns entered my room to speak of faith and hope. They gave me medals and spoke of when I would walk and leave this room; this whole feeling. They told me to pray. They smiled and laughed. But to me, smiling faces are only masks covering frightened mourners--mourners for those who have not yet departed.

I continued my thought. In awe, I watched the beauty of the world outside. The birds were chirping and the trees swayed softly with the gentle wind.

But I had to return to the inside, where all was real. "I am an old man," I thought; "My end is soon. I do not want to die in mourn, but in joy, with parties, and children, and goodness.

But the woman up the hall continued her screeching, the old man across the hall died, and the nuns were wrong--there is no hope--fate is the supreme ruler.

Throughout the building a silent whimpering could be heard. The women continued their cries.

CITY LIFE

The threadbare stairs creaked and groaned as the old man slowly made his way up them. Once upstairs he stopped to get his breath, thinking of the past and how he used to run up these same stairs.

He walked to his room and stood looking out onto a city now flooded with lights. It seemed odd to him that so many things stay the same, yet you don't notice them. You only notice the things that change.

He took the telegram out of his pocket and read it again. He had not, for a long time, even thought of his old friend. He wondered how they had gotten his address. He remembered that once he had called Mike and might of given him his address then.

He went and sat down on the edge of his bed, letting his mind drift back to the time when life held bright prospects, when everything was new and eagerly received. When life was shared.

But now he was tired of playing the foolish game. Now life was a swift and terrible race, with people never really knowing people, and never really caring. He was an old man, what could he do.

He got up and walked over to the window. How many times he had stood just like this, looking out onto the city. The city never seemed to change.

It had started to mist. A few lights went out. His along with them.

THE ACCIDENT

Pain is a horrible thing! Wrenching, unmerciful pain. What's wrong? Why is it that I ache so? What did I do to deserve this?
The light. Who shines those lights in my face? Where is my face? I am not blind, but I see nothing; I only feel . . . pain.

The sun shines so warmly on the water. Why is it that I cannot feel this warmth? Sea gulls. Waves. Sand castles. I walk, I run on sand covered beaches. My feet make imprints in the wet sand, but they remain only a short while. Washed away. Why do they disappear? I am still here. I have been here too long.

When I was a child, everything was small. I was big--important. I could not understand why the waves ruined my sand castles. But, it did not matter. The sun would set, and leave me in darkness, but I did not care--I had plenty of time to find out why.

I was alive--even though life was a question mark in my mind. What life would be, I didn't know. Furthermore, I didn't care. Things would work out. How? I didn't know that I was in charge of my life. Life to me was a sea gull floating on the waters of a very clammy ocean. I did not realize there were other gulls--only me.

As I grew older, I learned the answers to many questions. One still remained unanswered however. I may have been called a very learned man but even if that is true, why is it that the small questions plague me now. The questions which did not matter when I was young, now seemed important. I am no longer big. Very small.

I have stayed in this place too long. The waves now wash upon my footprints, wiping them out until I walk that path once more. I feel the sun, now. It warms my back--so that I am no longer cold.

The pain is lesser now.

UNKNOWN

It was said that the old Fuller mansion on Hilltop Drive was haunted. Most didn't believe this old tale, while others said that strange noises could be heard coming from behind its weather-beaten doors.

Marcus Gilmore, for one, did not believe in the supernatural. He would walk by the house every night on his way home without a second thought. So when his friend Bill Mason bet him $5.00 he wouldn't go into the house alone at the stroke of midnight, he was quick to accept.

The night was hot and muggy. A cold sweat was rolling down the faces of the two boys. The house loomed dark and silent before them.

The minutes that passed seemed more like hours. Then, at the first stroke of midnight, Marcus started walking up the long pathway. By the ninth stroke, he was at the top of the stairs. As he reached for the doorknob his heart started beating faster. At the last stroke, he slowly turned the knob and stepped inside.

Reaching in his pocket, he took out a candle and book of matches. Finding it difficult to light the candle, he walked over to a huge, dust-covered chair. He sat down to steady himself and he lit a candle. The room he was now in was a living room with a grand piano, several chairs and lamps, and a couch. All were covered with dust and looked as if they hadn't been touched in years. He rose from the chair slowly and walked into the next room. This was a dining room. In this room was a large table and about a dozen chairs. As he proceeded through the swinging doors, he found himself in a kitchen. Not being very interested with the kitchen, he passed through a heavy wooden door and found himself in front of the grand staircase.

He started to ascend the long, winding staircase. The thick, red carpeting beneath his feet made him think of the house in its time. When he reached the hallway at the top of the stairs, he saw five closed doors. He opened the first and saw just an ordinary bedroom. Closing that door, he moved toward the next door.

The clock struck one.

As Marcus opened the door, he decided to go inside and look around. As he glanced across the room, a soft breeze blew the candle out.

Then, the whole house was filled with a hysterical laughter. It continued for about five minutes.

Then, a dead silence.

The next day in the local newspaper:

In memory of Marcus F. Gilmore

> Marcus F. Gilmore, 15, son of Mr. and Mrs. Claire Gilmore, was found dead yesterday in the Fuller mansion. Cause of death; unknown.

"HELLO, MOTHER"

It was a good time to be alone. It was damp in the early dawn of that late May morning. The dense, New York fog had not yet settled and she could see the fast-fading light of a few twinkling stars as she drew her wet slicker about her.

She was considered pretty by most. Her complexion was often compared to the softness of a swan's down. Her eyes shone like emeralds. Her hair, a blazing red, provided a sharp contrast next to her cadium yellow slicker.

She had a host of friends and quite a few admirers. At times, she was headstrong and extremely unreasonable, though, usually, as now, she was quite logical and could understand most of her own feelings and thoughts. When in such a mood, she had an easy going personality and was often sought for advice.

Although, these past few weeks, she had been in such a tither, she hadn't known which way to turn. But she had hoped that this midnight stroll would help clear her head and help her to decide what course of action she should take.

She wasn't worried because of a shortage of money. She had an immense fortune her father had left her when he died. She was confused because of her mother.

Last week she had received a telegram from her mother informing her that she was coming on May twenty-sixth on the three o'clock flight from England. That was this afternoon! And she wasn't even prepared. She knew she wouldn't recognize her mother, she hadn't seen her for ten years.

That was her problem, she didn't know how to relate to her mother. She'd been at boarding school ever since she was twelve. She had only seen her mother on holidays and even then was glad when the visit was over. And to top that, she'd stopped seeing her mother all together when she was fifteen.

"But," she told herself, "you're all grown up now. Act like an adult, not a child."

She was going to the airport later to pick her mother up. But now the question uppermost in her mind was, "How should I approach her?" She couldn't very well go up to her mother like a timid little child asking forgiveness. That was preposterous! Nor could she go up to her as if they were old friends. After all, the arrangement of not seeing each other had been equally welcomed on both sides.

"No," she decided. She would meet her mother that afternoon as one woman meets another. Not as a daughter meets her mother.

"Yes," she thought to herself. That way a whole new relationship could begin, and maybe, this time, it would work better than the first one had.

"DIVORCE-DEATH"

The Peruvian mountainside was blanketed in a sheet of glistening white snow. Perfect for skiing. So thought the young New York stock broker who had come to Peru for only one purpose. That purpose was to kill the man who murdered his wife.

He remembers the painful ordeal of the divorce court. His wife's cutting accusations, the murmur of the court, and the sound of the judge's gavel restraining order rang clear in his ears. But she had won. She got the divorce. Then, three weeks after the divorce came through she was rushed to the hospital with a cerebal hemorrage. The surgeon had operated but the patient had died on the operating table. With his wife dead, he could only think of the surgeon who took her life. He soon became obsessed with ideas of killing the surgeon. His psychiatrist felt a vacation would be necessary. He took his vacation in Peru where the surgeon was attending a convention.

He remembered how it was, while standing alone on the mountain. Below him, the snow sparkled in the afternoon sunlight. The trees stood naked against the blue cloudless sky at the foot of the slope.

He pushed himself down the slope, feeling the wind rush through his fine red hair. Suddenly, he hit what seemed to be an invisible bump on the slope. He fell and rolled, entangled in his skis, down into the network of trees. He lay there, breathing heavily in the darkness. He lifted his right leg and groaned when a most unbearable pain ran through it.

Darkness was befalling the small valley in which he lay helpless. He had given up shouting for help long ago for no one was around to hear his cries. Coldness crept into his joints making them stiff. Thoughts of his wife and the man he was to kill returned to him. Nothing would stop him from doing what he had to do. Nothing. Not even a broken leg. He thought. As sunlight began to peek through the hills, a young man lay dying with pain in his eyes and hatred in his heart.

VEGETABLE GARDEN

Sitting on the cold park bench, the gray sky and drizzling rain seemed to reflect my thoughts. I couldn't understand why things were so unfair. People say that things always turn out right in the end. But do they, I thought. Do they ever?

I had just come from the military hospital where my brother lie, minus one leg and possibly his mind. Just like a vegetable.

I felt like I wanted to cry but I just sat there and stared, thinking.

Jim had just finished his four years of college when he told us that he had decided to enlist in the Army before going on to "med school." (He was going to be a doctor). He said it was something he felt he had to do.

So, he was sent to one of those Southern training camps for about three months. And then what we had feared for so long happened. Jim was sent to Viet Nam.

Well, away he went without any fuss, just like every red-blooded American boy should do. From his letters he said that although it was worse than he had expected and his outlook had changed, he was "surviving." And after a few months in the back lines Jim was sent up front. But still he survived. One day his best friend was shot and the next day he watched 10 women and children get bombed out of their homes. But still he survived, getting up at 5 every morning, doing his daily jobs, killing when he had to and dying with every one of them.

He survived right up until two weeks ago--two weeks before he was to come home. He had tried to save a little Viet Nameese girl from falling through a weak bridge but before Jim got to her he was shot in the back.

And, now he's "home." Lying in his own little bed in his own little row. Just like all the others. All lined up nice and neat.

And still he survives. Or does he?

CHARACTER ANALYSIS: O. HENRY'S SHORT STORIES

Sample 1

O. Henry, a humorous writer, is well known all over the world as a man that shows character and local color of all the people that he is trying to exhibit.

After having read other stories by this man, it has become quite evident that he writes as if he has lived through all these happenings himself.

The story "Witches' Loaves" was the first story I came upon. In this story a woman who works in a bakery takes interest in a man that comes to her bakery everyday and buys her greatly reduced, week-old, stale bread. Beginning to realize that that is probably all he eats, she decides to stick a pad of butter in-between the loaves that he buys one day. Later on this man comes back, reveals he is a painter and uses stale bread to refine his pencil sketches by rubbing stale bread on them. It is also revealed that by putting in the butter, she ruined a much-worked-on famous painting.

"Jimmy Hayes and Muriel", is a story in which Muriel is a frog. This man Jimmy and Muriel have a wonderful relationship that lasts a lifetime. Jim joins the Army and brings Muriel along with him. The men in the Army think that Jim is quite odd and they call him a coward, when he hasn't even had the chance to prove them wrong. Finally, a war began and Jim and his pet Muriel disappeared. All the men thought he had run away because of his cowardice, but in the end they take their words back. They are walking through the woods months after the twosome had disappeared and they came upon three bodies dead in a row. An evident struggle was shown. Yards away there was a skeleton of a man with their type of uniform and out from under it crawled Muriel, the frog.

The last story I read was, "Nemesis and the Candy Man." This story told of a very beautiful, snobby, cold, young, foolish woman, who treated men like dirt. Her lover asked her to go away with him, but after Nemesis acting coldly towards him, he stormed out of her house.

Later on that day a candy man came around and she began making passes at him and pretending a love that she really did not have for him. Day after day he would come to her house selling candy, only in the end to find out that she was really just a cold woman that had made him look foolish. She just coldly laughed at the humble candy man. Later that day her maid brought Nemesis a letter that said that her lover had left for good. She fainted of the shock and was never heard from again.

O. Henry is obviously showing moralization in every single story. This trait is one of his greatest that protrude with greatness over the others.

In the story, "Witches' Loaves" it is evident that he means that one should mind his own business and not meddle with other peoples affairs. In "Jimmy Hayes and Muriel" the moral there is simply don't judge someone before you've given them a chance to prove themselves worthy. With "Nemesis and the Candy Man" it is just the fact that you should never act cold towards someone after having supposedly loved him, especially when you don't really mean it. When you really love someone, don't ever let pride overcome your love for him and never let him go.

His vocabulary is quite simple and sentence structure may vary, but simplicity is overall dominant in his stories.

His descriptions do not go into great depth, but he does give much detail. It's interesting detail, though, not the kind you have to skip over just to pass it.

Conciseness is shown in his detail and the character of each person comes through because of this. In "Witches' Loaves" there is an excellent example. "He was a middle-aged man, wearing spectacles and a brown beard trimmed to a careful point."

He spoke English with a strong German accent. His clothes were worn and darned in places, and wrinkled and baggy in others. But he looked neat, and had very good manners."

Dialect is another of his many talents. Like Mark Twain, he distorts a word so that you understand how it is said. Examples of this are in "Jimmy Hayes and Muriel." "Brace up Muriel, old girl, we're 'most there now! Been a long ride for ye ain't it, ye old antediluvian handful of animated carpet tacks? Hey, now, quit a tryin' to kiss me. Don't hold on to my neck so tight--this here paint hoss ain't any too shore-footed, let me tell ye."

Third person-omniscient is usually his point of view. He's on the outside looking in, but usually some characters' views may be less limited than others' in the story. He seems to know more about the main person in the story than anyone else. Although he doesn't let the reader know any great, deep, dark, secrets about the innermost person, he lets you know just enough to keep you interested.

A characteristic I like of O. Henry's writing is the type of plot he sets. The climax is in the last few paragrpahs of the story. He leaves you dangling just enough, but you know what has happened. This type of effect creates an exciting suspense.

The only real type of symbolism he uses is using one person to represent all people of the world. There is no great depth or allegorical meanings that are actually shown in the stories I have read.

Last, but certainly not least, he seems to create a feeling of the setting that surrounds the story. One can actually picture the type of town or city where his stories take place. He paints a local color, shows habits and customs v ery well but in brevity. Showing the prejudice of a certain town, or its feelings and habits is quite frequent in his stories.

I find this type of man very impressing. He's imaginative, and he doesn't try to any great length to be humorous, but many passages seem to be very funny indeed. Evidently, brilliance and knowledge back him up and he'll continue to write till his death.

Response (2)

THE SAFECRACKER

Jimmy Valentine, an expert safe-cracker, is just getting out of prison. He gets his suitcase full of the best burglar equipment from a hotel where he was keeping it while he was in prison.

Jimmy steals some money from safes and goes to a small town in Arkansas. There he falls in love with Annabel Adams. He opens a shoe store and uses the name of Ralph D. Spencer. In a year he became an honest, successful owner of his shoe store. Then a famous detective, who had arrested him before, came into town. The detective knew that the minute he caught Jimmy he would send him back to jail. But one day he saw Jimmy being shown a new bank safe. A girl gets accidentally locked in the safe and Jimmy gets his tools and breaks open the safe and saves the girl. When he sees the detective, he expects to be arrested. Instead, the detective acted as if he didn't know him and walked away.

TWO THANKSGIVING DAY GENTLEMEN

On Thanksgiving Day every year, a bum named Pete waited for the Old Gentleman to come to the park and treat him to a good meal at a fine restaurant. But this year was different. On his way to the park, Pete is invited to a meal by two old ladies. Afterwards he was so full he could hardly walk to the park. When he met the old man, he wanted to tell him he was full, but he couldn't. So he went with him to the restaurant and when the meal was served he forced himself to eat it all. Then he thanked the old man and went on his way. Just a few steps out the door he passed out. Awakening in a hospital, he heard that the Old Gentleman was there, too. He heard the doctors saying that the old gentleman hadn't eaten in three days.

THE GREEN DOOR

Rudolf Steiner was a true adverturer. He worked in a piano store. Every evening he went looking for the unexpected. One night as he passed a dentist's office, a man was passing out cards. He gave one to Rudolf. When he passed the man again, he was given another card. But this one did not advertise the dentist's work. It said "The Green Door."

This puzzled him. So he started his search. He went inside the building that the dentist office was in. Two stories up, he found a green door in the dim light. Slightly afraid, he knocked on the door. A thin young woman opened the door. She fainted and fell to the floor. He picked her up and laid her on her couch. When she came to, she told him that she hadn't eaten in three days. Rudolf told her to wait until he came back. Her face was the one that he had been searching for. She was the reward for all his adventures.

He came back with food from a restaurant. She ate it like a starved animal. He told her he would be back tomorrow. As he went out the door he saw that every door on that floor was green. Every door in the whole building was green also.

As he left the building he saw the man with the cards was still there. Rudolf asked him about The Green Door. The man pointed to a theater called "The Green Door".

O. Henry has always been called the master of the surprise ending. He writes a lot about the life and hardships of New York City. The majority of his stories are simple little tales with a sudden unexpected change at the very end.

His sentences are not very long, and the words aren't usually fancy. This is a good thing because the plot of the stories sometimes are somewhat tricky. In his stories he makes ordinary men seem to be as important as anyone else in the world.

Sample 3

DRESSING UP
(and other stories)

O. Henry is a very simple writer, who tends to write in a pattern. All of his stories that I read were simple, and about unsophisticated people.

For instance his first story "Dressing Up" was about a man into some trouble and he gets a lot of cash all of a sudden. He and his girl walk into a store and spend $465. on clothes--only the best. He pays cash--then they go out and get drunk. A car pulls up and says he better leave the girl--Mike Bovois after him. He was drunk so he wouldn't go. The next day he got shot. The people in the story sounded like they were in New York. For example when Blue (the main character) walked into the store, he said "I'm buying an outfit, see, I'm gonna shed these rags and climb into something slick." The characters were very typical, but simple.

In the second story I read, "Gal Young Un" two hunters are hunting in the woods and run into a house. The lady (Matt) gives them a drink, and one of them gives her the quail they shot. They get mad at each other and split up. The man gets lost and finds his way back to the lady's house to ask her how to get back. The next day, Fran goes into town, and finds out that the 50 year old lady is rich, so he visits her all the time, and ends up marrying her. Fran was a bootlegger, so he left every day, sometimes he never came back for a week or two. Matt is too lonely to divorce him or push him out of her house. One day, Fran brought home a very young girl (probably around 14-16). Matt is furious. The fairly friendly girl thinks she is Fran's mother. Matt snaps at her, won't let her use the tub or wash basin, gives her the very minimum of food, and won't speak to her. Fran left Matt and Elly home for two weeks. When he came back, all his empty "ready for whiskey" bottles were broken. His new car is blown up, and Matt chases him out. She planned it all. She thought Elly went with him, but Fran abandoned her, too. Elly slept out in the cold all night and finally Matt let her in. Again, the characters are very typical and simple.

In the last story I read, "The White Circle" it was Tucker's 12th birthday and Tucker had a choice between any of the horses on the farm, but he picked the apple tree in the front yard for his birthday present. Anvil, the town bully, was sitting in the tree eating all 13 apples on the tree and stuffing a few in his shirt. Tucker ran over and told him to come down, and it ended up in a fight. Anvil wins of course, and Tucker gives up and wants to play. Anvil had used Tucker all his life and then there were flashbacks. They ended up in the barn, and there was a white circle on the floor. That was where you put the hay bales and the hayfork hauled it up. Anvil didn't know this, and Tucker told him that it was a game called prisoner's base. Anvil wanted to make trouble, but he finally agreed to play one game of prisoner's base. This was what he called a "sissy game." Tucker climbed up the stationary ladder and aimed the fork at Anvil to kill him as it did one of his horses a few years ago. Anvil took off, and never came back.

A SAMPLE AP ESSAY: HEART OF DARKNESS

Gloom is introduced at the outset of the story. As the story continues, the gloom grows with it until it evolves into the heart of darkness. The repetitious word "gloom" pervades the story and forces the reader to look for a deeper meaning of the word. Gloom is man--for man pretends he is a higher, civilized being who can be master over his destiny. Upon closer examination, one can see that man is akin to the beast in the den. He is callous and cunning. Greed and avarice are his constant companions. He takes all but gives nothing. Marlow's narrative depicts man's depravity, his evil ways, that create misery and gloom for those he touches; how in the gloom and darkness he has inspired, he is eventually crushed by his own devices.

Gloom extends from Gravesend to the women knitting the black wool. It seems symbolic of the death, the ever present darkness in the story as told by Marlow. He refers to his stumbling in the gloom as into an Inferno of Darkness, from which he cannot escape. The river, the wilderness, all are in profound darkness, with death lurking everywhere. The deeper the penetration into the wilderness, the more savage and fearful men become. Gloom and darkness is everywhere. The stations along the river route are also bathed in despair and gloom, only the ivory cluttering the hut bearing witness to man's evil genius, his folly and self-destruction.

Marlow tells his listeners that man can sink into the lowest depths of immorality and debasement. He can become possessed by the power of darkness. The need to possess material wealth no matter the cost, is to see oneself giving one's soul to the devil, to lose one's identity and become an agent of evil, of darkness. Here, in the story told by Marlow, the reader learns what can and does happen to man, the builder of empires. Man's inhumanity to man is a timeless and universal disease. To this add his insatiable greed and lust, contemptible in itself and horrifying in the extreme.

The gloom that abounds in the persual of man's grasping, bitter, demoniacal desire to own what others have, his methods used to obtain his means to those ends, are symptomatic of his wanton depravity, his gluttony, his disregard for humanity.

The word "gloom" is the string to which the story is tied. Darkness and gloom are the paths by which man must tread in his fruitless search for wealth and power. To lose one's soul to the devil is to be everlasting in impenetrable darkness. This is the price men, countries and empire builders exact from their victims. These are the men who are lost in the wilderness of evil intent. For the Kurtzes of the world, the gloom and the darkness ultimately seal their fate, for the darkness is in their own hearts.

Man must have the strength and fortitude to resist evil temptations. This is the real horror, that man can sink to the lowest level, that his normal instincts can be obscured by his need to own. Thus when man's conscience is awakened and he exposes himself to self scrutiny, he is appalled by the knowledge that he is the greatest contributor to his own downfall.

A SAMPLE AP ESSAY: WOMEN IN LITERATURE

The intrusion of women writers into the world of letters, hitherto the sanctum sanctorum of the self-styled nobility of the field, the superior mental giants, The Man! has been held a major disaster that befell man. This concept emerged in the dreary past and is still part of the dreary present. Women have resisted this state of affairs with every possible means open to them. They invaded and they conquered, and are here to stay.

According to Joan Goulianos, in her book, by a Woman Writt, this breakthrough has been fraught with heartbreak. Men could not conceive that a woman was more than a creature put upon our planet to satisfy every need, whim and want of the male. To admit that she might also possess a mind, and a talent, was not only incomprehensible, but considered absurd.

It took a great deal of courage and often subterfuge, for a woman to put on paper writings that came from her experiences. If she was so imprudent to bring her material to a significant male writer, she was told in no uncertain terms to conduct herself in a manner more becoming to a member of her sex--that is, rear her family, making sure that she keep herself ready to wait on her husband, embroider, perform her household duties, and destroy her writings before they destroy her.

This book is filled with the writings of bright, talented, unhappy women, women who were constantly subjected to repression, and who dared to overcome. Women were denied the freedom of self-expression. Creativity in the woman was equated with obscenity, immorality, and other adjectives, none of them flattering. The writings stressed the importance men gave to how well a woman could run her household, not how well she was able to write. Into the kingdom of the effete female she was summarily cast from whence she was not to try to escape.

The writings of these unsung heroines consist of diaries, poetry, letters, autobiographies, and letters of protest, women writers from the middle ages up to the present time. In all the writings the hue and cry is the same; how they were discriminated against, ridiculed by many of their own sex, and of course by the opposite sex; the pain inflicted upon them and the courage they needed to overcome the obstacles put in their path by men.

In pursuing the readings, I was more than chagrined, to read in Mary Wollstonecraft's selection from A Vindication of The Rights of Woman that Hugh Walpole refused to read it and referred to her as "a hyena in petticoats."

Charlotte Bronte also received negative criticism from Robert Southey, Poet Laureate of England. He averred that her literary dallyings would produce "a distempered state of mind." The bias and perverseness exhibited by well-known writers of their day to the women who had the mentality and sensitivity and the creativity to perform and achieve in the world of letters, stemmed from the age-old fear and trepidation that if they permitted women this freedom of expression it would reduce their power in the role assigned to them by divine right. To assess a woman's intellectuality being on a par with a man's, was tantamount to diminishing his status as a superior animal, and thus deprive him of the right to dominate and subjugate any woman hereafter--she would no longer agree to exist as his property or his slave.

The majority of the selections in Goulianos' book testify to the shameless humiliation they suffered at the hands of a male-dominated hierarchy. They tell with humility and candor how their art affected their lives. The writings touch on the state of marriage, motherhood, feminism, hopelessness and anger. The ignorance and absurdity of unfounded charges directed against them because they refused to be shut into a role designated to be the only role that sensible women accepted with equanimity and even pleasure. These are short stories and excerpts from novels and poetry. Each woman, in her specific writing, shows incredible intelligence and mastery of language, deep insight into the society she was born into, and a desire to break the bonds of tradition and convention and help to create a better world for herself and her children.

It is no secret that women writers have always had a difficult time getting their works published. Publishers were notorious anti-feminists and generally returned manuscripts labeled, "Not Good!" and reviling the authoress. Dorothy Richardson was one of those unfortunate writers who ran into such abuse. She made a great outcry in her thirteen volumes entitled, Pilgimage. I would like to give a few samples of the writings of several of these writers.

Alphra Behn: First woman to make money by writing, (seventeenth century) (1640-1698) wrote and produced a play, The Forced Marriage. She became the subject of praise and ridicule--both focusing as much on her sex as on her talent. She was alluded to as a "lewd harlot." In her Epistle to a Reader, she takes men down a few rungs of the ladder by informing them that they do not possess imagination or intelligence except to ridicule women who are much better able to write, given the same amount of education, and therefore of superior intelligence.

Mary Wollstonecraft: Besides calling her "a hyena in petticoats", Horace Walpole refused to read anything she wrote. Yet she was a brilliant woman, and in her Vindication she displays her very intelligent and remarkable talent. She accuses man of tyranny, of unjust criticism, of ignorance of what it means to be a woman. "How grossly they insult us." "Men, indeed, appear to me to act in a very unphilosophical manner, when they try to secure the good conduct of women by attempting to keep them always in a state of childhood." She spoke out against the audacity of men to refuse women the same rights granted to them by virture of their sex. She advanced arguments against Milton, Rousseau and the Bible itself. She did not hesitate to brand society as corrupt, husbands as blind, men as ignoble, contemptuous of the needs and rights of women. She wrote about women's oppression. She wrote about the enslavement of women and the hypocricy prevalent in the writings of famous men of letters. Wollstonecraft was a noted feminist of her time. She had an affair with an American, Gilbert Imlay, bore him a child, and was then deserted by him. She later married the philosopher, William Godwin, and bore him a daughter, Mary Shelley.

Charlotte Bronte: An attack against her by Southey, in which he wrote-- "that literature cannot be the business of a woman's life, and it ought not be. The more she is engaged in her proper duties, the less leisure will she have for it even as an accomplishment and a recreation."

Margery Kempe: Married at about twenty. After her first birth, which was a difficult one, she went mad. She saw visions, slandered her husband and her friends. She had a vision of Christ that restored her sanity. She bore thirteen more children, became a religious mystic. She traveled across England, on the continent and to the Holy Land. She was ridiculed, imprisoned, and called a whore. She denied the charge, claimed she tried to defend and help the poor. When she was aged, she had a scribe write the story of her life. In it she told of the hardships she endured as a woman, how women's bodies were used without their consent, of her resolve to love only God's creatures and foresake earthly acts. (1373-?)

> Alice Thornton: (1627-1707) As early as the seventeenth century, she was cognizant of the deficiency of the state of matrimony. She bore nine children, six of whom died. Widowed in middle age, she described her pregnancies, deliveries, still births and miscarriages. She writes of her sufferings during this period of her life.

There are too many articles and stories and writings to note here, but I must say in passing that all bear a resemblance to one another in their tales of trials and tribulations experienced as a women who chose careers or professions outside of marriage. Another talented writer of the seventeenth century, Margaret Cavendish, who was intelligent, ambitious, and unique in her time, was of the opinion that men were superior to women, although she believed in education for women. She wrote that women could not write "so wisely or wittily as men, being of the effeminate sex, whose brains nature has mixed with the coldest and softest elements, and to give my reason why we cannot be so wise as men, I take leave and ask pardon of my own sex, and present my reasons to the judgement of Truth." She made many derogatory remarks about women, not the least of which were that they had sharp tongues, could not make laws comparable to those of Moses, or Solomon; could not think like Socrates, or Euclid, etc. However, she also wrote that women were equal with men in birth but not in fact. She noted that women were enslaved, used like cattle, tyrannized by men, kept like slaves. Her contention was women could not be kept from thinking, because thoughts were free. She also notes that because men go to colleges and come home to their wives with their heads crammed full of knowledge, they ultimately pass it on to their wives. She goes on to say that men are oaks, women, willows; men made to rule, women to raise children. The scathing references and remarks about the inferiority of her sex would make any liberalized woman of today take a paddle and thrash her.

The names of women contributors to the book of Miss Goulianos, known and unknown, is outstanding, not only because of the subject material, but because of the manner in which it is presented. There are differences in point of view and also similarities. And one must remember that the women who wrote these articles range over six centuries. The complaints may differ, but only in degree. The underlying theme that prevails in all the writings, is based on the conviction that women are a downtrodden, abused, maligned and misused sex. But women are bright, articulate, sensitive to the needs of others around them. They yearn for a place in the sun, a place in which to warm themselves, to be respected and revered for what they are, for the contribution they have made in the past and to what they will bring in the future.

Amongst the many fine, understanding, sympathetic, women writers, I must include Kate Chopin. She wrote novels and short stories about Southern women. One fine story is "The Awakening" and it deals with the right of married women to think about themselves in the light of their roles as women; that even a married woman has the right to expect more from life than subservience to a man. The heroine has an 'awakening', she rebels against her society, the old conventions and traditions; she finds love and passion exists outside of her marriage.

The story created a furor, protests and criticisms against Chopin. Society objected to Chopin's idea of women freeing themselves of its mores. As far as the genteel society was concerned, women had no problems, no conflicts. They did what was expected of them, married, bore children, and made their husbands happy.

The material is cognitive as well as affective. It is fictionalized truth. The evaluation Chopin makes is based on her own experiences. She was an intelligent, perceptive woman. Her marriage ended in widowhood while she was still young, and she spent her time writing about things she saw and people she knew. She realized that many people lived in a cage and yearned to be free. From her perceptions she was in a position to see beneath the surface, and from this came her stories about love, sex, emancipation of women, and the desire for true identity. Her characters broke the bonds of traditional submissiveness, awakened to a need to be free.

The same holds true for Susanna Rowson's book, Charlotte Temple, a Tale of Truth. Rowson lived in the eighteenth century, born in 1762, in Portsmouth, England. Her book is about innocence wronged, male arrogance, aggressiveness, and deception and desertion. The heroine commits suicide and the male lives to regret his betrayal of the girl who loved him and died for him.

Another interesting work I found in Woman: An Issue, was in the section Women In Literature. It too deals with the subject of the abuse of women in the professions, namely literature. The position of women in this capacity is not an enviable one, and it is a reproach to men for their role in putting women down and trying to keep them down. I was not amused when I read this piece written by Abigail Adams to her husband at the Constitutional Convention:

> My dear John:
> By the way, in the new code of laws, I desire you would remember your ladies and be more generous and favorable to them than were your ancestors. Do not put such unlimited power in the hands of husbands. Remember, all men to be tyrants if they could.
> Your loving wife,
> Abigail

He replied:

> Depend on it, my dear wife, we know better than to repeal our masculine systems.
> John

There has not been any revolutionary change in the system. We still have a masculine system.

Elaine Showalter's excellent book, Women's Liberation and Literature bears out very strongly what I have tried to show thus far, that most women have experienced frustration and hostility in furthering their careers in the literary field. She quotes articles by leading feminists, among them Dorothy Parker, Mary Wollstronecraft, John Stuart Mill, the poets Elizabeth B. Browning, Anne Sexton, Sylvia Plath, Mary McCarthy, Betty Friedan, and Kate Millet.

There are more agreements than disagreements between the many authors of the books and articles herein noted. The consensus runs in the direction of affirmation, that is that women by and large have been kept out of the world of letters; that it's an area in which men claim they can be seen to be the superior sex in mind and matter. In this regard, Millet, in her doctoral dissertation, asserts that society is basically an oppressive one in which men become dominant and women submissive. Men regard women as limited in scope, over-emotional, inexperienced, therefore holding a narrow viewpoint about such relevant topics as politics, psychology, sociology, economics, history and related sciences.

John Stuart Mill's philosophical essay, "The Subjection of Women" agrees with the aforementioned writers that women, because of their accident of birth, continue to be excluded from pursuing their rightful employment in all areas in which mental performance was a requisite; it being therefore implied that men are born with higher mental faculties because they excel in politics, in education, in the arts, and in most areas of public interest. He went to great lengths to refute all the arguments on the nature of women, such as her weakness in a physical sense, the fact that they are better qualified to run a home than a government. He magnanimously contended that any women who was able to make a success in an open profession was qualified for it.

It is essential to note here that the times and the ideas shared by men and women in those times were aware of and open to the truth that women were deprived of functioning according to their ability and desire. This condition has existed since the story of Adam and Eve and The Fall. Women have been exploited, debased, maligned and abused in society, not only by philosophers, psychologists, educators, the church, and propaganda by the media in general, she has had to overcome her own fears of her inferiority and dependence on the approval of the 'fathers' in her life and her work.

My deep and, I am sure, lasting impression of these profound writings on the subject of women in literature, is due to the nature of the subject itself. I fully agree with Hortense Calisher that women who wrote books were alluded to as "women writers" while men in the same profession were simply referred to as "writers". Women were forced to adopt pseudonyms, such as the "George's" Eliot and Sand, or like Emily Dickinson wrote in a closet and hid her poetry in drawers.

There are apologists for famous women who write, but I cannot find any for men. Critics, more often than not, are patronizing about the value of books written for the reading public. Books written by men are criticized on content and or style, not belabored by accusation of sexuality as a ploy, or emotionalism, or imagination instead of experience.

I would like to see woman freed from stereotypes she has been associated with throughout the centuries. It is inimical to the stature of woman to accept with equanimity the back row seat in the literary field. It would be satisfying now for me to separate the myths from the facts, and to refute the Freudian theories regarding the biological and psychological reasons that makes the male superior to the female.

In closing, I would like to say that the information I was fortunate in getting in my readings, especially from Women's Liberation and Literature, has opened my eyes and my mind to the stupendous amount of material on the subject of women in literature. I would like to know whether women still have the problems with publishers that they once had. In view of the liberalization of women, will there be a real breakthrough in literary circles in the sense that a writer will finally lose her identification of sex, and will be judged for her ability to produce a work of art, or the platitude generally extended to her by her male competitor.

Some courageous men spoke up for women, men like Ibsen and Mill and George Henry Lewes (1817-1878). This last man was a journalist, editor, novelist and critic, and well acquainted with the literary society of his time. In his essay on "The Lady Novelists," he manages to use a complimentary tone, but it still smacks of undisguised assertions that men are better equipped to handle literature than women.

I read his essay with a feeling of indignation because he used a double approach to handle the situation of a woman who had a gift for writing, saying on the one hand that she ought not to be denied the opportunity which was given unhesitatingly to men, because it would be synonymous with putting a woman into a harem--shutting up her mind as well as her person; that a woman's intellectual life is not dissimilar from a man's. He went to great lengths to explain why the real destination of a woman was no longer thought to be that of a hand-maiden. He spoke about the female experience and the male experience; apologized for the male who felt uncomfortable in the presence of a "learned woman" and inquired whether it did not disturb a man when confronted with a woman of superior knowledge and intellect. But, and this is what annoyed me, Literature mirrors life--men can express it in a logical and profound manner--women express it through their emotions. That is their weakness, and it is also the reason that as writers of literature they fall short of their function.

He also finds that women are not original; they tend to imitate men, to mimic them as it were, to be able to adapt to masculine experiences and in that way write a great book. He states that a book written by a woman has a special tone, style, rhythm, and a definite womanly quality. Lewes was of the opinion that women had genius, insight, a certain rationale, a gift for characterization, and that in departments of literature, fiction is the one to which women are best adapted.

The problem besetting the professional woman today is moderate, compared to the hassle she had to contend with in the past. When one reads the stories, novels or essays of the literary geniuses of the centuries past, one is impressed by the sadness, the frustrations and the humiliation a woman was heir to. But there were rebels too. And the Wollstonecrafts, the Sands, women like Austen, Virginia Woolf, and contemporary women; all are collaborationists and because of them I feel that the hoax perpetrated and too long perpetuated by the myth of male supremacy in the field of literature is doomed.

These readings have been a revelation to me. Suddenly, I feel as though I have been freed through them. I have taken on a new identity--I am a whole being--I may now explore my own possibilities, and even be surprised. I do not have to accept any role I have distaste for. Now I can choose the role that suits me best.

Susanna Rowson's novel had not received too much rebuff from her critics. Some contended that it was written with a "basic sincerity and power" and considered her to be a feminist of her day.

Willa Cather also escaped derogatory criticism because her novel was based on the pioneering spirit of women, and told by a male narrator. Because she told a story of the land, that being the major theme of the work, she could write it "like a man" and this gave credence to her work plus saving her from the usual criticism of writing from the 'state of a woman's mind' where emotionalism prevails above all else.

I learned from these writings that to be considered a writer or an artist it is incumbent on women to be able to produce 'like a man' while living the experience allowable and suitable for a woman.

Bibliography

Baskin, Mary, Edwards, Lee S., Heath, Mary (eds.). Woman: An Issue. Book I, Boston-Toronto: Little, Brown & Co., 1972.

Cather, Willa. My Antonia. Boston: Houghton, Mifflin Co., 1949.

Chopin, Kate. The Awakening and Other Stories. New York: Holt, Rinehart & Winston, Inc., 1970.

Goulianos, Joan. by a Woman Writt. New York: The Bobbs-Merrill Co., 1973.

Rowson, Susanna. Charlotte Temple. New Haven, Conn., College & University Press, 1964.

Showalter, Elaine. Women's Liberation and Literature. New York: Harcourt Brace Jovanovich, Inc., 1971.

AP/CLEP ENGLISH EXAMINATION
DICTIONARY OF LITERARY TERMS

This is some of the language you're likely to see on your examination. You may not need to know all the words in this carefully prepared glossary, but if even a few appear, you'll be that much ahead of your competitors. Perhaps the greater benefit from this list is the frame of mind it can create for you. Without reading a lot of technical text you'll steep yourself in just the right atmosphere for high test marks.

ALLEGORY A poem or story in which the characters, objects, places, etc. may stand for certain ideas or ideals. For example, in The Pilgrim's Progress, a book by John Bunyan, the leading character, Christian, is really any man who struggles through life searching for goodness.

ALLITERATION Sometimes poets creat a certain effect when they use the same consonant in quick repetition. This is called alliteration. Usually, the consonant used appears as the first letter of the words, as you will see in the following examples:

"The mother of months in meadow or plain."
"And watching his luck was the girl he loved,
The lady that's known as Lou."

In the first example, the poet created an alliterative effect by the repetition of the letter "m" in "mother, " "months," and "meadow."

The second poet used the letter "l" to get an alliterative effect. Can you pick out the alliterative words?

APOSTROPHE a direct address to a dead or absent person or thing. Examples:

"O Spirit, that dost prefer the upright heart and pure."
"O Captain! my Captain! rise up and hear the bells."

ASSONANCE Assonance is a cousin to alliteration. It is the appearance of the same word vowel sounds in quick repetition. Here are examples:

"Mid hushed, cool-rooted flowers fragrant-eyed"
"A weed by the stream
Put forth a seed
And made a new breed"

In the first example, the sound of "oo" occurs twice. In the second example, the poet used the sound of "ee" and "ea" four times.

BALLAD A story in poetic form. Sometimes this form is called a narrative.

CLICHE A word or phrase which has been used so often in common speech that it has lost its freshness, its "spark."

COLLOQUIALISM A word or phrase that is identified with a certain locality. For example the phrase, "how you'all" is identified with the southern part of the United States.

DIRGE A sad poem in which the poet speaks of a dead friend, hero, or relative. Another term for dirge is elegy.

EUPHEMISM a substitution of a mild expression for a harsh one. Examples:

The departed (for the dead).
A slow student (for a stupid one).

FOOT a group of two or three syllables upon one of which the accent, or stress of the voice, falls in reading.

FREE VERSE Poetry that is not necessarily rhymed nor has any special meter.

HYPERBOLE An exaggeration which the reader knows is not true. Examples:

"He was the best card player that ever was or ever will be."
"We are immensely obliged."
"I'd walk a million miles for one of your smiles."

IMAGERY The poet often tries to arouse in the reader certain pictures of feelings, which is summed up as imagery. For example, when you read the lines,

The Owl and the Pussy-cat went to sea
    In a beautiful pea-green boat,

the poet hopes that you will see this ridiculous scene in your mind. Sometimes a poet may wish you to feel rather than to see. The poet wishes you to feel cold when you read the following lines:

Talk of your cold! Through the jacket's fold
It stabbed like a driven nail.
If our eyes we'd close, then the lashes froze
Till sometimes we couldn't see.

INVERSION The changing of the usual order of words. Usually this is done in order to maintain the meter of the poem. Examples of inversion are:

"Holy, fair, and wise is she"
(the usual order would be "She is holy, fair, and wise.")
"Let me not to the marriage of true minds
Admit impediments. . ."
(the usual order would be "Let me not admit there are impediments to the marriage of true minds.")

IRONY says something but means the opposite. Examples:

"Here's a pretty how-d'ye-do (if one gets a cold shoulder.)"
"You must love me (if one hates you.)"

LIMERICK A short humorous poem with a characteristic meter and rhyme structure:

There was a young lady of Niger
Who smiled as she rode on a tiger:
  They came back from the ride
  With the lady inside
And the smile on the face of the tiger.

LITOTES an understatement in which the negative of the opposite meaning is used: Examples:

Not bad at all.
A matter of no slight importance.
Not entirely unsatisfactory.

METAPHOR a comparison between persons or things without the use of like or as. Examples:

The road was a ribbon of moonlight.
He was a lion in strength.

METONYMY a figure by which a thing is designated, not by its own name, but by the name of something that resembles or suggests it. Examples:

glasses (for spectacles)
the knife (for surgery)

MONOLOGUE a story told by one person.

MOOD The feeling that the poet wishes the reader to achieve when reading his work. For example, the poet wishes you to have a feeling of well-being and happiness after you read

The year's at the spring.
And day's at the morn;
Morning's at seven;
The hill-side's dew-pearl'd;
The lark's on the wing;
The snail's on the thorn;
God's in His Heaven--
All's right with the world!

ONOMATOPOEIA Certain words are supposed to imitate the events they represent. Here are a few examples:

"Crack! was the sound of the rifle in the night!"
"The fire bells clanged their alarm."
"The ball plopped into the water."
"Crack!", "clanged", and "plopped" are examples of <u>onomatopoeia</u>.

OXYMORON   Words that seemingly are opposed, such as "a wickedly moral man" and "thunderous silence."

PARADOX   A statement which seems to contradict itself. However, upon close investigation, it turns out to have an element of truth.

PERSONIFICATION   a figure in which an inanimate object is given human qualities. Examples:

Old Sol is really shining today.
Death, be not proud!

SCAN A LINE   to mark the feet and tell what kind they are.

SIMILE   a comparison between persons or things with the use of like or as. Examples:

He is as restless as a windshield wiper.
The sky looks like a burning ship.

STANZA   a regularly recurring group of lines. For examples of stanzas, see Longfellow's "Psalm of Life" and "Village Blacksmith."

SYNECHDOCHE   a figure of speech in which a part is used for the whole. Examples:

The cutthroat (for murderer) was finally caught.
This ranch has sixty head (of cattle).

Part III

Essays

FREE-RESPONSE ESSAYS

Your essay will usually be given a high rating score by highly qualified AP English readers at the College Board. They "know their business", so be sure that you only write concisely about what you know and that you do not try to bluff them with inflated language. In this connection, it is well to recall what H. G. Wells said about his own writing style: "I write as I walk because I want to get somewhere, and I write as straight as I can, because that is the best way to get there." Your essay must be concise and straightforward to receive a high score. Beyond this there are four general standards by which your essay will be judged: content, technical English, style and organization.

The first of these, Content, is the validity of the ideas which you express and the manner in which you express them. Of course, the first requisite in writing an essay is to have expressible thoughts. You cannot express that which you do not know; you cannot be expected to write upon a subject unless you know something about it. Unless you think clearly, you cannot write concisely. Yet you already have a considerable store of knowledge. Take inventory of the interesting things in your "storehouse" - the great books that you have read, the colorful people that you have met, etc. By taking inventory you are exploring the possible content of your essay exam. The essay questions usually draw upon your inner "storehouse" of knowledge and experience.

The second, Technical English, usually involves the mechanics of grammar, word usage, sentence structure, punctuation, etc. It is in essence the technicalities of "standard written English". Through taking the previous sample exams you have become well aware of your weaknesses in this area. Go over them and correct them so that when you write your essay it will be technically excellent.

The third and fourth, Style and Organization, belong together. Weakness in these two areas cause most students to do poorly on essay examinations. Most of them simply do not know how to combine words into good sentences and then how to put sentences together into connected discourse. What is the result? The readers, who will be doing the grading, do not know exactly what the students mean, and evenutally lose respect for what they are reading. Poor Style and Organization inevitably result in a very low rating.

Good style is a creative and interesting manner of expression. Check to be sure that your sentences flow and are readable. Be sure that they are not too involved or too elementary. There should be variety in your writing. A wide vocabulary helps considerably in this regard. Good Organization is the expression of ideas in sequence. Unity is the key word here. If your essay has unity you will receive an assessment to be proud of.

HOW DO I PLAN THE WRITING OF MY ESSAY?

Before starting to write your essay, you are advised to take several preliminary steps. The first is to read the question at least twice, so that you will have a thorough idea of what the question consists of and what it is asking you. Then decide what mode of expression is most appropriate to the subject matter designated by the question. There are five major modes of expression to choose from, along with minor ones too numerous to mention. The first major mode is exposition, which explains how to do something, where to go, etc. The second is persuasion, which stimulates the reader to some kind of change in attitude or opinion. The third mode of expression is description. It presents that which is perceived by the senses such as people, places, colors, etc. The fourth mode is narration which recounts events. The fifth is argument which encourages the reader to agree with the writer.

Your decision as to the handling of the subject matter of your essay will probably involve a combination of these highly expressive modes. Once you have decided to persuade and describe, or to narrate and argue, while describing, you are ready for the final preliminary step of writing your essay--outlining.

HOW DO I OUTLINE MY ESSAY?

Have you ever opened an unfamiliar book and wondered what the book contains? In order to find out, you do not read it page by page. At the beginning of the book you find a "Table of Contents" which gives the order and contents of the book's divisions. You understand, then, that the author has taken pains to arrange his book in an orderly manner, so that you can readily find what you want.

If you read one of the chapters of the book, you will discover that the chapter is arranged in the same orderly fashion. It is divided into paragraphs. And, just as each chapter deals with a special subject, so each paragraph deals with a single thought concerning the subject. The arrangement of the paragraphs will be as careful and orderly as the arrangement of the chapters. Thus you can learn all that the author has to say about any particular thing without hunting all over the book for it.

Such a planned arrangement is equally necessary in an essay examination. A good writer always arranges his work in an orderly way. The best way to do this is to use an outline. It does not have to be an elaborate one; it may, for example, be a brief listing of the ideas which you expect to express in your essay. To further understand how to construct your outline, study the two following examples of essay questions and their brief outlines.

QUESTION ONE

"He who loves an old house never loves in vain."

Appreciation of one's home has been expressed in many ways, such as in the foregoing quotation. What is there in the make-up of the house or apartment that you return to at the end of the day that makes you like (or dislike) it. In answering this question, give a clear description of your "home" and its contribution to your life.

OUTLINE

1. Where is your home?
2. How large is it?
3. Of what material is it built?
4. What can you tell about the style of the structure?

5. How are the rooms furnished and arranged?
6. Does your home have a personality?
7. Who are the people living with you in your home?

QUESTION TWO

"The battle of Waterloo was won on the playing fields of Eton."

Rugby, a form of football, is the sport referred to by implication in this famous statement which explains the military success of the English over Napoleon. You probably like to play or watch some sport. Tell about it and emphasize its contributions to the life of your nation.

OUTLINE

1. What is the game or sport called?
2. What country did it originate in?
3. Does the sport challenge individuals or teams?
4. What equipment is required?
5. What physical prowess is instilled in its participants?
6. Does it have any personalities on the national scene?
7. Does it have spectators in all levels of the society?

HOW DO I INTRODUCE MY ESSAY?

The matter of introducing your essay is very simple. Every essay needs an introduction. Every writer owes it to his reader to let him know as soon as possible what he is going to write about.

The length and character of the introduction will, of course, vary considerably from essay to essay. If the subject you are writing about is well known, no introductory paragraph may be necessary; the first sentence of your opening paragraph may suffice. If the subject is less popular, more preliminary explanation will be required. In any case, pretend that you are walking with someone and you meet a third person whom you know, but whom your walking companion does not know. Be courteous. Introduce... with style...without delay.

HOW DO I ORGANIZE MY SENTENCES?

When you write your essay, you are not going to write it in one mass of sentences--you will divide the subject into sections. Almost every piece of prose is divided into these sections which are called paragraphs.

Each paragraph is a complete unit that deals with one particular division of the subject. If you want to test your essay for good paragraph division, try to give each paragraph a brief title. You could not do this if each were not a unit.

Each of your paragraphs should consist of well-arranged sentences. Your sentences should be ordered coherently and fitted together smoothly. They should create a flow of thought, a building of movement. If each of your paragraphs is constructed in this way your essay will achieve that unified organization that is essential to its success. You will succeed in touching the lives and inspiring the respect of your readers.

SAMPLE ESSAY QUESTIONS WITH EXPLANATORY ANSWERS

DIRECTIONS: Write an essay on each of the topics given below. Bear in mind that the quality of your writing is more important than the quantity. Be sure that you express yourself clearly and completely.

QUESTION ONE

"The word 'gadget' is slang in most dictionaries. Yet, it is frequently used in reference to a contrivance or device which has a special appeal."

Give your impression of gadgets. Do they have a special appeal for you. How do your friends feel about them. Tell about your experience or a friend's experience with a gadget. An illustration would be appropriate.

ANSWER

Gadgets! What a clever, yet all-inclusive word this one is. When we hear it we are reminded of devices which affect almost every phase of modern living and which range from the lowly jackknife to the highly sensitive electric eye. It is only after careful reflection that we realize how much actual influence these devices have on our daily lives.

First we should appreciate the wide diversification of interests which gadgets serve. During the course of the day we encounter gadgets at every turn. In the kitchen we find new-type can openers, apple corers, and cabbage choppers. The refrigerator has not escaped the inventive urge of the gadget scientists; lights that illuminate its interior and walls that clean themselves make the housewife's tasks easier. Our cars are distinguished by automatic direction indicators, window wipers, suction-type coat hangers. Truly we have come to regard gadgets almost as a part of up-to-date living.

It is this "up-to-datedness" that is another form of the "Keep Up With The Joneses" spirit of many Americans. The public's devotion to many fads and whims is now supplemented by the provocative appeal of gadgets of every description. It is sometimes the practical appeal which captivates the car buyer who admires many devices which make driving easier; more often it is his desire to proudly display the latest in gadgets. Here is the complacency of a Babbit at its worst.

Is it not also true that gadgets result in our dependence upon them. We feel lost without them, and that something is missing from the completeness of your day. Who has not felt a sense of inadequacy when he finds that one of his favorite gadgets is not functioning properly.

I realize my point of view is not a usual one, but let the reader ask himself as I have: Are gadgets really as insignificant as we think? I wonder.

ASSESSMENT: Approximate perfection in technique of composition. General plan clear and logical; good transitions shown. Firm grasp of sentences, grammatical correctness. Slight punctuation weakness. Paragraphs well-developed and unified. Correct spelling of difficult words. Introduction and conclusion effective. Superior vocabulary. Exceptional development of topic. Climactic arrangement of ideas. Thought mature.

QUESTION TWO

"The most effective way to envision history is to read fiction. Novels--if you choose with care--will often give you a clear picture of life in the past or life in the present in your own country of some other country."

Show the validity of this statement by referring to two novels that you have read. Give the titles and authors. Bring out specifically how each novel has given you a vivid understanding of some phase of history.

ANSWER

Part I

The Red Badge of Courage by Stephen Crane gives us a clear insight into the lives of the men who won the Civil War and preserved the nation. The author takes a youth of the Civil War period, Henry Fleming, and bares his soul to us. We meet Henry's comrades, live with them, fight with them, and sometimes die with them. Through Henry's eyes we see men in the heat of battle influenced by courage or cowardice that turns them into running sheep. We wait with Henry for his first engagement in battle and share his doubts of his courage and his dreams of heroic achievements. His fright is ours when he turns and flees during the battle and then experiences shame after the heat of the battle has left him. When he conquers his fear and returns to the battle, we can feel the surge of relief and almost happiness he experiences. Reading Mr. Crane's book gives us the feeling of sharing the hardships and rigors of the Union Army, from the viewpoint of the infantryman. Mr. Crane has painted a vivid picture for all of us. We often think of war in general terms and use the word casually, but through the author's penetrating analysis we are led to see its wastefulness and its tremendous psychological effect upon the individual soldier.

ASSESSMENT: Excellent choice of selection to meet requirements of question. Thorough knowledge of selection, supported by excellent references. Outstanding generalizations. Excellent application to personal experience; mature response. Excellent technique of composition.

Part II

To most of us, the early days of Christianity are far off in idea as well as in time, and we are inclined to regard them as part of the too-distant past which will always be vague to us. It is only through an author's imagination and vivid writing that these days come alive to us. In The Robe, by Lloyd C. Douglas, we read a tale of the spiritual regeneration of a soldier who eventually embraces Christianity. We meet a young Roman soldier, Marcellus, who commands the soldiers who crucified Jesus, and who wins the Robe in a dice game on Golgotha. Soon afterward Marcellus begins to realize the spiritual power in the Robe, and is sick at heart as he realizes his own personal guilt and unhappiness. Soon he investigates the Man who wore it. We travel with him to Greece and Asia Minor as he talks to many of the men who knew Jesus. He becomes a Christian himself, and we endure with him the many sufferings which the Romans imposed upon those who followed the new religion. Before he dies for his faith, he predicts Christianity will one day replace the Roman Empire. Throughout the entire story we are intrigued by Mr. Douglas' excellent descriptions of life at this time, and leave the book with a clearer understanding of the sublime nature of the early Christian martyrs and a sense of our comparative weakness in today's world.

ASSESSMENT: Excellent choice of selection. Excellent knowledge of selection. Forceful generalizations supported by specific references. Good application to personal experience. Excellent technique of composition. Slight punctuation weakness.

QUESTION THREE

"The moral standards of this country are sinking--and sinking lower day by day. It is high time that something was done about this deplorable situation."

If this statement is correct, we must agree that the situation is not only deplorable but quite serious. Give your own view in regard to the quotation.

ANSWER

I believe that the conclusion drawn by the writer of this quotation is just, and I shall try to illustrate its validity by discussing one aspect of the topic.

The morals of our public officials should be beyond reproach, since the faith of the public is vested in them. How much faith can the public have in its officials when important political and social decisions can be swayed by the price of a mink coat or a convertible car? The answer is quite clear.

The moral standards of our elected and appointed officials have been highly questionable in recent years. Many selfishly made decisions on the part of politicians have resulted in disadvantages to the people they are supposed to represent. Decisions for self-profit involving housing, for example, have directly or indirectly caused injury and death to many families. These cleverly neglected areas which we call slums or "underprivileged areas" are virtual death traps. The fact that these places exit, and huge profits are being made by their owners, suggests political corruption at its worst.

Recently city contracts were awarded by a now deposed elected official in return for "special favors" that included the redecorating of his home. Although this act had seemingly involved very little money, it turned out that the city had overpaid thousands of tax dollars by awarding contracts to that corrupt politician's associate.

This case is but one example of public plundering. Take this example and multiply it by other officials in other cities, in other states, and you have a very serious American trend toward immorality.

ASSESSMENT: Expertly organized. Facts expressed convincingly. Expression is correct and effective. Variety of style. Slight weakness in technical English.

QUESTION FOUR

Directions: You will have 20 minutes to plan and write an essay on the topic given below. YOU CANNOT BE GIVEN CREDIT FOR AN ESSAY ON ANY OTHER TOPIC.

Americans are often criticized for being excessively materialistic. We are faulted for pursuing money so that we can rush out to buy the latest model automobile or the most recent fashions or a larger television set. Critics say that we no sooner get these products that we become dissatisfied and anxious to buy even newer and better things that manufacturers produce every year. Yet, it seems only human for people to want to improve their position in life and to want to make their lives more comfortable and interesting.

What good do you see in people's desires to buy and own better things? Choose one or two examples from your own or another's experience that show this desire can be a benefit to an individual, to families, and even to society as a whole. Tell exactly what you consider the benefits of "materialistic desires" to be and tell how fulfilling these desires can be a positive good for people. Use specific examples to support your ideas.

You are expected to express your thoughts carefully, naturally, and effectively. Be specific. Remember that how well you write is much more important than how much you write.

Begin writing your essay now:

Sample Essay 1

An Excellent[a] Essay (Score = 12)

It seems only human for man to have "materialistic desires," to want to better himself and strive for a more luxurious life. Human nature encourages improvement. Progressive movement is normal when allowed.

If man were to be satisfied by his present position, and never work towards a better life style, then living would be very dull. Inventions were created by men looking to make their lives more comfortable and interesting. "Materialistic desires" caused man to use his brain, to figure out new ways and ideas to ease the burden of his work load. As a result, society benefitted as a whole.

---

[a]"Excellent" should be interpreted keeping in mind that students were given a topic they had not studied beforehand and allowed only twenty mintues to write.

Not only do "materialistic desires" encourage invention, but they also encourage industry and trade among nations. In man's quest for an easier life and in his pursuit of the "latest model," industry must always be in process to meet this demand. What man cannot find in his own country, he can receive through international trade, thus different societies of pepole can learn about each other because of their "materialistic desires."

Sample Essay 2

A Good Essay (Score = 10)

Earning a good living requires a certain amount of hard work, intelligence, and ambition. Granted wealth and social standing at birth as well as luck play a significant role but in general those who make the most money have utilized their intelligence and perseverance. They have pride in their ability to rise within the system of free enterprise and express this pride by purchasing material goods. These material items are a symbol of the hard work which brought them to their present position of affluence.

The pursuit of money and material things breeds competition, the cornerstone of the American economic system. "Keeping up with the Joneses" is an American ideal which keeps everyone working harder, striving to do better than the next man. A worker will perform better if he realizes there is an ambitious youngster right behind him who wants his job.

The quest for material goods also prevents stagnation of our culture. If people did not have the desire to buy the latest fashions or automobiles, perhaps designers would become complacent and show little desire to change their styles. Material desire creates competition, forward thinking in design and invention and ultimately growth of the American society as a whole.

Sample Essay 3

An Above Average Essay (Score = 8)

If Americans were not excessively materialistic the economy of the world would be much worse than it is today. The desire for better things causes jobs for many thousands of people in stores, manufacturing plants, or warehouses. Also, in order to purchase these products one must have money. People must go out and get jobs if they want to better themselves.

The desire for something, say a car, benefits the individual in various aspects of life. He must learn to save money. He must learn to pick merchandise wisely, lest he be cheated. Patience must be acquired for almost certainly the money will be saved over a period of months or years.

If one has waited a number of years to purchase a certain thing the self-satisfaction is tremendous. The person has achieved something acknowledged by the world as success. He can be proud of his life and his possessions. From the day of birth to the day of death the individual is trying to make materialistic gains. He cannot become complacent with his success or his neighbor might pass him. The friendly spirit of competition is shining through.

People's desires for material gains is definitely a plus for America. It causes growth in the individual, the community, and the world.

Sample Essay 4

An Average Essay (Score = 6)

In my opinion, when people buy and have the desire to buy better things, this shows us (the people) how quickly the environment is changing. Most people change along with the environment and the styles of life. The benefit of the materialistic desire, is self enjoyment. When a person buys something new this usually means one of a couple things. Either he needs the new piece of object to replace the old one, or he or she just want to keep with the styles of the changing generations. New kinds of materialistic objects are produced everyday, and the makers know that the product will sell. The buyer, or consumer, is very dependent on the makers to stay tuned with the times of the fast changing environment. The production of materialistic objects have come a long way and that what the people want and need. The consumers want it because it is sort of a conquest to have the best. Its also needed, because its a part of every day living.

Sample Essay 5

A Below Average Essay (Score = 4)

The people who criticize Americans for being materialistic most likely have three maids, a mansion and own half their country. It is quite natural for anyone to want advancement; since there is no one there to give you what you want, you must plan and struggle to take what you want. I know the world is full of people who have only materialistic values which is not good. But is anything absolute? For too much of anything ruins its beauty. For example, a person who love cars, which there is nothing wrong with. But a girl won't date a young man unless he has a car or excess to one? This is when the love of cars becomes filth. Take parents, wanting the best for their children. Most parents are over protective of their children, which is natural. But the father doesn't want his son to marry that girl because of her parents background? These are two good examples on how materialistic values control you. They are no longer nice things to have but essential to survive.

A 1976 SECTION II AP SAMPLE

The Advanced Placement Examination in English usually presupposes, but not necessarily so, the student's having had a special, full-year, college-level course in English in the senior year of high school, though the examination is open to students who pursue appropriate studies in other ways. A general description of high school courses is available in the booklet 1976-1977 Advanced Placement English; another publication, Beginning an Advanced Placement English Course, is also available. The AP Examination in English is offered every May and is no longer than three hours in length, though it may be shorter. It contains both objective (multiple-choice) and essay sections. The essay or free-response section traditionally forms the larger part of the examination.

The 1976 multiple-choice section consisted of 60 analytical questions based on several short literary passages reproduced in the examination. Most of these were passages of poetry, both contemporary and traditional; a few were prose. The second section consisted of three essay questions, reprinted in their entirety above. The time limits for each question were suggested, not mandated, and students were, of course, free to divide their time differently if they chose.

Question 1 asked the students to write an essay in which they discussed how Philip Larkin's diction reveals his attitude toward the two ways of living the poem implies. Question 2 asked students to select the work of an essayist in conflict with society, or to select a fictional character in conflict with society, and, in a critical essay, to analyze the conflict and discuss the moral and ethical implications for both the individual and the society. Question 3 presented students with a passage by John Gardner and asked them to characterize the world described in the passage, discuss the effect of the passage, and analyze those elements that achieved the effect. At the reading, Questions 2 and 3 were double-read; that is, each essay on those questions was scored independently by at least two readers. Question 1, more tightly structured, was read once but closely monitored, with readings constantly checked. Many essays, including all problem essays, were given two or three readings.

In the series of multiple-choice questions, the examination tested the students' ability to comprehend and analyze various kinds of poetry and some fairly difficult prose. The three essay questions examined their competence in writing and organizing ideas. Dealing firmly with method and technique, the examination tested critical intelligence, analytical powers, and perception, as well as knowledge of literature and proficiency in discussing literary works accurately and specifically.

The sample that follows is an actual student answer to the 1976 AP Examination; the student received a grade of 5, the best score possible. It should be remembered that AP candidates have a limited amount of time to read the questions and formulate their replies; even these best answers have weaknesses.

QUESTION 1

(Suggested time-30 minutes)

Read the Philip Larkin's "Poetry of Departures" (From The Less Deceived, Marvel Press, 1955) and then write a response in which you discuss how the poet's use of words (diction or choice of words) reveals his feeling toward the two ways of life's style recorded in the poem.

There are two contrasting lifestyles presented in this poem; one is the carefree, exhilarating life of a wanderer and the other is the well-ordered, limited life of a working man. From the opening lines, the speaker reveals his preference for the more adventurous type of life. The words "fifth-hand" suggest that the speaker very distant from the action, and one can sense that perhaps he would like to be the one who has just cleared off. He describes the sudden leaving of someone as "audacious" and "purifying". Audacious has a good connotation, for it suggests boldness in the sense of adventure. That move is "purifying" implies that man was made for a Robinson Crusoe - like existence, and his departure from his civilized, well-ordered life can only be for his good.

Larkin further emphasizes the desirability of an adventurer's life through the uses of words like "flushed" and "stirred". The mere mention of news that someone has walked out brings to the speaker's mind excitement much like he feels when he hears "Then she undid her dress" or "Take that you bastard". Both of these situations suggests a sense of daring and manliness. The adventurous life is further glorified through the uses of the word "swagger", and the inviting imagery of men whose lives are carefree, in the final stanza - to "crouch in the fo'c'sle stubbly with goodness".

Meanwhile, the speaker has rejected the home life as too well-ordered, and predictable. The second line of the 2nd stanza - "we all hate home" states this quite adequately. Home is pictured as "my room", "perfect order". The word "good" as used here conveys the impression of being too good and sugary sweet. "Room", "books", and "bed" imply a closed uneventful existence, and a perfectly ordered life suggests a life run by a clock, all predetermined and predictable. The word "sober" in stanza 3 implies seriousness and gravity, a life without impulsiveness and exhilaration.

There is an undertone of doubt in the poem however. In stanza 2, the words "I think" can be taken to mean that despite his approval, maybe it's not always right to leave a life with no cares or troubles. And in the last stanza, he refers to the wandering life as artificial. The idea of departing and leaving everything and everyone behind is seen as a mere pretense, a step backwards to try and create a new life. The speaker leaves us with the idea that although the adventure's life seems more attractive and stimulating, it is just an illusion and a life that contains "books" and "china" is "reprehensibly perfect" is preferred because it offers no shortcuts but just reality and the ways things really are.

QUESTION 2

(Suggested time-50 minutes)

"The conflict created when the will of an individual opposes the will of the majority is the recurring theme of many novels, plays, and essays."

Select an essayist who is in opposition to his or her society; or, from a work of recognized literary merit, select a fictional character who is in opposition to his or her society.

In a critical essay, analyze the conflict and discuss the moral and ethical implications for both the individual and the society. Do not summarize the plot or action of the work you choose.

The works below are listed as examples. Choose one from among them or select another appropriate work.

The Federalist	Crime and Punishment
Armies of the Night	An Enemy of the People
Civil Disobedience	Heart of Darkness
Moby-Dick	Murder in the Cathedral
The Crisis	Absalom, Absalom!
A Room of One's Own	A Portrait of the Artist as a Young Man
Moll Flanders	Letters from an American Farmer
Jude the Obscure	Invisible Man

Anyone who has read Eugene Ionesco's The Rhinoceros is left with an indelible impression of Beranger, the unlikely hero of the play. What makes Beranger unforgettable is not only the unusual struggle he's involved in, but the whole change in his character that comes with his self-realization of his strength to oppose a civilization gone haywire.

To understand more of Beranger's struggle, we must realize that The Rhinoceros is an allegory to the German occupation of France during WWII. The transformation of the people into rhinoceroses parallels the acceptance of the Nazis by the French. Beranger represents the rebel, the man who will not capitulate to the abnormal way of life being imposed on him. But before Beranger emerges as the lone holdout against an unreasoning society, he had to undergo many changes that gradually immersed him deeper and deeper into this conflict.

Our first view of Beranger is of a weak, cowardly apathetic man. He is unshaven, dirty, and is suffering from a hangover. Besides being an alcholic, Beranger has many doubts about himself and his meaning in life. He listens, unconcerned, as Jean, his best friend, berates his lackadaisial appearance. This first scene shows Beranger in opposition to the generally accepted norms set down by society, but it is characterized more by a lack of will, rather than Beranger's inner strength. It is Jean who plays the pivotal role in bringing Beranger directly involved in opposition to the drastic changes taking place. Beranger respects Jean as a tower of moral strength and good advice, but when Jean changes into a Rhinoceros before his eyes, Beranger is awakened to the fact that this mass deception of the invading rhinoceros has gone too far. His conviction is deep. It is definitely abnormal to have rhinoceroses around, and he doesn't subscribe to the "leave them alone, they won't hurt us" philosophy. It is perhaps ironic and intentional that Ionesco chose a black sheep society to represent the only sane hope of salvation. Beranger is now against society. His last desperate attempts to start a new society with Daisy, his girl friend, fail, and Beranger is left alone, castrated from human company and isolated in his despair. But in his heart he knows he's right, as even his momentary lapse into self-pity at the end of the play shows him that he can't change, and must travel the road alone.

The implications by the author are frightening, for to see a whole society change and readily accept a new life that is obviously wrong strikes us to the core. Beranger remains the hero, but the outlook for society is unnerving. Ionesco could be warning us to be wary of such invasions. The conflict between Beranger and the accepting attitude of the rest of the people is a grim foreshadowing of what can happen (and did happen) to a society that ceases to question.

QUESTION 3

(Suggested time-40 minutes)

"Read the passage carefully.* Then write an essay in which you characterize briefly the world and way of life described in the passage, discuss the effect of the passage and analyze those elements that achieve this effect."

The world as presented in the passage appears to be a mythical, fantastic world, although the identification of it to the northern countries is unmistakable. Both the people and the land appear cold, barren and colorless. It is a land of mystery, of an unknown culture, where people seemed to wait for something, a sign from the sky perhaps, to guide them.

The passage itself gives one an eerie feeling, a feeling that you're reading about a place where you've been before, but are now seeing if for the first time in a totally new and unexpected light. The use of the many unusual words to describe common astronomical phenomena, such as comets, or the motions of the planets, enhance this feeling. Everyday things take on a new meaning. Men dressed in wolfskins, a reasonable attire for arctic weather, take on a sinister appearance. Icebergs, through the use of personification, take on almost human qualities - "mournfully, groaning", but sound more like some strange primordial beast. The people themselves seem strange and aloof. This effect is brought about by the references to "the silent land" and "tall and stem". Also, the claim of the inhabitants that they come from outer space, and the large portion of their life directed by the "turning of planets and stars" give them a mystical appearance. The land as a whole is little-known, and the author emphasizes the scare contact between the 2 worlds. All these things combine to make**

*The actual passage is omitted here, but is available from any AP English Teacher.
**The student ran out of time, but received an AP grade of 5 on the test.

CLEP SAMPLE OPTIONAL ESSAYS
ANALYSIS AND INTERPRETATION OF LITERATURE EXAMINATION

INTRODUCTION

The CLEP Analysis and Interpretation of Literature Examination has an optional essay section that allows you the opportunity to demonstrate your ability to write well-organized critical essays on a given passage of poetry and on general literature questions. The assessment of your answer will take into account many items -- the quality of your writing (organization, sentence structure, diction, clarity, and general effectiveness), the relevance of your illustrations to the question asked, and the critical perception that your answers demonstrate. The following sample optional essays will provide a better understanding of this part of the CLEP Examination. Remember that in your responses you will be expected to discuss works of recognized literary merit and to avoid vague generalities, irrelevant philosophizing, and unnecessary plot summaries.

1. TRAVELS WITH CHARLEY

John Steinbeck's Travels With Charley, In Search of America, ably conveys a picture of the land we live in and the men who people it. Steinbeck traveled from one part of the country to the next, from east to the northeast, across the continent to the west, then down to the south and back to his starting point. This gave him an opportunity to relive the feelings and emotions of our early immigrants who, according to Crevecoeur, were a new breed of men in search of a new country, America.

Steinbeck admitted that he was a vagabond at heart and that he had long nursed a desire to learn more about America and the American people. A long, leisurely trip would give him the opportunity to re-examine and evaluate the character and the personality traits attributed to Americans by foreigners and by Americans at large. Writers, essayists, sociologists, and psychologists profess they know what we Americans are really like, and Steinbeck was determined to find out for himself if they had all the answers. He too had a desire to uncover the secret of what makes an American American. His book does help the reader get a more accurate picture of Americans in different regions of the country, how they live, what they expect from life and how they respond to certain events or ideas. Some indication of the character of Americans can be gleaned from their response.

According to Kouwenhoven, Americans are still trying to understand what it is to be American. He explains it in his essay clearly and concisely. We are, after all, a mixture of many peoples, but in the process of jelling we have taken on a little bit of the personality of the diverse groups of immigrants who have sought a refuge and a home in America. By the same token, a new man has emerged from this admixture.

In Lerner's essay he lists several opinions wherein Americans are described as being excessively childish mentally and yet having risen to excessive power; that Americans are sympathetic and unfeeling, idealistic, cynical, isolationists and leaders. Americans may be all these things and more, but essentially the American is human and vulnerable, despite the contradictions.

Steinbeck is aware of the traits attributed to the character of Americans for he meets Americans from all over the land as he pursues his quest to the answer of what lies behind the personality traits of Americans. The author sought out people in small towns so as to get a clearer picture of the individual, away from the bustle and noise of the city. He knew that the city dweller would be less inclined to talk to a stranger than the man in a small general store. What he discovered in these talks was that most of the people he interviewed had a strong urge to travel around, to be somewhere else. This urge does represent a large number of Americans as can be seen from the trips they are always making during vacations (Turner).

This coincides with the essayist Pierson who, like Turner, claims Americans are people on the move. Pierson gave this trait a name. He called it the M-Factor, the factor of movement, migration, mobility. Pierson states that this trait is inherent in the character of Americans, derived from the early settlers, whose very natures made possible the original crossing of the Atlantic. The search was on, a new land meant a new beginning, and this begot moving around to find the best place to build a house, find good land for farming, the right climate. Steinbeck's journey was taken to satisfy his own curiosity and to justify the opinions historians had and have of Americans.

In Travels With Charley, Steinbeck went in search of the new man Crevecoeur had written about. The traits Crevecoeur claimed Americans possessed, such as their ability to adjust to new surroundings, to cultivate the land in a profitable manner, to build roads, clear forests, work hard and enjoy the fruits of their labor; to mingle amongst people without the fear of having stepped out of one's social class. Although Steinbeck has earned fame and reknown as a writer, he did not divulge his name to anybody so that people would not be in awe of him and feel uncomfortable in his presence. His anonymity put him on an equal footing with people he met along the way and made his trip more meaningful.

Steinbeck was desirous of finding out how the individual American evaluates himself. Is he kind, helpful. courteous, or is he the man Schlesinger writes about; perhaps he is the man foreigners see. Steinbeck seemed to find a composite man in the American, possessing all the features both good and bad inherited from our forebears and blended with those developed in the building of America. If, as Schlesinger writes, the most foreigners' observance of Americans is superficial and that they do not take into account that the American experience had a direct bearing on the traits which they possess, then they are getting a blurred picture of Americans.

Naturally, Steinbeck does not look upon Americans with the eye of the stranger. Although he travelled through many sections of America and could observe people at close range he did find most Americans to be kind, helpful and courteous. Some were easy to talk to and enjoyed talking to him, others he found to be men of few words. But Steinbeck found that Americans from any part of America are characteristically alike, as had James Bryce found that to be true many years ago.

The traits that distinguish Americans as unique can be found in the author. He has the restive mobility of which Turner wrote, the intelligence and individuality which his democratic heritage supplied, as indicated in Tocqueville's writings, plus the fact that he is bold, adventurous, curious, religious, moral, educated, and highly resourceful. Tocqueville is quite articulate in his description of Americans and Steinbeck fits very snugly into these categories. Because he does possess these personality traits, he looks for them in the people he interviews as he travels around the country. Thus the reader is obliged to look for them too.

According to Bryce, Americans have many commendable attributes not the least of which are those described by Tocqueville, Lerner, and Potter, character traits such as being helpful, good-natured, charitable and philanthropic. Steinbeck did find these traits to be self-evident in many instances.

To mention a few that fit into this mold, I would like to tell about the incident which occurred as he travelled on to Oregon. As I mentioned earlier, Steinbeck's camper was well-stocked. Actually it was overloaded. One rainy morning he noticed that the truck was not riding properly. He got out to check it and discovered that the tires were losing air. He realized with a shock that it was Sunday, he was in a small town, and far from any service station. He decided to change the tires himself but could not because the weight of the camper made it impossible to get his jack under it. Steinbeck returned to his truck and slowly rolled along until by chance came upon a small service station that was open. The owner saw the predicament and informed him that he did not carry such big tires, but that he would try to obtain them for him. He called other service stations, got the tires, changed them, and earned Steinbeck's everlasting gratitude. The kind, helpful people Bryce writes about is borne out.

As Steinbeck travelled in search of America, he found that people were interested in their history, who their ancestors were, and how the present-day American fitted into the pattern set in motion by the men and women who came to this land seeking freedom and equality and opportunity. He noted small markers in most of the states he went through. They were historical markers commemorating various events or famous people. Americans take pride in their past and enjoy associating themselves with the immigrants who did so much to build this great land. Bryce remarked in his essay that Americans are proud of their history. He also called them inventive and experimental. Steinbeck fits that description, too, as I shall endeavor to show.

Steinbeck's ingenuity, inventiveness and originality asserts itself in an unusual manner. His camper, which he named "Rocinante," was densely packed with food, utensils, and miscellaneous items such as a fishing rod, gun plus other accourtrements necessary for a long trip. He noticed that the garbage was thorougly kneaded and mixed with he emptied the pail. By some fast thinking, he decided the natural motion of the car acted like an agitator in a washing machine, and lo, the pail became just that. His cooking utensils were disposable, so he discarded them when used -- no big cleanup after meals.

Motels afforded him a change of diet and a chance to get bathed. It also brought him into contact with local folks and presented him with an opportunity to listen to their talk or to talk to them. Most people were politically knowledgeable, had opinions to offer, but were open to change if that meant improvement for society and country.

Stopping at different farms as he progressed northeast he had a chance to talk to migrant crop-picking people of mixed backgrounds. Some came from Canada, some from Mexico, others from distant lands. They were brought here by farmers who needed additional help at harvesting time. These migrants came willingly, for pay, unlike the Negroes who were brought here against their will, as slaves. Steinbeck found them to be hard-working, friendly and humble. The early settlers were described in like manner by Crevecoeur, Tocqueville, and Bryce.

Steinbeck chose to make his trip during the fall and winter when vacationers were gone and he felt that men would have the time to chat with him. He found them happy to share a meal with him when invited to do so; admired his camper, did not mind sharing their thoughts, but were polite and mannerly and asked no personal questions, not even his name. This is a trait which was seen by Bryce. He wrote that Americans were a well-conducted people, like to chat round the store at the crossroads. And so they did, much to the delight of the author. They were eager to discuss with him their feelings about America.

Because no language barrier exists in any region of the country, Steinbeck had fun listening to the different regional accents, which he hoped would not disappear as time went on. He found people interesting in whatever mood they displayed, some serious or sullen, others gregarious or humorous. In short, Americans possess those personality traits Bryce, Tocqueville and Crevecoeur attributed to them. Steinbeck found a reticence to accept derision from outsiders or from other Americans as they formerly were wont to do. Kouwehoven's essay mentions that the modesty of Americans made it easy for them to accept criticism in good-natured approval, feeling that in the arts or literature or other media we were still inferior to Europeans.

One of his conversations with a rural farmer brings this new feeling he encountered thus, "What's the news on the radio?" "Well, Kruschev is at the United Nations, and he took off his shoe and pounded the table with it."

"Why did he do that?"

"Well, seems he didn't like something that was being said."

In the course of the conversation Steinbeck asked him how people in his area felt about that incident. The man could not tell him about the others, but he said, "Seems we're always having to defend ourselves, I'd like to see us do something so they had to talk back to us."

Steinbeck found people to be clanish, kind associating with kind; that is, people of particular occupations being inclined to be with others of their own industry. Truckers gathered in groups in restaurants speaking a special language of the road. Farmers had their associations because they too had a language pertaining to farming. People were joiners, he found, preferring group participation rather than being by themselves. Bryce noted that Americans are an associative people because they are a sympathetic people.

Bryce observed that people of native American stock are inclined to be religious, moral as well as charitable. This description also belongs to the author, for although constantly on the go, he managed to go to church on Sunday. That we enjoy religious freedom is apparent from Steinbeck's decision to visit churches of different demoninations and being accepted in each church he went to. Besides enjoying freedom of worship, Americans cherish the freedom to come and go wherever they choose, free from government restrictions. Steinbeck personifies this American personality in his vivid description of how annoyed he was when he was stopped at the border between Canada and New York state. The problem concerned his dog, Charley. Steinbeck had not crossed into Canada, but was on a bridge connecting both countries. The Canadian border guard advised him not to enter Canada because the U.S. border guards would not permit him to re-enter with Charley unless the dog was vaccinated. Because the dog could not be given the shot, he went back as he had come. Many words were spoken and much difficulty ensued before he was able to convince the guard that he had not left the U.S. Steinbeck wrote, "I admire all nations, and hate all governments."

It was Steinbeck's love of the country, rural America, that induced him to plan his trip to the west via the back roads so that he could retrace the progress the early immigrants made in their search of America. Love of the land is inherited from our descendants. Steinbeck attests to that as he describes the beauty of the countryside, the grandeur of nature. The vastness of the country came as a shocking revelation. Nor were the remote and desolate areas lacking in beauty for everything was bathed in dazzling color. He spoke about the clear streams and the purity of the air ... the untouched land where progress had failed to destroy it.

Crevecoeur said Americans loved the land, freedom to explore it. Tocqueville agreed and added to previous observations those of associativeness, equality of conditions, and their mobility, restlessness, materialism and generostiy. Turner accused Americans of wastefulness. Historians and essayists all agree that possessing so many contradictory traits, good and bad, make Americans a people unique in the world. Steinbeck makes mention of these attributes too, as when he writes with scorn about the present-day hunters. He claims that they do not measure up to the frontiersmen of old because they hunted for food and survival, not for the sake of hunting. They did not kill animals indiscriminately. By contrast, the present-day hunters kill for the sport of it, wasting animal life. Potter's article on Abundance exemplifies the wastefulness in our society.

Leaving the small towns and villages and going through the cities, Steinbeck noted that although the scenery and the skyline changed, the people seemed not to be so different from one another in the cities. They were surrounded by the same piles of rubbish, identical advertising signs, overcrowded streets, tall buildings, lots of stores displaying the abundance of goods. Americans live in a land of plenty, produce more than they can use, and because of materialistic well-being, tend to waste instead of conserve.

Steinbeck noticed that there were too many cars everywhere, their exhaust putrifying the air people breathe. He deplored the polluted rivers and lakes and the wasteful death of fish. But materialistic Americans are not paying heed. The author found that their indifference was more pronounced in the cities than in the rural areas of America. He found that the men who lived on and worked on the land loved it and were contented to remain where they were.

During his travels, Steinbeck came upon many trailer parks where mobile homes were set up in a semi-permanent fashion. He stopped at these parks because he was able to park his camper there too. This gave him a chance to talk to the park managers and owners of the mobile homes. Most agreed that living in a mobile home was comfortable and less expensive than buying a house. If economic factors made moving necessary, it was simple to either sell the home or move it to another location. It made little difference in maintenance costs if one's income went up or went down. The payments on the mobile home did not change. There were no taxes to pay. They enjoyed the freedom it afforded them. People were drawn together and communities developed within the trailer parks. Children continue their education as buses pick them up at the park and return them there. Thus the family car is left free for the needs of the family. And the family can live in the country instead of the overcrowded city. This brings the essays of Pierson, Turner, and Bryce into focus, for it shows the character of the American people in their associativeness, the need to be free to move by need or desire and the enjoyment of living outside of the cities.

Several things come to mind as I read and write about the character of Americans. One is that the restlessness of the people has not been eased. Another is that they still enjoy movement, mobility, and migration, and that the pioneering spirit has not altogether gone out of their blood. Americans are still in a state of exploring new places, new modes of living, always looking for bigger and better opportunities. They insist on privacy as Hsu pointed out in his essay. The author related that in conversations with these people, they say they enjoy their family relationships more because both parents and children can visit without intruding on one another's privacy. The older folks can rest undisturbed by crying children and irritating problems associated with in-laws are avoided and life is pleasant for all (Hsu).

Steinbeck asked how they felt about growing up rooted or unrooted due to constant moving. The answer was that very few people ever established roots because people no longer lived in the same houses where their grandparents lived in and died in. Roots are a sign of permanence, an unknown factor in America. Like the early settlers, if the land became unproductive, they pulled up stakes and on they went in search of better land (Turner).

Travelling as he did, Steinbeck discovered that the people differed in some respects from one another in different regions of the country. Yet there exists a uniformity in their behavior, wherever they live (Bryce). Whatever the differences were, all were alike in their Americanness. He found no strangers. One of his passages is worth copying, and I quote, "For all of our enormous geographic range, for all of our sectionalism, for all of our interwoven breeds drawn from every part of the ethnic world, we are a nation, a new breed." (Crevecoeur) "Americans are much more American than they are Northerner, Southerner, Westerner, or Easterner. And descendants of English, Irish, Italian, Jewish, German, Polish are essentially Americans."

Steinbeck visited friends in Texas and writes about the lavishly furnished homes, the expensive clothes, the unaffected ease in their way of living. This is quite indicitive of the material wealth that technology, industry and the abundance that America provides for Americans who are capable of harnessing these gifts, and resourceful enough to make them work for their betterment. Steinbeck manages to convey the fact that Americans feel that the accumulation of money and the possession of goods add to their social status (Potter).

The one shattering experience Steinbeck had in his long journey was his trip to the South. In Louisiana he came upon an ugly scene of screaming, rioting racist natives of that state during the school desegregation ordered by the government. He saw Southern sectionalism at its worst. He spoke to some people who were sick at heart at the cruelty and stupidity exhibited by the mob. Others, who while not condoning the violence and brutality, felt that Negroes had to know their place, and while they believed in segregation of the races, still thought of themselves as good, God fearing Christians. The articles on violence in American society claim and disclaim that violence is and is not natural to Americans. The Arendt article claims that racial violence was present in American society from the beginning of the American experience.

In closing, I must say that I earnestly hope that bigotry and malice will some day be stricken from the hearts of men everywhere. I hope that this country will be the country that our forefathers yearned to build, that freedom, equality and true brotherhood will be part of the character of Americans, and not just words on paper.

John Steinbeck's book Travels With Charley, In Search of America introduced me to parts of America I have never seen, introduced me to people I have never met, and whetted my appetite to find out more about America and Americans.

2. ANNA KARENINA

I feel justified in stating, without reservations, that Tolstoy's Anna Karenina is indeed a tremendous novel (outside of size) in the study of life in Russia in the mid-nineteenth century. The realism is alive and acute because it is written about people, how they feel, and what they think; how their lives are affected by every other person, the chain of events that bring them together, and tie them together, and the philosophy and the psychology that is the outcome of this meshing of mind and matter.

Biographers maintain that much of this book is autobiographical; that Levin is Tolstoy, and that the story concerning the suicide of Anna came about because a neighbor of Tolstoy's actually did commit suicide by throwing herself under the wheels of a train.

Be that as it may, the book is an experience in documenting people in different strata of society. In the beginning of the book the reader meets the head of the household of the Oblonskys. Stiva has a personality that matches his mentality. He lives outside of life, interested in the external values, loves his family in his own way, and lives one life with them and another with his friends and his mistresses.

It is his philosophy to extract from life every pearl, to worry about problems "tomorrow" and because of this attitude he is personable and affable and a welcome member of his society. As Tolstoy remarks, "With all his faults, one must do him justice. He has the true Russian, Slav nature!"

Tolstoy does not seem to be making a moral judgment but rather to tell it like it is. If man is made for life, then life is made for man. Stiva, like the rest of Tolstoy's many characters, is a product of his environment, and more than that, a product of Russian thought and life.

Tolstoy writes realistically about the human tragedy that is with us from birth to death. And he philosophizes about the inevitability of death. His novel is didactic. Tolstoy is aware of the double standard of men; of the subjugation and demeaning role assigned to women. He raises the question of the morality of marriages arranged by parents, or society. This, not Anna's infidelity, is immoral, and society must take the blame for the results of marriages arranged for convenience and status.

In this light, if one were to consider how the marraige of Kitty to Vronsky (had her mother been successful in her attempt to effect it) would have turned out; chances are that Vronsky would not have scorned peccadillos which were accepted by high society. In Anna's case, Karenin was not a philanderer, but what was just as sinful and immoral, he was the epitome of bureaucratic officialdom. Karenin was more concerned with outward appearances than facing facts truthfully. Tolstoy artfully shows how lacking Karenin is in showing compassion, although he professes he is adhering to Christian tenets of morality. To forgive is Christian, but Karenin interprets this axiom in his own parochial way.

Tolstoy, as others before him, saw city life as evil. The country represents decency and propriety. He sees physical work as the one thing that gives meaning and stability to life. Even admitting that the peasants can and do rob, are drunkards, refuse to learn anything about new methods of farming or machinery to ease the burden and produce more and better crops, he nevertheless extols them. From them one can learn simple truths and so restore one's faith in religion and in God.

The work is so grandiloquent, not only because it shows the author's compassion for and understanding of human nature, but because he shows the relation of man to life. This juxtaposition renders the work credible in the realm of realism. When Levin becomes engrossed in soul-searching, trying to become one with the peasants, engaging in the mowing with them, trying to emulate them in their simplicity, Tolstoy does not hypocritically imply that Levin can remove his aristocratic birth and background and intellectually and spiritually join them on their level.

Though Levin wants to help the peasants and does so, the peasants cannot forget that he is a member of the nobility and resent his working with them in the fields. Levin's brother Sergey suggests that the peasants should be educated, but Levin retorts that they have all the education that they require, and that they had their faith, whatever values they had, they were exclusively theirs. Tolstoy/Levin has ambivalent feelings about the Russian peasant and the intellectual -- about his conservative and liberal ideas -- about society as a whole. He denounces deceitfulness, lies, the Stahl brand of religion, the stupid and vapid social conventions high society paid attention to in their haughty and supercilious way.

Tolstoy is highly critical of his own class of the nobility in the manner in which they accept affairs of the heart as a frivolous pasting, eat and drink to excess, gamble away fortunes, live expensively and always in debt, exploit the peasants, and live idle lives filled with useless chatter. He paints a picture of the society of St. Petersburg and that of Moscow in a most unflattering light. The only characters he seems to have a real affinity for are Kitty and Levin, Dolly and her family. The family, in Tolstoy's belief, is sacrosanct.

He gives his characters freedom to think and to act according to their respective conscience. Thus one can peer into the inner recesses of Anna as she lives through the agonies of a woman who has broken her marriage vows, deserted her son and has become a slave to passion; who becomes so obsessed by jealousy, that ultimately she is victimized by her love and her frenzy drives her to self-destruction.

By contrast, the love of Kitty for Levin purifies that love and makes it great and enduring. And Dolly, in her wisdom and maturity, while acknowledging her Stiva's infidelity, and despising him for it, nevertheless decides that keeping the family and the home intact is the right thing, for in a sense the real heroine in this drama is Dolly. Her philosophy is not built on contradictions, but on facts, and she knows that Stiva with all his faults will never leave her and the children. She is also cognizant of the financial bind they are in.

It is ironical that Dolly has invited Anna to her home to talk to Stiva, Anna's brother, and help them put their marital difficulties to rights. She succeeds, but in the process meets Vronsky, and from that fateful meeting her own marriage fails; she becomes the "fallen woman" and ruins her life and Vronsky's. As for Karenin, Tolstoy sees him as a man without a soul, to whom duty is more important than love. He sees him as a religious hypocrite, an automaton, so devoid of emotional qualities of the spirit that he can understand how and why a woman like Anna could commit adultery with a man as dashing as Vronsky and leave both her son and Karenin.

Maybe Anna was imprudent, maybe she sinned, but the outmoded laws of divorce, the church, and society in general were more the sinners than the sinned against. Also there is substantial evidence that Anna did not capitulate to Vronsky immediately. She searched her conscience and admitted that what she was doing was wrong -- not only for her, but for Seryozha and even to Karenin. But once having made the step, she did not do it clandestinely. She made a full confession to Karenin and hoped he would not judge her or condemn her by taking her son from her. Society ostracized her. Truth was not a factor they were interested in. She flaunted society's mores, their conventions and was duly punished for it. Tolstoy finds their trasigence the greater of two evils. He does not fail to see the pitiable position Anna's public declaration of her love for Vronsky puts her in. Her suffering is intense.

Tolstoy has presented his ideas of life, his moral and philosophic principles in Levin, rather, through him. Levin finds God and faith through a simple remark made by one of his peasants. He has a conscious awakening that by omitting Reason from thought, Truth is revealed. He was agitated by the thought that he was an unbeliever, but he believed in humanity. His agony almost leads him to suicide. But he lives. When he finally finds what he is searching for, his agony become his ecstasy. He finds that God is Truth -- Truth is wisdom and beauty; Reason destroys Truth by inventing other things, beliefs that are only for the appetite not for the soul, producing lies and deceit. He has found that his philosophy is Faith, that Faith is God, and God the One Truth and Life.

The book has some profoundly marvelous scenes: the hunt, the race, and the harvest. The hunt provides a lesson in tolerance; the race provides the symbolic destruction of the mare Frou-Frou, and is the forerunner of what is to come; the harvest scene exudes the joy that Levin experiences in his work with the peasants. Tolstoy makes these passages alive with the completeness of selected detail. It is a study in character. The genius of Tolstoy allows him to see deep in the souls of men and women, divergent though they be, from peasants to landowners, from bureaucrats to mothers, from the shallow members of high society to creative and productive people.

Religion and morality pervade the story throughout. Tolstoy was not proselytizing but it is evident that he must have been going through a crisis in his own life. He could not abide the pseudo-religiosity of people like Karenin and the Countess Lidia. Karenin is cold, austere and inflexible, so orthodox, yet the ambiguity of his actions and his high Christian principles point to a moral lack in all areas of his life.

The traits of the characters are brought out through speech, through gestures, and mannerisms. Each character does certain things at certain times, such as Karenin cracking his knuckles; Stepan pulling his beard; or Anna squinting up her eyes or lowering her eyelids when under stress. Tolstoy's psychological insight is indeed limitless in range. He understood human nature, and he rejected conventional moral values because they had no moral qualities.

As a story about people, Anna Karenina has no peer. One gets a complete picture of the inner struggles of the dominant characters. Levin's philosophical quest is pursued to almost the end. He questions God, man's destiny; but he also cannot accept death -- Nikolai's. After violent mental aberration which almost destroys him, he sees the light and the truth which helps him resolve his conflicts. He finds that love can conquer what reason cannot -- it teaches humility and a reverence for life. Kitty is the embodiment of all that is gracious in love. Through her love Levin is able to face himself and accept what he had refuted as invalid. She gave to him what books, religion, and hard work could not. She saved his mind, his sanity. Tolstoy tells us that man must live for others, to sacrifice for others, to live for God.

Artistically, this work is sublime. Didactically, it gives a picture of a people living in a certain place in a certain time in history. We learn how they lived and what they thought, can gauge their moral values, their inconsistencies, but not the complexities of their "whys" . . .

3. THE GENTLEMAN FROM SAN FRANCISCO

This absorbing story, "The Gentleman from San Francisco," was written not by an American but paradoxically by a Russian writer, Ivan Bunin. The point of view belongs to the omniscient narrator, for he is telling the story and it is from his point of view that we learn the facts of the narrative.

Bunin's Gentleman is annonymous, which implies that he is a facsimile of all plutocrats, a man who has made his money exploiting others, in this case cheap coolie labor. Bunin is possibly making an indictment of the capitalist system which is an outgrowth of the materialistic nature inherent in western civilization. It is also a reminder of the civilization of the past, namely Babylon, which he mentions in the epigram at the very beginning of the story, and which also sets the tone for what follows.

Several readings bear out the fact that there is much that can be gleaned from this piece of writing. I believe that the author's work is more than a social satire. It is an expose of the spiritual rot with which man is infected and it is universal.

It is interesting to note that "The Gentleman from San Francisco" was written in 1915, a year when there was strife and turmoil in the world; when rebellion was a way of life in Europe. By way of comparison, this "Gentleman" is an American, a product of the New World, from a Republic, founded on the theory that all men are created equal. Herein lies the irony. The fact that a man like the "Gentleman" can be found here proves the theory false.

The "Gentleman" is a millionaire. He has kept his nose to the grindstone for most of his fifty-eight years, achieved what he had set out to do, and was ready to take a well-deserved vacation. They sail on the luxury liner "Atlantis" for Europe. Symbolically, the name of the ship is synonymous with the lost continent. Life is one long meal after another. Passengers spend hours at the table, gorge themselves with food and drink, wear beautiful clothes and flirt and dance, and seem not to have a care in the world. They are oblivious to the storm raging outside, and are quite convinced that their captain, who resembles an idol, will bring them safely through.

When the Gentleman and his family land in Capri they put up at a posh hotel and occupy a suite recently vacated by "an exalted personage -- Rais XVII" which fortifies the Gentleman's self-esteem. The Gentleman is accorded every comfort his money entitles him to. The servants and the manager are respectful and cordial, treat him with feigned humility. But when the Gentleman, this rich American, suddenly dies of a stroke before dinner, the attitude of the management and the servants changes drastically towards the body of the Gentleman and his widow and daughter.

They are not permitted to retain the special suite. A makeshift coffin is obtained and put into a small back room. Soon they are on the same little steamer on which they came to the island, returning after their brief stay. Back on the luxury liner "Atlantis," the body of the Gentleman is lying in the bowels of the ship. Thus man does not control his own destiny. The underlying theme in Bunin's work deals with man's vulnerability in the face of death.

Bunin's story is written with great insight regarding the nature of man. The Gentleman is animalistic in his instincts. He eats himself to death. Bunin, in long sentences, vividly draws a picture of the length of time the passengers spend in the dining room eating and drinking. He comments sarcastically that after partaking of all this food and drink the chamber maids were obliged to deposit "rubber bags with hot water to warm the stomachs." Again in this description of the Asiatic prince, "the fact that his skin showed through his coarse black mustache like that of a corpse..." Personification in his description of the "Atlantis" comparing the lights of the boat to "fiery eyes."

There is also much irony displayed when Bunin compares the generosity of the American while travelling with his aversion for the ragamuffins and the commissionaires, for the less fortunate in general. He makes a definitive appraisal of the world of the millionaires and the world of those who work for them. He is acutely aware of how the rich on the upper decks enjoy life to the fullest, in all manner of creature comforts, swathed in luxury, indolent, believing that this was meant for them alone, while "the lookouts up in their crow's-nest froze with the cold and grew dazed from straining their attention beyond their stern." Bunin goes on to contrast the condition of the men working in the furnace room, comparing them to the souls in Dante's Inferno, in the ninth circle, seeing the room as a womb; the men sweaty and filthy.

It is a pictorial masterpiece, eloquently stated, to say the least. Bunin can use nouns, verbs and adjectives with such finesse. He cites the injustice of a system that permits pernicious indifference, for he shows how relaxed and carefree the men are in the lounge on the upper part of the ship.

The art of characterization is another feat of this author. By descriptive facility, his characters become quite lifelike, therefore credible. One gets a feeling of meeting a gentleman who possesses the unattractive qualities inherent in a self-made millionaire who through ruthlessness and a lack of compassion for his fellow-man has become a symbol of power in his eyes.

Diction plays a very important part in this tale. It is concise, to the point, offering a technique unique to the author and his style. Imagery conveys a sense of what the reader may expect and it also helps to develop the character. From the description of the Gentleman, one sees a man of a certain type, which suggests in this case that he has the appetite of a beast and the analogy is in essence what the story is about. The writer's feelings about people like the Gentleman and the passengers on the ship are conveyed through diction.

The Gentleman's appearance is not pleasing at all. He looks like a Mongolian, has gold fillings, a bald head that gleams like ivory and a personality that matches his appearance. Food and creature comforts are life to him. Although he is a millionaire, he desires to hobnob with multi-millionaires, or with titled men. And where better than on this trip to Europe -- Capri -- where the Roman emperor lived and ruled. Bunin makes allusions to paganism and Christianity. He writes about the cruelty, the gluttony, the lasciviousness and miserliness of this power-mad man, and goes on to include a touching scene with the two pipers of Abruzzi, who, "coming down from Anacapri, stopped by a statue of the Holy Virgin, and bared their heads and raised their flutes to their lips -- praises poured forth, naive and humbly joyous, to the sun, to the morning, and to Her, the immaculate Intercessor for all the suffering in this wicked and beautiful world."

The story is shot through with irony. The title itself is ironical, for San Francisco was named for St. Francis, who was the giver of refuge to all living creatures, who preferred poverty to wealth. Bunin writes with keen insight about the world of the Gentleman and the world of man in general. He omits romanticism. Realistically, one sees the Gentleman's aversion to the ragamuffins and to "those greedy, garlic-stinking little wretches called Italians;" unlike St. Francis, he gave nothing. That city brought out the corrupt rich, who debased God's creatures (thereupon grew rich) exploiting them cruelly. He was a sinner, had no moral quality -- he loved money and power and these were his religion.

There are also some poignant moments to meditate about, the moral and philosophical meanings. The Gentleman was ready for life, but life was not ready for him. Symbolically the storm and gale the tourists encounter coincides with the obstacles man encounters, often monumental in degree, that he must fight in order to achieve a place in society. As Bunin goes on to describe the activities that these paragons of civilization engage in, he mentions the shooting of pigeons, and these birds are symbols of peace, which men shoot down and which act is an expression of the evil in man; the destruction wreaked on man by his own volition.

The author's mastery of language is apparent at all times. Direct narration is at a minimum while author description is at a maximum. Nor are the thoughts of the Gentleman revealed except for a few words which he utters when he beholds his image in the mirror and notices his aging appearance. The "Oh, its's dreadful! It's dreadful!" conveys a great deal to the reader about the egotistical nature of the Gentleman, yet not much of inner thoughts. Language is everything. His ability in this sphere is original and extraordinary.

There are similes scattered throughout, such as, "red-coated Negroes with eyeballs that looked like shelled hard-boiled eggs;" "the wind abated, becoming warmer and more fragrant, and golden snakes, gliding away from the lamp-posts on the quai, came floating on the subdued waves which gleamed like black oil;" "the small ship, lying like a beetle on the bright and delicate blue that filled the Bay of Naples..."

Describing the personality of the Gentleman, Bunin notes that he is generous while travelling, but this trait disappears as soon as the ship arrives at its destination. He looks with loathing upon the swarming poor; at their hovels, and he feels despair...but not for the less fortunate, rather that this scene intruded itself on the beauty and grandeur of Italy that he had come to see.

Bunin's detailed physical descriptions give the impression of stark realism, but the symbolism contributes a modicum of relief which rescues the story from heaviness in the extreme. He also uses much color, such as the old woman in gray; the color of skin resembling a corpse; the multi-colored waves of the Sea like the tail of a peacock; snowy-white crests. Another interesting observation are the museums, "lifelessly clean museums;" and the churches, "smelling of wax, which everywhere and always contain the same things: a majestic portal -- empty vastness, silence flames of a seven-branched candlestick glowing redly in the distant depths; and someone's "Descent from the Cross" the poetry and the articulation the author displays is uncommon.

The author does not use foreign words except to convey the foreign atmosphere in the story. The few phrases inserted are spoken by the servant Luigi, "Ha sonato, signore?" and "Gia e morto" plus words like the English shuffleboard, boullion, flirt, hotel, which are not Russian, but accepted as necessary to the story.

Bunin uses the circular plan in telling the story. It begins with a voyage and it ends with a voyage. The trip to Europe starts in luxury and comfort, the voyage akin to Heaven but the trip back is in the lowest level of the ship, in heat, sweat, fire, akin to Hell. The parallelism is seen in the actions of Luigi before and after the Gentleman's death; in the couple hired to simulate love on both trips; the reaction of the Management before and after the Gentleman's demise. It is a repetition in reverse order.

As for suspense, there is a foreboding, a premonition of some impending crisis in, "And everything went very well at first." Then the line, "On the day of departure, -- a most memorable one for the family from San Francisco." Also the image of the proprietor of the hotel was the same he had seen in his dream. These lines are written without emotion yet provide mood and atmosphere that sustains the feeling that all is not right.

The story is not meant to be didactic. It is, as I can ascertain, a study of people, man in relation to his environment. The author manages to contrast the practiced economies of the German youth and the Russians to the extravagance of the Americans and the reaction of the poor to them. However, he does not gloss over the fact that the workers too are guilty of hypocrisy and display the same greedy tendencies that the rich do.

In short, all men are motivated by a desire to get from life more than they need. They do not examine the means by which they obtain their ends. Thus civilization produces a Tiberius under whose rule human misery reached its zenith, including the crucifixtion of Christ, and a Gentleman, exhibiting love for money, power, and other excesses plus a conspicuous lack of compassion for his fellow-man.

4. THE STRANGER

In the novel The Stranger, the protagonist, Meursalt, was the twentieth century version of the existentialist hero. Existentialism is defined as a movement which claims to represent a middle way between traditional materialism and idealism. It stresses personal decisions made in a world without purpose. The behavior of Meursalt was an enduring testimony to his belief that life consisted of inescapable problems which could not be changed and were not worth agonizing hours of mental stress. One had to accept the unacceptable, learn to live with it, and make it feasible and worthwhile.

Life's absurdities were to Meursalt intrinsically related to society's concept of man's debt to universal man. Society based this concept on its evaluation of how it chose man to live within its moral precepts and then to conform to specific patterns made by man for man. (Paul Roubiczek, Existentialism For and Against, p. 121. To this concept Meursalt could not and did not subscribe. Nevertheless he did not deny life itself. He had his own set of values. Above all, he lived and exalted in the beauties of nature. Nature, unlike man, was infinite. For Meursalt the sun and the burning sands, the vast sea and the cool nights were more to be loved than material things. Nature spoke to him far more eloquently than ever could man.

Yet he did enjoy the physical relationship he had with Marie. Although he could not admit that he loved her, he did not object to marrying her if that was what she desired. As he was not the garrulous type, he did not discuss his feelings on that score. He acquiesced readily to suggestions, not bothering to ponder them for what they were worth. This indifference was instrumental in leading him into the affair that culminated in the murder of the Arab.

Meursalt's indifference did not render him incapable of human association. His was a gentle passive quality, devoid of emotion, yet affable and pleasing. He seemed to lack ambition, but was thought to be intelligent. He had no desire to change his mode of living. It was not important. He lived a dull and mechanical existence without any obvious links to a past. Meursalt's concern was only of the present and he did not dwell on the past. He existed in a world where life was purposeless and incomprehensible, unpredictable and incongruous. (Carol Petersen, Albert Camus, p. 45.) To the existentialist, however, the most realistic approach was to learn how to profitably live in the world, transforming it into a positive and creative state.

With clarity of perception, Camus' hero could reflect on the relation of man to live; of the meaningless struggle of man to be rational in a nonrational world. (Frederick Patka, Existentialist Thinkers and Thought, p. 129.) He saw man as a part of the whole, but not obliged to relinquish his individuality. In his quest of man in search of himself he never attempted to explain to himself why he was as he was. He did not intensify his need to know why he behaved as he did; it wasn't important. Neither did he absolve man from guilt in pursuing an archaic and didactic manner of living. It was essential for Meursalt to believe that man existed for himself and was therefore responsible for and to his own particular ideology.

As an existentialist philosopher, Meursalt did not consult the past to find his place in the present or in the immediate future. His needs were not contingent on society's code of ethics but solely on his own beliefs and his satisfaction in relation to his needs. Therefore he could not understand the reaction of the authorities when it was disclosed that he showed no emotion at the funeral of his mother. In actuality he was condemned not so much for the murder of the Arab as for the fact that he smoked at her funeral and did not shed a tear. He could not translate into words almost nonexistent feeling and so society felt the need to punish him in kind; it was necessary to have him pay with his life.

In the scheme of things in relation to man, Meursalt undeniably felt himself a stranger, for he was not like other men. He did not attach importance to certain things. He was not concerned with the mores of society. They were to him absurd. Their conventions and their concepts were alien to him. He did not live by their moral tenets. Meursalt felt that man had to live in a universe that was meaningless only if he chose to do so. He could not, in truthfulness and honesty, live by laws he had not helped to make. To be free was to rebel, to be true to oneself. Society's imposed restrictions did little to create happiness for man. It was this awareness of the part man was forced to play on the stage of life that estranged him from society. He had to live as he felt, a life based on the truth of being and feeling. (Henri Peyre, French Novelists of Today, p. 321.)

Meursalt's empathy for people and lack of questioning of motives and possible results led him to become involved in those events which were to have serious consequences. He willingly participated in whatever was asked of him. Since nothing really mattered anyway there was little reason to think about the effect one's actions might produce. It was that attitude that sealed his own fate. He lived a life uncomplicated by entanglements of an emotional nature. Not until the murder of the Arab and his subsequent arrest and incarceration did he evaluate his relationship to the world. (Peyre, p. 321.) Society denied him his importance as an individual. Rather was he judged by the old and outworn conventional values. Cognizant of his problem in the world of the absurd he did not desire to withdraw from the world or from day to day living. He realized that he wanted to live and that life, even with its absurdities, offers man the only chance for happiness. (Germaine Bree, Albert Camus, A Collection of Critical Essays, p. 32.)

Meursalt's preoccupation with the meaningless and the nothingness of life did not obscure the fact that life was the only thing that gave man dignity and that the life he lived did not take into account man's potentialities. Thus he came to realize that indifference to things created the nothingness. That Meursalt wanted to live was apparent to him when he had the loneliness and the time to keep him company. In that state of mind he became aware of the need to ask questions and to have them answered. To exist was really not enough.

Camus' hero awakened to reality too late. As he sat in the courtroom and listened to the prosecutor denounce him and liken him to a monster, he was struck by the hatred in the man. Yet Meursalt made no attempt to defend himself. Gradually his thoughts wandered away from the proceedings to other things and to other places. He remembered certain sounds of the town he loved -- sounds of the birds in the parks, the shouts of the newspaper boys, the screech of the streetcars as they sped along -- all faint and familiar sounds as the night stole over the town. Those were the things he missed most as he was returned to his lonely cell.

As the prosecutor droned on, Meursalt's thoughts faded more into the past. Suddenly he remembered a life which was no longer his. He reflected on the relation of man to life. Now he could see with clarity the meaningless struggle of man to protest those things which were not in his power to change. The futility of his position made him feel ill.

The existentialist's reaction to the absurdity of life did not include a disdain for life. To Meursalt life was meant to be lived and never was that as clear to him as when he found himself locked up and alone. He had spent his life searching for a meaning to life which he only discovered when he was near death. Society has crushed him in the end.

Meursalt refused to let the priest console him in his cell. He did not believe in God or in life after death. Therefore, religion was a farce, for the church did nothing to alleviate man's misery during his lifetime. By its laws and values, the church and society were responsible for his confinement. They had condemned him as a criminal and he had to accept their judgment. Their decision did not help to resolve his conflicts. The efforts of the priest to bring him back to God and reclaim his soul further alienated Meursalt and increased his indignation and contempt for the hypocrisy of organized orthodox religion. He accepted the inevitability of death, but not in a life beyond the grave. Meursalt came face to face with the stupidity inherent in the mind of man.

Camus' concept of existentialism differed from that of Sartre. Camus, unlike Sartre, refused to become enmeshed in violent political ideology. He was angered by his compatriots unconvincing attempt to use violence as a means of establishing a new order. (Philip Rhein, Albert Camus, p. 38.) Camus's refusal to defend a rigid socialist order based on violent revolution made his role an ambiguous one in the realm of the absolute existentialist writers and philosophers. He believed that man could not exist if not free. Coercion did not produce freedom or happiness. Man had to make his own decisions rather than be forced to accept at face value those principles foisted on him by sudden change. Sartre believed in communism as a lesser of two evils. (Rhein, p. 127.)

Sartre and Camus believed that man exists physically in history, but the latter believed that man can transcend history by participation in the human spirit. Sartre refuses any human nature and sees man as the sum total of his acts. Man cannot be separated from history and can come into being only through participation. (Henri Peyre, French Novelists of Today, p. 330.)

Camus was not indifferent to the absurdities of man's existence in a universe where life is ended by death, where there is no God, but ironically still a place where man can find happiness and dignity unique in the value of human life. Sartre's view was that man was brought into the universe not by design but by happenstance, forced to accept and adapt to laws not of his making. His opposition then was moral and ethical.

Camus was filled with the desire to bring to man the beauty and tranquility of nature. He loved and admired all that it afforded man. Nature, unlike man, could not be repressed or frustrated. Its horizons are broad, its dimensions limitless.

It would be impossible to evaluate the subject of existentialism by a simple yes or no on the basis of one reading. Fo although the reader can comprehend and sympathize with the philosophical theories pertaining to this movement, it is much too deep and complex a subject to eagerly accept or profoundly reject. However, I do agree in some measure with Camus when he states through his protagonist, Meursalt, that man is fraught with frustration because of the fact that he must conform or be annihilated. Society, not the individual, makes the rules. Man lives in a world not of his own making. He is considered an outcast, an alien, if he refuses to conform. If he challenges the existing rules of society, is he not then behaving in a criminal fashion? However, it is not expedient to remain aloof. Man must not be indifferent; he must question and be answered. He must not be ready to acquiesce, for that is the only way he can attain the state of happiness for which he strives. Man's saving grace is that he is the only animal who can use his intellect to some day enjoy freedom and peace.

5. ANDREW WYETH

The paintings of Andrew Wyeth are as American in subject matter and setting as the artist who painted them. His paintings are traditional in style. They are representational pictures of the geographic area in which Wyeth lives. His subjects are familiar neighbors and friends; also the objects and scenes he has been accustomed to looking at every day of his life has been reproduced in his paintings. The trees, brooks, ravines and ridges speak to him of the past and of the present. He is at home everywhere he roams for the people know him and are used to his figure as he walks alone looking and recording mentally ideas for his next picture. Wyeth is at ease with them, too, for he speaks their language, can sense their inner feelings, is a friend of all, black and white.

Wyeth is a realist, his trained eye taking in every aspect of the scene, depicting the mood, season and setting with expertise craftsmanship and artistic response. His paintings are loving reproductions of the countryside, its houses and fences, the barns, animals and insects; a solitary tree or a solitary person. A strong point in his pictures is his use of light and tone. It gives to his work movement and drama enabling the viewer to sense the heaviness of the snow upon the rooftop or the strength of the wind, the effect of time on man and his world.

Wyeth's world is the size of Brandywine Valley and the coast of Maine. His paintings are taken directly from the scenes nature provides. He paints America as he sees it through his own eyes. The legends he was acquainted with from early childhood served him well when he began to put the history of his country on canvas. His inventiveness and imagination were his greatest allies in depicting certain events the people he painted had lived through. Although Wyeth is a realist, he can produce paintings that contain psychological overtones. He not only portrays the contemplative side of the people he knows, the dreams of the young, he shows the innate loneliness of old age. His pictures of people are a study in character analysis. The paintings of Wyeth show his concern and sensitivity for his subjects. The artist can feel their emotions and their moods, for they are known to him. Wyeth is in everything he creates, for his pictures express him directly.

His originality is evident in the portrayal of rural America -- its landscapes, its dwellings, and its simple, unpretentious people. It is also part and parcel of his background, his Americanness in mind and matter. Wyeth's originality stems from his closeness to the soil and soul of the people and places he paints. He followed in the tradition of his father, reaching beyond him in his talent for originality. Because of his familiarity with the topography of Brandywine Valley as well as its American history and the area in Maine where he spent his summers, he is able, due to an acute memory of every stone and crag, to paint what he recalls, putting his experiences, moods, and emotions into each of his paintings.

Wyeth did not go beyond his world to find his themes and subjects for his paintings. They were on his doorstep in the Brandywine Valley and in the country in Maine. The people and the landscapes and seascapes were his models as were the lonely deserted farms and old dilapidated barns with perhaps a single animal near it. They supplied him with the narrative quality that is to be found in his pictures. The originality that Wyeth exhibits is due in no small measure to the fact that he was not tutored by artists who had themselves been trained by others who schooled in the European tradition. Wyeth's paintings are American in origin. They portray his knowledge of the land he has been familiar with since childhood.

The area Wyeth has lived in all his life abounds with American history. It is the history of the American Revolution. The buildings where the miller lived who ground the flour for the army's bread and the granary where it was stored are still standing and were a source of inspiration for Wyeth to do a series of paintings. His Americanness is keen and asserts itself in the antiquity and weatherbeaten look of buildings on farms which are steeped in history. One can see in his pictures rusting bits of metal, broken down fences, gnarled old trees, abandoned boats lying on the shore, a single bird in flight, or looking out of an old house's window through space. Everything related to people in time, past and present. He extracts bits and pieces of localism and puts the whole on canvas. Whatever he paints, it is all taken from the American scene and the figures are the American people. Wyeth's ability to fuse the past with the present confirms his knowledge of the periods of American growth and its relation to his art.

As an artist, he is considered a great watercolorist, perhaps the greatest we have. His tempera technique is also an indication of the discipline he exerts upon himself. The technique involves long, laborious and arduous hours of very carefully applied brush strokes. Each painting requires months of work before it is finished. To ease the work Wyeth paints in watercolor and in oils. His dry brush technique is neither as quick nor as fluid as watercolor. But it allows for the change of mood and tone before the finishing of a painting in tempera, for it is an intermediate step and helpful to the artist. Wyeth is a prodigious artist as can be seen from the amazingly realistic works he has produced.

The American school of watercolor painting is considered great by any standard. Many of our famous artists such as Himer, Sargent, Marin and others of their caliber are part of that school, yet Wyeth, although a product of it, differs from it because his is the tradition of Brandywine, handed down to him from his father. There is no influence of the European school in any of his works. The frills and fragility of portraiture or landscape is not within his style. His is the language of America, its rugged and peaceful beauty. It is not beauty for the sake of beauty. They speak of the realistic issues that confront humanity, therefore Wyeth can see something beautiful even in the mundane chores of man. Unlike the European artist he paints for himself, does not pander to the tastes and whims of this or that school of painting. His use of color is sombre but significant, whereas the European influences painter resorted to splashes of bright color. European culture is conspicuously absent in Wyeth's pictures.

Wyeth was not influenced in any way, shape or form by artists who emigrated to Europe to learn their craft and then returned to America to practice what they had learned. His training ground consisted of Chadds Ford, the Valley, and Maine. Wyeth did not paint surface appearances, he painted below the surface, coming face to face with the inner image which he capably transferred on to the canvas. The simplicity and vitality of his execution of scenes of nature in all her seasons is devoid of made-up prettiness usually found in paintings of American artists who could not see beauty in the uncultured, uncluttered American way of life, and so had to use Europe as a base for their period of training. Wyeth's deviation from the European tradition is complete.

Rural America comes alive under his brush. Rotting tree limbs alongside rotting barns are indicative of the life that once made itself felt living and working in the houses and the now abandoned rotting buildings. Wyeth lends his subjects a quiet dignity and a respect for their struggle to survive even in the face of adversity. His people show the ravages and scars of time, but in their faces he finds something wonderful and beautiful. Empty rooms or solitary figures or crude objects are depicted with compassion and understanding of what they denote. The pampered prettiness of European paintings of people or landscapes are nowhere to be seen in Weyth's pictures.

Wyeth can be classified as a realist-abstractionist. His pictures are not necessarily a pictorial cataloging of what he sees. However, the viewer will find the infinitely interesting bits of information of American tradition if he studies the paintings several times. The artist subtly entwines the old and the new, using color, mood, and light to convey what he is saying.

About the artist, Wyeth was born in Chadds Ford, Pennsylvania, 1917, son of Newell Convers Wyeth, a well-known illustrator, painter of the American tradition. Andrew Wyeth is one of America's best loved contemporary painters, has great public appeal, and is famous for his portrayals of rural America -- its inhabitants and its history. His one and only teacher has been his father. From him Wyeth received a rigorous training in the depiction of human anatomy. He also drew from casts and from still life as well as from a posed model. Later he did without the model and began to draw from memory. His flair for expressionism was already beginning to assert itself early in his career.

Wyeth experimented with watercolors when time allowed, especially when he painted outdoors. Nature supplied him with the effect of lights on the rooftop, the haze of distance, the reflection of the glitter of the sun on water. He sketched things on the ground, or the scene in the distance. He sketched tirelessly, learning to love everything he saw, committing to memory his experiences.

At the age of fourteen, he illustrated a series of children's books. He had his first one-man show at nineteen when members of the Arts and Program Committee of the Philadelphia Art Alliance invited him to exhibit in the Art Alliance galleries. At twenty he exhibited in the Macbeth Galleries in New York. At twenty-three he was launched on a career as a brilliant artist. He developed a meticulously detailed and realistic style in which he depicted nature and everyday experiences.

It was not until after World War II that he became known as a leader in the style called Magic Realism. This is a descendant of European Surrealism, which is characterized by the use of oblique angles of vision and juxtapositions of figures and objects to create pictures with psychological nuances.

Wyeth's paintings have an aura of loneliness about them. He spent much of his time by himself, observing and memorizing expressions and moods of the people he spent so much of his time with. His tempera studies have a stark, bare quality, often showing the drama of life unfolding. The colors are browns, greys, and whites, sometimes blues, ideally suited to his initmate portrayals of character.

He had a short formal education due to poor health. He was tutored at home which left him enough time to wander in the valley along the old Indian paths and the new paths which crisscrossed them when set up by the white man. Thus the world of nature was his to explore and to paint. He never had a desire to travel because he feared it might alter his taste and his mind and might be a detriment to him in his work.

He is married to Betsy Merle James and has two sons. The younger son is following in the footsteps of his father, and is already well-known as a painter. Wyeth's paintings speak for themselves. His reproductions of early America are an everlasting tribute to America by one of her famous sons.

His use of color is personal with symbolic overtones. His story of New England is unique in its portrayal and is a testimony to the people who made it what it is. In his pictures one senses a reverence for America and for its people.

SAMPLE ESSAY

Directions: A character's attempt to deal with the hypocrisies of life is important in a novel. Using a literary work such as Main Street, show with clear evidence from the work how the character's views on life support the author's theme.

"Carol Kennicott in Main Street"

Sinclair Lewis

Lewis possessed a natural affinity to probe beneath the surface, to take note of people in different walks of life, and to comment on what he found. His novels show his propinquity to events that affect the lives of men and women in society. This is evident in most of his writings. Lewis began his writing career as early as 1912. Although he did not achieve immediate success with his early works, he did add a dimension to the mind of his public by his conscious concern for the stultifying atmosphere in which Americans lived and worked. He was also mindful of the social inequities that existed in the land of plenty and opportunity for all. His travels through the United States enabled him to get a very close look at its people, his camera eye getting a clear view of the social and moral fibre of society just after the first World War.

But it would be unjust to depict him as the epitome of pessimism for he also had a sense of humor. Constance Rourke said of him, "Lewis is basically a teller of tall stories, a fabulist, a legend-maker, who in Main Street originated national archetypes. In his use of homely metaphors, in his passion for the monologue, he moves with the grain of native humor." (In Mark Schorer's Sinclair Lewis: An American Life , p. 37.) The official citation for the Nobel Prize read: "The 1930 Nobel Prize in Literature is awarded to Sinclair Lewis for his powerful and vivid art of description and 'his ability' to use wit and humor in the creation of original characters." (Also in Mark Schorer's Sinclair Lewis: An American Life, p. 37.)

Lewis collected notes on scores of essentials, the mores and manners of small town folk, their speech, their tastes in the cultural aspects, such as music, entertainment, their political beliefs and their gripes. His talent for reportage, which obtained for him jobs with newspapers where he was able to write on everything that was newsworthy, earned him the confidence that he could live by the pen, even though his articles were more essays than stories.

Lewis was not only a reporter and a novelist; he was a novelist of manners, the manners of his class. He studied every facet of American life, storing for future use what he did not need at the moment. When Main Street was published in 1920 it became an immediate success. The book was an expose of the myth that the small town was a good and a friendly place, where decency and morality were high on the list of priorities, where ethics were a known value, and characteristic of Americans' standards. Lewis's characters proved this to be otherwise. This produced adulation in some quarters and chagrin and anger in others.

The novel became as controversial as it was successful. In any case, Lewis's popularity during the 1920's was established. Lewis was certainly a critical realist, and he did not shirk from debunking the then prevalent myths and in a manner that both shocked and titilated. A motivating factor was his sense of truth as he saw it.

It is this commitment that paved the way for his tirade against the hypocrisy of society. Main Street shows how Carol Kennicott, the heroine of his story, runs into a brick wall in her attempt to upgrade the environment and the lives of the townspeople with whom she must live. Her ideals are lofty, her values those of an individual who is determined to be a reformer. She is adamant in her assault upon ugliness, she will remake the town somehow. She says, "I'll get my hands on one of those prairie towns and make it beautiful." (Main Street, pp. 37-92.) But, is she capable of doing this? What are her qualifications? She was a former librarian, and in this capacity had had access to a variety of books which gave her information she tried to put into workable patterns. Her disillusionment is total when Carol finds herself in an atmosphere devoid of what she thinks she believes in. She is idealizing life in the small town. But when she sees Gopher Prairie for the first time, she is disillusioned to a point of revulsion. This response to "small-town America" is Lewis's own reaction.

Lewis's novels examine American values, and American culture. He noted the change that had taken place in the world and its effect upon people. Suddenly, rural America was invaded by the automobile, as well as by other forms of utilitarian objects of progress, namely the radio and the telephone. Isolation was being attacked on all fronts as man's consciousness was awakened to the mode of living imposed on him by sundry other inventions; new gadgetry and new ideas for their use became a commonplace. Changes were needed and the time for them was ripe.

Women were awakening, seeking liberation in a male dominated world. Some politicians took their stand for what they considered normalcy instead of heroism. This fever of unrest, this departure from what had been to what is now, needed an interpreter to explain the new and startling changes and to tell people how to cope with them.

Lewis, the idealist, the reformer, although not a radical in the sense of ideological revolution, was certainly alive to those changes. He wrote: "This is America -- a town of a few thousand, in a region of wheat and corn and dairies and little groves. The town is, in our tale, called 'Gopher Prairie, Minnesota.' But its Main Street is the continuation of Main Streets everywhere. Main Street is the climax of civilization." (In Sheldon N. Grebstein, Sinclair Lewis, p. 64.)

Other writers of the period, namely Sherwood Anderson, Rebecca West, Theodore Dreiser, all imbued with a sense of liberty, made a sizable contribution to the literature of the new times in support of the new ideology that had taken hold of thinking men and women here and abroad. The dynamism was infectious -- but it also brought about pessimism, a theme which was apparent in Lewis's later works. Lewis introduced midwestern Americans to other sections of America, as seen through his eyes. He opened the windows of the houses that customarily were shut to the outside citizen and let the ordinary folk, yes, even the world, take a look inside.

What they saw was people caught in the complex web of life; a placid exterior hiding under it a seething interior. The issues were not national, but universal. Provincialism is a disease that has no geographical boundary. Lewis wrote that love, affection, understanding and mental stimulation claim priorities in the area of human worth.

This complexity embraces the heroine of Main Street, Carol Kennicott. Lewis gives the reader a picture of an individual with whom he is not entirely satisfied. He displays ambivalent feelings in his attitude towards her. At the outset he portrays her as a seeker of culture, albeit an imitation culture; for what she attempts to do is to bring the type of culture associated with the East to the Midwest, ignoring the fact that Gopher Prairie neither sought nor wanted to acquire a mode of life alien to it. (In Sheldon N. Grebstein, Sinclair Lewis, p. 295.)

Then he finds that Carol, as a woman with potentially good qualities for growth, does not develop sufficiently. She does not have the power of her convictions. Her husband Will opposes her ideas. He sees the towns as "good, hustling burgs." (Sheldon N. Grebstein, Sinclair Lewis, p. 64.) Carol finds the towns sordid, ugly, and repugnant in their architecture. Everywhere she sees the dirt and the shabbiness. She gets a lesson in education which turns out to be a counter-education, an "education in disillusionment." (Grebstein, p. 64.)

Lewis's attitude towards Carol is compatible with his attitudes towards small town people in all Main Streets in the United States. He reveals a state of moral indignation at the obtuseness of society in relation to change. Even though Carol is desirous of effecting drastic changes she cannot do so in light of the fact that prominent citizens of Gopher Prairie see her as an upstart, and refuse to support her in her endeavors. Because of their unwillingness to improve themselves or the town, Carol falls short of her optimistic plans. Lewis does not give Carol the necessary strength of purpose and determination to make her dreams become valid truths. When Carol and Will confront one another concerning the people and the town, Will remarks, "Is it your ambition to make this a better town, or isn't it?" Carol replies, "I don't know whether it is or not!" Will then tells her that she is a born reformer, to which Carol says, "I am not -- any more!" (Sinclair Lewis, Main Street, p. 96.)

Lewis permits his feelings to seep into his protagonist's mental state. Thus her good intentions culminate in gross disillusion, and he shows us a Carol who is unable to cope with the politics of her environment. She finds that human necessity is rewarded either by compromise or frustration. As her husband points out to her, "They think you're too frivolous." (Main Street, p. 96.) Lewis realizes that the people Carol must live with really do not understand her, nor do they try to do so. Instead they discuss her freely, each interpreting her behavior and her conversation is his own way.

The criticism cannot be ignored. This is what Lewis saw, and he wrote about people as he saw them. If one considers Lewis's remarks to be unflattering, that may be so; most candid opinions tend to be on the base side of flattery. Yet the book reveals the knowledge Lewis has about the psychological relationship that exists, the love-hate attitude of men caught in a closely related, insecure and highly competitive society. And Carol is no exception.

In his deep understanding of the small-town mentality could one say that Lewis's attitude towards them is in any way ambiguous? He knows them for what they are -- petty, small-minded, reluctant to accept any change in anything they look upon as traditional and therefore good and right for them. Lewis does not write as a romantic, but rather as a critical realist. He showed what historians showed, namely, that people are indifferent to and adamant against change. They are satisfied with retaining the status quo. Why change Gopher Prairie? Why change existing economic conditions, or the environment, or the status of women, or methods of education; what reason to rebel?

Lewis is here the social critic. Gopher Prairie is a microcosm in a macrocosm. It is a symbol of universal inertia. The surprising thing in this war of the people against themselves is that with or without their consent change does take place, albeit slowly and almost imperceptibly. With the technological and scientific changes comes the realization that time will not wait for approval. The Carols of this world will instigate a revolt for reform and a program to sustain it.

With economic and political changes in a constant state of flux, and with the reshuffling and the reshaping of the population from the east to the west, and from the cities to the rural areas and vice versa, and because Lewis had a sense of the political facts of life, he realized that the mentality of the Gopher Prairie citizens would be in line for an overhauling, whether or not the appetite for it was there.

In this climate of expectancy and stubborness on the part of the "cultural society" of Gopher Prairie, Carol, who sincerely and hopefully tried to apply her knowledge to that group of women who considered themselves the elite of the town, the denizens of respectability, found that society made her inadequate to the job; they listen to her proposals, but do not agree to institute any dramatic changes.

When Lewis wrote Main Street he did not write it in a spirit of ardent socialism, but more likely as an examination of the social structure in which men of vision had either to rebel against the system or live within it. Lewis evidently felt that it was better to rebel than to allow ennui and complacency to exist.

Where Carol feels disgust with and contempt for is the ineffectual arguments about the town being good enough for the local people because it was good enough for their parents. Lewis also shows the contrast between Carol and her husband Will. He sees nothing wrong with the town or with any other small town. Will is proud of the fact that within the last half of the century America had made remarkable progress, from a wilderness to the towns Carol denigrates. Lewis does not argue with the shortcomings that he finds in the small towns; he accedes to Carol's views in regard to the buildings that house the school, the city hall; that they are ugly, antiquated structures that show so plainly the slow growth and development of a town. It is again social comment.

He remarks more on this subject when he allows Carol to present her idealistic views to the Thanatopsis members. Overtly they agree with her but covertly thwart her every effort at improvement. Carol receives a lesson in deception from the town itself. She learns that the cultural club she belongs to is quite satisfied with things as they are. For them she is too sophisticated. At a meeting of the club Carol attempts to talk about the people in California who made significant changes in their town "which had changed itself from the barren brick fronts and slatternly frame sheds of a Main Street to a way which led the eye down a vista of arcades and gardens." (Main Street, p. 131.) She also lectures on the poets of the 19th century. The staid, 'cultured' ladies take offense at the writings of Swinburne, thinking him rather outspoken and not quite to their taste.

They also feel that her tastes in furnishing the clubhouse, the style of the architecture she proposes for the town's main buildings are too unconventional for the town. Her lesson in counter-education continues when the women remind her that children should be given more military training instead of pleasant recreation rooms, so that they will learn what duty and morality can do for them. It is these ideas of Carol's that annoy the older citizens of Gopher Prairie. As Mrs. Perry tells her when Carol airs her plans for the town, "Wish I could agree with you, dearie. When Champ and I came here we teamed-it with an ox-cart from Sauk Centre to Gopher Prairie, and there was nothing here but a stockade and a few soldiers and some log cabins." (Main Street, p. 135.)

In the episodes that follow one upon the other, Carol is more disillusioned than defeated. Lewis's treatment of Carol, showing her weakness and her strength, is symptomatic of all the Carols, Wills, clubwomen, in all the towns and villages across the nation. Lewis uses his characters to make his views sound sensible and plausible, arguing his theories like a true professional, a man who has studied the situation and come up with a valid complaint about society's inability to adopt true democracy and adapt it to themselves and themselves to it.

Throughout the book Lewis chides people for permitting social injustice and poverty and ugliness to be part of life. Lewis manages to make a moral comment about the situation, but he does not offer a solution to all the problems in America. Yet he opened the door to reform through his writings and to the consciousness in the minds of many people that a problem existed.

Lewis speaks through Carol; she is in effect Lewis, and Gopher Prairie is Sauk Centre, the town where Lewis was born and raised. Lewis speaks disdainfully of the provincialism that is part of the structure of middle western society. He had, by this time, travelled through much of the United States and made his comparisons through observation -- that is, he compared the Eastern section to the Midwestern section of the country, and found it wanting. He saw the bustling, restless, materialistic-minded society of the East as an area where people are progressive and enterprising; the small towns of America lack initiative, the drive and vigor needed to develop, and not enough interest to make equal improvements in style of living, in education or in real cultural endowments.

Lewis agrees that Carol's efforts to promote idealistic concepts and make them a reality could not be other than unsuccessful, because she could not convince the powerful men with small minds that traditions do not make great towns. All her attempts at modernizing the town ended in failure. The failures break her resolve, and in the process creates for her an unhappy atmosphere.

Carol's mental anguish manifests itself in her attitude to her husband and to the town in general. She ridicules the manners and the morals of the townspeople and becomes so alienated from them that she ends up by leaving Will. In one of his tirades against her he says, "Next thing, I suppose you'll be yapping about free speech. Free speech! There's too much free speech and free gas and free beer and free love and all the rest of your damned mouthy freedom, and if I had my way I'd make you folks live up to the established rules of decency even if I had to take you --." (Main Street, p. 420)

Rebellion and reform are words of an idealist -- but action along these roads can prove costly. Time does not remain static, but people must have patience with others as well as with themselves when they are trying to effect changes in society's mode of living. Neither Lewis nor Carol realized that history had much to do with the Gopher Prairies founded originally by the early pioneers; that they inhabited a land that gave them nothing if they did not work the land and develop a society suitable to their needs. Another important factor in the slow development of American small towns was the absence of a reputable past. Thus Lewis was forced to look outside of Sauk Centre for a more suitable atmosphere in which to cultivate his tastes and improve his life-style literally and culturally.

Part IV

Practice Examinations

1 Ⓐ Ⓑ Ⓒ Ⓓ Ⓔ	26 Ⓐ Ⓑ Ⓒ Ⓓ Ⓔ	51 Ⓐ Ⓑ Ⓒ Ⓓ Ⓔ	76 Ⓐ Ⓑ Ⓒ Ⓓ Ⓔ	101 Ⓐ Ⓑ Ⓒ Ⓓ Ⓔ	126 Ⓐ Ⓑ Ⓒ Ⓓ Ⓔ
2 Ⓐ Ⓑ Ⓒ Ⓓ Ⓔ	27 Ⓐ Ⓑ Ⓒ Ⓓ Ⓔ	52 Ⓐ Ⓑ Ⓒ Ⓓ Ⓔ	77 Ⓐ Ⓑ Ⓒ Ⓓ Ⓔ	102 Ⓐ Ⓑ Ⓒ Ⓓ Ⓔ	127 Ⓐ Ⓑ Ⓒ Ⓓ Ⓔ
3 Ⓐ Ⓑ Ⓒ Ⓓ Ⓔ	28 Ⓐ Ⓑ Ⓒ Ⓓ Ⓔ	53 Ⓐ Ⓑ Ⓒ Ⓓ Ⓔ	78 Ⓐ Ⓑ Ⓒ Ⓓ Ⓔ	103 Ⓐ Ⓑ Ⓒ Ⓓ Ⓔ	128 Ⓐ Ⓑ Ⓒ Ⓓ Ⓔ
4 Ⓐ Ⓑ Ⓒ Ⓓ Ⓔ	29 Ⓐ Ⓑ Ⓒ Ⓓ Ⓔ	54 Ⓐ Ⓑ Ⓒ Ⓓ Ⓔ	79 Ⓐ Ⓑ Ⓒ Ⓓ Ⓔ	104 Ⓐ Ⓑ Ⓒ Ⓓ Ⓔ	129 Ⓐ Ⓑ Ⓒ Ⓓ Ⓔ
5 Ⓐ Ⓑ Ⓒ Ⓓ Ⓔ	30 Ⓐ Ⓑ Ⓒ Ⓓ Ⓔ	55 Ⓐ Ⓑ Ⓒ Ⓓ Ⓔ	80 Ⓐ Ⓑ Ⓒ Ⓓ Ⓔ	105 Ⓐ Ⓑ Ⓒ Ⓓ Ⓔ	130 Ⓐ Ⓑ Ⓒ Ⓓ Ⓔ
6 Ⓐ Ⓑ Ⓒ Ⓓ Ⓔ	31 Ⓐ Ⓑ Ⓒ Ⓓ Ⓔ	56 Ⓐ Ⓑ Ⓒ Ⓓ Ⓔ	81 Ⓐ Ⓑ Ⓒ Ⓓ Ⓔ	106 Ⓐ Ⓑ Ⓒ Ⓓ Ⓔ	131 Ⓐ Ⓑ Ⓒ Ⓓ Ⓔ
7 Ⓐ Ⓑ Ⓒ Ⓓ Ⓔ	32 Ⓐ Ⓑ Ⓒ Ⓓ Ⓔ	57 Ⓐ Ⓑ Ⓒ Ⓓ Ⓔ	82 Ⓐ Ⓑ Ⓒ Ⓓ Ⓔ	107 Ⓐ Ⓑ Ⓒ Ⓓ Ⓔ	132 Ⓐ Ⓑ Ⓒ Ⓓ Ⓔ
8 Ⓐ Ⓑ Ⓒ Ⓓ Ⓔ	33 Ⓐ Ⓑ Ⓒ Ⓓ Ⓔ	58 Ⓐ Ⓑ Ⓒ Ⓓ Ⓔ	83 Ⓐ Ⓑ Ⓒ Ⓓ Ⓔ	108 Ⓐ Ⓑ Ⓒ Ⓓ Ⓔ	133 Ⓐ Ⓑ Ⓒ Ⓓ Ⓔ
9 Ⓐ Ⓑ Ⓒ Ⓓ Ⓔ	34 Ⓐ Ⓑ Ⓒ Ⓓ Ⓔ	59 Ⓐ Ⓑ Ⓒ Ⓓ Ⓔ	84 Ⓐ Ⓑ Ⓒ Ⓓ Ⓔ	109 Ⓐ Ⓑ Ⓒ Ⓓ Ⓔ	134 Ⓐ Ⓑ Ⓒ Ⓓ Ⓔ
10 Ⓐ Ⓑ Ⓒ Ⓓ Ⓔ	35 Ⓐ Ⓑ Ⓒ Ⓓ Ⓔ	60 Ⓐ Ⓑ Ⓒ Ⓓ Ⓔ	85 Ⓐ Ⓑ Ⓒ Ⓓ Ⓔ	110 Ⓐ Ⓑ Ⓒ Ⓓ Ⓔ	135 Ⓐ Ⓑ Ⓒ Ⓓ Ⓔ
11 Ⓐ Ⓑ Ⓒ Ⓓ Ⓔ	36 Ⓐ Ⓑ Ⓒ Ⓓ Ⓔ	61 Ⓐ Ⓑ Ⓒ Ⓓ Ⓔ	86 Ⓐ Ⓑ Ⓒ Ⓓ Ⓔ	111 Ⓐ Ⓑ Ⓒ Ⓓ Ⓔ	136 Ⓐ Ⓑ Ⓒ Ⓓ Ⓔ
12 Ⓐ Ⓑ Ⓒ Ⓓ Ⓔ	37 Ⓐ Ⓑ Ⓒ Ⓓ Ⓔ	62 Ⓐ Ⓑ Ⓒ Ⓓ Ⓔ	87 Ⓐ Ⓑ Ⓒ Ⓓ Ⓔ	112 Ⓐ Ⓑ Ⓒ Ⓓ Ⓔ	137 Ⓐ Ⓑ Ⓒ Ⓓ Ⓔ
13 Ⓐ Ⓑ Ⓒ Ⓓ Ⓔ	38 Ⓐ Ⓑ Ⓒ Ⓓ Ⓔ	63 Ⓐ Ⓑ Ⓒ Ⓓ Ⓔ	88 Ⓐ Ⓑ Ⓒ Ⓓ Ⓔ	113 Ⓐ Ⓑ Ⓒ Ⓓ Ⓔ	138 Ⓐ Ⓑ Ⓒ Ⓓ Ⓔ
14 Ⓐ Ⓑ Ⓒ Ⓓ Ⓔ	39 Ⓐ Ⓑ Ⓒ Ⓓ Ⓔ	64 Ⓐ Ⓑ Ⓒ Ⓓ Ⓔ	89 Ⓐ Ⓑ Ⓒ Ⓓ Ⓔ	114 Ⓐ Ⓑ Ⓒ Ⓓ Ⓔ	139 Ⓐ Ⓑ Ⓒ Ⓓ Ⓔ
15 Ⓐ Ⓑ Ⓒ Ⓓ Ⓔ	40 Ⓐ Ⓑ Ⓒ Ⓓ Ⓔ	65 Ⓐ Ⓑ Ⓒ Ⓓ Ⓔ	90 Ⓐ Ⓑ Ⓒ Ⓓ Ⓔ	115 Ⓐ Ⓑ Ⓒ Ⓓ Ⓔ	140 Ⓐ Ⓑ Ⓒ Ⓓ Ⓔ
16 Ⓐ Ⓑ Ⓒ Ⓓ Ⓔ	41 Ⓐ Ⓑ Ⓒ Ⓓ Ⓔ	66 Ⓐ Ⓑ Ⓒ Ⓓ Ⓔ	91 Ⓐ Ⓑ Ⓒ Ⓓ Ⓔ	116 Ⓐ Ⓑ Ⓒ Ⓓ Ⓔ	141 Ⓐ Ⓑ Ⓒ Ⓓ Ⓔ
17 Ⓐ Ⓑ Ⓒ Ⓓ Ⓔ	42 Ⓐ Ⓑ Ⓒ Ⓓ Ⓔ	67 Ⓐ Ⓑ Ⓒ Ⓓ Ⓔ	92 Ⓐ Ⓑ Ⓒ Ⓓ Ⓔ	117 Ⓐ Ⓑ Ⓒ Ⓓ Ⓔ	142 Ⓐ Ⓑ Ⓒ Ⓓ Ⓔ
18 Ⓐ Ⓑ Ⓒ Ⓓ Ⓔ	43 Ⓐ Ⓑ Ⓒ Ⓓ Ⓔ	68 Ⓐ Ⓑ Ⓒ Ⓓ Ⓔ	93 Ⓐ Ⓑ Ⓒ Ⓓ Ⓔ	118 Ⓐ Ⓑ Ⓒ Ⓓ Ⓔ	143 Ⓐ Ⓑ Ⓒ Ⓓ Ⓔ
19 Ⓐ Ⓑ Ⓒ Ⓓ Ⓔ	44 Ⓐ Ⓑ Ⓒ Ⓓ Ⓔ	69 Ⓐ Ⓑ Ⓒ Ⓓ Ⓔ	94 Ⓐ Ⓑ Ⓒ Ⓓ Ⓔ	119 Ⓐ Ⓑ Ⓒ Ⓓ Ⓔ	144 Ⓐ Ⓑ Ⓒ Ⓓ Ⓔ
20 Ⓐ Ⓑ Ⓒ Ⓓ Ⓔ	45 Ⓐ Ⓑ Ⓒ Ⓓ Ⓔ	70 Ⓐ Ⓑ Ⓒ Ⓓ Ⓔ	95 Ⓐ Ⓑ Ⓒ Ⓓ Ⓔ	120 Ⓐ Ⓑ Ⓒ Ⓓ Ⓔ	145 Ⓐ Ⓑ Ⓒ Ⓓ Ⓔ
21 Ⓐ Ⓑ Ⓒ Ⓓ Ⓔ	46 Ⓐ Ⓑ Ⓒ Ⓓ Ⓔ	71 Ⓐ Ⓑ Ⓒ Ⓓ Ⓔ	96 Ⓐ Ⓑ Ⓒ Ⓓ Ⓔ	121 Ⓐ Ⓑ Ⓒ Ⓓ Ⓔ	146 Ⓐ Ⓑ Ⓒ Ⓓ Ⓔ
22 Ⓐ Ⓑ Ⓒ Ⓓ Ⓔ	47 Ⓐ Ⓑ Ⓒ Ⓓ Ⓔ	72 Ⓐ Ⓑ Ⓒ Ⓓ Ⓔ	97 Ⓐ Ⓑ Ⓒ Ⓓ Ⓔ	122 Ⓐ Ⓑ Ⓒ Ⓓ Ⓔ	147 Ⓐ Ⓑ Ⓒ Ⓓ Ⓔ
23 Ⓐ Ⓑ Ⓒ Ⓓ Ⓔ	48 Ⓐ Ⓑ Ⓒ Ⓓ Ⓔ	73 Ⓐ Ⓑ Ⓒ Ⓓ Ⓔ	98 Ⓐ Ⓑ Ⓒ Ⓓ Ⓔ	123 Ⓐ Ⓑ Ⓒ Ⓓ Ⓔ	148 Ⓐ Ⓑ Ⓒ Ⓓ Ⓔ
24 Ⓐ Ⓑ Ⓒ Ⓓ Ⓔ	49 Ⓐ Ⓑ Ⓒ Ⓓ Ⓔ	74 Ⓐ Ⓑ Ⓒ Ⓓ Ⓔ	99 Ⓐ Ⓑ Ⓒ Ⓓ Ⓔ	124 Ⓐ Ⓑ Ⓒ Ⓓ Ⓔ	149 Ⓐ Ⓑ Ⓒ Ⓓ Ⓔ
25 Ⓐ Ⓑ Ⓒ Ⓓ Ⓔ	50 Ⓐ Ⓑ Ⓒ Ⓓ Ⓔ	75 Ⓐ Ⓑ Ⓒ Ⓓ Ⓔ	100 Ⓐ Ⓑ Ⓒ Ⓓ Ⓔ	125 Ⓐ Ⓑ Ⓒ Ⓓ Ⓔ	150 Ⓐ Ⓑ Ⓒ Ⓓ Ⓔ

1 Ⓐ Ⓑ Ⓒ Ⓓ Ⓔ	26 Ⓐ Ⓑ Ⓒ Ⓓ Ⓔ	51 Ⓐ Ⓑ Ⓒ Ⓓ Ⓔ	76 Ⓐ Ⓑ Ⓒ Ⓓ Ⓔ	101 Ⓐ Ⓑ Ⓒ Ⓓ Ⓔ	126 Ⓐ Ⓑ Ⓒ Ⓓ Ⓔ
2 Ⓐ Ⓑ Ⓒ Ⓓ Ⓔ	27 Ⓐ Ⓑ Ⓒ Ⓓ Ⓔ	52 Ⓐ Ⓑ Ⓒ Ⓓ Ⓔ	77 Ⓐ Ⓑ Ⓒ Ⓓ Ⓔ	102 Ⓐ Ⓑ Ⓒ Ⓓ Ⓔ	127 Ⓐ Ⓑ Ⓒ Ⓓ Ⓔ
3 Ⓐ Ⓑ Ⓒ Ⓓ Ⓔ	28 Ⓐ Ⓑ Ⓒ Ⓓ Ⓔ	53 Ⓐ Ⓑ Ⓒ Ⓓ Ⓔ	78 Ⓐ Ⓑ Ⓒ Ⓓ Ⓔ	103 Ⓐ Ⓑ Ⓒ Ⓓ Ⓔ	128 Ⓐ Ⓑ Ⓒ Ⓓ Ⓔ
4 Ⓐ Ⓑ Ⓒ Ⓓ Ⓔ	29 Ⓐ Ⓑ Ⓒ Ⓓ Ⓔ	54 Ⓐ Ⓑ Ⓒ Ⓓ Ⓔ	79 Ⓐ Ⓑ Ⓒ Ⓓ Ⓔ	104 Ⓐ Ⓑ Ⓒ Ⓓ Ⓔ	129 Ⓐ Ⓑ Ⓒ Ⓓ Ⓔ
5 Ⓐ Ⓑ Ⓒ Ⓓ Ⓔ	30 Ⓐ Ⓑ Ⓒ Ⓓ Ⓔ	55 Ⓐ Ⓑ Ⓒ Ⓓ Ⓔ	80 Ⓐ Ⓑ Ⓒ Ⓓ Ⓔ	105 Ⓐ Ⓑ Ⓒ Ⓓ Ⓔ	130 Ⓐ Ⓑ Ⓒ Ⓓ Ⓔ
6 Ⓐ Ⓑ Ⓒ Ⓓ Ⓔ	31 Ⓐ Ⓑ Ⓒ Ⓓ Ⓔ	56 Ⓐ Ⓑ Ⓒ Ⓓ Ⓔ	81 Ⓐ Ⓑ Ⓒ Ⓓ Ⓔ	106 Ⓐ Ⓑ Ⓒ Ⓓ Ⓔ	131 Ⓐ Ⓑ Ⓒ Ⓓ Ⓔ
7 Ⓐ Ⓑ Ⓒ Ⓓ Ⓔ	32 Ⓐ Ⓑ Ⓒ Ⓓ Ⓔ	57 Ⓐ Ⓑ Ⓒ Ⓓ Ⓔ	82 Ⓐ Ⓑ Ⓒ Ⓓ Ⓔ	107 Ⓐ Ⓑ Ⓒ Ⓓ Ⓔ	132 Ⓐ Ⓑ Ⓒ Ⓓ Ⓔ
8 Ⓐ Ⓑ Ⓒ Ⓓ Ⓔ	33 Ⓐ Ⓑ Ⓒ Ⓓ Ⓔ	58 Ⓐ Ⓑ Ⓒ Ⓓ Ⓔ	83 Ⓐ Ⓑ Ⓒ Ⓓ Ⓔ	108 Ⓐ Ⓑ Ⓒ Ⓓ Ⓔ	133 Ⓐ Ⓑ Ⓒ Ⓓ Ⓔ
9 Ⓐ Ⓑ Ⓒ Ⓓ Ⓔ	34 Ⓐ Ⓑ Ⓒ Ⓓ Ⓔ	59 Ⓐ Ⓑ Ⓒ Ⓓ Ⓔ	84 Ⓐ Ⓑ Ⓒ Ⓓ Ⓔ	109 Ⓐ Ⓑ Ⓒ Ⓓ Ⓔ	134 Ⓐ Ⓑ Ⓒ Ⓓ Ⓔ
10 Ⓐ Ⓑ Ⓒ Ⓓ Ⓔ	35 Ⓐ Ⓑ Ⓒ Ⓓ Ⓔ	60 Ⓐ Ⓑ Ⓒ Ⓓ Ⓔ	85 Ⓐ Ⓑ Ⓒ Ⓓ Ⓔ	110 Ⓐ Ⓑ Ⓒ Ⓓ Ⓔ	135 Ⓐ Ⓑ Ⓒ Ⓓ Ⓔ
11 Ⓐ Ⓑ Ⓒ Ⓓ Ⓔ	36 Ⓐ Ⓑ Ⓒ Ⓓ Ⓔ	61 Ⓐ Ⓑ Ⓒ Ⓓ Ⓔ	86 Ⓐ Ⓑ Ⓒ Ⓓ Ⓔ	111 Ⓐ Ⓑ Ⓒ Ⓓ Ⓔ	136 Ⓐ Ⓑ Ⓒ Ⓓ Ⓔ
12 Ⓐ Ⓑ Ⓒ Ⓓ Ⓔ	37 Ⓐ Ⓑ Ⓒ Ⓓ Ⓔ	62 Ⓐ Ⓑ Ⓒ Ⓓ Ⓔ	87 Ⓐ Ⓑ Ⓒ Ⓓ Ⓔ	112 Ⓐ Ⓑ Ⓒ Ⓓ Ⓔ	137 Ⓐ Ⓑ Ⓒ Ⓓ Ⓔ
13 Ⓐ Ⓑ Ⓒ Ⓓ Ⓔ	38 Ⓐ Ⓑ Ⓒ Ⓓ Ⓔ	63 Ⓐ Ⓑ Ⓒ Ⓓ Ⓔ	88 Ⓐ Ⓑ Ⓒ Ⓓ Ⓔ	113 Ⓐ Ⓑ Ⓒ Ⓓ Ⓔ	138 Ⓐ Ⓑ Ⓒ Ⓓ Ⓔ
14 Ⓐ Ⓑ Ⓒ Ⓓ Ⓔ	39 Ⓐ Ⓑ Ⓒ Ⓓ Ⓔ	64 Ⓐ Ⓑ Ⓒ Ⓓ Ⓔ	89 Ⓐ Ⓑ Ⓒ Ⓓ Ⓔ	114 Ⓐ Ⓑ Ⓒ Ⓓ Ⓔ	139 Ⓐ Ⓑ Ⓒ Ⓓ Ⓔ
15 Ⓐ Ⓑ Ⓒ Ⓓ Ⓔ	40 Ⓐ Ⓑ Ⓒ Ⓓ Ⓔ	65 Ⓐ Ⓑ Ⓒ Ⓓ Ⓔ	90 Ⓐ Ⓑ Ⓒ Ⓓ Ⓔ	115 Ⓐ Ⓑ Ⓒ Ⓓ Ⓔ	140 Ⓐ Ⓑ Ⓒ Ⓓ Ⓔ
16 Ⓐ Ⓑ Ⓒ Ⓓ Ⓔ	41 Ⓐ Ⓑ Ⓒ Ⓓ Ⓔ	66 Ⓐ Ⓑ Ⓒ Ⓓ Ⓔ	91 Ⓐ Ⓑ Ⓒ Ⓓ Ⓔ	116 Ⓐ Ⓑ Ⓒ Ⓓ Ⓔ	141 Ⓐ Ⓑ Ⓒ Ⓓ Ⓔ
17 Ⓐ Ⓑ Ⓒ Ⓓ Ⓔ	42 Ⓐ Ⓑ Ⓒ Ⓓ Ⓔ	67 Ⓐ Ⓑ Ⓒ Ⓓ Ⓔ	92 Ⓐ Ⓑ Ⓒ Ⓓ Ⓔ	117 Ⓐ Ⓑ Ⓒ Ⓓ Ⓔ	142 Ⓐ Ⓑ Ⓒ Ⓓ Ⓔ
18 Ⓐ Ⓑ Ⓒ Ⓓ Ⓔ	43 Ⓐ Ⓑ Ⓒ Ⓓ Ⓔ	68 Ⓐ Ⓑ Ⓒ Ⓓ Ⓔ	93 Ⓐ Ⓑ Ⓒ Ⓓ Ⓔ	118 Ⓐ Ⓑ Ⓒ Ⓓ Ⓔ	143 Ⓐ Ⓑ Ⓒ Ⓓ Ⓔ
19 Ⓐ Ⓑ Ⓒ Ⓓ Ⓔ	44 Ⓐ Ⓑ Ⓒ Ⓓ Ⓔ	69 Ⓐ Ⓑ Ⓒ Ⓓ Ⓔ	94 Ⓐ Ⓑ Ⓒ Ⓓ Ⓔ	119 Ⓐ Ⓑ Ⓒ Ⓓ Ⓔ	144 Ⓐ Ⓑ Ⓒ Ⓓ Ⓔ
20 Ⓐ Ⓑ Ⓒ Ⓓ Ⓔ	45 Ⓐ Ⓑ Ⓒ Ⓓ Ⓔ	70 Ⓐ Ⓑ Ⓒ Ⓓ Ⓔ	95 Ⓐ Ⓑ Ⓒ Ⓓ Ⓔ	120 Ⓐ Ⓑ Ⓒ Ⓓ Ⓔ	145 Ⓐ Ⓑ Ⓒ Ⓓ Ⓔ
21 Ⓐ Ⓑ Ⓒ Ⓓ Ⓔ	46 Ⓐ Ⓑ Ⓒ Ⓓ Ⓔ	71 Ⓐ Ⓑ Ⓒ Ⓓ Ⓔ	96 Ⓐ Ⓑ Ⓒ Ⓓ Ⓔ	121 Ⓐ Ⓑ Ⓒ Ⓓ Ⓔ	146 Ⓐ Ⓑ Ⓒ Ⓓ Ⓔ
22 Ⓐ Ⓑ Ⓒ Ⓓ Ⓔ	47 Ⓐ Ⓑ Ⓒ Ⓓ Ⓔ	72 Ⓐ Ⓑ Ⓒ Ⓓ Ⓔ	97 Ⓐ Ⓑ Ⓒ Ⓓ Ⓔ	122 Ⓐ Ⓑ Ⓒ Ⓓ Ⓔ	147 Ⓐ Ⓑ Ⓒ Ⓓ Ⓔ
23 Ⓐ Ⓑ Ⓒ Ⓓ Ⓔ	48 Ⓐ Ⓑ Ⓒ Ⓓ Ⓔ	73 Ⓐ Ⓑ Ⓒ Ⓓ Ⓔ	98 Ⓐ Ⓑ Ⓒ Ⓓ Ⓔ	123 Ⓐ Ⓑ Ⓒ Ⓓ Ⓔ	148 Ⓐ Ⓑ Ⓒ Ⓓ Ⓔ
24 Ⓐ Ⓑ Ⓒ Ⓓ Ⓔ	49 Ⓐ Ⓑ Ⓒ Ⓓ Ⓔ	74 Ⓐ Ⓑ Ⓒ Ⓓ Ⓔ	99 Ⓐ Ⓑ Ⓒ Ⓓ Ⓔ	124 Ⓐ Ⓑ Ⓒ Ⓓ Ⓔ	149 Ⓐ Ⓑ Ⓒ Ⓓ Ⓔ
25 Ⓐ Ⓑ Ⓒ Ⓓ Ⓔ	50 Ⓐ Ⓑ Ⓒ Ⓓ Ⓔ	75 Ⓐ Ⓑ Ⓒ Ⓓ Ⓔ	100 Ⓐ Ⓑ Ⓒ Ⓓ Ⓔ	125 Ⓐ Ⓑ Ⓒ Ⓓ Ⓔ	150 Ⓐ Ⓑ Ⓒ Ⓓ Ⓔ

SECOND PRACTICE AP/CLEP ENGLISH TEST
SECTION I

The ATP Achievement Test in Literature can have multiple-choice questions which require you to demonstrate knowledge of specific authors, styles and periods; these questions will give you the practice and review in this area.

Directions: Select from the lettered choices that choice which best completes the statement or answers the question. Indicate the letter of your choice on the answer sheet.

1. The Iliad of Homer is frequently referred to as

   (A) The Trojan Horse
   (B) The Wrath of Achilles
   (C) The Judgment of Paris
   (D) The Ten Years' War
   (E) The Speedy Victory

2. Each of the dialogues of Plato listed below is correctly paired with the subject with which it deals except

   (A) Lysis - the definition of friendship
   (B) Phaedo - immortality of the soul
   (C) The Symposium - the nature of love
   (D) Meno - the doctrine of recollection
   (E) The Apology - Plato's defense of idealism

3. The Arabian Nights is similar in form and structure to all of the following works except

   (A) The Decameron
   (B) Tales of a Wayside Inn
   (C) Lays of Ancient Rome
   (D) The Canterbury Tales
   (E) Fables of Bidpai

4. Author and book are correctly paired in all of the following except

   (A) William Gilmore Simms - Narrative of Davy Crockett
   (B) Charles Brockden Brown - Wieland
   (C) Washington Irving - Life of George Washington
   (D) Oliver Wendell Holmes - Elsie Venner
   (E) Joel Chandler Harris - Uncle Remus

5. The author of the The Innocents Abroad wrote all of the following except

   (A) Letters from the Earth
   (B) What Is Man?
   (C) The Mysterious Stranger
   (D) A Chance Acquaintance
   (E) The American Claimant

6. All of the following are quotations from the works of Ralph Waldo Emerson except

   (A) The only gift is a portion of thyself
   (B) Self-trust is the essence of heroism
   (C) Hitch your wagon to a star
   (D) All great truths begin as blasphemies
   (E) To be great is to be misunderstood

7. Fyodor Dostoyevsky's mystical anti-intellectualism is best exemplified in his portrayal of

(A) Raskolnikov
(B) Prince Myshkin
(C) Ivan Karamazov
(D) Pyotr Verhovensky
(E) Katerina Ivanovna

8. In Ibsen's An Enemy of the People, Dr. Stockmann sums up his political philosophy in the words,

(A) The common people have an instinct for justice
(B) The strongest man is he who stands alone
(C) There is no hope for man - the wisest is he who accepts despair
(D) We must never lose hope - the future belongs to the people
(E) We must be impartial in thought as well as in action

9. In Henry James's The Turn of the Screw, the actual existence of the two ghosts

(A) is never verified
(B) is established in the boy's statement at the close
(C) is established when the governess challenges the girl, Flora
(D) is verified by the narrator in his postscript to the story
(E) is disputed by a steward and a governess

10. Of the following statements, the one which may not be applied to Walt Whitman is that

(A) in the late 1840's and early 1850's he abandoned rhyme
(B) he was a male nurse during the Civil War
(C) he died in Camden, New Jersey
(D) he wrote for The Brooklyn Eagle
(E) he taught school for a while

11. John Galbraith has usually been identified with

(A) studies of contemporary society
(B) emancipation of the 20th Century Negro
(C) the Birch Society
(D) criticism of works by England's "angry young men"
(E) sociological and Marxist criticism

12. A teacher associated with the training of several prominent American playwrights was

(A) George Pierce Baker
(B) Joseph Warren Beach
(C) William Lyon Phelps
(D) Wallace Stegner
(E) William H. Kilpatrick

13. The author of The Plague wrote all of the following except

(A) The Stranger
(B) Caligula
(C) The Myth of Sisyphus
(D) Tiger at the Gates
(E) Wedding Feasts

14. The author of the screenplay, Lawrence of Arabia, also wrote the play,

(A) Ross
(B) A Man for All Seasons
(C) The Affair
(D) Beckett
(E) The Crisis

15. Who's Afraid of Virginia Woolf? is by the author of

(A) Waiting for Godot
(B) The Sand Box
(C) The Connection
(D) The Milk Train Doesn't Stop Here Anymore
(E) The Glass Menagerie

16. "I believe that man will not merely endure: he will prevail. He is immortal, not because he alone among creatures has an inexhaustible voice but because he has a soul," is part of a quotation from

(A) Carl Sandburg
(B) John Steinbeck
(C) T.S. Eliot
(D) Woodrow Wilson
(E) William Faulkner

17. The following characters are correctly paired according to the works in which they appear except

(A) Frederic Henry - Catherine Barkley
(B) Fleur Forsyte - Michael Mont
(C) Christopher Newman - Claire de Cintre
(D) Martin Arrowsmith - Antonia Shimerda
(E) Clyde Griffiths - Sondra Finchley

18. The author of The Rise and Fall of the Third Reich also wrote

(A) Into the Valley
(B) Shoes of the Fisherman
(C) Russia and the West
(D) The Berlin Wall
(E) Berlin Diary

19. The riddle of the Sphinx was answered by

(A) Alexander (C) Oedipus
(B) Odysseus (D) Solon
(E) Agamemnon

20. Of the following, the author who did not write an important book on American English is

(A) G. P. Krapp
(B) A. H. Marckwardt
(C) H. W. Fowler
(D) H. L. Mencken
(E) G. L. Kittredge

21. "A citizen of no mean city" is an illustration of

(A) hyperbole (C) litotes
(B) zeugma (D) tautology
(E) alliteration

22. Chaucer's line, "And gladly wolde he lerne and gladly teche," is a description of

(A) The Cook
(B) The Yeoman
(C) The Franklin
(D) The Pardoner
(E) The Clerk

23. The experience which William Shakespeare, Sir Philip Sidney, and Edmund Spenser had in common was the following:

(A) They all wrote poems on the subject of Venus and Adonis.
(B) They all wrote sonnet sequences.
(C) They all used Cleopatra as a subject for a major work.
(D) They all dedicated poems to the Earl of Southampton.
(E) They all wrote tragedies.

24. Of the following lines, the one not attributed to Shakespeare is

(A) As flies to wanton boys are we to th' gods
(B) Who steals my purse steals trash
(C) Stay a while, that we may make an end the sooner
(D) Leave her to heaven
(E) Let's carve him as a dish fit for the gods

25. Shakespeare's source for Romeo and Juliet was a poem by

(A) Arthur Brooke
(B) Michael Drayton
(C) Torquato Tasso
(D) Geoffrey Chaucer
(E) Sir Thomas Wyatt

26. Elinor Dashwood, Catherine Morland, and Anne Elliot are all characters from the works of

(A) Dickens
(B) Thackeray
(C) George Eliot
(D) Fielding
(E) Jane Austen

27. The essays comprising The Federalist were written by

(A) Franklin, Hamilton and Jefferson
(B) Hamilton, Madison and Jay
(C) Hamilton, Madison and Burr
(D) Hamilton, Jay and Adams
(E) Madison, Jay, Franklin

28. Dickens's last novel was

(A) Great Expectations
(B) Hard Times
(C) Oliver Twist
(D) Bleak House
(E) The Mystery of Edwin Drood

29. An accurate account of life in Europe in the fifteenth century is contained in

(A) Silas Marner
(B) The Pilgrims of the Rhine
(C) The Cloister and the Hearth
(D) Middlemarch
(E) Pride and Prejudice

30. Sir Patrick Spens

(A) was killed in the battle of Otterbourne
(B) was drowned on a mission for his king
(C) banished "the King's daughter to Noroway"
(D) slew the Black Douglas in hand-to-hand combat
(E) was sentenced to hang for disloyalty

31. Of the following titles of books the one which is not a phrase from Hamlet is

(A) In Dubious Battle
(B) This Above All
(C) The Bird of Dawning
(D) Mortal Coils
(E) Good Night, Sweet Prince

32. Of the following, the members of the group of which all wrote translations of Homer, are

(A) Pope, Cowper, Chapman
(B) Gray, Chapman, Pope
(C) Pope, Blake, Chapman
(D) Cowper, Arnold, Dryden
(E) Arnold, Pope, Gray

33. The 19th century American writer who produced a fine translation of Goethe's Faust was

(A) Bayard Taylor
(B) Sidney Lanier
(C) William Dean Howells
(D) Lew Wallace
(E) Henry James

34. In Hemingway's The Sun Also Rises Lady Brett Ashley

(A) commits suicide in Madrid
(B) marries Mike, her bankrupt fiance
(C) falls in love with a young bull-fighter
(D) dies in childbirth
(E) decides to live in the Orient

35. A style of writing is named by each of the following words except

(A) Gongorism
(B) Euphuism
(C) Marianism
(D) Metaphysical
(E) Fauvism

36. Chaucer's poem in which a group gather on St. Valentine's Day to select their mates is

(A) The House of Fame
(B) The Parliament of Fowls
(C) Book of the Duchess
(D) Canterbury Tales
(E) Troilus and Criseyde

37. A Novel Without a Hero is the subtitle of

(A) Jane Eyre
(B) Pamela
(C) Brave New World
(D) Vanity Fair
(E) War and Peace

38. Each of the following is a novel about World War I except

(A) The Naked and the Dead - Norman Mailer
(B) Under Fire - Henri Barbusse
(C) All Quiet on the Western Front - Erich Remarque
(D) Mr. Britling Sees It Through - H. G. Wells
(E) Command - William McFee

39. The breaking of some small glass figurines creates a dramatic scene in a play by

(A) William Inge
(B) Lillian Hellman
(C) Ben Hecht
(D) Tennessee Williams
(E) Edward Albee

40. In James Joyce's Ulysses, the character who represents the lost Ulysses is

(A) Stephen Dedalus
(B) Leopold Bloom
(C) Buck Mulligan
(D) Blazes Boylan
(E) Humphrey Earwicker

41. Of the following, The Screwtape Letters by C. S. Lewis resembles most closely

(A) Letters to his Son - Chesterfield
(B) Journal to Stella - Swift
(C) Journal of the Plague Year - Defoe
(D) Letters from the Earth - Clemens
(E) Letters - Walpole

42. Each of the following died a suicide except

(A) Anna Christie
(B) Emma Bovary
(C) Anna Karenina
(D) Hedda Gabler
(E) George Hurstwood

43. All of the following are characters in Pickwick Papers except

(A) Tony Weller
(B) Dodson and Fogg
(C) Alfred Jingle
(D) Dick Swiveller
(E) Rachel Wardle

44. Madame d'Arblay is better known as

(A) Charlotte Bronte
(B) Juliette Recamier
(C) Fanny Burney
(D) Mary Mitford
(E) George Eliot

45. The prevailing meter in Longfellow's Evangeline is

(A) trochaic
(B) dactylic
(C) anapestic
(D) iambic
(E) spondaic

46. The play which does not contain a play within a play is

(A) Hamlet
(B) The Second Shepherd's Play
(C) The Taming of the Shrew
(D) Man and Superman
(E) Gammer Gurton's Needle

47. All the following have written plays in verse except

(A) T. S. Eliot
(B) Christopher Fry
(C) John Millington Synge
(D) William Butler Yeats
(E) William Shakespeare

48. Fanfare for Elizabeth was written by

(A) Edith Sitwell
(B) Virginia Woolf
(C) Daphne du Maurier
(D) Katherine Mansfield
(E) Charlotte Bronte

49. Among the following, the one who was not also an artist is

(A) William Blake
(B) Dante Gabriel Rossetti
(C) Max Beerbohm
(D) Austin Dobson
(E) William Morris

50. As Tam O'Shanter returns home drunk, he loses

(A) his wallet
(B) his rosary
(C) his rabbit's foot
(D) his watch
(E) his mare's tail

51. The Waste Land is based on the legend of

(A) Beowulf
(B) Roland
(C) Faust
(D) the Grail
(E) Achilles

52. "Ah, what a tangled web we weave, When first we practise to deceive!" was written by

(A) Robert Burns
(B) Thomas Gray
(C) Sir Walter Scott
(D) Oliver Goldsmith
(E) Percy Bysshe Shelley

53. Some of the following statements correctly refer to the book, Innocents Abroad, by Mark Twain:

I. It shows the author's appreciation of art masterpieces on the continent
II. It is a factual record of travel on the continent
III. It relates the author's experience in Europe, Egypt, and the Holy Land in the 1860's
IV. It is based on a series of earlier letters by the author

The correct statements are

(A) I, II
(B) II, III
(C) III, IV
(D) I, IV
(E) I, III

54. In The Scarlet Letter, the Reverend Arthur Dimmesdale

(A) penitently marries Hester P Prynne
(B) accuses her of guilt as an adulteress
(C) rejects the narrow moral code of his society
(D) dies after an avowal of his sin
(E) changes his religion

55. The novelistic technique of projecting the narrative through feelings and thoughts of the characters, reached a perfected form in the works of

(A) Henry James
(B) William Dean Howells
(C) Theodore Dreiser
(D) Herman Melville
(E) James Joyce

56. Emily Dickinson's verse is most aptly characterized as

(A) showing an awareness of turbulent social forces
(B) paving the way for the following generation of vers libre poets
(C) expounding a philosophy akin to Emerson's
(D) expressing a brutal frankness about the evils of society
(E) exhibiting a sensitiveness to the symbolic implications of experience

57. A work which paved the way for the unsentimental and naturalistic treatment of life in small communities was

(A) The Hoosier Schoolmaster - Edward Eggleston
(B) Our Town - Thornton Wilder
(C) Winesburg, Ohio - Sherwood Anderson
(D) David Harum - Edward N. Westcott
(E) Huckleberry Finn - Mark Twain

58. The Nobel Prize for Literature was awarded in the year 1962 to

(A) Robert Frost
(B) Thomas Wolfe
(C) Carl Sandburg
(D) Ernest Hemingway
(E) John Steinbeck

59. In Babbitt, by Sinclair Lewis, George Babbitt

(A) remarries after his wife's death
(B) discovers that European culture is a veneer
(C) approves of his son's impulsive marriage
(D) bitterly denounces the mores of his town
(E) gives up his business

60. Birches, by Robert Frost, is best described as

(A) a free verse treatment of a pessimistic philosophy
(B) a lyrical appreciation of nature's forms
(C) a narrative poem with overtones of tragedy
(D) a didactic poem expressing the author's pantheism
(E) a nostalgic expression of longing for escape

61. Thornton Wilder's Bridge of San Luis Rey concludes with

(A) an affirmation of faith in divine justice
(B) a celebration in which estranged brothers become reconciled
(C) caustic rejection of the concept of divine justice
(D) an urbane objectivity with regard to the problem of divine justice
(E) doubt as to the existence of divine justice

62. An American poet who has exerted great influence on British poetry is

(A) Ezra Pound
(B) Joseph Auslander
(C) Edwin A. Robinson
(D) Carl Sandburg
(E) Vachel Lindsay

63. All of the following are plays by Tennessee Williams, except

(A) The Time of the Cuckoo
(B) Summer and Smoke
(C) The Glass Menagerie
(D) Camino Real
(E) A Streetcar Named Desire

64. "A man is rich in proportion to the number of things which he can afford to let alone" is a quotation from

(A) Emerson's Self-Reliance
(B) Thoreau's Walden
(C) Whitman's Democratic Vistas
(D) Mencken's Prejudices
(E) Bang's Southern Hospitality

65. Tennyson's The Princess was good-naturedly satirized by

(A) Robert Browning
(B) Rudyard Kipling
(C) Jerome K. Jerome
(D) Ernest Dowson
(E) W. S. Gilbert

66. That we reap what we sow, that "character is fate," is a dominant theme in the novels of

(A) Emily Brontë
(B) Charles Kingsley
(C) George Eliot
(D) Anthony Trollope
(E) William Thackeray

67. The title of John Gunther's book, Death Be Not Proud, is taken from

(A) a poem by John Donne
(B) a sonnet by Shakespeare
(C) a prose work by Thomas Browne
(D) an epitaph by George Herbert
(E) a speech by Lincoln

68. Dryden's All for Love deals with the same subject matter as

(A) Cymbeline
(B) Coriolanus
(C) Hamlet
(D) Romeo and Juliet
(E) Antony and Cleopatra

69. A tale of love and betrayal during the Trojan War is told by both

(A) John Lyly and George Moore
(B) Ben Jonson and Edmund Spenser
(C) Shakespeare and Chaucer
(D) Keats and Tennyson
(E) Marlowe and Bunyan

70. Robert Jordan, in For Whom the Bell Tolls, held on to life long enough to

(A) kill a lieutenant of the enemy forces
(B) marry Maria
(C) see his first-born son
(D) raise the flag of the Republic in Madrid
(E) write a confession

71. In Homeward Bound, James Fenimore Cooper, after his return from Europe,

(A) expressed pleasure at the liberal influences at work in the United States
(B) recounted adventures which he had had abroad
(C) painted a romantic picture of life at sea
(D) criticized the extension of suffrage to classes unprepared for it
(E) compared New World and Old World social customs

72. The titles, authors, and characters are correctly matched for each of the following except

(A) The Jungle, Upton Sinclair, Jurgis Rudkus
(B) Sister Carrie, Theodore Dreiser, George Hurstwood
(C) The Pit, Frank Norris, Curtis Jadwin
(D) Main Street, Sinclair Lewis, Gustaf Sondelius
(E) A Lost Lady, Willa Cather, Marian Forester

73. Isabel Archer, in The Portrait of a Lady, discovered that Pansy was really the daughter of

(A) Osmond's first wife
(B) Ralph Touchett
(C) Madame Merle
(D) Casper Goodwood
(E) Countess Gemini

74. The poetry of Walt Whitman may be characterized by all the following except

(A) an appreciation of nature
(B) a philosophy akin to Emerson's
(C) predominantly Anglo-Saxon language
(D) occasional extreme sensuality
(E) a deep feeling for the sufferings of laborers

75. Philip Freneau was

(A) one of the Connecticut Wits
(B) a Tory poet during the American Revolution
(C) a pro-revolutionary satirist and a nature poet
(D) a pro-Federalist journalist and a poet
(E) a diplomat who wrote poetry dealing with politics

76. The form of poetry whose composition most often includes a refrain at the end of each stanza, and an envoy, is called

(A) villanelle
(B) sestina
(C) rondel
(D) couplet
(E) ballade

77. Anchises was to Aeneas as was

(A) Zeus to Poseidon
(B) Agamemnon to Achilles
(C) Telemachus to Odysseus
(D) Priam to Paris
(E) Venus to Ceres

78. In the Divine Comedy, the sentiment expressed in the line, "The greatest sorrow of all is remembrance of past happiness in present woe," pertains to the episode of

(A) Paolo and Francesca
(B) Orpheus and Eurydice
(C) Petrarch and Laura
(D) Abelard and Heloise
(E) Dante and Beatrice

79. Samuel Butler's poem, Hudibras, satirizes

(A) Cavaliers
(B) Roman Catholics
(C) Puritans
(D) Lutherans
(E) The Established Church

80. Michael Drayton described the geography of England at great length in his poem

(A) Poly-Olbion
(B) Nymphidia
(C) Musophilus
(D) Arcadia
(E) The Ballad of Agincourt

81. All of the following were early works of their authors except

(A) History of New York - Washington Irving
(B) Fanshawe - Nathaniel Hawthorne
(C) Billy Budd - Herman Melville
(D) Sister Carrie - Theodore Dreiser
(E) The Harbor - Ernest Poole

82. Godey's Lady's Book was a

(A) periodical for women
(B) series of pamphlets remonstrating against denial of women's suffrage
(C) primer for governesses
(D) portfolio of paintings by women artists
(E) book of candy recipes

83. La Chartreuse de Parme was written by the author of

(A) Le Pere Goriot
(B) Le Rouge et le Noir
(C) Les Miserables
(D) Atala
(E) Madame Bovary

84. All of the following were educated at Harvard except

(A) T. S. Eliot
(B) George Santayana
(C) Ralph Waldo Emerson
(D) Herman Melville
(E) Oliver Wendell Holmes

85. All of the following authors wrote novels in the 1930's which were considered "revolutionary" in theme except

(A) John Steinbeck
(B) Andre Malraux
(C) Ignazio Silone
(D) John Dos Passos
(E) Hervey Allen

86. "All his novels present the losing struggle of individuals against the obscure power which moves the universe" best characterizes the work of

(A) George Meredith
(B) Arnold Bennett
(C) John Galsworthy
(D) Nathaniel Hawthorne
(E) Thomas Hardy

87. Conrad Richter's The Light in the Forest depicts

(A) the American pioneer in the West
(B) a white boy's life in Indian captivity
(C) beginnings of law and order in the western part of the United States
(D) the corrosion of loneliness endured by "mountain men"
(E) the search for a child lost in the woods

88. The title of the novel, Lord of the Flies, is derived from the name

(A) Belial
(B) Stan
(C) Lucifer
(D) Beelzebub
(E) Chaos

89. The period of the greatest influx of French words into the English language was

(A) the Anglo-Saxon
(B) the Elizabethan
(C) the Restoration
(D) the Middle English
(E) none of the above

90. Correctly matched with her field of special interest is each of the following Muses except

(A) Thalia - comedy
(B) Calliope - music
(C) Melpomene - tragedy
(D) Clio - history
(E) Terpsichore - dance

91. John Milton's tracts on divorce were believed to be the result of his unhappy experience with his wife,

(A) Catherine Woodcock
(B) Mary Powell
(C) Elizabeth Minshell
(D) Elizabeth Boyle
(E) Fanny Brawne

92. Matthew Arnold borrowed the phrase "sweetness and light" from a work by

(A) John Milton
(B) Edmund Spenser
(C) Michael Drayton
(D) John Bunyan
(E) Jonathan Swift

93. Of the following, the Samuel Butler characters resemble Don Quixote and Sancho Panza are

(A) Crites and Eugenius
(B) Hudibras and Ralpho
(C) Bajazet and Zabina
(D) Baranabe Riche and Jaques
(E) Nicodemon and Jochanan

94. The Spenserian stanza was used in all of the following except

(A) The Cotter's Saturday Night
(B) The Revolt of Islam
(C) Childe Harold
(D) Endymion
(E) The Castle of Indolence

95. "Sprung rhythm" describes the metrical pattern discernible in the poetry of

(A) Stephen Spender
(B) Oscar Wilde
(C) Gerard Manley Hopkins
(D) Amy Lowell
(E) Edna St. Vincent Millay

96. All of the following were used as source material by Shakespeare except

(A) Holinshed's Chronicle
(B) North's translation of Plutarch's Lives
(C) Ford's The Chronicle History of Perkin Warbeck
(D) Plautus's Menaechmi
(E) Daniel's Civil Wars

97. Prominent as practitioners of Imagism in American poetry were all of the following except

(A) Ezra Pound
(B) John Gould Fletcher
(C) Edwin Arlington Robinson
(D) Hilda Doolittle
(E) Richard Aldington

98. All of the following are associated with collections of American folklore or folk music except

(A) Benjamin Botkin
(B) Carl Sandburg
(C) Philip Barry
(D) John A. Lomax
(E) N. Howard Thorp

99. The local color writer and his literary work are correctly paired in all the following except

(A) Irwin Russell - Christmas-Night in the Quarters
(B) George Washington Cable - Old Creole Days
(C) Thomas Nelson Page - In Ole Virginia
(D) Erskine Caldwell - Tobacco Road
(E) Sarah Orne Jewett - The Old Dominion

100. Congreve's greatest skill as a dramatist is shown in his

(A) originality of plot
(B) sympathetic treatment of characters
(C) polished, brilliant dialogue
(D) blending of cynicism with sentiment
(E) bitterness and irony

ANSWER KEY

1. B
2. E
3. C
4. A
5. D
6. D
7. B
8. B
9. C
10. A
11. A
12. A
13. D
14. A
15. B
16. E
17. D
18. E
19. C
20. C
21. C
22. E
23. B
24. C
25. A
26. E
27. B
28. E
29. C
30. B
31. A
32. A
33. A
34. C
35. E
36. B
37. D
38. A
39. D
40. B
41. D
42. A
43. D
44. C
45. B
46. E
47. C
48. A
49. D
50. E
51. D
52. C
53. C
54. D
55. A
56. E
57. C
58. E
59. C
60. E
61. A
62. A
63. A
64. B
65. E
66. C
67. A
68. E
69. C
70. A
71. D
72. D
73. C
74. E
75. C
76. E
77. D
78. A
79. C
80. A
81. C
82. A
83. B
84. D
85. E
86. E
87. B
88. D
89. D
90. B
91. B
92. E
93. B
94. D
95. C
96. C
97. C
98. C
99. E
100. C

EXPLANATORY ANSWERS

1. (B) The Iliad, a Greek epic poem in twenty-four books, describes events connected with the tenth and final year of the Trojan War. However, the theme of the epic is the wrath of Achilles who leaves the battle and refuses to return until Agamemnon recognizes his wrath.

2. (E) Plato's Apology deals with the trial and conviction of Socrates. In this dialogue, Socrates, while answering the accusation that he has corrupted the youth of Athens, also sets forth his philosophy concerning human conduct, death, and man's relationship to the state. Here too he states that "The unexamined life is not worth living."

3. (C) Lays of Ancient Rome by Macaulay are translations from Livy. Macaulay attempts to reproduce the ballad style which Livy had used. All the other works are frame stories - that is, stories which are unified by some artificial device that brings the characters together and provides a story within a story. For example, Arabian Nights or A Thousand and One Nights uses as a frame the storytelling of Scheherazade, who avoids death by telling a story each night to her husband the king.

4. (A) Simms wrote novels set in South Carolina during the Revolutionary War. Although his writing resembles that of James Fenimore Cooper, his Indians are more credible, as for example in The Yemassee. The Narrative of Davy Crockett is autobiography.

5. (D) Mark Twain is the author of all these works except A Chance Acquaintance, which is a minor novel by William Dean Howells. Howells offers a pleasant description of Quebec and the area along the St. Lawrence in a work primarily intended as a study of the American class system.

6. (D) The quotations from Emerson illustrate his epigrammatic prose style. In essays such as Self-Reliance he offers practical application of his Transcendental philosophy.
   The other quotation is from George Bernard Shaw's Annajanska. It is typical of Shaw in the use of paradox for shock effect.

7. (B) The prince is the central character in The Idiot. He suffers from epilepsy as did Dostoevsky himself. Paradoxically, this disease is also attributed to Dostoevsky's most diabolical creation, Smerdyakov of The Brothers Karamazov.

8. (B) This play is one of a series of the naturalistic "problem" plays that began with The Pillars of Society. These plays caused considerable furor because they criticized such things as the subjection of women, corrupt politics, hereditary disease, and social hypocrisy.

9. (C) Although some critics have sought to interpret the ghosts as delusions of the governess's sex-starved imagination, the story itself shows the ghosts to be real not only to Flora and Miles, the two children, but also to Mrs. Grose, the housekeeper, and to the narrator-governess. The novelette is also an interesting exercise in point-of-view as the story is told at several removes from the reader through the use of an external-narrator and a reader-within-the-story.

10. (A) Although Whitman generally wrote in free verse, he showed an ability to compose in conventional prose patterns. As late as 1865 he wrote in regular meter <u>O Captain! My Captain!</u> in memory of the slain Lincoln. His greater poetic expression of grief over Lincoln's death is, however, <u>When Lilacs Last in the Dooryard Bloom'd,</u> written in free verse.

11. (A) John Kenneth Galbraith is a leading contemporary American economist, author of <u>The Affluent Society</u>. During the Kennedy administration he served as Ambassador to India. He is a leading force in such liberal organizations as Americans for Democratic Action.

12. (A) While at Harvard from 1905 to 1925, Baker organized and taught English 47 (usually known as the "47 Workshop"). Baker taught such writers as Eugene O'Neill, Thomas Wolfe, John Dos Passos, Philip Bary, Sidney Howard, and S. N. Behrman. In addition to its influence on important writers, Baker's course demonstrated a new faith in American drama.

13. (D) Albert Camus, the author of <u>The Plague</u>, is not strictly-speaking an Existentialist, but his view of the world is essentially existentialistic. <u>The Myth of Sisyphus</u> and <u>The Stranger</u> show that Camus is not so totally pessimistic as Sartre. In both, Camus argues that man should actively struggle.

14. (A) Both play and film are concerned with the great English adventurer T. E. Lawrence, whose <u>Seven Pilars of Wisdom</u> was the basis for the screenplay.

15. (B) Edward Albee, controversial dramatist of the present time, examines the psychological strains of a contemporary marriage in <u>Who's Afraid of Virginia Woolf</u>. In his one-act play <u>The Sand Box</u> he offers a highly unusual treatment of old age and death.

16. (E) These words are part of the speech made by Faulkner when he received the 1949 Nobel Prize for Literature. The optimism of Faulkner's address has appealed to millions who have never read his novels, and who, if they did, would quite likely find little there for optimism or faith in the future.

17. (D) Martin Arrowsmith is the central figure of Sinclair Lewis's novel <u>Arrowsmith</u>; Antonia Shimerda of Willa Chater's <u>My Antonia</u>. The other couples belong to the following works:
   A. Hemingway, <u>A Farewell to Arms</u>
   B. Galsworthy, <u>The Forsyte Saga</u>
   C. James, <u>The Americans</u>
   E. Dreiser, <u>An American Tragedy</u>.

18. (E) In <u>Berlin Diary</u> William L. Shirer, contemporary journalist and historian, offers an account of the days immediately preceding and following the declaration of World War II. <u>The Rise and Fall of the Third Reich</u>, a national best-seller, is an exhaustive study of the Nazi era.

19. (C) The Greek Sphinx had a winged lion's body except that from the waist up it had a woman's figure. The riddle was: What is it that walks on four feet and two feet and three feet and has one voice; when it walks on most feet it is weakest? The answer: Man. As a reward for answering the riddle, Oedipus was given the throne of Thebes and the hand of the queen, Jocasta, his mother. Earlier he had unwittingly killed his father, and thus fulfilled his fate.

20. (C) Fowler is the author A Dictionary of Modern English Usage and joint author with his brother, Francis George Fowler, of The Pocket Oxford Dictionary. Fowler's work on usage is widely accepted as the standard work on British English if not on American English.

21. (C) The phrase (taken from Acts of the Apostles, XXI, 39) is an example of litotes, a kind of understatement in which a thing is affirmed by stating the negative of its opposite. In this case, the intent is that the citizen is of a great and powerful city.

22. (E) The Clerk is described in the Prologue to The Canterbury Tales as lean of figure and sober of bearing. He preferred books to rich robes. A philosopher, "Yet hadde he but litel gold in cofre." He tells the story of Patient Griselda.

23. (B) Sonnet sequences were initiated by Petrarch and imitated by a number of Renaissance authors as well as by such modern poets as Edna St. Vincent Millay and W. H. Auden. The sonnet sequence or cycle is a series of sonnets linked to one other and dealing with a unified topic. Shakespeare's cycle of 154 sonnets does not have a particular title. Astrophel and Stella is by Spenser; Amoretti by Sidney.

24. (C) This line is from Sir Francis Bacon, Apothegms. The lines from Shakespeare are from the following plays:

   A. King Lear
   B. Othello
   D. Hamlet
   E. Julius Caesar

25. (A) In 1562 Brooke published The Tragicall History of Romeus and Juliet, and English poetical version of an Italian romance by Bandello. It is not clear whether Shakespeare had access to any version of the story other than Brooke's although it is possible there was already in existence a play on the same subject. And it is known that Shakespeare's usual practice was to make use of more than one source.

26. (E) Elinor Dashwood represents the sense aspect in Jane Austen's Sense and Sensibility; sensibility is represented by Marianne Dashwood. Catherine Morland appears in Northanger Abbey, Austen's anti-romantic novel which is critical of the Ann Radcliff style of romance. Anne Elliot is from Persuasion. Anne's love story may reflect Jane Austen's own life.

27. (B) These works, significant in American history and government, comprised an argument in favor of the proposed constitution and a defense of the conservative philosophy that marked the Federalist party.

28. (E) This unfinished but published mystery has been the subject of several attempts to create a plausible ending. The most serious difficulty revolves around Drood himself: Has he really been murdered? Who is Datchery? (He may be Drood.) Dickens left no hint of the solution he had planned.

29. (C) The life story and the "Colloquies" of Erasmus, as well as the works of Froissart and Luther, inspired Charles Reade to write this historical romance. The story tells of the ill-starred love of Gerard and Margaret and involves a series of realistic descriptions of fifteenth-century monasteries, palaces, and inns. The lovers are reunited happily at the end.

30. (B) This folk ballad is actually one of several on the same topic, all of which tell the same story in slightly different words. Like many other ballads, "Sir Patrick Spens" was probably written before 1700. One of the first to become interested in this literary form was Bishop Thomas Percy who published many ballads in his Reliques of Ancient English Poetry.

31. (A) Steinbeck's novel of strike violence and murder tells the story of Jim Nolan who, bitter because he is ill-treated by the police, joins the Communist Party, and is eventually killed. Although seeming to be a piece of Party propaganda, the novel actually shows that Party practices are often despicable. As a result, Communist critics found fault with the book.

32. (A) Pope translated both the Iliad and the Odyssey into heroic couplets. Although not an accurate translation, his Iliad is considered by many a great poem. Much of the less successful Odyssey translation was done by William Broome and Elijah Fenton.

Cowper's translations are generally inferior to Pope's.

Chapman's Iliad is written in fourteen-syllable riming lines; his Odyssey in heroic couplets. Both depart substantially from the original.

33. (A) Taylor, a lecturer, novelist, journalist, dramatist, and historian, was regarded as the greatest poet of his own day. However, his poetry is of little value. His novels Hannah Thurston and The Story of Kennett are better. His Faust is regarded as a fine translation; it retains the original meter.

34. (C) Before Brett Ashley falls in love with matador Pedro Romero, she has been living and loving with Bill Garton, Mike Campbell, and Robert Cohen. She finally abandons Romero, so as not to ruin his career, and marries Campbell.

35. (E) Fauvism is a style of painting associated with French artists of the early twentieth century and characterized by the use of vivid colors in immediate juxtaposition.

Gongorism, Euphuism, and Marianism are all styles characterized by great affection and extravagance of language. The Metaphysical style is marked by highly ingenious conceits.

36. (B) Written in rime royal, this vision poem tells of St. Valentine's Day, when every fowl chooses a mate at the Court of Nature. Three eagles advance their claim to a female, and a debate follows. Nature decides that the female may herself choose after a year's consideration. It is likely that the poem's animals have counterparts in English royalty.

37. (D) Thackeray's novel may not offer a hero, but in the person of Rebecca Sharp, it presents one of the great female figures in the English novel. Becky is the clever, ambitious, unscrupulous daughter of a penniless artist and a French opera-dancer. After rising to the heights of society, first in Paris, then in London, she compromises her honor, and is forced to spend her final years on the disreputable fringe of the society she once dominated.

38. (A) Mailer's work is indebted to such novels of the first World War as Remarque's All Quiet on the Western Front and Barbusse's Under Fire. But in Wells' novel, the setting is World War II. The soldiers depicted represent a cross-section of American life but the action takes place on the imaginary Pacific island of Anopopei. The use of "The Time Machine" to present flashbacks into civilian life is similar to Dos Passos' use of the "Camera Eye" in his trilogy U.S.A.

39. (D) In Williams' The Glass Menagerie, the crippled Laura has put all her love into a collection of miniature glass animals. When the Gentleman Caller, Jim O'Connor, accidentally breaks a part of the collection, Laura tries to dismiss it in her hope of having made a contact with another human being. But Jim is already engaged to another girl, and Laura is doomed to a life of loneliness.

40. (B) Leopold Bloom is a middle-aged Jew in the city of Dublin, whose day's wanderings through his native city are modern parallels of Ulysses' adventures. Telemachus is represented by Stephen Dedalus, and the faithful Penelope by the faithless, eternally-feminine Molly Bloom.

41. (D) Lewis's work, a moral tract so entertaining that it is a perennial best seller, offers letters by the devil Screwtape to his nephew Wormwood on how to proceed in the corruption of mankind. Twain's book is also a commentary on human fallability.

42. (A) Anna Christie is a play by Eugene O'Neil in which the central character, Anna finds moral regeneration in the end. The whole play ends on an optimistic note despite the commitment of Anna's father and husband, to return to the sea.

43. (D) Dick Swiveller is a character in Dickens' Old Curiosity Shop, the story of Little Nell, who lives in the gloomy atmosphere of her grandfather's shop. But the evil dwarf Daniel Quilp forces the old man and his grandfather to flee. The reversal of fortunes comes too late to save either from death.

44. (C) Madame d'Arblay - Fanny Burney - is best known for her first novel Evelina, an epistolary novel. After a second successful novel, Cecilia, Burney's career may be said to have stopped. Camilla and The Wanderer or Female Difficulties are tedious, dull narratives.

45. (B) The meter is datylic, the line primarily hexameter: "Fairer was she when, on Sunday morn, while the bell from its turret." A scanning of this line will show that it is not strictly dactyl or hexameter. However it is probably as close to pure dactylic hexameter as poets, writing English, can come.

46. (E) Gammer Gurton's Needle is the second English comedy in verse. (The first is Ralph Roister Doiser.) The farcical action concerns the losing and finding of the needle used to mend the clothing of Hodge, Gammer Gurton's servingman.

47. (C) Such plays by Synge as Playboy of the Western World and Riders to the Sea are written in a prose that shows the influence of Synge's visit to the Aran Isles. In his final, unfinished drama, Deirdre of the Sorrows, Synge's prose achieves such powerful rhythmic force as to obscure the traditional distinction between prose and verse.

48. (A) Edith Sitwell's verse shows the influence of the rhythms of contemporary music; indeed, some of her poetry is written to be recited to musical accompaniment. Despite a surface artificiality, her poems reveal a deep pathos verging on despair.

49. (D) Dobson was an accomplished writer of light verse and a serious student of the eighteenth century. He wrote prose biographies of such eighteenth-century figures as Goldsmith, Horace Walpole, and Fanny Burney.

50. (E) In Robert Burns' "Tam O' Shanter," the drunken farmer witnesses the dancing of witches and warlocks to the music of Old Nick's bagpipes. He gives himself away, and is lucky to escape with only the loss of the tail of his grey mare, Meg.

51. (D) T. S. Eliot derived much of the imagery and symbolism of the poem from Jessie L. Weston's From Ritual to Romance and Sir James Fraser's The Golden Bough. The story of the Grail concerns the barren land ruled over by a Fisher King, likewise barren. A wanderer or knight seeking the Holy Grail is the only means of restoring land and ruler to fertility.

52. (C) The lines are from Scott's Marmion, A Tale of Flodden Field, a poem in six cantos set during the reign of King Henry VIII. The well-known song "Lochinvar" occurs in the fifth canto.

53. (C) In this autobiographical account of his steamship tour of Europe and the Holy Land, Twain mocks many of the sights and manners of the Old World. The book is based on letters sent earlier to the San Franciso Alta California and the New York Herald and Tribune.

54. (D) In Hawthorne's novel of guilt and conscience, Hester Prynne is forced to wear on her bosom the red letter A that marks her an adultress. Her lover does not admit his own guilt for seven years. Then, on the edge of madness and death, he makes public confession at the pillory which was earlier the scene of Hester's humiliation.

55. (A) James' mastery of such technical aspects of the novel as "point of view" and characterization is to be seen in such late novels as The Wings of the Dove (1902), The Ambassadors (1903), and The Golden Bowl (1904).

56. (E) Emily Dickinson became a virtual recluse after the age of twenty-six, and only two of her poems were printed during her lifetime. Her openness to emotional experience is to be seen in such poems as "My life closed twice before its close" and "Hope is a subtle glutton."

57. (C) Winesburg, Ohio offers a set of connected sketches dealing with the lives of the inhabitants of a fictional Ohio town. Anderson shows antagonism to the traditional values of small-town life, and his most admirable characters are likely to be outcasts from respectable society.

58. (E) Although he did not receive the Nobel Prize until 1962, Steinbeck had done his greatest work in the thirties. He first won recognition with Tortilla Flat (1935). Of Mice and Men (1937) established his reputation. And in 1939 he published The Grapes of Wrath, a sympathetic account of the farmers who were driven from the Oklahoma dustbowl to seek prosperity in the promised land of California.

59. (C) Babbitt is a real-estate salesman in the midwestern city of Zenith. At the age of forty-six he begins to question the materialistic values by which he has lived. But afraid of social censure, he soon returns to a life of vulgar conventionality. He is able, however, to encourage his son to seek a better existence than his own.

60. (E) "Birches" describes the age-old New England game of climbing a birch tree to the very top, then swinging outward and down to the ground. The analogy is then drawn to life: the individual needs an occasional "climb toward heaven," but he also needs a return to the ordinary existence of this world. The poet knows that a balance between spiritual aspiration and material commitments is best; it is "good both going and coming back."

61. (A) The novel concerns a day in July, 1714, on which a bridge across a Peruvian gorge breaks, killing five people. Brother Juniper investigates the lives of the victims, and his findings lead him to a conviction of the benevolence of divine Providence.

62. (A) Pound played a large part in forming the style of T. S. Eliot and, by his own account, influenced the later poems of W. B. Yeats. His influence on such American poets as Hart Crane and Archibald MacLeish has also been considerable. Despite these influences on others, Pound's poetry remains distinctive, if only for its great erudition and technical brilliance.

63. (A) Williams is one of the most consistently successful of contemporary American dramatists. His recurring themes are perverted or

frustrated sexual passion and the loss of social stability in American life. In addition to the four plays mentioned in the question, he has written Cat on a Hot Tin Roof and The Rose Tattoo.

64. (B) In his rejection of sophisticated urban values and in his search for a life close to nature, Thoreau represents one of the deepest and most persistent themes in American life and letters. Walden is the account of his retreat to a forest hut, built by himself, and an expression of his desire "so to love wisdom as to live according to its dictates, a life of simplicity, independence, magnanimity, and trust."

65. (E) Tennyson's poem tells of Princess Ida, who becomes a champion of women's rights and founds a university to further the cause. In the end, the university is turned into a hospital and the princess into a lover. Gilbert and Sullivan's opera Princess Ida is based on Tennyson's work.

66. (C) George Eliot's emphasis on moral choice is to be seen in Adam Bede, Mill on the Floss, and Middlemarch. In each case, characters find themselves in situations which demand that they exercise their freedom to choose. In these novels, once a choice has been made there is no means of escaping the moral consequences.

67. (A) Donne's sonnet is typical of his concern with death and God and of his mastery of paradox and the conceit. Death is warned not to be proud; despite its apparent victory over men, it is death that dies when man is reborn into eternal life.

68. (E) Dryden's play, which has as subtitle The World Well Lost, is simpler and more concentrated than that by Shakespeare. Dryden confines the action to the last phase of Antony's career, and to the struggle between Cleopatra and the forces of Rome for the soul of Antony. Shakespeare's play offers more sweeping scenes and richer verse.

69. (C) Chaucer's poem Troilus and Cryseyde contributes to the legend the humorous figure of Pandarus and a subtle development of the character of Cressida into a sympathetic and serious woman. In the Shakespeare play Cressida is a faithless flirt and Pandarus a dirty old man. Shakespeare is also out of sympathy with Achilles in this bitter, mocking play.

70. (A) Hemingway's novel of the Spanish Civil War, Robert Jordan is an American teacher whose idealism leads him to fight for the Loyalists. The novel offers a study of men and women under the pressure of war. Some, like Pablo, prove to be moral cowards; others - Pilar, Jordan, Maria - find meaning in life and in death.

71. (D) Cooper was a patrician by birth and despite membership in the Democratic Party, he never relinquished belief in class distinctions and the right of the squirearchy to political rule. The American Democrat was a full statement of his social ideal of equality of right without equality of social conditions.

72. (D) In Main Street the chief characters are Carol Milford, an aspiring intellectual, and her husband, Dr. Will Kennicott. The young couple settles in Gopher Prairie, Minnesota, where Erik Valborg, the one townsman who would seem to promise any intellectual stimulation to Carol, proves to be a feckless nonentity.

73. (C) James' novel is a study of Isabel Archer's confrontation with European society. Inevitably, she comes to a recognition of the evil that surrounds her, but she is of sufficient strength of character to triumph over the cynicism and deviousness of those who oppose her.

74. (E) Whitman sings the glory and joy of physical labor as part of his theme of the greatness and diversity of America. In the group of nine poems known as "Calamus," he celebrates the concept of comradeship or "manly love."

75. (C) Freneau's revolutionary satires include "American Liberty," "A Political Litany," and "George the Third's Soliloquy." As a nature poet, he is best known for "To a Wild Honeysuckle" and "The Beauties of Santa Cruz."

76. (E) The ballade, a poetic form derived from the French, usually has three stanzas of seven, eight, or ten lines with only three or four rhymes, a recurrent rhyming pattern, and a refrain, and a concluding envoy of half the stanzaic length. The ballade is addressed to an individual. One of the best known English ballades is Rossetti's adaption of Francois Villon's "Ballade of Dead Ladies."

77. (D) Anchises was the father of the Trojan warrior Aeneas, who, after the fall of Troy, journeyed to Latium (Italy) so that his line could found Rome. King Priam of Troy was the father of Paris, whose abduction of Helen brought about the Trojan War.

78. (A) These lovers were contemporaries of Dante, Francesca fell in love with Paolo, her husband's brother, and as a result of their adulterous relationship the two were executed in 1289. In the fifth canto of the Inferno, Dante recounts his conversation with Francesca. She tells him that the adultery followed upon a reading of the romance of Lancelot and Guinevere.

79. (C) Butler ridicules the hypocrisy and self-seeking of Presbyterians and Independents. His work shows the influence of Cervantes and Rabelais; the title is taken from Spenser's The Faerie Queene. The verse consists of octosyllabic couplets in iambic tetrameter with many outrageous double and triple rhymes.

80. (A) Drayton's principal work is a patriotic poem indebted to Geoffrey of Monmouth. Of interminable length, it offers a catalogue of British saints, famous captains, and valiant seamen, as well as a genuine celebration of the beauties of the English countryside.

81. (C) At his death, Herman Melville left the unpublished manuscript of Billy Budd, which was not printed until 1924. This short novel is a consummate study of the conflict between natural justice and the laws of society. Captain Vere feels himself bound to order the execution of the innocent Billy whose last words are "God bless Captain Vere." In the struggle between Billy and Claggart, Melville returns to the theme of good and evil - a theme that preoccupied him in Moby Dick.

82. (A) This monthly periodical specialized in short fiction and enjoyed phenomenal success as an arbiter of fashion. It was edited by Sarah Josepha B. Hale from 1837 to 1877.

83. (B) The author is Stendhal, one of the earliest masters of the psychological novel. He lays bare the inner conflicts of his characters in a terse, clear style.

84. (D) Melville attended school in Albany, New York. After his father's death, he shipped as a cabin boy and spent most of the next few years at sea.

85. (E) In 1939 Steinbeck published Grapes of Wrath, a story of the sufferings of itinerant Oakies during the American depression.

La Condition Humaine (1933) by Malraux treats the beginnings of the communist struggle in China.

Ignazio Silone expressed his anti-Fascism in Fontamara (1933) and Bread and Wine (1936).

Dos Passos published his Marxian trilogy U.S.A. in the years 1930-36.

86. (E) Most of Hardy's novels are set in the imaginary but realistic county of Wessex in southern England. In such novels as The Return of the Native and Tess of the d'Urbervilles, the landscape represents a powerful force that dominates the characters.

87. (B) Richter won the Pulitzer Prize in 1960 for his trilogy, The Trees, The Fields, The Town. These novels trace the course of a family through several generations. Beginning with the family's Ohio pioneer days, Richter continues with its participation in the Civil War and ends with the urbanization of the family, their pioneer spirit spent.

88. (D) Beelzebub appears in various guises in myth and literature. The Hebrew word means "fly-lord" and it is in this sense that author William Golding uses the name. In the New Testament, Beelzebub is both lord of the underworld and prince of the devils. In Paradise Lost, Beelzebub is the most powerful angel after Satan.

89. (D) After the Norman Conquest many French-speaking nobles came to and remained in England. Because these nobles ruled the country, French became the language of official documents and court proceedings. Furthermore, the scribes were almost all Frenchmen, and there was no Old English-speaking upper class. As a result, Old English became colloquial, and throughout much of the Middle English period there was a good deal of borrowing from the French.

90. (B) The Muses, of whom there were nine, were initially the goddesses who inspired song. In later Roman times they became patrons of different kinds of poetry and of the arts and sciences. They were the daughters of Zeus and Mnemosyne. Calliope was associated with epic poetry, Euterpe with lyric poetry, Erato with erotic poetry, Polyhymnia with sacred music, and Urania with astronomy.

91. (B) Mary Powell, the daughter of Royalist parents, left her husband six weeks after her marriage to return to her parents' home. She refused to go back to her husband. Since Milton was a Puritan supporter, her refusal might have been connected with the outbreak of the Civil War. The following year the poet published a pamphlet in favor of divorce, which he followed by three more such pamphlets in the next few years. Mary eventually returned to her husband, and on her death in 1652 she left three daughters who, in later years, served as amanuenses to their blind father.

92. (E) In Battle of the Books Swift declares the two noblest things to be sweetness and light. Matthew Arnold used the phrase in Culture and Anarchy: "The pursuit of perfection, then, is the pursuit of sweetness and light united, works to make reason and the will of God prevail."

93. (B) Hudibras, in the poem by the same name, is pictured as a pedantic Presbyterian, who sets forth on a miserable horse to purify the world. His squire is the Independent Ralpho. The two are clearly modeled on Cervantes' characters; and in fact a number of Butler's incidents are parallels of events in Don Quixote.

94. (D) Endymion by Keats is written in rhymed couplets; however, The Eve of St. Agnes is in Spenserian stanza. This stanza consists of nine lines, the first eight in iambic pentameter, the ninth an iambic hexameter, also called an Alexandrine. The rhyme scheme is ababbcbcc. This type of stanza was first used by Spenser in The Faerie Queene.

95. (C) Hopkins "invented" the term to describe the meter of such poems as "The Windover," and "Spring." Unlike ordinary meter, sprung rhythm disregards unstressed syllables and is based on the number of stressed syllables in a verse. Hopkins believed that sprung rhythm "is nearest to the rhythm of prose."

96. (C) Perkin Warbeck was not written until after Shakespeare's death. However, Rod's play is considered the best historical drama, excluding those by Shakespeare, of the age. The chronicle plays are heavily indebted to Holinshed, less so to Daniel.

The Comedy of Errors owes much to Plautus, while Julius Casesar and Antony and Cleopatra come from North's translation of Plutarch.

97. (C) Unlike the Imagists, Robinson has shown a preference for long narrative poetry and rather traditional forms. He is a master of short epigrammatic characterizations of eccentric figures such as Richard Cory and Miniver Cheevy. His long poems include Ben Jonson Entertains a Man from Stratford and The Man Against the Sky.

98. (C) Barry is the author of such popular light comedies as The Animal Kingdom, The Philadelphia Story, and Paris Bound. But his experimental plays are probably more significant in their revolt against realism. White Wings and Hotel Universe are symbolic, even allegorical, with a stylization that is far removed from the naturalism that dominated the American drama during the years 1925-1935, when these works were produced.

99. (E) The Old Dominion is by Southern regionalist Thomas Nelson Page. Miss Jewett, a New England local colorist, recreated her native place and her neighbors in such novels as A Country Doctor, A Marsh Island, and The Tory Lover.

100. (C) Congreve was the supreme master of the comedy of manners that dominated the Restoration theatre. Two of his greatest comedies are The Way of the World and The Double Dealer, in which he displays the "great" world of fashion and gallantry by means of witty dialogue and satiric characterization.

SECOND PRACTICE AP/CLEP ENGLISH TEST
SECTION II

Question 1 (Suggested time - 40 minutes)

Directions: Read the following poems carefully and then write an essay in which you discuss how the two poems are similar, i.e., expressing the romantic mood.

KUBLA KHAN

Or, A Vision in a Dream

Samuel Taylor Coleridge

In Xanadu did Kubla Khan
A stately pleasure-dome decree:
Where Alph, the sacred river, ran
Through caverns measureless to man
  Down to a sunless sea.
So twice five miles of fertile ground
With walls and towers were girdled round:
And there were gardens bright with sinuous rills,
Where blossomed many an incense-bearing tree;
And here were forests ancient as the hills,
Enfolding sunny spots of greenery.

But oh! that deep romantic chasm which slanted
Down the green hill athwart a cedarn cover!
A savage place! as holy and enchanged
As e'er beneath a waning moon was haunted
By woman wailing for her demon-lover!
And from this chasm, with ceaseless turmoil seething,
As if this earth in fast thick pants were breathing,
A mighty fountain momently was forced:
Amid whose swift half-intermitted burst
Huge fragments vaulted like rebounding hail,
Or chaffy grain beneath the thresher's flail:
And 'mid these dancing rocks at once and ever
It flung up momently the sacred river.
Five miles meandering with a mazy motion
Through wood and dale the sacred river ran,

Then reached the caverns measureless to man,
And sank in tumult to a lifeless ocean:
And 'mid this tumult Kubla heard from far
Ancestral voices prophesying war!
  The shadow of the dome of pleasure
  Floated midway on the waves;
  Where was heard the mingled measure
  From the fountain and the caves.
It was a miracle of rare device,
A sunny pleasure-dome with caves of ice!

  A damsel with a dulcimer
  In a vision once I saw:
  It was an Abyssinian maid,
  And on her dulcimer she played,
  Singing of Mount Abora.
  Could I revive within me
  Her symphony and song,
  To such a deep delight 'twould win me,
That with music loud and long,
I would build that dome in air,
That sunny dome! those caves of ice!
And all who heard should see them there,
And all should cry, Beware! Beware!
His flashing eyes, his floating hair!
Weave a circle round him thrice,
And close your eyes with holy dread,
For he on honey-dew hath fed,
And drunk the milk of Paradise.

THE RAVEN

Edgar Allan Poe

Once upon a midnight dreary, while I pondered, weak and weary,
Over many a quaint and curious volume of forgotten lore --
While I nodded, nearly napping, suddenly there came a tapping,
As of some one gently rapping, rapping at my chamber door.
"'Tis some visiter," I muttered, "tapping at my chamber door --
    Only this and nothing more."

An, distinctly I remember it was in the bleak December;
And each separate dying ember wrought its ghost upon the floor.
Eagerly I wished the morrow; -- vainly I had sought to borrow
From my books surcease of sorrow -- sorrow for the lost Lenore --
For the rare and radiant maiden whom the angels name Lenore --
    Nameless <u>here</u> for evermore.

And the silken, sad, uncertain rustling of each purple curtain
Thrilled me -- filled me with fantastic terrors never felt before;
So that now, to still the beating of my heart, I stood repeating
"'Tis some visiter entreating entrance at my chamber door --
Some late visiter entreating entrance at my chamber door; --
    This it is and nothing more."

Presently my soul grew stronger; hesitating then no longer,
"Sir," said I, "or Madam, truly your forgiveness I implore;
But the fact is I was napping, and so gently you came rapping,
And so faintly you came tapping, tapping at my chamber door,
That I scarce was sure I heard you" -- here I opened wide the door; --
    Darkness there and nothing more.

Deep into that darkness peering, long I stood there wondering, fearing,
Doubting, dreaming dreams no mortal ever dared to dream before;
But the silence was unbroken, and the stillness gave no token,
And the only word there spoken was the whispered word, "Lenore!"
This I whispered, and an echo murmured back the word "Lenore!"
    Merely this and nothing more.

Back into the chamber turning, all my soul within me burning,
Soon again I heard a tapping somewhat louder than before.
"Surely," said I, "surely that is something at my window lattice;
Let me see, then, what thereat is, and this mystery explore --
Let my heart be still a moment and this mystery explore; --
    'Tis the wind and nothing more!"

Open here I flung the shutter, when, with many a flirt and flutter
In there stepped a stately Raven of the saintly days of yore.
Not the least obeisance made he; not a minute stopped or stayed he;
But, with mien of lord or lady, perched above my chamber door --
Perched upon a bust of Pallas just above my chamber door --
    Perched, and sat, and nothing more.

Then this ebony bird beguiling my sad fancy into smiling,
By the grave and stern decorum of the countenance it wore,
"Though thy crest be shorn and shave, thou," I said, "art sure no craven,
Ghastly grim and ancient Raven wandering from the Nightly shore --
Tell me what they lordly name is on the Night's Plutonian shore!"
    Quoth the Raven, "Nevermore."

Much I marvelled this ungainly fowl to hear discourse so plainly,
Though its answer little meaning -- little relevancy bore;
For we cannot help agreeing that no living human being
Ever yet was blessed with seeing bird above his chamber door --
Bird or beast upon the sculptured bust above his chamber door,
    With such name as "Nevermore."

But the Raven, sitting lonely on the placid bust, spoke only
That one word, as if his soul in that one word he did outpour.
Nothing farther then he uttered -- not a feather then he fluttered --
Till I scarcely more than muttered "Other friends have flown before --
On the morrow <u>he</u> will leave me, as my hopes have flown before."
    Then the bird said "Nevermore."

Startled at the stillness broken by reply so aptly spoken,
"Doubtless," said I, "what it utters is its only stock and store
Caught from some unhappy master whom unmerciful Disaster
Followed fast and followed faster till his songs one burden bore --
Till the dirges of his Hope that melancholy burden bore
    Of 'Never -- nevermore.'"

But the Raven still beguiling all my fancy into smiling,
Straight I wheeled a cushioned seat in front of bird, and bust and door;
Then, upon the velvet sinking, I betook myself to linking
Fancy unto fancy, thinking what this ominous bird of yore --
What this grim, ungainly, ghastly, gaunt, and ominous bird of yore
Meant in croaking "Nevermore."

This I sat engaged in guessing, but no syllable expressing
To the fowl whose fiery eyes now burned into my bosom's core;
This and more I sat divining, with my head at ease reclining
On the cushion's velvet lining that the lamplight gloated o'er,
But whose velvet violet lining with the lamplight gloating o'er,
She shall press, ah, nevermore!

Then, methought, the air grew denser, perfumed from an unseen censer
Swung by Seraphim whose foot-falls tinkled on the tufted floor.
"Wretch," I cried, "thy God hath lent thee -- by these angels he hath sent thee
Respite -- respite and nepenthe from they memories of Lenore;
Quaff, oh quaff this kind nepenthe and forget this lost Lenore!"
Quoth the Raven "Nevermore."

"Prophet!" said I, "thing of evil! prophet still, if bird or devil! --
Whether Tempter sent, or whether tempest tossed thee here ashore,
Desolate yet all undaunted, on this desert land enchanted --
On this home by Horror haunted -- tell me truly, I implore --
Is there -- is there balm in Gilead? -- tell me -- tell me, I implore!"
Quoth the Raven "Nevermore."

"Prophet!" said I, "thing of evil! -- prophet still, if bird or devil!
By that Heaven that bends above us -- by that God we both adore --
Tell this soul with sorrow laden if, within the distant Aidenn,
It shall clasp a sainted maiden whom the angels name Lenore --
Clasp a rare and radiant maiden whom the angels name Lenore."
Quoth the Raven "Nevermore."

"Be that word our sign of parting, bird or fiend!" I shrieked, upstarting --
"Get thee back into the tempest and the Night's Plutonian shore!
Leave no black plume as a token of that lie thy soul hath spoken!
Leave my loneliness unbroken! -- quit the bust above my door!
Take thy beak from out my heart, and take thy form from off my door!"
Quoth the Raven "Nevermore."

And the Raven, never flitting, still is sitting, still is sitting
On the pallid bust of Pallas just above my chamber door;
And his eyes have all the seeming of a demon's that is dreaming,
And the lamp-light o'er him streaming throws his shadow on the floor;
And my soul from out that shadow that lies floating on the floor
Shall be lifted -- nevermore!

Response (1):

"Kubla Kahn" and "The Raven": How are they Romantic?

Samuel Taylor Coleridge in "Kubla Khan" and Edgar Allen Poe in "The Raven" express Romantic tendencies. However, these tendencies are different in each poem.

According to A Handbook to Literature by C. Hugh Holman, there are certain characteristics of Romanticism. Among the aspects of Romanticism that may be listed are: sensibility, primitivism, love of nature, sympathetic interest in the past, mysticism, individualism, enthusiasm for the wild or grotesque, unrestrained imagination, enthusiasm for the uncivilized, sympathy with animal life, and sentimental melancholy. Not all of these characteristics are found in every piece of Romantic literature. This is the case with "The Raven" and "Kubla Khan" as well.

In "The Raven" Poe exhibits many Romantic qualities. He shows an enthusiasm for the wild in his choice of a subject. The raven is the least likely subject to write a poem about, however, it is this non-popularity that drew Poe to the raven. Poe has an insurpassable imagination. He hears the raven speak, the immortal word 'Nevermore.' At first Poe was enjoying the presence of the raven, in fact he was sympathetic. (Much I marvelled this ungainly fowl to hear discourse so plainly. line 49). This fascination with the raven ends when Poe discovers that the raven will be with him forever. (Take thy beak from out my heart, and take thy form from off my door!Quoth the Raven "Nevermore." lines 101-102). The predominating Romantic quality in "The Raven" is a sentimental melancholy. Poe is still trying to reconcile the loss of his beloved 'Lenore.' It is this melancholic mood that gives the poem its lasting quality.

"Kubla Kahn" is based on an interest in the past blended with other characteristics of Romanticism. The poem is about the land of China under the reign of the savage ruler Kubla Khan. (In Xanadu did Kubla Khan/a stately pleasure dome decree. lines 1-2). An enthusiasm for the mystic, grotesque, and uncivilized is found in one of Coleridge's strongest lines: "By woman wailing for her demon-lover!" line 16. The most effective word in this passage is 'wailing.' The word denotes an uncivilized cry, a cry used predominately by animals, not humans. The words 'demon-lover' imply some sort of relationship with a supernatural being. This type of savagery is evident throughout the images in "Kubla Khan."

"The Raven" with its melancholic mood and "Kubla Khan" with its images of savagery both exhibit Romantic qualities. This diversity in the different qualities illustrated in the two poems is what lends to the permanance of Romanticism through the centuries.

Response (2):

Coleridge vs. Poe
"Kubla Khan" vs. "The Raven"
What Makes Them Romantics?

Expressions of ecstacy, strangeness, and freedom begin to unfold the ideas shared among Romanticists. Two poets who breathe the romantic air are Samuel Taylor Coleridge and Edgar Allen Poe. From their various selections attention will center around two in particular. They are Coleridge's mystifying "Kubla Khan" and "The Raven" by Poe. Through these poems we will understand why both artists are classified as Romanticists.

We begin with, The Romantic Movement is a free movement. It allows the writer to make full use of his unlimited imagination. Coleridge certainly uses this source, for his poem is a recollection of a dream. He creates an enchanted land where a sacred river flows, gorgeous gardens grow, and radiant caves of ice exist. Idealism pours forth. Romanticism is therefore synonymous with idealism in the sense that extraordinary pictures are formed. Coleridge calls his utopia a "paradise." Certainly a utopia is far more wonderful than an ordinary world.

Poe's approach is slightly different. When dealing with the imagination, he tends to comprehend psychological truths; these truths that people cannot grasp in ordinary ways. His longing for Lenore throughout "The Raven" emphasizes this point.

The informal, wild, and irregular patterns of Romanticism also incorporate moments of restlessness. Both authors deal with this factor. When anomosity rares, Coleridge wails ". . . Beware, Beware!/His flashing eyes, his floating hair/Weaves a circle round him thrice." A definite wave of turbulence is implanted. This shakey atmosphere provides a source of adventure; also a characteristic of Romanticism. In Poe's case, uneasiness appears throughout "The Raven." First, when he jumps up to open the shutter after hearing an intruder tap, next as he becomes frustrated when the raven will utter no word but "Nevermore." Literally, the fact that Poe cannot sleep does suggest restlessness.

A staid and melancholic tone finalizes Poe's poem as he says, "And my soul from out that shadow that lies floating on the floor/Shall be lifted -- nevermore!" He alone adds this particular trait to his grave poem. Both Poe and Coleridge deal highly with emotions. Poe, in a grim manner, and the latter in a wild impressionate form. In regards to the second one, I am referring to the moment we read that a wild lady screeches for her lover. The shining moon lends an appropriate atmosphere to the scene.

Suggestions of beauty are evident in two different ways. Through word choices like "sinuous rills" and "dancing rocks," Coleridge suggests splendor. In turn Poe's constant use of internal rhyme has the same effect. Repetition is another tricky device that Poe takes full advantage of. By repeating a segment of the last line of each stanza, the work "Evermore" is converted to "Nothing More," then to "Nevermore." This illustrates another characteristic of Romanticism. It is the ability to smoothly shift moods. Poe's talent carried him through successfully.

Romanticists tend to be very subjective. So too are these poets. The land of Xanadu is Coleridge's personal creation. It is not simply an illustration of a borrowed idea. The sorrow and terror expressed in "The Raven" is very personalized.

Kubla Khan obeys the notion of presenting an idea that is remote in time and place. For example, it is rather unusual to hear of a woman howling like a coyote for her lover. Today such emotions are rather subdued. This illustration also introduces a sense of peculiarity. The excerpt that reads, "And 'mid this tumult Kubla Khan heard from far/Ancestral voices prophesying war," is rather ironic. For while Coleridge wishes to shut off all fears, his dreams are troubled by thoughts that encompass wars within his imaginary world. Poe addresses the Raven as he pleads for the return of Lenore. Yet the bird is a symbol of death.

As stated at the start, a favorable part of romanticism is expressed through highly ecstatic lines and phrases. Even though Poe chooses to omit this idea from his writings, Coleridge instinctively dreams of such happiness. To express his inner hope, he reverts to nature through the descriptions --- incense bearing trees, hills, waves, and caves. From free styles down to the use of odd subject matter, both poets live up to their names and both poets have broken the rigid expectations of Classicists. They are surely Romanticists.

Question 2 (Suggested time - 30 minutes)

Directions: Choose a literary work and discuss the relationships of the major characters. You may base your essay on work by one of the following authors, or you may choose a work of another author of comparable literary excellence.

Sophocles	William Butler Yeats
Harold Pinter	William Wordsworth
Anton Chekhov	Nathaniel Hawthorne
Robert Frost	Henrik Ibsen
T.S. Eliot	Alfred Lord Tennyson
Tennessee Williams	Leo Tolstoy
James Joyce	William Faulkner
George Orwell	Sylvia Plath
Dylan Thomas	Virginia Woolf
Charles Dickens	James Baldwin
John Keats	Miguel de Cervantes

Response:

"Foreshadowing in Anna Karenina"

The first chapter in any book is usually very important, providing insight into the characters as well as foreshadowing of what is to come. Such is the case with Anna Karenina. Tolstoy gives the reader descriptions of Anna, Levin, and Vronsky in Part I, which if taken at face value are detailed, accurate, and well-done. However, Tolstoy does not just want us to think how pretty Anna's gray misty eyes are but rather why they are misty and how this fact will affect the outcome of the novel. He wants us to make a connection between their looks and habits and the role they play or will play in the novel. To do this I have decided to concentrate on three main characters - Anna, Levin, and Vronsky - as they appear in Part I.

The first of the three characters to appear is Levin. Levin enters the novel in a customary burst of frankness and intense conviction.

> "Levin arrived in Moscow always excited and in a hurry, rather ill at ease and irritated by his own want of ease ... with a perfectly new unexpected view of things."

In this passage, Stiva's description of Levin, he appears to be headstrong but childish. From Levin's first physical description -- strongly built, broad-shouldered -- one would probably draw the conclusion that Levin was a grown mature man with responsibilities and burdens he must bear. In fact Levin and Oblonsky are almost the same age. But in truth Levin is immature and does not act like a man. The potential is there in the physical description but then Tolstoy says,

> "Levin suddenly blushed, not as grown up people blush ... but as boys blush."

This statement attests to the way Levin acts with Kitty. This childishness and immaturity is prominent throughout the novel. Early in Levin and Kitty's marriage Levin becomes jealous when Vassenka pays more attention than necessary to Kitty. However, it is because of his childish nature that he begins to realize that this married love is too changeable and delicate to base his whole life on. This foreshadows the moment when Levin finds supreme comfort in religion rather than in material happiness.

Count Vronsky is introduced in quite the opposite way implying Vronsky's attractiveness as well as his rigidity, Stiva characterizes him as "a perfect specimen of Petersburg's gilded youth." Vronsky's first appearance in the novel, however, is accompanied by a harsh remark from Prince Scherbatsky: "This one is a St. Petersburg dandy. They are all machine-made, all the same and all rubbish." This remark is not an accidental slip of the tongue, it will come to characterize Vronsky. Despite having intense interests -- horse racing, politics, his regiment -- Vronsky's life depends on various self-gratifications. He does not find anything "bad" in his behavior toward Kitty, although it has a "definite name: enticing young ladies without the intention of marriage." Vronsky does not understand this because seducing young ladies and other "bad" deeds are widespread occurences "among brilliant young people like him" and are not expected to elicit any sense of remorse or repentance. He has no inner core of identity as Levin has, for his career depends on winning favors from the "powerful in this world." Vronsky's supposed love for Kitty foreshadows his love for Anna, neither of which will endure. He is incapable of responsibility to others and it is this incapability which sets up his conflict with Anna.

We first hear of Anna in connection with her brother Stiva and his wife Dolly, where she intends to arrive at Moscow to repair their broken marriage. This is an ironic foreshadowing because as a result of the journey it is her own marriage she breaks up. The scene where she first meets Vronsky is at the railroad station. It is the place where she arrives and it is ultimately the place where she will depart. Once in Moscow Anna confronts a new destiny and enters a foreign world. As Anna is leaving the station there is an accident in which a man is killed under the train wheels. This "evil omen" which makes Anna shudder foreshadows her doom.

What is outstanding in Anna is her charm and fascination, apparent to Vronsky as their glances first met ... "Vronsky had time to notice the suppressed eagerness which played over her face and flitted between the brilliant eyes ... her shining grey eyes rested on his face as though she were recognizing him, and then promptly turned away as though she were looking for someone else ..." In this passage Anna realizes, when she sees Vronsky, that their relationship will be more than just that of passing acquaintances. But Anna tries to hide her feelings. The fact that the eagerness is suppressed shows that Anna is in control over Vronsky even from the very beginning. The smile that plays over her face and the allusion to her "shining grey eyes" suggests something almost diabolical in her nature and foreshadows her future with Vronsky. Anna, however, is too capable of deep and strong passions to keep her emotions hidden for long. "It was as though her nature were so brimming over with something that was against her will, it showed itself now in the flash of her eyes and smile. Deliberately she shrouded the light in her eyes." This passage indicates that her capacity for love has not yet been awakened. She is forcing herself to keep her exictement within herself and not let Vronsky realize its existence. The more she is in love the less she is visible to us. She begins to be a center of isolation and unreality. She becomes a symbol of this for Kitty, in the first part, who admired her so much and imagined her at the ball in a lilac dress. But instead she comes in black. This isolates her from Kitty and is the first step toward the life of isolation she will lead after her marriage to Vronsky.

What crushes Anna most at the end is her sense of isolation, as foreshadowed in Part I with Kitty. It is her sense of being outcast from the kind of society in which she is most naturally at home, and where at the beginning of the book she was at home, that gives Anna her final despair. Ordinary society has not so much excluded Anna as simply failed to see how much she needs it. She has become accepted as being a different sort of person, and to her this is the final loneliness.

Question 3 (Suggested time - 50 minutes)

Directions: Select a literary work of your choice and develop a single topic of interest.

Response (1):

"Birkin vs. Loerke: ART"

Through a vital conversation in one of the closing chapters of Women in Love, one may come to realize the importance of the question of art in relation to the rest of the work. Represented are principally two views on art: the Birkin/Ursula view and the Loerke/Gudrun view. Possibly one's entire understanding and basic interpretation of the work rests on his basic conception of art. Certainly Lawrence's view, as hypothetically represented by Birkin/Ursula, should be considered more important in this aspect. In this paper I intend to contrast the two views, placing more emphasis on the Birkin view.

If one is aware of it, one is able to observe Birkin's view of art throughout most of the work and is presented with no counter view until near the end of the book in a major confrontation between Loerke/Gudrun and even Gerald opposing Ursula. Throughout, Lawrence, as Birkin, has built up the idea of sensuality, without being obviously sexual, of spontaneity, of life as life itself without any deliberate controls. This applies to everything one does. In the chapter where the statue of the "savage woman in labor" first appears Gerald and Birkin are opposed in their views of the statue. Gerald hates it yet Birkin believes:

> 'It is art,' said Birkin.
> 'Why is it art?' Gerald asked.
> 'It conveys a complete truth ... it is an awful pitch of culture ... pure culture in sensation - in ultimate physical consciousness, mindless, utterly sensual. It is so sensual as to be final, supreme.' (p. 71)

This is Birkin's ultimate statement on art. In "A Chair," Birkin thinks a certain chair is beautiful, i.e., a work of art. An extremely sensual description is given of it. Its beauty "almost brought tears to the eyes." Again, Lawrence sees something behind the obvious beauty of the chair. The culture of a people, important in creating the statue of the "savage woman," is also prevalent in creating the chair. Birkin sighs, "My beloved country - it had something to express even when it made that chair." (p. 347). The obvious points Birkin made on art are: 1) sensuality; 2) mindlessness in the creating of the work of art; and 3) the influence of culture - background.

Birkin laments that true art isn't and can't be produced in the present day world. He states that "there is only sordid and foul mechanicalness." The people of today are too materialistic and mechanistic because there is nothing else for them to become. They are not capable of being anything else.

> "You've got to lapse into unknowingness, and give up your volition. You've got to learn no-to-be, before you can come into being." (p. 37)

This the modern man cannot do and he is therefore probably doomed in Lawrence's eyes.

All these qualities are to a greater or lesser degree present in Birkin. To him, they seem not just to represent qualities found in art, but those which must be present in one's life. Lawrence then must have believed that life, if lived wonderfully and correctly, was in itself an art.

As Ursula and Birkin become closer mentally and physically, Ursula gradually takes on more of Birkin's traits and ideas. This becomes obvious soon after their marriage. By the end of the book Birkin's visibility has shrunk so that at major confrontations among the prominent characters of the work, Birkin is generally supplanted by Ursula who represents both her's and Birkin's, and therefore Lawrence's, ideas. This is true in the aforementioned confrontation between Loerke/Gudrun and Ursula.

The portion of the scene which I am investigating opens with Gudrun and Loerke talking shop. It is interesting to note that they spend much time discussing technicalities - something which Birkin would never do. Loerke has strikingly different ideas of art:

> "Machinery and the acts of labour are extremely, maddeningly beautiful."
>
> "Art should interpret industry."
>
> "Sculpture and architecture must go together."

Loerke believes that a work of art should be planned and created not simply spun out of one's head. (Perhaps one can detect a note of irony here as the entire book <u>Women in Love</u> was rather quickly spun off the top of Lawrence's head.) Mechanics is beautiful, and there is nothing but mechanics and mechanics as work in the world today. He also, contradictory to Birkin, believes that any integral part of "a work of art has no relation to anything outside that work of art." (p. 420).

Loerke shows Gudrun an earlier, less mechanistic, more sensitive, work of his -- the bronze statuette. Ursula confronts him with the statement that it isn't sensitive at all and is horribly unrealistic. She furiously states that the horse is himself and the girl-rider one whom he had loved, etc. Loerke snorts:

> "It is a work of art, it is a picture - of absolutely nothing. It has nothing to do with anything but itself ... no relation with the everyday world of this and other ..."

Gudrun also says to Ursula, "<u>I</u> and my art, they have <u>nothing</u> to do with each other. My art stands in another world, I am in this world." (all on p. 420). These are the Loerke/Gudrun ultimate and radically different statements on art.

These very different attitudes on art reflect remarkably different personalities and attitudes on life. After seeing the relation of characters to attitude, perhaps you can see how this could relate to individual successes and failures in life. The Birkin/Ursula view is, in my eyes, more idealistic. But these two people are more willing to confront themselves in the things they do. More willing to know each other, and themselves through each other. It is these two, and only these two who find happiness, who are capable of creating happiness - a true art. Gudrun and Loerke are both personal failures. They fantasize about their lives the way they should be, but they do not seem to know what it is they want or how to obtain it. This is reflected in their concept of art. Failing to recognize their art as a part of themselves, they also fail to confront themselves in their art - and their life. Without recognizing this, like Birkin and Ursula, they will never even come close to being truly happy.

Response (2):

"Symbolism in Chapter XXVI: A Chair"

In this paper I will concentrate on how Gerald is symbolized by the young man and how the chair symbolizes Gerald and Birkin's relationship.

Throughout the scene, the young man if repeatedly likened to a rat. A rat is a water creature, a gutter presence.

> "He was impassive, abstract, like some dark suggestive presence, a gutter presence."

Gerald is often connected with water, e.g., the water party and his tragic death. He freezes to death in the snow. He is also connected with underground life. He is in charge of the mines and takes great satisfaction in improving and operating them.

Another aspect of the young man that leads one to feel he symbolizes Gerald is Ursula's impression of him. She is attracted to him.

> "He was a still mindless creature, hardly a man at all, ..., strangely purebred and fine in one sense, furtive, quick, subtle. ... He would be a dreadful, but wonderful lover to a woman, so marvellously contributed. ... he had some of the fineness and stillness and silkiness of a dark-eyed, silent rat."

This, in essence, is how Ursula regards Gerald. He is physical, mundane. He does not possess the spiritual aspects found in Birkin's character.

The young man is also regarded as one of the damned. Throughout his encounter with Ursula and Birkin and while his fiance bargains for a mattress, he stands aloof and if furtive. Birkin sympathizes with him. Gerald is also "one of the damned."

There are references throughout the novel to the brother he killed and that because of that accident, he is in some way "cursed," he stands apart from everyone else, he is aloof.

Death, for him, is tragic. It serves to illuminate the fact that his physical powers weren't wholly adequate to sustain a meaningful relationship with not only himself, but with others. So, in the end, he is damned because he cannot achieve an ultimate relationship on a more spiritual plane. Birkin also sympathizes with him and finally pities him when this relationship cannot exist.

One can see then that the young man represents Gerald not only in physical description and impressions he projects to others but in his mental attitude as well.

Gerald and Birkin's relationship is also discussed in this chapter; first symbolically, through the chair, and secondly, by Ursula and Gerald at the end of the chapter.

The description of the chair is one of beauty. The chair is graceful, square in shape, of the purest, slender lines. Birkin thinks it is very beautiful. He also thinks Gerald is beautiful. Gerald is fair, suntanned, well-made, he has clear northern flesh, and his hair "glistened like sunshine refracted through crystals of ice." He has a golden, bronzed look about him. The chair was once gilded and had a cane seat. Its symmetry matched Gerald's beauty.

However, it has one flaw -- and this symbolizes the flaw, the missing link, in Gerald and Birkin's relationship; it has a wooden seat someone had nailed in. The wooden seat ruins the perfect symmetry and delicateness of the chair. Gerald's inability to achieve a spiritual relationship with Birkin is the flaw in their relationship.

When Ursula rebels against the materialism the chair represents, she is actually rebelling against the two men's relationship. And when Birkin consents to giving up the chair, he is unconsciously giving up his ultimate relationship with Gerald. This act could be foreshadowing. He makes a choice between materialism and spiritualism, and in giving away the chair, chooses the latter. Later on, he must choose between Ursula and Gerald. With which one can he have a more perfect relationship? He chooses Ursula.

In conclusion, the description of the chair corresponds with Birkin's idea of Gerald's physical appearance. The chair is imperfect as is the two men's relationship, and by giving the chair to the young people, Birkin relinquishes their relationship. It is also symbolic that he gave the chair to the young man who symbolizes Gerald. It is as if he is withdrawing from his side of the relationship with Gerald and leaving the latter with the remnants of what "could have been." This is just what he does when he gives his preference to Ursula instead of Gerald.

1 Ⓐ Ⓑ Ⓒ Ⓓ Ⓔ	26 Ⓐ Ⓑ Ⓒ Ⓓ Ⓔ	51 Ⓐ Ⓑ Ⓒ Ⓓ Ⓔ	76 Ⓐ Ⓑ Ⓒ Ⓓ Ⓔ	101 Ⓐ Ⓑ Ⓒ Ⓓ Ⓔ	126 Ⓐ Ⓑ Ⓒ Ⓓ Ⓔ
2 Ⓐ Ⓑ Ⓒ Ⓓ Ⓔ	27 Ⓐ Ⓑ Ⓒ Ⓓ Ⓔ	52 Ⓐ Ⓑ Ⓒ Ⓓ Ⓔ	77 Ⓐ Ⓑ Ⓒ Ⓓ Ⓔ	102 Ⓐ Ⓑ Ⓒ Ⓓ Ⓔ	127 Ⓐ Ⓑ Ⓒ Ⓓ Ⓔ
3 Ⓐ Ⓑ Ⓒ Ⓓ Ⓔ	28 Ⓐ Ⓑ Ⓒ Ⓓ Ⓔ	53 Ⓐ Ⓑ Ⓒ Ⓓ Ⓔ	78 Ⓐ Ⓑ Ⓒ Ⓓ Ⓔ	103 Ⓐ Ⓑ Ⓒ Ⓓ Ⓔ	128 Ⓐ Ⓑ Ⓒ Ⓓ Ⓔ
4 Ⓐ Ⓑ Ⓒ Ⓓ Ⓔ	29 Ⓐ Ⓑ Ⓒ Ⓓ Ⓔ	54 Ⓐ Ⓑ Ⓒ Ⓓ Ⓔ	79 Ⓐ Ⓑ Ⓒ Ⓓ Ⓔ	104 Ⓐ Ⓑ Ⓒ Ⓓ Ⓔ	129 Ⓐ Ⓑ Ⓒ Ⓓ Ⓔ
5 Ⓐ Ⓑ Ⓒ Ⓓ Ⓔ	30 Ⓐ Ⓑ Ⓒ Ⓓ Ⓔ	55 Ⓐ Ⓑ Ⓒ Ⓓ Ⓔ	80 Ⓐ Ⓑ Ⓒ Ⓓ Ⓔ	105 Ⓐ Ⓑ Ⓒ Ⓓ Ⓔ	130 Ⓐ Ⓑ Ⓒ Ⓓ Ⓔ
6 Ⓐ Ⓑ Ⓒ Ⓓ Ⓔ	31 Ⓐ Ⓑ Ⓒ Ⓓ Ⓔ	56 Ⓐ Ⓑ Ⓒ Ⓓ Ⓔ	81 Ⓐ Ⓑ Ⓒ Ⓓ Ⓔ	106 Ⓐ Ⓑ Ⓒ Ⓓ Ⓔ	131 Ⓐ Ⓑ Ⓒ Ⓓ Ⓔ
7 Ⓐ Ⓑ Ⓒ Ⓓ Ⓔ	32 Ⓐ Ⓑ Ⓒ Ⓓ Ⓔ	57 Ⓐ Ⓑ Ⓒ Ⓓ Ⓔ	82 Ⓐ Ⓑ Ⓒ Ⓓ Ⓔ	107 Ⓐ Ⓑ Ⓒ Ⓓ Ⓔ	132 Ⓐ Ⓑ Ⓒ Ⓓ Ⓔ
8 Ⓐ Ⓑ Ⓒ Ⓓ Ⓔ	33 Ⓐ Ⓑ Ⓒ Ⓓ Ⓔ	58 Ⓐ Ⓑ Ⓒ Ⓓ Ⓔ	83 Ⓐ Ⓑ Ⓒ Ⓓ Ⓔ	108 Ⓐ Ⓑ Ⓒ Ⓓ Ⓔ	133 Ⓐ Ⓑ Ⓒ Ⓓ Ⓔ
9 Ⓐ Ⓑ Ⓒ Ⓓ Ⓔ	34 Ⓐ Ⓑ Ⓒ Ⓓ Ⓔ	59 Ⓐ Ⓑ Ⓒ Ⓓ Ⓔ	84 Ⓐ Ⓑ Ⓒ Ⓓ Ⓔ	109 Ⓐ Ⓑ Ⓒ Ⓓ Ⓔ	134 Ⓐ Ⓑ Ⓒ Ⓓ Ⓔ
10 Ⓐ Ⓑ Ⓒ Ⓓ Ⓔ	35 Ⓐ Ⓑ Ⓒ Ⓓ Ⓔ	60 Ⓐ Ⓑ Ⓒ Ⓓ Ⓔ	85 Ⓐ Ⓑ Ⓒ Ⓓ Ⓔ	110 Ⓐ Ⓑ Ⓒ Ⓓ Ⓔ	135 Ⓐ Ⓑ Ⓒ Ⓓ Ⓔ
11 Ⓐ Ⓑ Ⓒ Ⓓ Ⓔ	36 Ⓐ Ⓑ Ⓒ Ⓓ Ⓔ	61 Ⓐ Ⓑ Ⓒ Ⓓ Ⓔ	86 Ⓐ Ⓑ Ⓒ Ⓓ Ⓔ	111 Ⓐ Ⓑ Ⓒ Ⓓ Ⓔ	136 Ⓐ Ⓑ Ⓒ Ⓓ Ⓔ
12 Ⓐ Ⓑ Ⓒ Ⓓ Ⓔ	37 Ⓐ Ⓑ Ⓒ Ⓓ Ⓔ	62 Ⓐ Ⓑ Ⓒ Ⓓ Ⓔ	87 Ⓐ Ⓑ Ⓒ Ⓓ Ⓔ	112 Ⓐ Ⓑ Ⓒ Ⓓ Ⓔ	137 Ⓐ Ⓑ Ⓒ Ⓓ Ⓔ
13 Ⓐ Ⓑ Ⓒ Ⓓ Ⓔ	38 Ⓐ Ⓑ Ⓒ Ⓓ Ⓔ	63 Ⓐ Ⓑ Ⓒ Ⓓ Ⓔ	88 Ⓐ Ⓑ Ⓒ Ⓓ Ⓔ	113 Ⓐ Ⓑ Ⓒ Ⓓ Ⓔ	138 Ⓐ Ⓑ Ⓒ Ⓓ Ⓔ
14 Ⓐ Ⓑ Ⓒ Ⓓ Ⓔ	39 Ⓐ Ⓑ Ⓒ Ⓓ Ⓔ	64 Ⓐ Ⓑ Ⓒ Ⓓ Ⓔ	89 Ⓐ Ⓑ Ⓒ Ⓓ Ⓔ	114 Ⓐ Ⓑ Ⓒ Ⓓ Ⓔ	139 Ⓐ Ⓑ Ⓒ Ⓓ Ⓔ
15 Ⓐ Ⓑ Ⓒ Ⓓ Ⓔ	40 Ⓐ Ⓑ Ⓒ Ⓓ Ⓔ	65 Ⓐ Ⓑ Ⓒ Ⓓ Ⓔ	90 Ⓐ Ⓑ Ⓒ Ⓓ Ⓔ	115 Ⓐ Ⓑ Ⓒ Ⓓ Ⓔ	140 Ⓐ Ⓑ Ⓒ Ⓓ Ⓔ
16 Ⓐ Ⓑ Ⓒ Ⓓ Ⓔ	41 Ⓐ Ⓑ Ⓒ Ⓓ Ⓔ	66 Ⓐ Ⓑ Ⓒ Ⓓ Ⓔ	91 Ⓐ Ⓑ Ⓒ Ⓓ Ⓔ	116 Ⓐ Ⓑ Ⓒ Ⓓ Ⓔ	141 Ⓐ Ⓑ Ⓒ Ⓓ Ⓔ
17 Ⓐ Ⓑ Ⓒ Ⓓ Ⓔ	42 Ⓐ Ⓑ Ⓒ Ⓓ Ⓔ	67 Ⓐ Ⓑ Ⓒ Ⓓ Ⓔ	92 Ⓐ Ⓑ Ⓒ Ⓓ Ⓔ	117 Ⓐ Ⓑ Ⓒ Ⓓ Ⓔ	142 Ⓐ Ⓑ Ⓒ Ⓓ Ⓔ
18 Ⓐ Ⓑ Ⓒ Ⓓ Ⓔ	43 Ⓐ Ⓑ Ⓒ Ⓓ Ⓔ	68 Ⓐ Ⓑ Ⓒ Ⓓ Ⓔ	93 Ⓐ Ⓑ Ⓒ Ⓓ Ⓔ	118 Ⓐ Ⓑ Ⓒ Ⓓ Ⓔ	143 Ⓐ Ⓑ Ⓒ Ⓓ Ⓔ
19 Ⓐ Ⓑ Ⓒ Ⓓ Ⓔ	44 Ⓐ Ⓑ Ⓒ Ⓓ Ⓔ	69 Ⓐ Ⓑ Ⓒ Ⓓ Ⓔ	94 Ⓐ Ⓑ Ⓒ Ⓓ Ⓔ	119 Ⓐ Ⓑ Ⓒ Ⓓ Ⓔ	144 Ⓐ Ⓑ Ⓒ Ⓓ Ⓔ
20 Ⓐ Ⓑ Ⓒ Ⓓ Ⓔ	45 Ⓐ Ⓑ Ⓒ Ⓓ Ⓔ	70 Ⓐ Ⓑ Ⓒ Ⓓ Ⓔ	95 Ⓐ Ⓑ Ⓒ Ⓓ Ⓔ	120 Ⓐ Ⓑ Ⓒ Ⓓ Ⓔ	145 Ⓐ Ⓑ Ⓒ Ⓓ Ⓔ
21 Ⓐ Ⓑ Ⓒ Ⓓ Ⓔ	46 Ⓐ Ⓑ Ⓒ Ⓓ Ⓔ	71 Ⓐ Ⓑ Ⓒ Ⓓ Ⓔ	96 Ⓐ Ⓑ Ⓒ Ⓓ Ⓔ	121 Ⓐ Ⓑ Ⓒ Ⓓ Ⓔ	146 Ⓐ Ⓑ Ⓒ Ⓓ Ⓔ
22 Ⓐ Ⓑ Ⓒ Ⓓ Ⓔ	47 Ⓐ Ⓑ Ⓒ Ⓓ Ⓔ	72 Ⓐ Ⓑ Ⓒ Ⓓ Ⓔ	97 Ⓐ Ⓑ Ⓒ Ⓓ Ⓔ	122 Ⓐ Ⓑ Ⓒ Ⓓ Ⓔ	147 Ⓐ Ⓑ Ⓒ Ⓓ Ⓔ
23 Ⓐ Ⓑ Ⓒ Ⓓ Ⓔ	48 Ⓐ Ⓑ Ⓒ Ⓓ Ⓔ	73 Ⓐ Ⓑ Ⓒ Ⓓ Ⓔ	98 Ⓐ Ⓑ Ⓒ Ⓓ Ⓔ	123 Ⓐ Ⓑ Ⓒ Ⓓ Ⓔ	148 Ⓐ Ⓑ Ⓒ Ⓓ Ⓔ
24 Ⓐ Ⓑ Ⓒ Ⓓ Ⓔ	49 Ⓐ Ⓑ Ⓒ Ⓓ Ⓔ	74 Ⓐ Ⓑ Ⓒ Ⓓ Ⓔ	99 Ⓐ Ⓑ Ⓒ Ⓓ Ⓔ	124 Ⓐ Ⓑ Ⓒ Ⓓ Ⓔ	149 Ⓐ Ⓑ Ⓒ Ⓓ Ⓔ
25 Ⓐ Ⓑ Ⓒ Ⓓ Ⓔ	50 Ⓐ Ⓑ Ⓒ Ⓓ Ⓔ	75 Ⓐ Ⓑ Ⓒ Ⓓ Ⓔ	100 Ⓐ Ⓑ Ⓒ Ⓓ Ⓔ	125 Ⓐ Ⓑ Ⓒ Ⓓ Ⓔ	150 Ⓐ Ⓑ Ⓒ Ⓓ Ⓔ

1 (A) (B) (C) (D) (E)	26 (A) (B) (C) (D) (E)	51 (A) (B) (C) (D) (E)	76 (A) (B) (C) (D) (E)	101 (A) (B) (C) (D) (E)	126 (A) (B) (C) (D) (E)
2 (A) (B) (C) (D) (E)	27 (A) (B) (C) (D) (E)	52 (A) (B) (C) (D) (E)	77 (A) (B) (C) (D) (E)	102 (A) (B) (C) (D) (E)	127 (A) (B) (C) (D) (E)
3 (A) (B) (C) (D) (E)	28 (A) (B) (C) (D) (E)	53 (A) (B) (C) (D) (E)	78 (A) (B) (C) (D) (E)	103 (A) (B) (C) (D) (E)	128 (A) (B) (C) (D) (E)
4 (A) (B) (C) (D) (E)	29 (A) (B) (C) (D) (E)	54 (A) (B) (C) (D) (E)	79 (A) (B) (C) (D) (E)	104 (A) (B) (C) (D) (E)	129 (A) (B) (C) (D) (E)
5 (A) (B) (C) (D) (E)	30 (A) (B) (C) (D) (E)	55 (A) (B) (C) (D) (E)	80 (A) (B) (C) (D) (E)	105 (A) (B) (C) (D) (E)	130 (A) (B) (C) (D) (E)
6 (A) (B) (C) (D) (E)	31 (A) (B) (C) (D) (E)	56 (A) (B) (C) (D) (E)	81 (A) (B) (C) (D) (E)	106 (A) (B) (C) (D) (E)	131 (A) (B) (C) (D) (E)
7 (A) (B) (C) (D) (E)	32 (A) (B) (C) (D) (E)	57 (A) (B) (C) (D) (E)	82 (A) (B) (C) (D) (E)	107 (A) (B) (C) (D) (E)	132 (A) (B) (C) (D) (E)
8 (A) (B) (C) (D) (E)	33 (A) (B) (C) (D) (E)	58 (A) (B) (C) (D) (E)	83 (A) (B) (C) (D) (E)	108 (A) (B) (C) (D) (E)	133 (A) (B) (C) (D) (E)
9 (A) (B) (C) (D) (E)	34 (A) (B) (C) (D) (E)	59 (A) (B) (C) (D) (E)	84 (A) (B) (C) (D) (E)	109 (A) (B) (C) (D) (E)	134 (A) (B) (C) (D) (E)
10 (A) (B) (C) (D) (E)	35 (A) (B) (C) (D) (E)	60 (A) (B) (C) (D) (E)	85 (A) (B) (C) (D) (E)	110 (A) (B) (C) (D) (E)	135 (A) (B) (C) (D) (E)
11 (A) (B) (C) (D) (E)	36 (A) (B) (C) (D) (E)	61 (A) (B) (C) (D) (E)	86 (A) (B) (C) (D) (E)	111 (A) (B) (C) (D) (E)	136 (A) (B) (C) (D) (E)
12 (A) (B) (C) (D) (E)	37 (A) (B) (C) (D) (E)	62 (A) (B) (C) (D) (E)	87 (A) (B) (C) (D) (E)	112 (A) (B) (C) (D) (E)	137 (A) (B) (C) (D) (E)
13 (A) (B) (C) (D) (E)	38 (A) (B) (C) (D) (E)	63 (A) (B) (C) (D) (E)	88 (A) (B) (C) (D) (E)	113 (A) (B) (C) (D) (E)	138 (A) (B) (C) (D) (E)
14 (A) (B) (C) (D) (E)	39 (A) (B) (C) (D) (E)	64 (A) (B) (C) (D) (E)	89 (A) (B) (C) (D) (E)	114 (A) (B) (C) (D) (E)	139 (A) (B) (C) (D) (E)
15 (A) (B) (C) (D) (E)	40 (A) (B) (C) (D) (E)	65 (A) (B) (C) (D) (E)	90 (A) (B) (C) (D) (E)	115 (A) (B) (C) (D) (E)	140 (A) (B) (C) (D) (E)
16 (A) (B) (C) (D) (E)	41 (A) (B) (C) (D) (E)	66 (A) (B) (C) (D) (E)	91 (A) (B) (C) (D) (E)	116 (A) (B) (C) (D) (E)	141 (A) (B) (C) (D) (E)
17 (A) (B) (C) (D) (E)	42 (A) (B) (C) (D) (E)	67 (A) (B) (C) (D) (E)	92 (A) (B) (C) (D) (E)	117 (A) (B) (C) (D) (E)	142 (A) (B) (C) (D) (E)
18 (A) (B) (C) (D) (E)	43 (A) (B) (C) (D) (E)	68 (A) (B) (C) (D) (E)	93 (A) (B) (C) (D) (E)	118 (A) (B) (C) (D) (E)	143 (A) (B) (C) (D) (E)
19 (A) (B) (C) (D) (E)	44 (A) (B) (C) (D) (E)	69 (A) (B) (C) (D) (E)	94 (A) (B) (C) (D) (E)	119 (A) (B) (C) (D) (E)	144 (A) (B) (C) (D) (E)
20 (A) (B) (C) (D) (E)	45 (A) (B) (C) (D) (E)	70 (A) (B) (C) (D) (E)	95 (A) (B) (C) (D) (E)	120 (A) (B) (C) (D) (E)	145 (A) (B) (C) (D) (E)
21 (A) (B) (C) (D) (E)	46 (A) (B) (C) (D) (E)	71 (A) (B) (C) (D) (E)	96 (A) (B) (C) (D) (E)	121 (A) (B) (C) (D) (E)	146 (A) (B) (C) (D) (E)
22 (A) (B) (C) (D) (E)	47 (A) (B) (C) (D) (E)	72 (A) (B) (C) (D) (E)	97 (A) (B) (C) (D) (E)	122 (A) (B) (C) (D) (E)	147 (A) (B) (C) (D) (E)
23 (A) (B) (C) (D) (E)	48 (A) (B) (C) (D) (E)	73 (A) (B) (C) (D) (E)	98 (A) (B) (C) (D) (E)	123 (A) (B) (C) (D) (E)	148 (A) (B) (C) (D) (E)
24 (A) (B) (C) (D) (E)	49 (A) (B) (C) (D) (E)	74 (A) (B) (C) (D) (E)	99 (A) (B) (C) (D) (E)	124 (A) (B) (C) (D) (E)	149 (A) (B) (C) (D) (E)
25 (A) (B) (C) (D) (E)	50 (A) (B) (C) (D) (E)	75 (A) (B) (C) (D) (E)	100 (A) (B) (C) (D) (E)	125 (A) (B) (C) (D) (E)	150 (A) (B) (C) (D) (E)

THIRD PRACTICE AP/CLEP ENGLISH TEST
SECTION I

Directions: Select from the lettered choices that choice which best completes the statement or answers the question. Indicate the letter of your choice on the answer sheet.

1. "Why then, O brawling love! O loving hate!
   O anything! Of nothing first create.
   O heavy lightness! serious vanity!
   Misshapen chaos of well-seeming forms!"

   The above lines illustrate the use of

   (A) onomatopoeia
   (B) litotes
   (C) oxymoron
   (D) simile
   (E) hyperbole

2. In the <u>Book of Job</u>, Bildad the Shuhite

   (A) consoled Job
   (B) accompanied Job on his prilgrimage
   (C) justified Job's affliction at the hands of God
   (D) gloated over Job's misfortune
   (E) insulted Job

3. Each of the following groups of names is properly associated within the framework of a literary work except

   (A) Patroclus, Chryseis, Agamemnon
   (B) Scheherezade, Alladin, Sinbad
   (C) Franklin, Miller, Cook
   (D) Roland, Count Oliver, Griselda
   (E) Panurge, Pantagruel, Friar John

4. <u>Ancrene Riwle</u> was a

   (A) prose work written for the guidance of certain English recluses
   (B) forerunner of the medieval ballad
   (C) verse paraphrase of the Psalms
   (D) learned commentary on Genesis
   (E) set of monastic rules

5. Master Chaunticleer, Dame Pertelote, and Dan Russell, the Fox, all appear in Chaucer's

   (A) Wife of Bath's Tale
   (B) Friar's Tale
   (C) Pardoner's Tale
   (D) Squire's Tale
   (E) Nun's Priest's Tale

6. John Skelton's <u>Colin Cloute</u>, a satirical poem directed against ecclesiastical abuses, specifically attacks

   (A) Thomas Becket
   (B) Thomas More
   (C) Cardinal Wolsey
   (D) Archbishop Laud
   (E) St. Thomas Aquinas

7. In 1698, the license and obscenity of the English drama were attacked in a work entitled <u>Short View of the Immorality and Profaneness of the English Stage</u>, written by

   (A) Sir William D'Avenant
   (B) Sir Robert Walpole

(C) Jeremy Collier
(D) Jeremy Taylor
(E) Sir John Vanbrugh

8. The book most widely recognized as the best Arthurian story was done

(A) in free verse
(B) as a group of ballads
(C) in prose form
(D) partly in verse, partly in metrical form
(E) in none of the above

9. Navarre and Illyria are the locales respectively of

(A) Love's Labor Lost and Twelfth Night
(B) The Taming of the Shrew and The Merry Wives of Windsor
(C) Cymbeline and A Winter's Tale
(D) As You Like It and A Midsummer Night's Dream
(E) A Winter's Tale and As You Like It

10. "If thou be'est he-but oh how fallen! how unchanged
From him!-who in the happy realms of light,
Clothed with transcendent brightness, did'st outshine
Myriads, though bright..."

In Milton's <u>Paradise Lost</u>, the above lines are spoken to

(A) Beelzebub by Satan
(B) Satan by Michael
(C) Lucifer by Gabriel
(D) Baal by God
(E) Chaos by Baal

11. Edmund Spenser attacked some shortcomings of his society in

(A) Amoretti
(B) The Shepherd's Calendar
(C) Virgil's Gnat
(D) Astrophel
(E) The Faerie Queen

12. All of the following lines by John Milton are correctly paired with the titles of the works in which they appear except

(A) They hand in hand with wandring steps and slow,
Through Eden took their solitary way - Paradise Lost
(B) And calm of mind all passion spent - Samson Agonistes
(C) Or if Virtue feeble were
Heav'n itself would stoop to her - Paradise Regained
(D) At last he rose and twitched his Mantle blue
Tomorrow to fresh Woods, and Pastures new - Lycidas
(E) 'Tis Chastity, my brother, Chastity:
She that has that is clad in complete steel - Comus

13. The lines,
"He is a portion of the loveliness
Which once he made more lovely,"
are from a poem written as a tribute to

(A) Arthur Hugh Clough
(B) John Milton
(C) Percy Bysshe Shelley
(D) Thomas Chatterton
(E) John Keats

14. All of the following had strong elements of transcendentalism in their thinking except

(A) Walt Whitman
(B) Henry David Thoreau
(C) James Russell Lowell
(D) Theodore Parker
(E) Margaret Fuller

15. <u>Israfel</u> is an appellation associated with the author of the lines

(A) In Heaven a spirit doth dwell
Whose heartstrings are a lute
(B) Whither midst falling dew
While glow the heavens with the last steps of day
(C) This is the Arsenal. From floor to ceiling,
Like a huge organ, rise the burnished arms
(D) This is the ship of pearl, which, poets feign,
Sails the unshadowed main
(E) Her gentle limbs did she undress,
And lay down in her loveliness

16. Moliere's <u>Le Tartuffe</u> was intended as a satire on

 (A) snobbery
 (B) pedantry
 (C) religious hypocrisy
 (D) political treachery
 (E) quest for power

17. All of the following were known both as philosophers and as men of letters except

 (A) Louis Sullivan
 (B) George Santayana
 (C) Josiah Royce
 (D) William James
 (E) Ralph Waldo Emerson

18. The lines,
"The world stands out on either side
No wider than the heart is wide,"
are from the early poetry of

 (A) A. E. Housman
 (B) Siegfried Sassoon
 (C) Rupert Brooke
 (D) William Wordsworth
 (E) Edna St. Vincent Millay

19. All of the following American novels have their principal setting in Europe except

 (A) Dodsworth
 (B) The Golden Bowl
 (C) The Marble Faun
 (D) In Dubious Battle
 (E) The Sun Also Rises

20. <u>God's Angry Man</u>, by Leonard Ehrlich, is a fictionalized biography of

 (A) Daniel Webster
 (B) Paul Revere
 (C) Samuel Tilden
 (D) Martin Luther
 (E) John Brown

21. "I am bound by my own definition of criticism: a disinterested endeavor to learn and propagate the best that is known and thought in the world."

The line above is quoted from the work of

 (A) Herman Melville
 (B) Ralph Waldo Emerson
 (C) Edmund Wilson
 (D) Matthew Arnold
 (E) John Ruskin

22. All of the following one-act plays are correctly described except

 (A) The Valiant - A brother lies to his sister to put her mind at ease
 (B) Rider to the Sea - An American whaling captain tries to dissuade his sons from following in his footsteps
 (C) Spreading the News - A bit of gossip brings a humorous crisis to a village
 (D) Sorry, Wrong Number - A woman overhears the plan for her own murder
 (E) The Bet - A lawyer loses fifteen years of his life

23. Poems and their authors are correctly matched in all of the following except

 (A) The Rhodora - Ralph Waldo Emerson
 (B) Clarel - Herman Melville
 (C) Passage to India - Walt Whitman
 (D) Masque of Reason - Edwin Arlington Robinson
 (E) Anne Rutledge - Edgar Lee Masters

24. "'Warren?' she questioned.
'Dead,' was all he answered"
are the concluding lines of a poem written by the author of

 (A) The Whippoorwill
 (B) Hard Times
 (C) The Code
 (D) Western Star
 (E) Richard Cory

Directions for answering questions 25-32: The dots in each of the following poetry selections signify that a line has been omitted. Following each selection are suggested lines that may be substituted for the omitted line of poetry. For each suggested line, use the code below in order to arrive at your answer.

(A) appropriate
(B) not appropriate in rhythm or meter
(C) not appropriate in style or tone
(D) not appropriate in meaning
(E) ungrammatical

Then, too, alas! when she shall tear
  The lines some younger rival sends,
She'll give me leave to write, I
  fear,
  ....

25. And that's how our sad story ends.

26. Yet quicker youthful loving ends.

27. And we shall still continue friends.

28. Never more to be good friends.

How the robin feeds her young,
How the oriole's nest is hung;
Where the whitest lilies blow,
....

29. Where the weary farmers go.

30. Where bright-hued berries grow.

31. Where the berries grow and grow.

32. Where the freshest berries grow.

33. The story, Dr. Heidegger's Experiment, deals with a

(A) fatal landslide
(B) veil used as a mask
(C) search for the renewal of youth
(D) heart of stone
(E) a study of prehistoric monsters

34. The one of the following popularly known as Darwin's bulldog is

(A) Alfred Lord Tennyson
(B) Bertrand Russell
(C) Thomas Henry Huxley
(D) Pierre Simon LaPlace
(E) Henry Commager

35. "Art for art's sake" expresses the prevailing literary philosophy of

(A) Alfred Lord Tennyson
(B) Robert Browning
(C) Oscar Wilde
(D) John Davidson
(E) Thornton Wilder

36. The one of the following men of letters whose final days and burial place are clouded in obscurity is

(A) Edgar Allan Poe
(B) William Sidney Porter
(C) Ambrose Bierce
(D) Hamlin Garland
(E) Dylan Thomas

37. The metamorphosis of a man into a monstrous insect is the dominant theme of a work by

(A) Karel Capek
(B) Andre Malraux
(C) George Orwell
(D) Aldous Huxley
(E) Franz Kafka

38. The novel, One Day in the Life of Ivan Denisovich, by Alexander Solzhenitsyn, is concerned primarily with

(A) a Stalinish penal camp
(B) serfdom in Czarist Russia
(C) the execution of Nicholas II
(D) life on a collective farm
(E) the defeat of Hitler

39. "Treason doth never prosper; what's the reason?
Why, if it prosper, none dare call it treason"

The lines above illustrate

(A) a platitude
(B) a hokku
(C) an epigram
(D) a proverb
(E) a simile

40. A translation of the opening phrase of Virgil's "Aeneid" is the title of a play by

(A) Henrik Ibsen
(B) Edmond Rostand
(C) Ferenc Molnar
(D) George Bernard Shaw
(E) Elmer Rice

41. Each of the following mythical creatures has more than one head except

(A) Argus
(B) Hydra
(C) Cerberus
(D) Scylla
(E) Geryon

42. "Out of the eater came forth meat, and out the strong came forth sweetness" was a riddle put forth by

(A) Daniel
(B) Gideon
(C) Joshua
(D) Samson
(E) Samuel

43. The Pharsalia was

(A) an orgy
(B) an epic poem
(C) a religious rite
(D) a lighthouse
(E) a mystery ship

44. The York Plays, the Chester Plays, and the Townley Plays are all examples of

(A) interludes
(B) mystery cycles
(C) closet dramas
(D) morality plays
(E) dream plays

45. The host of the Tabard Inn where Chaucer and his fellow pilgrims assembled for their journey to Canterbury was named

(A) John Mandeville
(B) Harry Bailly
(C) Richard Holland
(D) George Turberville
(E) John Silver

46. Edward Hall, John Stow, and Raphael Holinshed were all

(A) members of Shakespeare's company
(B) historical chroniclers
(C) members of the "School of Night"
(D) writers of euphuistic poetry
(E) poets who wrote sonnets

47. The autobiographical story of John Bunyan's conversion and early experiences as a preacher is told in

(A) The Practice of Piety
(B) The Pilgrim's Progress
(C) Holy Living
(D) Grace Abounding
(E) Beauty and Love

48. "Man is born free, and everywhere he is in irons" was written by

(A) Thomas Paine
(B) Jean-Jacques Rousseau
(C) John Stuart Mill
(D) Benjamin Franklin
(E) Edmund Burke

49. Of the following combinations of Elizabethan plays and their authors, the one which is incorrectly paired is

(A) A Woman Killed With Kindness - Thomas Heywood
(B) The Duchess of Malfi - John Webster
(C) The Shoemaker's Holiday - Thomas Dekker
(D) The Changeling - Philip Massinger
(E) Taburlaine - Christopher Marlowe

50. Of the following, the play based on a murder actually committed in 1550 was

(A) Arden of Feversham
(B) Gorboduc
(C) Mother Bombie
(D) The Spanish Tragedy
(E) Judgment Day

51. Wyatt and Surrey's songs appeared in the well-known early collection of Elizabethan songs and sonnets, printed in 1557 and entitled

(A) Palladis Tamia
(B) England's Miscellany
(C) The Humming Bird

(D) The Passionate Pilgrim
(E) Tottel's Miscellany

52. "Faultily faultless, icily regular, splendidly null" is a criticism of one of his heroines by

(A) William Wordsworth
(B) Alfred Tennyson
(C) Rudyard Kipling
(D) Matthew Arnold
(E) Robert Browning

53. All of the following were Pulitzer Prize winners except

(A) The Caine Mutiny - Herman Wouk
(B) The Old Man and the Sea - Ernest Hemingway
(C) The Town - Conrad Richter
(D) Main Street - Sinclair Lewis
(E) The Reivers - William Faulkner

54. All of the following are based on the Arthurian legend except

(A) The Sword in the Stone
(B) Tom Thumb the Great
(C) Parsifal
(D) The Idylls of the King
(E) The Bride of Lammermoor

55. The only one of the following books that was not written by Thomas Love Peacock is

(A) Melincourt
(B) Gryll Grange
(C) The Misfortunes of Elphin
(D) Ravenshoe
(E) Crochet Castle

56. All of the following are traditional ballads of unknown authorship except

(A) The Two Sisters
(B) The King's Tragedy
(C) The Wife of Usher's Well
(D) Child Waters
(E) Kathrine Jaffray

57. Citizen of the World is a

(A) verse play about the American colonies
(B) satiric attack on George III
(C) translation from the Latin
(D) treatise on the deficiencies of democracy
(E) collection of letters professedly written by an imaginary Chinese philosopher

58. Of the following novels, the one that was not published in the 18th century is

(A) Evelina
(B) The Castle of Otranto
(C) Humphrey Clinker
(D) Old Mortality
(E) Gulliver's Travels

59. All of the following were actively associated with the Oxford English Dictionary except

(A) J. A. H. Murray
(B) Sir W. A. Craigie
(C) H. W. Fowler
(D) C. T. Onions
(E) H. Bradley

60. All of the following represent stories dealing with English school life except

(A) Thomas Hughes - Tom Brown's School Days
(B) James Hilton - Goodbye, Mr. Chips
(C) Rudyard Kipling - Salky & Co.
(D) George Meredith - Beauchamp's Career
(E) Dombey and Son - Charles Dickens

61. Floyd Ireson, in Skipper Ireson's Ride, was accused of

(A) ramming and sinking a fishing smack
(B) accepting a bribe to lose the cod race
(C) stealing his neighbor's cat
(D) setting fire to a rival establishment
(E) passing by a sinking ship

62. The lines,
"I warmed both hands before the fire of life;

It sinks, and I am ready to depart,
are a quotation from

(A) Walter Savage Landor
(B) Matthew Arnold
(C) Samuel T. Coleridge
(D) Lord Byron
(E) Christina Rossetti

63. The "graveyard" school of poetry included all of the following poets except

(A) William Cowper
(B) Thomas Gray
(C) Robert Blair
(D) Edward Young
(E) William Collins

64. "An immense poem in which one incident of Italian crime is shown reflected on a dozen mental facets," refer to Browning's work

(A) Sordello
(B) The Ring and the Book
(C) A Blot in the 'Scutcheon
(D) Asolando
(E) My Last Duchess

65. Savonarola appears as a character in

(A) The Inferno
(B) The Last of the Barons
(C) The Cenci
(D) Romola
(E) A Lost Lady

66. Among the following statements, the one which is not true is:

(A) Oliver Goldsmith studied medicine at Edinburgh University.
(B) General Wolfe is commonly believed to have recited Gray's Elegy to his officers on the way to the Battle of Quebec.
(C) Alfred, Frederick, and Charles Tennyson collaborated in the work, Poems by Two Brothers.
(D) The death of Sidney Lanier was the occasion for Whitman's "When Lilacs Last in the Dooryard Bloom'd."
(E) William Wordsworth's association with his neighbor, Coleridge, resulted in the joint volume, Lyrical Ballads.

67. Slawkenbergius is

(A) an 18th century Swedish philosopher
(B) an imaginary author in Sterne's Tristram Shandy
(C) an imaginary author in Burton's The Anatomy of Melancholy
(D) a Dutch captain in Knickerbocker's History of New York
(E) a German blacksmith who becomes a priest

68. "The poet's eye, in a fin frenzy
rolling,
Doth glance from heaven to earth,
from earth to heaven;
is a quotation from

(A) The Tempest
(B) The Merchant of Venice
(C) Pericles, Prince of Tyre
(D) Macbeth
(E) A Midsummer Night's Dream

69. The author of the line,
"Lest we forget - lest we forget!"
wrote all of the following except

(A) "Single men in barricks don't grow into plaster saints."
(B) "He travels the fastest who travels alone."
(C) "Experience is the name everyone gives to his mistakes."
(D) "Them that asks no questions isn't told a lie."
(E) "An' I learned about women from 'er."

70. James Gould Cozzens was awarded the Pultizer prize for his novel

(A) The Last Adam
(B) The Just and the Unjust
(C) S. S. San Pedro
(D) Guard Honor
(E) Castaway

71. Theories of time, as expounded by J. W. Dunne, are employed in several of the plays of

(A) Arthur Wing Pinero
(B) Laurence Housman
(C) John Boynton Priestly
(D) John Galsworth
(E) Eugene O'Neill

72. The pair not correctly associated is

(A) Keats - Fanny Brawne
(B) Shelley - Teresa Emilia Viviani
(C) Cowper - Mrs. Unwin
(D) Milton - Elizabeth Minshull
(E) Wordsworth - Caroline Bowles

73. All of the following were clergymen except

(A) Robert Herrick
(B) Thomas Percy
(C) George Crabbe
(D) William Blake
(E) John Henry Newman

74. The lines,
"O may I join the choir invisible
Of those immortal dead who live again,"
were written by

(A) James Thompson
(B) George Eliot
(C) Francis Thompson
(D) Isaac Watts
(E) William Cowper

75. The line,
"Here lies one whose name was writ in water,"
was written for his own tombstone by

(A) Shelley
(B) Chatterton
(C) Byron
(D) Keats
(E) Drayton

76. The sonnet form, originally Italian, was introduced into English verse by

(A) Sir Thomas Wyatt
(B) Thomas Sackville
(C) George Chapman
(D) Sir Philip Sidney
(E) John Lyly

77. The Rise of the Dutch Republic was written by

(A) William H. Prescott
(B) Lord Macaulay
(C) Henry Thomas Buckle
(D) Oswald Spengler
(E) John Lothrop Motley

78. Jeanie Deans is a character in

(A) The Mill on the Floss
(B) The Woman in White
(C) Vanity Fair
(D) The Ordeal of Richard Feverel
(E) The Heart of Midlothian

79. All of the following were poets laureate of England except

(A) Robert Southey
(B) Colley Cibber
(C) Thomas Hood
(D) Alfred Austin
(E) Ben Jonson

80. All of the following are written in the same poetical form except

(A) Amoretti
(B) Astrophel and Stella
(C) Epithalamion
(D) Delia
(E) House of Life

81. The lines,
"Fear death? - to feel the fog in my throat,
The mist in my face,"
are from

(A) Prospice
(B) Rabbi Ben Ezra
(C) Andrea del Sarto
(D) The Ring and the Book
(E) Home Thoughts from Abroad

82. Eugene Gant and Esther Jack are characters created by

(A) John Steinbeck
(B) Thomas Wolfe
(C) James Branch Cabell
(D) Joseph Hergesheimer
(E) Evelyn Waugh

Answer questions 83-87 in accordance with the following directions:

The dots in each of the following prose selections signify that a sentence has been omitted. Following each selection are suggested sentences that may be substituted for the omitted sentence. For each suggested sentence, use the code below in order to arrive at your answer.

(A) appropriate
(B) not appropriate in meaning
(C) not appropriate in tone or diction
(D) grammatically incorrect
(E) wordy or redundant

Think not, O thou guide of my mouth, that absence can impair my respect, or interposing trackless deserts blot your reverend figure from my memory. The farther I travel I feel the pain of separation with stronger force; those ties that bind me to my native country and you are still unbroken....................
....

83. The farther one travels, the closer they are brought back to their native land.

84. Howsoever I may roam, there be no place like home.

85. By every step away I only drag a greater length of chain.

86. Forsooth, the heart lieth where the foot remaineth planted.

87. I shall have fond memories and reminiscences of my native land in other clime.

88. A poet who has recreated Greek tragedy in contemporary verse drama is

(A) Dylan Thomas
(B) Robinson Jeffers
(C) e.e. cummings
(D) Marianne Moore
(E) Edward Fitzgerald

89. Lord Jim became a wanderer in primitive places because

(A) he was repelled by the shams of society
(B) he was moved by dreams of fortune
(C) he felt that among primitives one was close to God
(D) he wanted to expiate an act of cowardice
(E) he had a dream that changed his philosophy of life

90. The long romantic poem which chronicles the victory of the Scottish king at Bannockburn is

(A) John Barbour's The Brus
(B) Thomas Hoccleve's The Regement of Princes
(C) John Lydgate's The Temple of Glass
(D) William Caxton's The Golden Legend
(E) John Lyly's Cupid and Campaspe

91. In the denouément of The House of Mirth, Lily Bart

(A) accepts Rosedale's proposal
(B) decides to become an artist
(C) leaves New York to live in Europe
(D) takes up charitable work
(E) takes an overdose of sedative

92. Silent Spring has for its main theme

(A) the political awakening of Africa
(B) life on a South Sea island
(C) the challenge of frontier life
(D) the danger from pesticides
(E) the appreciation of natural beauty

93. A Moveable Feast by Ernest Hemingway gives an account of

(A) deep sea fishing off Florida's coast
(B) bull fighting in Mexico
(C) commercialism throughout America
(D) writing and writers in Paris
(E) cattle rustlers right after Civil War

94. "Old father, old artificer, stand me now in good stead" are the closing lines of the novel

(A) Rabble in Arms
(B) A Portrait of the Artist
(C) Rebel
(D) The Devil's Disciple
(E) Drums Along the Mohawk

95. "MacFlecknoe" is

(A) a reply by Swift to "Hudibras"
(B) a satire by Dryden ridiculing Thomas Shadwell
(C) a mock-heroic epic by Pope
(D) a defense by Addison of Sir Robert Walpole's foreign policy
(E) an attack upon the Scottish politicians

96. Incunabula, in book collecting, are books printed before

(A) 1500
(B) 1550
(C) 1600
(D) 1650
(E) 1700

97. Of the following places and names, all are correctly associated except

(A) Stoke Poges - Gray
(B) Strawberry Hill - Walpole
(C) Moor Park - Swift
(D) Missolonghi - Browning
(E) Manor Farm - Dickens

98. The student, Raskolnikov, is the protagonist in

(A) Chekhov's The Cherry Orchard
(B) Turgenev's Fathers and Sons
(C) Tolstoi's The Kreutzer Sonata
(D) Gorki's The Lower Depths
(E) Dostoevski's Crime and Punishment

99. Quotation and author are correctly paired in all the following except

(A) "To the glory that was Greece,
And the grandeur that was Rome" - Edgar Allan Poe
(B) "Whoso would be a man must be a nonconformist." - Ralph Waldo Emerson
(C) "Thou go not, like the quarry-slave at night,
Scourged to his dungeon" - John Greenleaf Whittier
(D) "The groves were God's first temples" - William Cullen Bryant
(E) "I think that I could turn and live with animals" - Walt Whitman

100. Best known for his novels about French provincial Catholic families is

(A) Andre Maurois
(B) Francois Mauriac
(C) Jacques Maritain
(D) Charles Maturin
(E) Andre Gide

ANSWER KEY

1. C
2. C
3. D
4. A
5. E
6. C
7. C
8. C
9. A
10. A
11. B
12. C
13. E
14. C
15. A
16. C
17. A
18. E
19. D
20. E
21. D
22. B
23. D
24. C
25. D
26. E
27. A
28. B
29. D
30. B
31. C
32. A
33. C
34. C
35. C
36. C
37. E
38. A
39. C
40. D
41. A
42. D
43. B
44. B
45. B
46. B
47. D
48. B
49. D
50. A
51. E
52. B
53. D
54. E
55. D
56. B
57. E
58. D
59. C
60. D
61. E
62. A
63. A
64. B
65. D
66. D
67. B
68. E
69. C
70. D
71. B
72. E
73. D
74. B
75. D
76. A
77. E
78. E
79. C
80. C
81. A
82. B
83. D
84. C
85. A
86. B
87. E
88. B
89. D
90. A
91. E
92. D
93. D
94. B
95. B
96. A
97. D
98. E
99. C
100. B

EXPLANATORY ANSWERS

1. (C) Oxymoron is a rhetorical antithesis which unites two contradictory terms for the sake of emphasis. Examples are: brawling love, loving hate, heavy lightness, serious vanity.

2. (C) Bildad the Shuhite, Eliphaz the Temanite, and Zophar the Naamathite are the ironically named "comforters" of Job. Their arguments are based on the idea that success is virtue. They attempt to destroy Job's faith, not in God, but in himself. For example, Bildad tells Job that "God will not reject the blameless man." Job rejects their views and advice and continues to insist on his own righteousness.

3. (D) Roland is the hero of Chanson de Roland (Song of Roland), a twelfth-century chanson de geste in medieval French. Count Oliver is Roland's brother in arms. The two are paladins of Charlemagne. Griselda is a character in Chaucer's "Clerk's Tale" and is known in this, in the Decameron, and in other tales at Patient Grissil.

4. (A) Known also as The Rule for Anchoresses or Nuns' Rule, this religious manual composed for three sisters belongs to the early Middle English period (c. 1200-1250). It is marked by inspiring morality, gentleness, and occasional touches of humor. Scholars label it the most significant English prose work between the time of Alfred and Malory.

5. (E) One of Chaucer's most charming tales, this work is a beast fable with elements of mock heroic and exemplum. It tells of Chanticleer's fall before the fox's flattery and of the fox's subsequent defeat by a similar ruse. The many classical allusions and the ironic parallels drawn between the animals and the heroes of myth and legend are typical of mock heroic verse.

6. (C) Colin Cloute is written in Skeltonics - a light verse form made up of short, usually six-syllable lines that repeat the rhyme many times in succession, as:

   And if ye stand in doubt
   Who brought this rime about,
   My name is Colin Clout,
   I purpose to shake out
   All my cunning bag...

   The attack on Wolsey, the Cardinal-Chancellor under Henry VIII, is veiled but unmistakable.

7. (C) Collier was a clergyman whose works on the immorality of the English drama attacks Congreve, Vanbrugh, and Wycherley. He accused their plays of bawdry and profaneness and of failing to instill morality, which he considered the only legitimate purpose of art.

8. (C) In the fifteenth century Sir Thomas Malory wrote in prison Morte d' Arthur, which collects the Arthurian legend into a unified narrative. Written in a supple prose style, Malory's work is tinged with the

melancholy of days already past. It inspired such later writers as Spenser and Tennyson.

9. (A) One of Shakespeare's earliest plays, Love's Labour's Lost, is a court comedy involving much word play and little dramatic action. Twelfth Night is notable for the character of Viola, its smoothly-complicated plot, and the famous lyric "Come away, come away, death."

10. (A) These are Satan's first words in the poem. Even Satan cannot fail to notice that his fellow angel has lost his heavenly brilliance. Satan goes on to declare that all is not lost and that war can still be waged against their enemy, God.

11. (B) The Shepherd's Calendar offers twelve eclogues, one for each month of the year, on the general theme of the unrequited love of Colin Clout (Spenser's name for himself) for Rosalind. Contemporary politics and religious abuses are attacked.

12. (C) These lines are actually from Comus (ll. 1022-23), which was first performed in 1634. Milton wrote the words and Henry Lawes wrote the music for this masque which has as theme dynamic rather than cloistered virtue. The usual elements of masque are present: rich song, classical setting, and polished complements to individual members of the audience.

13. (E) The lines, from Shelley's Adonais (XLIII), are a particularly fitting tribute to Keats, whose poetry celebrates the beautiful. Adonais is an elegy in Spenserian stanza that observes the pastoral conventions of Bion and Moschus. Shelley here laments the death of Keats, whom he knew only slightly, but he also reflects on his own life and poetry.

14. (C) Oliver Wendell Holmes, whose life spans most of the nineteenth century, was both doctor and poet. His poetry shows a certain grace and humor, but little of the deep religious or philosophical thought that characterized those writers who came under the influence of transcendentalism.

15. (A) The lines are from "Israfel," a poem by Edgar Allan Poe on the nature of the ideal poet. The stanza concludes:

> None sing so wildly well
> As the angel Israfel.

The poem epitomizes Poe's ability to manipulate vowel and consonant sounds in a pleasing manner.

16. (C) Tartuffe is the only play with a near-religious theme by the French neoclassic dramatist Moliere. In an early version Tartuffe is a member of the clergy, but Moliere was forced to make changes in order to have the play accepted by the society of his own day. The hypocrite Tartuffe does not appear until the play is well under way. His opening lines are: "Hang up my hairshirt, put my scourge in place."

17. (A) Sullivan (1856-1924) was a significant American architect who exerted a considerable influence on his disciple Frank Lloyd Wright.

18. (E) These lines are from Renascence, a poem written when Edna Millay was nineteen. In conventional iambic tetrameter couplets, the poetess reflects on the individual's closeness to infinity:

> The soul can split the sky in
>   two,
> And let the face of God shine
>   through.

19. (D) Steinbeck's novel In Dubious Battle glorifies the struggle of the American labor movement through a sympathetic account of a strike among itinerant applepickers on the West Coast. Although the hero is a member of the Communist party, the

book is not mere propaganda as party members are frequently seen to be fallible and destructive.

20. (E) John Brown believed himself chosen by God to destroy slavery by violent means. He led the attack on Harper's Ferry. Stephen Vincent Benet (1898-1943) has written a long narrative poem entitled John Brown's Body.

21. (D) Arnold set forth the purpose of criticism in The Function of Criticism at the Present Time. In The Study of Poetry he expounds his critical method of appraising literature by means of touchstones - that is, by reference to passages of acknowledged excellence.

22. (B) Riders to the Sea, by John Millington Synge, is a tragic study of an old Irish mother who loses an entire family to the sea. The sea itself plays an important role in creating the tragic atmosphere.

23. (D) In Masque of Reason, Robert Frost has written a poem that, in its questioning of human purpose, is quite different from his more popular works.

Robinson is best known for his short character poems "Miniver Cheevy" and "Richard Cory." He has also written on the Arthurian theme.

24. (C) In Death of the Hired Man, Robert Frost creates realistic characters and genuine feeling. In the one word, "Dead," the husband conveys to his wife his own deep emotion. Frost also uses dialogue and a farm setting in "The Code."

25. (D) The first three lines clearly show that the poet does not intend this as a "sad story" despite his playful use of the word "alas." This is confirmed by reference to the complete poem by Matthew Prior, "To a Child of Quality Five Years Old, The Author Forty."

26. (E) Quicker is the comparative form of the adjective quick. But this sentence demands an adverb to modify the verb ends - i.e., to tell how "youthful loving ends" - quickly.

27. (A) The poet lightly suggests that once the child is grown into a young lady who tears up the letters of would-be suitors, his letters will be acceptable - as those of an old family friend.

28. (B) The meter of the first three lines of the stanza is iambic tetrameter. The suggested line is not.

29. (D) The first two lines concern birds, the third flowers. The stanza's careful parallelism in meaning would be broken by the reference to a "weary farmer."

30. (B) The strong spondee of "bright-hued" does not conform to the basic iambic tetrameter of the stanza.

31. (C) The inane repetition of "grow and grow" is obviously inappropriate. Furthermore, the use of an adjective to modify lilies makes it likely that the parallel noun in the next line will also be modified.

32. (A) In this case the meter is identical with that of the preceding lines. Parallelism is observed in both syntax and meaning.

33. (C) This is one of Hawthorne's few farcical stories. The doctor and his friend drink the water of youth and grow younger. In this story, one of his many tales taken from witch lore, Hawthorne again shows his belief that an elixir of life would present to mankind more problems than it would solve.

34. (C) Huxley had the stylistic ability to popularize the theories of Darwin. He went beyond Darwin to suggest that the organism can alter its environment as a means of adaptation. Two of his most famous lectures are The Physical Basis of Life and On a Piece of Chalk.

35. (C) Wilde became the leading figure in the aesthetic movement of the close of the nineteenth century. He wrote a number of successful comedies, such as The Importance of Being Earnest and Lady Windermere's Fan, and the popular poem The Ballad of Reading Gaol.

36. (C) Ambrose Bierce, poet and short story writer, disappeared into Mexico in 1913 where he probably died a year later. His stories show a taste for the psychologically macabre.

37. (E) A minor theme throughout Kafka's writing is the parallel between man and other animals. Another theme is the overpowering sense of guilt. These themes are to be found in the short story Metamorphosis and also in Kafka's great novels The Trial, The Castle, and America.

38. (A) Having been falsely convicted of treason, Alexander Solzhenitsyn spent ten years in a Stalinist concentration camp. This autobiographical work describes one terrible, average day of his incarceration. First published in November, 1962, in the literary periodical Novy Mir, the book created an immediate literary and political furor.

39. (C) This epigram is from Sir John Harrington's Epigrams, Of Treason. The epigram is a short saying that is concise, pointed, clear and balanced. In Elizabethan England, the epigram was used primarily as satire. Ben Jonson tried to restore the classical meaning of the term by writing epigrammatic verses, epistles and epitaphs. After Jonson, the greatest epigrammatists in English were Alexander Pope and Walter Savage Landor.

40. (D) "I sing of arms and the man" wrote Virgil. From this line George Bernard Shaw took the title of his play Arms and the Man. The play is a satire on militarism, stupid courage, and chauvinism. Captain Bluntschili, an army officer, also known as the Chocolate Soldier, is the antithesis of the idealized soldier; in the end, his unheroic common sense wins out.

41. (A) Argus had only one head but one hundred eyes. Because of a fight between Zeus and Hera over Io, who had been turned into a cow which Argus guarded, Hermes beheaded Argus, and Hera transplanted his eyes to the tail of the peacock. Hydra was a nine-headed serpent killed by Hercules; Cerberus, a many-headed dog that guarded the entrance to Hades and which Hercules dragged to the upper world; Scylla, once a beautiful nymph, was changed to a six-headed monster by Circe and killed by Hercules; Geryon, also killed by Hercules, was a triple-headed monster.

42. (D) From Judges, XIV, 14. Samson wants to marry a Philistine woman, and at a prewedding feast he asks the riddle of thirty of her friends. They cannot answer, but they ask her to entice Samson into telling her so that she can tell them. When Samson discovers what has happened he kills thirty men.

43. (B) Pharsalia, the epic poem by Lucan on the civil war between Caesar and Pompey, was named after the battle of Pharsalus, fought in 48 B.C., in which Caesar was victorious.

44. (B) The mystery or miracle plays were medieval dramatic presentations of events from religious history or from the legendary lives of the saints. These plays reached their highest development in the fifteenth and sixteenth centuries. Collected into cycles, these plays were often performed under the supervision of the town corporation, with various episodes being assigned to local handicraft guilds.

45. (B) Bailly offers to accompany the company of some thirty pilgrims in order to show them the way to the

shrine of Thomas A. Becket. And it is he that proposes that each pilgrim shall tell two tales on the sixty-mile ride to Canterbury and two tales on the way back, with the best storyteller to be given a supper at the others' expense on the return to the Tabard. Of the contemplated hundred and more tales, Chaucer completed only twenty-four.

46. (B) Hall's chronical is notable for its account of the days of Henry VIII and its description of his court. Stow published, among other works, a study of Chaucer and an important Survey of London. Holinshed's Chronicles were utilized by Shakespeare and other dramatists.

47. (D) The full title of this autobiographical work reveals its character: Grace Abounding to the Chief of Sinners, or the brief Relation of the exceeding Mercy of God in Christ to his poor Servant John Bunyan. Written with deep sincerity, the book tells of the author's wicked youth, gradual awakening to religion, and final call to the ministry.

48. (B) These are the famous opening lines of The Social Contract, the work in which Rousseau sets forth his political philosophy. Although not particularly original in its proposal, this work had a profound influence on French thought, particularly during the years of the Revolution.

49. (D) The Changeling is a tragedy by Thomas Middleton and William Rowley. The complicated plot and subplot, the depiction of lust and exacerbated passions, is typical of the melodramatic tragedies of the Jacobean theater. Massinger's principal field was the romantic drama, of which The Duke of Milan and The Fatal Dowry are two good examples. His most popular play is the comedy A New Way to Pay Old Debts.

50. (A) The author of the play is unknown, but some have attributed it to Shakespeare. The actual murder is recorded by Holinshed. The same subject served as the basis of a play by Lillo.

51. (E) Richard Tottel printed the chief works of Wyatt and Surrey and other poets of the time in Song and Sonnets, which came to be known as Tottel's Miscellany. Its wide popularity is attested to by Slender, in Shakespeare's Merry Wives of Windsor, who would "rather than forty shillings" have had with him Tottel's "Book of Songs and Sonnets" when he went courting Anne Page.

52. (B) The poem is Maud, a monodrama in which the male narrator expresses his growing love for Maud, the daughter of the old lord who ruined the fortunes of the narrator's family. He wins her love but later suffers a spell of madness only to find a new meaning in life through service to his country. The poem contains some of Tennyson's best love lyrics.

53. (D) Lewis was offered the Pultizer Prize in 1926, but he refused it. In 1930 he accepted the Nobel Prize. Lewis's literary reputation rests on his novels of social criticism. His satire is broad and it covered almost every level of American society. Best known of his novels are Main Street, a study of small town conventionality and hypocrisy, and Babbitt, a satirical study of urban materialism.

54. (E) This historical novel by Sir Walter Scott is set at the time of William III. Considered to be a masterpiece of Gothic fiction, the novel tells of the tragic death of Lucy Ashton and Ravenswood. Italian composer Donizetti based his opera Lucia di Lammermoor on Scott's novel.

55. (D) A wit and satirist, Peacock wrote almost plotless novels in which characters and dialogue are all important. Peacock's satire is aimed at bigots and fanatics of all kinds. Ravenshoe is the work of Henry Kingsley, brother of the better-known Charles Kingsley.

56. (B) The King's Tragedy was one of Rosetti's last poems. It is a literary ballad written as a monologue. The other poems mentioned here are popular ballads.

57. (E) This collection of essays by Oliver Goldsmith is a collection of 123 pseudo-letters, supposedly written by a Chinese philosopher (living in London) to his friends in the Orient. The purpose of the essays-letters was to expose shady politics and to discuss the morals of the English. The central figure is Lien Chi Altangi, Chinese philosopher.

58. (D) One of Sir Walter Scott's lesser known novels, Old Mortality deals with the 1679-1689 rising of the Covenanters against the efforts of Charles II and James II to force episcopacy on them. Scott's sympathies were with the Covenanters. Evelina is by Fanny Burney; The Castle of Otranto by Horace Walpole; Humphrey Clinker by Smollett; Gulliver's Travels by Swift.

59. (C) Widely known as the O.E.D., this is the only definitive, historical dictionary of the English language ever compiled.

H. W. Fowler is best known for his "bible" of correctness, A Dictionary of Modern English Usage, which, though first published in 1926, is still a very useful guide.

60. (D) Politics and lovers are combined in this novel in which the hero, Beauchamp, a political radical, champions such things as universal suffrage, limitation of individual wealth, and state control. Other novels by Meredith include The Ordeal of Richard Feverel and The Egoist.

61. (E) One of John Greenleaf Whittier's best ballads, this poem deals with an incident that took place at Marblehead. It is rich in dialogue and humor. Ireson's ride is forced on him by the women of Marblehead, who tar and feather the Skipper and carry him out of town on a cart. Whittier's most important poem is Snow-Bound.

62. (A) Landor, in these lines from "Dying Speech of an Old Philosopher," exhibits his typical dissatisfaction with life and with his fellow man. A man of tempestuous temper, Landor was in trouble throughout his life. His lapidary verse includes tragedy, an historical trilogy, and short tales.

63. (A) The "graveyard" school poets wrote long, gloomy poems about death and the life to come. Gray's Elegy Written in a Country Churchyard is best known of the graveyard poems. Blair's The Grave and Young's Night Thoughts are typical of this poetic convention.

64. (B) Browning based his poem on the story of a Roman murder case. The poem tells the tale of the murder of Pompilia Comparini by her husband Count Guido Franceschini and of the Count's subsequent trial, conviction and execution. The poem is written as a series of dramatic monologues in which each speaker sheds some new light on the truth.

65. (D) George Eliot, pseudonym of Mary Anne Evans, wrote several novels of which Middlemarch and The Mill on the Floss are among the most important. Romola, unlike her other novels which are set in England, is set in Renaissance Italy. In their outlook, however, the characters of Romola are Victorian Englishmen and Englishwomen.

66. (D) Whitman's elegy was inspired by the death of Lincoln. Central to the poem is the idea of national unity inspired by grief. Also inspired by Lincoln's death was the poetically inferior but more popular O Captain! My Captain!

67. (B) Hafen Slawkenbergius is a German author of a Latin dissertation on noses. He is a minor member of a

group of esoteric humorous characters including Walter Shandy, Tristram's father, Uncle Toby whose hobby is war, and Corporal Trim, his batman.

68. (E) A Midsummer Night's Dream is one of Shakespeare's most charming romantic comedies. It is memorable for such humorous characters as Bottom, for its impossibly-complicated love plot, for the artisans' version of the Pyramus and Thisbe story, and for Theseus' grouping of lunatic, lover, and poet.

69. (C) This line from Lady Windermere's Fan is typical of Oscar Wilde's epigrammatic and ironic wit. All the other lines are by Kipling.

70. (D) Cozzen's novel deals with the moral and social problems of a U.S. Air Force general in World War II. Cozzens was highly praised for a later novel, By Love Possessed, the study of a man who cannot resolve the troubles that beset his life.

71. (B) Housman, brother of the better known A. E. Housman, was an author and artist. His more important works are the plays Prunelle, Angels and Ministers, and the satirical novels, The Duke of Flamborough and Trimblerigg.

72. (E) Fanny Brawne and Teresa Viviani were sources of inspiration to their respective Romantic poet-lovers. Mrs. Unwin, the subject of Cowper's poem "To Mary," cared for the poet during his illnesses. Elizabeth Minshull became Milton's third wife. Caroline Bowles was Southey's second wife. Principal women in Wordsworth's life were Annette Vallon, who bore his child, Mary Hutchinson who became his wife, and his ubiquitous sister Dorothy.

73. (D) Blake, though never a clergyman, had religious mystical visions throughout his life. As a child he met Ezekiel under a tree, and he also saw a tree filled with angels. The mystical quality of his personality he later expressed graphically in some of his engravings and paintings and also in such prophetic poems as Jerusalem and The Book of Thel.

74. (B) Although noted chiefly for her novels, George Eliot has written some rather good poetry. Her sonnet sequence Brother and Sister, consists of eleven poignant poems. A long dramatic poem The Spanish Gypsy is a lovers' tragedy that poses the dilemma of duty versus passion. The lines quoted are from a poem called "May I Join the Choir Invisible."

75. (D) The poet asked his good friend Joseph Severn, who was present at his death, to see that these words were his epitaph. Keats died in Rome in 1821 and is buried there.

76. (A) In the sixteenth century, Wyatt translated Patriarchan sonnets and also wrote more than thiry sonnets in English. Credit must also go to Henry Howard, Earl of Surrey, who modified the Patriarchan form to suit English prosody.

77. (E) Diplomat and novelist as well as historian, Motley has two novels to his credit, Morton's Hope and Merry-Mount. His popular histories include History of the United Netherlands and The Life and Death of John of Barneveld.

78. (E) Jeanie refuses to give false evidence that would save her sister Effie, who is accused of murdering her own child.

Authors of the other novels are:
A. George Eliot
B. Wilkie Collins
C. William M. Thackeray
D. George Meredith

79. (C) Thomas Hood was a minor poet of the first half of the nineteenth century. He is best remembered for his humorous verse, such as "Miss Kilmansegg," and for his poems of social protest, most notably "Song of the Shirt." His prose work Literary Reminiscences contains a famous account of a gathering at Charles Lamb's.

80. (C) Unlike the other works, which are sonnet cycles, Epithalamion is a nuptial hymn of twenty-three stanzas, followed by an envoy. The title is Greek for "upon the bridechamber," and the poem itself is thought to be the poet's celebration of his marriage to Elizabeth Boyle in 1594.

81. (A) These lines express Browning's belief that death is just one more adventure. He declares that he has always been a fighter
and welcomes the struggle with death:
I would hate that death bandaged
my eyes, and forbore,
And bade me creep past.

82. (B) Eugene Gant is the central figure of Wolfe's first two novels, Look Homeward Angel and Of Time and the River. Both works are highly autobiographical, with Eugene as the author himself.

Esther Jack figures prominently in Wolfe's two other novels. The Web and the Rock and You Can't Go Home Again. She is Jewish costume designer whose calm rationality is set against the hero's emotional intensity.

83. (D) Since one is singular, the use of they are and their are is incorrect. The main clause should read, "the closer one is brought back to his native land."

84. (C) Despite the attempt to "age" the proposed sentence, with howsoever and there be, the diction and tone are closer to that of a Western ballad than to the biblical style of the passage printed here.

85. (A) Here the meaning follows from what has gone before, and the style accords with the rest of the passage.

86. (B) The meaning of the proposed sentence is exactly opposite to the import of the passage in which the heart does not forget what is left behind.

87. (E) This could be put much more simply. In particular, the use of both fond memories and reminiscences is unnecessary.

88. (B) Jeffers has adapted Aeschylus and Euripides for presentation on the modern stage. He has also written a modern version of Medea. The concern with death, violence, passion, and incest that marks Jeffers' original poems has been attributed by the poet himself to the influence of classical tragedy.

89. (D) In Conrad's novel Lord Jim, the central figure, panic-stricken after his ship strikes a derelict and begins to sink, joins other officers in abandoning the ship and its several hundred Moslem pilgrims bound for Mecca. But the ship does not sink, and Jim spends the rest of his life attempting to redeem his honor.

90. (A) John Barbour was a Scottish poet of the fourteenth century. His poem The Brus or The Bruce celebrates the war of Scottish independence and the deeds of King Robert and James Douglas. He is also thought to be the author of the Legend of Troy and Legends of the Saints, translations from the Latin of Guido da Colonna.

91. (E) In this novel Edith Wharton depicts New York society at the turn of the century, but her chief interest is not social commentary but psychological analysis of character. In The Age of Innocence, Newland Archer rebels against conventional standards but is forced to live by them. In The Custom of the County, Undine Spragg is rootless and amoral in a society that is held together by tradition.

92. (D) Rachel Carson, the author of Silent Spring, is representative of a number of concerned American writers who have sought to awaken the public to the perils of indiscriminate use of pesticides and other chemicals. Her work has been a

factor in various efforts at Congressional investigation and legislation.

93. (D) Shortly after his death, Hemingway's A Moveable Feast, an account of his early years as a writer in Paris was published. A best-seller, the work offers a glimpse of such renowned figures of the twenties as Gertrude Stein and F. Scott Fitzgerald, but some critics have found a certain revengeful bitterness in these memories.

94. (B) James Joyce's novel A Portrait of the Artist as a Young Man is the story of Stephen Dedalus, who is to a large degree the author himself. By the end of the novel Stephen has given up both religion and the cause of Irish nationalism to dedicate himself to a life of art.

95. (B) Dryden's satire is a reply to Shadwell's The Medal of John Bayes. Flecknoe, an Irish writer of verse, is depicted as passing on to Shadwell his preeminence at dullness. Shadwell's right to the crown is clear:

The rest to some faint meaning make
  pretence,
But Shadwell never deviates into
  sense.

96. (A) Incunabula resemble medieval manuscripts in size, form, and general appearance. They also show similar artistic excellence. Among famous English examples are Caxton's edition of Chaucer's Canterbury Tales and Malory's Le Morte d'Arthur.

97. (D) In 1823, after having set forth to aid the cause of Greek independence, Byron died of fever at Missolonghi. Because of his wife's ill-health, Browning spent the middle years of his life in Italy - at Pisa, Florence, and Rome.

98. (E) In an effort to show his superioity to conventional moral standards, Raskolnikov brutally murders an old woman. In the end, Raskolnikov is redeemed by the love of a prostitue and purges his guilt by years of suffering in Siberia. Dostoevsky himself had spent long years in the Siberian mines.

99. (C) Bryant wrote the main parts of "Thanatopsis" at the age of seventeen. He was twenty-seven when the famous beginning, which makes nature the speaker, and the end were added. The poem shows Bryant to be something of a deist and stoic.

100. (B) Mauriac's principal novels are set in his native region of southwest France. His principal theme is sin, in particular the sin of sensuality. Among his most significant novels are Le Fleuve de Feu (The River of Fire), Le Baiser au Lepreux (The Kiss to the Leper), and Genitrix.

THIRD PRACTICE AP/CLEP ENGLISH TEST
SECTION II

Question 1 (Suggested time - 50 minutes)

Directions: Read the following poem of "Ulysses" by Alfred Lord Tennyson in which the poet takes his theme from Dante, who, in The Inferno, depicts the hero of The Odyssey as restless and eager to continue the search for knowledge and virtue. As you carefully read this poem, write an essay on Tennyson's use of adjectives in "Ulysses."

ULYSSES

Alfred Lord Tennyson

It little profits that an idle king,
By this still hearth, amont these barren crags,
Matches with an ages wife, I mete and dole
Unequal laws unto a savage race,
That hoard, and sleep, and feed, and know not me.
I cannot rest from travel; I will drink
Life to the lees. All times I have enjoyed
Greatly, have suffered greatly, both with those
That loved me, and alone; on shore, and when
Thro' scudding drifts the rainy Hyades
Vext the dim sea. I am become a name;
For always roaming with a hungry heart
Much have I seen and known, -- cities of men
And manners, climates, councils, governments,
Myself not least, but honored of them all, --
And drunk delight of battle with my peers,
Far on the ringing plains of windy Troy.
I am a part of all that I have met;
Yet all experience is an arch wherethro'
Gleams that untravelled world whose margin fades
For ever and for ever when I move.
How dull it is to pause, to make an end,
To rust unburnished, not to shine in use!
As tho' to breathe were life! Life piled on life
Were all to little, and of one to me

Little remains; but every hour is saved
From that eternal silence, something more,
A bringer of new things; and vile it were
For some three suns to store and hoard myself,
And this gray spirit yearning in desire
To follow knowledge like a sinking star,
Beyond the utmost bound of human thought.
  This is my son, mine own Telemachus,
To whom I leave the sceptre and the isle,
Well-loved of me, discerning to fulfill
This labor, by slow prudence to make mild
A rugged people, and thro' soft degrees
Subdue them to the useful and the good.
Most blameless is he, centred in the sphere
Of common duties, decent not to fail
In offices of tenderness, and pay
Meet adoration to my household gods,
When I am gone. He works his work, I mine.
  There lies the port; the vessel puffs her sail;
There gloom the dark, broad seas. My mariners,
Souls that have toiled, and wrought, and thought with me, --
That ever with a frolic welcome took
The thunder and the sunshine, and opposed
Free hearts, free foreheads, -- you and I are old;
Old age hath yet his honor and his toil.
Death closes all; but something ere the end,
Some work of noble note, may yet be done,
Not unbecoming men that strove with Gods.
The lights begin to twinkle from the rocks;
The long day wanes; the slow moon climbs; the deep
Moans round with many voices. Come, my friends.
'T is not too late to seek a newer world.
Push off, and sitting well in order smite
The sounding furrows; for my purpose holds
To sail beyond the sunset, and the baths
Of all the western stars, until I die.
It may be that the fuls will wash us down'
It may be we shall touch the Happy Isles,
And see the great Achilles, whom we knew.
Tho' much is taken, much abides; and tho'
We are not now that strength which in old days
Moved earth and heaven, that which we are, we are, --
One equal temper of heroic hearts,
Made weak by time and fate, but strong in will
To strive, to seek, to find, and not to yield.

Response (1):

In the poem Ulysses, Tennyson presents a different view of the Greek hero than one normally associates with him. He does this by giving Ulysses two characteristics that are not mentioned elsewhere. One is Ulysses' dislike for Ithaca and the other is his desire to travel. Both of these traits are brought out by Tennyson's use of adjectives in the poem.

Two types of adjectives are used to convey a certain tone in Ulysses. Negative adjectives are used at the beginning of the poem when Ulysses' situation at home is discussed.

It little profits that an idle king,
By this still hearth, among these barren crags,
Matched with an aged wife, I mete and dole
Unequal laws unto a savage race,
That hoard, and sleep, and feed, and know not me.

As can be seen in this passage, the words used to describe life on Ithaca are contrary to the belief that Ulysses was content at home. Words like "still," "barren," and "savage" do not convey the feeling of contentment one would expect to obtain from Ulysses, who has returned after such a long absence. Other adjectives also indicate displeasure at what he finds at home, like the words "idle," "aged," and "unequal." Consequently, the picture presented to the reader of Ithaca is bleak.

Another passage which uses negative adjectives to lead one to have a converse image of Ithaca is when Ulysses talks of his son Telemachus. In this section the use of words like "slow" and "rugged" again give the impression of the unappealingness of his home. Words like "common" and "household" accord Ithaca a lack of excitment or adventure.

An additional way in which the adjectives used present Ithaca as commonplace is the use of words in past tense. This type of word expresses an action that is completed and is in the past. Thus, no action is conveyed by such words as "aged," "untravelled," and "rugged." Again the idea of dissatisfaction is emphasized through the use of these adjectives.

However, to stress the second point brought out in the poem, namely Ulysses desire to travel, a different type of adjective must be employed. Therefore, Tennyson uses positive adjectives to accent the excitement of Ulysses at the thought of travel.

Come my friends,
'Tis not too late to seek a newer world.
Push off, and sitting well in order smite
The sounding furrows; for my purpose holds
To sail beyond the sunset, and the baths
Of all the western stars, until I die.

Here we see adjectives like "newer" and "sounding" which are not ordinary and seem to convey the strong feelings of Ulysses as he regards the life he would like to return to. The words used in this passage are bold and stirring and the adjectives underline the excitement of the Greek ruler at doing something which he feels in inspiring. Also, there are fewer adjectives as the nouns used carry more emotion than those found in other passages.

In another section Ulysses describes the adventures he has already had and uses adjectives like "rainy," "ringing," and "windy" to express the freedom and unrestraint that he feels while he is voyaging. The use of adjectives in present tense such as "scudding," "ringing," and "sounding" convey the feeling of more action and excitement. Again this reveals that Ulysses has a great desire to return to the life of a wanderer and seeker of adventures.

Using modifiers in the sections describing life at Ithaca slows down the action of the poem, while other sections with fewer modifiers go by more quickly. This emphasizes a lack of excitement in the former case and stimulation in the latter. One can see that the adjectives used by Tennyson have a great effect on the tone of the poem. They modify blank, unemotional nouns and convey exictement when coupled with others.

As a result one discovers that Tennyson has taken the famous epic Odyssey and modified it, giving us a unique picture of Ulysses. In Tennyson's poem the tone is more moderate than that of the Odyssey, where great adventure and excitement are disclosed. In Ulysses, more calm and less emotion is revealed. Also the character of Ulysses is changed slightly, from a strong hero yearning to reach home to an older ruler who yearns to travel and have still more experiences before his death.

Response (2):

To limit or describe a noun, or to specify or describe something as distinct from another -- This is a definition of an adjective, the tool Alfred Lord Tennyson uses so well in Ulysses. As a dramatic monologue, one of the qualities of Ulysses is that "the speaker demonstrates his character through the poem." Tennyson's word choice (mostly through abundant adjectives) is how the reader realizes just what the author's attitude is.

A dark and stagnant mood is established in lines 1-32 with phrases such as "idle king," "dim sea," "grey spirit," and "sinking star." Without adjectives, the nouns they describe would illustrate something completely different. In addition to distinguishing a definite attitude, these adjectives instill a clear picture in the mind of the reader. This allows the poet to convey the implications of his work more distinctly.

In contrast to the dim picture presented at the beginning of Ulysses, the end (lines 45-70) seems to break out of the darkness. This change is again accomplished by the use of adjectives. We are now confronted with a "frolic welcome," "free hearts," and "noble note." The "eternal silence" (line 27) has become "many voices" (line 56) and "sounding furrows" (line 59); a "sinking star" is now the "slow moon climbs" (line 55). Even Tennyson's view of mankind takes a definite turn. In line 4 he speaks of "Unequal laws unto a savage race," but by line 68 there is "One equal temper of heroic hearts." Descriptive wording speaks for itself as to the author's point of view. There is really no other way to express the feeling these phrases create except by using adjectives.

The drastic reversal of attitudes in the poem is probably due to the fact that it was written after the death of Tennyson's close friend. The beginning displays his regret at the loss of someone close, but builds to the main intention that no matter how unfair and dismal life sometimes seems we must push on. The closing lines emphasize this thought so well --

"Made weak by time and fate, but strong in will
To strive, to seek, to find, and not to yield."

Question 2 (Suggested time - 30 minutes)

Directions: Select a work of tragedy and discuss the defeat of a hero; this work should be of recognized literary value. Do not summarize the plot or action of the work you choose.

Response:

"Coriolanus"

Coriolanus is a Shakespearean tragedy. It follows the same sequence of events as all his other tragedies: Act 1 with the meeting of the hero; Act 2 with agitation and stirring up of mixed feelings towards the hero; Act 3 with the start of the downfall of the hero; Act 4 gives a spark of hope as the hero regains his feet; Act 5 sees the hero defeated. This drama is a tragedy because it is a sad story. Caius Marcius is not really a bad guy. His tragic flaw is that he doesn't really care for the lower class of people. Even this is good in him because he doesn't hide his feelings towards them. He may mock them, but he doesn't play the faker and flatter them in their presence but behind their backs discredit them.

The prevailing theme throughout Coriolanus is recognizable as a quest for power leading to an inevitable downfall. This universal theme is noted in another of Shakespeare's tragedies, Macbeth. Lady Macbeth pushes her husband into murdering the king. He may then become successor to the throne, and she then gets her wish and glory in being queen. Eventually, she goes mad with guilt and her plot is discovered. In the legend of King Midas, Midas wants only money; he thrives on riches. He is granted a wish that whatever he touches will turn to gold. This wish is followed to the letter, and Midas falls into a life of dispair because the power he gains by having money makes him lose all the joys of life -- the people and what little wealth he once had.

In Coriolanus, Caius Marcius is the renowned and honored war hero. His bravery and courage in battle against the Volscians have rewarded him with the oaken garland and scars of which he is proud. On his last attack, he was forced to retreat to the trenches. After a breather, he gave his troops a pep talk to arouse their weary bodies, then proceeded to charge again expecting his men to follow. He charged at the open gates of the city of Corioli, but was alone in his charge. Upon entering, the Volscians closed the gates. His troops thought him a goner for sure, but sure enough, the gates opened and out walked Marcius wounded in only two places, the shoulder and the left arm. For capturing the city, Caius Marcius was awarded his third oaken garland and the surname Coriolanus.

The people of Rome thought him a noble man. Even the common folk, whom he despised, considered him so. Many were content in thinking that Coriolanus performed these deeds of valor for his country, whereas, a few of the commoners who disliked him, said that he did them for his mother. He may be doing valorous deeds just to please his mother, but he has respect for his mother and shows it by doing justice to her wishes. He believes in her, and she plays a big part in the lives of the people in the story, first as a possible instigator of pride and life to Coriolanus, second as a savior to Rome. Volumnis edged her son into valient deeds - "I have lived to see inherited my very wishes and the buildings of my fancy: only there's one thing wanting, which I doubt not but Our Rome will case upon thee." Later in the drama, she begs him to stop his vengeance upon Rome for banishing him from the city, which he shamefully does, - "Oh my mother, mother! O! You have won a happy vistory to Rome." The citizens rejoice by saying - "Behold our patroness, the life of Rome."

At the same time Coriolanus was supposed to have been seeking his power, another group was seeking power also. As Coriolanus was in the process of being elected for consul, a conflict arose between himself and the common people and their elected tribunes Sicinius Velutus and Junius Brutus, who disliked Coriolanus. Even after he had won the Senate vote and had gone out to beg for the public's vote and won, Sicinius and Brutus went around to the people and told stories of how Coriolanus had mocked them and had made fools of them. They told the people that he was a traitor and that he wanted to be Consul to gain power and then take away some of their liberties. Of course the people revolted at these words and re-cast their votes against Coriolanus. They also voted to have him sentenced to death, but Coriolanus's best friend and aide, Menenius Agrippa, talked them down to only banishing him from the city of Rome.

The other group seeking power referred to earlier can now be disclosed as Sicinius and Brutus, the two tribunes. They had the backing of the lower class to give them the power to speak against an official or any recognized person. Both claimed they were speaking for the people, but they had the power of persuasion over them, so actually they were speaking for themselves. Their plan almost backfired when after having banished Coriolanus, he joined the Volscian forces and helped to stage an attack on Rome. The common people became very fearful when they heard this. They started saying things like they had always thought that Coriolanus would have made a fine Consul, and that they hadn't really wanted to banish him, but that Sicinius and Brutus forced them to do it. The crowd soon turned on the tribunes and said that they had better send Volumnia up to talk him out of attacking. If she couldn't get mercy from him, then both tribunes would be killed. Their downfall was nearing, but Volumnia returned in time with news that Coriolanus would spare their lives.

Still yet, the general of the Volscian army, Tullus Aufidius, was seeking power also. He wanted to be rid of Coriolanus so that he could be the greatest war hero and leader. However, when Coriolanus came to join his forces, he saw great conquering quests and leadership possibilities over others for himself; that is why he let Coriolanus join instead of slitting his throat. The Volscian troops accepted Coriolanus with ease. This made Aufidius jealous because it made him feel more of a follower of Coriolanus instead of a partner with him in governing it. Aufidius was resolved never to let Coriolanus beat him again so he had to have Coriolanus killed before his own downfall came, - "When, Caius, Rome is thine, then thou art poor'st of all; then shortly art thou mine." Aufidius has his men kill Coriolanus in the marketplace of Rome on the following day, after agreeing to Coriolanus's peace treaty with Rome. This gives him the power he had sought because he has finally defeated Coriolanus.

These last two power-seekers show that the quest for power exists on all levels of society. Not only do the noble want power and respect, but also the lower classes. The defeat of Coriolanus expresses the main objective of the paper, that a quest for power leads to an inevitable downfall. This work of Shakespeare has a statement to this effect in it. It reads:

> "And power unto itself most commendable,
> Hath not a tomb so evident as a chair
> to extol what it hath done."

This could be explained as -- power for the sake of power, has not so evident a tomb as a chairman telling what he has done.

Question 3 (Suggested time - 40 minutes)

Directions: Read the poem carefully and write an analysis.

"The Tiger"*

William Blake

Tiger! Tiger! burning bright
In the forest of the night,
What immortal hand or eye
Could frame thy fearful symmetry?

In what distant deeps or skies
Burnt the fire of thine eyes?
On what wings dare he aspire?
What the hand dare seize the fire?

And what shoulder, and what art,
Could twist the sinews of thy heart?
And when they heart began to beat,
What dread hand, and what dread feet?

What the hammer? what the chain?
In what furnace was thy brain?
What the anvil? what dread grasp
Dare its deadly terrors clasp?

When the stars threw down their spears,
And watered heaven with their tears,
Did he smile his work to see?
Did he who made the Lamb make thee?

Tiger! Tiger! burning bright
In the forest of the night,
What immortal hand or eye,
Dare frame they fearful symmetry?

Response(1):

"The Tiger" by William Blake is a lyrical poem. A lyrical poem is subjective, reflective poetry having a regular rhyme scheme and meter. This type of poem reveals the poet's thoughts and feelings to create a single, unique impression.

In this poem you find that the meter is trochaic-trimeter and regular. The poet applies two types of rhyme, end rhyme and assonance. End rhyme appears at the end of each line while assonance is found internally, such as in line 6, "Burnt the fire of thine eyes."

The theme is both subjective and reflective. The poet asks if it is possible for someone who creates good and is supposedly good to create evil at the same time. This question is found in line 20, "Did he who made the Lamb make thee." The lamb represents innocence, good, and purity as seen in Blake's poem, "The Lamb." It also tells us that the maker refers to himself as a lamb. The tiger on the other hand is the representation of evil. He is cruel, cunning, mysterious, and feared. How is it possible then, the poet asks, for something to be good but capable of evil?

*A modern spelling - the usual spelling is Tyger, not Tiger.

The evil in the theme dictates the tone of the poem. The reader finds that throughout this poem the tone of wonder and evil prevails. The poet as he speaks is somber and serious. Through his word selection the poet is able to put across to us the wonder and evil of the tiger. Words such as dare, dread, what, how, night, deadly, immortal and why all blend into the idea the poet has in mind.

The poem itself is a pattern of questions one following another, each reinforcing the wonder and evil instated. Who, how, what and why. Each question seems not to be about something human or created but made and inhuman. The questions are asked about the tiger; hard, cold, metal, unfeeling, with fire in its eyes.

As you read the poem it is evident how the tone and theme are developed and what the poet is trying to put across.

In stanza one of "The Tiger" we are immediately faced with wonder and evil. Tiger, who could have made you? You are feared and mysterious, "What immortal hand or eye could frame thy fearful symmetry." Here fearful images begin and the question "who" is posed by the author.

Next the question "where" is brought in. "In what distant deep or skies/Burnt the fire of thine eyes." The author asks from where the tiger came. Who dared to "seize the fire?" Who could create such a composite of evil force?

The content of the third stanza consists of the question "who." "What shoulder and what are/Could twist the sinews of thy heart." Who could twist every part of your heart to be so evil and heartless, cruel and cunning. The author here brings across the evil that lies within the heart of the tiger. He shows us through images produced by words that the tiger, as soon as created, is dreaded by all. The evil is combined with fear, cunning, coldness, and heartlessness, all of which are within him as soon as created.

Next we find concrete images being incorporated into the poem. The tiger, as implied by the poet, is not human or created but made. "What the hammer? What the chain? In what furnace was thy brain?" It is as if the tiger were made of cold, hard, metal, unfeeling. His brain is from the "furnace" which can be associated with evil and "hell." The anvil is also significant, metal is forged on an anvil. Could it be the poet wants us to see the tiger as forged out of metal according to a pattern, all the evil included.

In stanza five, images of the stars throwing spears and the skies crying are used. These images are used by the poet to put across to us the displeasure of the skies and heavens of God's creation. The poet asks, "Did smile his work to see." Could God be pleased with the evil he created? Next we find the poet comparing the lamb and the tiger asking again if something that creates good is capable of such evil.

Finally, we are faced with the last stanza. This stanza is a repeat of the first with much the same meaning. Once again the original question is posed in the reader's mind. "How can something who creates good and is supposedly good be capable of evil."

<u>Response (2)</u>:

Blake's poem "The Tiger" seems to be used as a contrast to his poem "The Lamb." In one poem Blake is asking who made such a gentle innocent lamb, while in the other he is wondering who made the tiger, who had the power and courage to create such a thing.

Blake knows it was something immortal that made the awesome animal. He asks where the fire in his eyes, which glows in the dark forest, came from. He wonders how he managed to handle and contain it. Lines 1 to 16 seem to deal with who made the Tiger and how he was made.

Blake speculated as to whether or not it was the same being that made the lamb. Was the being pleased with his creation, he wonders. It would seem weird that he should make such opposite animals. One of the animals is innocence, one of the animals is of a ferociousness that causes fear.

Taken on a deeper level, the tiger could be a symbol of evil. Evil that burns in the hearts of men like the eyes that burn in the forest. Blake seemed to use the lamb as a symbol of Christ so it seems logical that he would be using the tiger as a symbol also.

Blake wonders who could conceive such a thing as evilness. Could it indeed be the one who created the Christ symbol of goodness? He wants to know how one could create a thing like this. Whoever did, though, had to be powerful and great. There must have been a reason for this convention.

Lines 16 and 17 seem to be a symbol that evil could be overcome, and a greater peace would survive, giving the creator reason to smile about the creation.

One major difference in the poems is that in "The Lamb," Blake answers his question, while in "The Tiger" he never answers it. Because of his reference to the creator being immortal, and powerful, you would assume that he feels it was God who did the creating. In lines 19 and 20, Blake does not capitalize the word he, although he seems to be referring to God. This could be because he questions how great God is if he could create such a thing as evil.

In repeating the first stanza as his last, Blake seems to be underlining the idea that he can't really say or understand who created, or why they created such a thing. He does seem to say and understand that it is a part of a balance, hence the use of the word symmetry. Blake realizes that which the creator realized, that one must have a balance if his world is to survive and work.

1 Ⓐ Ⓑ Ⓒ Ⓓ Ⓔ	26 Ⓐ Ⓑ Ⓒ Ⓓ Ⓔ	51 Ⓐ Ⓑ Ⓒ Ⓓ Ⓔ	76 Ⓐ Ⓑ Ⓒ Ⓓ Ⓔ	101 Ⓐ Ⓑ Ⓒ Ⓓ Ⓔ	126 Ⓐ Ⓑ Ⓒ Ⓓ Ⓔ
2 Ⓐ Ⓑ Ⓒ Ⓓ Ⓔ	27 Ⓐ Ⓑ Ⓒ Ⓓ Ⓔ	52 Ⓐ Ⓑ Ⓒ Ⓓ Ⓔ	77 Ⓐ Ⓑ Ⓒ Ⓓ Ⓔ	102 Ⓐ Ⓑ Ⓒ Ⓓ Ⓔ	127 Ⓐ Ⓑ Ⓒ Ⓓ Ⓔ
3 Ⓐ Ⓑ Ⓒ Ⓓ Ⓔ	28 Ⓐ Ⓑ Ⓒ Ⓓ Ⓔ	53 Ⓐ Ⓑ Ⓒ Ⓓ Ⓔ	78 Ⓐ Ⓑ Ⓒ Ⓓ Ⓔ	103 Ⓐ Ⓑ Ⓒ Ⓓ Ⓔ	128 Ⓐ Ⓑ Ⓒ Ⓓ Ⓔ
4 Ⓐ Ⓑ Ⓒ Ⓓ Ⓔ	29 Ⓐ Ⓑ Ⓒ Ⓓ Ⓔ	54 Ⓐ Ⓑ Ⓒ Ⓓ Ⓔ	79 Ⓐ Ⓑ Ⓒ Ⓓ Ⓔ	104 Ⓐ Ⓑ Ⓒ Ⓓ Ⓔ	129 Ⓐ Ⓑ Ⓒ Ⓓ Ⓔ
5 Ⓐ Ⓑ Ⓒ Ⓓ Ⓔ	30 Ⓐ Ⓑ Ⓒ Ⓓ Ⓔ	55 Ⓐ Ⓑ Ⓒ Ⓓ Ⓔ	80 Ⓐ Ⓑ Ⓒ Ⓓ Ⓔ	105 Ⓐ Ⓑ Ⓒ Ⓓ Ⓔ	130 Ⓐ Ⓑ Ⓒ Ⓓ Ⓔ
6 Ⓐ Ⓑ Ⓒ Ⓓ Ⓔ	31 Ⓐ Ⓑ Ⓒ Ⓓ Ⓔ	56 Ⓐ Ⓑ Ⓒ Ⓓ Ⓔ	81 Ⓐ Ⓑ Ⓒ Ⓓ Ⓔ	106 Ⓐ Ⓑ Ⓒ Ⓓ Ⓔ	131 Ⓐ Ⓑ Ⓒ Ⓓ Ⓔ
7 Ⓐ Ⓑ Ⓒ Ⓓ Ⓔ	32 Ⓐ Ⓑ Ⓒ Ⓓ Ⓔ	57 Ⓐ Ⓑ Ⓒ Ⓓ Ⓔ	82 Ⓐ Ⓑ Ⓒ Ⓓ Ⓔ	107 Ⓐ Ⓑ Ⓒ Ⓓ Ⓔ	132 Ⓐ Ⓑ Ⓒ Ⓓ Ⓔ
8 Ⓐ Ⓑ Ⓒ Ⓓ Ⓔ	33 Ⓐ Ⓑ Ⓒ Ⓓ Ⓔ	58 Ⓐ Ⓑ Ⓒ Ⓓ Ⓔ	83 Ⓐ Ⓑ Ⓒ Ⓓ Ⓔ	108 Ⓐ Ⓑ Ⓒ Ⓓ Ⓔ	133 Ⓐ Ⓑ Ⓒ Ⓓ Ⓔ
9 Ⓐ Ⓑ Ⓒ Ⓓ Ⓔ	34 Ⓐ Ⓑ Ⓒ Ⓓ Ⓔ	59 Ⓐ Ⓑ Ⓒ Ⓓ Ⓔ	84 Ⓐ Ⓑ Ⓒ Ⓓ Ⓔ	109 Ⓐ Ⓑ Ⓒ Ⓓ Ⓔ	134 Ⓐ Ⓑ Ⓒ Ⓓ Ⓔ
10 Ⓐ Ⓑ Ⓒ Ⓓ Ⓔ	35 Ⓐ Ⓑ Ⓒ Ⓓ Ⓔ	60 Ⓐ Ⓑ Ⓒ Ⓓ Ⓔ	85 Ⓐ Ⓑ Ⓒ Ⓓ Ⓔ	110 Ⓐ Ⓑ Ⓒ Ⓓ Ⓔ	135 Ⓐ Ⓑ Ⓒ Ⓓ Ⓔ
11 Ⓐ Ⓑ Ⓒ Ⓓ Ⓔ	36 Ⓐ Ⓑ Ⓒ Ⓓ Ⓔ	61 Ⓐ Ⓑ Ⓒ Ⓓ Ⓔ	86 Ⓐ Ⓑ Ⓒ Ⓓ Ⓔ	111 Ⓐ Ⓑ Ⓒ Ⓓ Ⓔ	136 Ⓐ Ⓑ Ⓒ Ⓓ Ⓔ
12 Ⓐ Ⓑ Ⓒ Ⓓ Ⓔ	37 Ⓐ Ⓑ Ⓒ Ⓓ Ⓔ	62 Ⓐ Ⓑ Ⓒ Ⓓ Ⓔ	87 Ⓐ Ⓑ Ⓒ Ⓓ Ⓔ	112 Ⓐ Ⓑ Ⓒ Ⓓ Ⓔ	137 Ⓐ Ⓑ Ⓒ Ⓓ Ⓔ
13 Ⓐ Ⓑ Ⓒ Ⓓ Ⓔ	38 Ⓐ Ⓑ Ⓒ Ⓓ Ⓔ	63 Ⓐ Ⓑ Ⓒ Ⓓ Ⓔ	88 Ⓐ Ⓑ Ⓒ Ⓓ Ⓔ	113 Ⓐ Ⓑ Ⓒ Ⓓ Ⓔ	138 Ⓐ Ⓑ Ⓒ Ⓓ Ⓔ
14 Ⓐ Ⓑ Ⓒ Ⓓ Ⓔ	39 Ⓐ Ⓑ Ⓒ Ⓓ Ⓔ	64 Ⓐ Ⓑ Ⓒ Ⓓ Ⓔ	89 Ⓐ Ⓑ Ⓒ Ⓓ Ⓔ	114 Ⓐ Ⓑ Ⓒ Ⓓ Ⓔ	139 Ⓐ Ⓑ Ⓒ Ⓓ Ⓔ
15 Ⓐ Ⓑ Ⓒ Ⓓ Ⓔ	40 Ⓐ Ⓑ Ⓒ Ⓓ Ⓔ	65 Ⓐ Ⓑ Ⓒ Ⓓ Ⓔ	90 Ⓐ Ⓑ Ⓒ Ⓓ Ⓔ	115 Ⓐ Ⓑ Ⓒ Ⓓ Ⓔ	140 Ⓐ Ⓑ Ⓒ Ⓓ Ⓔ
16 Ⓐ Ⓑ Ⓒ Ⓓ Ⓔ	41 Ⓐ Ⓑ Ⓒ Ⓓ Ⓔ	66 Ⓐ Ⓑ Ⓒ Ⓓ Ⓔ	91 Ⓐ Ⓑ Ⓒ Ⓓ Ⓔ	116 Ⓐ Ⓑ Ⓒ Ⓓ Ⓔ	141 Ⓐ Ⓑ Ⓒ Ⓓ Ⓔ
17 Ⓐ Ⓑ Ⓒ Ⓓ Ⓔ	42 Ⓐ Ⓑ Ⓒ Ⓓ Ⓔ	67 Ⓐ Ⓑ Ⓒ Ⓓ Ⓔ	92 Ⓐ Ⓑ Ⓒ Ⓓ Ⓔ	117 Ⓐ Ⓑ Ⓒ Ⓓ Ⓔ	142 Ⓐ Ⓑ Ⓒ Ⓓ Ⓔ
18 Ⓐ Ⓑ Ⓒ Ⓓ Ⓔ	43 Ⓐ Ⓑ Ⓒ Ⓓ Ⓔ	68 Ⓐ Ⓑ Ⓒ Ⓓ Ⓔ	93 Ⓐ Ⓑ Ⓒ Ⓓ Ⓔ	118 Ⓐ Ⓑ Ⓒ Ⓓ Ⓔ	143 Ⓐ Ⓑ Ⓒ Ⓓ Ⓔ
19 Ⓐ Ⓑ Ⓒ Ⓓ Ⓔ	44 Ⓐ Ⓑ Ⓒ Ⓓ Ⓔ	69 Ⓐ Ⓑ Ⓒ Ⓓ Ⓔ	94 Ⓐ Ⓑ Ⓒ Ⓓ Ⓔ	119 Ⓐ Ⓑ Ⓒ Ⓓ Ⓔ	144 Ⓐ Ⓑ Ⓒ Ⓓ Ⓔ
20 Ⓐ Ⓑ Ⓒ Ⓓ Ⓔ	45 Ⓐ Ⓑ Ⓒ Ⓓ Ⓔ	70 Ⓐ Ⓑ Ⓒ Ⓓ Ⓔ	95 Ⓐ Ⓑ Ⓒ Ⓓ Ⓔ	120 Ⓐ Ⓑ Ⓒ Ⓓ Ⓔ	145 Ⓐ Ⓑ Ⓒ Ⓓ Ⓔ
21 Ⓐ Ⓑ Ⓒ Ⓓ Ⓔ	46 Ⓐ Ⓑ Ⓒ Ⓓ Ⓔ	71 Ⓐ Ⓑ Ⓒ Ⓓ Ⓔ	96 Ⓐ Ⓑ Ⓒ Ⓓ Ⓔ	121 Ⓐ Ⓑ Ⓒ Ⓓ Ⓔ	146 Ⓐ Ⓑ Ⓒ Ⓓ Ⓔ
22 Ⓐ Ⓑ Ⓒ Ⓓ Ⓔ	47 Ⓐ Ⓑ Ⓒ Ⓓ Ⓔ	72 Ⓐ Ⓑ Ⓒ Ⓓ Ⓔ	97 Ⓐ Ⓑ Ⓒ Ⓓ Ⓔ	122 Ⓐ Ⓑ Ⓒ Ⓓ Ⓔ	147 Ⓐ Ⓑ Ⓒ Ⓓ Ⓔ
23 Ⓐ Ⓑ Ⓒ Ⓓ Ⓔ	48 Ⓐ Ⓑ Ⓒ Ⓓ Ⓔ	73 Ⓐ Ⓑ Ⓒ Ⓓ Ⓔ	98 Ⓐ Ⓑ Ⓒ Ⓓ Ⓔ	123 Ⓐ Ⓑ Ⓒ Ⓓ Ⓔ	148 Ⓐ Ⓑ Ⓒ Ⓓ Ⓔ
24 Ⓐ Ⓑ Ⓒ Ⓓ Ⓔ	49 Ⓐ Ⓑ Ⓒ Ⓓ Ⓔ	74 Ⓐ Ⓑ Ⓒ Ⓓ Ⓔ	99 Ⓐ Ⓑ Ⓒ Ⓓ Ⓔ	124 Ⓐ Ⓑ Ⓒ Ⓓ Ⓔ	149 Ⓐ Ⓑ Ⓒ Ⓓ Ⓔ
25 Ⓐ Ⓑ Ⓒ Ⓓ Ⓔ	50 Ⓐ Ⓑ Ⓒ Ⓓ Ⓔ	75 Ⓐ Ⓑ Ⓒ Ⓓ Ⓔ	100 Ⓐ Ⓑ Ⓒ Ⓓ Ⓔ	125 Ⓐ Ⓑ Ⓒ Ⓓ Ⓔ	150 Ⓐ Ⓑ Ⓒ Ⓓ Ⓔ

1 Ⓐ Ⓑ Ⓒ Ⓓ Ⓔ	26 Ⓐ Ⓑ Ⓒ Ⓓ Ⓔ	51 Ⓐ Ⓑ Ⓒ Ⓓ Ⓔ	76 Ⓐ Ⓑ Ⓒ Ⓓ Ⓔ	101 Ⓐ Ⓑ Ⓒ Ⓓ Ⓔ	126 Ⓐ Ⓑ Ⓒ Ⓓ Ⓔ
2 Ⓐ Ⓑ Ⓒ Ⓓ Ⓔ	27 Ⓐ Ⓑ Ⓒ Ⓓ Ⓔ	52 Ⓐ Ⓑ Ⓒ Ⓓ Ⓔ	77 Ⓐ Ⓑ Ⓒ Ⓓ Ⓔ	102 Ⓐ Ⓑ Ⓒ Ⓓ Ⓔ	127 Ⓐ Ⓑ Ⓒ Ⓓ Ⓔ
3 Ⓐ Ⓑ Ⓒ Ⓓ Ⓔ	28 Ⓐ Ⓑ Ⓒ Ⓓ Ⓔ	53 Ⓐ Ⓑ Ⓒ Ⓓ Ⓔ	78 Ⓐ Ⓑ Ⓒ Ⓓ Ⓔ	103 Ⓐ Ⓑ Ⓒ Ⓓ Ⓔ	128 Ⓐ Ⓑ Ⓒ Ⓓ Ⓔ
4 Ⓐ Ⓑ Ⓒ Ⓓ Ⓔ	29 Ⓐ Ⓑ Ⓒ Ⓓ Ⓔ	54 Ⓐ Ⓑ Ⓒ Ⓓ Ⓔ	79 Ⓐ Ⓑ Ⓒ Ⓓ Ⓔ	104 Ⓐ Ⓑ Ⓒ Ⓓ Ⓔ	129 Ⓐ Ⓑ Ⓒ Ⓓ Ⓔ
5 Ⓐ Ⓑ Ⓒ Ⓓ Ⓔ	30 Ⓐ Ⓑ Ⓒ Ⓓ Ⓔ	55 Ⓐ Ⓑ Ⓒ Ⓓ Ⓔ	80 Ⓐ Ⓑ Ⓒ Ⓓ Ⓔ	105 Ⓐ Ⓑ Ⓒ Ⓓ Ⓔ	130 Ⓐ Ⓑ Ⓒ Ⓓ Ⓔ
6 Ⓐ Ⓑ Ⓒ Ⓓ Ⓔ	31 Ⓐ Ⓑ Ⓒ Ⓓ Ⓔ	56 Ⓐ Ⓑ Ⓒ Ⓓ Ⓔ	81 Ⓐ Ⓑ Ⓒ Ⓓ Ⓔ	106 Ⓐ Ⓑ Ⓒ Ⓓ Ⓔ	131 Ⓐ Ⓑ Ⓒ Ⓓ Ⓔ
7 Ⓐ Ⓑ Ⓒ Ⓓ Ⓔ	32 Ⓐ Ⓑ Ⓒ Ⓓ Ⓔ	57 Ⓐ Ⓑ Ⓒ Ⓓ Ⓔ	82 Ⓐ Ⓑ Ⓒ Ⓓ Ⓔ	107 Ⓐ Ⓑ Ⓒ Ⓓ Ⓔ	132 Ⓐ Ⓑ Ⓒ Ⓓ Ⓔ
8 Ⓐ Ⓑ Ⓒ Ⓓ Ⓔ	33 Ⓐ Ⓑ Ⓒ Ⓓ Ⓔ	58 Ⓐ Ⓑ Ⓒ Ⓓ Ⓔ	83 Ⓐ Ⓑ Ⓒ Ⓓ Ⓔ	108 Ⓐ Ⓑ Ⓒ Ⓓ Ⓔ	133 Ⓐ Ⓑ Ⓒ Ⓓ Ⓔ
9 Ⓐ Ⓑ Ⓒ Ⓓ Ⓔ	34 Ⓐ Ⓑ Ⓒ Ⓓ Ⓔ	59 Ⓐ Ⓑ Ⓒ Ⓓ Ⓔ	84 Ⓐ Ⓑ Ⓒ Ⓓ Ⓔ	109 Ⓐ Ⓑ Ⓒ Ⓓ Ⓔ	134 Ⓐ Ⓑ Ⓒ Ⓓ Ⓔ
10 Ⓐ Ⓑ Ⓒ Ⓓ Ⓔ	35 Ⓐ Ⓑ Ⓒ Ⓓ Ⓔ	60 Ⓐ Ⓑ Ⓒ Ⓓ Ⓔ	85 Ⓐ Ⓑ Ⓒ Ⓓ Ⓔ	110 Ⓐ Ⓑ Ⓒ Ⓓ Ⓔ	135 Ⓐ Ⓑ Ⓒ Ⓓ Ⓔ
11 Ⓐ Ⓑ Ⓒ Ⓓ Ⓔ	36 Ⓐ Ⓑ Ⓒ Ⓓ Ⓔ	61 Ⓐ Ⓑ Ⓒ Ⓓ Ⓔ	86 Ⓐ Ⓑ Ⓒ Ⓓ Ⓔ	111 Ⓐ Ⓑ Ⓒ Ⓓ Ⓔ	136 Ⓐ Ⓑ Ⓒ Ⓓ Ⓔ
12 Ⓐ Ⓑ Ⓒ Ⓓ Ⓔ	37 Ⓐ Ⓑ Ⓒ Ⓓ Ⓔ	62 Ⓐ Ⓑ Ⓒ Ⓓ Ⓔ	87 Ⓐ Ⓑ Ⓒ Ⓓ Ⓔ	112 Ⓐ Ⓑ Ⓒ Ⓓ Ⓔ	137 Ⓐ Ⓑ Ⓒ Ⓓ Ⓔ
13 Ⓐ Ⓑ Ⓒ Ⓓ Ⓔ	38 Ⓐ Ⓑ Ⓒ Ⓓ Ⓔ	63 Ⓐ Ⓑ Ⓒ Ⓓ Ⓔ	88 Ⓐ Ⓑ Ⓒ Ⓓ Ⓔ	113 Ⓐ Ⓑ Ⓒ Ⓓ Ⓔ	138 Ⓐ Ⓑ Ⓒ Ⓓ Ⓔ
14 Ⓐ Ⓑ Ⓒ Ⓓ Ⓔ	39 Ⓐ Ⓑ Ⓒ Ⓓ Ⓔ	64 Ⓐ Ⓑ Ⓒ Ⓓ Ⓔ	89 Ⓐ Ⓑ Ⓒ Ⓓ Ⓔ	114 Ⓐ Ⓑ Ⓒ Ⓓ Ⓔ	139 Ⓐ Ⓑ Ⓒ Ⓓ Ⓔ
15 Ⓐ Ⓑ Ⓒ Ⓓ Ⓔ	40 Ⓐ Ⓑ Ⓒ Ⓓ Ⓔ	65 Ⓐ Ⓑ Ⓒ Ⓓ Ⓔ	90 Ⓐ Ⓑ Ⓒ Ⓓ Ⓔ	115 Ⓐ Ⓑ Ⓒ Ⓓ Ⓔ	140 Ⓐ Ⓑ Ⓒ Ⓓ Ⓔ
16 Ⓐ Ⓑ Ⓒ Ⓓ Ⓔ	41 Ⓐ Ⓑ Ⓒ Ⓓ Ⓔ	66 Ⓐ Ⓑ Ⓒ Ⓓ Ⓔ	91 Ⓐ Ⓑ Ⓒ Ⓓ Ⓔ	116 Ⓐ Ⓑ Ⓒ Ⓓ Ⓔ	141 Ⓐ Ⓑ Ⓒ Ⓓ Ⓔ
17 Ⓐ Ⓑ Ⓒ Ⓓ Ⓔ	42 Ⓐ Ⓑ Ⓒ Ⓓ Ⓔ	67 Ⓐ Ⓑ Ⓒ Ⓓ Ⓔ	92 Ⓐ Ⓑ Ⓒ Ⓓ Ⓔ	117 Ⓐ Ⓑ Ⓒ Ⓓ Ⓔ	142 Ⓐ Ⓑ Ⓒ Ⓓ Ⓔ
18 Ⓐ Ⓑ Ⓒ Ⓓ Ⓔ	43 Ⓐ Ⓑ Ⓒ Ⓓ Ⓔ	68 Ⓐ Ⓑ Ⓒ Ⓓ Ⓔ	93 Ⓐ Ⓑ Ⓒ Ⓓ Ⓔ	118 Ⓐ Ⓑ Ⓒ Ⓓ Ⓔ	143 Ⓐ Ⓑ Ⓒ Ⓓ Ⓔ
19 Ⓐ Ⓑ Ⓒ Ⓓ Ⓔ	44 Ⓐ Ⓑ Ⓒ Ⓓ Ⓔ	69 Ⓐ Ⓑ Ⓒ Ⓓ Ⓔ	94 Ⓐ Ⓑ Ⓒ Ⓓ Ⓔ	119 Ⓐ Ⓑ Ⓒ Ⓓ Ⓔ	144 Ⓐ Ⓑ Ⓒ Ⓓ Ⓔ
20 Ⓐ Ⓑ Ⓒ Ⓓ Ⓔ	45 Ⓐ Ⓑ Ⓒ Ⓓ Ⓔ	70 Ⓐ Ⓑ Ⓒ Ⓓ Ⓔ	95 Ⓐ Ⓑ Ⓒ Ⓓ Ⓔ	120 Ⓐ Ⓑ Ⓒ Ⓓ Ⓔ	145 Ⓐ Ⓑ Ⓒ Ⓓ Ⓔ
21 Ⓐ Ⓑ Ⓒ Ⓓ Ⓔ	46 Ⓐ Ⓑ Ⓒ Ⓓ Ⓔ	71 Ⓐ Ⓑ Ⓒ Ⓓ Ⓔ	96 Ⓐ Ⓑ Ⓒ Ⓓ Ⓔ	121 Ⓐ Ⓑ Ⓒ Ⓓ Ⓔ	146 Ⓐ Ⓑ Ⓒ Ⓓ Ⓔ
22 Ⓐ Ⓑ Ⓒ Ⓓ Ⓔ	47 Ⓐ Ⓑ Ⓒ Ⓓ Ⓔ	72 Ⓐ Ⓑ Ⓒ Ⓓ Ⓔ	97 Ⓐ Ⓑ Ⓒ Ⓓ Ⓔ	122 Ⓐ Ⓑ Ⓒ Ⓓ Ⓔ	147 Ⓐ Ⓑ Ⓒ Ⓓ Ⓔ
23 Ⓐ Ⓑ Ⓒ Ⓓ Ⓔ	48 Ⓐ Ⓑ Ⓒ Ⓓ Ⓔ	73 Ⓐ Ⓑ Ⓒ Ⓓ Ⓔ	98 Ⓐ Ⓑ Ⓒ Ⓓ Ⓔ	123 Ⓐ Ⓑ Ⓒ Ⓓ Ⓔ	148 Ⓐ Ⓑ Ⓒ Ⓓ Ⓔ
24 Ⓐ Ⓑ Ⓒ Ⓓ Ⓔ	49 Ⓐ Ⓑ Ⓒ Ⓓ Ⓔ	74 Ⓐ Ⓑ Ⓒ Ⓓ Ⓔ	99 Ⓐ Ⓑ Ⓒ Ⓓ Ⓔ	124 Ⓐ Ⓑ Ⓒ Ⓓ Ⓔ	149 Ⓐ Ⓑ Ⓒ Ⓓ Ⓔ
25 Ⓐ Ⓑ Ⓒ Ⓓ Ⓔ	50 Ⓐ Ⓑ Ⓒ Ⓓ Ⓔ	75 Ⓐ Ⓑ Ⓒ Ⓓ Ⓔ	100 Ⓐ Ⓑ Ⓒ Ⓓ Ⓔ	125 Ⓐ Ⓑ Ⓒ Ⓓ Ⓔ	150 Ⓐ Ⓑ Ⓒ Ⓓ Ⓔ

FOURTH PRACTICE AP/CLEP ENGLISH TEST
SECTION I

1. The one of the following is not known as a dramatist:

   (A) William Butler Yeats
   (B) A. E. Housman
   (C) Lady Gregory
   (D) Lord Dunsany
   (E) Oliver St. John Gogarty

2. Dr. Primrose is a

   (A) magician
   (B) detective
   (C) counterfeit physician
   (D) vicar
   (E) dentist

3. Tono-Bungay is a(n)

   (A) village on a South Sea island
   (B) character in Erewhon
   (C) patent medicine
   (D) resident of Mars
   (E) Indian

4. Squire Allworthy is a character in

   (A) A Sentimental Journey
   (B) The History of Tom Jones, a Foundling
   (C) The Adventures of Roderick Random
   (D) Pamela
   (E) Peregrine Pickle

5. Drums Under the Window is the life story of

   (A) Elizabeth II
   (B) Gertrude Stein
   (C) Sean O'Casey
   (D) Sacheverell Sitwell
   (E) Edna St. Vincent Millay

6. Present Indicative is the autobiography of

   (A) Laurence Olivier
   (B) Lilli Palmer
   (C) Noel Coward
   (D) Beatrice Lillie
   (E) Richard Burton

7. A man becomes a hero because of a confessed murder in

   (A) A Night at an Inn
   (B) Loyalties
   (C) The Tragedy of Nan
   (D) Escape
   (E) The Playboy of the Western World

8. Four Quartets was written by

   (A) Somerset Maugham
   (B) D. H. Lawrence
   (C) T. S. Eliot
   (D) William Butler Yeats
   (E) G. K. Chesterton

9. The sonnet sequence, 1914, was written by

   (A) Rupert Brooke
   (B) Siegfried Sasson
   (C) Robert Bridges
   (D) Gerald Manley Hopkins
   (E) Francis Thompson

10. Areopagitica is

   (A) an heroic drama laid in Athens

(B) a plea for freedom of the press
(C) a collection of poetic translations from Greek writers
(D) an attack on the Catholic Church
(E) a novel about flying monsters

11. George Bernard Shaw says that because Joan was kept waiting by the Dauphin

(A) the hens did not lay
(B) the newly bottled wine soured
(C) the statue of the Virgin wept
(D) a pestilence fell upon the army
(E) the child could not fall asleep

12. The Tabard Inn is the setting for important parts of

(A) The Merry Wives of Windsor
(B) David Copperfield
(C) Henry IV
(D) Dr. Faustus
(E) The Canterbury Tales

13. Among the following statements, the one which is not true is

(A) Gloriana in The Faerie Queene refers to Queen Elizabeth
(B) Amoretti is a sonnet cycle
(C) the Spenserian stanza consists of nine iambic pentameter lines and three rhymes
(D) The Shepherd's Calendar is written in language imitative of Chaucer's
(E) Sir Walter Raleigh encouraged Edmund Spenser

14. The Houyhnhnms were

(A) a race of horses
(B) a group of monsters
(C) a Dutch family in England
(D) a group of poets, following World War II
(E) a lost tribe

15. In The Innocence of Father Brown, Father Brown is

(A) a missionary in South Africa
(B) the head of an Anglican order
(C) a renegade priest
(D) a detective
(E) a farmer

16. The earliest version in English of the Arthurian legend is found in

(A) Malory's Morte d'Arthur
(B) Geoffrey's Historia Regum Britanniae
(C) Mabinogian
(D) Lord Randal
(E) Layamon's Brut

17. Bartleby the Scrivener worked for a time in

(A) a steel factory
(B) a department store
(C) a dead-letter office
(D) a shipbuilder's concern
(E) none of the above

18. "A disinterested endeavor to learn and propogate the best that is known and thought in the world" is the definition of criticism offered by

(A) Matthew Arnold
(B) Walter Pater
(C) George Saintsbury
(D) John Ruskin
(E) Thomas Carlyle

19. That supernatural and fantastic stories call for "a willing suspension of disbelief" was a statement made by

(A) William Godwin
(B) Samuel Taylor Coleridge
(C) Sir Arthur Conan Doyle
(D) H. G. Wells
(E) Mary Shelley

20. "His best companions, innocence and health; And his best riches, ignorance of wealth" was written by

(A) Oliver Goldsmith
(B) Thomas Gray
(C) Alexander Pope
(D) Samuel Johnson
(E) John Dryden

21. "Alas for the rarity
Of Christian charity
Under the sun!"
was written by

(A) Elizabeth Barrett Browning
(B) Thomas Hood
(C) Charles Lamb
(D) George Eliot
(E) W. S. Gilbert

22. A French writer "remarkable for his highly finished style and for the impersonal, objective, carefully sculptured method of narrative which he introduced into the novel" is

(A) Andre Gide
(B) Henri Barbusse
(C) Anatole France
(D) Emile Zola
(E) Gustave Flaubert

23. Of the following, the one which does not embody a searching criticism of some aspect of the American scene is

(A) Garland - Main Traveled Roads
(B) Saroyan - The Human Comedy
(C) Anderson - Winesburg, Ohio
(D) Tarkington - The Turmoil
(E) Sinclair - The Jungle

24. Judging by The Education of Henry Adams, the author

(A) welcomed the challenges of the new age
(B) concluded that order is the law of nature
(C) found refuge from disillusionment in a quiet religious faith
(D) secluded himself from the influences of a hostile world
(E) faced his own chaotic era with a world-weary skepticism

25. In The Ambassadors, by Henry James, Strether

(A) with difficulty persuades Chad to return to America
(B) decisively rejects the puritanism of his background
(C) adds to his troubles by marrying a waitress
(D) condemns Chad for the laxity of his conduct
(E) comes to believe that Chad's experiences have enriched his life

26. Of the following works, all are based on imaginary premises except

(A) It Can't Happen Here - Sinclair Lewis
(B) A Connecticut Yankee - Samuel Clemens
(C) The Earth Abides - George Stewart
(D) Yankee from Olympus - Catherine D. Bowen
(E) Lost Horizon - James Hilton

27. All of the following writers have been awarded a Pultizer Prize in poetry except

(A) Archibald MacLeish
(B) Peter Vierick
(C) W. H. Auden
(D) Louis Untermeyer
(E) Phyllis McGinley

Directions for answering questions 28-35; Complete each of the following passages of poetry by supplying the appropriate line for the blank space from the four choices given below. Three of the four choices are not appropriate. On your answer sheet, mark each of the four choices according to the following code:

(A) appropriate
(B) not appropriate in rhythm or meter
(C) not appropriate in style or tone
(D) not appropriate in meaning
(E) ungrammatical

Ask of thy mother earth why oaks are made
Taller or stronger than the weeds they shade?
Or ask or yonder argent fields above
....

28. Why Jove's satellites are less than Jove.

29. Why man's charity is more than love.

30. Why eagles dominate the dove.

31. Why Heaven's rule commands e'en Jove.

I wandered lonely as a cloud
That floats on high o'er vales and
  hills,
When all at once I saw a crowd,
....

32. Rows after rows of pretty daffodils.

33. Of daffodils and daffodils.

34. A host of golden daffodils.

35. So many streams, so many rills.

36. The group in which the three characters do not appear in novels by the same author is

(A) Clem Spender, Mattie Silver, Newland Archer
(B) Natty Bumppo, Uncas, Chingachgook
(C) Eugene Grant, Francis Starwick, George Webber
(D) Judge Pyncheon, Count Donatello, Roger Chillingworth
(E) Captain Ahab, Billy Budd, Fletcher Christian

37. Of the following, the one in which the main action did not occur during American participation in World War II is

(A) Heller - Catch-22
(B) Wouk - The Caine Mutiny
(C) Shaw - The Young Lions
(D) Mailer - The Naked and the Dead
(E) Jones - From Here to Eternity

38. The play, The Heiress, was an adaptation of a novel by Henry James, entitled

(A) The Portrait of a Lady
(B) Washington Square
(C) The Wings of the Dove
(D) The Bostonians
(E) The Ambassadors

39. The author of the interpretative study of the age of Emerson and Whitman, entitled American Renaissance, is

(A) Lewis Mumford
(B) F. O. Matthiessen
(C) Paul Elmer More
(D) Stuart P. Sherman
(E) John Crowe Ransom

40. A notable columnist and sports writer is

(A) John Tunis
(B) Ring Lardner
(C) William R. Benet
(D) Wilber O. Steele
(E) Paul Green

41. Frank Norris's The Octopus ends with

(A) the triumph of the exploited farmers
(B) the loading of a relief ship in a Pacific port
(C) Annixter's realization that love compensates for personal failure
(D) the destruction of the railroad's monopoly
(E) the death of the head of the syndicate

42. In The Ordeal of Mark Twain, Van Wyck Brooks emphasizes Twain's

(A) attempt to undermine American complacency
(B) artistry in satirizing native types
(C) earthy humor and optimism
(D) rejection of contemporary social and esthetic values
(E) desire to justify formal religion

43. A play that dealt courageously with the relationship of parents and children was

(A) The Silver Cord
(B) The Little Foxes
(C) Saturday's Children
(D) The Fourposter
(E) The Anatomy of a Murder

44. "The world stands out on either side
No wider than the heart is wide;
Above the world is stretched the sky,
No higher than the soul is high."
is a quotation from

(A) Robinson's Flammonde
(B) Millay's Renascence
(C) Frost's The Road Not Taken
(D) Amy Lowell's Patterns
(E) Master's Lucinda Matlock

45. "The end of art is pleasure, not truth. In order that pleasure may be intense, the work of art must have unity and brevity" is a quotation from

(A) Bret Harte
(B) Edgar Allan Poe
(C) Edwin A. Robinson
(D) D. H. Lawrence
(E) William Allen White

46. An attack on Byron's early poetry was launched by the editors of

(A) Blackwood's Edinburgh Magazine
(B) The London Gazette
(C) The Manchester Guardian
(D) The Liverpool Press
(E) The Edinburgh Review

47. The Dial voiced the opinion of

(A) the Abolitionists
(B) the Transcendentalists
(C) the Mormons
(D) the Knickerbocker School
(E) the Naturalists

48. The expression, "an acute study in the consciousness of lost honor," is best applied to

(A) The Old Wives' Tale - Arnold Bennett
(B) Lord Jim - Joseph Conrad
(C) Justice - John Galsworthy
(D) The Beloved Vagabond - William Locke
(E) Tess of the D'Urbervilles - Thomas Hardy

49. A poet who frequently drew his material from ancient and medieval legends is

(A) Ralph Hodgson
(B) John Henry Newman
(C) William Morris
(D) James Thomson (1834-82)
(E) Osbert Sitwell

50. Character and novel are correctly matched in each of the following pairs except

(A) Sophia Western - Tom Jones
(B) Matthew Bramble - Humphrey Clinker
(C) Uncle Toby - Tristram Shandy
(D) Amy Robsart - The Vicar of Wakefield
(E) Godfrey Gauntlet - Peregrine Pickle

51. Milton's Comus is indebted in part to

(A) the story of Dido, from The Aeneid
(B) the Circe myth, in the Odyssey
(C) the Andromache episode, in The Iliad
(D) the tale of Paolo and Francesca, in The Divine Comedy
(E) the Prologue, from The Canterbury Tales

52. The Heart of the Matter, by Graham Greene, has as its main character a

(A) British official in a small African town
(B) missionary among the aborigines of the Amazon
(C) convict-settler in Australia
(D) wealthy planation owner in the new Indonesia
(E) guerilla fighter in Vietnam

53. Sir James M. Barrie gives his characters "a second chance" to relieve and improve their lives in

(A) The Little Minister
(B) Peter Pan
(C) The Twelve-Pound Look
(D) The Admirable Crichton
(E) Dear Brutus

54. Ruskin's Sesame: Of Kings' Treasuries deals principally with

(A) the value of an enlightened citizenry to a liberal monarch
(B) the questions of what to read and how to read
(C) the duty of governments to subsidize the production of the

true "kings" of a nation - its writers
(D) the effects of nineteenth century economic policies on the workers of the world
(E) the weaknesses of a democratic form of government

55. Nineteen Eighty-Four is

(A) an atomic scientist's vision of Armageddon
(B) H. G. Wells's last literary attempt to predict the future
(C) a novel depicting life in a completely authoritarian state
(D) a Blake-like poem replete with apocalyptic visions
(E) an account of an atomic war

56. The philosophy of The Rubaiyat of Omar Khayyan is directly antithetical to that of

(A) Herrick's To the Virgins to Make Much of Time
(B) Browning's Prospice
(C) Rossetti's Sister Helen
(D) Suckling's Why So Pale and Wan, Fond Lover?
(E) Eliot's The Wasteland

57. The Playboy of the Western World loses stature with the community when

(A) he tries to murder his father
(B) he betrays the love of Pegeen
(C) his father reappears
(D) he flees after the first attack on his father
(E) he forsakes his friends

58. The Wakefield Cycle is the name given to

(A) a series of medieval mystery plays
(B) a tapestry depicting England at the time of William the Conqueror
(C) a collection of plays with Wakefield as the setting
(D) folk ballads collected by Bishop Thomas Percy
(E) a group of 17th century comedies

Answer questions 59-73 in accordance with the following directions:

The dots in each of the following prose selections signify that a sentence has been omitted. Following each selection are suggested sentences that may be substituted for the omitted sentence. For each suggested sentence, use the code below in order to arrive at your answer.

(A) appropriate
(B) not appropriate in meaning
(C) not appropriate in tone or diction
(D) grammatically incorrect
(E) wordy or redundant

Here some one will interrupt me with the remark: "By the bye, where are we, and whither are we going? What has all this to do with a University? .... It is instructive doubtless; but still how much has it to do with your subject?

59. How does it fit into the total picture?

60. Who is going to give you their attention, if you persist in pursuing the irrelevant?

61. Explain clearly, if you will, in no uncertain terms, what is its purpose.

62. Why don't you first define your terms, your premises, your general assumptions?

63. At least what has it to do with education?

English writers, by diversity of time, have taken diverse matters in hand. In our fathers' time nothing was read but books of feigned chivalry, wherein a man by reading should be led to none other end but only to manslaughter and bawdry. .... For surely vain words do work no small thing thereunto of their own nature. These books, as I have heard say, were made the most part in abbeys and monasteries, a very likely and fit fruit of such an idle and blind kind of living.

64. If one were constrained or impelled to surmise or suppose they were worth the time and mind, he is deceived and mistaken.

65. If any man suppose they were good enough to pass the time withal, he is deceived.

66. In the main, they were idle and useless withal, and was in no way barely fit fruit of scholars and priests.

67. Since hereunto parchment and ink were scarce withal, such prodigality augmented God's grace none whatsoever.

68. In God's name, hath there ever been such a waste of time!

House martins are distinguished from their congeners by having their legs covered with soft down feathers down to their toes......................
....
During the time of breeding they are often greatly molested with fleas.

69. As songsters, they are not much; but twitter rather nicely and prettily in their temporary abodes.

70. They do not hardly ever sing; or do they do much less than twitter in a pretty, intimate way.

71. They are no songsters; but twitter in a pretty inward soft manner in their nests.

72. They are withal like bats; but sing not unpleasantly and are more comely to man.

73. They neither sing nor chant nor warble; but occasionally twitter in a soft, gentle manner from time to time.

74. "He was not of an age, but for all time!" was

(A) Wordsworth's tribute to Milton
(B) Jonson's tribute to Shakespeare
(C) Sandburg's tribute to Lincoln
(D) Keat's tribute to Homer
(E) Chesterton's tribute to Shaw

75. The quotation,
"What's time? Leave Now for dogs and apes!
Man has Forever,"
is from a poem by

(A) Tennyson (C) Browning
(B) Swinburne (D) Clough
(E) Southey

76. The expression, "between two worlds," comes from a famous poem by

(A) Elizabeth Barrett Browning
(B) Swinburne
(C) Dante Gabriel Rossetti
(D) Matthew Arnold
(E) Alfred Tennyson

77. A knowledge of sixteenth century mysticism is necessary for a thorough understanding of

(A) Darkness at Noon
(B) Emma
(C) Middlemarch
(D) A Mask of Mercy
(E) Four Quartets

78. An important scence laid in the vaults of a New York bank occurs in Marquand's

(A) The Late George Apley
(B) B. F.'s Daughter
(C) So Little Time
(D) Point of No Return
(E) H. M. Pulham, Esq.

79. M'Fingal is

(A) a novel about an Irish pioneer in the Mid-West
(B) an account of the author's college days at Yale
(C) a poem burlesquing American Tories

(D) a tract advocating armed rebellion in the South
(E) an essay decrying social injustice

80. Babbitt accepted his son's marriage philosophically because he

(A) needed capital which Eunice's father could provide
(B) was relieved to have gossip so silenced
(C) admired the boy's courage in defying the wishes of the two families
(D) had secretly engineered the romance
(E) realized his own shortcomings

81. Of the following novelists, the one whose stories are laid in pioneer days in Kentucky is

(A) Bess Streeter Aldrich
(B) Dorothy Canfield
(C) Ruth Suckow
(D) Elizabeth Madox Roberts
(E) Marjorie Kinnan Rawlings

82. The Golden Day, Lewis Mumford interprets American culture through

(A) its imaginative literature
(B) its art
(C) its pioneer movements
(D) its economic changes
(E) its recreational activities

83. Of the following statements, the one which can be associated most appropriately with Brahminism is

(A) literature should be the expression of the natural man
(B) true divinity dwells in the soul of each individual
(C) literature belongs in the drawing room and the library, and it must observe the drawing room amenities
(D) government should be the enactment of God's justice into human laws
(E) literature cannot be appraised as art and music can

84. Winesburg, Ohio is

(A) a collection of short stories about twisted village personalities
(B) a novel about a girl's escape from a small mill town
(C) the autobiography of Sherwood Anderson
(D) the story of the growth of a typical American town
(E) a play about small-town racketeers

85. In The Irresponsibles, Archibald MacLeish made an attack on

(A) rulers who inherit their power
(B) religious leaders throughout the world
(C) ordinary people who do not "bother" to vote
(D) authors and scholars who do not take an active stand for democracy
(E) politicians who make deals among themselves

86. Emerson's Phi Beta Kappa address, The American Scholar,

(A) deplored the lack of American culture
(B) called upon the intellectual Americans to take an active part in the life of their times
(C) urged a continuation of European standards
(D) denied the educational value of books of fiction
(E) raised the question. "what is loyalty?"

87. Melville's Billy Budd

(A) was hanged after having been accused of mutiny
(B) was flogged to death for killing an officer
(C) was drowned in a whale-hunt
(D) jumped ship in the Marquesas
(E) was acquitted after trial

88. Of the following books, the one whose author best represents the "lost generation" of the twenties in his writings is

(A) The Bulwark
(B) This Side of Paradise
(C) The City of Trembling Leaves
(D) The Grand Design
(E) Dodsworth

89. Gerard Manley Hopkins is an exemplar of the poetic technique known as

(A) antiphonal verse
(B) sprung rhythm
(C) polyphonic prose
(D) asymmetric verse
(E) wrenched accent

90. Of the following, the selection incorrectly quoted is

(A) I must go down to the seas again, for the call of the running tide,
Is a sweet call and a wild call I cannot turn aside
(B) Go down to Kew in lilac-time, in lilac-time, in lilac-time;
Go down to Kew in lilac-time (it isn't far from London!)
And you shall wander hand in hand with love in summer's wonderland
(C) Break, break, break
On thy cold gray stones, O Sea!
And I would that my tongue could utter
The thoughts that arise in me
(D) Oh, to be in England
Now that April's there,
And whoever wakes in England
Sees, some morning, unaware,
That the lowest boughs and the brushwood sheaf
Round the elm-tree bole are in tiny leaf
(E) A little learning is a dangerous thing;
Drink deep, or taste not the Pierian spring.

91. Gotthold Lessing's essay, Laokoon, deals chiefly with

(A) Greek sculpture and its defects
(B) the difference between the art of poetry and the plastic arts
(C) dramatic poetry versus epic poetry
(D) source material for Greek tragedies
(E) the relationship between Greek and Renaissance art

92. All of the following have written several novels about the South except

(A) Ellen Glasgow
(B) Robert Penn Warren
(C) George Washington Cable
(D) William Faulkner
(E) Dorothy Canfield Fisher

93. A noted literary critic who has done considerable work in the area of semantics is

(A) Malcom Cowley
(B) I. A. Richards
(C) Granville Hicks
(D) John Ciardi
(E) M. C. Beardsley

94. Constantine P. Cavafy, the poet, is identified with the city of

(A) Alexandria
(B) Smyrna
(C) Athens
(D) Istanbul
(E) Rome

95. The titles and their sources listed below are all incorrectly matched except

(A) Look Homeward Angel - Milton
(B) So Red the Rose - Fitzgerald
(C) Time Remembered - Swinburne
(D) Generation of Vipers - Wylie
(E) Where Angles Fear to Tread - Pope

96. George Crabbe's twenty-four letters in poetry describing life in Aldeburgh, Suffolk were titled

(A) The Borough
(B) The Village
(C) The Parish Register
(D) Tales of the Hall
(E) The Town

97. The lines,
"You are old, Father William,' the young man cried,

'The few locks which are left you
are gray',"
were written by

(A) Edward Lear
(B) Lewis Carroll
(C) Oliver Wendell Holmes
(D) W. S. Gilbert
(E) Robert Southey

98. The long romantic poem which chronicles the victory of the Scottish king at Bannockburn is

(A) John Barbour's The Brus
(B) Thomas Hoccleve's The Regement of Princes
(C) John Lydgate's The Temple of Glass
(D) William Caxton's The Golden Legend
(E) John Lyly's Cupid and Campaspe

99. The author of The Advancement of Learning, also wrote

(A) The Anatomy of Melancholy
(B) Confessions of an Opium Eater
(C) The Gull's Hornbook
(D) A Short View of Tragedy
(E) The New Atlantis

100. Of the following definitions of poetry, the one which is incorrectly paired with its author is

(A) The spontaneous overflow of powerful feelings; it takes its origin from emotion recollected in tranquillity - E. A. Poe
(B) The record of the best and happiest moments of the happiest and best minds - P. B. Shelley
(C) If I feel physically as if the top of my head were taken off, I know that it is poetry - Emily Dickinson
(D) Poetry - the best words in their best order - Samuel Talor Coleridge
(E) Poetry is the most beautiful and effective mode of saying things - Matthew Arnold

ANSWER KEY

1. E
2. D
3. C
4. B
5. C
6. C
7. E
8. C
9. A
10. B
11. A
12. E
13. C
14. A
15. D
16. E
17. C
18. A
19. B
20. A
21. B
22. E
23. B
24. E
25. E
26. D
27. D
28. A
29. D
30. C
31. B
32. B
33. C
34. A
35. D
36. E
37. E
38. B
39. B
40. B
41. B
42. D
43. A
44. B
45. B
46. E
47. B
48. B
49. C
50. D
51. B
52. A
53. E
54. B
55. C
56. B
57. C
58. A
59. C
60. D
61. E
62 B
63. A
64. E
65. A
66. D
67. B
68. C
69. C
70. D
71. A
72. B
73. E
74. B
75. C
76. D
77. E
78. D
79. C
80. C
81. D
82. A
83. C
84. A
85. D
86. B
87. A
88. B
89. B
90. A
91. B
92. E
93. B
94. A
95. D
96. A
97. E
98. A
99. E
100. A

EXPLANATORY ANSWERS

1. (E) Gogarty, a minor poet and entertaining wit, was a friend and schoolmate of James Joyce, Yeats, George Russell (A.E.), Lady Gregory, and Lord Dunsany were all involved in the renaissance of Irish drama in the early decades of the twentieth century.

2. (D) Dr. Primrose is the hero of Goldsmith's Vicar of Wakefield and the narrator of the story. The work includes the famous adventures of Moses Primrose and the gross of green spectacles, as well as the lyric "When lovely woman stoops to folly."

3. (C) Tony Bungay is one of the most notable works of H. G. Wells. Published in 1909, it offers a picture of English society in dissolution at the close of the nineteenth century and the rise of a new class of the wealthy.

4. (B) Considered Henry Fielding's greatest work, Tom Jones tells of the foundling discovered one night by Mr. Allworthy, a wealthy, virtuous and benevolent country squire. For a time Tom suffers from the machinations of Blifil, but in the end he is discovered to be the son of Allworthy's sister and wins the hand of Sophia, daughter of the bluff Squire Western.

5. (C) Sean O'Casey, Irish playwright, is the author of such plays as Juno and the Paycock and The Plough and the Stars. In his autobiographical writings as in his plays, O'Casey shows his commitment to pacifism and socialism.

6. (C) Born in 1899, Noel Coward is an English playwright and actor who has also enjoyed considerable success as author and composer.

7. (E) In Synge's play, Christopher Mahon arrives cold and hungry at a country pub on the west coast of Ireland. He brags of slaying his own father with a single blow and is accepted by the villagers' praise turns to angry scorn. In the end Christy declares, "I'll go romancing through a romping lifetime from this hour to the dawning of the judgment day."

8. (C) Four Quartets is the title given to Eliot's poems "Burnt Norton," "East Coker," "The Dry Salvages," and "Little Gidding." The four are unified by a common theme and by intertwining imagery and rhythms. The total work is acclaimed by some as Eliot's greatest achievement; certainly it is an impressive affirmation of belief in orthodox Christianity.

9. (A) Brooke's 1914 group of sonnets was published in the posthumous Collected Poems of 1918. Brooke himself died in the second year of the war and was buried at Skyros. The publication of his poems was interpreted as evidence that his premature death was a serious loss to English letters.

10. (B) Areopagitica is the eloquent appeal to Parliament by John Milton for the liberty of unlicensed printing. He pleads: "Give me the liberty to know, to utter, and to argue freely, according to conscience, above all liberties."

11. (A) Shaw's play Saint Joan is an iconoclastic portrayal of the famous French martyr of the fifteenth century. The author's point is the artificiality of organized religion in contrast to the simple directness of the individual conscience.

12. (E) The Tabard Inn is the point at which the thirty odd pilgrims assemble for their trip to Canterbury. The host of the inn, Harry Bailly, proposes that each traveler tell two stories on the way to Canterbury and two on the way back. Thus does Chaucer construct the frame which enables him to tell a variety of tales.

13. (C) Spenserian stanza consists of nine lines, the first eight in iambic pentameter, the last in iambic hexameter. The rhyme scheme is ababbcbcc. In addition to The Faerie Queene, such famous works as The Eve of St. Agnes and Childe Harold are written in Spenserian stanza.

14. (A) Houyhnhnms are the talking horses in the fourth part of Gulliver's Travels. Here Swift contrasts the simplicity and virtue of the rational horses with the disgusting brutality of the Yahoos, who represent beast-like humans.

15. (D) G. K. Chesterton is the author of the popular Father Brown tales, in addition to poems such as The Ballad of the White Horse and biographies on Robert Browning and Charles Dickens.

16. (E) Layamon amplified and expanded the Arthurian legend that came down to him. He tells of the origin and purpose of the founding of the Round Table, and to a degree turns the Anglo-Norman Arthur of earlier minstrels into a strong English monarch. Layamon is also significant as the first source in English for the stories of Lear, Cymbeline, Sabrina - stories that were to be used by Shakespeare and Milton among others.

17. (C) In Herman Melville's short-story of the same title, Bartleby the Scrivener once served as a subordinate clerk in the Washington dead-letter office. The hopelessness symbolized by the dead letters - "On errands of life, these letters speed to death" - characterizes the life of Bartleby himself.

18. (A) In Essays in Criticism Arnold extended literary criticism to include an attack on the philistinism which he considered to be the dominant note of contemporary English society. Other significant critical prose writings by Arnold are: Culture and Anarchy, On Translating Homer, and The Study of Celtic Literature.

19. (B) The phrase appears in Coleridge's Biographia Literaria, where the poet is recalling the plan of the Lyrical Ballads. It was agreed between Wordsworth and him that his compositions would endeavor "to transfer from our inward nature a human interest and a semblance of truth sufficient to procure for these shadows of imagination that willing suspension of disbelief for the moment, which constitutes poetic faith."

20. (A) The lines are from Goldsmith's The Deserted Village. The theme of the poem is the superiority of rural to urban life, of agriculture to trade. On a return to the village of Auburn, the poet decries the state of society in which "wealth accumulates and men decay."

21. (B) The lines are from The Bridge of Sighs, one of Hood's most popular works. The subject is the discovery of the body of a drowned woman, a

social outcast, and the treatment shows Hood's mastery of pathos.

22. (E) Flaubert's most famous novel is Madame Bovary, a realistically sordid tale of bourgeois life in the French provinces. It demonstrates his dedication to the search for the precise word, le mot juste.

23. (B) Saroyan has achieved popularity as novelist, playwright, and short-story writer. In The Human Comedy he offers a pleasantly sentimentalized picture of American life. The most famous of his short stories is probably "The Daring Young Man on the Flying Trapeze."

24. (E) Henry Adams' intellectual autobiography attempts to achieve a synthesis of all human knowledge and to show a continuity between European medievalism and American industrialism. He seeks to reconcile the Virgin of the thirteenth century and the Dynamo of the twentieth.

25. (E) In this novel, Henry James shows the various reactions of different Americans to European culture. Chadwick Newsome succumbs completely; Strether is captivated but returns to America out of a sense of duty; Sarah Peacock remains indifferent.

26. (D) Catherine Drinker Bowen is a popular contemporary biographer of such figures as the American jurist Oliver Wendell Holmes and the English essayist and philosopher Sir Francis Bacon.

27. (D) MacLeish received the award in 1933 for Conquistador; Auden in 1948 for The Age of Anxiety; Viereck in 1949 for Terror and Decorum; Phyllis McGinley in 1961 for Times Three: Selected Verse from Three Decades.

28. (A) These lines from Alexander Pope point to the presumption of man's questioning the wisdom of God. Man might equally well ask the skies above why the satellites that circle the planet Jupiter are smaller than Jupiter itself.

29. (D) There is no connection between turning to the skies and seeking an answer to a question regarding man's charity.

30. (C) The tone of the passage demands a grander question.

31. (B) This line shows almost total disregard of the iambic pentameter that is demanded to complete the heroic couplet.

32. (B) This line is not written in the iambic tetrameter of the rest of the quatrain.

33. (C) The proposed line has no discernible style.

34. (A) This, the line actually written by Wordsworth, combines the simplicity of "golden daffodils" with the impressiveness of "host." This combination of simplicity and dignity makes the entire poem.

35. (D) Streams and rills can hardly be referred to as a crowd.

36. (E) Captain Ahab and Billy Budd appear in Herman Melville's Moby Dick and Billy Budd, respectively. Fletcher Christian is the central figure of Mutiny on the Bounty by Nordhoff and Hall.

37. (E) James Jones' novel is set in Hawaii in the period immediately preceding the attack on Pearl Harbor. Jones has also written The Pistol and The Thin Red Line.

38. (B) The heiress is Catherine Sloper, plain, honest, but determined, who falls in love with the penniless fortune-hunter Morris Townsend. Virtually disinherited by her father, she accepts her fate graciously and in later life refuses a second chance to marry Townsend.

39. (B) Matthiessen's book was and still is a milestone in the development of literary criticism in the United States. In this work Matthiessen

analyzes five major writers who influenced them. The five writers are Emerson, Thoreau, Hawthorne, Melville, and Whitman.

40. (B) Lardner is also noted as a humorist and short-story writer. Two of his most famous short story collections are How to Write Short Stories (1924) and The Love Nest (1926).

41. (B) The Octopus is the first work in Norris' projected trilogy on the "Epic of the Wheat." At the end of the novel, the natural force of the wheat is seen as the eternal victor over the puny power of individual men. The representative of the railroad, S. Behrman, falls into the ship's hold and is buried alive under the flood of wheat that roars out of the loading chute.

42. (D) The biographical study was published in 1920 and is widely regarded as one of the pioneer studies in psychological criticism. Another biographer who has taken the psychological approach to literary criticism is Joseph Wood Krutch, whose Edgar Allan Poe: A Study in Genius applies Freudian theories to the poet's life.

43. (A) Sidney Howard's play of 1926 is a harsh picture of a mother who smothers her two sons in neurotic love. The older son finally breaks free, but the younger man renounces his engagement for the bondage of "the silver cord." Other works by Howard include They Knew What They Wanted and Christopher Bean.

44. (B) Miss Millay wrote "Renascence" at the age of nineteen. Its popular success made her a symbol and legend of the bohemian Twenties. Her love sonnets include "What Lips My Lips Have Kissed" and "Oh, Sleep Forever in the Latmian Cave."

45. (B) Poe was convinced that only a short lyric can sustain a high level of poetic vision. He was fascinated with the emotive power of particular words and worked tirelessly to find the precise word to produce in the reader the psychological or emotional reaction that the poem demanded. In his essay "The Philosophy of Composition," he tells of his choice of the word nevermore as the structural basis of his famous poem "The Raven."

46. (E) While a student at Cambridge, Byron published a collection of poems under the title Hours of Idleness. The caustic criticism of this work by the Edinburgh Review led Bryon to reply in English Bards and Scotch Reviewers, a satirical poem in heroic couplets. Byron attacked not only Jeffrey, the editor of the Review but the Lake poets and Scott. His praise is reserved for the neoclassicists Dryden and Pope.

47. (B) The Dial appeared for a few years in the 1840's and for a time was edited by Ralph Waldo Emerson. Henry David Thoreau was one of the contributors.

48. (B) Lord Jim is the story of a young Englishman who in a moment of panic deserts his apparently sinking ship. He finally redeems his honor by a noble death. Other novels by Conrad are The Nigger of the Narcissus and Heart of Darkness.

49. (C) Morris' works, Life and Death of Jason and Earthly Paradise, show his love of myth and legends. Sigurd the Volsung is probably his finest poem. Based on the Volsunga Saga, it is an epic in four books written in anapestic couplets.

50. (D) Amy Robsart, in real life the wife of Robert Dudley, Earl of Leicester, appears in Scott's Kenilworth. The leading character in Goldsmith's The Vicar of Wakefield is Dr. Primrose.

51. (B) In Milton's masque Comus, Comus is the son of Bacchus and Circe. He waylays travelers and tempts them to taste a magic drink that changes

their facial appearance to that of wild beasts. Sabrina, goddess of the river Severn, frees a lady who has been entrapped by Comus.

52. (A) Greene's novel is a study of the conflict between religious duty and human pity in the heart of Scobie. Other novels by the same author are The End of the Affair, The Quiet American, A Burned-Out Case.

53. (E) In Dear Brutus, each character has an opportunity at a second chance at life by visiting the magic wood just outside old Lob's house. The inevitable awakening that occurs in the third act is carefully kept within the comic vein. The title is indebted to the line from Julius Caesar: "The fault, dear Brutus, is not in our stars, but in ourselves."

54. (B) In this first essay from Sesame and Lilies Ruskin urges the diffusion of the literature as "conferring the purest kingship that can exist among men." In the second essay "Lilies: of Queen's Gardens," he considers the education and duties of women of the upper class.

55. (C) Orwell's novel envisions a time when the nations of the world are reduced to three super-states - Eurasia, Eastasia and Oceania - and was has become permanent. Big Brother is the symbol of the state's eternal vigilance and of the end of of personal freedom. In the end Winston Smith, who has attempted rebellion, is broken in mind and body.

56. (B) The theme of The Rubaiyat is to live for the day, to indulge the senses, for the meaning of life is doubtful but death is certain. In his poem, Browning asks "Fear death?" and answers that he has always fought his way through life and he will not be defeated by death.

57. (C) In Synge's play Christy Mahon has bragged of killing his father, but when his father reappears the two go off together, leaving behind Pegeen Mike who has fallen in love with the Playboy. Other plays by Synge are Riders to the Sea and In the Shadow of the Glen.

58. (A) The Wakefield Cycle, also known as the Towneley plays, is one of the four great collections of extant English mystery or miracle plays. These plays were drawn from the legendary lives of the saints and from the Old and New Testament, but the religious themes did not prevent large sprinklings of humor, as in the Second Shepherd's Play in the Wakefield Cycle.

59. (C) The proposed sentence is too colloquial for the rest of the passage.

60. (D) The plural their does not agree with the singular Who is.

61. (E) It is redundant to use both explain clearly and in no uncertain terms.

62. (B) The passage does not imply a discussion that could lead the present speaker to make such a demand.

63. (A) This question provides the link between the one that precedes and the one that follows.

64. (E) Constrained, surmise, deceived, would be much better if not yoked to impelled, suppose, mistaken, respectively.

65. (A) In this line the style and meaning accord with the rest of the passage.

66. (D) There are two errors: the use of was instead of were, and the double negative that results from using no and barely in the same phrase.

67. (B) The passage indicates strong disapproval of the monastic life, but the proposed sentence implies a belief that the monks did seek to augment God's grace.

68. (C) Despite the use of hath, this sentence is obviously in the style of a period considerably later than that of the passage.

69. (C) The phrases"they are not much" and"temporary abodes"do not suit the rather elegant style of the rest of the passage.

70. (D) The double negative and the double do are extremely gauche.

71. (A) Here the style, meaning and grammar are all acceptable.

72. (B) Bats do not have "their legs covered with soft down feathers down to their toes."

73. (E) The sentence is generally wordy, but the combination of occasionally and from time to time is particularly offensive.

74. (B) In his tribute to Shakespeare, Jonson invoked his fellow dramatist:

Thou are a monument, without a tomb,
And art alive still, while thy book
  doth live
And we have wits to read, and praise
  to give.

This same poem is also remembered for its slight at Shakespeare's education - "small Latin and less Greek" and the epithet "Sweet Swan of Avon."

75. (C) Even if the lines themselves are not familiar, the style and meaning clearly point to Browning. The rhetorical question "What's time?" has its counterpart in "Fear death?" from "Prospice." The optimistic affirmation in life - "Man has forever" - is to be found in other Browning poems - e.g., "Rabbi Ben Ezra."

76. (D) The phrase occurs in Arnold's "Stanzas from the Grande Chartreuse." The poet sees his generation.

Wandering between two worlds, one
  dead,
The other powerless to be born.

The theme is very similar to that of "Dover Beach," in which the Sea of Faith is heard retreating from earth's shore.

77. (E) Four Quartets is T. S. Eliot's great testimony to his belief in Anglo-Catholicism. This belief is set forth also in the prose work The Idea of a Christian Society.

78. (D) In this novel, published in 1949, Charles Gray is a successful banker who pauses in mid-life to question the worth of his life. Eventually he decides that it is too late, that he has passed "the point of no return."

79. (C) John Trumbull's satire is founded on Samuel Butler's Hudibras and Churchill's The Ghost. The protagonist is a Scotsman instead of a native American. Instead of satirical bite, the work offers good-natured entertainment.

80. (C) In Babbitt, Sinclair Lewis is satirizing the conventionality of American suburban life, just as he satirizes the medical profession in Arrowsmith, organized religion in Elmer Gantry, big business in Dodsworth, and small-town limitations in Main Street.

81. (D) Novels by Mrs. Roberts include The Time of Man (1926), My Heart and My Flesh (1927), and The Great Meadow (1930). She has also published two short-story collections: The Haunted Mirror and Not by Strange Gods.

82. (A) Editor and critic, Lewis Mumford has published a number of important studies of American life and culture. In addition to The Golden Day, these include Technics and Civilization, The South in Architecture, and most recently The City in History.

83. (C) In India, a Brahmin or Brahman is a member of the highest or the priestly caste among the Hindus. As used in the West, the word may mean

a highly cultured person, but frequently it implies social exclusiveness and intellectual snobbery.

84. (A) The central figure of Sherwood Anderson's story cycle is George Willard, reporter on the Winesburg Eagle. Two of the best-known sketches are "Hands," a study of repressed homosexuality, and "Godliness," a modern version of the Biblical tale of David and Jesse.

85. (D) At least since the inception of the New Deal era, MacLeish has been a poet actively engaged in political and social issues. During Roosevelt's administration he held public office and sought to use his artistic ability in support of American democracy and in opposition to facism. His verse play for radio The Fall of the City is an allegory on fascism.

86. (B) Delivered in 1837, The American Scholar was the most influential demand for American independence from Europe in thought and artistic creation. Emerson declares, "We have listened too long to the courtly muses of Europe." He urges the thinking man to participation and leadership.

87. (A) Set during the Napoleonic era, Billy Budd tells of a young seaman impressed into the British navy. Accused of mutiny by the evil master-at-arms Claggart, Billy in a flash of anger strikes his accuser. Captain Vere recognizes Billy's innocence before the eyes of God, but feels it necessary to execute him lest the other sailors use the incident as an excuse to mutiny.

88. (B) F. Scott Fitzgerald is, for many readers, the chronicler of the Jazz Age. The themes that dominate his novels are also to be found in his short stories. "Babylon Revisited" is a sensitive study of the passing of an era; "Winter Dream" and "The Rich Boy" are tales of social ambition.

89. (B) Sprung rhythm was a term invented by Hopkins to describe meter which depends on the number of stressed syllables and disregards unstressed syllables. In each foot the first syllable is always accented. The meter is to be found in "The Windhover," "Spring," "God's Grandeur" and other poems by Hopkins.

90. (A) The second stanza of John Masefield's poem "Sea-Fever" actually reads:

I must down to the seas again, or
  the call of the running tide
Is a wild call and a clear call that
  may not be denied.

The other poets are as follows:
- B. Alfred Noyes
- C. Alfred Tennyson
- D. Robert Browning
- E. Alexander Pope

91. (B) Lessing is a German dramatist and critic of the eighteenth century. In his most famous essay he sought to define the basic laws of aesthetic perception. As a critic of the drama he has been ranked second only to Aristotle.

92. (E) Dorothy Canfield Fisher (1879-1958) wrote a number of novels, including The Bent Twig and The Brimming Cup, in addition to essays and studies in literature and in education.

93. (B) Richards is one of the experts on language who provided the theoretical basis for the New Criticism. With C. K. Ogden he wrote The Meaning of Meaning. In 1926 his Principles of Literary Criticism appeared. Here he advances the thesis that poetic images are designed rather to arouse emotional attitudes than to convey information.

94. (A) Cavafy is the pen name used by C. P. Kavafis, 1863-1933, who wrote narrative poems about the past of Greece, and personal lyrical poems that often dealt with homosexual love. He published only one book of poems.

95. (D) Generation of Vipers, by Philip Wylie, derives its title from the Bible: "Oh generation of vipers, who hath warned you to flee from the wrath to come?" (Matthew. I, 7) Wylie is a satirist and critic of such aspects of American society as female dominance.

96. (A) All these poems are by Crabbe. The Village and The Borough are his longest works. The former is a somber, realistic picture of the rural poor; the latter contains some notable tales, especially "Peter Grimes," "Ellen Orford," and "Clelia." Crabbe always strove for accurate, unadorned description.

97. (E) Southey's poem "The Old Man's Comforts, and How He Gained Them," a rather silly poem, is known only because of Lewis Carroll's excellent parody. Southey wrote a number of long poems, "Thalaba," "Madoc," and "The Curse of Kehama." He is now better known for such shorter poems as "The Battle of Blenheim," "The Holly Tree," and "The Inchcape Rock."

98. (A) John Barbour was a Scottish poet of the fourteenth century. His poem The Brus or The Bruce celebrates the war of Scottish independence and the deeds of King Robert and James Douglas. He is also thought to be the author of the Legend of Troy and Legends of the Saints, translations from the Latin of Guido da Colonna.

99. (E) The Advancement of Learning is unlike most of Francois Bacon's philosophical studies in that it was written in English rather than Latin. Bacon examines the various methods of advancing knowledge and analyzes the three divisions of knowledge, history, poetry, and philosophy.

The New Atlantis is Bacon's unfinished treatise on political philosophy in the form of a fable.

100. (A) In the Preface to Lyrical Ballads, Wordsworth insisted on poetry as the record of powerful emotions. Poe, on the other hand, emphasizes the careful, meticulous artistry of the poet, who must search until he finds the precise word to communicate a single mood.

FOURTH PRACTICE AP/CLEP ENGLISH TEST
SECTION II

Question 1 (Suggested time - 30 minutes)

Directions: Discuss the "moral christian tradition" found in the character of Hamlet or some other acknowledged literary work.

Response:

Hamlet possessed qualities and abilities that endeared him to the populace. He had a compassionate concern for mankind. He was learned and witty, skilled with the sword, and had a taste for music and drama. On the credit side of his character were his moral standards, which were high and consistent. Although he was an idealist, he was also a realist and given to thoughtful rather than impulsive actions.

His mother's hasty marriage to his uncle, King Claudius, disgusted Hamlet for he felt it was an act that was immoral in its very nature. The Church did not approve of marriage between a woman and her brother-in-law, and in view of the tenets of the Church, they were living together without the blessings of the Church. Hamlet claimed it was an incestuous relationship and pleaded with his mother to end the marriage. The plea had Christian moral overtones.

The ghost's entreaty to Hamlet to avenge his death did not bring about instant retaliation because Hamlet had to decide whether the ghost was sent by the devil or in reality the spirit of his dead father. This too shows concern for moral tradition. Hamlet's reaction was contemplative, because he realized that he would have to set right the evils around him in a manner not to his liking.

The revelation that Hamlet had about his two friends, Rosencrantz and Guildenstern, their hypocrisy and willingness to spy on him in order to ingratiate themselves with Claudius, brings forth the remarkable speech, thus:

> "What a piece of work is a man, how noble in reason, how
> infinite in faculties, in form and moving how express and
> admirable, in action how like an angel, in apprehension
> how like a god: the beauty of the world, the paragon of
> animals! And yet to me what is this quintessence of dust?
> Man delights not me - nor woman neither."

He knew well the vagaries of man.

According to Christian beliefs at that time, it was improper not to avenge murder of one's kin, yet in Hamlet's case it was difficult for him to carry out such a deed even when presented with a perfect opportunity. His uncle kneeling at prayer would have made it easy, but in Hamlet's mind the fact that he was at prayer would have erased the sin from his foul act and his soul escape damnation. The moment for revenge passed.

Another aspect of his moral values was the fact that he could not commit suicide, for that was against Christian principals, and the lines from the play here bear this out as follows:

> "Or that the everlasting had not fixed His canon 'gainst
> self-slaughter."

He could not damn his soul to perdition.

Hamlet's affection for Horatio was sincere and on a high moral plane, as evidenced by his refusal to allow him to drink of the poison. Also his feeling for Yorick when he was handed his skull in the graveyard is another example of his feeling for mankind in general.

Hamlet was well aware of the inequities of his position and of the plot upon his life by his uncle, yet he did consent to the duel with Laertes. He felt he had a moral obligation to himself to submit to the request.

Forging the signature of Claudius on a letter sent to England requesting that Hamlet be killed, and changing the name to Rosencrantz and Guildenstern, did not upset Hamlet, but should have according to Christian moral tradition. He felt that their deaths were justified, and in that case morally right. Finally, his mother's death from a drink intended for him spurs him on to kill the king for his treachery. Hamlet eventually acted and thus upheld his honor as he discharged his filial duty.

Question 2 (Suggested time - 50 minutes)

Directions: Literary giants have written about other literary figures (even their critics); write an essay of such a happening. Select a work of acknowledged literary merit and in a well-written essay show how the character is developed. You may wish to choose your illustration from the list of authors provided below, but you may use any work of comparable literary excellence.

Sophocles	William Butler Yeats
Harold Pinter	William Wordsworth
Anton Chekhov	Nathaniel Hawthorne
Robert Frost	Henrik Ibsen
T.S. Eliot	Alfred Lord Tennyson
Tennessee Williams	William Faulkner
James Joyce	Sylvia Plath
George Orwell	Virginia Woolf
Dylan Thomas	James Baldwin
Charles Dickens	Miguel de Cervantes
John Keats	Alexander Pope

Response (1):

"Portrait of Addison"

Joseph Addison was an English poet, essayist, and critic. He was also a friend and contemporary of Alexander Pope. In 1715, the two had a bitter quarrel because Addison supported a rival translation of Homer (instead of Pope's translation). He tried to discredit Pope. Addison had the misfortune of crossing one of England's greatest satirists.

"Portrait of Addison" appeared in a long poem, "Epistle to Dr. Arbuthnot," which contained many character descriptions. Pope's "Portrait" consists of eleven heroic couplets, most of which are separate attacks within themselves. The purpose of this paper will be to primarily explain these attacks and references Pope drew upon in the poem.

Overall, Pope's portrayal of Addison is of the good boy gone bad. He opens up with the "nice" description of Addison, the idea that he is (or was) blessed with talent and art. The implication that follows, though, is that Addison, because of other existing rivalries, has developed a complex. Although one time friends, the fact that Addison belonged to Addison's literary society and Pope belonged to Swift's probably didn't help matters.

"Shou'd such a man, too fond to rule alone,
Bear, like the Turk, no brother near the throne."

Pope is saying that Addison has put himself on a pedestal, and thinks no one else can compare with him. He attacks anyone (in this case Pope) who he considers a rival. The Turkish monarchs had a reputation for murdering off relatives who were considered rivals to the throne. Addison is paranoid, and likewise does the same as the Turk.

Lines 199-200 would have us believe that Addison is seething with jealousy and envy. It is here that Pope starts to make use of the heroic couplet showing Addison with contradictory actions; or to state it simply, that Addison is "wishy-washy." Pope says that Addison scorns, yet only because he is jealous. It is the only way

Addison can save his ego. It's his only defense.

"Damn with faint praise, assent with civil leer,
And without sneering, teach the rest to sneer;
Willing to sound, and yet afraid to strike,
Just hint a fault, and hesitate dislike;"

Pope is claiming here that Addison outwardly supports him, yet this is what is most damaging to Pope; "Damn with faint praise." It's with "civil leer" and "faint praise" that Addison generates the opposition. It is like in modern times a criminal supporting a political candidate; in reality he is damaging that candidate. The only difference is that Addison is consciously doing it. It is in this way that Addison teaches "the rest to sneer" without sneering himself.

The second couplet appearing above again points to the fact that Addison is indecisive, "wishy-washy." It would seem that Addison has no real motivation or capacity to do anything effective, and that if he could, he'd be too apprehensive to do it anyway. He accents this with "strong" words (in implication) like wound and strike, and then uses weaker words like fault and dislike.

"Dreading ev'n fools, by Flatterers besieg'd
And so obliging that he ne'er oblig'd;
Like Cato, give his little Senate laws.
And sit attentive to his own applause;"

"Dreading ev'n fools" implies that Addison doesn't even have enough brainpower to confront a fool; that all he can handle are the flatterers and he loves every minute of it. Cato was a Roman patriot and hero (whom Addison wrote a play about); the Senate refers to Addison's literary society. Pope insinuates that Addison sits on his pedestal all day drinking in the flattery, "sitting attentive to his own applause." The literary coterie is merely a fan club.

The Wits and Templers mentioned in line 211 refer to literary people of the day. Pope says that while they support and praise Addison they really know not why. Atticus was a Roman philosopher known for his love of truth. Pope concluded by saying that men of truth would weep at what Addison stood for.

Response (2):

"Analyzation of Pope's 'Epistle to Mr. Addison'"

Alexander Pope's "Epistle V, To Mr. Addison," was 'occasioned by his dialogue on medals,' that is, Joseph Addison's "Dialogues Upon the Usefulness of Ancient Medals." It was another in a series of attacks on the person and literary capabilities of Addison; the feud dated back to 1712, when he suggested to Pope that he lengthen "The Rape of the Lock." Previous to this episode they had been good friends; when Pope first came to London to earn his living as a writer he joined Addison's set of literary cronies. However, Pope was as vain as he was physically short, and although he revised most of his works frequently in his search for poetic precision and perfection, apparently the revisions were all of his own initiative.

One of the results of this quarrel, fed by many other incidents and vituperative attacks on both sides, was the "Epistle to Mr. Addison." It was written in 1715 during the subject's lifetime, but not published until later, when Pope tacked it on to his four Moral Essays, written in the form of epistles. A thorough satirization of Addison, in the character of Atticus, is found in the Epistle to Dr. Arbruthnot, published in 1732.

In the epistle to Addison, Pope is seemingly very polite to him and he appears to praise his dialogue. He restates Addison's theme that ancient buildings and monuments soon crumble into dust, whereas coins of the civilizations are a more lasting and venerable symbol of the culture. Beneath the polite exterior, however, is concealed a rather clever satire on the reasoning behind Mr. Addison's claim to the superiority of coins in his Dialogues. The wording in the coupled,

> "Convinced, she [Ambition] not contracts her vast design,
> And all her triumphs shrink into a coin"

gives one the impression that a small piece of metal is not large enough to disclose the might and glory displayed in monuments. By using the images of triumph shrinking and ambition contracting, he leads one to feel that the old glory has become ignobled by being squeezed so small. The power and glory of ages past seems diminished and even ridiculed by being forced to fit the narrow bounds of the coin, seen in the phrases "Scantier limits the proud Arch Confine," "A small Euphrates," and "And Little Eagles."

The last 'paragraph' of the work is a supposed longing for England to coin its Tributaries and heros for future generations to admire. He even suggests a series of coins commemorating poets.

> "Or in fair series laurelled Bards be shown
> A Virgil there, and here an Addison."

But knowing how Pope felt about Addison, the couplet appears to be extremely tongue-in-cheek by mentioning him and Virgil in the same breath. To Pope, Addison was a fool, and he proceeded from satirizing his intellectual follies, i.e., his Dialogues, to his person.

Of course, this epistle is not an actual letter delivered to Mr. Addison for his private edification. Like almost all of Pope's works, it is a poem written in heroic couplets. As was mentioned before, he was a perfectionist in classical polish and restraint, and this shows up plainly in his iambic pentameter. The reader feels no Romantic emotion from the description of the proud monuments sacked by infidels and pagans, or pity that "Beneath her palms sad Judea weeps." This poem, like all of his verse, appeals solely to the intellect, as it is interesting and even slightly amusing, but not passionate. Yet he was the master at form, and so Pope constrived to keep the couplets from being tedious through poetic devices such as variations in tempo and careful alliteration. The couplet

> "In one short view subjected to our eye
> Gods, Emp'rors, Heroes, Sages, Beauties lie"

is an excellent example of his variations of tempo and slight deviations from iambic pentameter.

Taken as a whole, the poem is certainly not a great original moral essay; in truth, it is not a moral essay at all, rather a retaliation against poor Mr. Addison. However, within it Pope clearly exhibits his cleverness as a satirist and skill as a technician, for which he has always been regarded as great.

Response (3):

"In the Age of Reason"

"Epistle to Mr. Addison" was written in 1715 (Joseph Addison was one of the authors of "The Spectator" and "The Tatler." His essays were to give birth to the idea of the magazine.) At this time Addison and Pope were still friends. It was occasioned by the publication of Addison's "Dialogues on Medals."

This poem as all of Pope's works is a perfect embodyment of eighteenth-century poetic rules and regulations. "Epistle to Mr. Addison" is a masterpiece of Pope's brilliant manipulations of the heroic couplet (pairs of rhyming iambic pentameter lines). Every two lines are perfectly blended to gain their maximum effect.

Pope opens his Epistle with a statement of his fear of time, which causes culture and civilization to degenerate.

"See the wild Waste of all devouring years."

This line vividly conveyed his fear. He then pictures the ruins of Greece and Rome. These were perhaps the two greatest civilizations of all times, yet today they are nothing. Only their ruins remain.

"With nodding arches, broken temples spread."

Somewhere buried in the ruins a name or story is preserved. This is a reminder of the culture. Historians argue over the who and why behind the name. They mistakedly give credit of one man's deeds to another. Pope's choice of emperors, Titus and Vespasian, displays his demand of perfection in his couplet. Titus is believed to have ruled while his father was still alive; in this way Titus is given credit for work which might have been his father's. Also, Titus' reign was at the time considered a great and glorious one, but it had no lasting value. His reign is a symbol of Rome for it too has been devoured by time.

In opening his second section he begins with the ambitions of man. Ambition, Pope says, is worthless for all will someday be gone as is the Roman Empire.

"Ambition sigh's, She found it vain to trust."

The victories, the agonies of Rome and all other great cultures are vanished with their great men. We remember of Rome only what we see in a coin.

"And all her Trumphs shrink into a coin."

Confined in the coin you can see Rome's proud temples, Egypt's Nile. How they seem so small; their grandeur is forgotten. It is suggested that the coins of which Pope writes are symbolic of literature. This theory is later proven by his references to Plato and Virgil as coin makers. Through literature we gain a picture of the times as they were. So medals (literature) brings to us the ages before. Through them we meet the great men and women of the past for here alone do they live.

He refers to antiquarians who discover these antique objects. He calls them dull and says they view their discovery only for their age not for their significance.

"Th' inscription value, but the rust adore."

True learned men see the remains of great civilization as a means to reveal historical truths which they in turn tell the world. Through these learned men Rome, her heros, and her gods live again.

"Touch'd by thy hand, again Rome's glories shine."

Pope then states clearly that the medals of which he speaks are art.

"The verse and sculpture bore and equal part."

Here he also relates art to literature. To Pope all arts blend into one center, that center being writing.

In the last section, Pope merges into Patriotism. England, he proclaims, should imitate Greece and Rome and make her own medals.

"Stan Emulous to Greek and Roman fame."

This would be done through writing so future generations could see the greatness of England along with that of Greece and Rome. He states this admiration of the English culture by comparing her great men to those of Greece and Rome. Plato, a Greek philosopher and mathematician, is compared to Bacon, an English philosopher and Newton, an English scientist. These men, says Pope, will someday all be regarded in the same light.

"How Plato's Bacon's Newton's looks agree."

He also compared Addison to Virgil, the greatest of all Roman poets.

The poem ends on a positive note. In commendation for good sense and true learning. A fitting ending for a poem written by the master of the Age of Reason.

Question 3 (Suggested time - 40 minutes)

Directions: Read the following poem carefully and then write an essay in which you discuss how the poet uses the functions of dramatic monologue.

"My Last Duchess"

Robert Browning

That's my last Duchess painted on the wall,
looking as if she were alive. I call
That piece a wonder, now; Frà Pandolf's hands
Worked busily a day, and there she stands.
Wil't please you sit and look at her? I said
"Frà Pandolf" by design, for never read
Strangers like you that pictured countenance,
the depth and passion of its earnest glance,
But to myself they turned (since none puts by
The curtain I have drawn for you, but I)
And seemed as they would ask me, if they durst,
How such a glance came there; so, not the first
Are you to turn and ask thus. Sir, 'twas not
Her husband's presence only, called that spot
Of joy into the Duchess' cheek: perhaps
Frà Pandolf chanced to say, "Her mantle laps
Over my lady's wrist too much," or "Paint
Must never hope to reproduce the faint
Half-flush that dies along her throat." Such stuff
Was courtesy, she thought, and cause enough
For calling up that spot of joy. She had
A heart-how shall I say?-too soon made glad,
Too easily impressed; she like whate'er
She looked on, and her looks went everywhere.
Sir, 'was all one! My favor at her breast,
The dropping of the daylight in the west,
The bough of cherries some officious fool
Broke in the orchard for her, the white mule
She rode with round the terrace-all and each
Would draw from her alike the approving speech,
Or blush, at least. She thanked men, - good! but thanked
Somehow - I know not how - as if she ranked
My gift of a nine-hundred-years-old name
With anybody's gift. Who'd stoop to blame
This sort of trifling? Even had you skill
In speech - (which I have not) - to make your will
Quite clear to such an one, and say, "Just this
Or that in you disgusts me; here you miss,
Or there exceed the mark" - and, if she let
Herself be lessoned so, nor plainly set
Her wits to yours, forsooth, and made excuse,
- E'en then would be some stooping; and I choose
Never to stoop. Oh sir, she smiled, no doubt,
Whene'er I passed her; but who passed without
Much the same smile? This grew; I gave commands;
Then all smiles stopped together. There she stands
As if alive. Will't please you rise? We'll meet

The company below, then. I repeat,
The Count your master's known munificence
Is ample warrant that no just pretense
Of mine for dowry will be disallowed;
Though his daughter's self, as I avowed;
At starting, is my object. Nay, we'll go
Together down, sir. Notice Neptune, though,
Taming a sea-horse, thought a rarity,
Which Claus of Innsbruck cast in bronze for me!

Response (1):

In "My Last Duchess" by Robert Browning, dramatic monologue brings out the Duke's character. It doesn't seem to be his true nature throughout the poem, though. I think his true nature comes out more clearly in the lines in which he speaks about his former wife. In the other lines he seems to be covering something up.

The Duke begins and ends his monologue with art. In the beginning he talks about how beautiful the picture of his last Duchess is; then he goes on to explain how his presence did not have anything to do with her look of joy. In the end he is talking about Neptune taming a sea-horse. It is ironic that he has this cast in bronze because he could never "tame" his wife.

I get the impression that the Duke tells these stories to show the reason for his bad marriage. He feels hurt because his wife didn't regard him as something special. In marrying again he hopes to get someone who will look up to him and whom he can be dominate over.

The Duke wants to show that the Duchess is shallow. She treats everyone who is nice to her the same way. When he talks about the way she annoys him you can see his jealousy coming through. He is very jealous of the men she pays attention to, because she doesn't set him apart from them. In the end when he can't take it anymore he commands her to stop what she's doing, but this doesn't really help because not only does she stop paying attention to the other men, she also ignores him.

You can see different moods when the Duke talks about the Duchess and when he talks about art. In the beginning when he talks about her his tone is impersonal. He mostly mentions how beautiful the portrait is done. When he starts telling the stories you can see his mood change. He is very involved, like he was living them all over again. In the end he realizes what he is saying and changes the conversation. His tone becomes impersonal again and he talks about trivial things.

Through dramatic monologue the author was able to bring out the Duke's character as well as the subject of the poem. Through the words and tone he uses you can pick out the Duke's true nature.

Response (2):

In his dramatic monologue "My Last Duchess," Robert Borwning relates the life of the Duke of Este and his last wife. The Duke is speaking to the representative of a family wishing to make an alliance with the Duke through the marriage of their daughter and the Duke.

A dramatic monologue "is a poem told by one speaker about a significant event. The speaker reveals in his own words some dramatic situation in which he is involved. He demonstrates his character through the poem. And, the speaker addresses a listener who does not engage in dialogue but still helps to develop the speech." (Nadel, Mas and Sherrer, Arthur, Jr., "How to Prepare for the Advanced Placement Examination in English, page 117.)

The dramatic situation discussed in this poem concerns the prospective marriage of the Duke of Este and the daughter of a count. The Duke reveals his character vividly as he relates the fate of his last duchess. Este is a very proud man and very proud of his artistic tastes, such as his "last duchess painted on the wall" and his "Neptune ... taming a sea horse." The line, "Will't please you sit and look at her" (5) expresses this notion of pride. Here the Duke asks his visitor to regard the painting, and he does so in a very arrogant manner. He subtly forces his guest to observe the painting as he recounts the memories it conjures up.

"-as if she ranked/My gift of a nine-hundred-years-old name/With anybody's gift" expresses the Duke's dismay at his duchess' slighting of his name. Este is obviously of royal descendance, but this wife does not seem to care. She included his position with any of the gifts she received from the men she came in contact with. This trait of the duchess upset the Duke very much but he was against taking any action against his wife because he chose "never to stoop" (43) to such degradation.

Este is also a possessive husband. When the duchess' smiles grew the same for him as for every other man, he "-gave commands;/Then all smiles stopped together." (44-45) When the Duke grew too domineering, his wife disregarded him from then on. But even though he has lost this lady, the Duke has her forever on the wall "as if alive." (47).

The listener to whom the Duke of Este addresses himself helps to develop the monologue. When the Duke says "I said/Frà Pandolf" (5-6), he is emphasizing the expression of the duchess' face. As these words are spoken, a sense of perplexion fills the guest. This puzzlement causes the Duke to continue his story of how the Duchess came to have that unequaled expression on her face. Without the listener questioning the Duke through expressions these features would never be included in the poem.

Towards the end of the poem, the Duke uses his guest to express his reasons for wanting to marry the Count's daughter. The dowry has nothing to do with the union; "his fair daughter's self" was the sole reason for the Duke's love. He cares not for money, or more generally, material possessions, yet he insists on exhibiting his "objects d'arts."

It is clearly seen why this poem ranks as the best example of a dramatic monologue. The speaker describes a situation; he reveals his character; and the speaker clearly addresses the unseen guest. Dramatic monologue is the appropriate genre for this poem because Browning allows the Duke to describe himself as he describes everything else in his home.

<u>Response (3)</u>:

Robert Browning's greatest talent is his ability to portray human character. His main contribution to literature is the dramatic monologue, a form through which Browning reveals the true spirit and personality of the narrator, fitting the speech and thought appropriately to the character speaking. The dramatic monologue has three characteristics: it presents a dramatic moment in the life of the speaker; it reveals his character; and it includes a listener who does not speak but who affects the development of the monologue.

"My Last Duchess" is perhaps Browning's most famous use of dramatic monologue.

In this paper I would like to illustrate Browning's technique as he reveals the repulsive character of the speaker.

The setting is the city of Ferrara in northern Italy during the Renaissance. The speaker is the Duke of Ferrara, who is negotiating with an envoy from a count about marrying the Count's daughter. At the moment, the Duke is showing his collection of paintings to the messenger. They stop at a portrait of the Duke's late wife, and drawing the curtain before it, the Duke begins to describe the painting. Already the reader is receiving an impression of the Duke. We notice how he very subtly drops the name of the painter, Frà Pandolf, into the conversation to impress his listener. He also adds importance to himself by including the fact that he is the only person who ever draws the curtain to this painting.

The Duke begins to explain the look of joy on the Duchess' face. He tells the envoy that such a look was common to her face, and begins to describe the cause of it.

> "Sir, t'was not her husband's presence only that called that spot of joy into the Duchess' cheek. Perhaps Frà Pandolf chanced to say, 'Her mantle laps over my lady's wrist too much,' or 'Paint cannot hope to reproduce the faint half flush that dies along her throat.'"

The Duke complains,

> "She had a heart too soon made glad."

Through this passage Browning shows us how the Duke is offended by his wife's politeness and transforms this kindness into infidelity to him.

We are told that everything pleased the Duchess.

> "She liked whate'er she looked on and her looks went everywhere."

The Duchess was good to all, including the least of her servants, and this disturbs the Duke who is quite aware of his social position. He finds it unbearable that she ranked everything the same and puts the same value on a bowl of cherries brought to her by a servant as on the gift of his nine-hundred-year-old name.

> "... all and each would draw from her alike the approving speech, or blush at least. She thanked men-good! but - I know not how - as if she ranked my gift of a nine-hundred-years-old name with anybody's gift."

The Duke does not reprove his wife or blame her in any way for he says that,

> "E'en that would be stooping and I choose never to stoop."

The Duke tells the envoy that the situation grew until he,

> "gave commands; then all smiles stopped together. There she stands as if alive."

"Commands" obviously means an order for the Duchess' execution.

The two men leave the portrait and the Duke expresses his confidence that the Count will grant any reasonable request for an ample dowry, quickly adding,

> "Though his fair daughter's self, as I avowed at
> starting, is my object."

As the men begin to go downstairs the Duke remarks,

> "Notice Neptune, though, taming a sea-horse, thought
> a rarity, ..."

Through the repeated use of the word "though," the Duke is subtly comparing himself to Neptune, god of the sea, and warning the envoy that the Count's daughter had better be "tame," for "taming a sea-horse" is not such a rarity.

In fifty-six lines, Browning has revealed to us a character so jealous, greedy, and cold that he was unable to understand or appreciate the warmth of a kind, courteous woman like the Duchess.

1 Ⓐ Ⓑ Ⓒ Ⓓ Ⓔ	26 Ⓐ Ⓑ Ⓒ Ⓓ Ⓔ	51 Ⓐ Ⓑ Ⓒ Ⓓ Ⓔ	76 Ⓐ Ⓑ Ⓒ Ⓓ Ⓔ	101 Ⓐ Ⓑ Ⓒ Ⓓ Ⓔ	126 Ⓐ Ⓑ Ⓒ Ⓓ Ⓔ
2 Ⓐ Ⓑ Ⓒ Ⓓ Ⓔ	27 Ⓐ Ⓑ Ⓒ Ⓓ Ⓔ	52 Ⓐ Ⓑ Ⓒ Ⓓ Ⓔ	77 Ⓐ Ⓑ Ⓒ Ⓓ Ⓔ	102 Ⓐ Ⓑ Ⓒ Ⓓ Ⓔ	127 Ⓐ Ⓑ Ⓒ Ⓓ Ⓔ
3 Ⓐ Ⓑ Ⓒ Ⓓ Ⓔ	28 Ⓐ Ⓑ Ⓒ Ⓓ Ⓔ	53 Ⓐ Ⓑ Ⓒ Ⓓ Ⓔ	78 Ⓐ Ⓑ Ⓒ Ⓓ Ⓔ	103 Ⓐ Ⓑ Ⓒ Ⓓ Ⓔ	128 Ⓐ Ⓑ Ⓒ Ⓓ Ⓔ
4 Ⓐ Ⓑ Ⓒ Ⓓ Ⓔ	29 Ⓐ Ⓑ Ⓒ Ⓓ Ⓔ	54 Ⓐ Ⓑ Ⓒ Ⓓ Ⓔ	79 Ⓐ Ⓑ Ⓒ Ⓓ Ⓔ	104 Ⓐ Ⓑ Ⓒ Ⓓ Ⓔ	129 Ⓐ Ⓑ Ⓒ Ⓓ Ⓔ
5 Ⓐ Ⓑ Ⓒ Ⓓ Ⓔ	30 Ⓐ Ⓑ Ⓒ Ⓓ Ⓔ	55 Ⓐ Ⓑ Ⓒ Ⓓ Ⓔ	80 Ⓐ Ⓑ Ⓒ Ⓓ Ⓔ	105 Ⓐ Ⓑ Ⓒ Ⓓ Ⓔ	130 Ⓐ Ⓑ Ⓒ Ⓓ Ⓔ
6 Ⓐ Ⓑ Ⓒ Ⓓ Ⓔ	31 Ⓐ Ⓑ Ⓒ Ⓓ Ⓔ	56 Ⓐ Ⓑ Ⓒ Ⓓ Ⓔ	81 Ⓐ Ⓑ Ⓒ Ⓓ Ⓔ	106 Ⓐ Ⓑ Ⓒ Ⓓ Ⓔ	131 Ⓐ Ⓑ Ⓒ Ⓓ Ⓔ
7 Ⓐ Ⓑ Ⓒ Ⓓ Ⓔ	32 Ⓐ Ⓑ Ⓒ Ⓓ Ⓔ	57 Ⓐ Ⓑ Ⓒ Ⓓ Ⓔ	82 Ⓐ Ⓑ Ⓒ Ⓓ Ⓔ	107 Ⓐ Ⓑ Ⓒ Ⓓ Ⓔ	132 Ⓐ Ⓑ Ⓒ Ⓓ Ⓔ
8 Ⓐ Ⓑ Ⓒ Ⓓ Ⓔ	33 Ⓐ Ⓑ Ⓒ Ⓓ Ⓔ	58 Ⓐ Ⓑ Ⓒ Ⓓ Ⓔ	83 Ⓐ Ⓑ Ⓒ Ⓓ Ⓔ	108 Ⓐ Ⓑ Ⓒ Ⓓ Ⓔ	133 Ⓐ Ⓑ Ⓒ Ⓓ Ⓔ
9 Ⓐ Ⓑ Ⓒ Ⓓ Ⓔ	34 Ⓐ Ⓑ Ⓒ Ⓓ Ⓔ	59 Ⓐ Ⓑ Ⓒ Ⓓ Ⓔ	84 Ⓐ Ⓑ Ⓒ Ⓓ Ⓔ	109 Ⓐ Ⓑ Ⓒ Ⓓ Ⓔ	134 Ⓐ Ⓑ Ⓒ Ⓓ Ⓔ
10 Ⓐ Ⓑ Ⓒ Ⓓ Ⓔ	35 Ⓐ Ⓑ Ⓒ Ⓓ Ⓔ	60 Ⓐ Ⓑ Ⓒ Ⓓ Ⓔ	85 Ⓐ Ⓑ Ⓒ Ⓓ Ⓔ	110 Ⓐ Ⓑ Ⓒ Ⓓ Ⓔ	135 Ⓐ Ⓑ Ⓒ Ⓓ Ⓔ
11 Ⓐ Ⓑ Ⓒ Ⓓ Ⓔ	36 Ⓐ Ⓑ Ⓒ Ⓓ Ⓔ	61 Ⓐ Ⓑ Ⓒ Ⓓ Ⓔ	86 Ⓐ Ⓑ Ⓒ Ⓓ Ⓔ	111 Ⓐ Ⓑ Ⓒ Ⓓ Ⓔ	136 Ⓐ Ⓑ Ⓒ Ⓓ Ⓔ
12 Ⓐ Ⓑ Ⓒ Ⓓ Ⓔ	37 Ⓐ Ⓑ Ⓒ Ⓓ Ⓔ	62 Ⓐ Ⓑ Ⓒ Ⓓ Ⓔ	87 Ⓐ Ⓑ Ⓒ Ⓓ Ⓔ	112 Ⓐ Ⓑ Ⓒ Ⓓ Ⓔ	137 Ⓐ Ⓑ Ⓒ Ⓓ Ⓔ
13 Ⓐ Ⓑ Ⓒ Ⓓ Ⓔ	38 Ⓐ Ⓑ Ⓒ Ⓓ Ⓔ	63 Ⓐ Ⓑ Ⓒ Ⓓ Ⓔ	88 Ⓐ Ⓑ Ⓒ Ⓓ Ⓔ	113 Ⓐ Ⓑ Ⓒ Ⓓ Ⓔ	138 Ⓐ Ⓑ Ⓒ Ⓓ Ⓔ
14 Ⓐ Ⓑ Ⓒ Ⓓ Ⓔ	39 Ⓐ Ⓑ Ⓒ Ⓓ Ⓔ	64 Ⓐ Ⓑ Ⓒ Ⓓ Ⓔ	89 Ⓐ Ⓑ Ⓒ Ⓓ Ⓔ	114 Ⓐ Ⓑ Ⓒ Ⓓ Ⓔ	139 Ⓐ Ⓑ Ⓒ Ⓓ Ⓔ
15 Ⓐ Ⓑ Ⓒ Ⓓ Ⓔ	40 Ⓐ Ⓑ Ⓒ Ⓓ Ⓔ	65 Ⓐ Ⓑ Ⓒ Ⓓ Ⓔ	90 Ⓐ Ⓑ Ⓒ Ⓓ Ⓔ	115 Ⓐ Ⓑ Ⓒ Ⓓ Ⓔ	140 Ⓐ Ⓑ Ⓒ Ⓓ Ⓔ
16 Ⓐ Ⓑ Ⓒ Ⓓ Ⓔ	41 Ⓐ Ⓑ Ⓒ Ⓓ Ⓔ	66 Ⓐ Ⓑ Ⓒ Ⓓ Ⓔ	91 Ⓐ Ⓑ Ⓒ Ⓓ Ⓔ	116 Ⓐ Ⓑ Ⓒ Ⓓ Ⓔ	141 Ⓐ Ⓑ Ⓒ Ⓓ Ⓔ
17 Ⓐ Ⓑ Ⓒ Ⓓ Ⓔ	42 Ⓐ Ⓑ Ⓒ Ⓓ Ⓔ	67 Ⓐ Ⓑ Ⓒ Ⓓ Ⓔ	92 Ⓐ Ⓑ Ⓒ Ⓓ Ⓔ	117 Ⓐ Ⓑ Ⓒ Ⓓ Ⓔ	142 Ⓐ Ⓑ Ⓒ Ⓓ Ⓔ
18 Ⓐ Ⓑ Ⓒ Ⓓ Ⓔ	43 Ⓐ Ⓑ Ⓒ Ⓓ Ⓔ	68 Ⓐ Ⓑ Ⓒ Ⓓ Ⓔ	93 Ⓐ Ⓑ Ⓒ Ⓓ Ⓔ	118 Ⓐ Ⓑ Ⓒ Ⓓ Ⓔ	143 Ⓐ Ⓑ Ⓒ Ⓓ Ⓔ
19 Ⓐ Ⓑ Ⓒ Ⓓ Ⓔ	44 Ⓐ Ⓑ Ⓒ Ⓓ Ⓔ	69 Ⓐ Ⓑ Ⓒ Ⓓ Ⓔ	94 Ⓐ Ⓑ Ⓒ Ⓓ Ⓔ	119 Ⓐ Ⓑ Ⓒ Ⓓ Ⓔ	144 Ⓐ Ⓑ Ⓒ Ⓓ Ⓔ
20 Ⓐ Ⓑ Ⓒ Ⓓ Ⓔ	45 Ⓐ Ⓑ Ⓒ Ⓓ Ⓔ	70 Ⓐ Ⓑ Ⓒ Ⓓ Ⓔ	95 Ⓐ Ⓑ Ⓒ Ⓓ Ⓔ	120 Ⓐ Ⓑ Ⓒ Ⓓ Ⓔ	145 Ⓐ Ⓑ Ⓒ Ⓓ Ⓔ
21 Ⓐ Ⓑ Ⓒ Ⓓ Ⓔ	46 Ⓐ Ⓑ Ⓒ Ⓓ Ⓔ	71 Ⓐ Ⓑ Ⓒ Ⓓ Ⓔ	96 Ⓐ Ⓑ Ⓒ Ⓓ Ⓔ	121 Ⓐ Ⓑ Ⓒ Ⓓ Ⓔ	146 Ⓐ Ⓑ Ⓒ Ⓓ Ⓔ
22 Ⓐ Ⓑ Ⓒ Ⓓ Ⓔ	47 Ⓐ Ⓑ Ⓒ Ⓓ Ⓔ	72 Ⓐ Ⓑ Ⓒ Ⓓ Ⓔ	97 Ⓐ Ⓑ Ⓒ Ⓓ Ⓔ	122 Ⓐ Ⓑ Ⓒ Ⓓ Ⓔ	147 Ⓐ Ⓑ Ⓒ Ⓓ Ⓔ
23 Ⓐ Ⓑ Ⓒ Ⓓ Ⓔ	48 Ⓐ Ⓑ Ⓒ Ⓓ Ⓔ	73 Ⓐ Ⓑ Ⓒ Ⓓ Ⓔ	98 Ⓐ Ⓑ Ⓒ Ⓓ Ⓔ	123 Ⓐ Ⓑ Ⓒ Ⓓ Ⓔ	148 Ⓐ Ⓑ Ⓒ Ⓓ Ⓔ
24 Ⓐ Ⓑ Ⓒ Ⓓ Ⓔ	49 Ⓐ Ⓑ Ⓒ Ⓓ Ⓔ	74 Ⓐ Ⓑ Ⓒ Ⓓ Ⓔ	99 Ⓐ Ⓑ Ⓒ Ⓓ Ⓔ	124 Ⓐ Ⓑ Ⓒ Ⓓ Ⓔ	149 Ⓐ Ⓑ Ⓒ Ⓓ Ⓔ
25 Ⓐ Ⓑ Ⓒ Ⓓ Ⓔ	50 Ⓐ Ⓑ Ⓒ Ⓓ Ⓔ	75 Ⓐ Ⓑ Ⓒ Ⓓ Ⓔ	100 Ⓐ Ⓑ Ⓒ Ⓓ Ⓔ	125 Ⓐ Ⓑ Ⓒ Ⓓ Ⓔ	150 Ⓐ Ⓑ Ⓒ Ⓓ Ⓔ

1 Ⓐ Ⓑ Ⓒ Ⓓ Ⓔ	26 Ⓐ Ⓑ Ⓒ Ⓓ Ⓔ	51 Ⓐ Ⓑ Ⓒ Ⓓ Ⓔ	76 Ⓐ Ⓑ Ⓒ Ⓓ Ⓔ	101 Ⓐ Ⓑ Ⓒ Ⓓ Ⓔ	126 Ⓐ Ⓑ Ⓒ Ⓓ Ⓔ
2 Ⓐ Ⓑ Ⓒ Ⓓ Ⓔ	27 Ⓐ Ⓑ Ⓒ Ⓓ Ⓔ	52 Ⓐ Ⓑ Ⓒ Ⓓ Ⓔ	77 Ⓐ Ⓑ Ⓒ Ⓓ Ⓔ	102 Ⓐ Ⓑ Ⓒ Ⓓ Ⓔ	127 Ⓐ Ⓑ Ⓒ Ⓓ Ⓔ
3 Ⓐ Ⓑ Ⓒ Ⓓ Ⓔ	28 Ⓐ Ⓑ Ⓒ Ⓓ Ⓔ	53 Ⓐ Ⓑ Ⓒ Ⓓ Ⓔ	78 Ⓐ Ⓑ Ⓒ Ⓓ Ⓔ	103 Ⓐ Ⓑ Ⓒ Ⓓ Ⓔ	128 Ⓐ Ⓑ Ⓒ Ⓓ Ⓔ
4 Ⓐ Ⓑ Ⓒ Ⓓ Ⓔ	29 Ⓐ Ⓑ Ⓒ Ⓓ Ⓔ	54 Ⓐ Ⓑ Ⓒ Ⓓ Ⓔ	79 Ⓐ Ⓑ Ⓒ Ⓓ Ⓔ	104 Ⓐ Ⓑ Ⓒ Ⓓ Ⓔ	129 Ⓐ Ⓑ Ⓒ Ⓓ Ⓔ
5 Ⓐ Ⓑ Ⓒ Ⓓ Ⓔ	30 Ⓐ Ⓑ Ⓒ Ⓓ Ⓔ	55 Ⓐ Ⓑ Ⓒ Ⓓ Ⓔ	80 Ⓐ Ⓑ Ⓒ Ⓓ Ⓔ	105 Ⓐ Ⓑ Ⓒ Ⓓ Ⓔ	130 Ⓐ Ⓑ Ⓒ Ⓓ Ⓔ
6 Ⓐ Ⓑ Ⓒ Ⓓ Ⓔ	31 Ⓐ Ⓑ Ⓒ Ⓓ Ⓔ	56 Ⓐ Ⓑ Ⓒ Ⓓ Ⓔ	81 Ⓐ Ⓑ Ⓒ Ⓓ Ⓔ	106 Ⓐ Ⓑ Ⓒ Ⓓ Ⓔ	131 Ⓐ Ⓑ Ⓒ Ⓓ Ⓔ
7 Ⓐ Ⓑ Ⓒ Ⓓ Ⓔ	32 Ⓐ Ⓑ Ⓒ Ⓓ Ⓔ	57 Ⓐ Ⓑ Ⓒ Ⓓ Ⓔ	82 Ⓐ Ⓑ Ⓒ Ⓓ Ⓔ	107 Ⓐ Ⓑ Ⓒ Ⓓ Ⓔ	132 Ⓐ Ⓑ Ⓒ Ⓓ Ⓔ
8 Ⓐ Ⓑ Ⓒ Ⓓ Ⓔ	33 Ⓐ Ⓑ Ⓒ Ⓓ Ⓔ	58 Ⓐ Ⓑ Ⓒ Ⓓ Ⓔ	83 Ⓐ Ⓑ Ⓒ Ⓓ Ⓔ	108 Ⓐ Ⓑ Ⓒ Ⓓ Ⓔ	133 Ⓐ Ⓑ Ⓒ Ⓓ Ⓔ
9 Ⓐ Ⓑ Ⓒ Ⓓ Ⓔ	34 Ⓐ Ⓑ Ⓒ Ⓓ Ⓔ	59 Ⓐ Ⓑ Ⓒ Ⓓ Ⓔ	84 Ⓐ Ⓑ Ⓒ Ⓓ Ⓔ	109 Ⓐ Ⓑ Ⓒ Ⓓ Ⓔ	134 Ⓐ Ⓑ Ⓒ Ⓓ Ⓔ
10 Ⓐ Ⓑ Ⓒ Ⓓ Ⓔ	35 Ⓐ Ⓑ Ⓒ Ⓓ Ⓔ	60 Ⓐ Ⓑ Ⓒ Ⓓ Ⓔ	85 Ⓐ Ⓑ Ⓒ Ⓓ Ⓔ	110 Ⓐ Ⓑ Ⓒ Ⓓ Ⓔ	135 Ⓐ Ⓑ Ⓒ Ⓓ Ⓔ
11 Ⓐ Ⓑ Ⓒ Ⓓ Ⓔ	36 Ⓐ Ⓑ Ⓒ Ⓓ Ⓔ	61 Ⓐ Ⓑ Ⓒ Ⓓ Ⓔ	86 Ⓐ Ⓑ Ⓒ Ⓓ Ⓔ	111 Ⓐ Ⓑ Ⓒ Ⓓ Ⓔ	136 Ⓐ Ⓑ Ⓒ Ⓓ Ⓔ
12 Ⓐ Ⓑ Ⓒ Ⓓ Ⓔ	37 Ⓐ Ⓑ Ⓒ Ⓓ Ⓔ	62 Ⓐ Ⓑ Ⓒ Ⓓ Ⓔ	87 Ⓐ Ⓑ Ⓒ Ⓓ Ⓔ	112 Ⓐ Ⓑ Ⓒ Ⓓ Ⓔ	137 Ⓐ Ⓑ Ⓒ Ⓓ Ⓔ
13 Ⓐ Ⓑ Ⓒ Ⓓ Ⓔ	38 Ⓐ Ⓑ Ⓒ Ⓓ Ⓔ	63 Ⓐ Ⓑ Ⓒ Ⓓ Ⓔ	88 Ⓐ Ⓑ Ⓒ Ⓓ Ⓔ	113 Ⓐ Ⓑ Ⓒ Ⓓ Ⓔ	138 Ⓐ Ⓑ Ⓒ Ⓓ Ⓔ
14 Ⓐ Ⓑ Ⓒ Ⓓ Ⓔ	39 Ⓐ Ⓑ Ⓒ Ⓓ Ⓔ	64 Ⓐ Ⓑ Ⓒ Ⓓ Ⓔ	89 Ⓐ Ⓑ Ⓒ Ⓓ Ⓔ	114 Ⓐ Ⓑ Ⓒ Ⓓ Ⓔ	139 Ⓐ Ⓑ Ⓒ Ⓓ Ⓔ
15 Ⓐ Ⓑ Ⓒ Ⓓ Ⓔ	40 Ⓐ Ⓑ Ⓒ Ⓓ Ⓔ	65 Ⓐ Ⓑ Ⓒ Ⓓ Ⓔ	90 Ⓐ Ⓑ Ⓒ Ⓓ Ⓔ	115 Ⓐ Ⓑ Ⓒ Ⓓ Ⓔ	140 Ⓐ Ⓑ Ⓒ Ⓓ Ⓔ
16 Ⓐ Ⓑ Ⓒ Ⓓ Ⓔ	41 Ⓐ Ⓑ Ⓒ Ⓓ Ⓔ	66 Ⓐ Ⓑ Ⓒ Ⓓ Ⓔ	91 Ⓐ Ⓑ Ⓒ Ⓓ Ⓔ	116 Ⓐ Ⓑ Ⓒ Ⓓ Ⓔ	141 Ⓐ Ⓑ Ⓒ Ⓓ Ⓔ
17 Ⓐ Ⓑ Ⓒ Ⓓ Ⓔ	42 Ⓐ Ⓑ Ⓒ Ⓓ Ⓔ	67 Ⓐ Ⓑ Ⓒ Ⓓ Ⓔ	92 Ⓐ Ⓑ Ⓒ Ⓓ Ⓔ	117 Ⓐ Ⓑ Ⓒ Ⓓ Ⓔ	142 Ⓐ Ⓑ Ⓒ Ⓓ Ⓔ
18 Ⓐ Ⓑ Ⓒ Ⓓ Ⓔ	43 Ⓐ Ⓑ Ⓒ Ⓓ Ⓔ	68 Ⓐ Ⓑ Ⓒ Ⓓ Ⓔ	93 Ⓐ Ⓑ Ⓒ Ⓓ Ⓔ	118 Ⓐ Ⓑ Ⓒ Ⓓ Ⓔ	143 Ⓐ Ⓑ Ⓒ Ⓓ Ⓔ
19 Ⓐ Ⓑ Ⓒ Ⓓ Ⓔ	44 Ⓐ Ⓑ Ⓒ Ⓓ Ⓔ	69 Ⓐ Ⓑ Ⓒ Ⓓ Ⓔ	94 Ⓐ Ⓑ Ⓒ Ⓓ Ⓔ	119 Ⓐ Ⓑ Ⓒ Ⓓ Ⓔ	144 Ⓐ Ⓑ Ⓒ Ⓓ Ⓔ
20 Ⓐ Ⓑ Ⓒ Ⓓ Ⓔ	45 Ⓐ Ⓑ Ⓒ Ⓓ Ⓔ	70 Ⓐ Ⓑ Ⓒ Ⓓ Ⓔ	95 Ⓐ Ⓑ Ⓒ Ⓓ Ⓔ	120 Ⓐ Ⓑ Ⓒ Ⓓ Ⓔ	145 Ⓐ Ⓑ Ⓒ Ⓓ Ⓔ
21 Ⓐ Ⓑ Ⓒ Ⓓ Ⓔ	46 Ⓐ Ⓑ Ⓒ Ⓓ Ⓔ	71 Ⓐ Ⓑ Ⓒ Ⓓ Ⓔ	96 Ⓐ Ⓑ Ⓒ Ⓓ Ⓔ	121 Ⓐ Ⓑ Ⓒ Ⓓ Ⓔ	146 Ⓐ Ⓑ Ⓒ Ⓓ Ⓔ
22 Ⓐ Ⓑ Ⓒ Ⓓ Ⓔ	47 Ⓐ Ⓑ Ⓒ Ⓓ Ⓔ	72 Ⓐ Ⓑ Ⓒ Ⓓ Ⓔ	97 Ⓐ Ⓑ Ⓒ Ⓓ Ⓔ	122 Ⓐ Ⓑ Ⓒ Ⓓ Ⓔ	147 Ⓐ Ⓑ Ⓒ Ⓓ Ⓔ
23 Ⓐ Ⓑ Ⓒ Ⓓ Ⓔ	48 Ⓐ Ⓑ Ⓒ Ⓓ Ⓔ	73 Ⓐ Ⓑ Ⓒ Ⓓ Ⓔ	98 Ⓐ Ⓑ Ⓒ Ⓓ Ⓔ	123 Ⓐ Ⓑ Ⓒ Ⓓ Ⓔ	148 Ⓐ Ⓑ Ⓒ Ⓓ Ⓔ
24 Ⓐ Ⓑ Ⓒ Ⓓ Ⓔ	49 Ⓐ Ⓑ Ⓒ Ⓓ Ⓔ	74 Ⓐ Ⓑ Ⓒ Ⓓ Ⓔ	99 Ⓐ Ⓑ Ⓒ Ⓓ Ⓔ	124 Ⓐ Ⓑ Ⓒ Ⓓ Ⓔ	149 Ⓐ Ⓑ Ⓒ Ⓓ Ⓔ
25 Ⓐ Ⓑ Ⓒ Ⓓ Ⓔ	50 Ⓐ Ⓑ Ⓒ Ⓓ Ⓔ	75 Ⓐ Ⓑ Ⓒ Ⓓ Ⓔ	100 Ⓐ Ⓑ Ⓒ Ⓓ Ⓔ	125 Ⓐ Ⓑ Ⓒ Ⓓ Ⓔ	150 Ⓐ Ⓑ Ⓒ Ⓓ Ⓔ

FINAL PRACTICE AP/CLEP ENGLISH TEST
SECTION I

Answer questions 1 - 5 by referring to the following selections:

"Love of your selfe," she saide, "and deare constraint,
Lets me not sleepe, but waste the wearie night
In secret anguish and unpittied plaint,
Whiles you in carelesse sleepe are drowned quight."
Her doubtfull words made that redoubted knight
Suspect her truth; yet since no' untruth he knew,
Her fawning love with foule disdaineful spight
He would not shend, but said, "Deare dame, I rew,
That for my sake unknowne such griefe unto you grew."

1. The verse shows

   (A) a kinship with the old metrical romances and with morality plays
   (B) a feeling of tolerance toward fellowmen
   (C) an appreciation of architecture and painting
   (D) evidence of existentialism
   (E) none of the above

2. The words "constraint" (line 1) and "shend" (line 8) mean, respectively,

   (A) strain and flinch
   (B) consternation and reveal
   (C) resistance and flaunt
   (D) distress and reproach
   (E) contention and show

3. Throughout the stanza there is a tone of

   (A) the Victorian Period
   (B) skepticism
   (C) the Age of Chivalry
   (D) levity
   (E) sarcasm

Thou still unravish'd bride of quietness,
Thou foster-child of silence and slow time,
Sylvan historian, who canst thus express
A flowery tale more sweetly than our rhyme:
What leaf-fringed legend haunts about they shape
Of deities or mortals, or of both,
In Tempe or the dales of Arcady?
What men or gods are these? What maidens loath?
What mad pursuit? What struggle to escape?
What pipes and timbrels? What wild ecstasy?

4. The references to Tempe and Arcady are

(A) Italian
(B) Teutonic
(C) Greek
(D) Persian
(E) none of the above

5. The individuals mentioned

(A) appear on a vase
(B) appear in the poet's nightmare
(C) pass the poet's window while he is musing
(D) are gods in the shape of human things
(E) are acquaintances of the poet

Answer questions 6 - 7 by referring to the following selection:

Hence, loathed Melancholy,
Of Cerberus and blackest Midnight born
In Stygian cave forlorn
Mongst horrid shapes, and shrieks, and sights unholy!
Find out some uncouth cell,
Where brooding Darkness spreads his jealous wings,
And the night-raven sings:
There, under ebon shades and low-browed rocks,
As ragged as they locks,
In dark Cimmerian desert ever dwell.

6. The poet is attempting to

(A) enter a spiritual domain
(B) create a mood of despair
(C) dispel unpleasant thoughts
(D) equate men with animals
(E) do none of the above

7. It is obvious that these lines contain

(A) a wealth of allusion
(B) references to pantheism
(C) some mixed metaphors
(D) implications of atheism
(E) none of the above

Answer questions 8 - 13 by referring to the following selections:

I saw Eternity the other night,
Like a great ring of pure and endless light,
All calm, as it was bright;
And round beneath it, Time, in hours, days, years,
Driv'n by the spheres,
Like a vast shadow moved, in which the world
And all her train were hurled.
The doting lover in his quaintest strain
Did there complain;
Near him, his lute, his fancy, and his flights,
Wit's four delights,
With gloves, and knots, the silly snares of pleasure.

Yet his dear treasure,
All scattered lay, while he his eyes did pour
Upon a flower.

8. It has been said that this poet could have been a great one if he had been able to maintain the elevation of

(A) lines 1-3
(B) lines 4-7
(C) lines 8-9
(D) lines 10-12
(E) lines 13-15

9. This poetry is, in essence,

(A) orgiastic
(B) querulous
(C) argumentative
(D) mystical
(E) melodic

Out upon it, I have loved
Three whole days together!
And am like to love three more,
If it prove fair weather.

Time shall moult away his wings,
Ere he shall discover
In the whole wide world again
Such a constant lover.

But the spite on't is, no praise
Is due at all to me:
Love with me had made no stays,
Had it any been but she.

Had it any been but she,
And that very face,
There had been at least ere this
A dozen dozen in her place.

10. The tone of the poem is one of

(A) angry pessimism
(B) deep disappointment
(C) vengeful sneering
(D) smiling cynicism
(E) questioning innocence

11. This poet belonged to a group called the Caroline poets, also called the

(A) Cavalier poets
(B) Graveyard poets
(C) Metaphysical poets
(D) Pre-Raphaelite poets
(E) Impressionist poets

Full many a gem of purest ray serene,
The dark unfathom'd caves of ocean bear:
Full many a flower is born to blush unseen,
And waste its sweetness on the desert air.

Some village-Hampden, that with dauntless breast
The little Tyrant of his fields withstood;
Some mute inglorious Milton here may rest,
Some Cromwell guiltless of his country's blood.

Far from the madding crowd's ignoble strife,
Their sober wishes never learn'd to stray;
Along the cool sequester'd vale of life
They kept the noiseless tenor of their way.

12. These stanzas reveal a(n)

(A) originality of thought
(B) marked pessimism
(C) plea for human kindness
(D) mastery of form
(E) subtle irony

13. Among the lines is the source of a title used by the novelist

(A) Steinbeck
(B) Hardy
(C) James
(D) Dreiser
(E) Hemingway

Answer questions 14 - 17 with reference to the following passage:

These historical investigations will shed a great deal of light on processes of modern lexicography. No one man can be given credit as the great innovator; dictionaries have been built upon previous models and vocabularies a piece at a time. Over 150 years of experimentation took place before the publication of Johnson's Dictionary in 1755. Some of the innovations of the seventeenth century were word classification by field of knowledge, usage labels, biographical sketches, inclusion of cant and dialect, etymology, and citations (usually of proverbs). Eighteenth-century contributions include expansion of vocabulary beyond hard words, abridgments and portable editions, use of accent marks as an aid to pronunciation, discriminated definitions, idiomatic phrases, advances in etymology and explanation of etymons, more extensive use of citations, winnowing of archaic and inkhorn words, and grammatical designation of entries. Perhaps the most significant advance, however, is the development of a comprehensive plan for a dictionary, attributed especially to Nathan Bailey, Benjamin Martin, and Samuel Johnson.

14. The first English lexicon appeared in

(A) 1550
(B) 1604
(C) 1702
(D) 1755
(E) 1798

15. It is not true that Samuel Johnson

(A) hoped that his dictionary would purify and regulate the English language
(B) composed the first English "hard-word" lexicon
(C) borrowed freely from early lexicographers
(D) had a ponderous style of writing
(E) was very eccentric

16. An inkhorn word is one which

(A) is bookish and pedantic
(B) is commonly used
(C) is contrived and smacks of jargon
(D) has a banal or entimental implication
(E) has obscene implications

17. An etymon is

(A) the etymological explanation of a word
(B) the obsolete meaning of a word
(C) the earliest known form of a word
(D) an idiomatic phrase
(E) none of the above

Answer questions 18 - 21 by referring to the following selections:

Break, break, break,
  On thy cold grey stones, O Sea!
And I would that my tongue
  The thoughts that arise in me.

O well for the fisherman's boy,
  That he shouts with his sister at play!
O well for the sailor lad,
  That he sings in his boat on the bay!

And the stately ships go on
  To their haven under the hill;
But O for the touch of a vanish'd hand.
  And the sound of a voice that is still!

Break, break, break,
  At the foot of thy crags, O Sea!
But the tender grace of a day that is dead
  Will never come back to me.

18. This may be described as a

(A) call to the sea in ships
(B) hope for the return of a lost one
(C) sea chantey without music
(D) lyric on the loss of youth, innocence, and happiness
(E) plea for an era of good will

19. The style of the poem is marked for its

(A) allegory
(B) powerful appeal to hope for the best
(C) description of sea life
(D) smoothness of rhythm
(E) similes and metaphors

  Alas! what boots it with uncessant care
To tend the homely, slighted, shepherd's trade,
And strictly meditate the thankless Muse?
Were it not better done, as others use,
To sport with Amaryllis in the shade,
Or with the tangles of Neaera's hair?
Fame is the spur that the clear spirit doth raise
(That last infirmity of noble mind)
To scorn delights and live laborious days.

20. The meaning of the last three lines ("Fame is the spur...laborious days") is that

(A) one will give up comfort for prestige
(B) true wit and madness are quite near allied
(C) fame may, since it is fleeting, be compared to a runaway horse
(D) it is not easy to give up material pleasures
(E) the paths of glory lead to the grave

21. The Amaryllis referred to is

(A) a flower
(B) a woman of ill-repute
(C) a dance
(D) a country girl
(E) none of the above

Answer questions 22 - 24 with reference to the following passage:

That the most minute singularities which belonged to him, and made very observable parts of his appearance and manner, may not be omitted it is requisite to mention that while talking or even musing as he sat in his chair, he commonly held his head to one side toward his right shoulder, and shook it in a tremulous manner, moving his body backward and forward, and rubbing his left knee in the same direction, with the palm of his hand. In the intervals of articulating he made various sounds with his mouth; sometimes giving a half whistle, sometimes as if ruminating, or what is called chewing the cud, sometimes making his tongue play backward from the roof of his mouth, as if clucking like a hen, and sometimes protruding it against his upper gums in front, as if pronouncing quickly under his breath, too, too, too: all this accompanied sometimes with a thoughtful look, but more frequently with a smile. Generally when he had concluded a period, in the course of a dispute, by which time he was a good deal exhausted by violence and vociferation, he used to blow out his breath like a whale. This I suppose was a relief to his lungs; and seemed in him to be a contemptuous mode of expression, as if he had made the arguments of his opponents fly like chaff before the wind.

22. The expression "clucking like a hen" is an example of both

(A) alliteration and metaphor
(B) hyperbole and oxymoron
(C) personification and metonymy
(D) onomatopoeia and simile
(E) antithesis and litotes

23. This passage may appropriately be titled

(A) Dr. Johnson's Perculiarities
(B) A Wheeze and a Cough
(C) Dr. Johnson - A Genius
(D) Animal Sounds
(E) Backwards and Forwards

24. The style of the writer may be described as

(A) ingenuous and articulate
(B) pompous and obscure
(C) colorful and balanced
(D) figurative and labored
(E) freighted and irregular

Answer questions 25 - 27 with reference to the following passage:

The characteristic peculiarity of the Pilgrim's Progress is that it is the only work of its kind which possesses a strong human interest. Other allegories only amuse the fancy. The allegory of Bunyan has been read by many thousands with tears. There are some good allegories in Johnson's works, and some of still higher merit by Addison. In these performances there is, perhaps, as much wit and ingenuity as in the Pilgrim's Progress. But the pleasure which is produced by the Vision of Mirza, the Vision of Theodore, the Genealogy of Wit, or the Contest between Rest and Labour, is exactly similar to the pleasure which we derive from one of Cowley's odes, or from a canto of Hudibras. It is a pleasure which belongs wholly to the understanding, and in which the feelings have no part whatever. Nay, even Spenser himself, though assuredly one of the greatest poets that ever lived, could not succeed in the attempt to make allegory interesting. It was in vain that he lavished the riches of his mind on the House of Pride and the House of Temperance. One unpardonable fault, the fault of tediousness, pervades the whole of the Faerie Queene. We become sick of cardinal virtues and deadly sins, and long for the society of plain men and women. Of the persons who read the first canto, not one in ten reaches the end of the first book, and not one in a hundred perseveres to the end of the poem. Very few and very weary are those who are in at the death of the Blatant Beast. If the last six books, which are said to have been destroyed in Ireland, had been preserved we doubt whether any heart less stout than that of a commentator would have held out to the end.

25. The writer's style is marked by

(A) obscure allusions and involved sentence structure
(B) a richness of imagery and long sentences which occasionally obscure the thought
(C) a deep religious feeling and considerable polemic ability
(D) frequent sentence inversion and a highly imaginative quality
(E) variety in sentence structure and skillful use of antithesis and contrast

26. The passage does not imply that

(A) The Faerie Queene deals with unreal people
(B) Bunyan is a superior poet
(C) The Faerie Queene is uninteresting
(D) Spenser is a mediocre craftsman
(E) most readers complete the Faerie Queene at one sitting

27. Life and Death of Mr. Badman was written by

(A) Butler
(B) Cowley
(C) Johnson
(D) Bunyan
(E) none of the above

Answer questions 28 - 30 by referring to the following selection:

I was asking for something specific and perfect for my
    city,
Whereupon lo! upsprang the aboriginal name.
Now I see what there is in a name, a word, liquid,
    sane, unruly, musical, self-sufficient
I see that the word of my city is that word from of old,
Because I see that word nested in nests of water-bays,
    superb,
Rich, hemmed thick all around with sailships and
    steamships, an island sixteen miles long, solid-
    founded,
Numberless crowded streets, high growths of iron,
    slender, strong, light, splendidly uprising toward
    clear skies,

Tides swift and ample, well-loved by me, toward
    sundown,
The flowing sea-currents, the little islands,
    larger adjoining islands, the heights, the
    villas,
The countless masts, the white shore-steamers,
    the lighters, the ferry-boats, the black
    sea-steamers well modeled,
The down-town streets, the jobbers' houses of
    business, the houses of business of the ship-
    merchants and money-brokers, the river-streets,
Immigrants arriving, fifteen or twenty thousand in
    a week,
The carts hauling goods, the manly race of drivers
    of horses, the brown-faced sailors,
The summer air, the bright sun shining, and the
    sailing clouds aloft,
The winter snows, the sleigh-bells, the broken ice
    in the river, passing along up or down with the
    flood-tide or ebb-tide.
The merchanics of the city, the masters, well-in-
    formed,beautiful-faced, looking you straight in
    the eyes,
Trottoirs thronged, vehicles, Broadway, the women,
    the shows,
A million people-manners free and superb-open voices
    -hospitality - the most courageous and friendly
    young men,
City of hurried and sparkling waters! city of spires
    and masts!
City nested in bays! my city!

28. The style of the poem reveals that it was written by

(A) Robert Frost
(B) Alexander Pope
(C) Emily Dickinson
(D) Edgar Lee Masters
(E) Walt Whitman

29. The subject is

(A) a village nestled between two mountains
(B) a deserted village
(C) an archipelago
(D) a very large city
(E) none of the above

30. The type of verse is

(A) blank
(B) free
(C) rhymed
(D) a combination of all three
(E) none of the above

Answer questions 31 and 32 by referring to the following selection:

Much have I travell'd in the realms of gold,
  And many goodly states and kingdoms seen;
  Round many western islands have I been
Which bards in fealty to Apollo hold.
Oft of one wide expanse had I been told.
  That deep-brow'd Home ruled as his demesne:
  Yet did I never breathe its pure serene
Till I heard Chapman speak out loud and bold:
Then I felt like some watcher of the skies
  When a new planet swims into his ken:
Or like stout Cortez when with eagle eyes
  He stared at the Pacific-and all his men
Look'd at each other with a wild surmise-
  Silent, upon a peak in Darien.

31. The Homer referred to here is

(A) an animal
(B) an explorer
(C) a monarch
(D) a farmer
(E) a soldier

32. For historical correctness, Cortez should be replaced by

(A) Magellan
(B) Balboa
(C) Vespucci
(D) Drake
(E) Columbus

Answer questions 33 - 35 with reference to the following passage:

One final convention of the Greek theatre deserves notice. Since the stories were traditional, Sophocles was obliged to sacrifice the easy effects of sensational incident: the result of the action was known to the audience at the outset. But like other limitations of the Greek drama, this one resulted in a sophistication of dramatic technique. The attention is shifted from what happens to how what is known to have happened will occur. The very fact of the audience's foreknowledge-itself an underscoring of the inevitability of the action-was used to great ironic effect. This irony can be distinguished as of two sorts-an irony of action and dramatic irony proper. This "transformation of an experience into its contrary," to use the language of the Poetics, is the major pattern of the play. Oedipus' attempt to better the plight of Thebes results in a worsening of his own: as he had delivered Thebes from the plague of the Sphinx earlier by solving her riddle of himself. Dramatic irony occurs when an actor uses words in one sense which the spectator knows to be true in another. Oedipus' remark that the man who killed Laius may well be his enemy too is but one of many examples in the play. Not the least effect of this irony is the reinstatement of suspense into the play. But it is not the suspense of the mystery story. The grosser uses of melodrama are outlawed; in their place we see subtlety and power. The subtlety is that of a chess master deploying his forces: Sophocles now hints (Creon's first speeches), now states (Teiresias' prophecy) the outcome. The virtuosity lies in the establishment of a situation which, while remaining realistic, forbids the characters to see the truth. The spectator who is alive to the irony must keep the whole story in mind, and the effort to do so engages him both emotionally and intellectually in the action.

33. The following was not a convention of the Greek theatre:

(A) The play was staged in a large amphitheatre.
(B) The performance was held out-of-doors.
(C) The actors wore no masks.
(D) The chorus seldom took part in the plot action.
(E) Characters were often supernatural.

34. We may imply from the passage that, in comparison with Greek drama, modern drama

(A) is of a higher intellectual level
(B) is of a lower intellectual level
(C) is of a similar intellectual level
(D) stresses sensationalism more than Greek drama did
(E) contains fewer "theatre of the absurdtype" plays

35. When Oedipus says

"I intend to fight (Laius') battle
As though he were my father, I will leave
Nothing undone to find his murderer.."

we have what is known as

(A) irony of action
(B) foreshadowing
(C) catharis
(D) dramatic irony
(E) none of the above

Answer questions 36 - 38 with reference to the following passage:

In the Yeats poem, "Ballad of Moll Magee," the persona is not the poet but the chief character in the drama; and ostensible intention is announced by her in the first and last stanzas: "pity Moll Magee." Human cruelty and crushing work are in the foreground of "The Ballad of Moll Magee." The children do not have "sweet" faces; we meet them in the first quatrain stoning the outcast. The daily work of the Magees is long and cruel; hard work is indeed the abstract villain of the piece, the direct cause of the death of the baby. The husband is brutalized. Even Charity, when it appears, has a "pityin', scornin' eye." And work must go on, in spite of bereavement and "solitude" (seen here for what, usually, "solitude" really is). Thus a significant change in the Art of the Naive and the Romantic conception of nature is wrought by Yeats in his "Ballad": only Moll is naive, and naive only in her inability to draw any conclusion from her experience beyond her hymn-book fancy in the next-to-last quatrain and the innocent appeal for pity. The poet is not naive-he knows what the score is; and he has no Wordsworthian conception of a "healing" nature. Does he believe that God really "looks upon the poor"? It doesn't matter; it is enough that Moll thinks so and depends on the thought for comfort. Does the personal voice of the poet ever break through the take over from Moll? Probably once: "But gather with your shinin' looks": regeneration of the cruel children of the first stanza, Innocence Regained in the child; a hint of Blake (whom Yeats admired) supplying a link with the earlier Romanticism. Is it a sentimental poem? Perhaps only in the relentless pathos of the suffering woman's story.

36. You would expect a poem which exemplifies the Art of the Naive to

    (A) place primary emphasis on man's inhumanity to man
    (B) demonstrate the appeal of the simple and the natural in complex and artificial societies
    (C) stress the importance of living without complaining
    (D) express the existentialist philosophy-there is no purpose in life
    (E) do none of the above

37. One may infer that Yeats

    (A) was not a strong advocate of organized religion
    (B) had a philosophy that bespoke optimism
    (C) was a romantic poet
    (D) shared Emerson's philosophy of compensation
    (E) was a great admirer of Queen Victoria

38. Into which category would you place "Ballad of Moll Magee"?

    (A) Poems of Social Conscience
    (B) War Poems
    (C) Poems of Fantasy
    (D) Esoteric Poetry
    (E) Romantic Poetry

Answer questions 39 - 44 by referring to the following selections:

Let me not to the marriage of true minds
Admit impediments. Love is not love
Which alters when it alteration finds,
Or bends with the remover to remove.
Oh, no! it is an ever-fixed mark,
That looks on tempests and is never shaken;
It is the star to every wandering bark,
Whose worth's unknown, although his height be
    taken.
Love's not Time's fool, though rosy lips and cheeks
Within his bending sickle's compass come;
Love alters not with his brief hours and weeks,
But bears it out even to the edge of doom.
    If this be error and upon me proved,
    I never writ, nor no man ever loved.

39. The verse form is

    (A) epic
    (B) sonnet
    (C) ballad
    (D) dramatic monologue
    (E) none of the above

40. The poem is remarkable for its

    (A) clever satire on love
    (B) alliterative quality combined with a definite rhythmic flow
    (C) clearcut and incontrovertible philosophy
    (D) its penetration into the weaknesses of humanity
    (E) beauty and suggestiveness of phrasing

God made the country, and man made the town.
What wonder then that health and virtue, gifts
That can alone make sweet the bitter draught
That life holds out to all, should most abound
And least be threatened in the fields and groves?
Possess ye, therefore, ye who, borne about
In chariots and sedans, know no fatigue
But that of idleness and taste no scenes
But such as art contrives, possess ye still
Your element; there only can ye shine,
There only minds like yours can do no harm.

41. These lines are outstanding for their

(A) symbolism
(B) irony
(C) variety of mood
(D) rhythmic effect
(E) simplicity and naturalness of style

42. It is clear that the poet is

(A) wealthy
(B) inventive
(C) physically strong
(D) nature-loving
(E) none of the above

43. The philosophy of this poet is much like the philosophy expressed by another poet in

(A) "Leaves of Grass"
(B) "The Wasteland"
(C) "Spoon River Anthology"
(D) "The People, Yes"
(E) "Endymion"

Market of Trinidad
in the warm moist morning!
Tropical golds of wings and fruits,
ocean greens edged by pelicans,
seas of coral, fires of mother-of-pearl in the sun.

44. The poet's approach is

(A) euphuistic
(B) epochal
(C) ironic
(D) impressionistic
(E) none of the above

Answer questions 45 - 47 with reference to the following passage:

Approaching the question of meaning from the direction of the whole sentence will make it easy to emphasize the fact that the meaning of a word (in the broad sense of a dictionary entry) is not something which it inalienably has (as a dog has hair or a house has walls) but is something which it contributes to the sentences in which it appears. This introduces the all-important notion of the place of context in meaning. It is impossible to tell what a word like round "means" in isolation; in fact, it doesn't mean anything until it takes a position in a larger structure. The context of any appearance of a word is simply all the rest of the structure in which it appears. As soon as we have one of the following, we can begin to talk about the meaning of round:

They sat at a round table.
The fighter was knocked out in the third round.
We watched the car round the corner on two wheels.

Note that there is an interaction between context and individual word. We select from a large area of possible meanings the one which makes sensible and acceptable contribution to the total structure; this in turn allows us to gather what the total structure means. The circularity of this process is what makes ambiguity possible. Ambiguity may be informally defined as a state of affairs in which more than one meaning makes a sensible contribution to a context and there is nothing in the context to indicate which is to be chosen.

45. The writer would agree that

(A) careful study of any sentence will result in arriving at the correct meanings of the words in the sentence
(B) the words of a sentence are not in themselves important - it is the sentence as a whole that is significant
(C) every word in a sentence has more than one meaning
(D) by context we mean not only a phrase or a sentence, but also a whole passage
(E) one need not know grammar to write well

46. In the sentence - Smith was hit hard and finally knocked out. - the context may likely be

(A) baseball as well as tennis
(B) boxing as well as tennis
(C) baseball as well as boxing
(D) tennis as well as volley ball
(E) football as well as handball

47. If one states "It is raining after a long drought and on the day of a planned picnic", his statement has, for the most part,

(A) linguistic context
(B) physical context
(C) social context
(D) economic context
(E) psychological context

Answer questions 48 - 50 with reference to the following passage:

Now this is the point. You fancy me mad. Madmen know nothing. But you should have seen me. You should have seen how wisely I proceeded - with what caution - with what foresight - with what dissimulation I went to work! I was never kinder to the old man than during the whole week before I killed him. And every night, about midnight, I turned the latch of his door and opened it so gently! And then, when I had made an opening sufficient for my head, I put in a dark lantern, all closed, closed, so that no light shone out, and then I thrust in my head. Oh, you would have laughed to see how cunningly I thrust it in! I moved slowly - very, very slowly, so that I might not disturb the old man's sleep. It took me an hour to place my whole head within the opening so far that I could see him as he lay upon his bed. Ha! - would a madman have been so wise as this? And then, when my head was well in the room, I undid the lantern cautiously (for the hinges creaked) - I undid it just so much that a single thin ray fell upon the vulture eye. And this I did for seven long nights - every night just at midnight - but I found the eye always closed; and so it was impossible to do work; for it was not the old man who vexed me, but his Evil Eye. And every morning, when the day broke, I went boldly into the chamber, and spoke courageously to him, calling him by name in a hearty tone, and inquiring how he had passed the night. So you see he would have been a very profound old man, indeed, to suspect that every night, just at twelve, I looked in upon him while he slept.

48. It is clear from this passage that the author writes in such a way that

 (A) its effectiveness is attributable, in great measure, to local color
 (B) almost each word has been selected for the purpose of building up a single effect
 (C) there is an irony between the lines - you can almost see a slight smile bespeaking incredibility on the face of the writer
 (D) there is both subtlety and warmth in the lines
 (E) none of the above statements is true

49. This passage is largely an appeal to

 (A) the intellect
 (B) one's prejudices
 (C) the emotions
 (D) one's social conscience
 (E) one's loyalty

50. The writer wants the reader to interpret the character in the story as one who

 (A) is violently insane
 (B) wrongfully accused
 (C) is of below-normal intelligence
 (D) intelligent but seriously disturbed
 (E) is cruel and vengeful

Answer questions 51 - 56 by referring to the following selections:

My heart leaps up when I behold
    A rainbow in the sky:
So was it when my life began;
So is it now I am a man;
So be it when I shall grow old,
    Or let me die!
The Child is father of the Man;
And I could wish my days to be
Bound each to each by natural piety.

51. The style is marked by its

 (A) pessimism
 (B) effect through repetition
 (C) egocentricism
 (D) optimism
 (E) simplicity and sincerity

52. The words concluding the verse - "natural piety" - refer to

 (A) a deep religious conviction
 (B) inherited religious leanings
 (C) a filial reverence for nature
 (D) love of man
 (E) none of the above

All Nature is but Art, unknown to thee;
All Chance, Direction, which thou canst not see;
All Discord, Harmony not understood;
All partial Evil, universal Good:
And, spite of Pride, in erring Reason's spite,
One truth is clear, Whatever is, is right.

53. The lines indicate that the poet is

(A) in full agreement with Emerson's philosophy of compensation
(B) impressed by the orderliness of the universe
(C) a deeply religious man
(D) of the belief that honesty is the best policy
(E) vainly seeking an acceptable philosophy of life

54. A philosophy expressed in this verse is that of

(A) escapism
(B) agnosticism
(C) materialism
(D) Confucianism
(E) pragmatism

Answer questions 55 - 57 with reference to the following passage:

"I have considered the structure of all volant animals, and find the folding continuity of the bat's wings most easily accommodated to the human form. Upon this model I shall begin my task tomorrow, and in a year expect to tower into the air beyond the malice or pursuit of man. But I will work only on this condition, that the art shall not be divulged, and that you shall not require me to make wings for any but ourselves."

"Why, " said Rasselas, "should you envy others so great an advantage? All skill ought to be exerted for universal good; every man has owed much to others, and ought to repay the kindness that he has received."

"If men were all virtuous," returned the artist, "I should with great alacrity teach them all to fly. But what would be the security of the good, if the bad could at pleasure invade them from the sky? Against an army sailing through the clouds neither wall, nor mountains, nor seas, could afford any security. A flight of northern savages might hover in the wind, and light at once with irresistible violence upon the capital of a fruitful region that was rolling under them. Even this valley, the retreat of princes, the abode of happiness, might be violated by the sudden descent of some of the naked nations that swarm on the coast of the southern sea."

55. The person whom Rasselas is speaking to is

(A) a tailor
(B) a gambler
(C) a bat
(D) an artist
(E) a biologist

56. The attitude of the person giving his point of view is one of

(A) optimism
(B) sprightliness
(C) distrust
(D) innocence
(E) sarcasm

57. In this selection, the author is employing the literary device of

(A) onomatopoeia
(B) symbolism
(C) flashback
(D) alliteration
(E) irony

Answer questions 58 - 60 with reference to the following passage:

However important we may regard school life to be, there is no gainsaying the fact that children spend more time at home than in the classroom. Therefore, the great influence of parents cannot be ignored or discounted by the teacher. They can become strong allies of the school personnel or they can consciously or unconsciously hinder and thwart curricular objectives.

Administrators have been aware of the need to keep parents apprised of the newer methods used in schools. Many principals have conducted workshops explaining such matters as the reading readiness program, manuscript writing and developmental mathematics.

Moreover, the classroom teacher, with the permission of the supervisors, can also play an important role in enlightening parents. The informal tea and the many interviews carried on during the year, as well as new ways of reporting pupils' progress, can significantly aid in achieving a harmonious interplay between school and home.

To illustrate, suppose that a father has been drilling Junior in arithmetic processes night after night. In a friendly interview, the teacher can help the parent sublimate his natural paternal interest into productive channels. He might be persuaded to let Junior participate in discussing the family budget, buying the food, using a yardstick or measuring cup at home, setting the clock, calculating mileage on a trip and engaging in scores of other activities that have a mathematical basis.

If the father follows the advice, it is reasonable to assume that he will soon realize his son is making satisfactory progress in mathematics, and at the same time, enjoying the work.

Too often, however, teachers conferences with parents are devoted to petty accounts of children's misdemeanors, complaints about laziness and poor work habits, and suggestion for penalties and rewards at home.

What is needed is a more creative approach in which the teacher, as a professional adviser, plants ideas in parents' minds for the best utilization of the many hours that the child spends out of the classroom.

In this way, the school and the home join forces in fostering the fullest development of youngsters' capacities.

58. It can be inferred that the author

(A) is satisfied with present relationships between home and school
(B) feels that the traditional program in mathematics is slightly superior to the developmental program
(C) believes that schools are woefully lacking in guidance personnel
(D) feels that parent-teacher interviews can be made more constructive than they are at present
(E) is of the opinion that teachers of this generation are inferior to those of the last generation

59. The author's attitude toward supervisors is one of

(A) disdain (B) indifference
(C) indecision (D) suspicion
(E) approval

60. The author implies that

(A) participation in interesting activities relating to a subject improves one's achievement in that area
(B) too many children are lazy and have poor work habits
(C) school principals do more than their share in interpreting the curriculum to the parents
(D) only a small part of the school day should be set apart for drilling in arithmetic
(E) teachers should occasionally make home visits to parents

ANSWER KEY

1. A	16. A	31. C	46. C
2. D	17. C	32. B	47. E
3. C	18. D	33. C	48. B
4. C	19. D	34. B	49. C
5. A	20. A	35. D	50. D
6. C	21. D	36. B	51. E
7. A	22. D	37. A	52. C
8. A	23. A	38. A	53. B
9. D	24. C	39. B	54. E
10. D	25. E	40. E	55. D
11. A	26. D	41. E	56. C
12. D	27. D	42. D	57. B
13. B	28. E	43. A	58. D
14. B	29. D	44. D	59. E
15. B	30. B	45. D	60. A

FINAL PRACTICE AP/CLEP ENGLISH TEST
SECTION II

Question 1 (Suggested time - 30 minutes)

Directions: Write an essay on one or more of the books by Rabelais or some other work of acknowledged literary merit.

Response:

"Gargantua and Pantagruel"

Gargantua and Pantagruel are actually two books, but are usually thought of as one. They are the books that established Rabelais' fame in the literary field and made known to the world a unique form of humor -- Rabelaisian humor.

Gargantua and Pantagruel can be viewed in two ways, as a mock epic and as a satire.

An epic, according to the Oxford Companion to English Literature, is "a poem that celebrates in the form of a continuous narrative, the achievements of one or more heroic personages of history, tradition, or imagination."

Gargantua and Pantagruel is not a poem, but it does deal with heroes and it is a continuous narrative. The factor that makes it a "mock" epic is the subject matter involved. Most classical epics deal with lofty and elevated subjects. Although Gargantua and Pantagruel is of "gigantic" proportions, the characters seem to be preoccupied with nothing but sex, excretion, and feasting. The form that the narrative takes, being usually so restrained, serves to make the antics of the characters even more ludicrous in comparison.

The main characters in the two books are Gargantua, Grangousier (his father), and Pantagruel (Gargantua's son). They are very jovial giants who reside in the kingdom of Utopia and spend most of their time imbibing wine. The name "Pantagruel," in fact, actually means "the all-thirsty one."

Although very fond of carousing, these giants were not totally devoid of intelligence and affection. There are many instances in the story where one or the other of them proves to be wise, gentle, or intelligent. Grangousier provides proof for this statement in his manner of handling Utopia's war with Lerne which will be discussed later in this paper.

In the realm of satire, Rabelais criticizes many of the elements of his society. The three largest of these are religion, wars, and education.

Francois Rabelais shows the uselessness of the educational system of his day by using Gargantua as an example. Under many scholars, Gargantua's intelligence is seen to deteriorate rather than flourish. Grangousier, seeing that his son is becoming a simple-minded idiot, sends him to Paris to study under Ponocrates, a scholar of a totally different pattern. Ponocrates' system of education is actually the one that Rabelais is proposing as a reform. The main principle of this system is to be always occupied from the moment of awakening to the moment of sleep with some worthwhile project. Moderation in eating and drinking were also advocated.

Through his book, Rabelais also illustrates the trivial causes that might (and do!) give rise to devastating wars. The example itself is a hyperbole, but it is a simple matter to see what Rabelais is really trying to say. A war is seen to take place between the countries of Utopia and Lerne. The cause of the war was the theft of five dozen cakes from the cake-bakers of Lerne on the part of some Utopian subjects. The two countries had been allies for many years, and, because of this, Grangousier tried to avoid war. He repaid the loss many times but it was to no avail. Picrochole (the king of Lerne) was determined to take revenge. The war did take place, but not as Picrochole had anticipated: Utopia was victorious. The entire war, and all the deaths incurred because of it, could have been avoided if Picrochole had been more diplomatic.

Monastic life and, indeed, all aspects of religion are satirized by Rabelais in Gargantua and Pantagruel. As with education, he suggests what he considers to be a better system. In Rabelais' modernized monastary, men and women would live together and be lavishly adorned and entertained. Moreover, they would all be well-bred and handsome in appearance. This is in total opposition to the actual monestaries of the time which seemed to be full of miserable criminals from the gutters. Rabelais questioned, and rightly so, the purity of monestaries that took as their inmates society's outcasts. He thought that the better off people were, the better able they would be to serve God.

Thus, Francois Rabelais, by use of the epic form and a satirizing view, brings home his ideas. One must certainly look for these views, because Rabelais himself points the way. He says in the prologue, "... in the perusal of this treatise, you shall find another kind of tase, and a doctrine of a more profound and obtruse consideration ...". This one must definately do to see the worth of Gargantua and Pantagruel, which would otherwise seem a stupid and grotesque piece of work.

Question 2 (Suggested time - 40 minutes)

Directions: Read Richard Wilbur's "Death of a Toad" and comment on the poet's idea of human death.

Response (1):

This poem is the author's analysis of the death of a toad. In three very different ways, the author describes the toad's death. The toad's death is stated very simply in the first stanza to very complexly in the third stanza.

The first stanza mainly describes what happened to the toad and what the toad's reaction was when it happened. The toad got caught in the lawn mower, then hopped over to hide under the dead leaves under the ash trees to die.

The second stanza goes into what the author sees as the toad dies. The author describes the thin blood of the toad, how it flows onto the ground, onto the toad's body and into his eyes. The toad, which looks as still as a statue, dies.

The third stanza is the most complex part of the poem. The stanzas of this poem seem to go in an increasing order of complexity. The first stanza is simply what happened. The second is a little more complicated. The reader has to think a little more to understand it. The third stanza is really deep. It starts out with a lot of imagery. The images which appear in the first two lines of the third stanza are what could be considered as a kind of toad's heaven. Or where the toad goes after it dies. The author can see the light fading from the toad's eyes even though the eyes still appear as if they are watching the daylight across the lawn.

The adjectives and images in the poem all have to do with death. Such as, "cineraria leaves" in the fourth line, which means ashes or remains of dead leaves. Also, in the sixth line, the "final glade." These are sort of a foreshadowing that the toad is dying. And in the third stanza, in the third line, "day swindles, drowning" is a sign of death. The word "antique" in the next line also suggests dying or the dead.

The tone of the poem seems to be death, sadness. The author shows no feeling towards the death of the toad. In a way, the author is saying that the toad's death is nothing. No one cares that the toad died.

The three stanzas are alike in some ways but are very different in others. They have the same rhyme scheme which is a a b c b c. The first stanza deals with the facts. The second deals with the physical dying of the toad while the third deals with the afterlife or what the author thinks happens to the toad after it dies. The author tries to imagine what happens to the toad after death, whether it just dies or whether it has a Heaven or an "Amphibia's emperies" of its own. That might be the peak of the poem. First the toad dies but what becomes of the toad is what the author is talking about in the third stanza.

This poem seems to open the reader's mind about death. By using a toad as the subject of the poem the author is implying that all things die -- even the smallest things. In the third stanza, the author compares the end of the day to the toad. The light went out of the toad's eye just like the light goes out of the day. Also the end of the day can go unnoticed just like the death of the toad and like the deaths of some people.

Response (2):

In this poem, Richard Wilbur writes about death, and uses the death of a toad as his example of how a creature feels as it awaits death and whatever comes after.

His example begins by dealing specifically with the toad and then proceeds to become more universal, discussing feelings common to all creatures - man included.

In the first stanza of the poem, we learn that the toad has been caught in the power mower and has lost a leg - a fatal injury. He hobbles to the edge of the garden and takes refuge under the leaves of a cineveria plant where it is dim and quiet and he can be alone and wait to die.

In stanza two, we see that as the toad's blood seeps into the ground under him, his life slowly ebbs. He becomes weak and unmoving, losing his individualness along with his life; he becomes more and more like stone. Death is the great equalizer on the earth. It is inevitable that all creatures will die and when they do, the qualities and characteristics that distinguished them as individuals disappear.

The toad's life flows away to somewhere or something that is intangible and unknown and he accepts this and does not try to struggle against the force of death which is taking him.

In the third stanza, the toad passes from this world to some suggested after-world.

The end of the poem leaves us with the image of the toad, under the cinevaria leaves, seemingly unchanged, although actually he has gone through a great change - he is now dead.

I think Wilbur is saying that our lives are fairly short - they dwindle like days - and death can overtake us whether or not we are expecting it. It is something we must face alone. Our lives will pass, and to us the passing will be significant, but the rest of the world may not notice we are gone.

Question 3 (Suggested time - 50 minutes)

Directions: Write an essay on the use of dramatic devices employed by Aeschylus or other classical playwright. The work you choose should be of acknowledged literary merit.

Response:

"Oresteia"

Many and varied are the dramatic devices employed by Aeschylus in the trilogy, Oresteia. The first play's dramatic portent is Agamemnon's signal that he is returning. The chorus is used to proclaim here the King's exploits and then to Clytaemestra as she tells of the curse on the House of Atreus. The dramatic impact builds from the beginning and lines spoken in this vein are a device which insures audience interest, as it prepares them for the suspense in the drama.

Clytaemestra's outpouring of grief for her lost child, those long years without Agamemnon, her goodness and loyalty to her Lord, dramatize her feeling for the events past and present.

Persuading Agamemnon to tread on the carpet as though he were a God is very dramatic in its meaning and is another device used to propel the play to the next event. It has purpose and meaning and contributes to the tragic overtones apparent in the conversation between Agamemnon and Clytaemestra. Another dramatic scene is Agamemnon's refusal to tread on the carpet, his fear of incurring the wrath of the Gods should he, a mortal, behave like a God. Clytaemestra's innuendo concerning his earned right to tread on it is another high point of dramatic interest.

An analysis of the dramatic devices employed in the plays would help set the stage for the methods used to obtain the ends each character has set for his or her goals. Certain words bespeak positive actions which the characters will ultimately carry out. This adds tragic dimensions to the actions and the results of these actions on the characters.

Aeschylus is adept at using words to stimulate the excitement the audience feels. The scene between Clytaemestra and Agamemnon concerning his sacking of Troy, the pillage and murder of its people, is another of the devices the author uses for dramatic purpose. Another important dramatic high spot is Cassandra's prophecy of the death of Agamemnon and her own death which she is powerless to avoid since it is so fated and therefore must be accepted. She tells the chorus that a net is prepared to entangle Agamemnon and to slay him. Each act brings closer to a climax the dreadful events the curse on the House of Atreus has brought its occupants. The plays have religious and moral aspects. Evil and good are properly dealt with throughout. The subtlety of the language is useful in making the story clear to the audience. The drama builds in intensity. Agamemnon's captive mistress, Cassandra, inspires sympathy for she is but a tool in the hand of Fate.

Each dramatic action can be analyzed as an important step to the next event. Tying together the narrative, the moral issues, the hate-in-love, the jealousy between mother and daughter, son-mother, crime and punishment, does take imagination, restraint and convistion. The dream device wherein Clytaemestra is bitten by a snake, and that snake is Orestes who comes to kill her and avenge his father's death, is another example of dramatic purpose to define tragedy. The homicide is the last act of the tragic consequences of the curse on the House of Atreus.

Murder begets murder, but if it avenges a father's death, then it will be absolved by the Gods and the court defends the verdict.

Part V

Supplementary Material

AP ENGLISH READING LIST

Poets and Poetry (Most frequently found in AP Tests)

Ballads, Chaucer, Wyatt, Sidney, Spenser, Shakespeare, Ben Jonson, Donne, Herrick, Herbert, Milton, Marvell, Pope, Dryden, Blake, Burns, Wordsworth, Byron, Shelley, Keats, Poe, Tennyson, Browning, Arnold, Whitman, Dickinson, Hardy, Hopkins, Housman, Yeats, Frost, T.S. Eliot, Theodore Roethke, Robert Lowell, Marianne Moore, W.H. Auden, e.e. cummings, Dylan Thomas, Wallace Stevens, Philip Larkin, W.S. Merwin, Randall Jarrell, Richard Wilbur, Anne Sexton, Sylvia Plath, and other modern poets

Authors of Short Stories

Hawthorne, Poe, Conrad, Crane, Maupassant, Henry James, Joyce, Lawrence, Mann, Mansfield, Chekhov, Katherine Anne Porter, Sherwood Anderson, Kafka, Flannery O'Connor, Eudora Welty, John Updike, Bernard Malamud, Peter Taylor, and J.L. Borges

Novels

Defoe	Moll Flanders
Swift	Gulliver's Travels
Fielding	Joseph Andrews
Austen	Pride and Prejudice Emma
Thackeray	Vanity Fair
Balzac	Pere Goriot
Dickens	Hard Times Great Expectations Our Mutual Friend
Hawthorne	The Scarlet Letter
Charlotte Brontë	Jane Eyre
Emily Brontë	Wuthering Heights
Turgenev	Fathers and Sons
Melville	Moby Dick

Flaubert	Madame Bovary
Dostoevsky	Crime and Punishment
Mark Twain	Huckleberry Finn
George Eliot	The Mill on the Floss
Hardy	Tess of the D'Urbervilles The Return of the Native The Mayor of Casterbridge
Crane	Red Badge of Courage
James	Portrait of a Lady The American
Conrad	Victory Heart of Darkness Lord Jim
Joyce	Portrait of the Artist as a Young Man
Lawrence	Sons and Lovers Women in Love
Woolf	Mrs. Dalloway To the Lighthouse
Dreiser	Sister Carrie
Kafka	The Castle
Fitzgerald	The Great Gatsby
Faulkner	Light in August The Sound and the Fury
Hemingway	A Farewell to Arms The Sun Also Rises
E.M. Forster	A Passage to India
Graham Greene	The Power and the Glory The Heart of the Matter Brighton Rock
Robert Penn Warren	All the King's Men
Camus	The Stranger
Bernard Malamud	The Natural
Ralph Ellison	Invisible Man
Richard Wright	Native Son

John Updike	Rabbit, Run
John Fowles	The French Lieutenant's Woman

Drama - Plays

Aeschylus	Agamemnon
Sophocles	Antigone Oedipus Rex
Aristophanes	The Frogs
Euripides	Medea Everyman The Second Shepherds' Play
Marlowe	Dr. Faustus
Shakespeare	(Almost any play will be rewarding.)
Ben Jonson	Volpone
Moliere	The Doctor in Spite of Himself Tartuffe
Congreve	The Way of the World
Sheridan	The School for Scandal
Goldsmith	She Stoops to Conquer
Ibsen	A Doll's House Ghosts
Wilde	The Importance of Being Earnest
Shaw	Saint Joan Major Barbara The Devil's Disciple
Chekhov	The Cherry Orchard The Sea Gull
Pirandello	Six Characters in Search of an Author
Synge	The Playboy of the Western World
O'Casey	Juno and the Paycock
T.S. Eliot	Murder in the Cathedral
O'Neill	The Hairy Ape A Long Day's Journey into Night

Brecht	*Galileo* *The Caucasian Chalk Circle*
Sartre	*No Exit* *The Flies*
Tennessee Williams	*The Glass Menagerie* *A Streetcar Named Desire*
Miller	*Death of a Salesman* *The Crucible*
Pinter	*The Homecoming* *The Birthday Party*
Stoppard	*Rosencrantz and Guildenstern Are Dead*
Albee	*Who's Afraid of Virginia Woolf?*
MacLeish	*J.B.*
Beckett	*Waiting for Godot*
Ionesco	*The Lesson* *Rhinoceros*

Writers of the Essay

Bacon, Montaigne, Milton, Defoe, Swift, Chesterfield, Addison, Johnson, Franklin, Jefferson, Madison, Coleridge, Lamb, Carlyle, Emerson, J.S. Mill, Thoreau, Arnold, Pater, Stevenson, Thomas Huxley, Yeats, T.S. Eliot, Orwell, Virginia Woolf, Forster, Mencken, Krutch, Edmund Wilson, Lionel Trilling, Margaret Mead, Mary MaCarthy, Susan Sontag, Simone de Beauvoir, and other contemporary writers

RECOMMENDED AP ENGLISH MATERIALS
READING AND STUDY GUIDES

Poetry (Works frequently used in AP courses)

Brooks, Cleanth, and Warren, Robert Penn. Understanding Poetry. New York: Holt, Rhinehart and Winston, 1960.

Ciardi, John. How Does a Poem Mean? Boston: Houghton, Mifflin Co., 1960.

Perrine, Lawrence. Sound and Sense: An Introduction to Poetry. New York: Harcourt Brace Jovanovich, 1973.

Short Story (collections of short stories)

Bloom, Edward A., and Bloom, Lillian, eds. The Variety of Fiction: A Critical Anthology. Indianapolis: Odyssey Press, 1969.

Brooks, Cleanth, and Warren, Robert Penn. Understanding Fiction. New York: Appleton-Century-Crofts, 1959.

Lesser, M.X., and Morris, J.N. Modern Short Stories: The Fiction of Experience. New York: McGraw-Hill, 1962.

MacKenzie, Barbara. The Process of Fiction. Second ed. New York: Harcourt Brace Jovanovich, 1974.

Prigozy, Ruth, and Thune, Ensaf. The Short Story: A Critical Anthology. New York: Macmillan, 1973.

West, Ray, and Stallman, Robert. Art of Modern Fiction. New York: Holt, Rinehart and Winston, 1956.

Novel (Useful Novel Reference Books)

Booth, Wayne C. The Rhetoric of Fiction. Chicago: University of Chicago Press, 1961.

Drew, Elizabeth. The Novel. New York: Dell, 1963.

Forster, E.M. Aspects of the Novel. London: Edward Arnold, 1927, 1953.

Frye, Northrop. Anatomy of Criticism. Princeton, NJ: Princeton U. Press, 1957.

Scholes, Robert. Elements of Fiction. New York: Oxford, 1968.

Stevick, Philip, ed. The Theory of the Novel. New York: The Free Press, 1967.

Drama (Suggested texts on drama)

Boynton, Robert, and Mack, Maynard. Introduction to the Play. Rochelle Park, NJ: Hayden, 1969.

Brooks, Cleanth, and Heilman, William. Understanding Drama. New York: Holt, Rinehart and Winston, 1948.

Cubeta, Paul. Modern Drama for Analysis. Third ed. New York: Holt, Rinehart and Winston, 1962.

Felheim, Marvin, ed. Comedy: Plays, Theories, and Criticism. New York: Harcourt Brace and World, 1962.

Kernan, Alvin. Character and Conflict: An Introduction to Drama. New York: Harcourt Brace Jovanovich, 1969.

Levin, Richard, ed. Tragedy: Plays, Theory, and Criticism. New York: Harcourt Brace and World, 1960.

Language and Composition (Most frequently used publications)

Altick, Richard. Preface to Critical Reading. Fifth ed. New York: Holt, Rinehart and Winston, 1969.

Baker, Sheridan. The Practical Stylist. Third ed. New York: Crowell, 1969.

Brooks, Cleanth, and Warren, Robert Penn. Modern Rhetoric. Third ed. New York: Harcourt Brace Jovanovich, 1970.

Cohen, Benjamin B. Writing about Literature. Glenville, IL: Scott, Foresman, 1973.

Diederich, Paul. Measuring Growth in English. 104pp., 1974.
End-of-Year Examinations in English for College-Bound Students. 193 pp., 1963.
Evaluating a Theme. 16 pp., 1958.
NOTE Guide to Teaching Materials for English. 1974-75 and Supplements.

Francis, Nelson. The English Language: An Introduction. New York: Norton, 1965.

Hayakawa, S. I. Language in Action. New York: Harcourt, Brace, 1941.

Kane, Thomas, and Peters, Leonard. Writing Prose. Third ed. New York: Oxford, 1969.

McCrimmon, James. Writing with a Purpose. Boston: Houghton, Mifflin, 1973.

Purves, Alan C., and Rippere, Victoria. Elements of Writing about a Literary Work. 90 pp., 1968.

Roberts, Edgar. Writing Themes about Literature. Third ed. New York: Prentice-Hall, 1973.

Sister Judine, I.H.M., ed. A Guide for Evaluating Student Composition. 162 pp., 1965.

12,000 Students and Their English Teachers. 389 pp., 1968.

Strunk, W. and White, E. B. Elements of Style. Second ed. New York: The Macmillan Co., 1972.

Warriner, John E., Ludwig, Richard, and Connolly, F. X. Advanced Composition. New York: Harcourt Brace Jovanovich, 1968.

SYNOPSES OF SHAKESPEARE'S PLAYS

ALL'S WELL THAT ENDS WELL

ALL'S WELL THAT ENDS WELL is a play, the story of which came to the poet from Boccaccio, through Paynter's 'Palace of Pleasure,' although he introduces variations. It tells how Helen de Narbon, a physician's daughter, and orphaned, forced her love on a handsome and birth-proud young French nobleman, Bertram de Rousillon, with whom she had been brought up from childhood. It is a tale of husband-catching by a curious kind of trick. To most *men* the play is repellent. Yet Shakespeare has treated the theme again in 'Twelfth Night' (Olivia), and in 'Midsummer Night's Dream' (Helena). Many women woo in courtship—by word, glance, or gesture at least; and among the lower orders the courting is quite undisguised. Shakespeare endows Helena with such virtues that we excuse and applaud. All's well that ends well. She heals the king with her father's receipt, asks for and accepts Bertram as her reward, and is married. But the proud boy flies to the Florentine wars on his wedding-day, leaving his marriage unconsummated. Helen returns sorrowfully to Rousillon; and finds there a letter from her husband, to the effect that when she gets his ring upon her finger and shows him a child begotten of his body, then he will acknowledge her as his wife. She undertakes to outwit him and reclaim him. Leaving Rousillon on pretense of a pilgrimage to the shrine of Saint Jacques le Grand, she presently contrives to have it thought she is dead. In reality she goes to Italy, and becomes Bertram's wife in fact and not mere name, by the secret substitution of herself for the pretty Diana, with whom he has an assignation arranged. There is an entanglement of petty accidents and incidents connected with an exchange of rings, etc. But, finally, Helen makes good before the King her claim of having fulfilled Bertram's conditions; and she having vowed obedience, he takes her to his heart, and we may suppose they live happily together «till there comes to them the destroyer of delights and the sunderer of societies.» One's heart warms to the noble old Countess of Rousillon, who loves Helen as her own daughter. She is wise and ware in worldly matters, and yet full of sympathy, remembering her own youth. Parolles is a cross between Thersites and Pistol,—a volte-faced scoundrel who has to pull the devil by the tail for a living. His pretense of fetching off his drum, and his trial blindfolded before the soldiers, raises a laugh; but the humor is much inferior to that of 'Henry IV.'

ANTONY AND CLEOPATRA

ANTONY AND CLEOPATRA, written about 1607, is the second of Shakespeare's Roman plays. 'Julius Cæsar' being the first. For breadth of treatment and richness of canvas it excels the latter. There is a splendid audacity and self-conscious strength, almost diablerie, in it all. In Cleopatra, the gipsy sorceress queen, the gorgeous Oriental voluptuousness is embodied; in the strong-thewed Antony, the stern soldier-power of Rome weakened by indulgence in lust. There is no more affecting scene in Shakespeare than the death, from remorse, of Enobarbus. In the whole play the poet follows North's 'Plutarch' for his facts. The three rulers of the Roman world are Mark Antony, Octavius Cæsar, and their weak tool, Lepidus. While Antony is idling away the days in Alexandria with Cleopatra, and giving audience to Eastern kings, in Italy things are all askew. His wife Fulvia has died. Pompey is in revolt with a strong force on the high seas. At last Antony is shamed home to Rome. Lepidus and other friends patch up a truce between him and Cæsar, and it is cemented by Antony marrying Cæsar's sister Octavia, to the boundless vexation of Cleopatra. What a contrast between the imperial Circe, self-willed, wanton, spell-weaving, and the sweet, gentle Octavia, wifely and loyal! From the time when Antony first met his «serpent of old Nile,» in that rich Venetian barge of beaten gold, wafted by purple sails along the banks of the Cydnus, up to the fatal day of Actium, when in her great trireme she fled from Cæsar's ships, and he shamefully fled after her, he was infatuated over her, and she led him to his death. After the great defeat at Actium, Enobarbus and other intimate followers deserted the waning fortunes of Antony. Yet once more he tried the fortune of battle, and on the first day was victorious, but on the second was defeated by sea and land. Being falsely told that Cleopatra is dead, Antony falls on his sword. Cleopatra has taken refuge in her monument, and she and her women draw up the dying lover to its top. But the monument is forced by Cæsar's men, and the queen put under a guard. She has poisonous asps smuggled in a basket of figs, and applies one to her breast and another to her arm, and so dies, looking in death «like sleep,» and

> "As she would catch another Antony
> In her strong toil of grace."

AS YOU LIKE IT

As You Like It.—In this happiest of his middle-period comedies, Shakespeare is at no pains to avoid a tinge of the fantastical and ideal. Its realism lies in its gay riant feeling, the fresh woodland sentiment, the exhilaration of spirits that attend the escape from the artificialities of urban society. For one reason or another all the characters get exiled, and all meet in the Forest of Arden, where «as you like it» is the order of the day. There is the manly young Orlando, his villainous elder brother Oliver, and their servant Adam. At court is the reigning duke, his daughter Celia, her cousin Rosalind, and Touchstone the clown. In the forest, the banished elder duke (father of Rosalind) and the melancholy Jacques, and other lords who are blowzed with sun and wind a-chasing the dappled deer under the greenwood tree; the pealing bugle, the leaping arrow, the *al fresco* table loaded with the juicy roast of venison, and long idle summer hours of leisurely converse. On the outskirts of the forest are shepherd swains and lasses,—old Corin, Silvius (in love with Phebe), and the wench Audrey. Orlando has had to fly from his murderous brother. Rosalind has been banished the court by her uncle, and she and Celia disguised as shepherd men have slipped away with Touchstone. Now Rosalind has been deeply smitten with Orlando since she saw him overcome the duke's wrestler, and he is equally in love with her. We may imagine her as «a nut-brown maid, tall, strong, rustically clad in rough forest garments,» and possessing a perennial flow of cheerful spirits, a humor of the freshest and kindliest. Touchstone is a fellow of twinkling eye and dry and caustic wit, his face as solemn as a church-yard while his hearers are all agrin. He and Jacques look at life with a cynical squint. Jacques is a blasé libertine, who is pleased when things run counter and athwart with people, but is after all not so bad as he feigns to be. Like a series of dissolving views, scene after scene is glimpsed through the forest glades,—here the forester lords singing, and bearing the antlers of the stag; there love-sick Orlando carving verses on the bark of trees, or rescuing his brother from the lion. The youth Ganymede (really Rosalind) pretends she can cure Orlando of his love-sickness by teaching him to woo him as if he were Rosalind, all of which makes a pretty pastoral picture. Anon Touchstone passes by, leading by the hand the captive of his spear, Audrey, who has never heard of poetry; or in another part of the woodland he is busy mystifying and guying the shepherd Corin. Ganymede gets the heartless coquette Phebe to promise that if she ever refuses to wed him (with whom she is smitten) she will wed her scorned and despairing admirer Silvius, and makes her father promise to give Rosalind to Orlando; then retires and comes back in her own garments as Rosalind. The play ends with a fourfold marriage and a dance under the trees.

THE COMEDY OF ERRORS

The Comedy of Errors, by its irresistibly laughable plot (and it is all plot), is perennially popular. It is the shortest of the plays, and one of the very earliest written. The main story is from the ‹Menæchmi› of Plautus. The Syracusans and the men of Ephesus have mutually decreed death to a citizen of one city caught in the other, unless he can pay a heavy ransom. Ægeon of Syracuse is doomed to death by the Duke of Ephesus. He tells the duke his story,—how at Epidamnum many years ago his wife had borne male twins, and at the same hour a meaner woman near by had also twin boys; how he had bought and brought up the latter; and how he and his wife had become separated by shipwreck, she with one of each pair of twins and he with one of each; and how five years ago his boy and servant had set out in search of their twin brothers, and he himself was now searching them and his wife. Of these twins, one Antipholus and one Dromio live in Ephesus as master and servant respectively, the former being married to Adriana, whose sister Luciana dwells with her. By chance the Syracusan Antipholus and his Dromio are at this time in Ephesus. The mother Æmilia is abbess of a priory in the town. Through a labyrinth of errors they all finally discover each other. Antipholus of Syracuse sends his Dromio to the inn with a bag of gold, and presently meets Dromio of Ephesus, who mistaking him, urges him to come at once to dinner: his wife and sister are waiting. In no mood for joking, he beats his supposed servant. The other Dromio also gets a beating for denying that he had just talked about dinner and wife. In the mean time, Adriana and her sister meet the Syracusans on the street, and amaze them by their reproaches. As in a dream the men follow them home, and Dromio of Syracuse is bid keep the door. Now comes home the rightful owner with guests, and knocks in vain for admittance. So he goes off in a rage to an inn to dine. At his home the coil thickens. There Antipholus of Syracuse makes love to Luciana, and down-stairs the amazed Dromio of Syracuse flies from the greasy kitchen wench who claims him as her own. Master and man finally resolve to set sail at once from this place of enchantment. After a great many more laughable puzzles and *contretemps*, comes Adriana, with a conjurer — Doctor Pinch — and others, who bind her husband and servant as madmen and send them away. Presently enter the bewildered Syracusans with drawn swords, and away flies Adriana, crying, «They are loose again!» The Syracusans take refuge in the abbey. Along comes the duke leading Ægeon to execution. Meantime the real husband and slave have really broken loose, bound Doctor Pinch, singed off his beard, and nicked his hair with scissors. At last both pairs of twins meet face to face, and Ægeon and Æmilia solve all puzzles.

CORIOLANUS

CORIOLANUS, a powerful drama of Shakespeare's later years (written about 1609), retells from North's ‹Plutarch,› in terse sinewy English, the fate that overtook the too haughty pride of a Roman patrician,— generous, brave, filial, but a mere boy in discretion, his soul a dynamo always overcharged with a voltage current of scorn and rage, and playing out its live lightnings on the least provocation. See his fierce temper reflected in his little boy, grinding his teeth as he tears a butterfly to pieces: «Oh, I warrant how he mammocked it!» Mark his strength: «Death, that dark spirit, in's nervy arm doth lie.» «What an arm he has! he turned me about with his finger and thumb as one would set up a top.» In battle «he was a thing of blood, whose every motion was timed with dying cries.» In the Volscian war, at the gates of Corioli, this Caius Marcius performed such deeds of derring-do that he was nigh worshiped; and there he got his addition of ‹Coriolanus.› His scorn of the rabble, their cowardice, vacillation, dirty faces, and uncleaned teeth, was boundless. The patricians were with him: if the plebeians rose in riot, accusing the senatorial party of «still cupboarding the viand,» but never bearing labor like the rest, Menenius could put them down with the apologue of the belly and the members,— the belly, like the Senate, indeed receiving all, but only to distribute it to the rest. Coriolanus goes further, and angers the tribunes by roundly denying the right of the cowardly plebs to a distribution of grain in time of scarcity. The tribunes stir up the people against him; and when he returns from the war, wearing the oaken garland and covered with wounds, and seeks the consulship, they successfully tempt his temper by taunts, accuse him of treason, and get him banished by decree. In a towering rage he cries, «You common cry of curs, I banish you!» and taking an affecting farewell of his wife, and of Volumnia his mother (type of the stern and proud Roman matron), he goes disguised to Antium and offers his services against Rome to his hitherto mortal foe and rival, Tullus Sufidius. The scene with the servants forms the sole piece of humor in the play. But his destiny pursues him still: his worser genius, like the Little Master in 'Sintram,' whispers him to his ruin; his old stiff-necked arrogance of manner again appears. The eyes of all the admirant Volscians are on him. Sufidius, now bitterly jealous, regrets his sharing of the command; and when, softened by the entreaties of weeping wife and mother, Coriolanus spares Rome and returns with the Volscians to Antium, his rival and a band of conspirators «stain all their edges» in his blood, and he falls, like the great Julius, the victim of his own willful spirit.

CYMBELINE

CYMBELINE was written by Shakespeare late in his life, probably about 1609. A few facts about Cymbeline and his sons he took from Holinshed; but the story of Imogen forms the ninth novel of the second day of Boccaccio's 'Decameron.' These two stories Shakespeare has interwoven; and the atmosphere of the two is not dissimilar: there is a tonic moral quality in Imogen's unassailable virtue like the bracing mountain air in which the royal youths have been brought up. The beautiful song 'Fear No More the Heat o' the Sun' was a great favorite with Tennyson. Cymbeline wanted his daughter Imogen to marry his stepson Cloten, a boorish lout and cruel villain, but she has secretly married a brave and loyal private gentleman, Posthumus Leonatus, and he is banished for it. In Italy one Iachimo wagers him ten thousand ducats to his diamond ring that he can seduce the honor of Imogen. He miserably fails, even by the aid of lies as to the disloyalty of Posthumus, and then pretends he was but testing her virtue for her husband's sake. She pardons him, and receives into her chamber, for safe-keeping, a trunk, supposed to contain costly plate and jewels, but which really contains Iachimo himself, who emerges from it in the dead of night; slips the bracelet from her arm; observes the mole, cinque-spotted with crimson, on her breast; and notes down in his book the furniture and ornaments of the room. He returns to Italy. Posthumus despairingly yields himself beaten, and writes to his servant Pisanio to kill Imogen; to facilitate the deed, he sends her word to meet him at Milford Haven. Thither she flies with Pisanio, who discloses all, gets her to disguise herself in men's clothes and seek to enter the service of Lucius, the Roman ambassador. She loses her way, and arrives at the mountain cave in Wales where dwell, unknown to her, her two brothers, Guiderius and Arviragus, stolen in infancy. Imogen is hospitably received by them under the name of Fidele. While they are at the chase she partakes of a box of drugged medicine which the wicked queen had prepared, and sinks into a trance resembling death. Her brothers sing her requiem. In the end Cloten is killed, the paternity of the youths revealed, Iachimo confesses his crime, and Imogen recovers both her husband and her brothers.

HAMLET

HAMLET is Shakespeare's longest and most famous play. It draws when acted as full a house to-day as it ever did. It is the drama of the intellect, of the soul, of man, of domestic tragedy. Five quarto editions appeared during the poet's life, the first in 1603. The story, Shakespeare got from an old black-letter quarto, 'The Historie of Hamblet,' translated from the French of Belleforest, who in turn translated it from the Danish History of Saxo Grammaticus. Some time in winter («'tis bitter cold»), the scene opens on a terrace in front of the castle of Kronberg in Elsinore, Denmark. The ghost of his father appears to Hamlet,—moody and depressed over his mother's marriage with Claudius, her brother-in-law. Hamlet learns from his father the fatal secret of his death at the hands of Claudius. He devises the court-play as a trap in which to catch his uncle's conscience; breaks his engagement with Ophelia; kills the wary old counselor Polonius; and is sent off to England under the escort of the treacherous courtiers Rosencrantz and Guildenstern, to be put to death. On the way he rises in the night, unseals their murderous commission, rewrites it, and seals it with his father's ring, having worded it so that they themselves shall be the victims when they reach England. In a fight with pirates Hamlet boards their ship, and is conveyed by them back to Denmark, where he tells his adventures to his faithful friend Horatio. At Ophelia's grave he encounters Laertes, her brother; and presently, in a fencing bout with him, is killed by Laertes's poisoned sword, but not before he has stabbed his treacherous uncle and forced the fatal cup of poison down his throat. His mother Gertrude has just died from accidentally drinking the same poison, prepared by the King for Hamlet. The old threadbare question, «Was Hamlet insane?» is hardly an open question nowadays. The verdict is that he was not. The strain upon his nerves of discovering his father's murderer, yet in such a manner that he could not prove it (*i. e.*, by the agency of a ghost), was so great that he verges on insanity, and this suggests to him the feigning of it. But if you deprive him wholly of reason, you destroy our interest in the play.

HENRY IV, Part I

King Henry IV., Part i., stands at the head of all Shakespeare's historical comedies, as Falstaff is by far his best humorous character. The two parts of the drama were first published in 1598 and 1600 respectively, the source-texts for both being Holinshed's ‹Chronicles› and the old play, ‹The famous Victories of Henry the Fifth.› The contrasted portraits of the impetuous Hotspur (Henry Percy) and the chivalric Prince Henry in Part i., are masterly done. King Henry, with the crime of Richard II.'s death on his conscience, was going on a crusade, to divert attention from himself; but Glendower and Hotspur give him his hands full at home. Hotspur has refused to deliver up certain prisoners taken on Holmedon field: «My liege, I did deny no prisoners,» he says in the well-known speech painting to the life the perfumed dandy on the field of battle. However, the Percys revolt from the too haughty monarch; and at Shrewsbury the Hotspur faction, greatly outnumbered by the King's glittering host, is defeated, and Percy himself slain by Prince Harry. For the humorous portions we have first the broad talk of the carriers in the inn-yard at Rochester; then the night robbery at Gadshill, where old Jack frets like a gummed varlet, and lards the earth with perspiration as he seeks his horse hidden by Bardolph behind a hedge. Prince Hal and Poins rob the robbers. Falstaff and his men hack their swords, and tickle their noses with grass to make them bleed. Then after supper, at the Boar's Head, in slink the disappointed Falstaffians, and Jack regales the Prince and Poins with his amusing whoppers about the dozen or so of rogues in Kendal green that set upon them at Gadshill. Hal puts him down with a plain tale. Great hilarity all around. Hal and Jack are in the midst of a mutual mock-judicial examination when the sheriff knocks at the door. The fat knight falls asleep behind the arras, and has his pockets picked by the Prince. Next day the latter has the money paid back, and he and Falstaff set off for the seat of war, Jack marching by Coventry with his regiment of tattered prodigals. Attacked by Douglas in the battle, Falstaff falls, feigning death. He sees the Prince kill Hotspur, and afterwards rises, gives the corpse a fresh stab, lugs it off on his back, and swears he and Hotspur fought a good hour by Shrewsbury clock, and that he himself killed him. The prince magnanimously agrees to gild the lie with the happiest terms he has, if it will do his old friend any grace.

HENRY IV, Part II

King Henry IV., Part ii., forms a dramatic whole with the preceding. The serious parts are more of the nature of dramatized chronicle; but the humorous scenes are fully as delightful and varied as in the first part. Hotspur is dead, and King Henry is afflicted with insomnia and nearing his end. «Uneasy lies the head that wears a crown,» he says in the fine apostrophe to sleep. At Gaultree Forest his son Prince John tricks his enemies into surrender, and sends the leaders to execution. The death-bed speeches of the King and Prince Henry are deservedly famous. All the low-comedy characters reappear in this sequel. Dame Quickly appears, with officers Snare and Fang, to arrest Falstaff, who has put all her substance into that great belly of his. In Part i. we found him already in her debt: for one thing, she had bought him a dozen of shirts to his back. Further, sitting in the Dolphin chamber by a sea-coal fire, had he not sworn upon a parcel-gilt goblet to marry her? But the merry old villain deludes her still more, and she now pawns her plate and tapestry for him. Now enter Prince Hal and Poins from the wars, and ribald and coarse are the scenes unveiled. Dame Quickly has deteriorated: in the last act of this play she is shown being dragged to prison with Doll Tearsheet, to answer the death of a man at her inn. The accounts of the trull Doll, and her billingsgate talk with Pistol, are too unsavory to be entirely pleasant reading; and one gladly turns from the atmosphere of the slums to the fresh country air of Gloucestershire, where, at Justice Shallow's manse, Falstaff is «pricking down» his new recruits,—Mouldy, Feeble, Wart, etc. Shallow is like a forked radish with a beard carved on it, or a man made out of a cheese-paring. He is given to telling big stories about what a wild rake he was at Clement's Inn in his youth. Sir John swindles the poor fellow out of a thousand pounds. But listen to Shallow: «Let me see, Davy; let me see, Davy; let me see.» «Sow the headland with red wheat, Davy;» «Let the smith's note for shoeing and plough-irons be cast and paid.» «Nay, Sir John, you shall see my orchard, where, in an arbor, we shall eat a last year's pippin of my own graffing, with a dish of caraways and so forth.» Amid right merry chaffing and drinking enters Pistol with news of the crowning of Henry V. «Away, Bardolph! saddle my horse; we'll ride all night; boot, boot, Master Shallow, I know the King is sick for me,» shouts old Jack. Alas for his hopes! he and his companions are banished the new King's presence, although provided with the means to live.

HENRY V

King Henry V. is the last of Shakespeare's ten great war dramas. It was first printed in 1600, the materials being derived from Holinshed and the old play on the same subject. Henry IV. is dead, and bluff King Hal is showing himself to be every inch a king. His claim to the crown of France is solemnly sanctioned. The Dauphin has sent him his merry mock of tennis balls, and got his stern answer. The traitors —Cambridge, Scroop, and Grey—have been sent to their death. The choice youth of England (and some riff-raff, too, such as Bardolph, Nym, and Pistol) have embarked at Southampton, and the threaden sails have drawn the huge bottoms through the sea to France. The third act opens in the very heat of an attack upon the walls of the seaport of Harfleur, and King Harry is urging on his men in that impassioned speech —«Once more unto the breach, dear friends»—which thrills the heart like a slogan in battle. We also catch glimpses of the army in Picardy, and finally see it on the eve of Agincourt. The night is rainy and dark, the hostile camps are closely joined. King Henry, cheerful and strong, goes disguised through his camp, and finds that whatever the issue of the war may be, he is expected to bear all the responsibility. A private soldier—Williams—impeaches the King's good faith, and the disguised Henry accepts his glove as a gauge and challenge for the morrow. Day dawns, the fight is on, the dogged English win the day. Then, as a relief to his nerves, Henry has his bit of fun with Williams, who has sworn to box the ear of the man caught wearing the mate of his glove. The wooing by King Henry of Kate, the French King's daughter, ends the play. But all through the drama runs also a comic vein. The humorous characters are Pistol,—now married to Nell Quickly,—Bardolph, Nym, and Fluellen. Falstaff, his heart «fracted and corroborate» by the King's casting of him off, and babbling o' green fields, has «gone to Arthur's bosom.» His followers are off for the wars. At Harfleur, Bardolph, of the purple and bubukled nose, cries, «On to the breach!» very valorously, but is soon hanged for robbing a church. Le grand Capitaine Pistol so awes a poor Johnny Crapaud of a prisoner that he offers him two hundred crowns in ransom. Pistol fires off some stinging bullets of wit at the Saint Tavy's day leek in the cap of Fluellen, who presently makes him eat a leek, giving him the cudgel over the head for sauce. The blackguard hies him home to London to swear he got his scalp wound in the wars.

HENRY VI, Parts I, II, III

Henry VI., Parts i., ii., iii. Of the eight closely linked Shakespeare historical plays, these three are the last but one. The eight cover nearly all of the fifteenth century in this order:

‹Richard II.›; ‹Henry IV.,› Parts i. and ii.; ‹Henry V.›; ‹Henry VI.› (three parts); and ‹Richard III.›—Henry IV. grasped the crown from Richard II., the rightful owner, and became the founder of the house of Lancaster. About 1455 began the Wars of the Roses. (The Lancastrians wore as a badge the white rose, the Yorkists the red; Shakespeare gives the origin of the custom in Henry VI., Part i., Act ii., Scene 4, adherents of each party chancing in the Temple Garden, London, to pluck each a rose of this color or that as symbol of his adherency.) In 1485 the Lancastrian Henry VII., the conqueror of Richard III., ended these disastrous wars, and reconciled the rival houses by marriage with Elizabeth of York. The three parts of ‹Henry VI.,› like ‹Richard II.,› present a picture of a king too weak-willed to properly defend the dignity of the throne. They are reeking with blood and echoing with the clash of arms. They are sensationally and bombastically written, and such parts of them as are by Shakespeare are known to be his earliest work. In Part i. the scene lies chiefly in France, where the brave Talbot and Exeter and the savage York and Warwick are fighting the French. Joan of Arc is here represented by the poet (who only followed English chronicle and tradition) as a charlatan, a witch, and a strumpet. The picture is an absurd caricature of the truth. In Part ii., the leading character is Margaret, whom the Duke of Suffolk has brought over from France and married to the weak and nerveless poltroon King Henry VI., but is himself her guilty lover. He and Buckingham and Margaret conspire successfully against the life of the Protector, Duke Humphrey, and Suffolk is killed during the rebellion of Jack Cade,—an uprising of the people which the play merely burlesques. Part iii. is taken up with the horrible murders done by fiendish Gloster (afterward Richard III.), the defeat and imprisonment of Henry VI. and his assassination in prison by Gloster, and the seating of Gloster's brother Edward (IV.) on the throne. The brothers, including Clarence, stab Queen Margaret's son and imprison her. She appears again as a subordinate character in ‹Richard III.› In 1476 she renounced her claim to the throne and returned to the Continent.

HENRY VIII

HENRY VIII., a historical drama by Shakespeare, based on Edward Hall's ‹Union of the Families of Lancaster and York,› Holinshed's ‹Chronicles,› and Fox's ‹Acts and Monuments of the Church.› The key-idea is the mutability of earthly grandeur, and by one or another turn of Fortune's wheel, the overthrow of the mighty—*i. e.*, of the Duke of Buckingham, of Cardinal Wolsey, and of Queen Katharine. The action covers a period of sixteen years, from the Field of the Cloth of Gold, in 1520, described in the opening pages, to the death of Queen Katharine in 1536. It is the trial and divorce of this patient, queenly, and unfortunate woman, that forms the main subject of the drama. She was the daughter of Ferdinand and Isabella of Castile, and born in 1485. She had been married when seventeen to Arthur, eldest son of Henry VII. Arthur lived only five months after his marriage, and when at seventeen years Henry VIII. came to the throne (that «most hateful ruffian and tyrant»), he married Katharine, then twenty-four. She bore him children, and he never lost his respect for her and her unblemished life. But twenty years after his marriage he met Anne Bullen at a merry ball at Cardinal Wolsey's palace, and fell in love with her, and immediately conceived conscientious scruples against the legality of his marriage. Queen Katharine is brought to trial before a solemn council of nobles and churchmen. With fine dignity she appeals to the Pope and leaves the council, refusing then and ever after to attend «any of their courts.» The speeches are masterpieces of pathetic and noble defense. In all his facts the poet follows history very faithfully. The Pope goes against her, and she is divorced and sequestered at Kimbolton, where presently she dies heart-broken, sending a dying message of love to Henry. Intertwined with the sad fortunes of the queen are the equally crushing calamities that overtake Cardinal Wolsey. His high-blown pride, his oppressive exactions in amassing wealth greater than the king's, his *ego et rex meus*, his double dealing with Henry in securing the Pope's sanction to the divorce,—these and other things are the means whereby his many enemies work his ruin. He is stripped of all his dignities and offices, and wanders away, an old man broken with the storms of State, to lay his bones in Leicester Abbey. The episode of the trial of Archbishop Cranmer is so pathetically handled as to excite tears. He is brought to trial for heresy by his enemy Gardiner, bishop of Winchester, but has previously been moved to tears of gratitude by Henry's secretly bidding him be of good cheer, and giving him his signet ring as a talisman to conjure with if too hard pressed by his enemies. Henry is so placed as to oversee (himself unseen) Cranmer's trial and the arrogant persecution of Gardiner. Cranmer produces the ring just as they are commanding him to be led away to the Tower; and Henry steps forth to first rebuke his enemies and then command them to be at peace. He does Cranmer the high honor of asking him to become a godfather to the daughter (Elizabeth) of Anne Bullen; and after Cranmer's eloquent prophecy at the christening, the curtain falls. The setting of this play is full of rich and magnificent scenery and spectacular pomp.

JULIUS CAESAR

JULIUS CÆSAR.—The material for this stately drama, the noblest of Shakespeare's historical plays, was taken from Plutarch. The action covers nearly two years,—44 to 42 B. C. The dramatic treatment, and all the splendid portraiture and ornamentation, cluster around two points or nodes,—the passing of Cæsar to the Capitol and his assassination there, and the battle of Philippi. Of the three chief conspirators,—Brutus, Cassius, and Casca,—Brutus had the purest motives: «all the conspirators, save only he, did that they did in envy of great Cæsar»; but Brutus, while loving him, slew him for his ambition and to serve his country. His very virtues wrought Brutus's ruin: he was too generous and unsuspecting. The lean-faced Cassius gave him good practical advice:—first, to take off Antony too; and second, not to allow him to make an oration over Cæsar's body. Brutus overruled him: he spoke to the fickle populace first, and told them that Antony spoke only by permission of the patriots. The eloquent and subtle Antony seized the advantage of the last word, and swayed all hearts to his will. There lay the body of the world-conqueror and winner of hearts, now a mere piece of bleeding earth, with none so poor to do him reverence. Antony had but to hold up the toga with its dagger-rents and show the pitiful spectacle of the hacked body, and read the will of Cæsar,—giving each citizen a neat sum of money, and to all a beautiful park for their recreations,—to excite them to a frenzy of rage against the patriots. These fly from Rome, and, drawing their forces to a head at Philippi, are beaten by Octavius Cæsar and Antony. Both Brutus and Cassius fall upon their swords. The great «show» passages of the play are the speech of the tribune Marullus («O you hard hearts, you cruel men of Rome»); the speeches of Antony by Pompey's statue («O mighty Cæsar! dost thou lie so low?»—«Here wast thou bayed, brave hart.»—«Over thy wounds now do I prophesy»); and of Brutus and Antony in the rostrum («Not that I loved Cæsar less, but that I loved Rome more»; and «I come to bury Cæsar, not to praise him»),—these, together with the quarrel and reconciliation of Brutus and Cassius in the tent at Philippi. Certain episodes, too, are deservedly famous: such as the description by blunt-speaking, superstitious Casca of the night-storm of thunder and lightning and rain (the ghosts, the surly-glaring lion, and other portents); the dispute at Brutus's house about the points of the compass («Yon grey lines that fret the clouds are messengers of day»); the scenes in which that type of loyal wifeliness, Portia, appears (the wound she gave herself to prove her fortitude, and her sad death by swallowing fire); and finally the pretty scene in the last act, of the little page falling asleep over his musical instrument, in the tent in the dead silence of the small hours of morning, when by the waning taper as he read, Brutus saw the ghost of murdered Cæsar glide before him, a premonition of his death on the morrow at Philippi.

KING JOHN

KING JOHN, a drama, the source of which is an older play published in 1591. The date of the action is 1200 A. D. John is on the throne of England, but without right; his brother, Richard the Lion-Hearted, had made his nephew Arthur of Bretagne his heir. Arthur is a pure and amiable lad of fourteen, the pride and hope of his mother Constance. The maternal affection and the sorrows of this lady form a central feature of the drama. Arthur's father Geoffrey has long been dead, but his mother has enlisted in his behalf the kings of Austria and of France. Their forces engage King John's army under the walls of Angiers. While the day is still undecided, peace is made, and a match formed between Lewis, dauphin of France, and John's niece Blanche. The young couple are scarcely married when the pope's legate causes the league to be broken. The armies again clash in arms, and John is victorious, and carries off Prince Arthur to England, where he is confined in a castle and confided to one Hubert. John secretly gives a written warrant to Hubert to put him to death. The scene in which the executioners appear with red-hot irons to put out the boy's eyes, and his innocent and affectionate prattle with Hubert, reminding him how he had watched by him when ill, is one of the most famous and pathetic in all the Shakespearian historical dramas. Hubert relents; but the frightened boy disguises himself as a sailor lad, and leaping down from the walls of the castle, is killed. Many of the powerful lords of England are so infuriated by this pitiful event (virtually a murder, and really thought to be such by them), that they join the Dauphin, who has landed to claim England's crown in the name of his wife. King John meets him on the battle-field, but is taken ill, and forced to retire to Swinstead Abbey. He has been poisoned by a monk, and dies in the orchard of the abbey in great agony. His right-hand man in his wars and in counsel has been a bastard son of Richard I., by Lady Faulconbridge. The bastard figures conspicuously in the play as braggart and ranter; yet he is withal brave and patriotic to the last. Lewis, the dauphin, it should be said, makes peace and retires to France.

KING LEAR

LEAR. — Shakespeare's great drama, ‹King Lear,› was written between 1603 and 1606. The bare historical outline of the story of the King he got probably from Holinshed or from an old play, the ‹Chronicle History of Leir›; the sad story of Gloster was found in Sir Philip Sidney's ‹Arcadia.› The motifs of the drama are the wronging of children by parents and of parents by children. With the fortunes of the King are interwoven those of Gloster. Lear has she-devils for daughters (Goneril and Regan), and one ministering angel, Cordelia; Gloster has a he-devil for son (Edmund), and one faithful son, Edgar. The lustre of goodness in Cordelia, Edgar, Albany, loyal Kent, and the faithful Fool, redeems human nature, redresses the balance. At the time the play opens, Lear is magnanimously dividing his kingdom between his sons-in-law Cornwall and Albany. But he has already a predisposition to madness, shown by his furious wrath over trifles, his childish bids for affection, and his dowering of his favorite daughter Cordelia with poverty and a perpetual curse, simply for a little willful reserve in expressing her really profound love for him. Blind impulse alone sways him; his passions are like inflammable gas; for a mere whim he banishes his best friend, Kent. Coming into the palace of Goneril, after a day's hunt with his retinue of a hundred knights, his daughter (a fortnight after her father's abdication) calls his men riotous and asks him to dismiss half of them. Exasperated to the point of fury, he rushes out tired and supperless into a wild night storm; he is cut to the heart by her ingratitude. And there before the hovel, in the presence of Kent, the disguised Edgar, and the Fool, insanity sets in and never leaves him until he dies at Dover by the dead body of Cordelia. In a hurricane of fearful events the action now rushes on: Gloster's eyes are plucked out, and he wanders away to Dover, where Cordelia, now Queen of France, has landed with an army to restore her father to his rights. Thither, too, the stricken Lear is borne at night. The joint queens, most delicate friends, lust after Edmund. Regan, made a widow by the death of Cornwall, is poisoned by Goneril. Cordelia and Lear are taken prisoner, and Cordelia is hanged by Edmund's order. Edmund is slain in the trial by combat. Lear dies; Gloster and Kent are broken-hearted and dying; Regan has stabbed herself; Edgar and Albany alone survive. The Fool in ‹Lear› is a man of tender feeling, and clings to his old comrade, the King, as to a brother. His jests are like smiles seen through tears; they relieve the terrible strain on our feelings. Edmund is a shade better than Iago; his bastardy, with its rankling humiliations, is an assignable cause, though hardly a palliation of his guilt.

LOVE'S LABOUR'S LOST

Shakespeare's Plays. LOVE'S LABOUR'S LOST is Shakespeare's first dramatic production, written about 1588 or '89, and has all the marks of immature style; yet its repartees and witticisms give it a sprightly cast, and its constant good-humor and good-nature make it readable. The plot, as far as is known, is Shakespeare's own. There is an air of unreality about it, as if all the characters had eaten of the insane root, or were at least light-headed with champagne. Incessant are their quick venues of wit,—«snip, snap, quick, and home.» In a nutshell, the play is a satire of utopias, of all thwarting of natural instincts. Ferdinand, King of Navarre, and his three associate lords, Biron, Dumain, and Longaville, have taken oath to form themselves into a kind of monastic academy for study. They swear to fast, to eat but one meal a day, and for three years not to look on the face of woman; all of which «is flat treason against the kingly state of youth.» But, alas! the King had forgotten that he was about to see the Princess of France and three of her ladies, come on a matter of State business. However, he will not admit them into his palace, but has pavilions pitched in the park. At the first glance all four men fall violently in love, each with one of the ladies,—the king with the princess, Biron with Rosaline, etc.: Cupid has thumped them all «with his bird-bolt under the left pap.» They write sentimental verses, and while reading them aloud in the park, all find each other out, each assuming a stern severity with the perjured ones until he himself is detected. One of the humorous characters is Don Adriano de Armado, «who draweth out the thread of his verbosity finer than the staple of his argument.» In him, and in the preposterous pedant Holofernes, and the curate Sir Nathaniel, the poet satirizes the euphuistic affectations of the time,—the taffeta phrases, three-piled hyperboles, and foreign language scraps, ever on the tongues of these fashionable dudes. The «pathetical nit,» Moth, is Armado's page, a keen-witted rogueling. Dull is a constable of «twice-sodden simplicity,» and Costard the witty clown. Rosaline is the Beatrice of the comedy, brilliant and caustic in her wit. Boyet is an old courtier who serves as a kind of usher or male lady's-maid to the princess and her retinue. The loves of the *noblesse* are parodied in those of Costard and of the country wench Jaquenetta. The gentlemen devise, to entertain the ladies, a Muscovite masque and a play by the clown and pedants. The ladies get wind of the masque, and, being masked themselves, guy the Muscovites who go off «all dry-beaten with pure scoff»; Rosaline suggests that maybe they are sea-sick with coming from Muscovy. The burlesque play tallies that in ‹Midsummer Night's Dream,› the great folk making satirical remarks on the clown's performances. Costard is cast for Pompey the Huge, and it transpires that the Don has no shirt on when he challenges Costard to a duel. While the fun is at its height comes word that sobers all: the princess's father is dead. As a test of their love the princess and Rosaline impose a year's severe penance on their lovers, and if their love proves true, promise to have them; and so do the other ladies promise to their wooers. Thus love's labor is, for the present, lost. The comedy ends with two fine lyrics,—the cuckoo song (‹Spring›), and the ‹Tu-whit, tu-whoo› song of the owl (‹Winter›).

MACBETH

MACBETH, one of Shakespeare's great tragedies of passion, which owes its great power of fascination to the supernatural element, was written about 1605. The prose story used was found in Holinshed's ‹Chronicles.› The sombre passions of the soul are painted with a brush dipped in blood and darkness. In every scene there is the horror and redness of blood. The faces of the murdered King Duncan's guards are smeared with it, it stains the spectral robes of Banquo, flows from the wounds of the pretty children of Macduff, and will not off from the little hand of the sleep-walking Lady Macbeth. Banquo and

Macbeth have just returned from a successful campaign in the north. On the road they meet three weird sisters, who predicted for Macbeth kingship, and for Banquo that his issue should be kings. 'Tis very late; the owl has shrieked good-night; only the lord and lady of the castle are awake. He, alone and waiting her signal, sees a vision of a phantasmal dagger in the air before him. He enters the chamber. «Hark! it was but the owl.»—«Who's there? what ho!»—«I have done the deed: didst thou not hear a noise?» In the dead silence, as day dawns, comes now a loud knocking at the south entry, and the coarse grumbling of the half-awakened porter brings back the commonplace realities of the day. Macbeth is crowned at Scone. But his fears stick deep in Banquo, and at a state banquet one of his hired murderers whispers him that Banquo lies dead in a ditch outside. As he turns he sees the ghost of that nobleman in his seat. «Prithee, see there! behold! look!»—«Avaunt! and quit my sight! Thy bones are marrowless, thy blood is cold; thou hast no speculation in those eyes which thou dost glare with.»—«Gentlemen, rise, his Highness is not well.» Macbeth, deep in crime, has no resource but to go deeper yet and becomes a bloody tyrant; but ends his career at Dunsinane Castle, where the slain king's sons, Malcolm and Macduff, and ten thousand stout English soldiers, meet their friends the Scottish patriot forces. The tyrant is fortified in the castle. The witches have told him he shall not perish till Birnam wood shall come to Dunsinane, and that no one of woman born shall have mortal power over him. But the enemy, as they approach, cut branches from Birnam wood «to shadow the number of their host.» This strikes terror to Macbeth's heart; but relying on the other assurance of the witches, he rushes forth to battle. He meets the enraged Macduff, learns from him that he (Macduff) was ripped untimely from his mother's womb, and so is not strictly of woman born. With the energy of despair Macbeth attacks him, but is overcome and beheaded.

MEASURE FOR MEASURE

Measure for Measure is one of Shakespeare's later tragi-comedies, the outline of the plot taken from the Italian novelist Cinthio and from Whetstone's tragedy of 'Promos and Cassandra.' License has now for a long while in Vienna run by the hideous law, as mice by lions; and the sagacious but eccentric duke attempts to enforce it, especially against sins of lust. The scenes that follow are gloomy and painful, and search deep into the conscience; yet all ends happily after all. The motif is mercy; a meting unto others, measure for measure, as we would wish them to mete unto us. The duke feigns a desire to travel, and appoints as deputies Angelo and Escalus. They begin at once to deal with sexual immorality: Escalus none too severely with a loathsome set of disreputable folk; but Angelo most mercilessly with young Claudio, who, in order to secure dower for his betrothed, had put off legal avowal of their irregular relation until her condition had brought the truth to light. Angelo condemns Claudio to death. His sister Isabella, about to enter a nunnery of the votarists of Saint Clare, is induced to plead for his life. As pure as snow, yet, as her «cheek-roses» show, not cold-blooded, her beauty ensnares the outward-sainted deputy and «seemer,» who proposes the release of her brother to her as the price of her chastity. Isabella has plenty of hot blood and moral indignation. She refuses with noble scorn; and when her brother begs his life at her hands, bids him die rather than see her dishonored. The duke, disguised as a friar, has overheard in the prison her splendid defense of virtue, and proposes a plan for saving her virtue and her brother's life too. It is this: There dwells alone, in a certain moated grange, forgotten and forlorn now these five years, Mariana, legally affianced to Lord Angelo, and who loves him still, although owing to the loss of her dowry he has cast her off. The friar-duke proposes that Isabella shall feign compliance, make an appointment, and then send Mariana in her place. Isabella agrees to risk her reputation, and the dejected grass-widow is easily won over to meet Angelo by night in his brick-walled garden. The base deputy, fearing Claudio's revenge if he frees him, breaks his promise and sends word to have him executed. The duke and the provost of the prison send Angelo the head of a prisoner (much like Claudio) who has died overnight:

Isabella supposes her brother to be dead. The duke, entering the city gates in state, *in propria persona*, hears her petition for justice. Angelo confesses; and after (by the duke's order) marrying Mariana, is pardoned. Indeed, there is a general amnesty; and the duke takes to wife Isabella, who thus enters upon a wider sphere of usefulness than that of a cloister.

MERRY WIVES OF WINDSOR

MERRY WIVES OF WINDSOR (printed 1602) is a play written at the request of Queen Elizabeth, who wanted to see Falstaff in love. With its air of village domesticity and out-o'-doorness is united the quintessential spirit of fun and waggery. Its gay humor never fails, and its readers always wish it five times as long as it is. The figures on this rich old tapestry resolve themselves, on inspection, into groups: The jolly ranter and bottle-rinser, mine host of the Garter Inn, with Sir John Falstaff and his men, Bardolph, Nym, and Pistol; the merry wives, Mrs. Ford and Mrs. Page, and their families; then Shallow (the country justice), with his cousin of the «wee little face and little yellow beard» (Slender), and the latter's man Simple; further Dr. Caius, the French physician, who speaks broken English, as does Parson Hugh Evans, the Welshman; lastly Dame Quickly (the doctor's housekeeper), and Master Fenton, in love with sweet Anne Page. Shallow has a grievance against Sir John for killing his deer; and Slender has matter in his head against him, for Sir John broke it. But Falstaff and his men outface the two cheese-parings, and they forget their «pribbles and prabbles» in the parson's scheme of marrying Slender to Anne Page. But the irascible doctor has looked that way too, and sends a «shallenge» to Evans. Mine host fools them both by sending each to a separate place for the duel. They make friends, and avenge themselves on the Boniface by getting his horses run off with. Falstaff sends identically worded love-letters to Mrs. Ford and Mrs. Page, hoping to replenish his purse from their husbands gold. But Pistol and Nym, in revenge for dismissal, peach to said husbands. The jealous Ford visits Falstaff under the name of Brook, and offers him a bag of gold if he will seduce Mrs. Ford for him. Jack assures him that he has an appointment with her that very day. And so he has. But the two wives punish him badly, and he gets nothing from them but a cast out of a buck-basket into a dirty ditch, and a sound beating from Ford. The midnight scene in Windsor Park, where Falstaff, disguised as Herne the Hunter, with stag-horns on his head, is guyed by the wives and their husbands and pinched and burned by the fairies' tapers, is most amusing. During the fairies' song Fenton steals away Anne Page and marries her. The doctor, by previous arrangement with mother Ford, leads away a fairy in green to a priest, only to discover that he has married a boy. And Slender barely escapes the same fate; for he leads off to Eton Church another «great lubberly boy,» dressed in white as agreed with Mr. Page. Anne has given the slip to both father and mother, having promised her father to wear white for Slender and her mother to dress in green for the doctor. But she dressed boy substitutes in white and green, and fooled them all.

THE MERCHANT OF VENICE

THE MERCHANT OF VENICE is a drama of Shakespeare's middle period (1594). The story of the bond and that of the caskets are both found in the old Gesta Romanorum, but the poet used especially Fiorentino's ‹Il Pecorone› (Milan, 1558). An atmosphere of high breeding and noble manners enwraps this most popular of Shakespeare's plays. The merchant Antonio is the ideal friend, his magnificent generosity a foil against which Shylock's avarice glows with a more baleful lustre. Shylock has long hated him, both for personal insults and for lending money gratis. Now, some twenty and odd miles away, at Belmont, lives Portia, with her golden hair and golden ducats; and Bassanio asks his friend Antonio for a loan, that he may go that way a-wooing. Antonio seeks the money of Shylock, who bethinks him now of a possible revenge. He offers three thousand ducats gratis for three months, if Antonio will seal to a merry bond pledging that if he shall fail his day of payment, the Jew may cut from his breast, nearest the heart, a pound of flesh. Antonio expects ships home a month before the day, and signs. While

Shylock is feeding at the Christian's expense, Lorenzo runs away with sweet Jessica, his dark-eyed daughter, and sundry bags of ducats and jewels. Bassanio is off to Belmont. Portia is to be won by him who, out of three caskets, —of gold, silver, and lead, respectively,—shall choose that containing her portrait. Bassanio makes the right choice. But at once comes word that blanches his cheeks: all of Antonio's ships are reported lost at sea; his day of payment has passed, and Shylock clamors for his dreadful forfeit. Bassanio, and his follower Gratiano, only tarry to be married, the one to Portia, and the other to her maid Nerissa; and then, with money furnished by Portia, they speed away toward Venice. Portia follows, diguised as a young doctor-at-law, and Nerissa as her clerk. Arrived in Venice, they are ushered into court, where Shylock, fell as a famished tiger, is snapping out fierce calls for justice and his pound of flesh, Antonio pale and hopeless, and Bassanio in vain offering him thrice the value of his bond. Portia, too, in vain pleads with him for mercy. Well, says Portia, the law must take its course. Then, «A Daniel come to judgment!» cries the Jew; «Come, prepare, prepare.» Stop, says the young doctor, your bond gives you flesh, but no blood; if you shed one drop of blood you die, and your lands and goods are confiscate to the State. The Jew cringes, and offers to accept Bassanio's offer of thrice the value of the bond in cash; but learns that for plotting against the life of a citizen of Venice all his property is forfeited, half to Antonio and half to the State. As the play closes, the little band of friends are grouped on Portia's lawn in the moonlight, under the vast blue dome of stars. The poet, however, excites our pity for the baited Jew.

A MIDSUMMER NIGHT'S DREAM

MIDSUMMER NIGHT'S DREAM was written previous to 1598; the poet drawing for materials on Plutarch, Ovid, and Chaucer. The roguish sprite Puck, or Robin Goodfellow, is a sort of half-brother of Ariel, and obeys Oberon as Ariel obeys Prospero. The theme of this joyous comedy is love and marriage. Duke Theseus is about to wed the fair Hippolyta. Lysander is in love with Hermia, and so is Demetrius; though in the end, Demetrius, by the aid of Oberon, is led back to his first love Helena. The scene lies chiefly in the enchanted wood near the duke's palace in Athens. In this wood Lysander and Hermia, and Demetrius and Helena, wander all night and meet with strange adventures at the hands of Puck and the tiny fairies of Queen Titania's train. Like her namesake in ‹All's Well,› Helena is here the wooer: «Apollo flies and Daphne leads the chase.» Oberon pities her, and sprinkling the juice of the magic flower love-in-idleness in Demetrius's eyes, restores his love for her; but not before Puck, by a mistake in anointing the wrong man's eyes, has caused a train of woes and perplexities to attend the footsteps of the wandering lovers. Puck, for fun, claps an ass's head on to weaver Bottom's shoulders, who thereupon calls for oats and a bottle of hay. By the same flower juice, sprinkled in her eyes, Oberon leads Titania to dote on Bottom, whose hairy head she has garlanded with flowers, and stuck musk roses behind his ears. Everybody seems to dream: Titania, in her bower carpeted with violets and canopied with honeysuckle and sweet-briar, dreamed she was enamored of an ass, and Bottom dared not say aloud what he dreamed he was; while in the fresh morning the lovers felt the fumes of the sleepy enchantment still about them.

But we must introduce the immortal players of ‹Pyramus and Thisbe.› Bottom is a first cousin of Dogberry, his drollery the richer for being partly self-conscious. With good strings to their beards and new ribbons for their pumps, he and his men meet at the palace, «on the duke's wedding-day at night.» Snout presents Wall; in one hand he holds some lime, some plaster and a stone, and with the open fingers of the other makes a cranny through which the lovers whisper. A fellow with lantern and thorn-bush stands for Moon. The actors kindly and in detail explain to the audience what each one personates; and the lion bids them not to be afeard, for he is only Snug the joiner, who roars extempore. The master of the revels laughs at the delicious humor till the tears run down his cheeks (and you don't wonder), and the lords and ladies keep up the fun by a running fire of witticisms when they can keep their faces straight. Theseus is an idealized

English gentleman, large-molded, gracious, and wise. His greatness is shown in his genuine kindness to the poor players in their attempt to please him.

MUCH ADO ABOUT NOTHING

MUCH ADO ABOUT NOTHING was first published in 1600. The mere skeleton of the serious portions of the drama he took from Bandello, through Belleforest's translation; the comic scenes are all his own. In the portrayal of Beatrice, Benedick, and Dogberry, he lavishes all his skill. The constable Dogberry is hit off to the life, with his irresistibly funny malapropisms. He is a lovable old heart-of-gold, who is always taking off his hat to himself and his office, and absurdly pardons every crime except the calling of himself an ass. The scene is laid in Messina. Benedick is just home from the wars. He and Beatrice have had some sparring matches before, and thick and fast now fly the tart and merry witticisms between them,—she «the sauciest, most piquant madcap girl that Shakespeare ever drew,» yet genuinely sympathetic; he a genial wit who tempts fate by his oaths that he will never marry. From the wars comes too Claudio, brave, but a light-weight fop, selfish, and touchy about his honor. He loves Hero, daughter of Leonato. Beatrice is the latter's niece, and in his house and orchard the action mostly takes place. The gentlemen lay a merry plot to ensnare Beatrice and Benedick. The latter is reading in the orchard, and overhears their talk about the violent love of Beatrice for him, and how (Hero has said) she would rather die than confess it. The bait is eagerly swallowed. Next Beatrice, hearing that Hero and Ursula are talking about her in the garden, runs, stooping like a lapwing, and hides her in the honeysuckle arbor. With a strange fire in her ears she overhears how desperately in love with her is Benedick. The bird is limed; she swears to herself to requite his devotion. Hero's wedding-day is fixed: Claudio is the lucky man. But the villain Don John concocts a plot which has most painful results—for twenty-four hours at least. He takes Claudio and his friend Don Pedro to the orchard, and shows them, as it seemed, Hero bidding John's follower Borachio a thousand good-nights: it is really her maid Margaret in her garments. Claudio in a rage allows her to go to church, but before the altar scornfully rejects her. Her father is in despair, Beatrice nobly indignant and incredulous. Hero swoons, and the officiating friar advises the giving out that she is dead from the shock. Claudio believes it, and hangs verses on her tomb. Meantime Dogberry's famous night-watch have overheard Borachio confess the villainous practice of John and himself. Then Hero's joyful friends plan a little surprise for Claudio. Leonato makes him promise, in reparation, to marry a cousin of Hero's, who turns out to be Hero herself come to life. A double wedding follows, for Benedick willingly suffers himself to be chaffed for eating his words and becoming «the married man.» Yet both he and Beatrice vow they take each other only out of pity.

OTHELLO

OTHELLO, THE MOOR OF VENICE, ranks with 'Hamlet,' 'Lear,' and 'Macbeth,' as one of Shakespeare's four great masterpieces of tragedy. The bare outline of the story came to him from Cinthio's 'Il Moro di Venezia.' It is the story of «one who loved not wisely, but too well; of one not easily jealous, but being wrought, perplexed in the extreme.» Othello has a rich exotic nature, a heroic tenderness, quick sense of honor, childlike trust, yet fiercest passion when wronged in his soul. In Iago we have a werewolf's face behind a mask of stoutest honesty; he is one to whom goodness is sheer silliness and cruel craft a fine prudence. The Moor has wedded Desdemona, and from Venice sailed to Cyprus, followed by Roderigo, who is in love with her and is a tool of Iago. Iago hates Othello for appointing Cassio his lieutenant, leaving him to be his humble standard-bearer. He also suspects him of having cuckolded him, and for mere suspicion in that kind will diet his revenge by trying to pay him off wife for wife, or failing that, to poison his happiness forever by jealousy. And he wants Cassio's place. He persuades Roderigo that Cassio and Desdemona are in love, and that if he is to prosper, Cassio must be degraded from office or killed. The loyal Cassio has a poor brain for drink, Iago gets him tipsy and involved in a fray, and then has the garrison alarmed by the bell. Othello dismisses

Cassio from office. The poor man, smitten with deep shame and despair, is advised by «honest» Iago to seek the mediation of the divine Desdemona, and out of this he will work his ruin; for he craftily instills into the mind of Othello that his wife intercedes for Cassio as for a paramour, and brings him where he sees Cassio making his suit to her, but retiring when he perceives Othello in the distance. «Ha! I like not that,» says Iago. And then, forced to disclose his thought, he reminds the Moor that Desdemona deceived her father by her secret marriage, and may deceive him; also tells a diabolically false tale of his sleeping with Cassio, and how he talked in his sleep about his amour with Desdemona. Othello had given his wife a talismanic embroidered handkerchief, sewed by a sibyl in her prophetic fury. Iago had often urged his wife Emilia to steal this «napkin,» and when he gets it he drops it in Cassio's chamber. The Moor sees it in his lieutenant's hands, and further sees him laughing and gesturing about Bianca, a common strumpet, and is told by Iago that Desdemona and his adventures with her were Cassio's theme. When, finally, the «honest,» «trusty» Iago tells him that Cassio had confessed all to him, the tortured man throws his last doubt to the winds, and resolves on the death of Cassio and Desdemona both. Cassio is only wounded; but the gentle Desdemona, who, all heart-broken and foreboding, has retired, is awaked by Othello's last kisses (for his love is not wholly quenched), and after a terrible talk, is smothered by him where she lies,—reviving for a moment, after the entrance of Emilia, to assert that Othello is innocent and that she killed herself. The Moor avows the deed, however, both to Emilia and to two Venetian officials, who have just arrived on State business. In the conversation Iago's villainy comes to light through Emilia's telling the truth about the handkerchief; she is stabbed to death by Iago, while Othello in bitter remorse stabs himself, and as he dies imprints a convulsive kiss on the cold lips of Desdemona. Iago is led away to torture and death.

PERICLES

Pericles, Prince of Tyre, a play written in part by Shakespeare. His part in it begins with the magnificent storm scene in Act iii.,—«Thou god of this great vast, rebuke these surges,»—«The seaman's whistle is as a whisper in the ears of death, unheard,» etc. The play was very popular with the masses for a hundred years. Indeed the romantic plot is enough to make it perennially interesting and pathetic; the deepest springs of emotion and of tears are touched by the scenes in which Pericles recovers his lost wife and his daughter. —After certain strange adventures Pericles, Prince of Tyre, arrives with ships loaded with grain at Tarsus, and feeds the starving subjects of King Cleon and Queen Dionyza. Afterwards shipwrecked by Pentapolis, he recovers from the waves his suit of armor, and buying a horse with a jewel, goes to King Simonides's court and jousts for his daughter Thaïsa's love. He marries her, and in returning to Tyre his wife gives birth, in the midst of a terrible storm, to a daughter whom he names Marina. The mother, supposed dead, is laid by Pericles in a water-tight bitumened chest, with jewels and spices, etc., and is thrown overboard by the sailors, but cast ashore at Ephesus and restored to life by the wise and good physician Cerimon. Pericles lands with his infant daughter at Tarsus, where he leaves her with his old friends Cleon and Dionyza. The pretty Marina grows up, and so excites the hatred of the queen by outshining her own daughter, that she tries to kill her; but the girl is rescued by pirates, who carry her to Mitylene, where she is bought by the owner of a disreputable house, but escapes to take service as a kind of companion in an honest family. The fame of her beauty and accomplishments spreads through the city. One festal day comes Pericles, sad and ill, in his ship to Mitylene, and meeting with Marina, learns from her her story. His joy is so great that he fears death. By Diana's command, revealed to him in a vision, he goes to Ephesus to confess before the people and before her priestess the story of his life. The officiating priestess turns out to be his wife Thaïsa, who went from the physician's house to become a ministrant in the temple of the goddess of chastity.

RICHARD II

Richard II. (Compare 'Henry VI.') This drama (based on Holinshed's

‹Chronicle›) tells the story of the supplanting, on the throne of England, of the handsome and sweet-natured, but weak-willed Richard II., by the politic Bolingbroke (Henry IV.). The land is impoverished by Richard's extravagances. He is surrounded by flatterers and boon companions (Bushy, Bagot, and Green), and has lost the good-will of his people. The central idea of ‹Richard II.› is that the kingly office cannot be maintained without strength of brain and hand. Old John of Gaunt (or Ghent) is loyal to Richard; but on his death-bed sermons him severely, and dying, prophesies of England, — «this seat of Mars,»

> «This fortress built by Nature for herself
> Against infection and the hand of war,
> This happy breed of men, this little world.»

Richard lets him talk; but no sooner is the breath out of his body than he seizes all his movable or personal wealth and that of his banished son Bolingbroke, to get money for his Irish wars. This step costs Richard his throne. While absent in Ireland Bolingbroke lands with a French force, to regain his property and legal rights as a nobleman and open the purple testament of bleeding war. The country rises to welcome him. Even a force in Wales, tired of waiting for Richard, who was detained by contrary winds, disperses just a day before he landed. Entirely destitute of troops, he humbly submits, and in London a little later gives up his crown to Henry IV. Richard is imprisoned at Pomfret Castle. Here, one day, he is visited by a man who was formerly a poor groom of his stable, and who tells him how it irked him to see his roan Barbary with Bolingbroke on his back on coronation day, stepping along as if proud of his new master. Just then one Exton appears, in obedience to a hint from Henry IV., with men armed to kill. Richard at last (but too late) shows a manly spirit; and snatching a weapon from one of the assassins, kills him and then another, but is at once struck dead by Exton. Henry IV. lamented this bloody deed to the day of his death, and it cost him dear in the censures of his people.

RICHARD III

Richard III., the last of a closely linked group of historical tragedies. (See ‹Henry VI.›) Still a popular play on the boards; Edwin Booth as Richard will long be remembered. As the drama opens, Clarence, the brother of Richard (or Gloster as he is called) is being led away to the Tower, where, through Gloster's intrigues, he is soon murdered on a royal warrant. The dream of Clarence is a famous passage, — how he thought Richard drowned him at sea; and in hell the shade of Prince Edward, whom he himself had helped to assassinate at Tewkesbury, wandered by, its bright hair dabbled in blood, and crying: —

> «Clarence is come; false, fleeting, perjured Clarence.»

Gloster also imprisons the son of Clarence, and meanly matches Clarence's daughter. The Prince Edward mentioned was son of the gentle Henry VI., whom Richard stabbed in the Tower. This hunch-backed devil next had the effrontery to woo to wife Anne, widow of the Edward he had slain. She had not a moment's happiness with him, and deserved none. He soon killed her, and announced his intention of seeking the hand of Elizabeth, his niece, after having hired one Tyrrel to murder her brothers, the tender young princes, sons of Edward IV., in the Tower. Tyrrel employed two hardened villains to smother these pretty boys; and even the murderers wept as they told how they lay asleep, «girdling one another within their innocent alabaster arms,» a prayer-book on their pillow, and their red lips almost touching. The savage boar also stained himself with the blood of Lord Hastings, of the brother and son of Edward IV.'s widow, and of Buckingham, who, almost as remorseless as himself, had helped him to the crown, but fell from him when he asked him to murder the young princes. At length at Bosworth Field the monster met his match in the person of Richmond, afterward Henry VII. On the night before the battle, the poet represents each leader as visited by dreams, — Richmond seeing pass before him the ghosts of all whom Richard has murdered, who encourage him and bid him be conqueror on the morrow; and Richard seeing the same ghosts pass menacingly by him, bidding him despair and promising to sit heavy on his soul on the day of battle. He awakes, cold drops of sweat standing on his brow; the lights burn blue in his tent: «Is there a murderer here? No. Yes, I am: then fly. What, from myself?» Day breaks; the battle is joined; Richard fights with fury, and his horse is killed under him: «A horse! a horse! my kingdom for a horse!» But soon brave Richmond has him down, crying, «The day is ours: the bloody dog is dead.»

The story of Richard III. reads more like that of an Oriental or African despot than that of an English monarch.

ROMEO AND JULIET

Romeo and Juliet was first published in 1597. The plot was taken from a poem by Arthur Brooke, and from the prose story in Paynter's ‹Palace of Pleasure.› The comical underplot of the servants of Capulet *vs.* those of Montagu; the fatal duels, the deaths of Mercutio and Tybalt; the ball where Romeo, a Montagu, falls in love with Juliet; the impassioned love-scenes in the orchard; the encounter of the Nurse and Peter with the mocking gallants; the meetings at Friar Laurence's cell, and the marriage of Juliet there; Romeo's banishment; the attempt to force Juliet to marry the County Paris; the Friar's device of the sleeping-potion; the night scene at the tomb, Romeo first unwillingly killing Paris and then taking poison; the waking of Juliet, who stabs herself by her husband's body; the reconciliation of the rival families,—such are the incidents in this old Italian story, which has touched the hearts of men now for six hundred years. It is the drama of youth, «the first bewildered stammering interview of the heart,» with the delicious passion, pure as dew, of first love, but love thwarted by fate and death. Sampson bites his thumb at a Montagu; Tybalt and Mercutio fall. Friar John is delayed; Romeo and Juliet die. Such is the irony of destiny. The mediæval manners at once fierce and polished,—Benvenuto limns them. We are in the warm south: the dense gray dew on leaf and grass at morn, the cicada's song, the nightingale, the half-closed flower-cups, the drifting perfume of the orange blossom, stars burning dilated in the blue vault. Then the deep melancholy of the story. And yet there is a kind of triumph in the death of the lovers: for in four or five days they had lived an eternity; death made them immortal. On fire, both, with impatience, in vain the Friar warns them that violent delights have violent ends. Blinded by love, they only half note the prescience of their own souls. 'Twas written in the stars that Romeo was to be unlucky: at the supper he makes a mortal enemy; his interference in a duel gets Mercutio killed; his over-haste to poison himself leads on to Juliet's death. As for the garrulous old Nurse, foul-mouthed and tantalizing, she is too close to nature not to be a portrait from life; her advice to «marry Paris» reveals the full depth of her banality. Old Capulet is an Italian Squire Western, a chough of lands and houses, who treats this exquisite daughter just as the Squire treats Sophia. Mercutio is everybody's favorite: the gallant loyal gentleman, of infinite teeming fancy, in all his raillery not an unkind word, brave as a lion, tender-hearted as a girl, his quips and sparkles of wit ceasing not even when his eyes are glazing in death.

THE TAMING OF THE SHREW

The Taming of the Shrew, partly by Shakespeare and partly by an unknown hand, is a witty comedy of intrigue, founded on an old play about «the taming of the shrew» and on Ariosto's ‹I Suppositi›; and is preceded by another briefer bit of dramatic fun (the «induction») on a different topic,—*i. e.*, how a drunken tinker, picked up on a heath before an alehouse by a lord and his huntsmen, is carried unconscious to the castle, and put to bed, and waited on by obsequious servants, treated to sumptuous fare, and music, and perfumes, and told that for many years he has been out of his head, and imagining that he was a poor tinker. «What! am I not Christopher Sly, old Sly's son of Burton Heath? . . . ask Marian Hacket, the fat ale-wife of Wincot, if she know me not.» At length this Sancho Panza, who still retains his fondness for small ale, sits down to see the laughter-moving comedy ‹The Taming of the Shrew,› enacted for his sole benefit by some strolling players. The brainless sot found its delicious humor dull; not so the public. Baptista, a rich old gentleman of Padua, has two daughters. The fair Katharina has a bit of a devil in her, is curst with a shrewish temper; but this is partly due to envy of the good fortune of the mincing artificial beauty,

Bianca, her sister, whose demure gentle ways make the men mad over her. Yet Kate, when «tamed,» proves after all to be the best wife. The other gallants will none of her; but the whimsical Petruchio of Verona has come «to wive it wealthily in Padua,» and nothing daunted, wooes and wives the young shrew in astonishing fashion. The law of the time made the wife the chattel of her husband, otherwise even Petruchio might have failed. His method was to conquer her will, «to kill her in her own humor.» He comes very late to the wedding, clothed like a scarecrow, an old rusty sword by his side, and riding a sunken-backed spavined horse with rotten saddle and bridle. His waggish man Grumio is similarly accoutred. At the altar he gives the priest a terrible box on the ear, refuses to stay to the wedding dinner, and on the way to his country-house acts like a madman. Arrived home, he storms at and beats the servants, allows Kate not a morsel of food for two days, preaches continence to her, throws the pillows around the chamber, and raises Cain a-nights generally so that she can get no sleep, denies her the bonnet and dress the tailor has brought, and so manages things as to seem to do all out of love to her and regard for her health, and without once losing his good-humor. In short he subdues her, breaks her will, and makes his supreme; so that at the end she makes a speech to the other wives about the duty of obedience, that would make the «new woman» of our time smile in scorn. Of Bianca's three suitors the youngest, Lucentio, gets the prize by a series of smart tricks. Disguised as a tutor of languages he gets her love as they study, while his rivals, «like a gemini of baboons,» blow their nails out in the cold and whistle. Lucentio at the very start gets his servant Tranio to personate himself, and an old pedant is hired to stand for his father; and while Baptista, the father of Bianca, is gone to arrange for the dower with this precious pair of humbugs, Lucentio and his sweetheart run off to church and get married. The arrival of the real father of Lucentio makes the plot verily crackle with life and sensation.

THE TEMPEST

THE TEMPEST, one of Shakespeare's very latest plays (1611), written in the mellow maturity of his genius, is probably based on a lost Italian *novella* or play, though certain incidents are borrowed from three pamphlets on the Bermudas and Virginia and from Florio's Montaigne. The scene is said to be laid in the haunted island of Lampedusa in the Mediterranean. In the opening lines we see a ship laboring in heavy seas near the shore of an island, whose sole inhabitants, besides the spirits of earth and air typified in the dainty yet powerful sprite Ariel, are Prospero and his lovely daughter Miranda, and their slave, the deformed boor Caliban, an aborigine of the island. The grave and good Prospero is a luckier castaway than Robinson Crusoe, in that his old friend Gonzalo put into the boat with him not only his infant daughter, but clothes, and some books of magic, by the aid of which both men and spirits, and the very elements, are subject to the beck of his wand. He was the rightful Duke of Milan, but was supplanted by his brother Antonio, who with his confederate, the king of Naples, and the latter's son Ferdinand and others, is cast ashore on the island. The shipwreck occurs full in the sight of the weeping Miranda; but all hands are saved, and the ship too. The humorous characters are the butler Stephano, and the court jester Trinculo, both semi-drunk, their speech and songs caught from the sailors, and savoring of salt and tar. Throughout the play the three groups of personages,—the royal retinue with the irrepressible and malapropos old Gonzalo, the drunken fellows and Caliban, and Prospero with his daughter and Ferdinand,—move leisurely to and fro, the whole action taking up only three hours. The three boors, fuddled with their fine liquor and bearing the bark bottle, rove about the enchanted island, fall into the filthy-mantled pool, and are stoutly pinched by Prospero's goblins for theft. The murderous plot of Antonio and the courtier Sebastian is exposed at the phantom banquet of the harpies. Spellbound in the linden grove, all the guilty parties come forward into a charmed circle and take a lecture from Prospero. General reconciliation. Then finally, Miranda and Ferdinand are discovered playing chess before Prospero's cell, and learn that to-morrow they set sail for Naples to be married.

TIMON OF ATHENS

Timon of Athens is by Shakespeare, either in whole or in part. It is a bitter satire on friendship and society, written in the stern sarcastic vein of Juvenal. The sources of the plot seem to have been Paynter's 'Palace of Pleasure,' Plutarch's 'Life of Antony,' and Lucian's 'Dialogue on Timon.' Shakespeare's 'Timon' is unique both in his ostentations and indiscriminate prodigality and in the bitterness of his misanthropy after his wealth was gone. Yet he was of the noblest heart. His sublime faith that his friends were as generous as he, and that they were all brothers, commanding one another's fortunes, was a practical error, that was all. Men were selfish wolves; he thought them angels. His bounty was measureless: if a friend praised a horse 'twas his; if one wanted a little loan of £5,000 or so, 'twas a trifle; he portioned his servants and paid his friends' debts; his vaults wept with drunken spilth of wine, and every room blazed with lights and brayed with minstrelsy; at parting each guest received some jewel as a keepsake. When all was gone, full of cheerful faith he sent out to his friends to borrow, and they all with one accord began to make excuse. Not a penny could he get. Feast won, fast lost. The smiling, smooth, detested parasites left him to his clamorous creditors and to ruin. The crushing blow to his ideals maddened him; his blood turned to gall and vinegar. Yet he determined on one last banquet. The surprised sycophants thought he was on his feet again, and with profuse apologies assembled at his house. The covered dishes are brought in. «Uncover dogs, and lap!» cries the enraged Timon. The dishes are found to be full of warm water, which he throws in their faces, then pelts them with stones and drives them forth with execrations, and rushes away to the woods to henceforth live in a cave and subsist on roots and berries and curse mankind. In digging he finds gold. His old acquaintances visit him in turn, —Alcibiades, the cynical dog Apemantus, his faithful steward Flavius, a poet, a painter, senators of Athens. He curses them all, flings gold at them, telling them he gives it that they may use it for the bale of man, pronounces his weeping steward the only honest man in the world, builds «his everlasting mansion on the beached verge of the salt flood,» where «vast Neptune may weep for aye on his low grave, on faults forgiven,» writes his epitaph, and lies down in the tomb and dies.

TITUS ANDRONICUS

Titus Andronicus.—A most repulsive drama of bloodshed and unnatural crimes, not written by Shakespeare, but probably touched up for the stage by him when a young man. It is included in the original Folio Edition of 1623. No one who has once supped on its horrors will care to read it again. Here is a specimen of them: Titus Andronicus, a Roman noble, in revenge for the ravishing of his daughter Lavinia and the cutting off of her hands and tongue, cuts the throats of the two ravishers, while his daughter holds between the stumps of her arms a basin to catch the blood. The father then makes a paste of the ground bones and blood of the slain men, and in that paste bakes their two heads, and serving them up at a feast, causes their mother to eat of the dish. Iago seems a gentleman beside the hellish Moor, Aaron, of this blood-soaked tragedy.

TROILUS AND CRESSIDA

Troilus and Cressida is one of the later products of Shakespeare's pen. Whether he got his facts from Chaucer, or from mediæval tales about Troy, is uncertain. The drama is his wisest play, and yet the least pleasing as a whole, owing to the free talk of the detestable Pandarus and the licentiousness of the false Cressid. Some have thought the piece to be an ironical and satirical burlesque of Homer. There is very little plot. The young Trojan, Troilus, in love with Cressida, is brave as a lion in battle and green as a goose in knowledge of women. (But «to be wise and love exceeds man's might.») His amour, furthered by Cressida's uncle, Pandarus, is scarcely begun when Cressida is exchanged for a Trojan prisoner and led off by Diomed to the Greek camp. On arriving, she allows herself to be kissed by the Greek generals, whom she sees for the first time; as Ulysses says, «There's language in her eye, her cheek, her lip.» She has just vowed eternal loyalty to Troilus too. But she is anybody's Cressid; and with anguish unspeakable, Troilus later overhears her making an appointment with Diomed, and sees her give him his own remembrance pledge. By gross flattery of the beef-witted Ajax, the wily Greek leaders get him to fight Hector. But Hector and he are related by blood, and after some sparring and hewing they shake hands. Hector is then feasted in the Grecian tents. The big conceited bully Achilles, «having his ear full of his airy fame,» has grown «dainty of his worth»; and finding his reputation «shrewdly gored» by his long inactivity, and by the praise Ajax is getting, and especially spurred on by the death of Patroclus, at length comes into the field, but plays the contemptible coward's part by surprising Hector with his armor off and having his Myrmidons butcher him. Thersites is a scurvy, foul-mouthed fellow, who does nothing but rail, exhausting the language of vile epithets, and hitting off very shrewdly the weak points of his betters, who give him frequent fist-beatings for his pains. The great speeches of Ulysses, Agamemnon, and Nestor all breathe the selfsame tone of profound sagacity and insight into human nature. They have the mint-stamp of but one soul, and that Shakespeare's. Homer's sketches of the Greek leaders are the merest Flaxman outlines; but Shakespeare throws the Röntgen rays of his powerful analysis quite through their souls, endowing them with the subtlest thoughts, and through their masks utters such sentences as these:—

« The ample proposition that hope makes
In all designs begun on earth below,
Fails in the promised largeness.»

« *One* touch of nature makes the whole world kin,—
That all with one consent praise new-born gauds.»

« Keep then the path;
For emulation hath a thousand sons
That one by one pursue: if you give way,
Or hedge aside from the direct forthright,
Like to an entered tide they all rush by
And leave you hindmost.»

There are no other scenes in Shakespeare so packed with sound and seasoned wisdom as the third of Act i. and the third of Act iii. in ‹Troilus and Cressida.›

TWELFTH NIGHT

TWELFTH NIGHT, OR WHAT YOU WILL, is a delightfully humorous comedy. An item in the manuscript diary of John Manningham shows that it was played February 2d, 1601, in the fine old hall of the Middle Temple, London,—a hall still in existence. The twelfth night after Christmas was anciently given up to sport and games; hence the name. The fresh, gay feeling of a whistling plowboy in June was the mood of the writer of ‹Twelfth Night.› Tipsy Sir Toby's humor is catching; his brain is like a bottle of champagne; his heels are as light as his head, and one feels he could cut a pigeon-wing with capering Sir Andrew «to make all split,» or sing a song «to make the welkin dance.» The scene is a seaport city of Illyria, where a sentimental young duke is fallen into a love-melancholy over the pitiless lady Olivia. Now the fair Viola and her brother Sebastian,—strikingly alike in feature,—unknown to each other reach the same city, Sebastian in company with his friend Captain Antonio. Viola enters the service of the duke as a page, in garments such as her brother wore. With the rich Olivia dwell her Puritanical steward Malvolio, her kinsman Sir Toby Belch, and her maid Maria, and other servants. Olivia has a suitor, and Sir Toby an echo, in the lean-witted Sir Andrew Aguecheek. Malvolio is unpopular: he thinks because he is virtuous there shall be no more cakes and ale; but Maria lays a trap for his vanity, which is fathoms deep. She drops a mysterious letter in Malvolio's path, penned in Olivia's hand («her very C's, her U's, and her T's»). The letter begins with «M O A I doth sway my life,» bids him be opposite with a kinsman and surly with servants, recall who commended his yellow stockings and wished to see him cross-gartered, and remember that some have greatness thrust upon them. He swallows the bait, and makes himself such a ridiculous ass that Olivia thinks him out of his wits, and Sir Toby has him bound and put into a dark room. Malvolio has called the clown «a barren rascal,» and this keen-witted lovable fellow now has a delicious bit of retaliation. Assuming the voice of the curate Sir Topas, he assures him that until he can hold the opinion of Pythagoras that the soul of his grandam might haply inhabit a bird, he shall not advise his release. Then resuming his own voice he indulges in more excellent fooling. When last seen Malvolio is free, and bolting out of the room swears he will be «revenged on the whole pack» of them. To return: Viola (as «Cesario») becomes the duke's messenger to woo Olivia by proxy. Olivia falls desperately in love with the messenger; and when Aguecheek spies her showing him favors, he is egged on by roguish Sir Toby to write him a challenge. But Cesario is afraid of the very sight of naked steel, and Sir Andrew is an arrant coward. Sir Toby, after frightening each nearly out of his wits with stories of the other's ferocity, at length gets them for form's sake to draw their swords; when in comes Captain Antonio, and mistaking Cesario for Sebastian, takes his part. In the mean time, Olivia has married Sebastian by mistake for Cesario, and the two knights both get their heads broken through a similar misunderstanding; for however it may be with Cesario, Sebastian is «a very devil incardinate» with his sword. Presently Sebastian and Cesario meet, and the mystery is solved: Viola avows her sex, and marries the duke, whom she ardently loves.

THE TWO GENTLEMEN OF VERONA

TWO GENTLEMEN OF VERONA, one of Shakespeare's earliest and least attractive comedies, for the plot of which he was slightly indebted to Bandello, to Sidney's 'Arcadia,' and to Montemayor's 'Diana Enamorada.' The scene is laid alternately in Verona and in Milan. The noble Valentine of Verona remarks to his friend Proteus that «home-keeping youths have ever homely wits»; hence he will travel to Milan, with his servant Speed. Proteus, a mean-souled, treacherous, fickle young sprig, is in love with Julia, or thinks he is. His servant's name is Launce, a droll fellow who is as rich in humor as Launcelot Gobbo of the 'Merchant of Venice.' Julia is the heroine of the piece; a pretty, faithful girl. Proteus soon posts after Valentine to Milan, and at once forgets Julia and falls «over boots in love» with Silvia. Julia also goes to Milan, disguised as a boy, and takes service with Proteus. The latter treacherously betrayed Valentine's plan of elopement with Silvia to the duke her father, who met Valentine, pulled the rope ladder from under his cloak, and then banished him. As in the play of 'As You Like It,' all the parties finally meet in the forest, where Valentine has been chosen leader by a band of respectable outlaws. Julia confesses her identity; Valentine, with a maudlin, milk-sop charity, not only forgives Proteus (whom he has just overheard avowing to Silvia that he will outrage her if he cannot get her love), but, on Proteus repenting, actually offers to give up Silvia to him. But Julia swoons, and Proteus's love for her returns. A double marriage ends this huddled-up finale. Launce affines with Touchstone, Grumio, Autolycus, and the Dromios. He is irresistibly funny in the enumeration of his milkmaid's «points,» and in the scenes with his dog Crab. This cruel-hearted cur, when all at home were weeping over Launce's departure, and the very cat was wringing her hands, shed not a tear; and when, in Madam Silvia's dining-room, he stole a chicken-leg from the trencher and misbehaved in an unmentionable manner, Launce manfully took a whipping for him. Nay, he stood on the pillory for geese he had killed, and stood in the stocks for puddings he had stolen. Crab enjoys the honor of being the only dog that sat to Shakespeare for his portrait, although others are mentioned in his works.

A WINTER'S TALE

A WINTER'S TALE, probably the last dramatic piece from Shakespeare's pen, has the serene and cheerful wisdom of 'Cymbeline' and 'The Tempest.' It is based on Greene's 'Pandosto' (1588). In this story, as in Shakespeare, Bohemia is made a maritime country and Delphos an island. The name 'Winter's Tale' derives partly from the fact that the play opens in winter, and partly from the resemblance of the story to a marvelous tale told by a winter's fire. Like 'Othello,' it depicts the tragic results of jealousy,—in this case long years of suffering for both husband and wife, and the purification of the soul of the former through remorse, and his final reconciliation with his wronged queen. Leontes, king of Sicily, unlike Othello, has a natural bent toward jealousy; he suspects without good cause, and is grossly tyrannical in his persecutions of the innocent. Hermione, in her sweet patience and sorrow, is the most divinely compassionate matron Shakespeare has delineated. Polixenes, king of Bohemia, has been nine months a guest of his boyhood's friend Leontes, and is warmly urged by both king and queen to stay longer. Hermione's warm hospitality and her lingering hand pressures are construed by the king as proof of criminality: he sees himself laughed at for a cuckold; a deep fire of rage burns in his heart; he wants Camillo to poison Polixenes; but this good man flies with him to Bohemia. Leontes puts his wife in prison, where she is delivered of a daughter. He compels Antigonus to swear to expose it in a desert place, and then proceeds with the formal trial of his wife. His messengers to Delphi report her guiltless. She swoons away, and Paulina gives out that she is dead. But she is secretly conveyed away, after the funeral, and revived. Her little son dies from grief. Sixteen years now elapse, and we are across seas in Bohemia, near the palace of Polixenes, and near where Hermione's infant daughter was exposed, but rescued (with a bundle containing rich bearing cloth, gold, jewels, etc.) by an old shepherd. Antigonus and his ship's crew were all lost, so no trace of the infant could be found. But here she is, the sweetest girl in Bohemia and named Perdita («the lost one»). A sheep-shearing feast at the old shepherd's cottage is in progress. His son has gone for sugar and spices and rice, and had his pocket picked by that rogue of rogues, that snapper-up of unconsidered trifles, Autolycus. The dainty Perdita moves about under the green trees as the hostess of the occasion, giving to each guest a bunch of sweet flowers and a welcome. Polixenes and Camillo are here in disguise, to look after Polixenes's son Florizel. After dancing, and some songs from peddler Autolycus, Florizel and Perdita are about to be betrothed when Polixenes discovers himself and threatens direst punishment to the rustics. The lovers fly to Sicily, with a feigned story for the ear of Leontes; and the old shepherd and his son get aboard Florizel's ship to show the bundle and «fairy gold» found with Perdita, expecting thus to save their lives by proving that they are not responsible for her doings. Polixenes and Camillo follow the fugitives, and at Leontes's court is great rejoicing at the discovery of the king's daughter; which joy is increased tenfold by Paulina, who restores Hermione to her repentant husband's arms. Her device for gradually and gently possessing him of the idea of Hermione's being alive, is curious and shrewd. She gives out that she has in her gallery a marvelous statue of Hermione by Julio Romano, so recently finished that the red paint on the lips is yet wet. When the curtain is drawn by Paulina, husband and daughter gaze greedily on the statue, and to their amazement it is made to step down from its pedestal and speak. They perceive it to be warm with life, and to be indeed Hermione herself,—let us hope, to have less strain on her charity thereafter.